Franciscus de Vitoria
1486–1546

THE CATHOLIC CONCEPTION OF INTERNATIONAL LAW

FRANCISCO DE VITORIA, FOUNDER OF THE MODERN LAW OF NATIONS

FRANCISCO SUÁREZ, FOUNDER OF THE MODERN PHILOSOPHY OF LAW IN GENERAL AND IN PARTICULAR OF THE LAW OF NATIONS

A Critical Examination and a Justified Appreciation

BY

JAMES BROWN SCOTT

Trustee and Secretary of the Carnegie Endowment for International Peace; Professor of International Law, Roman Law and Jurisprudence in Georgetown University; President of the American Society of International Law; President of the American Institute of Law; Member and former President of the Institut de Droit International

---

With a new introduction by
William E. Butler

John Edward Fowler Distinguished Professor of Law, Penn State School of Law; Emeritus Professor of Comparative Law, University of London; Foreign Member, National Academy of Sciences of Ukraine and National Academy of Legal Sciences of Ukraine

---

THE LAWBOOK EXCHANGE, LTD.
Clark, New Jersey

ISBN 978-1-58477-821-9 (hardcover)
ISBN 978-1-61619-452-9 (paperback)

Lawbook Exchange edition 2008, 2014

The quality of this reprint is equivalent to the quality of the original work.

THE LAWBOOK EXCHANGE, LTD.
33 Terminal Avenue
Clark, New Jersey 07066-1321

Please see our website for a selection of our other publications and fine facsimile reprints of classic works of legal history:
www.lawbookexchange.com

Library of Congress Cataloging-in-Publication Data

Scott, James Brown, 1866-1943.
The Catholic conception of international law : Francisco de Vitoria, founder of the modern law of nations, Francisco Suarez, founder of the modern philosophy of law in general and in particular of the law of nations : a critical examination and a justified appreciation ; with a new introduction by William E. Butler / James Brown Scott.
p. cm.
Originally published: Washington, D.C. : Georgetown university press, 1934.
ISBN-13: 978-1-58477-821-9 (cloth : alk. paper)
ISBN-10: 1-58477-821-0 (cloth : alk. paper)
1. International law--History--20th century. 2. Catholic Church. 3. Vitoria, Francisco de, 1486?-1546. 4. Suárez, Francisco, 1548-1617. I. Title.
KZ1242.S26 2008
341--dc22

2006100179

Printed in the United States of America on acid-free paper

James Brown Scott and the "Spanish School" of International Law

A week or so before Christmas 1927 an American international lawyer of Scottish descent, Canadian birth, and Presbyterian faith processed down the aisle of an edifice in the University of Salamanca to receive an honorary doctor of laws – only the third individual in five centuries to be so recognized in this manner by the University. By then James Brown Scott (1866-1943) was well-established as the leading specialist on the "Spanish School" of international law in the English language and the role of those jurists in laying the foundations of the modern doctrine of international law.

The Book

Although the present volume is merely one of several which James Brown Scott devoted to the Spanish School generally[1] and to Francisco de Vitoria (also spelled Vittoria and Victoria – the last not without amusing consequences)[2] and Francisco Suarez (1548-1617) most especially, it occupied a special place and

---

1. See J. B. Scott, *The Spanish Origin of International Law* (Washington D. C., Georgetown University School of Foreign Service, 1928), published in Spanish as Scott, *El origen español del derecho international moderno* ([Valladolid], 1928), later enlarged into his volume of 1934; id, *The Spanish Origin of International Law* (1934; reprinted Lawbook Exchange 2000); *Selections from Three Works of Francisco Suarez, S. J.* (1944), with an Introduction by J. B. Scott and in press when he died; id, *The Spanish Conception of International Law and of Sanctions* (1934), a pamphlet slightly revised from the initial version published in the *Georgetown Law Journal* for January and March 1934 and then incorporated into the present volume.
2. The *New York Times* was among those misled by the spelling when reporting on the unveiling of the mural panels in the United States Department of Justice in November 1937. Their correspondent wrote: "Some people may

purpose in the author's thinking. To fully appreciate that place and purpose, one must turn to an episode nearly three decades previously, when the then Solicitor for the Department of State wrote a letter to Robert S. Woodward, President of the Carnegie Institution Washington, suggesting that the said Institution undertake a project to republish the "classics of international law" with new translations, annotations, and introductions. Included in the proposal was a substantial list of candidates for inclusion in the project, among them Vitoria and Suarez.[3] The Project won the endorsement and financial support of the Carnegie Institution and matured into the famed "Classics of International Law" series issued between 1913 and 1950.[4]

Having created in his classics series the foundation of Vitoria studies in English with a facsimile version of the original texts of

---

wonder that Queen Victoria is included. She is the only head of State on the list since ancient Egypt and Babylonia. Perhaps it was [the artist's] idea that in the great Victorian reign the British democracy made big strides forward, and the self-governing dominions got their Constitutions". *New York Times*, 21 November 1937, Section E, p. 8. The artist, Boardman Robinson, wrote to correct the error: "May I call your attention to a slight error of identification in Topics of the Times? Victoria in the mural is not a portrait of the late Regina, but of Francisco de Victoria (1480-1546), a Dominican monk of Salamanca, one of the 'fathers' of spelling – perhaps inadvisedly – in conformity with the general custom". *New York Times*, 8 December 1937, p. 24. Vitoria is believed to have been born c. 1483 by modern scholars.

3. See [James Brown Scott], *The Classics of International Law: Letter from James Brown Scott, Solicitor for the Department of State, to R. S. Woodward, President of the Carnegie Institution of Washington relative to a Project for the Republication of the Classics of International Law* [Washington DC (Printed for the Carnegie Institution, January 1907). 13 p. Prepared for the Trustees of the Institution, the "Letter" was printed on magnificent handmade paper, fore-edge untrimmed, in sewn wrappers. A more elegant proposal can hardly be imagined.

4. The series comprised 22 volumes in 40. All have been reprinted by Oceana Publications (1964) and by William S. Hein (1995), among others. The series commenced in 1911 and concluded in 1950, initially published by the Carnegie Institution in Washington D. C. As from 1 January 1917 the series was transferred to the Carnegie Endowment for International Peace.

Vitoria and, in due course, Suarez, a new translation by an acknowledged Latin scholar, and a learned scholarly introduction,[5] Scott produced the present volume with which he hoped that he could persuade the senior establishment of the Roman Catholic Church to incorporate international law into the approved courses of study in all Catholic educational institutions from secondary school upwards. He also aspired to convince the Holy Father to issue an Encyclical that would declare "... the international doctrines of St. Augustine, Father, Saint, and Doctor, of St. Thomas Aquinas, as developed and applied to international relations by Francisco de Vitoria, by Francisco Suarez, and by Robert Bellarmine, Saint and Doctor, to be the doctrines of the Church Universal and as such to be taught in Catholic institutions of learning".[6] *The Catholic Conception of International Law* is that volume.

The book was printed and delivered during the summer of 1934. By late September of that year James Brown Scott was in Rome, armed with copies and a letter of introduction that he hoped would secure an audience with the Pope himself. Although that audience was not to be, Scott wrote on 29 September 1934 to the "Very Reverend Father General of the Society of Jesus" to report: "Thursday morning I waited upon Monseigneur Pizzardo, who also graciously received me, accepting for himself a copy of The Catholic Conception of International Law and volunteering to present a copy of the volume to the Holy Father". The volume, Scott continued, "... was not intended to be and it is not a textbook. It is *une oeuvre de propaganda*, an attempt on my part to show

---

5. Vitoria, F. de, *Franciscus de Victoria De Indis et De iure belli relectiones.Being Part of 'Relectiones theologicae XII'*, introduction by Ernest Nys, translated by John Pawley Bate, edited by Herbert Francis Wright (1917). A superior translation appears in A. Pagden and J. Lawrance (eds.), *Vitoria. Political Writings* (1991).

6. Quoted from a Memorandum prepared by James Brown Scott and entitled "Suggestions Relating to Encyclical" (undated) and held in the James Brown Scott Papers, Box 52, Folder 1, Georgetown University Library, Special Collections Division, Washington D. C., p. 3.

that the Catholic conception of International Law should be and therefore must be, the accepted Law of Nations of the future if not of the present, if the intercourse of nations is to be, as it must be, both moral and Christian".[7]

Scott pursued his goal in a letter to the Head of the Vatican Library of ca. 5 December 1934. Enclosing copies of both *The Spanish Origins of International Law* and of *The Catholic Conception of International Law*, he expressed the hope that "... through these various publications, and others which are in the course of preparation, to have the international law of St. Augustine and St. Thomas, and of Vitoria and Suarez, with certain contributions of St. Robert Bellarmine, introduced into institutions of learning, including, of course, the law schools". If, he added, "opportunity arises, I should be deeply grateful to you if you would present this delicate matter to the Holy Father, in the hope that he might be willing, if it meet with his approbation, to recommend, in some appropriate manner, the teaching of the scholastic conception of law, of international law, and of their philosophy, in Catholic institutions at large".[8]

In connection with his European visit and contacts with Vatican officials James Brown Scott prepared and constantly reworked lengthy memoranda in support of his proposal in the English and French languages. What appears to be a close to final, if not final, draft is preserved in his personal papers under the title "Memorandum on the Catholic Conception of International Law", with sections as follows: "I. St. Augustine; II. St. Thomas Aquinas; III. Francois de Vitoria; IV. Francisco Suarez; V. St. Robert Bellarmine; VI. Suggestions for a Proposed Encyclical; VII. Teaching of the Catholic Conception of International Law; VIII. Bibliography; IX. Annex of Historical Acts of Sovereigns and Pontiffs in Support of Peace".

---

7. A typed copy of the letter, undated but ascribed to 29 September 1934, is in the James Brown Scott Papers, Box 52, Folder 2, Georgetown University Library, Special Collections Division, Washington D. C..
8. Ibid., Box 52, Folder 4.

He made a detailed case for further studies, placing *The Catholic Conception of International Law* in the context of the existing literature:[9]

> Obviously, there is a need of further translations … there should also be complete translations in at least four other cultural languages – French, German, Spanish, and Italian. It is believed that these could be issued in the near future under the guidance of competent scholars of the Church. French translations, for example, could be prepared under the direction of Abbé de la Brière of the Faculté libre de Droit de Paris. Translations into other languages could be entrusted to scholars of similar standing in different countries. The result would be a body of source texts suitable for use in all parts of the world.
>
> …
>
> The Latin treatises, and translations of them, should be supplemented by at least two textbooks, one to serve as an introduction to the subject, and another for more advanced students. The recently issued volume, *The Catholic Conception of International Law*, might, until it is replaced by one more adequate, serve as an introductory work. As a more advanced textbook there is now being prepared a volume which will contain the international law of Victoria and of Suarez set forth in numbered articles in the form of an elaborate code, with extensive commentaries on each article, and with appendices containing the Latin and English texts from which the articles are taken.

Armed with these materials, it would be possible, he suggested, that a "… course of international law be required not only for students in law schools, but also for all students of the arts and sciences in Jesuit institutions in which courses the Suarezian philosophy of law should be stressed".

---

9. Ibid., Box 52, Folder 1 (undated Memorandum).

In another draft memorandum (undated) containing "Suggestions Relating to Encyclical", Scott counseled that:[10]

> The growth of international law must be a controlled growth if it is to be orderly, and the control must be by that high standard of reason which, distinguishing between right and wrong, is immanent in the contributions of the great Churchmen responsible for what may be called the Catholic conception of international law. For a law thus controlled becomes a science. A law that is not a science can not have a philosophy, but if it become a science, it requires ... a philosophy and that philosophy is jurisprudence, set forth in fullness and meticulous detail in the masterly tractate of Suarez, *De Legibus ac Deo Legislatore*. It is not, then too much to say that upon the legal philosophy of Suarez, the teaching of modern jurisprudence could and should be based, so that it may have a moral and a spiritual content always lacking where jurisprudence is exclusively the product of the layman.

Publication details of *The Catholic Conception of International Law* are not disclosed in the Scott Papers. One assumes that either the Carnegie Institution and/or the author himself took much of the print run for distribution, and that the print run was not large. The title is uncommon, although not rare, in its original version, and probably was not marketed widely. Only a couple of reviews were published.[11]

Neither is the relationship, if any, disclosed in the Scott Papers between *The Catholic Conception of International Law* and another work supported, indeed published, by the Carnegie

10. Ibid., Box 52, Folder 1.

11. See *American Journal of International Law*, XXIX (1935), 183-184 (Charles G. Fenwick); *Revista de derecho internacional*, XIII, vol. XXVI, no. 52 (31 December 1934), p. 298 (Antonio S. de Bustamante y Sirven), who gave it a cursory note.

Endowment for International Peace a year after the present volume appeared: Eppstein's (1895-19?) work on the Catholic tradition in the law of nations.[12] Eppstein undertook to provide, as related in his Preface, "... what until now has not been available in the English language – a compendium of the teaching and tradition of Catholic Christianity upon international morality" (p. xvii). The originator of Eppstein's work was not James Brown Scott, but James Thomson Shotwell (1874-1965), who at the time was the Director of the Division of History and Economics at the Carnegie Endowment. The present work was available at least a year in advance of Eppstein's; Scott is not mentioned in the Acknowledgements, but is cited in passing twice in footnotes (pp. 116, 260).

The Author

James Brown Scott was born near Kincardine, Canada, on 3 June 1866, the youngest child of John Scott (1830-1885) and Jeannette Brown (1831-1901). His father was a stone cutter, and his mother the daughter of a weaver. Both had emigrated in 1849 from Scotland to New York, where they met and married in 1853 before moving to Canada. There were four other children in the family, three girls and a boy: Mary, Margaret, John, and Jeannette. John died in childhood, aged 15. Three years after the birth of James, the family left Canada for Philadelphia, returned to Canada in 1871, and relocated permanently to Philadelphia in 1876.

James and his sisters were provided with a good education. When their father passed away they were left with sufficient funds

---

12. John Eppstein, *The Catholic Tradition of the Law of Nations* (1935; reprinted by Lawbook Exchange, 2008). Eppstein had published in 1929, a year or so before his volume was commissioned, *Ten Years' Life of the League of Nations: A History of the Origins of the League and its Development from A. D. 1919 to 1929* (1929). Vitoria also was given attention at the time in William Francis Roemer (1894-19?), *The Ethical Basis of International Law* (1929; reprinted Lawbook Exchange 2007).

to complete their studies until they became self-supporting. All the Scott children excelled in their schooling and completed their education in Europe. Mary, the eldest, studied in Berlin, Vienna, and Munich after graduating from the Women's Medical College in Philadelphia; she was among the first women to be admitted to the Institut Pasteur (Paris). Upon her return to the United States, she became a specialist in children's diseases, an interest aroused by the boyhood death of her brother John.

Margaret became a professor of romance languages upon completing her studies in France and Germany at initially the University of Illinois and then Syracuse University. She outlived the other members of the family.

Jeannette, the youngest sister, studied art and followed the career of a painter. Upon graduation from the School of Design in Philadelphia, she attended the Pennsylvania Academy of Fine Arts and then studied in Europe for five years, from 1889 to 1894. Returning to the United States, she accepted a position as instructor in painting at Syracuse University, retiring in 1927 as head of the Department of Painting with the degree of Doctor of Fine Arts.[13] She was interested in women's rights and helped to finance the Inter American Commission of Women, created by the Sixth Pan American Conference (Havana, 1928), the first juridical Commission of Women ever established by governments acting in concert.

James Brown Scott completed his secondary schooling in Philadelphia and was admitted to Harvard College and graduated *summa cum laude* in 1890 with his B.A., staying on a further year to complete his A. M. (1891).[14] His career as an international

---

13. Drawn from the unpublished biography of James Brown Scott by George Finch, in the James Brown Scott Papers, Box 69, Folder 1, Georgetown University Library, Special Collections Division, Washington D. C.

14. For biographical materials on Scott, I have had the benefit of the James Brown Scott Papers held at Georgetown University, which contain the manuscript biography by George Finch and numerous curriculum vitas prepared by Scott himself for various occasions. Among printed materials, see obituaries in the *American Journal of International Law*, XXXVII (1943), 508 (G. A.

lawyer commenced with his being selected for a Parker Fellowship at Harvard which he held for three years. He did not attend law school, but instead spent a year at Heidelberg University, where he was awarded the *juris utriusque doctor*. Upon returning to the United States, he pursued the practice of law in California. He was not distracted from academic legal life for long. In 1896 he organized the Law School at Los Angeles (now the University of Southern California School of Law) and was then enticed to become the Dean of the University of Illinois Law School (1899-1903). The Columbia Law School persuaded him to come to New York (1903-06),[15] and he might have remained there had he not written a letter to the United States Secretary of State suggesting that a legal advisor might be appointed to the Department and that he might be considered a candidate for the position.

His interview made an excellent impression, and he moved to the nation's capital, where he remained until 1940, when he retired to his summer home in nearby Annapolis. He married Adele Cooper Scott in 1901.

During the years 1905-06 he was actively involved with others in forming the American Society of International Law.[16] From 1895 to 1914 members of what many regard as the United States "foreign policy establishment" assembled each year at Lake Mohonk in upstate New York to discuss the preservation of peace and, more particularly, the perceived importance of international

---

Finch); XXXVII (1943), 559-561 (F. R. Coudert); XXXVIII (1944), 183-217 (G. A. Finch); *Transactions of the Grotius Society*, XXIX (1943), vii-viii (Cecil J. B. Hurst); and D. Stevens, *Paintings & Drawings of Jeannette Scott 1864-1937* (1940).

15. While at Columbia he produced J. B. Scott (ed.), *Cases on Quasi-Contracts* (1905) and the following year, having removed to George Washington University, Scott (ed.), *Cases on Equity Jurisdiction* (1906), in two volumes; and Scott (ed.), *Cases on International Law, Selected from Decisions of English and American Courts* (1902), revised and published in 1906 by West Publishing Co., and revised throughout the interwar period

16. See F. L. Kirgis, *The American Society of International Law's First Century 1906-2006* [(2006)].

arbitration as an alternative to war. James Brown Scott was present at the eleventh conference from 31 May to 2 June 1905, where the American Society of International Law was conceived. He acted as one of an informal committee of three[17] which decided to put the proposal for the Society to those in attendance at the Conference and then as the secretary of the meeting of twenty-four Conference participants who supported the proposal unanimously and appointed a committee of seven to draft a constitution for the Society. When the Society constitution was ultimately adopted, Scott was appointed Recording Secretary and a member of the Executive Council of the Society. An integral part of the scheme to organize the Society was the establishment of a journal, and at the twelfth meeting at Lake Mohonk on 1 June 1906 the Executive Council appointed Scott as Managing Editor of the *American Journal of International Law*. The journal has appeared quarterly thereafter; Scott advanced from his own pocket the funds necessary to print the first two issues, being later reimbursed.

While acting as the Solicitor for the Department of State, he took a dual appointment at the George Washington University Law School (1906-11) and also lectured at The Johns Hopkins University (1906-16). After service during the First World War and involvement in the negotiations of the postwar settlements, he accepted appointment to the School of Foreign Service at Georgetown University from 1921 until his retirement. He acted as an exchange professor at various times at the Universities of Chile, Havana, Montevideo, Salamanca, Berlin, Frankfurt, Göttingen, Kiel, and Munich, among others.

He received seventeen honorary degrees: (Syracuse, Salamanca, Paris (Sorbonne), Universidad Mayor de San Marcos (Peru), George Washington, St. John's College (Annapolis), University of Chile, Warsaw University, University of Habana,

---

17. The other two members being Robert Lansing, later the United States Secretary of State, and Professor G. W. Kirchwey, sometime President of the American Peace Society.

Cambridge University, Michigan, Oberlin, Lyon, Queen's University (Ontario), Athens, Georgetown, and Southern California).

Elected an Associate of the Institut de droit international in 1908, he became a full member in 1910 and eventually served as President. He was elected to the Royal Academy of Sciences in Belgium (1919), to the Institut de France (1921), to the American Academy of Arts and Sciences (1935), among a number of distinctions of this kind. A number of countries (Belgium, Yugoslavia, Serbia, Chile, Italy, Ecuador, Romania, Netherlands, and Cuba included) conferred decorations upon him.

Having, as noted above, persuaded the Carnegie Institution to support his Project on the classics of international law, he accepted appointment as secretary of what became the Carnegie Endowment for International Peace and director of the Division of International Law. In both capacities for more than three decades, to borrow the apt phrase of Manley Ottmer Hudson (1886-1960), he "... fathered and fostered the development of international law during the greatest period of its history".[18]

Sixteenth-century Catholic doctrinal writings continued to constitute a significant portion of his scholarly writings. Not long after receiving his honorary degree from Salamanca University, he initiated measures to arrange a celebration of the 400th anniversary of Vitoria's lectures at the University, dated by common consent to 1532. In 1930 he was awarded a gold and silver plaque for his original research in "establishing the title of Francisco de Vittoria ... a Dominican priest, as the founder of modern International Law".[19]

At a luncheon of the members of the Institut de droit international in 1932 it was decided to form the International

---

18. See the Remarks of Manley O. Hudson, in "Portrait of Dr. James Brown Scott", *Harvard Alumni Bulletin*, XXXIII, no. 14 (1 January 1931), p. 419.
19. Press Release, dated 5 April 1930, James Brown Scott Papers, Box 63, Folder 8, Georgetown University Library, Special Collections Division, Washington D. C.

Association of Francis of Vitoria and of Suarez.[20] The 30 or so members present were regarded as charter members, with a ceiling on membership of 100 and local societies to be formed in nations accepting and abiding by the principle of international law in their mutual relations. No country could have more than ten members on the international body. Dr. Nicolas Politis (1872-1942) was elected the President and Dr. Alfred Verdross (1890-19?), the Secretary-General. The Statutes of the International Association Vitoria-Suarez were approved by the Constitutive General Assembly at Oslo on 17 August 1932 (the Association actually operating within the framework of meetings of the Institut de droit international). James Brown Scott was elected First Vice President of the Association in 1936 and recruited a number of his close professional colleagues to be elected among the maximum quota of ten in the International Association. Members of the international association were active throughout the 1930s in propagating the doctrines of Vitoria, and the association itself identified with a number of publications.[21]

Diplomacy played an important role in his career. In 1907 he was a technical delegate to the Second Hague Peace Conference. From 1914 to 1917 he was the Chairman of the United States Neutrality Board, and in 1919 acted as the legal adviser to the delegation of the United States at the Paris Peace Conference. During 1922-23 he was the legal adviser to the American delegates at the Washington Conference on the Limitation of Armaments. In 1927 he was a member of the Inter-American Commission of Jurists which met at Rio de Janeiro. The following year he served as delegate to the Sixth International Conference of American States at Havana.

---

20. In effect this was to be an international "umbrella" association for national societies such as the Asociacion Francisco de Vitoria, established in 1928 as related by James Brown Scott, "Asociacion Francisco de Vitoria", *American Journal of International Law*, XXII (1928), 136-139. It was the same pattern he used when creating the American Institute of International Law.

21. Among them *Vitoria et Suarez: contribution des théologiens au droit international moderne*, Preface by James Brown Scott (1939).

The Chichele Chair of International Law

Upon the retirement of Professor Sir Thomas Erskine Holland (1835-1926), the Chichele Chair of International Law became vacant at Oxford University in 1910. To the surprise of many, James Brown Scott decided to make application for the position. The application itself is a remarkable document – a printed booklet of considerable length setting out Dr. Scott's credentials and containing testimonials of his qualifications and character from leading figures throughout Europe and the United States.

The Scott Papers do not disclose whether Erskine persuaded or encouraged Scott to apply for the position or not.[22] The electors took a considerable time to come to a view on who should be appointed, perhaps because they were divided. Scott was kept in contact with what was happening by Professor Lassa Oppenheim (1858-1919), who held the Whewell Chair at Cambridge University. On 22 November 1910 Oppenheim wrote from Whewell House in Cambridge:

> ... As regards the Oxford chair, I have heard nothing which would indicate how matters are going on. Everybody knows that you are Holland's candidate, and people who discuss you may be divided into two camps, although everybody agrees that you are the best candidate. To the one camp belong Pollock [Sir Frederick Pollock (1845-1937) – WEB], Whittuck [Edward Arthur Whittuck (1844-1924)] – WEB], and others, with a wide horizon, who say that the best man ought to have it no matter whether he be an English subject or not. To the other camp belong a number of small minded people who say that to appoint an American would be awkward in view of the possibility of an Anglo-

22. Scott had persuaded Erskine to edit the works of Richard Zouche (1590-1661) for the Classics of International Law series. The volumes appeared in 1911. On Erskine's tenure in the Chair, see T. E. Erskine, *A Valedictory Retrospect (1874-1910)* (1910).

> American conflict. Since the more influential people belong to the first mentioned class I trust that your election is certain. But so much is absolutely certain that if you fail to be elected the only matter which bared [sic] your election is that you are not an English subject. I shall send a wire anyhow as soon as I hear of the result.

On 16 December 1910 Oppenheim wrote:[23]

> ... I suppose that Holland provides you with news in this matter. I hear very little, but the following may be of interest: I hear from a good source that the President of the Admiralty Court who is one of the electors stands firm for Macdonnell [Sir John Macdonnell (1846-1921 – WEB]. Westlake [John Westlake (1828-1913) – WEB] works hard – so Whittuck writes me – for Higgins [Alexander Pearce Higgins (1865-1935) – WEB]. There is also a rumour that Fromageot is supported by one of the electors. Another rumour is that the election is postponed on account of the political crisis, and there is also a rumour that the postponement is due to the fact that the electors have not yet come to an agreement ...

It was perhaps the example of Professor Oppenheim which Scott followed in developing his application for the Chair. Oppenheim supplied Scott with a copy of his own application for the Whewell Chair, printed by the University Press Cambridge and dated 6 July 1908.

Scott was not elected to the Chair, impressive as his credentials were.

---

23. Both letters are in the James Brown Scott Papers Box 57, Folder 12, Georgetown University Library, Special Collections Division, Washington D. C.

American Institute of International Law

Scott's predilection towards encouraging the development of international law in the Western hemisphere is evident in his untiring efforts to encourage the formation of learned societies of international law throughout the Americas. In the summer of 1911 he met with Alejandro Alvarez (1868-1960) of Chile to discuss means for bringing together international lawyers to discuss problems of mutual interest and to develop principles of law for the settlement of disputes by judicial methods. These discussions matured into a formal proposal circulated on 10 October 1911 to a leading jurist in each Latin American country. The enthusiasm encountered led the proposers to seek European assent, which was warmly forthcoming. On 12 October 1912 a temporary organization was formed with James Brown Scott elected as President and Alvarez as Secretary-General. A pre-condition to the permanent establishment of the American Institute was the formation of individual societies of international law in each of the American countries. Scott and Alvarez were untiring in their efforts in this direction, such that by December 1915 the first meeting of the American Institute could be convened in Washington D. C. in connection with the Second Pan American Scientific Congress of representatives from twenty-one international law societies in the American republics.[24]

James Brown Scott was elected the first President of the American Institute and was the principal author of the "Declaration of the Rights and Duties of Nations" adopted unanimously on 6 January 1916 at a session of the Institute and the accompanying commentary. He remained the major moving force in this organization until his retirement in 1940.

---

24. The early history of the American Institute of International Law is recorded in J. B. Scott, *The American Institute of International Law: Its Declaration of the Rights and Duties of Nations* (1916).

American Society for Judicial Settlement of International Disputes

Scott's unflagging efforts in support of the establishment of an international court of justice were pursued partly through diplomatic channels and partly through the generation of popular public support in favor of such an institution. To the latter end he played the key part in creating the American Society for Judicial Settlement of International Disputes, of which he was elected the first president. The first international conference of the Society was held at Washington D. C. on 15-17 December 1910 and attended principally by businessmen, educators, diplomats, and federal and state legislators.

The reference to "judicial" settlement was narrowly understood; arbitration was not included, as Scott made clear in his opening remarks to the constitutive conference: The purposes of the Society are "... limited to a discussion of the judicial determination, as distinguished from the arbitral adjustment, of international controversies. It seeks to strengthen sentiment where existing, and to create sentiment where it does not exist, in favor of judicial settlement. It stands for a permanent court, as distinguished from a temporary tribunal ... It stands for judicial decision according to principles of law, not compromise according to the standards of diplomacy ... We are not opposed to arbitration. On the contrary, we favor it individually, but arbitration as such falls beyond the scope of our labors".[25]

There were six conferences of the American Society in all, the last in 1916. They greatly informed efforts following the First World War to create the Permanent Court of International Justice.

---

25. *Proceedings of the Conference on the Judicial Settlement of International Disputes* (1910), p. 3.

Court of Arbitral Justice

James Brown Scott's energies in support of the judicial settlement of disputes as the exclusive concern of the American Society for the Judicial Settlement of International Disputes reflected no disenchantment with arbitration as an alternative method of dispute resolution – to use a term in fashion today but not at the time. Having been appointed as technical expert of the United States to the Second Hague Peace Conference of 1907 after merely a year or so of service as Solicitor for the Department of State, Scott took "… a conspicuous, one may even say the leading part, in preparing and urging the adoption of the draft for a convention for a Court of Arbitral Justice, and was extremely active and useful in promoting all the conventions adopted by the Conference".[26]

Scott was selected by the Second Hague Peace Conference to prepare the official report to the Conference in respect of the draft Convention for the Establishment of a Court of Arbitral Justice. It was he who explained to the Conference what the draft intended, article by article, and urged its adoption with great eloquence. Although in the end the Conference merely recommended the draft convention to the signatory powers rather then adopting the text itself, it was felt that considerable progress had been made in the right direction. At the Naval Conference in London during 1908-09, which was to agree the law to be applied by a proposed International Prize Court, Scott urged that the United States propose the International Prize Court be vested with the jurisdiction and functions of the Court of Arbitral Justice and, when sitting, should be guided by the draft convention for the establishment of the Arbitral Court. The proposal was made, but for sundry reasons which culminated in the refusal of the United Kingdom to ratify the Prize Court Convention, the Court of Arbitral Justice never came into being. The United States did ratify, but

26. Letter of David Jayne Hill, 18 January 1917, quoted in note 27 below, p. 18.

that action did not move the United Kingdom to like action. The proposal ultimately came to an end. Scott persisted with initiatives to revive the scheme in some way. These were ultimately overtaken by the outbreak of the First World War.

The Nobel Peace Prize

James Brown Scott was nominated on at least six occasions for the Nobel Peace Prize. The first and most concerted effort on his behalf was undertaken in late 1916 for presumably the Prize awarded in 1917. A substantial printed Memorial, dated 29 December 1916, was submitted on his behalf.[27]

A junior Norwegian diplomat and great admirer of Scott, Gregers W. Gram, informed Scott on 2 January 1923 that he had twice proposed him for the Nobel Prize and intended to do so a third time.[28]

On 13 February 1927 the eminent French international lawyer, Gilbert Gidel (1880-1958), wrote Scott to say: "I believe that no one other than you deserves the Nobel Peace Prize and I shall take advantage of my right of nomination to put forward your candidacy".[29]

Professor Karl Strupp (1886-1940) wrote to Scott on New Year's Day of 1937 informing him of his nomination:[30]

---

27. See *Memorial in Support of the Nomination of James Brown Scott for the Nobel Peace Prize* [n.p., 1917]. [iv], 71 p. Copies are held in the James Brown Scott Papers, Box 59, Folder 5, Georgetown Univesity Library, Special Collections Division, Washington D. C.

28. James Brown Scott Papers, Box 59, Folder 6.

29. James Brown Scott Paper, Box 59, Folder 6: "j'ai estime que nul plus que vous n'etait digne du Prix Nobel de la Paix et j'ai profite de mon droit de presentation pour poser votre candidature".

30. James Brown Scott Papers, Box 59, Folder 6. Strupp wrote in German; Scott had the letter translated, and I have quoted the translation supplied to him.

> Permit me to say that I have proposed you, the father of the Permanent Court of International Justice, for the Nobel Prize; and may I dedicate to you, in the same capacity, my Commentary on the Status and Reglement of this court, which I hope to finish by the end of 1937?

Other Publications

James Brown Scott awaits his proper bibliographer. He published extensively (one would imagine well over 1,000 books, articles, reviews, and translations),[31] but both the volume and nature of his publications were skewed by his association with the Carnegie Institution and later the Carnegie Endowment for International Peace and as the principal moving force behind the *American Journal of International Law*. From 1907 to 1916 inclusive Scott published 266 editorial comments, mostly concerned with topics bearing upon international relations from the standpoint of an international lawyer dedicated to international peace, fourteen leading articles, and 58 book reviews. The series of volumes published as "Classics of International Law", all under his general editorship and many containing a learned introduction by his hand, came to twenty-two titles in forty volumes. A "spin-off" of this project was a two-volume work: Scott (ed.), *The Armed Neutralities of 1780 and 1800: A Collection of Official Documents Preceded by the Views of Representative Publicists* (1918).

He was a popular lecturer frequently invited throughout the country and Europe to deliver not merely single addresses but an entire *cours* dedicated to a particular subject, such as the Hague peace conferences,[32] or dispute settlement. Many found their way

---

31. The Harvard Law School Library records more than 200 books and pamphlets under his name.

32. See Scott, *The Hague Peace Conferences of 1899 and 1907: A Series of Lectures Delivered Before the Johns Hopkins University in the Year 1908* (1909);

into print as monographs or special issues of student law reviews. A number were translated into Spanish or French, usually under Carnegie Endowment auspices.

A considerable portion of his larger works comprised edited, translated, and thoroughly annotated collections of documents which in his day could not have been commercially published without Carnegie Endowment support. All without exception have retained their value for legal scholarship, as their frequent reprinting by commercial publishers demonstrates. Among the titles, usually self-explanatory if not brief, are: Scott (ed. & intro.), *Texts of the Peace Conferences at the Hague, 1899 and 1907 with English Translation and Appendix of Related Documents* (1908); Scott (ed. & intro.), *Instructions to the American Delegates to the Hague Peace Conferences and Their Official Reports* (1916); Scott (ed. & intro.), *The Hague Court Reports Comprising the Awards, Accompanied by Syllabi, the Agreements for Arbitration, and Other Documents in Each Case Submitted to the Permanent Court of Arbitration and to Commissions of Inquiry Under the Provisions of the Conventions of 1899 and 1907 for the Pacific Settlement of International Disputes* (1916-1932) in two series; Scott, *The Status of the International Court of Justice with an Appendix of Addresses and Official Documents* (1916); Scott (collected & ed.), *Judicial Settlement of Controversies Between States of the American Union: Cases Decided in the Supreme Court of the United States* (1918). 3 vols.; Scott, *James Madison's Notes of Debates in the Federal Convention of 1787 and Their Relation to a More Perfect Society of Nations* (1918); Scott (ed.), *The Declaration of London February 26, 1909: A Collection of Official Papers and Documents Relating to the International Naval Conference Held in London December, 1908 – February, 1909* (1919); Scott, *The United States of America: A Study in International Organization* (1920); Scott, *Observations on Nationality with*

Scott, *The Judicial Settlement of International Disputes: Addresses at the Geneva Institute of International Relations August 16th and 17th, 1926* (1927).

Especial Reference to the Hague Convention of April 12th, 1930: A Plea for a Single and Impersonal Standard of Nationality in the Law and Practice of Nations (1931).

With particular reference to the western hemisphere he prepared: Scott, *The American Institute of International Law: Its Declaration of the Rights and Duties of Nations* (1916); Scott (ed. & intro.), *The International Conference of American States 1889-1926: A Collection of the Conventions, Recommendations, Resolutions, Reports, and Motions adopted by the First Six International Conferences of the American States, and Documents relating to the Organization of the Conferences* (1931).

His casebooks, alluded to above, dominated the teaching of international law in the United States for nearly four decades. The first edition of 1902 was succeeded by another in 1906 (with a change of publisher) and contributed to his serving for a number of years as one of the general editors of a casebook series for West Publishing Co. in St. Paul Minnesota. The last edition appeared in 1937 in collaboration with Walter H. E. Jaeger, then Professor of Law and Director of Graduate Research at Georgetown University as the junior author.

Scott's final major work of this genre appeared in two volumes under the title: *Law, The State, and The International Community* (1939-40), volume one of which constituted "A Commentary on the Development of Legal, Political, and International Ideals" and volume two a collection of quotations from the writings of those political and legal thinkers whose ideas were discussed in the first volume, all arranged in a subject order of his own making. Volume two he called in the looser meaning of the term a "codification" of political and legal conceptions influential in the modern world. His personal archive contains a large body of working papers and drafts drawn up over the years in connection with various activities, not least the preparation of *The Catholic Conception of International Law*. Whether he was able to take full advantage of this material when approaching the Vatican about incorporating international law into the syllabi of Catholic secondary and higher education or not, he made good and extensive use of these materials in this, his last, major work.

A chapter is devoted in the Commentary to Vitoria ("the founder, in the opinion of many, of the modern law of nations") and Suarez ("the prince of modern jurists"), but the influence of the progenitors of the "Spanish School" in this study is much larger when the chapter is read against the accompanying volume of documents. When Scott sent the volume to press, the Suarez works had not yet appeared in the "Classics of International Law" series and indeed were published in 1944 shortly after James Brown Scott died. But he had the manuscript of Suarez by then and was disposed to use that resource extensively: "It may ... seem, especially to those who are not familiar with Francisco Suarez, that the number of quotations from his writings is disproportionately large. And it is quite true that more passages have been drawn from Suarez than from any other writer" (p. ix). The reason for this, Scott says, is not his partiality on his part towards the Catholic jurists, but to the fact that "... in certain of his writings, especially in his great *Tractatus de legibus ac Deo legislatore*, there is summed up and blended into a philosophic whole the best of our legal and our political heritage from the ancient and medieval worlds".

The Catholic Conception of International Law as a star in the larger cosmos of the intellectual legacy of James Brown Scott represents his most considered and comprehensive attempt to make the practical importance of the law of nations accessible and relevant to the layman. He believed, and his work is predicated upon this conviction, that the principles of Christian morality have informed and must continue to inform the articulation and "codification" of the legal and political principles fundamental to the existence of the State and the international community.

The Portraits

When the new building for the Department of Justice was being completed in Washington D. C., the decision was taken to embellish the ceremonial entrance leading from the court of honor with a series of murals depicting the great law-givers of history, commencing with Menes, a ruler of ancient Egypt. As part of his support for and admiration of the Spanish School of international law, Scott succeeded in persuading those who chose the figures to be portrayed in the murals to include Vitoria. The artist commissioned to undertake the murals was Boardman Robinson (1876-1952).[33] As he completed his work it was discovered that no likeness of Vitoria was known. At the suggestion of Doris Stevens, it was decided to use the visage of James Brown Scott. When Scott appeared, Boardman made a quick pencil-sketch, and from that developed the portrait that in fact exists.[34]

James Brown Scott as Vitoria, painted by Boardman Robinson, 1937, for the Department of Justice

---

33. Boardman Robinson, illustrator, cartoonist, painter, journalist, teacher, and muralist. His murals are to be found in the Rockefeller Center, Department of Justice, and other buildings. From 1936 to 1947 he was Director of the Colorado Springs Fine Arts Center.
34. What transpired was related by a journalist from the local Washington newspaper. See "Jovial Artist of Justice Building Here to 'Hang' 16 Law-Givers", *The Washington Post*, 11 November 1937.

Scott was overwhelmed. He wrote to Robinson on 10 December 1937:[35]

> Words fails me to express my appreciation of the magnificent mural of Franciscus de Vitoria ... I do not think there could have been conceived a finer setting for this founder of the law of nations and from the bottom of his heart the unworthy one whose likeness Victoria bears on the walls of the Department of Justice thanks you for the most perfect portrait which he has ever had, painted by you at the suggestion, I am happy and proud to say, of the always thoughtful and gracious Doris Stevens, who never, as you know, fails a friend.

For reasons unfathomable, when James Brown Scott died on 25 June 1943 the local press took the occasion to "solve a mystery" of an important work of art in the Capital. Once again what had transpired in 1937 was disclosed, that Dr. Scott's face appeared as Vitoria in the mural.[36]

In due course a painting of Vitoria surfaced, but not in the lifetime of James Brown Scott. The Scott Papers contain an advertising brochure announcing a German reprint and translation of Vitoria's celebrated works on the law of nations. Depicted on the front of the brochure and in the book itself is a portrait of Vitoria, but with no source given for the painting.[37] In the interim another portrait of the young Vitoria has been identified and used on a Spanish banknote.

James Brown Scott's own portrait, painted by his sister Jeannette (1864-1937), was formally presented to the Harvard Law School on 28 October 1930 to join the portraits in the International Law Seminar Room of Langdell Hall of Henry

---

35. James Brown Scott Papers, Box 63, Folder 10.

36. James Waldo Fawcett, "Dr. James Brown Scott's Death Reveals Solution of Art Mystery", *The Evening Star*, 28 June 1943.

37. See W. Schätzel (ed.), *De Indis Recenter Inventis et de Jure Belli Hispanoturm in Barbaros Relectiones* (Tubingen, 1952).

Wheaton (1785-1848) and Richard Henry Dana (1815-1882). Professor Manley O. Hudson made the presentation on behalf of the Scott family to Dean Roscoe Pound (1870-1964). It is one of six known to have survived. One hung at the Washington headquarters of the Carnegie Endowment for International Peace and was the favorite of those done by the artist. Another is owned by the Law School of Georgetown University, and a third was given to the University of Southern California. The whereabouts of a painting done by Jeannette when she was a student in Paris is unknown, but it depicts James Brown Scott in a colonel's uniform, his rank and attire while serving during the Spanish-American War.

William E. Butler
September 2008

THE CATHOLIC CONCEPTION OF INTERNATIONAL LAW

FRANCISCO DE VITORIA, FOUNDER OF THE MODERN LAW OF NATIONS

FRANCISCO SUÁREZ, FOUNDER OF THE MODERN PHILOSOPHY OF LAW IN GENERAL AND IN PARTICULAR OF THE LAW OF NATIONS

A Critical Examination and a Justified Appreciation

BY

JAMES BROWN SCOTT

Trustee and Secretary of the Carnegie Endowment for International Peace; Professor of International Law, Roman Law and Jurisprudence in Georgetown University; President of the American Society of International Law; President of the American Institute of Law; Member and former President of the Institut de Droit International

GEORGETOWN UNIVERSITY PRESS
WASHINGTON, D. C.
1934

PRESS OF RANSDELL, INC.

FOREWORD

THE present volume owes its origin, like so many things, to the discovery of America by Columbus. The western adventure opened up a new world to the exploitation of the old, and immediately there sprang up rivalry between the seagoing nations of Europe, in their eagerness to make discoveries of their own and thus subject the regions discovered beyond the seas to their colonization.

Two great and indeed fundamental questions arose. The first, what right discovery gave to the discoverer, and the second, the rules and regulations which the discoverer might impose upon the aborigines of the newly found territories. Because of the first question there might be and there was many a conflict between discoverers of different portions of the Western World, which, if not settled by rule of law, would ultimately be settled by the rule of force. Because of the second question, the European colonizers had to determine the right, if any, which the Europeans, on account of what they called their superior civilization, could properly exercise over the "barbarian principalities," to use an expression of their day: whether it should be the right of equals or the right of superiors. The questions thus raised involved fundamental principles of international law, and they are still fundamental principles.

Now it happened that a young and enterprising man by the name of Bartolomé de las Casas took part in one of the early western voyages—Diego Velasquez's "colonizing expedition to Cuba in 1511-12"—and seeing how the natives were systematically deprived of rights which the Europeans themselves claimed and exercised, he made it his life mission to plead the cause of the oppressed both in Spain and in the Spanish settlements of the New World. He entered the Church, becoming a member of the Dominican Order, known as the Order of Preachers, the Dominicans of his day, anticipating the Jesuits of a later day, having devoted themselves to missionary labors in the Western World. The accounts which the missionaries gave of the brutality and lawlessness of the *Conquistadores* reached Spain and found a permanent lodgement in the mind and the heart of one Francisco de Vitoria, *prima* professor of theology at the University of Salamanca.

He too became a missionary—a "home missionary," as we might say—maintaining from his chair in Salamanca that all human beings, irrespective of race, irrespective of geography, irrespective of religion, should have the same rights and perform the same duties.

We do not need to speculate on the circumstances which led Francisco de Vitoria to the conclusions set forth in his two Readings, *On the Indians Lately Discovered* and *On the Law of War;* he informs us himself in the opening lines of the Reading *On the Indians:* "The whole of this controversy and discussion was started on account of the aborigines of the New World, commonly called Indians, who came forty years ago into the power of the Spaniards, not having been previously known to our world." And he added for the information of his audience—then assembled in a classroom, but today including the civilized world: "In the first part we shall inquire by what right these Indian natives came under Spanish sway. In the second part, what rights the Spanish sovereigns obtained over them in temporal and civil matters. In the third part, what rights these sovereigns or the Church obtained over them in matters spiritual and touching religion, . . ."

Here we have not merely the origin of the readings but the date at which they were composed. Columbus had discovered America on the 12th of October, 1492, and forty years thereafter —then as now—would be 1532, which date we may confidently assign to their composition. These readings were subsequently delivered by Victoria during the course of his professorate at Salamanca, it being the duty of the *prima* professor to deliver public readings in each of the years of his professorate; and in these two readings Francisco de Vitoria, we veritably believe, formulated the modern law of nations.

Fortunately we do not need to ask the intelligent reader to accept a personal statement regarding this epoch-making contribution, inasmuch as on the 23d day of December of the year of our Lord one thousand nine hundred and thirty-three, the representatives of the American Republics unanimously accorded to Victoria the position of founder of the modern law of nations by adopting the following resolution:

> The Seventh International Conference of American States,
> *Resolves*: To recommend that a bust of the Spanish theologian, Francisco de Vitoria, be placed in the headquarters of the Pan American Union, in Washington, as a tribute to the professor of Salamanca who, in the sixteenth century, established the foundations of modern international law.

Now Victoria's principles, which the Seventh of the Pan American Conferences declared to be the modern law of nations, are set forth in the opening section of the present volume.

In the following sections the philosophy of international law and the philosophy of law in its entirety are set forth in analyses of the works of Francisco Suárez, said by the outstanding jurist of our day to be the "prince of modern jurists."

The subsequent writers on international law are but their successors and debtors.

A word as to the method of presentation. We draw aside, as it were, the veil which, century after century, has hidden these two high-minded and noble Spaniards, in order that they may speak to the world as from their respective chairs at Salamanca and Coimbra. Comment, perhaps over-generous comment, has been added, but only with the purpose of drawing the modern implications from the express statements of these two leaders of the Spanish School.

Would that Victoria's law of nations and Suárez' philosophy of international law were taught in every seat of learning in the wide, wide world, for then law, to be binding, would have to be moral as well as social, equitable as well as just and always and everywhere consistent with the nature and the dignity of the human being.

August 15, 1934, being the 400th anniversary of the founding of the Jesuit Order at Paris, August 15, 1534.

JAMES BROWN SCOTT.

CONTENTS

CONTENTS

CONTENTS

CONTENTS

THE LAW OF NATIONS

Its Application and Philosophy

La séptima Conferencia Internacional Americana,
RESUELVE:

Recomendar la colocación en la sede central de la Unión Panamericana de Wáshington, del busto del teólogo español Francisco de Vitoria en homenaje a quien en el siglo XVI, y desde la cátedra de Salamanca, echó las bases del Derecho Internacional moderno. (Aprobada el 23 de diciembre de 1933)

[ENGLISH TRANSLATION]

The Seventh International Conference of American States,
RESOLVES:

To recommend that a bust of the Spanish theologian, Francisco de Vitoria, be placed in the headquarters of the Pan American Union, in Washington, as a tribute to the professor of Salamanca who, in the sixteenth century established the foundations of modern international law. (Approved December 23, 1933)

CHAPTER I

FRANCISCO DE VITORIA'S LAW OF NATIONS

The disquisitions, usually termed readings, of Francisco de Vitoria[1] which treat at length of the *Jus gentium*—or, in our modern parlance, international law—are two in number. The first, frequently referred to as *De Indis,* is concerned with that law as it could and should be applied to "the Indians lately discovered," under normal conditions, while the second deals with the law to be applied under abnormal conditions, that is to say, in time of war and is entitled, *De Indis, Siue de Iure Belli Hispanorum in Barbaros.*

The reading *De Indis* has three sections, dealing with what may be called the law of peace. The first section, after a general introduction, discusses the important question of the legal status of the Indians, that is to say, whether they were, as human beings, possessed of the same rights as the Spaniards, however much they might differ from their "discoverers" in intellectual capacity, religion, manners and customs.

The second section deals with what Victoria calls "the illegitimate titles for the reduction of the aborigines of the New World into the power of the Spaniards." There are seven of these titles, but for the moment we need mention but two, that is to say, the claim to lordship over the world advanced in behalf of the Emperor, who, be it said, was none other than Charles I, King of Spain, and who as Charles V, Holy Roman Emperor, was alleged to be sovereign of the world; and the claim put forth in behalf of the Pope to both temporal and spiritual sovereignty over the world and therefore over the Americas and the Americans.

1 When the full name is used, the Spanish form, Francisco de Vitoria is employed. But when the last name only is given the Latinized (and Englished) form, Victoria, has been adopted as being more familiar to the English-speaking world.

The third section deals with what Victoria calls "lawful and adequate" titles, the meaning of which phrase is that, supposing the facts to be as the Spaniards stated them, they might have the right, under these titles, to take possession of and exercise their sovereignty over the Indians. It is to be observed that the appositeness of the titles in question depends on the facts as such.

FIRST SECTION OF THE FIRST READING

In considering the first section, it is only necessary, for the present purpose, to mention with a careful comment some of the questions which Victoria raises, and which, if decided against the Indians would deprive their "princes and overlords" of that exclusive jurisdiction in their respective lands, of which Catholic sovereigns were rightfully possessed in their own lands.

After disposing of certain preliminary matters, Victoria raises the question whether the Indian aborigines before the arrival of the Spaniards "were true owners in both public and private law"; and whether there were among them any "true princes and overlords."[2] Victoria's answer is in the affirmative. They were owners under public law; they were owners under their private law; there were princes among them, and they therefore lived under the governments of princes and overlords, not governments such as that of Spain, but governments which met

[2] *De Indis et de Iure Belli,* p. 120. The English translation of the two Readings *On the Indians* and *On the Law of War* used for the present analysis is that by John Pawley Bate as published in *De Indis et de Iure Belli Relectiones; Being Parts of Relectiones Theologicae XII,* with an introduction by Ernest Nys (The Classics of International Law, published by the Carnegie Institution of Washington, 1917). The edition in question also contains a reproduction of the Latin text, preceded by an exhaustive editorial commentary and a carefully revised and extended text prepared by Herbert Francis Wright, both of which are of much interest and value, especially in connection with Victoria's references. For the sake of brevity, this edition of Victoria's two readings will be referred to in subsequent footnotes simply as *De Indis* or as *De Iure Belli,* depending on the which of the two Readings is cited.

For a scholarly reproduction of the first and second editions of Victoria's *Relectiones* (Lyons, 1557, and Salamanca, 1565) as well as of the manuscripts of the *Relectiones* as taken down by Victoria's students, see the first volume of the *Relectiones Teológicas del Maestro Fray Francisco de Vitoria,* edited by P. Mtro. Fr. Luis G. Alonso Getino (Madrid, 1933). A second volume has just been issued containing a critical edition of several Readings of Victoria together with an admirable Spanish translation.

adequately enough the requirements of international law as understood and expounded by the great Dominican.

The question of religion looms large with Victoria, as it did with Europeans of that day. Before the Reformation, which happened in Victoria's time, there were two great divisions: Christendom on the one hand, made up of the European states; and non-Christians, including the rest of the world. Victoria's view on this matter, as on so many others, was one which would be commended even in a writer of the present day, the belief "that it is not justifiable to take anything that they possess from either Saracens or Jews or other unbelievers as such, that is, because they are unbelievers; but the act would be theft or robbery no less than if it were done to Christians." [3] But there are unbelievers and there are non-believers; and finally there is the brand of Christians known as heretics, that is to say, persons once of the true faith, but who have left it. The classical definition of a heretic is a person who, being a Christian, renounces the Catholic faith, or does not subscribe to the full doctrine; in other words, members of the various Protestant groups were not to be looked upon as unbelievers, as were the Indians, but rather as erring children. They were subject to punishment because they had withdrawn from communion with the Church, and the temporal penalty, the one with which we are concerned, was likely to be a serious one, as it involved, or might involve, the loss of property and the property rights which they had possessed when members of the Church, and which were forfeited or might be forfeited by the law of the Church against heretics. The Indians were not heretics, because they had not been Christians. If they became Christians, then the rule would apply to Indian converts who withdrew from the Church as it did to converts of other races in the same condition. However, it must be said that Victoria, a broad-minded, high-minded and charitable person, refused to hold too closely to these views, saying that "if some heretic were in Germany, a Catholic could lawfully buy from him. For it would be oppressive if a Catholic could not buy land from a heretic or sell land to him in a Lutheran state;

[3] *De Indis,* p. 123.

yet it would be necessary to say this, if a heretic were utterly disabled from ownership in the forum of conscience."[4]

To deal further with the subject would be to dwell upon religious doctrine, whereas our purpose is with the Indians as non-believers and the law of nations. Neither as Indians nor as unbelievers were they to "be barred from being true owners, alike in public and in private law, by reason of the sin of unbelief or any other mortal sin, nor does such sin entitle Christians to seize their goods and lands, as Cajetan proves at some length and neatly (*Secunda Secundae,* qu. 66, art. 8)."[5]

This doctrine of Victoria seems to be as sound in logic as it is sound in morality and, therefore, sound in law. It is a doctrine tried and proved by time, with the result that it is embodied in the law of today. This being the case, we can but agree with the closing lines of Victoria's first section, that "the conclusion stands sure, that the aborigines in question were true owners, before the Spaniards came among them, both from the public and the private point of view."

SECOND SECTION

The second part of the first reading consists, as has been stated, of two sections: the first dealing with "the titles which might be alleged, but which are not adequate or legitimate," and the second with the "legitimate titles under which the aborigines could have come under the sway of the Spaniards."[6]

The first illegitimate title whereby the Indians might be alleged to have come under the sway of the Spaniards, is that the Holy Roman Emperor as such, "is lord of the whole world and therefore of these barbarians also."[7] If it be granted that the Emperor was lord of the earth, it would follow that he was likewise overlord of Spain and he could therefore authorize the Spaniards to take possession of the land of the barbarians, since the Americans also would lie within his world-wide domain. But Victoria denounced this contention as baseless, denying its

[4] *De Indis,* p. 125.
[5] *Ibid.*
[6] *Ibid.,* p. 129.
[7] *Ibid.,* p. 130.

fundamental premise, and asserting roundly that "the Emperor is not the lord of the whole earth."

There were, however, other arguments advanced in behalf of this title which he felt should be specifically dealt with. It was also claimed, for example, that there was "one Emperor over the world by express grant of Christ," and that "just as He left on earth one vicar in matters spiritual, so also in matters temporal, and in the latter case it is the Emperor," which statement Victoria brands as "quite inadmissible." [8] Again there was the argument that, even if the Emperor was not the lord of all the world, the Kingdom of Spain might nevertheless be subject to the Emperor, since the Holy Roman Emperor insisted that the states of Europe were so subject, including Spain—an argument which Victoria denied for Spain and also for France, and which England denied for itself.

Had the state of affairs thus denied actually existed, the Christian states of Europe would have been united in a loose confederation under the headship of the Emperor. The refusal to accept this unity, even in a loose form, has resulted in the nations of Europe being independent of each other, and in the development of a nationalism which still keeps them apart.

But, to return to the Indians, Victoria ends his discussion of the first illegitimate title by denying that the Emperor "could seize the provinces of the Indian aborigines" even if he "were the lord of the world." [9] The reason by which Victoria justifies this denial is that "even those who attribute lordship over the world to the Emperor do not claim that he is lord in ownership, but only in jurisdiction," which right, if admitted, does not "warrant him in converting provinces to his own use or in giving towns or even estates away at his pleasure"; therefore, Victoria concludes "that the Spaniards can not justify on this ground their seizure of the provinces in question."

This is strong language from a subject of Spain, for it should be remembered that the Emperor, whose title to overlordship Victoria somewhat curtly, if not brutally, denied, was himself

[8] *Ibid.*, p. 132.
[9] *Ibid.*, p. 134.

the King of Spain by direct inheritance through Ferdinand and Isabella; but Victoria was one of the few elect who could see wrong, even in his own country, and who was possessed of the courage to state and denounce it boldly and in unmistakable terms, when the so-called prudent would have maintained a discreet silence. Had he been merely discreet instead of courageous, had he kept silence where others feared to speak, he would not be looked upon today as the founder of the modern law of nations.

Let us now take up the second part of the claim, based upon another alleged title, namely, that "the Pope is temporal monarch, too, over all the world and that he could consequently make the Kings of Spain sovereign over the aborigines in question, and that so it has been done."[10]

In behalf of this contention, the authority of jurists could be invoked—jurists who held that the Pope "has full jurisdiction in temporal matters over the whole earth" and who even added "that the power of all secular princes comes to them from the Pope." If this were so, then the Pope could, because of his temporal overlordship "make the Kings of Spain rulers over the Indian aborigines," or he could require direct recognition of his temporal power by the Indians, and a refusal on their part to admit his power "would warrant him in making war on them and in putting rulers over them." Now both of these things had been done, for had not "the Supreme Pontiff granted the provinces in question to the Kings of Spain," and had not the aborigines been "notified that the Pope is the vicar of God and His vicegerent on earth" and that they should, therefore "recognize him as their superior?" And finally, it was specifically claimed that "their refusal furnishes a good ground for making war on them and seizing their lands."[11] To each of these contentions Victoria made an unequivocal denial. "The Pope"—he said—"is not civil or temporal lord of the whole world in the proper sense of the words 'lordship' and 'civil power.'" The distinguished Spanish theologian Torquemada, he pointed out, had

[10] *De Indis*, p. 134.
[11] *Ibid.*, p. 135.

already reached this conclusion, and the distinguished canonist, who became Pope under the title of Innocent III, admitted that the Pope had no "temporal power over the Kingdom of France." Therefore, to adopt the logic of the schoolman, if the Pope did not have civil or temporal power over Spain or France, he could not be lord of the whole world, for Spain and France were then, and still are, integral parts of the world, and if Christ, the Lord, did not have temporal power over the whole world, as St. Thomas Aquinas maintained, it would have to be accepted that the Pope, being Christ's vicar, could not have it, as his power was not original, but derivative. Indeed, Victoria adds that the Pope himself never claimed this supremacy with which the advocates of temporal power had vested him.

Victoria might have rested his case here, but he wanted apparently to settle the matter once and for all, in order to be able to test the rights of the Spaniards to the Western World, freed from the exaggerated claims of the Emperor and of the Pope, set forth by their sycophants, in the matter of temporal power—and indeed in the matter of both spiritual and temporal power, as claimed by the advocates of the Pope—a claim which, if carried to the breaking point, would deprive the Pope of one, as well as the other. Therefore, "even assuming that the Supreme Pontiff had this secular power over the whole world"—which Victoria did not concede—"he could not give it to secular princes." Why? Because, if the assumption were correct, the power would be in the office of the Pope, but not in his person, and consequently not at his disposition to grant to this prince or that. It would be, as Victoria says, "annexed to the Papacy" and the Pope could not "sever it from the office of Supreme Pontiff or deprive his successor of that power, for the succeeding Supreme Pontiff can not be less than his predecessor; and, if some one Pontiff had made a gift of this power, either the grant would be null or the succeeding Pontiff could cancel it." [12]

This does not mean that the Pope, possessed of spiritual attributes, could not exercise temporal power, but it does mean that he could do it only "so far as it is in subservience to matters

[12] *Ibid.*, p. 136.

spiritual," that is, as Victoria adds, "as far as is necessary for the administration of spiritual affairs." This is the doctrine of the indirect power of the Pope, later to be expressed so perfectly, as we shall see, by the Cardinal—now Saint and Doctor—Robert Bellarmine.[12a] What was the authority for this view, which has been of vast importance in the history not merely of the Papacy but of the Christian world in general? The answer, which must be given in the words of Victoria, indicates that authority—indeed, the best of authority—was at hand. "This is also the view of Torquemada," he declares, "and of all the doctors."

In a united Christendom, the temporal power in aid of the spiritual was admitted, grudgingly perhaps, by temporal sovereigns, and a logical consequence was that "when princes are at variance with one another about some right of sovereignty and are rushing into war, he [the Pope] can act as judge and inquire into the claims of the parties and deliver judgment, a judgment which the princes are bound to respect, lest those numerous spiritual evils should befall which are the inevitable results of a war between Christian princes." [13]

This exercise of temporal power was possible only in a united Christendom, where it might, and at times did, render a valuable service to faithful princes and peoples of the Catholic community. But the power in question was, in point of fact, infrequently asserted and applied, not because the Pope lacked authority, but "for fear of scandal," as Victoria informs us, because it was the desire of the Supreme Pontiff "to prevent the princes from thinking his motive is ambition or because he is afraid of a revolt from the Apostolic See on the part of the princes." The same view was later set forth by Suárez in his disquisition on war.[14] It may be said in passing that it would have been better for the world if the Pope had been free to act as arbiter oftener than

[12a] See *infra,* chap. x.

[13] *De Indis,* p. 137.

[14] *De bello,* being Disputation 13 of the tractate *De charitate* in Suárez' work *De triplici virtute theologica.* In this Disputation the view of Suarez on the matter under consideration is succinctly stated in a single sentence: "But sometimes the Pope does not interpose his authority, lest perchance greater evils result."—Sec. II. 5. For an analysis of this disputation, see *infra,* chap. xii.

he did, and I venture to say—Protestant though I be—that it would make greatly for the peace of the world if today the Pope, sovereign of the little state of the Vatican, should be called upon as arbiter in disputes between nations, irrespective of religion, inasmuch as he is the only sovereign in the world who can not be taxed with territorial ambition.

What, then, is the conclusion of Victoria on this phase of the matter? We shall state it in his own language, to show the logic of the schoolman and how he used it on behalf of human freedom, as well as to uphold the doctrines of his Church. Here is the premise and here is the conclusion, not acceptable then perhaps, but acceptable now, as is so often the case with Victoria's convictions. The whole matter, of immense importance to the world of his day, and of as great, if not greater, importance in the days to come, is expressed in four simple sentences:

1. The Pope has no temporal power over the Indian aborigines or over other unbelievers.
2. For he has no temporal power save such as subserves spiritual matters.
3. But he has no spiritual power over them (I. *Corinth.* ch. 5, v. 12).
4. Therefore he has no temporal power either.

To this unanswerable syllogism, there is a corollary, equally unanswerable, and equally on behalf of religious and civil liberty, "that even if the barbarians refuse to recognize any lordship of the Pope, that furnishes no ground for making war on them and seizing their property." The reason? "Because he has no such lordship."[15]

So much for the first two titles, those based on the powers accredited by some to the Emperor and the Pope. Concerning the third title, that of discovery, Victoria says, "no other title was originally set up, and it was in virtue of this title alone that Columbus . . . first set sail. And"—Victoria continues—"this seems to be an adequate title because those regions which are deserted become, by the law of nations and the natural law, the property of the first occupant,"[16] citing the Justinian *Institutes*

[15] *De Indis,* p. 137.
[16] *Ibid.,* pp. 138-9.

(2. 1. 12) in this behalf. Therefore, in the opinion of those supporting this view, "as the Spaniards were the first to discover and occupy the provinces in question, they are in lawful possession thereof, just as if they had discovered some lonely and thitherto uninhabited region."[17] But it is to be observed from the very language of Victoria, that the doctrine applies to a region uninhabited and therefore unoccupied and without ownership. The question immediately presents itself: Was America inhabited in fact, uninhabited in law? It is this point which shows Victoria to be as versed in law as he was in theology, and a realist at the same time, with whom morality and Christian charity counted greatly: "Not much, however, need be said about this third title of ours, because, as proved above, the barbarians were true owners, both from the public and from the private standpoint."[18] What, then, becomes of this discovery, and what was Victoria's law of nations on this point? "Now the rule of the law of nations is that what belongs to nobody is granted to the first occupant, as is expressly laid down in the aforementioned passage of the *Institutes*. And so, as the object in question was not without an owner, it does not fall under the title which we are discussing."[19] And his conclusion is that this title, in and by itself, "gives no support to a seizure of the aborigines any more than if it had been they who had discovered us."[20]

The fourth and subsequent illegitimate titles deal with the spiritual phases of the subject, and are even more interesting and more important, than the first two illegitimate titles, because in connection with these further titles the consequences of the premises which Victoria has already stated, are made evident in terms of a continent and, indeed, are shown to be applicable to the entire world.

The fourth illegitimate title is the refusal of the barbarians "to accept the faith of Christ, although it is set before them and

[17] *De Indis*, p. 139.
[18] *Ibid.*
[19] *Ibid.*
[20] *Ibid.*

although they have been adjured and advised to accept it."[21] In answer to this statement of the claim, Victoria replies with a proposition to the effect that "before the barbarians heard anything about Christianity, they did not commit the sin of unbelief by not believing in Christ."[22] A second proposition carries the argument still further. "The Indians in question are not bound, directly the Christian faith is announced to them, to believe it, in such a way that they commit mortal sin by not believing it."[23] In a word, the mere announcement of the faith, "without miracle or any other proof or persuasion" is not likely to make converts or "to induce belief." The fault in such circumstances would lie, not with the Indians, but with the method of presentation. From this proposition, therefore, Victoria draws a corollary: "If the faith be presented to the Indians in the way named only and they do not receive it, the Spaniards can not make this a reason for waging war on them or for proceeding against them under the law of war."[24] The reason? "Because they are innocent in this respect and have done no wrong to the Spaniards."[25]

As this is the crux of the question, as it is a denial of the right of the Spaniards to wage war, Victoria's views in the matter should be stated in his own words, based upon two great authorities and Saints of the Church, and confirmed by one whose authority was very great at the time of the discovery of America. First, he invokes the authority of St. Thomas, who "lays it down (*Secunda Secundae,* qu. 40, art. I), [that] for a just war 'there must be a just cause, namely, they who are attacked for some fault must deserve the attack.' "[26] Next, he appeals to St. Augustine, the great and unquestioned authority of all Christians, who says *(Liber 83 Quaestionum):* "It is involved in the definition of a just war that some wrong is being avenged, as where a people or state is to be punished for neglect to exact amends

21 *Ibid.*

22 *Ibid.,* p. 140.

23 *Ibid.,* pp. 142-3.

24 *Ibid.,* p. 143.

25 *Ibid.*

26 *Ibid.*

from its citizens for their wrongdoing or to restore what has been wrongfully taken away."[27] Upon these two authorities, Victoria concludes: "Where, then, no wrong has previously been committeed by the Indians, there is no cause of just war." This is, indeed, much and sufficient, but it is not all, for "this is"—Victoria continues—"the received opinion of all the doctors, not only of the theologians, but also of the jurists." Cajetan, likewise, a theologian and a great authority of his day, "lays it down clearly (*Secunda Secundae,* qu. 66, art. 8)," and Victoria adds, "and I know of no doctor whose opinion is to the contrary."[28]

Victoria admits that the Indians should listen to the Christian missionaries, and that the Christian faith, put before the aborigines, not perfunctorily, but intelligently and zealously, accompanied by an upright life, should be accepted by the aborigines "under penalty of mortal sin;" but, speaking in his own person and on his own authority, which in these matters certainly was equal to any which he could invoke, he remarks: "It is not sufficiently clear to me that the Christian faith has yet been so put before the aborigines and announced to them that they are bound to believe it or commit fresh sin." Continuing to speak in the first person, and he knew whereof he spoke, Victoria observes somewhat bluntly: "I hear of no miracles or signs or religious patterns of life; nay, on the other hand, I hear of many scandals and cruel crimes and acts of impiety."

But suppose that the Christian faith had been "announced to the Indians with adequate demonstration" and that they had "refused to receive it." Even this, the noble Spaniard concludes, "is not a reason which justifies making war on them and depriving them of their property." Such a statement was bound to encounter opposition in his day—a day when tolerance had as yet poured but little oil on the stormy waters of religious controversy. Knowing this, Victoria decided to meet in advance the arguments of the fanatical, the bigoted and those who sought to justify wrong actions by religious casuistries. For this purpose he chose an unanswerable authority, that of St. Thomas (*Secunda*

[27] *De Indis,* p. 143.

[28] *Ibid.,* p. 144.

Secundae, qu. 10, art. 8), "where he says that unbelievers who have never received the faith, like Gentiles and Jews, are in no wise to be compelled to do so."[29] And Victoria adds, by way of confirmation, although the word St. Thomas, now, as then, was sufficient: "This is the received conclusion of the doctors alike in the canon law and the civil law."[30] What was the proof which supported this conclusion? The "fact that belief is an operation of the will." Now it had been pointed out by no less a philosopher than Aristotle that fear and the free exercise of the will were incompatible. Therefore the forceful imposition of the faith was not likely to produce a belief which would be, to repeat the language of Victoria, "an operation of the will."

It would seem that there was nothing further to be said by Victoria, but wishing to establish his contention so clearly, that religious warfare, that terrible scourge, could not be carried from the Old to the New World, he added: "Our proposition receives further proof from the use and custom of the Church. For never have Christian Emperors, who had as advisors the most holy and wise Pontiffs, made war on unbelievers for their refusal to accept the Christian religion."

This is, however, a statement of fact, and the facts of history are ever open to dispute by doubting and argumentative Thomases. Victoria ends the possibility of argument of that kind by a statement—which no enlightened person might reasonably dispute—that "war is no argument for the truth of the Christian faith," or, indeed, we should like to add in our own behalf, for anything else. Having thus, as it were, silenced his opponents, Victoria disposes once and for all of the fourth title by declaring roundly that "the Indians can not be induced by war to believe, but rather to feign belief and reception of the Christian faith, which is monstrous and a sacrilege."

Now the fifth illegitimate title "seriously put forward" is "the sins of these Indian aborigines," and the sins in question are

---

[29] *Ibid.,* pp. 144-5.

[30] *Ibid.,* p. 145.

those which are considered as "against the law of nature." [31] Without entering into the argument on this point, for which Victoria, in his fair-minded way, quoted authority, we may content ourselves here by noting his answer to the claim put forth under this title—an answer in which he speaks again in the first person: "I, however, assert the following proposition: Christian princes can not, even by the authorization of the Pope, restrain the Indians from sins against the law of nature or punish them because of those sins." [32] Proofs in plenty are marshalled to support this proposition, but for present purposes two will suffice. "My first proof," affirms Victoria, "is that the writers in question build on a false hypothesis, namely, that the Pope has jurisdiction over the Indian aborigines." Of course, if this be denied, they are, as we would say, out of court—and Victoria had already denied, with overwhelming proofs, this "false hypothesis." A further proof, scattering the "writers," so to speak, in full flight, was that non-Christians can not "be subjected to the judgment of the Pope, for the Pope has no other right to condemn or punish them than as vicar of Christ. But, the writers in question admit . . . that they can not be punished because they do not receive Christ. Therefore not because they do not receive the judgment of the Pope, for the latter presupposes the former." [33]

The sixth illegitimate title is that of "voluntary choice," and in support of this claim it was stated that the King of Spain had sent the Spaniards to the New World for the good of the aborigines. Indeed, it would seem that the latter were admonished by the newcomers "to receive and accept" the Spanish monarch "as lord and king; and the aborigines replied that they were content to do so." [34]

Supposing that they did, should this be taken as a true renunciation of sovereignty on the part of the Indians—a renunciation which passed title over them and their lands to the

[31] *De Indis,* p. 145.
[32] *Ibid.,* p. 146.
[33] *Ibid.,* p. 147.
[34] *Ibid.,* p. 148.

Spaniards? Again Victoria replies in the first person, "I, however, assert the proposition that this title, too, is insufficient." Why? Victoria's argument on this point, asserting that government is by the consent of the governed, is so convincing, that it should be given in his own words and in entirety; and in order that each objection to the claim may stand out, his sentences are numbered and stated as paragraphs:

1. This appears, in the first place, because fear and ignorance, which vitiate every choice, ought to be absent.

2. But they (fear and ignorance) were markedly operative in the cases of choice and acceptance under consideration for the Indians did not know what they were doing; nay, they may not have understood what the Spaniards were seeking.

3. Further we find the Spaniards seeking it in armed array from an unwarlike and timid crowd.

4. Further, inasmuch as the aborigines, as said above, had real lords and princes, the populace could not procure new lords without other reasonable cause, this being to the hurt of their former lords.

5. Further, on the other hand, these lords themselves could not appoint a new prince without the assent of the populace.

And now for Victoria's logical conclusion:

6. Seeing, then, that in such cases of choice and acceptance as these there are not present all the requisite elements of a valid choice, the title under review is utterly inadequate and unlawful for seizing and retaining the provinces in question.[35]

There was a seventh ill-established claim—the last of the "false and inadequate titles" advanced by the Spaniards in order "to seize the lands of the Indians,"[36] a title set forth by the advocates of the Spanish cause, as being "by special grant from God." Victoria was unaffected by this title, indeed, it seemed to annoy him: "For some (I know not who) assert that the Lord by His especial judgment condemned all the barbarians in question to perdition because of their abominations and delivered them into the hands of the Spaniards, just as of old He delivered the Canaanites into the hands of the Jews."[37] His

[35] *Ibid.*, p. 148.
[36] *Ibid.*, p. 149.
[37] *Ibid.*, p. 148.

answer, doubtless irritating to his opponents, is conclusive: "I am loath to dispute hereon at any length, for it would be hazardous to give credence to one who asserts a prophecy against the common law and against the rules of Scripture, unless his doctrine were confirmed by miracles." And the miracles were wanting, as Victoria asserts in a short, but bitter passage: "No such are adduced by prophets of this type." [38] Moreover, even if the Lord had determined to bring the barbarians to perdition, "it would not follow"—in Victoria's opinion—"that he who wrought their ruin would be blameless." With a final outburst which does him infinite credit, he exclaims, "And, would that, apart from the sin of unbelief, there might be no greater sins in morals among certain Christians than there are among those barbarians!"

Concerning these illegitimate titles, we may say with Victoria, "let this suffice." [39]

THIRD SECTION

If this were the ending of the Reading *On the Indians Recently Discovered,* it might be looked upon as negative, in that Victoria sets up, as it were, a man of straw, only to annihilate him. But in the third section of the first reading, Victoria speaks affirmatively, stating what he believes to be the rights and duties alike of Spaniards and Europeans on the one hand, and the Indians on the other, admitting the claim of the Spaniards only when the barbarians had violated a right, which it would have been wrong on the part of the Spaniards and the French to have violated under the same conditions. These rights and duties are the very warp and woof of the modern law of nations, applicable alike to the barbarians and to the Spaniards, and to all other peoples whether Christians or not.

The first lawful and adequate title "whereby the Indians might have come under the sway of the Spaniards" is, in the conception and language of Victoria, "that of natural society and fellowship," [40] the mere statement of this title implying that

[38] *De Indis,* p. 148.
[39] *Ibid.,* p. 149.
[40] *Ibid.,* p. 151.

what was natural to the Spaniards was natural to the Indians, and that the rights and duties, inherent in society and fellowship, applied to both peoples, as we shall see, upon equal terms.

In the previous sections, Victoria has been dealing with the abnormal; from now on he deals with what may be considered the normal, and by normal we mean the condition of peace under the law of peaceful intercourse which, if violated, may involve the use of force. The third section, therefore, is a statement of the law of peace, and of the right to redress the wrongs committed under that law. The second reading covers the actual redress of such wrongs by the use of force on that large scale which is called war, so that we have in the last section of the first reading and in the second reading, what the people of our day are inclined to consider the modern law of nations, in peace, and in war.

As the one fundamental conception of the law of nations is society and fellowship within a group or state, it is natural that Victoria should begin with this phase of the subject, and that he should consider the violation of the rights and duties arising from this society and fellowship to be a violation of the law of nations.

And the first statement of a right under the modern international law is that "the Spaniards have a right to travel into the lands in question and to sojourn there, provided they do no harm to the natives, and the natives may not prevent them." [41]

This, however, is not a special right of the Spaniards in their relations with the Indians. It is a universal rule, Victoria expressly saying that "it would not be lawful for the French to prevent the Spanish from traveling or even from living in France, or vice versa, provided this in no way enured to their hurt and the visitors did no injury." Having thus universalized the rule by showing that it applied equally and impartially in the Old World as well as the New, he brought the rule to bear upon the matter in hand by adding that it would be unlawful for the Indians to violate it.

---

41 *Ibid.*, p. 151.

Here we have the recognition on the part of Victoria that the Indians were entitled to the same rights that the French and the Spaniards enjoyed, and that the violation of a right by the French or the Spaniards is exactly the same, in fact and in law, as the violation by the Indians of a right of the Spanish, the French, or the peoples of any and every civilized community.

Now for the particular right in question—that of travel and sojourn. Upon what is this right of the Spaniards based, and also the like right of the Indians? Upon none other than the law of nations *(jus gentium)*. And what is this law? It "either is natural law or is derived from natural law"; and what is the authority for this statement? The *Institutes* (I. 2. 1) of Justinian: "What natural reason has established among all nations is called the *jus gentium." (Quod naturalis ratio inter omnes gentes constituit, vocatur ius gentium.)*

Upon consulting the *Institutes* it will be observed that Victoria has modified the statement in order to meet his purpose. The original wording is: *"Quod vero naturalis ratio inter omnes homines constituit, id apud omnes populos peraeque custoditur vocaturque ius gentium, quasi quo iure omnes gentes utuntur."*

His purpose undoubtedly was to make the *jus gentium* apply to nations, instead of merely to individuals, as appears not only from the shifting of terms and the words omitted but also from the statement immediately following, in the nature of a corollary, where the word *nationes* is used, indicating that Victoria regarded *gentes* to be synonymous with *nationes,* that is, nations; by so doing, he made an adequate definition of the law of nations, and by the sense in which he applied it, of our modern law of nations.[42] What, then, is this corollary? "For, congruently herewith, it is reckoned among all nations inhumane to treat visitors and foreigners badly without some special cause,

---

[42] *Vide* Professor Ernest Nys in his admirable Introduction to the edition of *De Indis et de Iure Belli Relectiones* above cited, pp. 42-3. *Vide* also J. Barthélemy in *Les Fondateurs du Droit International* (Paris, 1904), p. 7; Herbert Francis Wright, *Francisci de Victoria, De Iure Belli Relectio* (Washington, 1916), pp. 15-16; and the statement by the distinguished Cuban statesman, publicist, and judge of the Permanent Court of International Justice, Antonio Sánchez de Bustamante y Sirvén, in his *Derecho Internacional Público* (Habana, 1933), p. 21.

while, on the other hand, it is humane and correct to treat visitors well." But Victoria, although a reformer, was nevertheless a reasonable man. "The case would be different, he said, "if the foreigners were to misbehave when visiting other nations." [43]

Here we have a definition of the law of nations, which is as a background for the balance of this reading, and for the reading on war.

Now the right of visiting other lands is, as we have seen, a right under the law of nations, and so, common to all. But Victoria looked upon that law as either identical with or derived from natural law, and by natural law all things were originally held in common, each individual having an equal but undivided right therein. And among the original common rights was that of travel. In the very next paragraph he says, "it was permissible from the beginning of the world (when everything was in common) for any one to set forth and travel wheresoever he would."

It might be maintained, however, that all rights in common ceased to exist when property was divided. Not so, in the opinion of Victoria, for he says expressly that the right in question survived, it being "never the intention of peoples to destroy by that division the reciprocity and common user which prevailed among men." [44]

These would seem to be sufficient proofs of the validity of the first lawful title invoked by Victoria—that of natural society and fellowship—but the matter was so important that he wished to make assurance doubly sure by further proofs. Therefore he quoted *Ecclesiasticus* (ch. 15), "Every animal loveth its kind," from which he very properly concludes that "friendship among men exists by natural law and it is against nature to shun the society of harmless folk." [45]

Hitherto, Victoria has been speaking of *terra firma*, but to reach a new world, the Spaniards had to cross vast waters and enter rivers and harbors. These waterways, he felt, should like-

[43] *De Indis,* p. 151.
[44] *Ibid.,* p. 151.
[45] *Ibid.,* p. 152.

wise be free and common to all under an adequate system of international law, just as they were originally under the law natural. Therefore he adds, "by natural law running water and the sea are common to all, so are rivers and harbors, and by the law of nations ships from all parts may be moored there." What is the authority for this? Again the *Institutes* (2. 1. 1 *et seq.*) of Justinian. And because the waterways in question are common to all, they are what is called public things, so that it is not lawful "to keep any one from them." Here we have the freedom of the seas, one of the great fundamental principles with the establishment of which in modern times Grotius is credited, but which he actually took from the third section of Victoria's first reading, as may be seen by anyone who cares to read the first chapter of Grotius tractate on the *Freedom of the Seas.* Here Grotius in the opening paragraph, and without mentioning Victoria, lays down the latter's doctrine as the very foundation of his argument. If this were all it might be argued that Grotius had arrived at these conclusions without the aid of the theologian of Salamanca. But in a later part of the same chapter he expressly mentions Victoria, referring specifically to the passage under consideration.[46]

There was still another proof at hand, familiar to us under the guise of the favored nation clause, the simple and unadorned significance of which is that one nation claims from a sister nation the same treatment and privileges as those accorded to another nation or nations. Now the barbarians admitted other barbarians to their shores. Therefore it followed, upon these premises, that "the aborigines would be doing a wrong to the Spaniards, if they were to keep them from their territories."

Thus it appears that from these few paragraphs, the right is established for all peoples to travel upon the high seas, common to all, and to visit and to settle in territories of other peoples,

---

[46] Grotius's citation is actually of Section II of the *De Indis,* but there can be no doubt that this was a mere slip and that his reference is to the *third* section, for he speaks specifically of Victoria's discussion of the right of "traveling or sojourning," a subject which is treated, as we have just seen, in Section III. *Vide The Freedom of the Seas,* translation by Ralph van Deman Magoffin, issued with the Latin text by the Carnegie Endowment for International Peace (New York, 1916), pp. 7 and 9.

provided, to paraphrase Victoria, that they do not "misbehave" when visiting foreign parts. Now, Victoria regarded these rights as so fundamental—and well he might—that he proceeds to make this doubly, or indeed trebly, sure, by saying that "if it were not lawful for the Spaniards to travel among them"—meaning the Indians—"this would be either by natural law or by divine law or by human law. Now, it is certainly lawful by natural and by divine law." [47] This he does not argue, because it is unarguable, but what of human law, that is to say, law which is not natural and divine; law which differs from that which is natural and divine, because, unlike these two categories, it is made by human beings? Let us suppose that there was some "human law which without any cause took away rights conferred by natural and divine law." What would be the result? It would be, Victoria answers, "inhumane and unreasonable and consequently would not have the force of law."

Here, then, we have the three great categories of law embodying every rule and precept of human conduct; natural and divine law, and human law in so far as it does not conflict with natural or divine law.

We may grant that Victoria's arguments as a man of law are unanswerable, but as a theologian and a moralist he was not content to rest his case on law alone. Therefore he now invokes first the New Testament and then St. Augustine to show that, since "the Spaniards are the neighbors of the barbarians . . . they are bound to love their neighbors as themselves," and therefore, "they may not keep them away from their country without cause." But who are our neighbors? The answer is from St. Augustine's *De Doctrina Christiana:* "When it is said 'Love thy neighbor,' it is clear that every man is our neighbor." The meaning of this is that if all human beings are neighbors, all human beings have the right, which Victoria has set forth to demonstrate, to visit and settle among any and all peoples of the known world.

This is Victoria's first proposition, which recognizes the right to travel in foreign lands and to sojourn there. In his second

[47] *De Indis,* p. 152.

proposition he amplifies this right by declaring that "the Spaniards may lawfully carry on trade among the native Indians, so long as they do no harm to their country, as, for instance, by importing thither wares which the natives lack and by exporting thence either gold or silver or other wares of which the natives have abundance." [48]

The right, however, is here, as elsewhere, equal, Victoria immediately adding: "Neither may the native princes hinder their subjects from carrying on trade with the Spanish; nor, on the other hand, may the princes of Spain prevent commerce with the natives."

Here we have the threefold right of visiting, sojourning in and trading with foreign countries, with the necessary right of using the high seas, common to all, as well as rivers and harbors.

Of course, although Victoria uses as illustrations gold and silver, in which his countrymen were particularly interested, he was careful to add "other wares," so that the right to trade is as unlimited as it is universal. If further proof be needed to establish these rights, it is the proverb which Victoria quotes, "Thou shalt not do to another what thou wouldest not wish done to thyself." [49]

It is clear from what Victoria has said, that he treats Christians and non-Christians, Europeans and non-Europeans, upon a like footing, but the matter is so important, that he should speak for himself without the intervention of a third person. "And, in sum," he says "it is certain that the aborigines can no more keep off the Spaniards from trade than Christians can keep off other Christians. Now, it is clear that if the Spaniards kept off the French from trade with the Spaniards, and this not for the good of Spain, but in order to prevent the French from sharing in some advantage, that practice would offend against righteousness and charity."

It is evident that Spain and France are stock examples for Victoria, the reason being that those are the two countries of the world with which he was most familiar. A born subject

[48] *De Indis,* p. 152.
[49] *Ibid.,* p. 153.

of Spain, he spent some eighteen years of his life as student and teacher in Paris, so that France became to him a second country. Therefore, having an affection for both, he apparently considered himself justified in taking liberties with either, and in speaking of Spain he is gracious enough in his examples to allow his own country to be at fault, which is the way to prevent foreign persons and countries from feeling injured.

What is his authority, for Victoria bristles with authorities? As is said in the *Digest* of Justinian (I. 1. 3), "Nature has established a bond of relationship between all men";[50] therefore, "it is contrary to natural law for one man to dissociate himself from another without good reason. 'Man,' says Ovid"—although due diligence has failed to locate the passage—" 'is not a wolf to his fellow man, but a man.' "

We now come to the third proposition, which, with the three paragraphs with which Victoria ends his reading *On the Law of War,* would suffice for the glory of any internationalist, if he had nothing else to his credit.

The first part of this proposition is a further application of the favored nation clause, with which international lawyers are familiar. "If there are among the Indians any things which are treated as common both to citizens and to strangers, the Indians may not prevent the Spaniards from a communication and participation in them." This was the general principle, but general principles are never the worse off for an apt illustration or two. "If, for example"—Victoria therefore continues—"other foreigners are allowed to dig for gold in the land of the community or in rivers, or to fish for pearls in the sea or in a river, the natives can not prevent the Spaniards from doing this, but they have the same right to do it as others have, so long as the citizens and indigenous population are not hurt thereby." In proof of this, he refers to what he has previously said: "For if the Spaniards may travel and trade among them, they may consequently make use of the laws and advantages enjoyed by all foreigners."

It is to be observed that here, as elsewhere, Victoria insists

50 *Ibid.*, p. 153.

upon the limitation or condition that the act of the foreigner shall not be to the injury of the native. "Inasmuch as things that belong to nobody are acquired by the first occupant according to the law of nations," for which Victoria's authority is the *Institutes* (2. 1. 12), it follows, in his opinion, that "if there be in the earth gold or in the sea pearls or in a river anything else which is not appropriated by the law of nations those will vest in the first occupant, just as the fish in the sea do. And, indeed" —Victoria adds without a break—"there are many things in this connection which issue from the law of nations, which, because it has a sufficient derivation from natural law, is clearly capable of conferring rights and creating obligations." [51]

Here we have again natural law as the source of the law of nations, and the law of nations, thus conceived, creates both rights and duties, for the existence of the right clearly necessitates the existence of an obligation to protect its exercise. In a word, with the right there is implied the duty which is its appropriate sanction.

But to continue with Victoria: "even if we grant that it"— meaning the law of nations—"is not always derived from natural law"—we interpolate, what then? Here we are upon the very threshold of the modern law of nations, as well as that of an unending future—"yet there exists clearly enough a consensus of the greater part of the whole world, especially in behalf of the common good of all."

It will be observed that these brief but pregnant passages contain more than the germ of a complete system of international law, because it may be completed. The consensus of all is not necessary, but the greater part of the whole world suffices,—just as Victoria had said that the minority within a state could not bind the state, and that therefore, the majority could,—especially if the consensus is for the common good of all. This is an illustration in advance of the Benthamite formula, the greatest good to the greatest number, and even more than that, the pursuit of individual and collective happiness, a conception with which we of the United States are necessarily familiar, as it stands out in

[51] *De Indis*, p. 153.

our Declaration of Independence, the first public document in which the term "the United States of America" is to be found.

Victoria did not content himself with abstractions. Dealing with them in behalf of the concrete, he sought always to reduce them to concrete terms. He therefore indulges in an illustration, in order to make that concrete which was abstract. "For" —he continues—"if after the early days of the creation of the world or its recovery from the flood the majority of mankind decided that ambassadors should everywhere be reckoned inviolable and that the sea should be common and that prisoners of war should be made slaves"—a reference to the one time rule of the law of nations whereby slavery and servitude were as a means of preserving the lines of captives—"and if this, namely, that strangers should not be driven out, were deemed a desirable principle, it would certainly have the force of law, even though the rest of mankind objected thereto." [52]

Thus we have international law as synonymous with, or largely derived from, the law of nature, and we have a majority of mankind possessing the right to incorporate in the law of nations existing at any time further rules or principles, in order to adapt it to newer conditions, when and as they arise. It was not merely the international law of Victoria's day or of the morrow, but of an incalculable future; not merely the modern, but the newer international law. With this passage we have reached a turning point in the world's history.

Hitherto Victoria has spoken of Spaniards who visited, sojourned and traded with the Indians. However, it might be that children were born to the Spaniards during their residence. What was to be their nationality? "If children of any Spaniard be born there and they wish to acquire citizenship, it seems they can not be barred either from citizenship or from the advantages enjoyed by other citizens," [53]—Victoria says referring to the case where the parents were domiciled in the lands of the Indians. Under what law? "The rule of the law of nations"—Victoria answers—"that he is to be called and is a citizen who is born

[52] *Ibid.*, p. 153.
[53] *Ibid.*

within the state."[54] What is his authority? The *Codex* of Justinian (7. 62. 11). For us, the authority is the Fourteenth Amendment to the Constitution of the United States, that "all persons born or naturalized in the United States, and subject to the jurisdiction thereof, are citizens of the United States and of the State wherein they reside." But let us revert to Victoria, who says that "the confirmation lies in the fact that, as man is a civil animal, whoever is born in any one state is not a citizen of another state," which is as much as to say that Victoria had in mind the doctrine of *jus soli,* the predominating doctrine of the Americas. "Therefore," Victoria continues, "if he were not a citizen of the state referred to, he would not be a citizen of any state, to the prejudice of his rights under both natural law and the law of nations."

This doctrine of Victoria obviates dual, triple or quadruple nationality, or nationality to the nth degree if that were possible to the ingenuity of man, as well as that embarrassing condition known as statelessness. But Victoria does not deal merely with nationality by birth; he contemplates a nationality by what we would call naturalization, saying: "Aye, if there be any persons who wish to acquire a domicile in some state of the Indians, as by marriage or in virtue of any other fact whereby other foreigners are wont to become citizens, they can not be impeded any more than others."

Here again, we have the favored nation clause, as well as an unmistakable implication that rights and duties are correlative: "Consequently they enjoy the privileges of citizens just as others do, provided they also submit to the burdens to which others submit."

What should the Spaniards do upon the violation of their rights by the Indians? If the Indians prevented the Spaniards from enjoying any of the above mentioned rights, which Victoria says they possessed "under the law of nations," the Spaniards should not use force in the first instance, but "reason and persuasion in order to remove scandal . . .; and ought to show" that they intend no harm to the Indians, "not only by word,

[54] *De Indis,* p. 154.

but also by reason, according to the saying, 'It behoveth the prudent to make trial of everything by words first.'" If, however, "the barbarians decline to agree and propose to use force, then," Victoria says, "the Spaniards can defend themselves and do all that consists with their own safety, it being lawful to repel force by force."[55] For if the Indians deny "the Spaniards their rights under the law of nations they do them a wrong," and the conclusion follows: "Therefore, if it be necessary, in order to preserve their right, that they should go to war, they may lawfully do so."

Now just as Victoria had said, in a passage relating to the acceptance of the Christian belief, that the Indians might well be afraid of the Spaniards who were strangers, so here he adds a note of warning to the Spaniards to be careful and hesitant in the use of their rights, saying that "the Spaniards ought to defend themselves, but so far as possible with the least damage to the natives, the war being a purely defensive one."[56] However, if the Spaniards cannot otherwise maintain their rights against the Indians, they may lawfully seize "their cities" and reduce "them to subjection," for does not St. Augustine say "peace and safety are the end and aim of war?"

The second title which Victoria considers as possible is the "propagation of Christianity," as to which we may say what Madame Roland is reported to have said of another and even greater right: "O Liberty! Liberty! how many crimes are committed in thy name!"

From what has previously been said, it might be divined that in Victoria's opinion and, indeed, in that of our day, Christians "have a right to preach and declare the Gospel in barbarian lands."[57] Among his various arguments, as applicable now as then, Victoria declares that if, as he has already proved, "the Spaniards have a right to travel and trade among the Indians, they can teach the truth to those willing to hear them, especially as regards matters pertaining to salvation and happiness, much

---

55 *Ibid.*

56 *Ibid.*, p. 155.

57 *Ibid.*, p. 156.

more than as regards matters pertaining to any human subject of instruction."

The doctrine of the "good neighbor" is also invoked, in language which is as acceptable today as it was then. "They are our neighbors . . . Therefore it concerns Christians to instruct those who are ignorant of these supremely vital matters."

It may be said that this was the duty of a Christian, and therefore a duty of all Christians, or, as Victoria says, "a task common and permitted to all," yet he adds, "the Pope might entrust it to the Spaniards and forbid it to all others." This would seem to be an appropriate action for him, although as Victoria said "the Pope is not temporal lord, yet he has power in matters temporal when this would subserve matters spiritual." This is assuredly one of the most convincing statements which could be made of the appropriate exercise of the twofold power; inasmuch as the Pope, possessing the spiritual power, could "entrust it to the Spaniards" to the exclusion of all others if he believed that the Spaniards were the best fitted for the task; nor is this all, he could forbid subjects of other nations to preach in the New World, and Victoria adds, "also to trade there . . . for he can order temporal matters in the manner which is most helpful to spiritual matters." Victoria had doubtless had experience with competing orders of the Church, just as we are familiar with the competition of missionaries of the various sects of Christendom in foreign parts. In any event he advocated the choice of missionaries of one nationality as "the course most conducive to spiritual welfare, because, if there was to be an indiscriminate inrush of Christians from other parts . . . , they might easily hinder one another and develop quarrels, to the banishment of tranquility."[58]

The high-minded and spiritual Dominican here resorts for the time to a material reason and in so doing expresses a preference for his countrymen: "Inasmuch as it was the sovereigns of Spain who were the first to patronize and pay for the navigation of the intermediate ocean, and as they then had the good fortune to discover the New World, it is just that this travel should be for-

[58] *De Indis,* p. 157.

bidden to others and that the Spaniards should enjoy alone the fruits of their discovery."

We now come to Victoria's conclusion, and we can divine, indeed, we know, what it is to be from what he has already said: "If the Indians allow the Spaniards freely and without hindrance to preach the Gospel, then whether they do or do not receive the faith, this furnishes no lawful ground for making war on them and seizing in any other way their lands"; and a little later he says that this is self-evident, "seeing that there can not be a just war where no wrong has previously been done (*Secunda Secundae,* qu. 40, art. 1)." The most, then, that Victoria allows is the right to preach the Gospel, leaving the natives free to accept or not to accept the doctrine of Christ. The right, however, to preach is unquestioned. Hence opposition to the preaching on the part of the Indians would justify a resort to force, even war, until they—meaning the Spaniards—"succeed in obtaining facilities and safety for preaching the Gospel," and the same right would accrue to the Spaniards if the Indians "allow preaching, but hinder conversion." However, the purpose of the missionaries must not be their own advantage, but solely that of the Indians. "What we have been showing"—Victoria says—"is what is lawful in itself," and speaking in the first person, he continues: "I personally have no doubt that the Spaniards were bound to employ force and arms in order to continue their work there, but I fear measures were adopted in excess of what is allowed by human and divine law." [59]

The third title, which Victoria now takes up, deals with the converts and the protection which should be accorded to them. And the conclusion which he reaches is that if such protection is not accorded, this "would justify the Spaniards, should other methods fail, in making war and in compelling the barbarians by force to stop such misconduct."

The fourth possible title is a continuation of the third and, indeed, of the second, on the supposition that the Indians converted formed a large part of the natives. In this case, Victoria concedes to the Pope "for a reasonable cause," which the Pope

---

[59] *Ibid.,* p. 158.

would decide, "either with or without a request" from the natives, the right to "give them a Christian sovereign and depose their other unbelieving rulers."

This would seem to be stretching the doctrine of the "indirect power" to the breaking point.

The fifth title is founded "either on the tyranny of those who bear rule among the aborigines of America or on the tyrannical laws which work wrong to innocent folk there, such as that which allows the sacrifice of innocent people or the killing in other ways of uncondemned people for cannibalistic purposes." [60]

Victoria considers intervention under such circumstances as a right based on human welfare, a right which authorizes the Spaniards, without the Pope's sanction, to "stop all such nefarious usage and ritual among the aborigines," and likewise "to rescue innocent people from an unjust death." [61] Indeed, Victoria goes further, saying that, if the Indians refuse to cease such practices, "it is a good ground for making war on them and proceeding against them under the law of war, and if such sacrilegious rites can not otherwise be stopped, for changing their rulers and creating a new sovereignty over them." To Victoria "it is immaterial that all the Indians assent to rules and sacrifices of this kind and do not wish the Spaniards to champion them, for herein they are not of such legal independence as to be able to consign themselves or their children to death."

To the question: Am I my brother's keeper? Victoria's answer would be in the affirmative.

The sixth lawful title is the voluntary choice of the Indians, that is to say, "if the Indians, aware alike of the prudent administration and the humanity of the Spaniards, were of their own motion, both rulers and ruled, to accept the King of Spain as their sovereign." [62] This could lawfully be done if a majority should be in favor of so doing for, as Victoria has already said, "in matters touching the good of the State the decisions of the majority bind even when the rest are of a contrary mind; other-

---

[60] *De Indis*, p. 159.
[61] *Ibid.*
[62] *Ibid.*, pp. 159-60.

wise naught could be done for the welfare of the State, it being difficult to get all of the same way of thinking."[63]

The seventh and the last of the titles which Victoria considered adequate is the espousal of "the cause of allies and friends," for there is no doubt, "as Cajetan also asserts (*Secunda Secundae,* qu. 40, art. 1), that the cause of allies and friends is a just cause of war, a State being quite properly able, as against foreign wrongdoers, to summon foreigners to punish its enemies."

History is, indeed, full of examples of this doctrine, but it has often happened that friends who intervened on behalf of those who sought their intervention, as in the case of the Romans, remained in possession of the territories which they had been invited to protect.

There was, however, an eighth title, which in the present instance Victoria said he dared not affirm nor entirely condemn; it is none other than what we of today call the mandate as exercised under the League of Nations, which many people will be surprised to learn was not merely foreshadowed, but expressly stated by Victoria: "Although the aborigines in question are . . . not wholly unintelligent, yet they are little short of that condition, and so are unfit to found or administer a lawful State up to the standard required by human and civil claims. . . . It might, therefore, be maintained that in their own interests"—Victoria continues after a none too flattering discussion of some of the American barbarians—"the sovereigns of Spain might undertake the administration of their country. . . . And surely this might be founded on the precept of charity, they being our neighbors."[64] But here, as elsewhere, Victoria sounds a word of warning, and none more humanitarian than on this occasion. "Let this, however, . . . be put forward without dogmatism and subject also to the limitation that any such interposition be for the welfare and in the interests of the Indians and not merely for the profit of the Spaniards. For this is"—again sounding a note of warning—"the respect in which all the danger to soul and salvation lies."

[63] *Ibid.,* p. 160.
[64] *Ibid.,* p. 161.

SECOND READING

It has been observed in the course of the preceding sections, that the violation of a right is to be redressed, if need be, in appropriate cases, by a resort to force which, in itself, is or may be considered an act of war. Now Victoria felt that his first reading would be incomplete if it were not followed by something on war as such, and he therefore supplemented "the foregoing discussion of the titles, some just and some unjust, which the Spaniards may allege for their hold on the lands in question, by a short discussion of the law of war, so as to give more completeness to that *relectio.*" [65]

The discussion was, however, much shorter than the preceding reading, the claims on his time not allowing him to deal with the subject as he would have liked to do. Because of "the shortness of the time" at his disposal, he could, therefore, only "note the main propositions . . . with very brief proofs," and in consequence he was obliged to abstain from "many doubtful matters which might otherwise be brought into this discussion." He singled out, however, four principal questions: "First, Whether Christians may make war at all; secondly, Where does the authority to declare or wage war repose; thirdly, What may and ought to furnish causes of just war; fourthly, What and how extensive measures may be taken in a just war against the enemy?" [66]

To the first question, whether Christians may make war at all, Victoria roundly answered, "Christians may serve in war and make war," [67] and the authorities whom he cited were the greatest of the Fathers, St. Augustine, and St. John the Baptist, the forerunner of Christ. The passage supporting the answer is short, so short that it can not be shortened by a summary, and so important that not a word should be omitted; it, therefore, follows in full and without interruption: "This is the conclusion of St. Augustine in the many passages where he thoroughly considers the question, such as: (*a*) in his *Contra Faustum,* (*b*), in

[65] *De Iure Belli,* p. 165.
[66] *Ibid.*
[67] *Ibid.,* p. 166.

his *Liber 83 Quaestionum*, (*c*), in his *De verbis Domini*, in his *Contra Secundinum Manichaeum*, (*d*), in his sermon on the Centurion's son, and (*e*) in his Letter to Boniface. And, as St. Augustine shows, this is proved by the words of John the Baptist to the soldiers (*St. Luke*, ch. 3), 'Do violence to no man, neither accuse any falsely.' 'But,' says St. Augustine, (*f*) 'if Christian doctrine condemned war altogether, those looking for counsels of salvation in the Gospel would be told to throw away their arms and give up soldiering altogether; but what is said to them is: Do violence to no man and be content with your wages.' "[68]

The second proof is the "reason of the thing," taken from St. Thomas' *Secunda Secundae* (qu. 40, art. 1): "To draw the sword and use arms against internal wrongdoers and seditious citizens is lawful. . . . Therefore it is lawful also to use the sword and arms against external enemies." Next, the *Digest* (I, i, 3) of Justinian is invoked to supply legal proof: "In a defensive war force may be employed to repel force . . . , this is also proved with regard to an offensive war, that is, a war where we are not only defending ourselves or seeking to repossess ourselves of property, but also where we are trying to avenge ourselves for some wrong done to us";[69] and the great authority of St. Augustine (*Liber 83 Quaestionum*) is again invoked, describing those wars as just "which are waged in order to avenge a wrong done, as where punishment has to be meted out to a city or state because it has itself neglected to exact punishment for an offense committed by its citizens or subjects or to return what has been wrongfully taken away." [70]

Here we have the state responsible for the acts of its citizens which it has not punished, or for not returning that which had been wrongfully taken away. Here we also have two of the questions which, we shall shortly see, arise in a lawsuit: those of due diligence and a denial of justice. In addition, vengeance

---

68 *Ibid.*, p. 166.
69 *Ibid.*, pp. 166-7.
70 *Ibid.*, p. 167.

is to be exacted, because if there were no fear of "retribution," states, like people, could not be kept from "wrongdoing."

Moreover, there was another proof at hand, for "as St. Augustine says *(De verbo Domini and Ad Bonifacium)*, the end and aim of war is the peace and security of the State." [71] And a final and all-embracing consideration was the "good of the whole world."

The second question is: "In whose hands lies the authority to declare and to make war?" To this Victoria replies that "any one, even a private person, can accept and wage a defensive war." This has already been shown by the fact that "force may be repelled by force," which may be used "without authority from any one else, for the defense not only of his person, but also of his property and goods." Can one who is attacked by a robber or enemy attack his assailant if escape by flight is possible? To this question, Bartolus, with whom Victoria agrees, replies "that self-defense is lawful and that there is no obligation to fly, the putting to flight being itself a wrong." [72] Now self-defense applies not merely to life, but to property, although defensive war by individuals is justified only by dire necessity, and should not be employed when the danger has passed.

Who has authority to declare public war? "Every State." Now there is a distinction in the matter of war between the action of a private person and that of a state; for the private person, as we have seen, can defend himself and prevent an injury only at the very moment of danger, whereas "a State is within its rights not only in defending itself"—which is as far as the individual may go—"but also in avenging itself and its subjects and in redressing wrongs" even after the injury has been inflicted.

When the state is mentioned, the prince is likewise included, and when the prince is mentioned, the state is implied. This is in accordance with the opinion of St. Augustine *(Contra Faustum)*: "The natural order, best adapted to secure the peace of mankind, requires that the authority to make war and the advisability of it should be in the hands of the sovereign

[71] *De Iure Belli*, p. 167.

[72] *Ibid.*, p. 168.

prince." [73] Victoria adds in his own behalf that "reason supports this, for the prince only holds his position by the election of the State. Therefore he is its representative and wields its authority."

But, "what is a State, and who can properly be called a sovereign prince?" To his own question, Victoria replies that the state is a "perfect community," but what, then, is a perfect community, for the same difficulty confronts us whether we speak of the state or the community? Victoria endeavors to meet the difficulty by saying that "a thing is called perfect when it is a completed whole, for that is imperfect in which there is something wanting, and, on the other hand, that is perfect from which nothing is wanting." [74] Admitting this, the question still arises, what is a perfect state or community? To which Victoria, having carefully chosen his ground, at last replies directly: "one which is complete in itself, that is, which is not a part of another community, but has its own laws and its own council and its own magistrates." If he had stopped there, he might be accused of dealing in the abstract, but his weakness, if he had any, was for the concrete; therefore, he furnished examples such as "the Kingdom of Castile and Aragon and the Republic of Venice and other the like."

It is to be observed that although he was in favor of monarchy, nevertheless in the matter of "perfection" Victoria apparently makes no distinction between a kingdom and a republic. And finally he enlarged his definition to include confederations by adding that "there is no obstacle to many principalities and perfect States being under one prince. Such a State, then, or the prince thereof, has authority to declare war, and no one else."

The state of today is the state of Victoria.

Suppose, however, that a "number of States of this kind or a number of princes have one common lord or prince," can they, of themselves, and without the authorization of their superior lord, make war? Victoria's answer is that "they can do so undoubtedly, just as the kings who are subordinate to the Emperor can make war on one another without waiting for the Emperor's

[73] *Ibid.*, p. 169.
[74] *Ibid.*

authorization, for . . . a State ought to be self-sufficient, and this it would not be, if it had not the faculty in question."

But there are states and states. Petty rulers and princes are not the heads of perfect states, but as Victoria rightfully says, "are parts of another State," and therefore, they "can not begin to carry on a war." [75] Had he stopped here, we would be left to conjecture, but Victoria never leaves us in the dark; therefore he again gives examples, such as "the Duke of Alva or the Count of Benevento." Why are the Duke and the Count not heads of perfect states? Because "they are parts of the Kingdom of Castile and consequently have not perfect States."

How are we to know when a state is or is not sufficient unto itself? The answer of Victoria is that "these matters are for a great part governed by the law of nations or by human law." It may be, however, that the petty state or prince has, by ancient custom, the right to make war, and "this authority can not be gainsaid, even if in other respects the State be not a perfect one." Here we have usage making international law. In addition, "necessity can confer this license and authority."

An example of the imperfect state in matters of war would be, in our part of the world, a State of the American Union, which cannot, unless actually invaded or in imminent danger, declare war to defend itself if attacked, for, if the danger were not imminent, it should under the Constitution call upon the Government of the United States and not take action on its own initiative. If, however, the danger were imminent, the "necessity" to which Victoria refers would confer the "license and authority" to act directly.

The third question which Victoria treats is the "reason and cause of just war," [76]—a matter than which none could be more important and about which there has been much difference of opinion, a difference which will exist until war as an instrument of national and international policy no longer exists. Victoria was fully aware of the importance of the question, for he rightly said that it was "particularly necessary to ask this in connection

[75] *De Iure Belli*, p. 169.
[76] *Ibid.*, p. 170.

with the case of the Indian aborigines," which was then before him and his audience. The learned professor indulges in a series of propositions of á general nature. The first is: "Difference of religion is not a cause of just war." It is natural that he should commence with this; for the Reading itself was delivered because of the Indians and one of the chief matters of contention between them and the Spaniards, his countrymen, was difference of religion. Apparently he was pleased with the previous Reading *On the Indians Newly Discovered,* since he states roundly, without circumlocution, that "we demolished the fourth alleged title for taking possession of the Indians, namely, their refusal to accept Christianity," and he repeats in a single sentence his own view—which happened to be the opinion of St. Thomas "and the common opinion of the doctors"—speaking in the first person, as he did when his cause ran away with him, "indeed, I know of no one of the opposite way of thinking." But Victoria had in mind not only the Indians. He was thinking of Charles V, the Holy Roman Emperor, who was specializing in religious wars, and Victoria was—it can not be too often said —a subject of that Spain whereof the Holy Roman Emperor was the monarch.

The second proposition is material and political: "Extension of empire is not a just cause of war." [77] We do not need to discuss this, as every right-minded person admits it. It is, however, a comfort to have the authority of Victoria, his statement being more pleasing to us than it was to Charles V, who made a specialty of extending empire by means of war. Here again, it is to be said, Victoria was as much a Spaniard as Charles himself, and not every Spaniard denied the alleged rights of his sovereign.

The third proposition is: "Neither the personal glory of the prince nor any other advantage to him is a just cause of war." [78] Victoria's comment is almost brutal: "This, too, is notorious. For," he continues, after this curt statement, "a prince ought to subordinate both peace and war to the common weal of his

[77] *Ibid.*
[78] *Ibid.*

State and not spend public revenues in quest of his own glory or gain, much less expose his subjects to danger on that account." And he adds: "Herein, indeed, is the difference between a lawful king and a tyrant, that the latter directs his government towards his individual profit and advantage, but a king to the public welfare, . . ."—a definition as old as Aristotle, whose authority is invoked, although none was needed. We are tempted to dwell on the question of tyrants, but we may not, as the question is elaborately treated in the section on Suárez.[79]

As Charles V, Holy Roman Emperor and King of Spain, was the most warlike monarch of his day, it can readily be believed that His Imperial and Royal Majesty did not relish this sort of comment on his various undertakings. Indeed he indicated his displeasure by an imperial and royal letter to the University of Salamanca, forbidding the discussion of certain questions concerning the Indians.

So far the statements of Victoria have been negative. His fourth proposition is positive, defining the cause of a just war within the compass of a single sentence,—indeed, in two or three words of a sentence—as "a wrong received." [80] When people have pondered a subject and have reached definite convictions, they have a way of stating them so that they can be neither misunderstood nor forgotten. The definition of Victoria is a case in point. Moreover, it was a definition based on the highest authority for it was in accord with St. Augustine's opinion, St. Thomas' opinion, and, Victoria adds, "the opinion of all the doctors." It would also follow that offensive war for the purpose of avenging a wrong received and of taking punitive measures against the enemy who had committed the wrong would fall within the definition of a just war. This definition was perhaps the severest condemnation of Charles Fifth's conduct which could be imagined, for his wars were largely wars of ambition, and rarely waged because of wrongs received.

But Victoria, now speaking for himself, without reference to authority, expresses his own opinion, revealing in the fifth propo-

---

[79] *Infra*, p. 261.
[80] *De Iure Belli*, p. 170.

sition his own innermost thought on the subject, saying that "not every kind and degree of wrong can suffice for commencing a war."[81] The two proofs which he invokes should be given in his own language,—"not even upon one's own fellow-countrymen is it lawful for every offense to exact atrocious punishments, such as death or banishment or confiscation of property." If that be so within a restricted area, when nations are involved, "it is not lawful for slight wrongs to pursue the authors of the wrongs with war, seeing that the degree of the punishment ought to correspond to the measure of the offense,"—and the evils inflicted in war were of a severe and "atrocious" character.

Here he puts the question, which he later considers at greater length, "what kind and degree of stress is lawful in a just war"; and he answers it with reference to the end and aim of war, which he describes as "the defense and preservation of the State." Wherefore, "in war everything is lawful which the defense of the common weal requires."[82]

Is it permissible "to recapt everything that has been lost?" Victoria's answers to questions of this kind are laconic: "This is too notorious to need proof." Why? "For war is begun or undertaken with this object."[83]

Is it "lawful to make good out of enemy property the expenses of the war and all damages wrongfully caused by the enemy?" Yes; "for the enemy who has done the wrong is bound to give all this redress"; and "therefore the prince can claim it all and exact it all by war."[84]

It is probably evident by this time that it was as necessary for a theologian to be a jurist as it was for a jurist to be a theologian, —at least in the days of Victoria; for the statements just quoted suggest a lawsuit, Victoria's conception and the conception of his school—indeed of their predecessors—being that war was a means of executing a judgment in behalf of a state or people suffering a legal wrong.

---

[81] *Ibid.*, p. 171.
[82] *Ibid.*
[83] *Ibid.*
[84] *Ibid.*

But clear as this would seem to be, Victoria would have no doubt in the matter. Therefore he says expressly that "if there were any competent judge over the two belligerents, he would have to condemn the unjust aggressors and authors of wrong, not only to make restitution of what they have carried off, but also to make good the expenses of the war to the other side, and also all damages."

Now these are exactly the remedies arising from the just cause of a private litigant, given definite form and shape in a court of the prince within the state of which the litigants are subjects.

There is a just cause of suit, that is to say, "a wrong received."[85] Within the state the wrong is to be made good at the expense of the defendant; in terms international, by the guilty state or people. However, why argue the analogy, when Victoria himself states it? "A prince who is carrying on a just war is as it were his own judge in matters touching the war,"—to which the necessary and logical conclusion is that "he can enforce all these claims upon his enemy."

In a lawsuit the wrong is not merely redressed but security for the future is given, just as under criminal law the defendant may be bound over to keep the peace. This apparently was Victoria's view of the suit between states: "Not only are the things just named allowable, but a prince may go even further in a just war and do whatever is necessary in order to obtain peace and security from the enemy."[86] By way of example, Victoria says that he may "destroy an enemy's fortress and even build one on enemy soil, if this be necessary in order to avert a dangerous attack of the enemy"; for "the end and aim of war is peace and security."[87] Now these are external guaranties; but they are justified by the fact that "all measures of this kind may be taken against internal foes, that is, against bad citizens"—for just as such measures are the proper consequences of a lawsuit, so they would also be lawful in force suits against external foes.

Within the state, a defendant may be required to give bond or

---

[85] *De Iure Belli*, p. 170.
[86] *Ibid.*, p. 171.
[87] *Ibid.*, p. 172.

to quit the state. Therefore, by analogy, in force suits "the enemy may be made to give hostages, ships, arms, and other things," in order that the successful litigant—whom we will suppose is the plaintiff state—may live in peace and security.

Now there are two kinds of defendants: the defendant within and the defendant beyond the state. There is little difficulty in serving process upon a defendant within, and indeed attaching his person; for the prince—that is to say, the government of the state—has undoubted, indeed unquestionable, jurisdiction. But how is the jurisdiction to be obtained by a prince in his force suit with a defendant state? The process is simple within the state. Why? Because the people of the state have organized themselves into a society, with adequate rules of conduct and the provision of damages for their violation, to be ascertained by a court of justice, and with the further provision that the judgment is to be executed by the appropriate authority of the state against the defendant. Here jurisdiction is conferred by statute.

But, as Victoria has elsewhere said, the world is, "in a way, one single state," [88] with power to make laws and to secure their enforcement, instancing in this connection the immunity of ambassadors and saying that such immunity arises under the law of nations, which is made by the entire world. Therefore in disputes between states, jurisdiction may be said to be conferred by international law.

Now how is the wrong which a state has suffered at the hands of another state to be redressed? A wrong has been committed under international law and there should be a remedy for this wrong; otherwise international law is imperfect. The process is that within the state, but on a larger scale. The plaintiff in matters international is the monarch or chief executive (generally called the "prince" by Victoria), who acts in behalf of his state, whether the injury has been to the state or to the subjects of the state. He is the representative or, as we would say in law, the agent, both of the state and of its subjects. What is the

[88] *De Potestate Civili,* sec. 21. For an English translation of this *Relectio,* see James Brown Scott, *The Spanish Origin of International Law, Part I, Francisco de Vitoria and his Law of Nations* (Oxford, 1934), p. lxxi *et seq.*

procedure? It is in essentials that of the private lawsuit. The private litigant consults counsel in order to ascertain whether he has a case under the law, to be laid before a court of justice and to be tried in the presence of the defendant, or in his absence if, duly summoned, he fails to appear. In like manner, the prince confers with his counsellors, and, being informed that he has a case, he assumes, as it were, the office of judge and delivers judgment which with a demand for satisfaction, is presented, through appropriate channels, to the prince of the state which has committed the alleged wrong. The defendant prince should likewise consult his counsel, just as the individual defendant would consult counsellors at law. If the defendant prince complies with the demand, then the case is said to be settled. If, on the other hand, he does not comply, further steps are to be taken. After judgment had by an individual within a state, the defendant might be deprived of his liberty by the sheriff or appropriate officer. In the case of a defendant state, the judgment is executed by the prince against the defendant state by such force of arms as may be necessary to secure compliance.

But to return to the specific question of jurisdiction. Let us examine several propositions, showing the way in which Victoria has the injured state, intent on securing redress for the wrongs it has suffered, obtain jurisdiction of the foreign state and of its people, and thus, in the absence of a municipal remedy, secure compliance with its rightful demands. Victoria begins by saying "that princes have authority not only over their own subjects, but also over foreigners, so far as to prevent them from committing wrongs." What is the authority which granted this jurisdiction. It is granted "by the law of nations and by the authority of the whole world."[89] In a single state there are laws prescribing rights, and their correlative duties, and a means of protecting those rights and enforcing the performance of those duties. This is, as he shows in the Reading *On the Civil Power,* by natural law, because—man being a social and political animal—if this were not done, Victoria expressly says that individuals grouped together in society would fall apart and

[89] *De Iure Belli,* p. 172.

the state would be dissolved. Therefore, the preservation of the state ultimately depends upon natural law. In Victoria's words, "otherwise society could not hold together unless there was somewhere a power and authority to deter wrongdoers and prevent them from injuring the good and innocent"; and he continues that "everything needed for the government and preservation of society exists by natural law, and in no other way can we show that a State has by natural law authority to inflict pains and penalties on its citizens who are dangerous to it." [90]

If this is so of the small society which we call the state, it must also be so of the larger society which we call the international community, of which the states are members; and the law of this international community is the law of nations and made "by the authority of the whole world," as Victoria has said. "But if a State," he continues, "can do this to its own citizens, society at large no doubt can do it to all wicked and dangerous folk, and this can only be"—in Victoria's day—"through the instrumentality of princes." Here is the lawsuit on a larger scale,—but the lawsuit without a court between states. It is therefore a force suit until a mixed commission or a temporary tribunal is, upon the proposal of the plaintiff state, accepted by the defendant state; or until the mixed commission or temporary tribunal has been replaced by a permanent tribunal, with the agreement of all those states by whose pact or agreement or treaty this tribunal has been formed, thus furnishing the international community with its court and thereby removing the only justification of war, which Victoria and his theological predecessors would permit.

Now let us take the balance of Victoria's statement in this connection. "It is, therefore, certain that princes can punish enemies who have done a wrong to their State and that after a war has been duly and justly undertaken the enemy are just as much within the jurisdiction of the prince who undertakes it as if he were their proper judge." The justification? "In reality peace and tranquility, which are the end and aim of war, can not be had unless evils and damages be visited on the

[90] *Ibid.*

enemy in order to deter them from the like conduct in the future."[91]

The court within the state has preserved peace and tranquility; the court of the international community will likewise preserve peace and tranquility.

Perhaps the clearest example of what Victoria had in mind is furnished by reprisals. "If the enemy," he says, "refuse to restore things wrongfully seized by them and the injured party can not otherwise properly recoup himself, he may do so wherever satisfaction is obtainable, whether from guilty or from innocent. For instance, if French brigands"—Victoria in this particular instance makes the French the aggressors, rather than his own people, contrary to his custom—"made a raid into Spanish territory and the French King would not, though able, compel them to restore their booty, the Spanish might, on the authorization of their sovereign, despoil French merchants or farmers, however innocent these might be."[92] Why should this be done or permitted by the law of nations? "Because, although the French State or Sovereign might initially be blameless, yet it is a breach of duty, as St. Augustine says, for them to neglect to vindicate the right against the wrongdoing of their subjects, and the injured sovereign can take satisfaction from every member and portion of their State."

The right of reprisal, which the Spanish could exercise, was through "letters of marque and reprisal," which princes, meaning chiefs of state, were wont to issue in accordance with a long established and unfortunate custom, "on account"—as Victoria says—"of the neglect and breach of duty of the other prince," and it was to overcome the neglect or breach "that the prince of the injured party grants him this right to recoup himself even from innocent folk."[93] The high mindedness and the foresight of Victoria are as conspicuously evident here as elsewhere, for he unhesitatingly characterized letters of marque and reprisal as "hazardous" and opening "the way to plunder," a

[91] *De Iure Belli,* p. 172.
[92] *Ibid.,* p. 181.
[93] *Ibid.,* p. 181.

view which was justified in 1856 by the Treaty of Paris, ending the Crimean War, and expressly repudiating letters of marque and reprisal on the part of the signatory parties. The renunciation is today universal.

Now war is limited to a just cause, but there are two tests by which the cause is found to be just and both should be applied. It is not enough that the prince, who is the plaintiff in our international dispute, is advised by his counsel just as the ordinary litigant would be advised by his counsellor at law, that his cause is just. To be sure, the decision of the prince, rendered as if a judge, binds the state, inasmuch as he is its representative; but what of the people, who, as it were, supply the second test? Must the cause appear just to them, or must they be content with "my country, right or wrong"? Generally the latter, if history is to be believed. But what of the court of conscience, the court before which prince and pauper alike must appear? If the subject believes that the cause is unjust, he should not serve in the war; if he has not reached a definite conclusion, he may serve, because in such a case he is justified in accepting the judgment of his prince. And Victoria allows that, in general, the command of the prince is sufficient, inasmuch as he has advice which the private person can not have and, therefore, the individual may trust to the justness of the decision without committing a mortal sin, although through ignorance he may happen to be in the wrong.

Now the right of the subject to decide for himself that a war is unjust and to refuse to take part in it is none other than the doctrine of the conscientious objector, which made its appearance on a large scale during the World War, and which is likely to assume vast importance in the future, for today the people are not pawns and can not forever be considered as dumb, driven cattle.

Mercenaries who hired themselves out in Victoria's day were conscienceless persons, and they no longer exist—at least under that name.

It may happen, however, that a case arises where the justice of the war may be doubtful, that is, "when there are"—Victoria says—"apparent and probable reasons on both sides." In this case, neither of the belligerents would be at fault, and if the dispute involved property the party in possession would under such circumstances be entitled to retain possession.

Victoria gives a series of examples taken from his day, as we would expect in one who had made the subject of his two readings the rights and duties of the Spaniards toward the Americans recently discovered; and although Victoria very properly draws many illustrations from the Fathers and the Doctors of the Church, it is to be said that, by actual count, Victoria devoted a greater proportion of the references in his brief readings to concrete examples of his day than did many other writers on international law, not excluding the Italian, Gentili, who made a specialty of concrete examples, nor Grotius, the Netherlander, whose large treatise bristles with examples from the past.[94]

In the present case, Victoria says: "Suppose the King of France to be in lawful possession of Burgundy and that it be doubtful whether he has or has not right thereto." [95] "Lawful possession" would seem here to be possession under a claim of law. In such a case "the Emperor may not try to oust him by arms."

Victoria, however, was impartial in his criticisms and praises. Therefore, he immediately invokes an example against the French and in favor of the Emperor, "nor on the other hand may the French King seize Naples or Milan, if there be doubt who is entitled to it." [96]

The reason? "In the suits and causes of private persons it is

---

[94] The examples of "modern" events with which Victoria illustrates his text are not, however, of quite the same type as Grotius'. Many references in Victoria are built upon hypothetical cases, the persons and places concerned in which are, nevertheless, real and historical. Grotius' examples are illustrations drawn from history, showing what did occur in a given set of circumstances. Victoria, on the other hand, supposing the circumstances, shows what the legal result of an action on these circumstances should be.

Considering the great length of Grotius' treatise, and the shortness of Victoria's, the latter's "modern" events do, in mathematical ratio, greatly outnumber the former's.

[95] *De Iure Belli*, p. 174.

[96] *Ibid.*, pp. 174-5.

never permissible in a doubtful matter to dispossess a lawful possessor." [97]

Suppose, however, that a city or province is claimed by the King of Spain or the King of France and neither is in possession, each claiming by inheritance, and the point is of a doubtful nature. In such a case, Victoria supposes that one or the other of the claimants proposes "a division or compromise as to part of the claim." What is the duty of the other? "To accept his proposal, even if that other be the stronger and able to seize the whole by armed force." The reason? "When the merits of a quarrel are equal, one side does no wrong by claiming an equal part of the thing in dispute." And a further reason: "In private disputes also, where the matter is in doubt, one party may not seize the whole thing."

In this class of cases, there are two considerations which weigh with Victoria. First a war, by its definition, must have a just cause, and second, if the cause be doubtful, the war may appear to both sides to be just. But Victoria pursues a claim as a hunter his game: to the bitter end. He therefore presupposes that a person in peaceable possession has doubt as to his title; what, then, should he do? "Examine carefully into the cause and give a quiet hearing to the arguments of the other side." [98] Here as elsewhere Victoria's method is so judicial that he has the prince acting as judge, even against himself, because of the absence of a superior. "Also, princes are judges in their own cases, inasmuch as they have no superior. But"—he continues—"if any one raises any objection to a lawful possessor, the judge is bound to examine the case. Therefore the princes are bound to examine their own case."

Victoria's boldness is shown in a criticism of Adrian, who maintained that a subject doubting the justice of the war "may not serve in such a war, even at the command of his prince"; for if he does, according to Adrian "he exposes himself to the danger of mortal sin." [99] Victoria takes the opposite side, observ-

[97] *Ibid.*, p. 175.
[98] *Ibid.*
[99] *Ibid.*, p. 176.

ing that a lictor of Rome, under Roman law "is bound to carry out the decree of the judge, even though he has his doubts about its justice, for there would be serious danger in the opposite course." Victoria also invokes the authority of St. Augustine. Now, the Adrian in question was none other than Adrian who had been a Pope and, indeed, Pope in Victoria's day, and one would need to be very bold indeed, in that day and generation, although Adrian was no longer living, to say in a chair at Salamanca, that "however Adrian may twist and turn, he can not free himself from the authority of St. Augustine, for our proposition is, beyond cavil, the conclusion at which St. Augustine arrives."

We now come to another phase of the question whether a war can be just on both sides. According to the definition of the fathers, from St. Augustine down, the only just cause of war was a wrong suffered. This gives rise to the lawsuit, and if both parties were right in the litigation, there would be no judgment. Applying the analogy to litigation between states, the war would be unjust if both were right, because in either case, the lawsuit or the force suit is to redress an injury by the person or the state which has been injured, and if both be right, there is no injury to be redressed; "hence"—as Victoria now and then says without completing the syllogysm. But in the present instance Victoria answers specifically that "apart from ignorance the case clearly can not occur, for if the right and justice of each side be certain, it is unlawful to fight against it, either in offense or in defense."[100] Yet it may happen that there is what is called "invincible" ignorance, that is, excusable ignorance, in which event the war would still be wrong, but the subject being ignorant and without the means at his disposal to enlighten himself is justified in going to war, and Victoria, summing up the case, says: "on the side of the subjects at any rate, this may often occur; for even if we assume that a prince who is carrying on an unjust war knows about its injustice, still . . . subjects may in good faith follow their prince, and in this way the sub-

[100] *De Iure Belli*, p. 177.

jects on both sides may be doing what is lawful when they fight."

Victoria next takes up the situation of a person ignorant of the wrong of war, but who "subsequently is convinced of its injustice." This may happen alike to prince or subject. What should then be done according to Victoria's law of nations? Here Victoria gives a very material illustration, as unexpected as it is apposite. He supposes that if proof of the injustice of the war had been "within reach," the prince should when he learns of the injustice "give back what he has taken away and not yet consumed, that is, to the extent to which he has been enriched." Now for the reason, "but he need make no amends as regards what he has consumed, because"—Victoria says—"the rule of law is that a person who is not in fault ought not to be damnified." And now for the surprising but effective illustration: "just as one who in good faith attended a sumptuous banquet given by a thief where stolen things were consumed would be under no obligation to give redress therefor, save perhaps up to the amount that his meal would have cost him at home."

This doctrine applies to both of the contending parties. But a war may be just and lawful as regards the letter of the law, and yet it may actually be unlawful. A prince "may be entitled to recapture a city or a province and yet . . . because of some scandal, this may become quite unlawful."[101] The example? Wars, Victoria has said more than once, should only be waged "for the common good." If the evil consequences of the war be much greater than its advantages, it is, in Victoria's conception, "indubitable that the prince is bound rather to give up his own rights and abstain from war." This is in the abstract; now for the concrete: "if the King of France, for example, had a right to retake Milan,"—then in the possession of Charles V, the Holy Roman Emperor—"but by the war both the Kingdom of France and the Duchy of Milan would suffer intolerable ills and heavy woes, it would not be right for him to retake it."[102] In this

[101] *Ibid.*, p. 178.
[102] *Ibid.*

case the harm done would exceed the gain on either side, and in Victoria's opinion this alone could make a war unjust.

So much for the causes of wars and the innocence or guilt of those who take part in them.

The degree of stress permissible on the part of combatants, even if the war be just, raises many doubts. Is it lawful in the war to kill the innocent? To which question Victoria replies, "The deliberate slaughter of the innocent is never lawful."

For war is only permissible to redress a wrong, and here the person is innocent, and within the state, as between states, only the guilty are to be punished; even in the storming of a city, the Old Testament excepted women and little ones on the theory that they were innocent. On the same ground Victoria would spare the children of the Turks—at that time mortal enemies of the Christians, it should be said; for when the Reading *On the Law of War* was prepared the battle of Lepanto in 1571, in which the power of the Turks in Europe was forever checked, was more than a generation in the future. Victoria's reference to the Turks is only another example of his humanitarianism. Not only the children, but the women of the unbelievers were to be spared, unless they had taken part in the hostilities. These observations are followed by three short sentences of immense consequence:

> 1. Aye, and this same pronouncement must be made among Christians with regard to harmless agricultural folk, and also with regard to the rest of the peaceable civilian population, for all these are presumed innocent until the contrary is shown.
>
> 2. On this principle it follows that it is not lawful to slay either foreigners or guests who are sojourning among the enemy, for they are presumed innocent, and in truth they are not enemies.
>
> 3. The same principle applies to clerics and members of a religious order, for they are presumed innocent unless the contrary be shown, as when they engage in actual fighting.[103]

Why? The presumption is in each case that they are innocent, and only the guilty, and, as we shall see, not all of those, are liable to slaughter. Sometimes, however, it would seem right to

---

[103] *De Iure Belli,* p. 179.

slay even the innocent, "as when a fortress or city is stormed in a just war," [104] for their presence could not be availed of as an excuse to prevent what was universally admitted in Victoria's day to be legitimate warfare. In the same way, if a town were "wrongfully besieged and rightfully defended," the besieged would not be prevented from returning the fire, although there happened to be "children and innocent people" in the hostile camp. In this connection, Victoria again refers to what he has already said: "the obligation to see that greater evils do not arise out of the war than the war would avert"—and he continues: "In sum, it is never right to slay the guiltless, even as an indirect and unintended result, except when there is no other means of carrying on the operations of a just war."

There were those in Victoria's time who permitted the killing of guiltless persons, such as "the children of Saracens," as there was "good reason to fear" that if they were spared, later when grown up they would attack the Christians, to which argument Victoria's noble answer is, speaking in the first person: "I believe that it is in no wise right, seeing that evil is not to be done in order to avoid greater evil still, and it is intolerable"—he adds—"that any one should be killed for a future fault." [105]

Victoria now passes to the question whether it is lawful "to despoil the innocent of goods and things which the enemy would use against us, such as arms, ships, and engines of war." We would call these things today contraband of war and they were and still are subject to capture as a means to "the victory" which, Victoria agrees, "is the aim of war." Also, it is lawful "to take the money of the innocent and to burn and destroy their grain and kill their horses"; but Victoria was opposed to "the spoliation of the agricultural population" for "they ought not to be despoiled." However, he was of the opinion that what is lawfully seized in war is not "subject to restitution," [106] although he admits there is an opposite view; but there unquestionably is one class who should not be despoiled, "foreigners and travelers on

---

[104] *Ibid.*

[105] *Ibid.*, p. 180.

[106] *Ibid.*

enemy soil, unless they are obviously at fault."[107] The reason? They are not "enemies." Victoria would seem here to be more liberal with the neutral than we of today.

If properties have been seized by the enemy, and can not be recovered from the seizors, the previous owner may recoup himself from enemy subjects generally "wherever satisfaction is obtainable, whether from guilty or from innocent." This is permitted under the law of reprisals, already discussed.

Victoria correctly notes that it is unlawful to kill children and other innocent parties, but "is it permissible"—he asks—"to carry them off into captivity and slavery?" Yes; it is just as permissible "to carry the innocent off into captivity as to despoil them, liberty and slavery being included among the good things of Fortune." In extreme cases, it is indeed "justifiable to carry all enemy-subjects off into captivity, whether they be guilty or guiltless." Such was the case with the Saracens, with whom war was regarded in Victoria's day as perpetual and therefore it was permissible "to carry off both the children and the women of the Saracens into captivity and slavery." This was the law of the barbarians and, in wars with them became the law of the Christians by retaliation. As we have seen, however, the enslaving of Christians was not permitted in a war between Christians, but they might be held captives in order to "receive a money-ransom for them." This was an extreme measure and "must not be pushed"—he said—"beyond what the necessity of the war may demand and what the custom of lawful belligerents has allowed." Today a further step has been taken, for prisoners are exchanged, they are no longer held for ransom.

Victoria now considers the question of exchanging hostages, common in his day, but no longer practised. However, in Victoria's time hostages were sureties for good faith, either in truce or at the conclusion of the war. But was it lawful to kill hostages? "My answer"—Victoria says *in propria persona*—"is in a single proposition: If the hostages are in other respects among the guilty, as, for instance, because they have borne arms, they may rightfully be killed in that case; if, however, they are

[107] *De Iure Belli,* p. 181.

innocent, as, for instance, if they be children or women or other innocent folk, it is obvious . . . that they can not be killed." [108]

Now we come to the guilty. May they all be killed in a just war? In this connection, Victoria summarizes the purposes for which war is waged: "Firstly, in defense of ourselves and what belongs to us; secondly, to recover things taken from us; thirdly, to avenge a wrong suffered by us; fourthly, to secure peace and security." [109]

Each of these purposes of war is considered in answering the question concerning the treatment of the guilty. First of the letter of the law, which Victoria states only to temper it with humanity. In the heat and stress of battle, all may be killed who resist. But may this be done after the victory when the enemy is no longer dangerous? According to *Deuteronomy*, ch. 20, "manifestly, yes," and indeed, after "victory has been won and no danger remains, it is lawful to kill the guilty." The reason is that "a prince when at war has by right of war the same authority over the enemy as if he were their lawful judge and prince. And a further reason is that . . . security for the future can not be had, unless the enemy be restrained by fear of punishment."

If the case be one of avenging a wrong, it would not always be lawful, "even among citizens . . . , not even where the wrong was done by the whole city or district, to kill all the delinquents; nor in a common rebellion would it be permissible to slay and destroy the whole population. . . . For such conduct would not be for the public good, which is nevertheless the end and aim of both war and peace." And the punishment, as Cicero says, "must be such as equity and humanity allow." Sometimes, apparently, it is both "lawful and expedient to kill all the guilty." However, this can not be the ordinary rule, and can only be availed of in special cases, as "against unbelievers, from whom it is useless ever to hope for a just peace on any terms," the unbelievers doubtless being the Turks, for "in a war with Christians"—Victoria says—"I do not think this would be allow-

[108] *Ibid.*, pp. 181-2.
[109] *Ibid.*, p. 182.

able." And in this connection he expresses himself with that largeness of view which those who have followed us thus far have become accustomed to expect: "it would involve"—he says —"the ruin of mankind and of Christianity if the victor always slew all his enemies, and the world would soon be reduced to solitude, and wars would not be waged for the public good, but to the utter ruin of the public." [110] Another reason is that "the measure of the punishment . . . must be proportionate to the offense, and vengeance ought to go no further." Moreover the punishing prince should remember that the enemy subjects may in fact be ignorant of the true cause of the war, having been deceived by their own prince and having fought "in reliance on his authority and on public counsels."

Heretofore, Victoria has been dealing with five doubtful points. There are four more, and of one and all of this group he says that "sometimes, nay, frequently, not only subjects, but princes, too, who in reality have no just cause of war, may nevertheless be waging war in good faith, with such good faith, I say, as to free them from fault; as, for instance, if the war is made after a careful examination and in accordance with the opinion of learned and upright men." [111]

These last four doubts are:

6. Whether it is lawful to slay those who have surrendered or been captured supposing them also to have been guilty." [112]

7. Whether everything that is captured in a just war becomes the property of the captor and seizor.[113]

8. Whether it is lawful to impose a tribute on conquered enemies.[114]

9. Whether it is lawful to depose the princes of the enemy and appoint new ones or keep the princedom for oneself.[115]

The sixth doubt is soon resolved by Victoria. The letter of the law of war might justify the wholesale slaughter of guilty captives, but custom, entering through the law of nations, had

[110] *De Iure Belli*, p. 183.
[111] *Ibid.*, pp. 186-7.
[112] *Ibid.*, p. 183.
[113] *Ibid.*, p. 184.
[114] *Ibid.*, p. 186.
[115] *Ibid.*, p. 186.

tempered the old and savage rules of warfare, so that captives were no longer to be butchered after victory had been won. As for those who surrendered, their treatment should be in accordance with the conditions of capitulation; or, if they surrendered unconditionally, the more "notorious offenders" among them might be put to death "on the order of the prince or judge."

Under the seventh doubt above, Victoria deals with things captured in war, such as movables (like money, garments, silver and gold) or immovables (like lands, cities and fortresses), concluding that "All movables vest in the seizor by the law of nations, even if in amount they exceed what will compensate for damages sustained."[116] But Victoria tempers legal right with Christian mercy, saying: "it is not to be imagined that, if the French have ravaged some one district or insignificant town in Spain, the Spanish might also, if they could, ravage the whole of France; they can only retort in a manner proportionate in kind and degree to the wrong done, according to the estimate of a good man."[117] In this connection Victoria adverts to the sacking of a city, having in mind, although he does not mention the city by name, the sacking of Rome by the troops of Charles V, Holy Roman Emperor, in 1527, an act indescribably appalling, everything that a brutal victorious army, relapsed into barbarism, would dare to perpetrate. Admitting the right of soldiery to sack, "Nevertheless"—Victoria says—"inasmuch as such authorization to sack results in many horrors and cruelties, enacted beyond all humane limits by a barbarous soldiery, such as slaughter and torture of the innocent, rape of virgins, dishonor of matrons, and looting of temples, it is undoubtedly unjust in the extreme to deliver up a city, especially a Christian city, to be sacked, without the greatest necessity and weightiest reason."

"If, however,"—he goes on to say—"the necessities of war require it, it is not unlawful, even if it be likely that the troops will perpetrate foul misdeeds of this kind, which their generals

[116] *Ibid.*, p. 184.
[117] *Ibid.*

are none the less bound to forbid and, as far as they can, to prevent." [118]

As regards immovable property, it may be seized and held, including lands, fortresses and towns "so far is necessary to obtain compensation for the damages . . . caused," [119] and Victoria continues: "For if it is lawful to exact compensation from the enemy for the things of ours which he has taken, it is certain that by the divine law and natural law it is not more lawful to take recompense therefor in movables than in immovables." [120]

As a matter of security, Victoria considers it "lawful to seize and hold a fortress or city belonging to him"—the enemy—"which is necessary for our defense or for taking away from him an opportunity of hurting us." Likewise, it is lawful, by way of punishment for a wrong received, "that is, in revenge, to mulct the enemy of a part of his territory in proportion to the character of the wrong, or even on this ground to seize a fortress or town." This should be done, however, "within due limits" and not "as far as our strength and armed force enable us to go in seizing and storming" and, in any event only so much should be "retained as is just, in way of compensation for damages caused and expenses incurred and of vengeance for wrongs done, and with due regard for equity and humanity, seeing that punishment ought to be proportionate to the fault"; and recurring to an illustration which he has used on more than one occasion, "it would be intolerable that, if the French raided the flocks of the Spanish or burnt a single district, the latter should be allowed to seize the whole Kingdom of France." The argument in behalf of this doctrine is that "internal wrongdoers may be punished in this way, that is, they may be deprived of house or land or a fortress, in proportion to the character of the circumstances"—and if this be so—"Therefore foreign wrongdoers also." How does Victoria legally justify the mulcting of the enemy under these circumstances? He looks upon a victorious prince as judge—in his own suit, to be sure, but having

---

118 *De Iure Belli*, pp. 184-5.
119 *Ibid.*, p. 185.
120 *Ibid.*

nevertheless all the rights of a judge against the defendant prince; "a superior judge has competence to mulct the author of a wrong by taking away from him a city (for instance) or a fortress. Therefore"—he adds without a pause—"a prince who has suffered wrong can do this too, because by the law of war he is put in the position of a judge." [121]

We come now to the eighth doubt, "whether it is lawful to impose a tribute on conquered enemies." Victoria's answer in this connection should be taken, however, with his general comment—which has been quoted above—on doubts six to nine, inclusive. "It is undoubtedly lawful, not only in order to recoup damages, but also as a punishment and by way of revenge." His authority? *Deuteronomy,* ch. 20.

The last and ninth doubt is "whether it is lawful to depose the prince of the enemy and appoint a new one or keep the princedom for oneself." [122] This is, indeed, a very serious matter and neither is, nor can be, as Victoria says, "unqualifiedly permissible," lest it conflict with the rule repeatedly laid down that "punishment should not exceed the degree and nature of the offense." Moreover, as he here adds, "punishments should be awarded restrictively, and rewards extensively," which is not a rule of human law only, but also of natural and divine law." Therefore, his conclusion is that "even assuming that the enemy's offense is a sufficient cause of war, it will not always suffice to justify the overthrow of the enemy's sovereignty and the deposition of lawful and natural princes; for these would be utterly savage and inhumane measures." But Victoria was willing to and did admit "that there may sometimes arise sufficient and lawful cause for effecting a change of princes or for seizing a sovereignty . . . because of the number and aggravated quality of the damages and wrongs which have been wrought or, especially, when security and peace can not otherwise be had of the enemy and grave danger from them would threaten the State if this were not done." It is evident, however, that the redress grudgingly allowed under this doubtful doubt, as we may almost

121 *Ibid.,* p. 186.
122 *Ibid.*

call it, is repugnant to him, although its application to the Indians recently discovered might endow the Spaniards with innumerable principalities in the New World.

Victoria has abounded in specific instances, which have enabled him to formulate general rules, but these general rules he merged in a canon, indeed in three canons, which he believes the God of justice and of mercy would Himself approve in the wars to which His feeble and often erring children have resorted:

> . . . First canon: Assuming that a prince has authority to make war, he should first of all not go seeking occasions and causes of war, but should, if possible, live in peace with all men, as St. Paul enjoins on us (*Romans,* ch. 12). Moreover, he should reflect that others are his neighbors, whom we are bound to love as ourselves, and that we all have one common Lord, before whose tribunal we shall have to render our account. For it is the extreme of savagery to seek for and rejoice in grounds for killing and destroying men whom God has created and for whom Christ died. But only under compulsion and reluctantly should he come to the necessity of war.
>
> Second canon: When war for a just cause has broken out, it must not be waged so as to ruin the people against whom it is directed, but only so as to obtain one's rights and the defense of one's country and in order that from that war peace and security may in time result.
>
> Third canon: When victory has been won and the war is over, the victory should be utilized with moderation and Christian humility, and the victor ought to deem that he is sitting as judge between two States, the one which has been wronged and the one which has done the wrong, so that it will be as judge and not as accuser that he will deliver the judgment whereby the injured state can obtain satisfaction, and this, so far as possible should involve the offending state in the least degree of calamity and misfortune, the offending individuals being chastised within lawful limits; and an especial reason for this is that in general among Christian all the fault is to be laid at the door of their princes, for subjects when fighting for their princes act in good faith and it is thoroughly unjust, in the words of the poet, that—
>
> Quidquid delirant reges, plectantur Achivi.[124]

124 "For every folly their Kings commit the punishment should fall upon the Greeks."

CHAPTER II

THE MODERN LAW OF NATIONS AND ITS MUNICIPAL SANCTIONS[1]

In conformity with the practice of the schoolmen, with at least two of whom I feel almost personally acquainted, and for whose writings I have a profound respect, I propose a text and a thesis. The text is from Victoria's *Relectio De Potestate Civili.*[2]

> International law has not only the force of a pact and agreement among men, but also the force of a law; for the world as a whole, being in a way one single State, has the power to create laws that are just and fitting for all persons, as are the rules of international law. Consequently, it is clear that they who violate these international rules, whether in peace or in war, commit a mortal sin; moreover, in the gravest matters, such as the inviolability of ambassadors, it is not permissible for one country to refuse to be bound by international law, the latter having been established by the authority of the whole world.

The thesis is as a corollary from Victoria's text which is itself a corollary to his Reading *On the Civil Power of the State.*

And the conclusions flowing, as I conceive, from this text are that every rule of international law has a municipal sanction *in esse* or *in posse,* and that a failure to enact a municipal statute for that purpose—or to apply it if enacted—renders the state in default liable in damages.

In 1492, on the 12th day of October, Columbus landed on American soil, of which he took possession in the name of the Spanish sovereigns, and, returning to Spain in the following year, laid a New World at the feet of their Catholic Majesties, Isabella of León and Castile, and Ferdinand of Aragon.

---

[1] Reprinted with slight modifications from the *Georgetown Law Journal,* January, 1934, pp. 139-206.

[2] Francisco de Vitoria, *De Potestate Civili,* a *relectio* dated Christmas, 1528. Latin text, Simon's Edition of the *Relectiones Morales,* Cologne and Frankfort (1696), § 21, p. 219 *et seq.* For an English translation see Scott, *op. cit., supra,* p. 41.

Forty years after the discovery of the New World, a professor of theology in the University of Salamanca, extended to the problems arising through Spanish colonization of the New World the principles of that enlightened justice which the Spanish theologians applied to the relations of the nations and states of Christian civilization.

Thus a Christendom, broken by the Reformation, was replaced by an international community, today universal and embracing all peoples of all continents; the law applicable to members of the Christian community was found to be applicable to non-Christians; and the law of nations, once confined to Christendom, has become international. Without ceasing to be Christian in fact, the law of nations became laicized in form; and from century to century it has enlarged its content to meet new conditions by making that express which previously was implicit. Through Francisco de Vitoria it became a science—the science of the rules of social conduct; a moral science, because it applies to moral beings. It was endowed with its philosophy by Francisco Suárez; and it was given its literary form by Grotius in his *Commentary on the Law of Prize*—first written in 1604-5, and revised from time to time, but which unfortunately remained in manuscript until 1868—and its classic and over-elaborated form in his Three Books on the *Law of War and Peace,* published for the first time in 1625, in the midst of a Thirty Years' War.

Thus the discovery of America gave birth to a modern law of nations, Spanish in origin, lay in form, but Catholic in fact and capable of continued development under the control of that Christian morality of which all peoples, and therefore all nations, are the beneficiaries.

The Spanish school came into being and passed out within the course of a century, but it has to its credit the modern law of nations—not merely as law but as a philosophy—Grotius himself saying that "the theologians," and not the professional "jurists," are the ones who "follow natural reason." [3]

[3] GROTIUS, *De iure praedae,* chapter vii, ms. p. 51: "Qua in parte theologorum magis sententiae, quam jurisperitorum standum est. Illi enim rationem sequuntur naturalem, hi vero instituta civilia, quae utilitatis alicujus causa permittunt fieri saepe, quod alioqui facere non licet." The manuscript of the *De iure praedae,* edited, with

Francisco de Vitoria was a Dominican—a member of the Order of Preachers—and he preached to the best of purposes. Before the Society of Jesus came into being, the Dominicans specialized in foreign missions, following in the wake of Columbus, and in this field of beneficent and humanitarian activity Bartolomé de Las Casas stands out—and justly—as the Apostle to the Indians, and one whose noble example the Jesuits were later to imitate.

As a Dominican, Victoria was naturally interested in their missions to the New World, which then perhaps loomed larger on the western horizon than now; letters from the brethren beyond the seas passed from hand to hand, and tales of improper conduct on the part of the brethren themselves were not wanting. Victoria's idea was to treat the Indians as brothers and as equals, to help them in their worldly affairs, to instruct them in spiritual matters and lead them to the altar by the persuasion of a Christian life on the part of the missionary. Or, as Chaucer puts it:

> But Cristes lore, and his apostles twelve
> He taught, but first he folwed it himselve.

Deeply versed in the lore of the Church, through his attendance at the University of Paris—then without question the international center—and his contact with thousands of foreigners who, like himself, were completing their studies, lodged in quarters appropriately known as their "nations," and who could not fail to see themselves in their fellow students, it was inevitable that Victoria should make of Aquinas the guide of his life, for St. Thomas was also a Dominican; he had also studied in the University of Paris, and had even been its Rector. To be sure, the *Sentences* of Peter Lombard were still in vogue, but they were being replaced in matters spiritual by the theology of St. Thomas Aquinas—then and today the doctrine of the Church—and, in matters national and international, by conceptions of

an introduction, by H. G. Hamaker, was published at The Hague in 1868 by Martinus Nijhoff. An English translation and a collotype reproduction of the Latin text are now being prepared by the Carnegie Endowment for International Peace and will be published in its series of the *Classics of International Law*.

St. Thomas, which gave permanent form to the views of Aristotle on the nature of the state, and to the views of St. Augustine on the two great questions which interest and baffle us today—war and peace.

When Victoria became *prima* professor of theology in Salamanca in 1526, the conceptions of St. Thomas also made their appearance, and when Victoria died twenty years later, the doctrine, spiritual and temporal, of St. Thomas remained as a monument of Victoria's foresight and influence.

When in 1532 Victoria prepared his public Reading *On the Indians Lately Discovered,*[4] he appropriately discarded the Old for the New Testament, for was not his text— "Teach all nations, baptizing them in the name of the Father, and of the Son and of the Holy Spirit." We have already examined this Reading at length, but for present purposes a further word or two concerning it is essential. The text involved the baptism of children of tender age, of unbelievers, without the consent of their parents. The authorities which he invoked were Peter Lombard and of course St. Thomas Aquinas, Doctors of the Church—The *Sententiae* (Dist. 4) of the former, and the *Secunda Secundae* (Question 10, Art. 12), and the *Tertia Pars* (Question 68, Art. 10), of the latter. Here a casual reader turning the page might perhaps lay the Reading aside without troubling himself further with Victoria, his text or his authorities; but if he were a Spaniard, the next sentence would hold him spellbound as Coleridge's Ancient Mariner held the unwilling wedding guest.

"The whole of this controversy and discussion," Victoria declares, "was started"—as we already know—"on account of the aborigines of the New World, commonly called Indians, who came forty years ago into the power of the Spaniards not having been previously known to our world." Here we have Victoria's own statement that the controversy of which he was to discourse had arisen not merely on account of the discovery of the New World, but because of the Indians coming into the power of the Spaniards. There is power and there is power. There is the

[4] For details concerning reproductions of Victoria's *Relectiones* see *supra*, p. 2, note 2.

power of justice; there is, unfortunately, the power of injustice. The question which confronted and deeply concerned Victoria, who insisted that the conduct of his government should be right, and that the duty of right-minded men was to set it aright —or at least endeavor to do so—was whether the Spaniards, his countrymen, were justified in taking possession of the territories of the aborigines of the New World, commonly called Indians, and, if so, on what grounds; if not—to use an academic expression—why not? And the question being one of right, which may be and often is different from law—since the conventional view is that right is a moral, whereas law is a legal conception—caused Victoria to state that "it is not for jurists to settle this question or at any rate not for jurists only," for "since the barbarians in question . . . were not in subjection by human law; it is not by human, but by divine law that questions concerning them are to be determined." Why was this so? Because, Victoria adds, and very properly, in terms applicable to our day as well: "Jurists are not skilled enough in the divine law to be able by themselves to settle questions of this sort"; nor was he sure that "in the discussion and determination of this question theologians have ever been called competent to pronounce on so grave a matter." Why was the matter so grave? "And as the issue," he continued, "concerns the forum of conscience, its settlement belongs to the priests, that is, to the Church."

We have just referred to the conventional view that law and right may differ, that the legal conception and the moral conception are things apart. But is this true? Are not the two sets of terms, in fact, complementary. What is morality without rules? And what is law without the moral guide of justice? If we insist that law be moral, instead of a mere command of an artificial superior, then we shall make morality the test of law and find ourselves in accord with Victoria and the Spanish School.

But Victoria had in mind an additional purpose, which he reveals by asking: "In order that the whole of the matter be adequately examined and assured, is it not possible that so weighty a business may produce other special doubts deserving of discussion?" He answered that he thought that he would be "doing something which is not only not futile and useless, but well worth the trouble, if"—speaking in the first person—"I am enabled to discuss this question in a manner befitting its importance." He did discuss, in its various aspects, this international event which, in its material aspect, is supposed to be the most important event of modern history—indeed, it separates the medieval from the modern world. And the discussion, conducted "in a manner befitting its importance," was not only "not futile and useless, but well worth the trouble," as it resulted in the modern law of nations, which is also, in no slight degree, the law of nations of the future.

To come, however to the opening paragraph of Victoria's Reading *On the Indians Lately Discovered*.[5] The "disputation about them" was to fall into three parts. It did. In the first he inquired "by what right these Indian natives came under Spanish sway." This phase of the subject required an examination not merely from the national but from the international point of view, leading him to state those principles of right and wrong in international relations, which he himself, as a high-minded son of the Church, with a legal training as sound as his conception of morality, considered applicable.

But the question was even larger, for the second part dealt with the rights which "the Spanish sovereigns obtained over them"—the Indians recently discovered—"in temporal and civil matters"—these rights, of course, to be tested by right, not might. But the question was even broader than this, involving not only the rights of the sovereigns, but those which "the Church obtained over them"—meaning, of course, the American barbarians—"in matters spiritual and touching religion." These questions required an answer equally broad in scope—an answer involving the law of international relations: the right of a foreign nation to impose itself on equals as well as on inferior nations; and also the spiritual relations of nations and their peoples to one

[5] *De Indis*, p. 116.

another. Under three headings we have the program of the modern international law.

As the relations of the Spaniards and the Indians were relations, to use Victoria's own phrase, "of Indian principalities" with the Spanish monarch—in other words, relations of state with state—it is not merely advisable, but essential that we consider the state, its origin and its purpose, from within, before proceeding to its external relations and discussing whether, either as a mere state, or as a single state in an association of states, it possesses a municipal sanction, *in esse* or *in posse,* for every rule of the law of nations.

Victoria, as we have said, was elected *prima* professor of theology in the University of Salamanca in 1526, having been previously appointed professor and also director of studies in the University of Vallodolid, in the then capital of Spain. The method at that time of choosing a professor was interesting and bids fair to make its appearance again—a competition with public disquisitions of the candidates upon set subjects, in the presence of the students, who would choose from among the candidates for the chair the one who seemed best to meet requirements. Assuredly in Victoria's case the choice has met with the approval of succeeding centuries. It gave him the opportunity which he no doubt had in mind, since his eighteen years in France in the formative period of his life had confirmed him in internationalism—for who, belonging to a church which was international, could help but be an internationalist?

Now there were two professors of theology in the University of Salamanca—the *prima* and the *vespera*—the holder of the *prima* chair—the more coveted—meeting his class at six o'clock in the morning, when the student body was not worn out by the day's task, as was probably the case when its members came together at vespers in the afternoon. Probably also that was the reason why the morning class was but an hour and a half in duration, whereas in the afternoon it sat in continuous session at the feet of the *vespera* master for two full hours. The later period seems to us more attractive, although perhaps early or late Victoria would draw today as he did at Salamanca, where his auditors were said to number a round thousand.

It was the duty of the *prima* professor, in addition to his teaching, to deliver at least once a year a public address or disquisition, ordinarily based upon the course which he had professed throughout an academic term. The course consisted of *lectiones* or daily readings and the *Publicum* (the term in vogue in Germany) was called a *relectio,* which would be considered not as a re-reading of the entire course but as a re-statement of the views which had been set forth more at length.

As the international law of Victoria, as well as of other persons learned in the subject, is the law applicable to states and their peoples, it is necessary, as we have said to discuss in some detail Victoria's conception of the origin and nature of the state and its government. And as a prelude to this discussion it will be advisable to give an outline of his conception in summary form. Victoria's view on the origin and nature of the state is the Aristotelian view that man, as a social and political animal, must live in organized society; and this, Victoria holds, by both divine and natural law. There must be government, for the people would fall apart if the rights of each were not accompanied by the correlative duties. In this government the source of power is twofold. It is divine, in that, according to a text adopted by Victoria, "all power is from God"; and it is human in that the form and exercise of that power depend upon the will of the majority of the people.

The introductory remarks to Victoria's *Relectio* on the State (*De Potestate Civili*) are in the nature of a justification, not merely of the topic which he had chosen, but of the method of its presentation. In the words of Victoria:

> The duties and functions of the theologian extend over a field so vast, that no argument, no discussion, no text, seem alien to the practice and purpose of theology. And this may account for the fact that the lack of able and sound theologians is as great as—not to say greater than—the lack of orators which is mentioned by Cicero, and which he explains by saying that men who are distinguished and skilled in every science and

in all the arts are very rare. Theology, indeed, is the first of all those sciences and studies which the Greeks call Θεολογία.

Consequently, there is no occasion for surprise, if very few are found who are competent in a subject so difficult. In this immense domain, then, and in the extensive field composed of the writings of all scholars, an infinite number of possibilities present themselves; but I have selected one passage for special notice: surely if it merits my consideration and treatment of it, it is worthy—most illustrious and learned gentlemen—of your attention. The passage, then, concerns the State: a matter with regard to which many points remain to be considered, although earnest and erudite men have already accorded it extensive treatment. Since the topic is too broad to be disposed of in a single discussion, I have chosen as the subject for today the public and private power by which States are governed.

The passage to be read and commented upon is from the 'Master of the Sentences' (2d. 44), and is based upon the words of Paul (*Romans,* 13:1): 'There is no power but of God.' Although a multitude of topics might be brought up in connection with this passage, nevertheless, our entire discussion shall be limited for the present to laic or secular power, in order that we may not be more discursive and rambling than is needful.

Victoria was not merely a master of the scholastic method, but through him the old scholastic method was renewed so as to apply to the newer theology whereof he was also the accredited master. The favorite authorities of Victoria's day in matters of the state were Aristotle and Cicero, and through Victoria we hear, as it were, their voices. As a Christian the New Testament was his guide, and just as in the case of the Reading *On the Indians Lately Discovered,* he took his text, in the Reading *On the Civil Power,* from the *Sentences* of Peter Lombard, from St. Augustine and from the *Summa* of St. Thomas Aquinas.

But to the state. The first question which confronted Victoria was the source of power; and the power "by which the secular state is governed"—the words are those of Victoria, for his concern was the secular state—"is not only just and legitimate, but is so surely ordained of God, that not even by the consent of the whole world can it be destroyed or annulled."

Now power, he says, "is twofold—public and private"—and Victoria's first anxiety was to state "the causes of civil laic power," as it was to be, he says, "the subject of the whole lecture." He here invokes the authority of Aristotle, to the effect that " 'necessity' should be considered from the viewpoint of purpose," the first, as Aristotle holds, "of all causes, and the principal one."

What, then, of "the purpose that underlies the establishment of the power which we are about to consider?" Mother Nature looked after the animal world, supplying it with the means of protection. "To man alone," Victoria says, "she granted reason and virtue," and man being endowed with reason, could not live in solitude, either for his own comfort or for the perpetuation of the species; and he was likewise endowed with speech, "the messenger of the understanding," inasmuch as, in the famous phrase of Aristotle, he is a civil and sociable animal. For justice—"and the same is true of friendship"—"cannot be practised except by the multitude" (to be understood in this connection as meaning, it is believed, "more than one").

"Therefore," says Victoria, "since human societies have been established for this purpose—namely, that we should bear one another's burdens—and civil society is of all societies that which best provides for the needs of men, it follows that the community is, so to speak, an exceedingly natural form of intercommunication."

But "a single family is not self-sufficing." If society is in accord with nature, then it follows that states and commonwealths are not the invention of man, but of nature, "who produced this method of protecting and preserving mortals."

What is the conclusion which Victoria draws from these premises? That "the same purpose and necessity underlie the existence of public powers," and that hence, public powers are in accord with nature, and therefore "the use and the utility of public power, and of the community, and of society are absolutely the same." Why this identity? "For if all were equal," Victoria says, "and subject to no power, each individual would draw away from the others in accordance with his own opinions and will." What would be the consequence? "The commonwealth would of necessity be torn apart; and the State would be dissolved."

These observations are of the utmost importance, lying as they do at the root of government. Victoria was apparently of this opinion, because he invoked the authority of the New Testament, contained in substantially the same wording in three of the Gospels: "Every kingdom divided against itself shall be brought to desolation"; and "where there is no ruler . . . the people shall perish." The conclusion of Victoria on this phase of the subject is that "if States and societies are established in accordance with divine or natural law, the same is true of power, without which States could not exist." This is design in nature, according to the Greeks; according to the Christians, God in action.

In the Victorian conception, government must be according to the law natural and divine, but the form of the government must depend upon the state, that is, the people united in a community, "which by its very nature is competent to govern and administer itself, and to order all its powers for the common good." In this connection, Victoria reverts to the statement he has already made—that if the state were without a head, "the commonwealth would of necessity be torn apart"—to use again his language. For if all were equal, there would be no superior, and consequently in an assembly no "one individual" could of himself assume authority, "in view of the fact that every man has by natural law the power and the right to defend himself, there being nothing more natural than to repel force by force." But if the state were not, so to speak, "beheaded," the situation would be otherwise, since the community or state might protect the right of each individual, "in order to preserve the integrity of the whole, and in a spirit of devotion to the public good."

What should be the governing will—that of a single person—as in a monarchy (which Victoria prefers); or the authority vested in a select few (as in an aristocracy); or vested in the many (as in the case of a democracy)? We of today must supply our own answer to this question.

But whatever the form, it is necessary that the administration of the state should be entrusted to the care of some person or persons (and it matters not whether this power is entrusted to one or to many). If this were not so, Victoria would be sore pressed to acknowledge that "princes and other magistrates found among pagans are legitimate."

What, then, is the Victorian definition of public secular power? It is "the faculty, authority, or right to govern the civil State," whether it be Christian or pagan; but be the government a monarchy, an aristocracy, or a democracy there need be no less liberty in one than in another, and the ruler of one or the other binds the state, which "as a whole may rightfully be punished for the sin of the monarch"—meaning thereby the chief executive. To such an extent is this true that, in Victoria's words, "if any king make unjust war upon another ruler, the injured party may plunder and make lawful war upon and slay the subjects of the unjust king, even if all these subjects be innocent; for when the king"—or other agency—"has once been set up by the State, any immoderate act of his is charged against the State."

That the head of the state—whatever the name, whether consisting of one or of a number—is to be chosen by a majority of the people, and is to be subject to the government which has been established, is clear from the illustrations which Victoria gives. "Just as the majority of members of a State may set up a king over the whole State, although other members are unwilling," so "in free States such as Venice and Florence, the majority may elect a king even though the rest of the citizens be opposed." The proof in either case betrays a subtlety on the part of the great Dominican which would seem to be more natural to Suárez than to Victoria. "It suffices," Victoria says, "in order to do anything legitimately, that the majority should agree on the course in question." "This point," he observes, much to our pleasure, "can be satisfactorily demonstrated," adding by way of illustration: "For if two parties disagree, it must necessarily result that the sentiment of one party should prevail; and inasmuch as their desires conflict, the sentiment of the party which is in the minority ought not to prevail; therefore it is the sentiment of the majority which should dominate." Victoria, although not given to hairsplitting, as is the wont of the philosopher, adds:

"If the consent of all is required in order to create the king, why is it not also required in order that he be not so created? Why is unanimous consent more to be required in an affirmative than in a negative matter?"—a doctrine which applies, it would seem, in the unmaking as well as in the making of an agent of the state.

The dethroning of a monarch is thus the prerogative of the majority, and a revolt is justifiable if only it has the support of the majority in its behalf.

In short, governments are made by peoples, not by princes. The state has the power of self-government, as in the case of the Venice and Florence of Victoria's day—not to speak of this Western World of ours; "for the State," he says, "has the power of self-government, and the act of the greater part is the act of the whole; therefore, the State may accept the form of government that it desires, even if this be not the best form. Rome, for example, possessed an aristocratic government, which is not the best type." In this we agree, preferring a representative democracy.

At the beginning of his public address *On the Civil Power,* Victoria stated that the Reading would be restricted to certain conclusions. Having disposed of various preliminary matters, he devotes the balance of the Reading to a final and all important conclusion: "the laws and constitutions of princes are binding in such a way as to render transgressors guilty in the court of conscience." This is indeed a weighty subject, about which there was a difference of opinion. The importance of the conclusion was not lost upon Victoria; otherwise he would not have assigned it, as it were, the place of honor. "If time permitted," he said, "many points neither futile nor unworthy of mention might be brought up in this connection and in support of this conclusion. But inasmuch as a lengthy discussion would be inopportune," doubtless out of consideration for his audience, "I shall dispose of the whole matter in as few words as possible." We shall follow his example. First he stated the view of his opponents, who held that "the laws possess no force which, renders trangressors guilty in the court of conscience," admitting, however, that "princes and magistrates may justly punish the violators of said laws." The concession in this matter is immaterial, inasmuch as the violations of the laws of the state are punishable by the appropriate authorities of the state.

However, it seemed to Victoria "indubitable that civil laws are binding in the court of conscience." His authority? The Apostle Paul: "Wherefore ye must needs be subject, not only for wrath, but also for conscience sake." Victoria adds: "And Peter says: 'Submit yourselves to every ordinance of man for the Lord's sake: whether it be to the king, as supreme . . .,' an admonition,"[7] Victoria adds, "which would seem entirely unintelligible if laws were binding only in the courts of civil contentions and not in the court of conscience." Victoria then says "that civil laws are binding under pain of sin and guilt, in the same manner as ecclesiastical laws."

The two kinds of law he finds in agreement, for "divine law so endows a thing with the quality of a virtue or a vice that anything which is in accordance with the mandates of divine law is rendered good and serviceable, although it would not otherwise be possessed of these characteristics; whereas that which is prohibited by divine law has in it something evil and vicious which it would not otherwise have."

A little later he adds: "In like manner, human law has this same power to endow anything with the quality of a virtue, and its opposite with the quality of a vice." Therefore he states his opinion in two short sentences: "There is no difference in this respect between human and divine law. For in both cases, just as there is merit in an act of virtue, so guilt attends a vicious act."

The violation of divine law is a mortal, not a venial, sin. To the objection that the human law does not state whether the violation is a mortal or a venial sin, Victoria answers that "not even in divine law, and especially not in natural law, is a statement always included as to whether a given precept concerns mortal or venial sin." In each case, the question of mortal or venial sin "must be decided according to the particular case involved." Perhaps even today it is not superfluous to add that

[7] *Romans*, xiii. 5; *Peter*, ii. 13.

taxation is necessary for the well-being of the state. Victoria says roundly indeed, that "if any one should fail to pay his taxes, he would be committing a mortal sin," and among other illustrations he more than intimates that "if it is prohibited that any one should carry money out of the country, all those who do so are committing a mortal sin," from which it appears that Victoria was a man of the world as well as a theologian.

There are two questions of more than passing importance which Victoria discusses and which have greatly perplexed the past: "Has the king power to exempt one from liability to guilt, if he should so desire"—meaning, may the king, or, as we would say, the chief executive, issue a pardon of an offense and remit a punishment? His answer is "that without doubt he is empowered to do so." This is universal practice, after trial and conviction, although the right should be and is only sparingly used. The next question is whether the laws of the state are binding upon the members of the legislature who enact them and upon kings—meaning, of course, chief executives as well. There was a difference of opinion on this matter in his time, and it was that difference of opinion in the English-speaking world which brought the head of Charles Stewart to the block. Victoria was clear about the matter, maintaining against opposition that both legislators and executives are bound—for a reason which is worth while noting: "although the act of creating the law be voluntary on the part of the king; nevertheless, the fact that he is thereby bound or not bound, does not depend upon his own will: just as in the case of pacts; for he who enters into a pact of his own free will, is nevertheless bound thereby."

The assimilation of a pact to a law, binding those who have entered into it voluntarily, can not be passed over, for, although Victoria is dealing with the state—that is, men, women and children in association, and therefore forming a society—he had also in mind the association of the states and their peoples in a larger community extending beyond the narrow confines of Europe and embracing in our day the entire world, which society, being composed of natural persons, would disintegrate and the association dissolve, if, although equal, its members did not vest their governments with authority to make laws, to compel their execution and to punish their violation. So also the larger community composed of these states would fall asunder, if there were not laws, and pacts having the force of laws, whereby the states forming the international community should conform their actions to the laws and pacts of their making. Therefore, to quote again Victoria's conclusion in his own language, as it was and still is the goal toward which the forward-looking and far-seeing are directed:

> From all that has been said, a corollary may be inferred, namely: that international law has not only the force of a pact and agreement among men, but also the force of a law; for the world as a whole, being in a way one single State, has the power to create laws that are just and fitting for all persons, as are the rules of international law. Consequently, it is clear that they who violate these international rules, whether in peace or in war, commit a mortal sin; moreover, in the gravest matters, such as the inviolability of ambassadors, it is not permissible for one country to refuse to be bound by international law, the latter having been established by the authority of the whole world.

For the violation of this law—which is a mortal sin—there exists the court of conscience. There is also, now existing at The Hague—and, appropriately in the Peace Palace—a Permanent Court of International Justice, in which the violations of the law of nations can be determined and righted. We can see the court at The Hague with our own eyes, but the court of conscience is none the less existent, although invisible, and it was to this court to which no less an internationalist than Grotius appealed in behalf of the rights of the Netherlands against the opposition of the Portuguese to Dutch navigation on the high seas and to trade without let or hindrance in the islands and territories of the Indian Ocean.

After saying that courts within nations take charge of violations of the law committed within their jurisdictions, and that the Creator of the Universe reserved to Himself punishment of the offenses of nations and their rulers, Grotius adds that there is one tribunal which even the luckiest of sinners does not escape, namely, conscience, or the estimation of one's self, and public opinion, or the estimation of others. "To this double tribunal," he says, "we bring a new case. It is in truth no petty case . . . No! It is a case which concerns practically the entire expanse of the high seas, the right of navigation, the freedom of trade . . . . In this controversy"—between Spain and the Netherlands—"we appeal to those jurists among the Spanish themselves who are especially skilled in both divine and human law; we actually invoke the very laws of Spain itself." [8]

Hitherto, in dealing with the Reading *On the Civil Power* we have been considering the "state" of Victoria, since the state is as a person in this larger state which we call the international community. And just as the inhabitants of a state, such as Spain, his own country, were bound by its national law, so his country, as a "person" of the international community of states, was and is bound hand and foot, as it were, by the law of nations.

Now, "the law of nations," in the Victorian conception, either is natural law or is "derived from natural law," and quoting the *Institutes* of Justinian, Victoria adds: "What natural reason has established among all nations is called the *jus gentium.*"

It should be observed that he remarks, in what we would call a sort of offhand way, that a large part at least of this *jus gentium* is synonymous in content with natural law, and that natural law is the source from which it flows. As we have seen, later on in the third section of the Reading *On the Indians,* in the opening paragraph of which the definition of international law is given, he completes his idea: "Indeed, there are many things in this connection which issue from the law of nations, which, because it has a sufficient derivation from natural law, is clearly capable of conferring rights and creating obligations." Here we catch a glimpse in the offing, but nevertheless a glimpse, of the impending sanction.

But to continue Victoria's enlargement of his definition: "even if we grant that it [the law of nations] is not always derived from natural law, yet there exists clearly enough"—What? Nothing more or less than "a consensus of the greater part of the whole world, especially in behalf of the common good of

[8] *Mare Liberum,* Carnegie Endowment Edition (New York, 1916), p. 4.

all." This, in short, defines not only the law but the standard of the law.

Again to continue with Victoria's illustration. "For," he says, "if after the early days of the creation of the world or its recovery from the flood the majority of mankind decided that ambassadors should everywhere be reckoned inviolable and that the sea should be common and that prisoners of war should be made slaves"—at one time they were killed, later enslaved, later still ransomed, and in our day exchanged—"and if this, namely, that strangers should not be driven out, were deemed a desirable principle, it would certainly have the force of law, even though the rest of mankind objected thereto." This is not merely Victoria's law of nations, but the process by which that law of nations may be developed to meet the changing conditions of a changing world.

But Victoria immediately indulges in a further example, which will be peculiarly pleasing to our fellow-countrymen, for in advance he commends their adoption of the rule of *jus soli* in determining nationality: "If children of any Spaniard be born there," he says, meaning in our America, "and they wish to acquire citizenship, it seems they can not be barred either from citizenship or from the advantages enjoyed by other citizens—I refer to the case where the parents had their domicile there." The proof thereof is the law of nations, and one of its rules he now proceeds to apply. "He is to be called and is a citizen who is born within the state."[9] However, the authority is not enough. As a schoolman, he felt the necessity for it to be confirmed, and he says that "the confirmation lies in the fact that, as man is a civil animal, whoever is born in any one state is not a citizen of another state." So reasonable was the enlightened Spaniard that he eliminated by a stroke of his pen, or by a stress of his voice, the stateless person, saying immediately: "Therefore, if he were not a citizen of the state referred to, he would not be a citizen of any state, to the prejudice of his rights under both natural law and the law of nations."

Yet this is not all. The sojourner in the Americas who does

[9] JUSTINIAN, INST. lib. VIII, tit. 62, § 11.

not have the good fortune to be born in our part of the world, may become an American by naturalization. "Aye," Victoria continues, "and if there be any persons who wish to acquire a domicile in some state of the Indians, as by marriage or in virtue of any other fact whereby other foreigners are wont to become citizens, they can not be impeded any more than others"—here we have the favored nation clause—"and consequently they enjoy the privileges of citizens just as others do"; and the proviso is the law of our day, as well as of his—"provided they also submit to the burdens to which others submit." And though it be against the present immigration law of the United States, which would have excluded many of us were we or our forbears not fortunate enough to have arrived before it was passed, Victoria says expressely that "refusal to receive strangers and foreigners is wrong in itself."

This is a sample of what the Spaniard could say in a couple of paragraphs, and it is therefore no wonder that in two short disquisitions he set forth in essence the law of nations as it was in his day, as it now is, and as it will be in generations, if not centuries, hence.

But what of rights and obligations—or, rather, obligations which are correlative with rights? The matter was one for which Victoria had a predilection, so that he considered it not only in his *Relectio,* but also in his daily lectures to his classes, which, it may be added, are in the course of publication at the present time, several volumes already having appeared containing Victoria's commentaries on the *Secunda Secundae* of St. Thomas.[10]

A certain lecture consisted of a commentary or discussion of Question 40 of the *Secunda Secundae* of St. Thomas on the subject of war; and it is interesting to note—although we may not dwell upon it here—that therein are implied, where not expressed, all of Victoria's views on the subject of war, as set forth in his later formal Reading. For our present purpose,

[10] Edited by R. P. Vicente Beltrán de Heredia, O.P., under the title *Francisco de Vitoria, O.P., Comentarios a la Secunda secundae de Santo Tomás,* and published in the collection *Biblioteca de Teólogos Españoles* issued at Salamanca, Spain. Four volumes of the *Comentarios* have now been published (1932-1934).

however, we can choose but a single passage from the lecture—one which contains not merely the seed but the budding flower of the Victorian conception of sanctions.

"In the case of defensive warfare," Victoria says, "any king whatsoever and any commonwealth whatsoever—for example, this city [meaning the city in which he was lecturing]—may defend themselves"; and the passage which we are quoting is an admirable example of Victoria's method—first in the abstract, then a concrete example: "If the inhabitants of Toledo attack the inhabitants of Salamanca, the latter may defend themselves on their own authority. There can be no doubt on this point. Secondly, I hold," he says, "that the power of the prince is derived from the state. Therefore, in cases in which it is permissible for a state to wage war, it is in like manner permissible for a king to wage war." In our own behalf, we may add, by way of comment, that kings are, as it were, agents of an organized community. "Thirdly," speaking again in the first person, he continues, "I hold that there is a distinction between private persons and states; for, granting that a private person may defend himself and his property, it is nevertheless impermissible for him to avenge himself or to reclaim his own property save through the judge." Here we have the very heart and soul of Victoria's system. Within the state there is a court of the prince, to which every injured person must resort, unless he is obliged on the instant to defend his life or to maintain his property against the immediate danger of an overwhelming attack. On other occasions the resort must be to law through a court of justice. In a word, Victoria's system is law with a court to interpret the law and to declare the sanction to be applied.

To recur again to Victoria: "For if it were permissible for him to do so in a different manner, that is, if any person whatsoever were the judge of his own cause, it would not be possible to govern the world." Why must this be so? Victoria replies: "For such [a state of affairs] would be contrary not only to divine law, but also to natural law," both of which permit—and indeed require—the organization of a state, under a "prince" or other magistrate, in order to keep peace and tranquility within the borders of the community. "The state, on the other hand," he goes on to say, "has complete power to avenge itself, to recover its own property, and to punish its enemies," the truth whereof is demonstrated by the fact that, "if the state had not this power, there would be disorder in the world, and injury would be suffered at the hands of the wicked." What, then, is to be done? "Wherefore it follows, that, with respect to these three points—namely, avenging itself upon its enemies, recovering its property, and punishing its enemies—the state possesses the same power over its enemies as that which it possesses over its subjects." And the conclusion? "And if the state has this power, so also has the prince; for he draws his power from the state."

In the association of the artificial persons which we call states of the international community, the international court, in Victoria's day, was lacking, although the process of remedying right and wrong was in its nature and essence judicial.

So much by way of introduction, taken from Victoria's commentary on Question 40 of the *Secunda Secundae* of St. Thomas.

And now a passage—already referred to, but well worth many a careful examination—from Victoria's Reading *On the Law of War,*[11] in which the sanction makes its material appearance. To begin with, Victoria says: "Princes have authority not only over their own subjects, but also over foreigners, so far as to prevent them from committing wrongs." How can this be so? "By the law of nations and by the authority of the whole world." In the next passage, Victoria adds: "By natural law also, seeing that otherwise society could not hold together unless there was somewhere a power and authority to deter wrongdoers and prevent them from injuring the good and innocent." This power must exist, and because it must exist and is essential to the existence of every organized society, whether group, state or the international community, it is power under the natural law. "Now," declares Victoria, "everything needed for the government and preservation of society exists by natural law, and in no other

[11] See *supra*, p. 32. The Latin text of the Reading is to be found in Getino, *op. cit.*, and the Carnegie Institution edition of Victoria, *op. cit.* An English translation is also printed in the latter volume.

way"—he is bold enough to say—"can we show that a State has by natural law authority to inflict pains and penalties on its citizens who are dangerous to it." In this passage, Victoria is speaking, of course, of a single and organized state for which he has in a sentence provided the sanction, based on natural law, to be used within its borders. Turning to the international community, he says: "But if a state can do this to its own citizens, society at large"—including in the term "society" that largest of communities which embraces the world at large—"can do it to all wicked and dangerous folk, and this can only be through the instrumentality of princes"—or the agency of the state, as we would say today. "It is, therefore, certain," he continues, "that princes can punish enemies who have done a wrong to their State and that after a war has been duly and justly undertaken the enemy are just as much within the jurisdiction of the prince who undertakes it as if he were their proper judge." Here we have the judicial conception of international law applied not merely to the state but to the society of states, requiring for its development and application a court of the prince in the midst of equal states.

"For instance," to use Victoria's own example in a later passage of the same Reading *On War*: "If French brigands made a raid into Spanish territory and the French king would not, though able"—note the word "able"—"compel them to restore their booty, the Spanish might, on the authorization of their sovereign, despoil French merchants or farmers, however innocent these might be." We are in the presence of a law and the authorization of the sovereign to apply it as against persons who, in judicial terms, would be called the defendant state. Why does this right of reprisals exist? "Because," Victoria informs us, "although the French State or Sovereign might initially be blameless, yet it is a breach of duty, as St. Augustine says, for them [the French State or Sovereign] to neglect"—note the word "neglect"—"to vindicate the right against the wrongdoing of their subjects"—not in their own behalf, but in behalf of the state and of its people—"and the injured sovereign can take satisfaction from every member and portion of their State." What is the inner meaning of this, implicit, if not express? That the defendant king has failed to provide a sanction and a law to carry it into effect, thus manifesting a lamentable lack of that "due diligence" required of both prince and state in international relations.

"An evil and adulterous generation seeketh after a"—sanction; but none other need be given than that of Victoria.

It is universally admitted that there must be relations between nations, for no nation, however large and powerful and possessed of material wealth, is sufficient unto itself. It is also admitted that there should be a law upon which these relations should be based. It is generally—although not universally—admitted that the law in such cases is the law of nations; but there is doubt among the modern "doctors" whether the law international or the law of nations can properly be called law because it lacks a "something," and that "something" is called a "sanction."

Perhaps the simplest way to settle the difference of opinion would be to suggest that there are various kinds of law which culminate in the law of nations. There is what is called "natural law"; there is what is called "divine law"; there is the law of the state, which we call in English "municipal law"; and there is something indefinable and intangible, and yet vastly important—the law, or, as we generally say, the rule of reason, synonymous, in a sense, with what is called natural law and at the same time a source of law.

As we are dealing with law, it is best to rely upon adjudged cases in which law, recognized as such, has been applied. On the question of sanction, we cite first *The Prometheus,*[12] decided in the Supreme Court of Hongkong, in 1906, by Sir Henry Spencer Berkeley, Acting Chief Justice, which case was made, as it were, for our present purpose. It was stated that the owners of the *Prometheus*—a Norwegian vessel—took aboard, in the war between Russia and Japan, a cargo to be delivered to a Japanese port. The question involved was whether food-stuffs were, or were not, contraband under the laws of nations. In the language of the learned Chief Justice, "it was contended on behalf of the owners of the *Prometheus* that the term 'law,' as applied to

[12] 2 Hongkong Law Reports 207 (1906).

this recognized system of principles and rules known as international law, is an inexact expression, that there is, in other words, no such thing as international law; that there can be no such law binding upon all nations, inasmuch as there is no sanction for such law, that is to say, that there is no means by which obedience to such law can be imposed upon any given nation refusing obedience thereto."

What did the Chief Justice, a lawyer to his fingertips and engaged in the administration of the law, say to this? He did not concur: "In my opinion a law may be established and become international, that is to say binding upon all nations, by the agreement of such nations to be bound thereby, although it may be impossible to enforce obedience thereto by any given nation party to the agreement." Why should this be so? Because "the resistance of a nation to a law to which it has agreed does not derogate from the authority of the law because that resistance can not, perhaps, be overcome." What, then, is the effect? "Such resistance merely makes the resisting nation a breaker of the law to which it has given its adherence, but it leaves the law, to the establishment of which the resisting nation was a party, still subsisting." With this he might have stopped, but he added two further sentences, one a question and the other an answer. The question: "Could it be successfully contended that because any given person or body of persons possessed for the time being power to resist an established municipal law, such law had no existence?" And "the answer to such a contention would be that the law still existed, though it might not for the time being be possible to enforce obedience to it."

It is to be observed that the learned Chief Justice—and he was indeed learned—was speaking of international law of our day, which he did not define, but it is very material to the present purpose that we have a definition of our day, and what definition could be better than that of Sir Charles Russell, later to be known as Lord Russell of Killowen, a very distinguished practitioner at the bar? He had had experience in international affairs—as had a Chief Justice of the Supreme Court of the United States, who, before his appointment to the Bench, was counsel in the *Alabama* case,[18] and whose authority we shall presently invoke in behalf of municipal sanctions for international law. Sir Charles was counsel for Great Britain in the Bering Sea Arbitration at Paris in 1892, and shortly thereafter he became Lord Chief Justice of Great Britain—the first Catholic raised to that position since the reign of Mary Tudor.

In an address before the American Bar Association in 1896, His Lordship asked the question: "What, then, is international law?"—to which his reply was (and he was not a theorist, but a hard-headed lawyer as well as a distinguished judge upon the Bench): "I know no better definition of it" (meaning international law) "than that it is the sum of the rules or usages which civilized states have agreed shall be binding upon them in their dealings with one another."

The distinguished *prima* professor of theology in the University of Salamanca could not have done better; indeed, it was his view as well as that of the learned Lord Chief Justice, that an "agreement is a pact"; and that a pact is a law which binds both the conscience and the conduct of individuals as well as nations. The difference is a mere question of wording. Writers on law have usually had in mind law as applied to the subjects of a state in their relation to the state and with one another, and that law is generally held to be the command of the superior, that is, of the state, or rather, the sovereign, to the subject—with a material penalty for violation of the law, whether it be fine or imprisonment.

In international relations we are, however, dealing not with a superior and an inferior—as is said to be the case with municipal law (that is, the law of a particular state), but with equals, the theory being that as each state is the equal of the other, there is no superior to prescribe a law to an inferior. Therefore international law—if law be a command of a superior—can not be law. This conclusion, however, does not follow from such a premise; for there may be one kind of law in the case of a state—that of a superior to an inferior—and another kind of law between nations,

18 The Alabama Case, S. Ex. Doc. No. 21, 44th Con., 2d Sess., Report from the Secretary of State, with Accompanying Papers, relating to the Court of Commissioners of Alabama Claims (Washington, 1877), pp. 147, 148.

in which the relationship of superior and inferior does not exist.

Admitting for the sake of argument—although we do not admit it as a fact—that law is a command by the sovereign power in a state (as the analytical school of English jurisprudence insists), it must nevertheless be pointed out that there is a kind of law even within states which is not a command; for indeed, the common law of England was not a comand from the sovereign, although its violation is subject to a penalty. If that be so, it follows that a command is not a necessary element either to a law or to its sanction. It is therefore very material to inquire, then: what is common law? It is frequent usage developing into a custom which, accepted as law, is applied as law through and by courts of justice. The analytical school, however, goes on the theory that what the king permits he commands; hence, the common law, being permitted by the king, is commanded by the king and therefore enforced through the king's courts of justice. Permission, it is to be said, is, however, not a command but is in fact a recognition and acceptance of the custom. Therefore, in the manner of the schoolmen, we may take it as proved that the common law, at least, is not a command.

If there can be law within a state without command, may there not be a law between states without a command? May we not say that in the latter, as in the case of the common law, command is absent, since between and among equals there can be no superior?

Now as there is a common law of the state, so there may be a common law of the states or nations, but between the states there can not be, even upon the basis of the arguments of the analytical school, a common law which is a command, because among equals there can be no superior whose permission can be distorted into a command. How does this common law of nations arise? Frequent usage of nations becomes hardened into the custom of nations, and through the adoption by nations of these universal customs, they become the common law of nations by the tacit agreement of the nations, evidenced by their application of customs in their mutual relations.

Just as the common law in England assumed definite form and

shape through the decisions of courts, so the common law of nations has, in the course of centuries, assumed definite form and shape through the practice of nations. The process, differing in form, is essentially the same in each case; therefore the result should be and is the same. The only difference is that courts of justice exist within the state to apply the customary law in question in suits brought in such courts, the cases being thus decided by judges learned in the law; while on the other hand there has been until recently no court between the nations, although from antiquity to the present day, there have been temporary mixed commissions or tribunals of arbitration created by *agreement* of the parties—that is to say, the states—to decide disputes which have arisen between them and which it has been the desire of the states to settle without a resort to war. In these tribunals, as well as in the Permanent Court of International Justice at The Hague, we have a court without a superior, created by the *agreement* of nations, with a law which it administers, whether it be custom, "as evidence of a general practice accepted as law,"[14] or agreements in the form of pacts, "having the force of law," according to Victoria's statement.

The definition of law as the command of a sovereign—a command which does not exist in customary law, forming a large part of the law of England—can not be said to be essential to the existence of law; and the common law of nations, consisting of generally recognized customs, is even less the command of superiors than are the customs of England. Pacts of equal states—for what state ever voluntarily recognizes itself as inferior to another—are agreements. According to Victoria, pacts are laws and bind those who have entered into them voluntarily. In short, not only customs but pacts, are voluntarily, without the necessary intervention of a sovereign within the state or between the states except as agent of the respective peoples.

But there is another kind of law—positive law, as it is called. This is the law of a king or other ruler, possessed of the right to make law, or of a legislature, having the power to enact laws.

---

[14] Statute of the Permanent Court of International Justice at The Hague, Article 38 (2).

Therefore it is said to be the law of the sovereign. Assuredly, however, it is not the law of a personal sovereign, for such a sovereign no longer makes law in civilized states or communities. He is, for instance, a party to the law-making power in Great Britain, with the right to veto an act of Parliament, which right to veto has not been exercised these many years. In the United States, the Congress, composed of a Senate and a House of Representatives, enacts a law, which, to become effective, requires the approval of the President of the United States; or, to be passed over his veto, it requires the vote of two-thirds of both houses. It is only as a legal fiction, therefore, that the acts of the British Parliament and the acts of the American Congress can be said to be positive law in the sense of a command. But to speak only of the United States, we know that the source of power in each of the American states is vested in the people—men and women—of the states. We know that the legislators who pass acts do so as representatives of the people and that the legislator is their agent, not their master.

Thus it is that the members of the Senate—ninety-six in number—are elected by the men and women of the different states of the American Union, and the members of the House are elected by the states in proportion to their respective populations and within what are called Congressional districts of the individual states. The senators are therefore the representatives of the people of the individual states and the members of the House of Representatives—there is an argument in the very name—are the authorized agents of the voters within their districts—men and women, without distinction of sex, exercising the right to vote. How can it be said that an act of Congress is a command, unless it be a command of the people—from below, not above? The theory of positive law as a command is not only monarchical but it is also archaic. Law in this modern world of ours is not a command; it is the authority and consent of the people given in advance to the enactment of laws which, in the opinion of their chosen agents are necessary for the common good within the state. Whether the laws be national or local, the process is the same, for the legislatures of each state are composed of a lower and an upper house corresponding to the Senate and the House of Representatives of the United States, with the right on the part of the Governor to veto, which veto can be overridden by the two houses of each of the states.

Suppose, however, the act within the state is passed by the legislature and approved by the Governor, but is displeasing to the people of the state. The act will be repealed, because the agency is subject to the principal.

In the same way, the Congress is but the agency of the people of the different states, and an act of Congress which is obnoxious to the people in their united capacity will be repealed. Indeed, the most solemn of laws—an amendment to the Constitution of the United States—which meets with the disapproval of the people of the states is subject to repeal; and within the past year the eighteenth amendment to the Constitution of the United States, forbidding the manufacture and sale of intoxicating liquors, was repealed on the 5th day of December, 1933. The repeal of an amendment requires the concurrence of three-fourths of the states, either by their respective legislatures or by conventions especially called and elected for this purpose, as in the case at hand. This is indeed the consent of the governed; this is the Declaration of Independence in action—of government by the consent of the governed.

If this be the case within every republic of the Western World—of which there are twenty-one—we are justified in believing that it either is or will be the case with every other modern state, so that even if we argue by analogy, there is no need for us to change or attempt to change the conception of international law as a thing of custom or pact, because the law within the state, where once a sovereign power above and beyond the people was exercised by a personal sovereign, has given way to government "of the people, by the people and for the people." Government by command involves a power superior to that of those who are commanded. Government by consent is the only form of government consistent with the nature and dignity of human beings.

Victoria does not express himself on this aspect of law in such definite terms; but what is his government by majorities except government by consent? And therefore within his state, as between nations, there is consent—which is not a command—and between states there are agreements, which negative a command. Therefore we need not trouble ourselves about the definitions of theorists of our day or of writers of the past, who insist that law is a command of a sovereign power above the people forming the state.

Let us consider the statement of Victoria in reference to the international community—"the world as a whole, being in a way one single State." He has proved, as we have seen, that laws are made in the state and that they bind both the legislature and the king even though the act of creating the law be voluntary on the part of the king—and I add, the chief executive, to bring his statement up to date; and that it does not depend upon the will of the legislature or the chief executive that one or the other is bound. Also in the case of pacts, one who enters into a pact of his own free will is nevertheless bound thereby. The pact is an agreement, and a first principle of natural law is that pacts, although entered into voluntarily—and they should be so entered into—are to be kept. *Pacta sunt servanda.*

Proceeding from the group forming the state to the group of states forming the international community, Victoria infers a corollary: "that international law has not only the force of a pact and agreement among men, but also the force of a law." The reason is that "the world as a whole, being in a way one single State, has the power to create laws that are just and fitting for all persons"—that is to say, for all members of each and every group of individuals and of all states forming the international community—"as are the rules of international law." Here we have the groups of individuals associated for a political and social and moral purpose to form a state, and the states in turn forming the international community; and as the state represents the individuals and the group within state lines, so the international community represents the individuals and the states composing the international community.

It is easy enough for us to see all this today. It was not an easy thing for Victoria in his day and generation. Yet he divined the international community, although he did not create it. Indeed, he not only recognized the existence of, but defined, the community which existed of itself, irrespective of the will or the action of any man or of any group; for the international community existed *ex jure necessitatis*.

Now let us suppose that a person residing within a state violates the law of the state. According to Victoria, if the case be one of sufficient gravity, he commits a mortal sin, cognizable in the court of conscience. It is also cognizable in a court of justice; for the law of the state has a double sanction—the one spiritual, in the court of conscience, and the other material, in a court of justice. The great Grotius recognized this and stated it in unmistakable and incontrovertible terms in his address to the Christian Princes, prefixed to his tractate on the *Freedom of the Seas*.[15] What, then, of international rules, applying to each and every state? "Consequently," Victoria says, "it is clear that they who violate these international rules, whether in peace or in war, commit a mortal sin"; and he adds that "in the gravest matters, such as the inviolability of ambassadors, it is not permissible for one country to refuse to be bound by international law." Why? "The latter having been established by the authority of the whole world."

Let us analyze this sentence—for it is but a sentence. We have international rules. But whether they be customs or agreements, or whether the violations of them be in peace or in war, in the cases which we have in mind, there is no command involved. These rules have arisen from customs; or they are express agreements as in the case of pacts. Now, in the Victorian conception, these customary rules, although they are not agreements, in the sense of pacts, are binding, as are pacts, because Victoria selects as his example the inviolability of ambassadors, which inviolability arose from the custom and the practice of nations, and not by municipal statute or by pact; and the custom being general, no country can refuse to be bound by the rule concerning the inviolability of ambassadors—and therefore,

[15] *Supra*, p. 74.

the state being bound by international law, its agents commit a mortal sin if they violate the immunity of ambassadors, a sin cognizable alike in the court of conscience and in a court of justice.

What is the implication of all this? If, by the constitutional law of a state, an act of the legislative body be required in order to carry out the rule of international law, then it is the duty of the nation in question to pass such a municipal statute, and if it does not pass the municipal act, it is liable for damages to the nation or to the individual who may have suffered by its failure so to do. As Victoria frequently chooses the immunity of ambassadors in order to make his meaning clear—inasmuch as the immunities of diplomatic agents are universal and may therefore be considered as "established by the authority of the whole world"—let us test the appositeness of the illustration by a few decisions of municipal courts dealing with such immunities.

The first case is one of more than passing interest.[16] It happened in the lifetime of Peter the Great, Czar of all the Russias, whose empire had formally made its entry into the international community. One Andrew Artemonowitz Mattueof had been appointed "ambassador extraordinary of his czarish majesty, emperor of Great Russia, her majesty's [Queen Anne's] good friend and ally." It appeared that his excellency was arrested and taken "by violence, out of his coach in the public street," and "he was detained in custody for several hours, in contempt of the protection granted by her majesty, contrary to the law of nations and in prejudice of the rights and privileges which ambassadors and other public ministers, authorized and received as such, have at all times been thereby possessed of, and ought to be kept sacred and inviolable."

As a result of this incident there was an act of Parliament passed in the year 1708, to carry into effect the law of nations relating to the immunity of ambassadors and public ministers, an immunity under the law of nations which had been recognized time out of mind. When the case of the Ambassa-

[16] The Case of Andrew Artemonowitz Mattueof, Ambassador of Muscovy, 8 Queen Anne 598, 10 Mod. 5 (1710).

dor of Muscovy—for so he was called in the suit—was tried in the eighth year of the reign of Queen Anne, that is, in 1710, in the Queen's Bench, before Lord Chief Justice Holt, the question before the court was whether an ambassador could lawfully be arrested for debt—or for any other cause. The case was argued by the Attorney-General, Sir James Montague (later Chief Baron of the Exchequer), in behalf of the ambassador, and the Attorney-General said roundly that the ambassador could not be arrested, and then proceeded to state the reasons, as applicable then as they are today: "If the privileges of an ambassador may by law be broken in upon and invaded for the preservation of the property of a private subject, princes will be cautious of sending ambassadors to us; ours must expect the like treatment." This we consider to be a question of general right—not merely immunity from suit for indebtedness. After stating that "few will be prevailed with to take that character [of ambassador] upon them," the Attorney-General continued, "should an ambassador be liable to the restraints of the law of the land to which he goes, how easy would it be, upon an emergency, to take off his attendance upon his master's business." Here we have two reasons: that ambassadors would be unwilling to subject themselves to arrest or restraint; and that, under such circumstances, not merely the ambassador, but the business of his master, would or might suffer. The practice of nations was clearly in favor of immunity; for "the person of an ambassador," the Attorney-General continued, "has ever been held sacred and inviolable by the law of nations." Neither his property nor his person is liable to arrest. There should, however, be a remedy available to prevent abuse of the inviolability; otherwise unscrupulous ambassadors, or other diplomatic agents, might avail themselves of their immunity to violate the laws of the country to which they were accredited. What, then, is the way of preventing this? "An ambassador must be intreated," the Attorney-General further continued, "and upon refusal sent back to his master," the theory being that the country which he represents still exercises exclusive jurisdiction over his person and property, so that, in case he commits an offense or a crime within the country to which he is accredited, he should be returned to the jurisdiction of the country whereof he is the diplomatic agent.

The Attorney-General next dwells upon the representative character of the ambassador, asserting that nobody would say that "the Czar himself might have been arrested," and that "the same fiction of law that makes him [the ambassador] represent the person of his master, makes him extraparochial, and quasi, in the dominions of his master." And, finally, that "the ill treatment of ambassadors is a thing of dangerous consequence, for it may involve the nation in a war, and it would be very inconvenient that this should be in the power of any private person whatsoever."

The persons implicated were arrested, examined before the privy council, and seventeen were committed to prison. They were tried and convicted on the facts by the jury, but no sentence was rendered.

The case of *Triquet* v. *Bath*[17] involved also the question of diplomatic immunities. It was tried in 1764, in the Court of King's Bench, before Lord Chief Justice Mansfield, who decided that "the privilege of foreign ministers and their domestic servants depends upon the law of nations," and that, to quote his exact words, "all that is new in this act[18] is the clause which gives a summary jurisdiction for the punishment of the infractors of this law."

His Lordship then proceeded to recount in an interesting and indeed, entertaining way, for his judgments were literature as well as law, the facts in the case of the Ambassador from Muscovy—the wrath of the Czar and the humiliation of Great Britain, resulting in a special embassy and an illuminated apology to his "czarish majesty." His exact language we quote, lest inadvertently we do an injustice to my Lord Mansfield or to the Czar:

> . . . The act of Parliament was made upon occasion of the Czar's ambassador being arrested. If proper application had been immediately made for his discharge from the arrest, the matter might and doubtless

[17] 3 Burr. 1478 (1764).
[18] 7 Anne, c. 12 (1708).

would have been set right. Instead of that, bail was put in, before any complaint was made. An information was filed by the then Attorney-General against the persons who were thus concerned, as infractors of the law of nations, and they were found guilty, but never brought up to judgment.

The Czar took the matter up, highly. No punishment would have been thought, by him, an adequate reparation. Such a sentence as the court could have given, he might have thought a fresh insult.

Another expedient was fallen upon and agreed to; this Act of Parliament passed, as an apology and humiliation from the whole nation. It was sent to the Czar, finely illuminated, by an ambassador extraordinary, who made excuses in a solemn oration.

A great deal relative to this transaction and negotiation appears in the annals of that time; and from a correspondence of the Secretary of State there printed.

But the Act was not occasioned by any doubt 'whether the law of nations, particularly the part relative to public ministers, was not part of the law of England, and the infraction, criminal; nor intended to vary an iota from it.'

In an earlier case on the subject—that of *Buvot* v. *Barbut*,[20] decided in 1736 by Lord Chancellor Talbot—Lord Mansfield, then known as William Murray and practising at the London bar, appeared as counsel in the case. As Lord Mansfield said, in the course of his opinion in the case of *Triquet* v. *Bath*, that he "was counsel in this case," and had "a full note of it," preference should naturally be given to his statement of the matter. "These questions arose," he said, "and were discussed. 'Whether a minister could, by any act or acts, waive his privilege.' 'Whether being a trader was any objection against allowing privilege to a minister, personally.' 'Whether an agent of commerce, or even a consul, was entitled to the privileges of a public minister.' 'What was the rule of decision: the act of Parliament or the law of nations.'" His lordship continued: "Lord Talbot declared a clear opinion—'That the law of nations, in its full extent, was part of the law of England.' 'That the act of Parliament was declaratory, and occasioned by a particular incident.' 'That the law of nations was to be collected from the practice of different nations, and the authority of writers.' Accordingly, he argued and

[20] Cas. *temp.* Talbot 281, 25 E. R. 777 (1736).

determined from such instances, and the authority of Grotius, Barbeyrac, Binkershoek, Wiquefort, &c.; there being no English writer of eminence upon the subject."

Three years after the case of *Triquet* v. *Bath,* Lord Mansfield considered a like question in *Heathfield* v. *Chilton,*[21] in part confirming what he had said in the previous case, making, however, a very precious addition: "The privileges of public ministers and their retinue depend upon the law of nations;[22] which is part of the common law of England. And the act of Parliament of 7 Anne, c. 12, did not intend to alter, nor can alter the law of nations."

What conclusions are to be drawn from these three leading cases, each dealing with the nature and extent of diplomatic immunity? In the first place, it is to be observed that the immunity was that of the law of nations—a law existing previously to the statute of Queen Anne. In the second place, it is to be further observed, that the law of nations was the law of England—not statute law, but common law—resulting from the practice of nations. In the third place, that it was a law superior to any other law in England, in that it could not be modified by an act of Parliament. And finally, that the statute was expressly passed to provide the rule of the law of nations with a municipal sanction, and that, in so doing, it recognized the law of nations as an existing and obligatory law. The right to immunity, and the duty of England to protect that right, existed. The duty was not created by the statute; it existed under international law, and, because the statute had not theretofore existed, Great Britain passed it, in order that the violation of the immunity of diplomatic agents under international law should not happen again.

21 4 Burr. 2015 (1767).

22 The law of nations which Lord Mansfield had in mind was stated in the report of the Law Officers of the Crown in the famous diplomatic case of the Silesian loan to which his Lordship, as William Murray, then Solicitor-General, affixed his name—if the definition did not actually come from his hand: "The Law of Nations is founded upon Justice, Equity, Convenience, and the Reason of the Thing, and confirmed by long Usage, . . ."—Rt. Hon. Sir Ernest Satow, *The Silesian Loan and Frederick the Great* (Oxford, 1915), p. 82.

It is to be observed that the three cases are English cases. But, as the common law of England became the law of the Colonies and was continued without modification when they became States, in so far as international law is concerned, the English cases were American precedents. An early and a leading and an interesting case is that of *Nathan* v. *Commonwealth of Virginia*,[23] tried in the Court of Common Pleas of Philadelphia County, in the State of Pennsylvania, in the September Term of 1781, when our Washington, to whom reference is made, was paying his respects to Cornwallis, temporarily residing at Yorktown. It appears that a quantity of clothing belonging to the Commonwealth of Virginia was imported from France, and one Simon Nathan, claiming an interest in the property, caused a foreign attachment to be issued against Virginia, and the clothing was attached in Philadelphia. "The delegates in Congress from Virginia,"—then sitting in Pennsylvania—"conceiving this a violation of the laws of nations, applied to the Supreme Executive Council of Pennsylvania, by whom the sheriff was ordered to give up the goods."

The case was elaborately argued by the Attorney-General of the Commonwealth of Pennsylvania and by counsel for the plaintiff. The court decided that the property of a sister state was not liable to attachment in Philadelphia. As the judgment was rendered without an opinion and in accordance with the views of the Attorney-General, only the material portion of his argument dealing with the principle in question will be considered. "He premised, that though the several states which form our federal republic, had, by the confederation,"—which had gone into effect on the 1st day of March, 1781—"ceded many of the prerogatives of sovereignty to the United States, yet these voluntary engagements did not injure their independence of each other; but that each was a sovereign, 'with every power, jurisdiction, and right, not expressly given up.'" His argument consisted of two points: "First: that every kind of process, issued against a sovereign, is a violation of the laws of nations; and is in itself

23 1 Dall. 77 note (1781).

null and void. Second: that a sheriff cannot be compelled to serve or return a void writ."

The first point the Attorney-General "endeavoured to prove, by considering, first, the nature of sovereignty, and, secondly, the rules of law, relative to process issued against ambassadors, the representatives of sovereigns," relying upon Vattel, who was before, and apparently still is after, their independence, the principal authority on international law in the United States—and in the Supreme Court since its organization.

Having stated there was no instance in our law books of a process against a sovereign, the Attorney-General considered suits against their representatives. The stock example, of course, was the immunity of diplomatic officers, existing by the law of nations, the violation of which was to be punished [in England] under the famous statute of 7 Queen Anne, Chap. 12, "which statute," he said, "did not introduce the immunity of diplomatic agents, but was merely declaratory of the law of nations, with nothing new in it, except the clause prescribing a summary mode of punishment"; and he concluded, under this heading, that this statute was a "part of the common law of the land before, and consequently extended to Pennsylvania." His authorities were Blackstone's *Commentaries,*[24] and the cases of *Triquet* v. *Bath, and Healthfield* v. *Chilton.*

Since the writ of the sheriff was null and void against a representative, as against the sovereign, it followed that the sheriff attaching the goods in question was liable to punishment, and to show the "inconveniences" were this not so, the Attorney-General referred to the calamity which might happen to the body politic, if the sheriff could lawfully attach the goods addressed to a sovereign or its representative: "that any disaffected person, who happened to be a creditor of the United States might injure our public defence, and retard or ruin the operations of a campaign; that he might issue an attachment against the cannon of General Washington, or seize the public money designed for the payment of his army."

[24] Bl. Comm. 67.

The allusion to Washington was not accidental. As appears by his diary, his army, marching toward Yorktown, arrived in Philadelphia on the 31st of August, and on the 5th of September there is an entry concerning "the rear of the French Army having reached Philadelphia and the American's having passed it." [27]

There is a later case in Pennsylvania which is even more interesting. It is that of *Respublica* v. *de Longchamps* [28] in the Court of Oyer and Terminer at Philadelphia in 1784. The facts were that the Chevalier de Longchamps, an officer of the French Army in America, was indicted on the charge that he "unlawfully and insolently did threaten and menace bodily harm and violence to the person of . . . François Barbé-Marbois" in the residence of the French Minister Plenipotentiary. M. Barbé-Marbois was then Secretary of the French Legation and Consul General of France to the United States. It was specifically stated in the indictment that M. Barbé-Marbois was at the time "under the protection of the laws of nations, and this commonwealth"; and that, on the 19th of May, the Chevalier de Longchamps, in the public street, "unlawfully, premeditatedly and violently" assaulted M. Barbé-Marbois, striking him "in violation of the laws of nations, against the peace and dignity of the United States and of the Commonwealth of Pennsylvania."

The Attorney-General, assisted by none other than the famous James Wilson, a signer of the Declaration of Independence, soon to be a member from Pennsylvania of the Federal Convention in Philadelphia, to the success of which he largely contributed, and still later to be an original member of the Supreme Court appointed by President Washington, appeared for the prosecution. They advocated "the necessity of sustaining the law of nations, of protecting and securing the persons and privileges of ambassadors";—to quote the exact language of the report—"the connection between the law of nations and the municipal law, and

[27] *The Diaries of George Washington* (1748-1799), ed. by John Fitzpatrick (Boston and New York, 1925), vol. ii, p. 258.

[28] 1 Dall. 111 (1784).

the effect which the decision of this case must have upon the honor of Pennsylvania, and the safety of her citizens abroad."

In support of their contention, they invoked the authority of *Triquet* v. *Bath;*[29] Blackstone's *Commentaries,*[30] and Vattel's

[29] In this case, Lord Mansfield, after saying, "I was counsel in this case"—meaning that of Buvot *v.* Barbut, before Lord Talbot (*supra,* p. 93)—"and have a full note of it," continues without a break: "I remember, too, Lord Hardwicke's declaring his opinion to the same effect; and denying that Lord Chief Justice Holt ever had any doubt as to the law of nations being part of the law of England, upon the occasion of the arrest of the Russian ambassador."

Chief Justice McKean refers in the decision of Republica *v.* De Longchamps to "the case of the Russian ambassador": "A wrong opinion has been entertained concerning the conduct of Lord Chief Justice Holt and the court of king's bench, in England, in the noted case of the Russian ambassador. They detained the offenders, after conviction, in prison, from term to term, until the Czar Peter was satisfied, without ever proceeding to judgment; and from this, it has been inferred, that the court doubted, whether they could inflict any punishment for an infraction of the law of nations. But this was not the reason. The court never doubted, that the law of nations formed a part of the law of England, and that a violation of this general law could be punished by them; but no punishment less than death would have been thought by the Czar an adequate reparation for the arrest of his ambassador. This punishment they could not inflict, and such a sentence as they could have given, he might have thought a fresh insult. Another expedient was, therefore, fallen upon. However, the princes of the world, at this day, are more enlightened, and do not require impracticable nor unreasonable reparations for injuries of this kind."

The above passage from Chief Justice McKean's opinion pronouncing judgment is here reproduced, in order to show the care with which the case of Respublica *v.* De Longchamps was considered and the judicial precedents examined and mastered regarding the law of nations as the law universal and therefore the law of each and every state.

There is an incident appearing in APPLETON'S ENCYCLOPEDIA OF AMERICAN BIOGRAPHY (1st ed. 1888), vol. iv, p. 199, in the article on "François de Barbé-Marbois," which shows that time left undimmed the Marquis de Barbé-Marbois' interest in things American:

"Just before Lafayette's death Marbois invited him, with the American minister and several of the latter's compatriots, including Col. Nicolas Fish, to dine with him. Before the repast the company was shown into a room that was in strong contrast with the other elegant apartments. It looked like a large room in a Dutch or Belgian farmhouse. On a long, rough table was spread a dinner in keeping with the room: a single dish of meat, uncouth pastry, and wine in bottles and decanters, accompanied by glasses and silver goblets. 'Do you know where we are?' said Marbois to Lafayette and the other guests. The marquis looked at the low ceiling with its heavy, bare beams, and, after a brief pause, exclaimed: 'Ah! the seven doors, and the one window, and the silver goblets, such as the marshal of France used in my youth! My friends, we are in Washington's headquarters, on the Hudson fifty years ago.'"

[30] 1 BL. COMM. 253.

Law of Nature and of Nations.[31] Upon these authorities they stated that M. Barbé-Marbois "must have been prevented from paying a proper attention to his appointments, which is certainly a violation of the law of nations," citing in this respect Vattel.[32] "Upon the same principle"—to quote from the argument as reported—"that the infringement of a statute is an indictable offence, though the mode of punishment is not pointed out in the act itself, an offence against the laws of nations, while they compose a part of the law of the land, must necessarily be indictable."

Chief Justice McKean, a man of large political and judicial experience and himself a signer of the Declaration of Independence, stated the trial to be a case of "first impression in the United States"; that it was to be determined "on the principles of the laws of nations, which form a part of the municipal law of Pennsylvania."

The jury returned a verdict of "guilty," first on the assault count and later on both counts.

The case being considered of "first impression in the United States," the sentence of the court of first instance was suspended and the case stayed for the opinion of the judges. It was very carefully argued, as appears from the report and from the opinion rendered by Mr. Chief Justice McKean, in the course of which, after stating that the crime was an infraction of the law of nations, he added that "this law, in its full extent, is a part of the law of this state, and is to be collected from the practice of different nations, and the authority of writers"; that "the person of a public minister is sacred and inviolable"; and that "whoever offers any violence to him, not only affronts the sovereign he represents, but also hurts the common safety and well-being of nations"; and such being the case, that "he is guilty of a crime against the whole world."

The *Longchamps* case was not a whit less interesting than *Triquet* v. *Bath,* and it makes an even stronger appeal to us of America, not merely because of its historical associations, but be-

[31] VATTEL, LAW OF NATIONS (1760), pref. 6, p. 203; *id.,* lib. 1, § 6; *id.* lib. 4, §§ 80, 84.

[32] *Id.,* lib. 2, § 218.

cause of the argument of counsel and the opinion of the Chief Justice.

In passing, it may be said that it is also the first case, so far as is known, of a request for extradition from the United States on the part of a foreign government—in this instance, France, and de Longchamps the person to be extradited—which the court, after grave deliberation, refused on the ground that the offense was committed in the United States and should be tried where committed. In the argument, as we have seen, it was maintained that the law of nations being a part of the law of the land, the offense was as indictable as if under a statute, in that the law of nations, being the law of the land, had the effect of a statute, and that a person violating the law of nations was guilty of a crime against the whole world, and that not merely the law of the state in which the offense was committed was violated, but the right of every state of the civilized world was violated by the violation of international law, wherever it took place.

We are indeed deeply indebted to the argument of James Wilson and to the opinion of Thomas W. McKean, Chief Justice of Pennsylvania.

But important as the case is, and interesting as it must be admitted to be, it is perhaps more interesting by virtue of the persons involved; more so, perhaps, than any other case decided in our courts. François, Marquis de Barbé-Marbois was not merely Consul General and Secretary of the Legation, who, as such, performed his duties to the satisfaction of his government during the period of our Revolution, but later he it was who advised M. de Vergennes, then Minister of Foreign Affairs of France, not to recommend a foreigner as the first Bishop of the Catholic Church in the United States and (if he recommended anybody) to name one John Carroll, who would be most acceptable because highly thought of in the United States.[35] In addition, it was through the same Marquis de Barbé-Marbois, Minister of State of the great Napoleon, that the proposition was

[35] See the article by the Rev. Jules A. Baisnée entitled, *The Myth of the "French Scheme for the Enslavement of American Catholics" (1783-1784)*, published in the Catholic Historical Review, vol. xix, No. 4, January, 1934, pp. 437-459.

made to Robert R. Livingston, then our Minister to France, to cede the vast territory of Louisiana to the United States.

If we now turn to the Constitution of the United States,[36] we find that Congress has the power "to define and punish," let us say, without quoting, offenses against international law, specifying some and including all others by the words, "offenses against the law of nations."[37] The word "piracy" is used. But what if it is not defined? Then, of course, it is piracy against the law of nations. If, however, it is defined by Congress, it is still according to the law of nations, for if the definition of the United States differs from the meaning under the law of nations, the statute is an attempt to set up a definition inconsistent with the law of nations and is, to the extent of the inconsistency, null and void as against the nations. Why is this so? Because a statute of the United States, even if dealing with the law of nations, is an unilateral act and therefore can only bind the United States and be exercised within their jurisdiction.

The best case, perhaps, on the subject is *United States* v. *Smith*,[38] decided in 1820. The defendant Smith was indicted for piracy under an act of Congress of March 3, 1819,[39] providing "that if any person or persons whatsoever, shall, on the high seas, commit the crime of piracy, as defined by the law of nations, and such offender or offenders shall afterwards be brought into, or found in, the United States, every such offender or offenders shall, upon conviction thereof, before the circuit court of the United States for the district into which he or they may be brought, or in which he or they shall be found, be punished with death." Here we have the exact case of the Constitution, by virtue of which Congress is authorized "to define and punish . . . Piracies," etc. So much for the first question raised.

[36] The text from this point to the discussion of the Arjona case (*infra*, p. 118), is reproduced by permission, with an occasional modification, from a presidential address entitled "International Law, Municipal Law, and Their Sanctions," delivered before the American Society of International Law on April 27, 1933, and printed in the Proceedings of the Society for 1933, pp. 5-33.

[37] Art. viii, § 10.

[38] 5 Wheat. 153 (1820).

[39] An Act to protect the commerce of the United States and punish the crime of piracy. 3 STAT. 513 (1819), 33 U. S. C. § 383 (1926).

The second was whether the crime of piracy was defined by the law of nations with reasonable accuracy. The opinion in the case was that of the learned Justice Story, who said in this connection: "What the law of nations on this subject is, may be ascertained by consulting the works of jurists, writing professedly on public laws; or by the general usage and practice of nations; or by judicial decisions recognizing and enforcing that law." What, then, was the definition under the law of nations? "Robbery, or forcible depredations upon the sea, *animo furandi,* is piracy." Then, too, he says, great writers on maritime law profess the same doctrine, and the common law to which he refers "recognises and punishes piracy as an offence, not against its own municipal code, but as an offence against the law of nations (which is part of the common law)"—it is Justice Story who is speaking—and "as an offence against the universal law of society, a pirate being deemed an enemy of the human race." [41] Here we have the law of nations considered as an integral part of the law of the United States, and the offense or the felony is sufficiently defined, "whether we advert to writers on the common law, or the maritime law, or the law of nations"; that is to say, the law of nations binding upon every nation is a part of

[41] For a more elaborate statement of Justice Story's conception of the law of nations and its sources see La Jeune Eugénie, 2 Mason, 409, Fed. Cas. No. 15,551 (1822). Arranged in seven numbered parts, the statement reads:

"(1) Now the law of nations may be deduced, first, from the general principles of right and justice, applied to the concerns of individuals, and thence to the relations and duties of nations; or (2) secondly, in things indifferent or questionable, from the customary observances and recognitions of civilized nations; or, (3) lastly, from the conventional or positive law, that regulates the intercourse between states. (4) What, therefore, the law of the nations is, does not rest upon mere theory, but may be considered, as modfied by practice, or ascertained by the treaties of nations at different periods. (5) It does not follow, therefore, that because a principle cannot be found settled by the consent or practice of nations at one time, it is to be concluded, that at no subsequent period the principle can be considered as incorporated into the public code of nations. (6) Nor is it to be admitted, that no principle belongs to the law of nations, which is not universally recognized, as such, by all civilized communities, or even by those constituting what may be called, the Christian states of Europe. . . . (7) But I think it may be unequivocally affirmed, that every doctrine that may be fairly deduced by correct reasoning from the rights and duties of nations, and the nature of moral obligation, may theoretically be said to exist in the law of nations; and unless it be relaxed or waived by the consent of nations, which may be evidenced by their general practice and customs, it may be enforced by a court of justice, whenever it arises in judgment. . . ."

the municipal law of every nation, to be rendered effective in case of need by a municipal statute, the offense being under international law and the punishment under a municipal statute. A case of piracy, however, is of a very general nature. Although a pirate's acts may bring him under the definition of piracy under the law of nations, he is regarded as not acting under the law of any country and is to be tried for the offense in any country within whose jurisdiction he may be brought.

There are many interesting cases of an international nature punishable by a municipal sanction. Speaking within the jurisdiction of the United States, it will suffice for us to cite a few American cases dealing with neutrality. The law of neutrality used to confer an equal right upon both belligerents. Thus in the time of Grotius it was stated by that great man to be within the right of neutral nations to allow a belligerent to cross its territory on condition that the same right were accorded to the other belligerent. But Grotius also allowed the neutral to grant preferred treatment to the belligerent whose cause was just as against the belligerent with an unjust cause. This latter conception of neutrality, however, has been disregarded, as it involves the exercise, on the part of the neutral, of the function of a judge, deciding the cause of the war, one or the other of the belligerents to be adjudged right or wrong, according to the view of the neutral. This was not the American conception, which was that the neutral should be "neuter" in the sense that he should take no part in the contest and that, if an American citizen did so, it was at his peril; and a statute of the United States to that effect was passed in 1794,[42] the first municipal statute upon this international right or duty. President Washington's administration was of the opinion that the offense was under international law and that, as international law was the law of the land, it did not require a statute. However, to remove any possible doubt on the question, and to provide definite penalties, the statute was passed making the violation of neutrality a municipal offense and creating a municipal punishment for the violation of international law thus specifically recognized by the statute of the United States.

42 Neutrality Act of 1794, 1 STAT. 381 (1794).

The neutrality statute in question warned American citizens against trading in contraband and blockade, in that they might be captured by the belligerent whose cause was injured by such trade, even though the offense were committed on the high seas outside of the jurisdiction of any nation.

Let us consider two situations, with which we are familiar—perhaps too familiar, as they are taken from the so-called law of war—for I have often wondered how an illegal thing can claim to be a thing of law. The first deals with the law of neutrality, and the second, with an offense upon the high seas, without reference to neutrality.

Let us suppose that a belligerent vessel is lying within the territorial waters of the United States and that an individual, native or foreign, enlists himself as a member of the foreign crew. This is a violation of a statute of the United States designed to carry into effect what President Washington's government believed to be the neutral duty of the United States, and therefore of its citizens. It was not a law passed at random; it was passed because of the fear in many quarters that the rule of international law did not carry with it a municipal penalty. Therefore the Neutrality Act of June 5, 1794, was passed for the express purpose of making a municipal duty by statute what President Washington and his advisers considered an international duty without statute. Here we have a municipal sanction of an admitted principle of the law of nations.

Let us take as an illustration an early case in the history of the United States. It is that of Gideon Henfield,[43] who in 1793 was charged with having illegally enlisted on a French privateer, the *Citizen Genet,* at Charleston, South Carolina, and with having taken part in the capture of a British vessel at a time when the United States was at peace with Great Britain. The trial took place before the Circuit Court of the United States for the Pennsylvania District, and the case was argued before Judges Wilson, Iredell and Peters. The former, in his charge to the jury, said:

> It is the joint and unanimous opinion of the Court, that the United States, being in a state of neutrality relative to the present war, the acts

[43] Francis Wharton, STATE TRIALS (Philadelphia, 1849), pp. 49, 84.

of hostility committed by Gideon Henfield are an offence against this country, and punishable by its laws.

It has been asked by his counsel, in their address to you, against what law has he offended? The answer is, against many and binding laws. As a citizen of the United States, he was bound to act no part which could injure the nation; he was bound to keep the peace in regard to all nations with whom we are at peace. This is the law of nations; not an *ex post facto* law, but a law that was in existence long before Gideon Henfield existed.

But this was not all. "There are, also," the learned judge continued, "positive laws, existing previous to the offence committed, and expressly declared to be part of the supreme law of the land." He had in mind treaties, and he referred, among others, to the definitive treaty of peace with Great Britain, which declared, he stated, "that there shall be a firm and perpetual peace between His Britannic Majesty and the United States, and between the subjects of the one and the citizens of the other." [44] It was clearly the opinion of the court that Gideon Henfield had offended against the law of nations in general and in particular, and that, since the law of nations was acknowledged by the United States, he had committed "an offence against this country" and was "punishable by its laws."

A second illustration is that of a war vessel of a foreign belligerent country being fitted out within the United States. A year after the Gideon Henfield case the Neutrality Act, to which I have referred, was passed. Its provision on this phase of the question is that any person who, within the "waters of the United States," fitted out and armed or was knowingly "concerned in the furnishing, fitting out or arming of any ship or vessel" for employment "in the service of any foreign prince or state . . . with whom the United States are at peace," or who issued "a commission within the territory or jurisdiction of the United States for any ship or vessel to the intent that she may be employed as aforesaid," should, if convicted, "be adjudged guilty of a high misdemeanor, and shall be fined and imprisoned at the discretion of the court," the fine to be in no case "more than

[44] *Id.*, at p. 85.

five thousand dollars" and the imprisonment not to "exceed three years . . ."[46]

The statute further provided that a person engaged in augmenting the force of any armed vessel or any cruiser of a foreign country within the jurisdiction of the United States, the country to which it belongs being at peace with the United States, should "upon conviction be adjudged guilty of a misdemeanor," and should "be fined and imprisoned at the discretion of the court," with the further proviso that the fine should "not exceed one thousand dollars, nor the term of imprisonment be more than one year."[47]

It would be supposed that if any person within the jurisdiction of the United States were to be punished for enlisting in the crew of a foreign belligerent vessel, and if any individual were to be punished for issuing commissions within the United States, and if any individual were to be punished for augmenting the force of any ship, that any group of individuals setting on foot expeditions against the "territory or dominions of any foreign prince or state with whom the United States are at peace"[48] would likewise be fined; and such, indeed, was the case, the statute providing for this offense a fine not to "exceed three thousand dollars," and imprisonment for not more than three years. Nor should it astonish us, given the above provisions of the Neutrality Act, that captures made by a belligerent "within the waters of the United States or within a marine league of the coasts or shores thereof"[49] should be declared unlawful, as, indeed, they were.

And finally, the statute, to be complete, would not merely need to define the offense and the punishment, but the court in which the person or persons guilty of the offense should be tried. It was to be the district court of the United States of the jurisdiction in which the offense was committed.[50]

---

[46] Act of June 5, 1794—An Act in addition to the act for the punishment of certain crimes against the United States, 1 Stat. 383, § 3.

[47] *Id.*, § 4.

[48] *Id.*, § 5.

[49] *Id.*, § 6.

[50] For a judicial confirmation of this principle see Justice Johnson's opinion in behalf of a unanimous court in *United States* v. *Hudson*, 7 Cranch 32 (1812).

It is to be observed that in all these provisions the offense is committed within the jurisdiction of the United States. But if the same offense should be committed in a foreign country, the offense should be punishable by the laws of that country as in the case of the United States, and if the offense should not be so punished, it would be as a liability under international law, to be the subject of diplomatic negotiations, and, failing in them, to be submitted to an international tribunal.

Let us say a word of contraband and of blockade. It is admitted to be a right of the citizens of each and every state under the customary law of nations to trade in certain articles, called contraband articles, which help a belligerent in prosecuting its real or alleged right under international law. But it is also the right of the belligerent to seize the commodities under certain conditions and to prevent the entry of a neutral vessel and cargo into a blockaded port of the enemy. The carriage of contraband is permitted to the neutral, however, only if it has not been declared a punishable wrong in the proclamations of neutrality which the neutral states are accustomed to issue after the outbreak of a war. Their citizens are warned in these proclamations that in carrying contraband and in seeking to enter a blockaded port, they do so at their peril. When in the future the carriage of contraband or the running of blockades is made a legal wrong by international law, there will then be a municipal duty on the part of the neutral to provide a penalty for the offense in either case.

I have already referred to piracy, but it is here a last and crowning example. It is robbery or theft committed by force upon the high seas. The flag which the pirate vessel may fly is not regarded as that of any country; and such vessel has no protection from its flag, if it engage in an act of piracy, for piracy is an offense against each and every nation of the international community and the pirate is looked upon as an enemy of the human race. Therefore it is that, wherever the act be committed, the pirate vessel coming into any port is subject to seizure and the crew liable to the punishment of death, which is the international punishment for the international crime of piracy. This is an extreme example, in that any vessel guilty of piracy, without reference to the nationality of the vessel or of the equipment of the crew, may be proceeded against in any port of any nation to which one or the other is brought.

Is it not possible to assimilate to piracy an act which the nations have agreed should be treated as piracy? We do not need to argue the question. It is not theoretical; it is practical, inasmuch as this very step was taken in the matter of belligerent attacks upon merchant vessels in the treaty signed at Washington February 6, 1922,[51] of which ratification was advised by the Senate of the United States on March 22 of the same year. The provision in question of this treaty, which assimilated to piracy acts in contravention "of the humane rules of existing law," was adopted by the Conference for the Limitation of Armament, held at Washington in 1922, upon the proposal, it should be said, of no less a person than Mr. Elihu Root.

Thus we have instances of municipal laws passed in order to punish violations of international law, whether they take place within the exclusive jurisdiction of the state in question or upon the high seas, outside of the exclusive jurisdiction of any state—as in the case of piracy, which, being an offense against humanity, is triable within any jurisdiction within which the vessel or the members of the piratical crew be found.

In the English-speaking world, crime is punishable within and according to the laws of the country where it is committed. Non-English-speaking countries also punish violations of their law which take place within a country according to the law of the particular country; but, as a general rule, the law follows their nationals, whithersoever they go, to such a degree that an offense against the law of their own country, although committed within a foreign jurisdiction, is punishable when the national returns to the homeland. But there is a tendency, even in the English-speaking world, to pass laws for the punishment of an increasing number of offenses committed in foreign parts, upon the na-

[51] Treaty relating to the use of submarines and noxious gases (Conference on the Limitation of Armament, Washington, 1922), Art. III, p. 1608.

tional being found within the jurisdiction of the country whereof he is a subject or citizen.

* * * * * * *

Let us consider certain international cases which involved violations of the law of nations, and which gave rise to extended diplomatic negotiations, but which were fortunately settled without a resort to force. We may, indeed we should, begin with a case in which the United States violated international law to the detriment of Great Britain and the world at large. It is the *Trent* case,[52] almost as well known as the *Alabama* case.[53]

Now the *Trent* was a British packet, and therefore a neutral ship, in the Civil War between the states of the American Union. It was a mail steamer, entirely neutral in its action, plying as it was on its regular voyage between two neutral ports, Vera Cruz (Mexico) and St. Thomas (Danish West Indies), by way of Havana. It had aboard among its passengers two civil agents of the Southern Confederacy (Messrs. Mason and Slidell), the one of Virginia, the other of Louisiana, both members of the Confederacy, who were on their way to St. Thomas to embark on a British steamer for Southampton, England. As passengers on the *Trent* they were on a British, and therefore neutral, steamer, sailing under the British flag, on a scheduled voyage between neutral points. The *San Jacinto* was a man-of-war of the United States, commanded by a "man of war," Charles Wilkes,[53] who nearly precipitated a war between the two countries. He hailed the *Trent* on November 8, 1861, had it boarded, and removed Messrs. Mason and Slidell, taking them aboard his vessel and landing them in Boston harbor, where he found himself a popu-

[52] On the *Trent* case see John Bassett Moore's *Digest of International Law* (Washington, 1906), vol. vii, pp. 768-779. Judge Moore observes (p. 775), that "the fullest and most satisfactory discussion of the *Trent case* is that given in the monograph of Dr. Heinrich Marquardsen, the preface to which is dated at Erlangen, February, 1862." The title of the monograph is *Der Trent-Fall.*

[53] For Captain Wilkes' report, in defense of his conduct, to the Secretary of the Navy, written aboard the San Jacinto, "At sea, November 16, 1861," see Senate Ex. Doc. 1, 37th Cong., 2d Sess., vol. 3, p. 123.

For the protests of Great Britain and France, see Sen. Ex. Doc. 8, 37th Cong., 2d sess., vol. 4, pp. 2-16. The protest of Austria is to be found in Sen. Ex. Doc. 14, pp. 1-2, and of Prussia in Sen. Ex. Doc. 18, pp. 1-3.

lar hero, with his digestion threatened by banquets in his honor.

As confirmed by his official reports of the affair,[54] Captain Wilkes had acted without orders from his government, indeed without knowledge of the authorities in Washington.[55] Each government involved found itself in an embarrassing position. What Captain Wilkes had done was in accordance with the principles of international law as laid down by my Lord Stowell in his prize court decisions and, therefore, in accordance with British practice,[56] of which the United States had formerly and repeatedly complained. Therefore, the Government of the United States after the event could not well approve Captain Wilkes' action, without at the same time accepting that British policy, which had been one of the causes of the War of 1812.

The Government of Great Britain, on its part, was no doubt inwardly pleased that, in opposing Captain Wilkes' action, it was upholding the contention of the United States in earlier days, when the American Government had insisted that American merchant vessels, in a war in which the United States were neutral, should not be subject to visit and search, and the removal of civilians from American merchantmen. President Lincoln himself warned against inconsistency:

> We must stick to American principles concerning the rights of neutrals. We fought Great Britain for insisting, by theory and practice, on the right to do precisely what Captain Wilkes has done. If Great Britain

[54] Gideon Welles, "The Capture and Release of Mason and Slidell," *The Galaxy* (New York, 1873), Vol. XV, p. 647.

[55] Ephraim Douglass Adams, *Great Britain and the American Civil War* (New York and London, 1925), Vol. I, p. 205. Secretary Seward to Mr. Adams, November 27, 1861—John G. Nicolay and John Hay, *Abraham Lincoln* (New York, 1890), Vol. 5, p. 32. In further reference to this point, see the statement of Miss Slidell, one of the *Trent* passengers, summarized on p. 517 of the *Proceedings of the Massachusetts Historical Society* (1911-1912), Vol. 45 (Richard Henry Dana's paper on "The Trent Affair—An Aftermath"), that "the American officer who boarded the *Trent* took pains to state that the commander of the *San Jacinto* had no instructions from his Government, but was acting on his own responsibility."

[56] See letter of Lord Palmerston to Mr. Delane, editor of the London *Times*, Nov. 11, 1861, involving the very point at issue, in which his Lordship admitted that the right of a belligerent "to stop and search any neutral not being a ship of war, and being found on the high seas and being suspected of carrying enemy's despatches" was "according to the principles of international law laid down in our courts by Lord Stowell, and practised and enforced by us." E. D. Adams, *op. cit. supra,* at p. 208. See also *The Galaxy,* at p. 650 column 1, lines 3-5, *op. cit. supra.*

shall now protest against the act, and demand their release, we must give them up, apologize for the act as a violation of our doctrines, and thus forever bind her over to keep the peace in relation to neutrals, and so acknowledge that she has been wrong for sixty years.[57]

What was to be done? Her Majesty, Queen Victoria, and the Prince Consort were opposed to any war with the United States. Secretary Seward, in behalf of the American Government, declared, in what is described as "one of his chief literary triumphs,"[58] that Captain Wilkes had acted on his own responsibility and that his action was not approved; and likewise in behalf of the government, he expressed regret at the incident.[59] Great Britain was willing to and did accept the *amende honorable.* The two commissioners were therefore returned to British custody. But their usefulness, as it turned out, had ended.

The result of the incident was that the governments of the two countries admitted in principle that the early practice of Great Britain and the unauthorized action of Captain Wilkes were opposed to the principles of international law.

If this were all, we should not be citing the incident on this occasion. Of course, Great Britain had the right to protest, and it was in our interest as well as Great Britain's that Her Majesty's Government did so. But Prussia protested, Austria protested, and France protested. Each was right; and every member of the

[57] Nicolay and Hay, at pp. 25, 26, *op. cit. supra.* President Lincoln was in the habit of referring to Messrs. Mason and Slidell as calculated "to be white elephants."

[58] *Id.*, at p. 38. Concerning this document, the authors say: "That long and remarkably able document must be read in full, both to understand the wide range of the subject which he treated and the clearness and force of his language and arguments. It constitutes one of his chief literary triumphs. There is room here only to indicate the conclusions arrived at in his examination. First, he held that the four persons seized and their dispatches were contraband of war; second, that Captain Wilkes had a right by the law of nations to detain and search the *Trent;* third, that he exercised the right in a lawful proper manner; fourth, that he had a right to capture the contraband found. The real issue of the case centered in the fifth question: 'Did Captain Wilkes exercise the right of capturing the contraband in conformity with the law of nations?' Reciting the deficiency of recognized rules on this point, Mr. Seward held that only by taking the vessel before a prize court could the existence of contraband be lawfully established; and that Captain Wilkes having released the vessel from capture, the necessary judicial examination was prevented, and the capture left unfinished or abandoned."

[59] See comment of Secretary Welles, *Diary of Gideon Welles* (Boston, 1911), Vol. I, p. 299.

international community would have been right if each had protested. For if it was a right of Great Britain, as a neutral, to protest the unneutral action of the United States, it was the right of each and every member of the international community to protest.[60] It was indeed a threefold right: a right in behalf of Great Britain as the nation directly injured; the right of Prussia, of Austria, and of France as subject to a prospective injury; and the right of each and every one directly or prospectively injured to protest not only in behalf of the law common to each of the neutral nations, but also in behalf of the international community of which each was a member.

If the ministers of foreign affairs of Prussia, Austria and France were today to contemplate such action, they would be able to invoke the unimpeachable authority of a great American statesman, Elihu Root, himself once a Secretary of State:

> . . . it follows necessarily that when one sovereign state is dealing not with its internal affairs but with its international relations and violates the rule of right as aganist another equal and independent state, all other equally independent states have a right to insist that the international rule shall be observed, and such insistence is not interfering with the quarrels of others but is an assertion of their own rights. In each case every state must be guided by its own circumstances and interests in determining how far it will go in supporting its interference. There can, however, be no doubt of the international right to interfere in behalf of the maintenance of the law.[61]

Let us hold the scales of justice even and now take a case in which Great Britain violated international law to the detriment of the United States and the world at large.

---

[60] The correspondence of Russia and Italy on the *Trent* case is published in Sen. Ex. Docs. 22 (pp. 1-3) and 30 (pp. 1-3), respectively. From these documents it will be seen that Russia expresses its satisfaction over the maintenance, instead of the repudiation, of the early American doctrine; while Italy, also expressing its satisfaction at the peaceful solution reached through the conciliatory attitude of the United States, stated its own attachment to the freedom of the seas, and added that "we hesitated to believe that it [the Government of the United States] desired to change its character all at once and become the champion of theories which history has shown to be calamitous, and which public opinion has condemned forever."

[61] From an address of April 27, 1916, before the American Society of International Law on "The Declaration of the Rights and Duties of Nations of the American Institute of International Law," published in *Addresses on International Law Subjects* by Elihu Root (1916), pp. 421, 422.

The classic example of this phase of the question is that of the *Alabama*,[62] a cruiser built in a British shipyard in Liverpool, at the request of agents of the Government of the Confederate States of America, and to be used by the authorities of the Confederate States to commit hostilities against the United States. The case of the *Alabama* is not only the classic case, but the arbitration is the classic arbitration of the nineteenth century. The case was in a way an accident, very unfortunate for Great Britain. The arbitration, however, was in the interest of Great Britain, as well as of the United States and of the world at large, because it showed that arbitration might stop the hand of war in a case which threatened to plunge the two English-speaking nations into what we may call a fratricidal, if not a civil, war.

The case was, as I have said, accidental. The American Minister, Charles Francis Adams, of the classic Adams family of the United States, had informed the British Government that a certain vessel (No. 290) was being built in behalf of the Confederate Government in the British shipyard of Lairds at Liverpool. Her Majesty's principal Secretary of State for Foreign Affairs, the Earl of Russell, formerly and affectionately known as Lord John Russell, was unwilling to undertake the action which Mr. Adams requested, namely, to take steps so that the vessel should not be permitted to depart from British waters. However, he recognized, and well he might, the gravity of the affair and submitted the question in the usual course to the Queen's Advocate, Sir John Harding. Now the Queen's Advocate happened to be mentally incapacitated, a fact which his devoted wife concealed from the authorities, so that the request for the information lay unanswered upon his desk.[63] Finally, when Mr. Adams persisted in his statement that the vessel was being built for the Confederate Government and that it would soon take the seas, his Lordship bestirred himself, and, learning of Sir John Harding's situation, submitted the question to the other law officers of the Crown, the Attorney General, Sir Wil-

[62] Sen. Ex. Doc. No. 21, 44th Con. 2d Sess.

[63] See John Bassett Moore, *Principles of American Diplomacy* (New York, 1918), pp. 50-51.

liam Atherton, and the then Solicitor General, Sir Roundell Palmer, later, as Lord Selborne, to be Lord High Chancellor, who advised that the vessel be seized and not permitted to depart from British jurisdiction. However, the vessel had that very morning—July 28, 1862—taken the seas, which fact Lord Russell should have known and prevented. Mr. Adams knew that the vessel was to depart and His Lordship, with better means of knowledge at his disposal, should also have known and should have prevented its leaving British jurisdiction.

In addition, the shipbuilding Lairds had under construction for the Confederate States certain vessels known as "iron rams," "designed to raise the blockade" of the Southern ports. In September, 1863, the rams were about to put to sea, Lord Russell announcing that the British authorities "advise that they cannot interfere in any way with these vessels." Whereupon Mr. Adams countered with: "My lord, it would be superfluous in me to point out to your Lordship that this is war."[64] The "rams" did not sail.

The tension produced by the "unneutral" conduct of Great Britain in the matter of Confederate vessels was the source of immense irritation in the United States, and irritation in Great Britain because of the irritation in America. Incidents such as these all too often generate war.

Now it so happened—and this is the fortunate part of the incident—that Mr. Gladstone later became Prime Minister, and he accepted the suggestion of a peaceful settlement in the form of arbitration by an arbitral tribunal. Thus it was that the treaty of May 8, 1871, in its first article, provided "that all the said claims, growing out of acts committed by the aforesaid vessels, and generally known as the 'Alabama Claims,' shall be referred to a tribunal of arbitration to be composed of five Arbitrators," one to be "named" by the President of the United States; one by Her Britannic Majesty; one by His Majesty the King of

[64] Charles Francis Adams, "Memoir of Hon. Charles Francis Adams, LL. D." *Proceedings of the Massachusetts Historical Society,* Second Series (Boston, 1900), Vol. XIII, p. 205.

Italy; one by the President of the Swiss Confederation; and finally, one by His Majesty the Emperor of Brazil.[65]

It is to be observed that there were three "Majesties" and two "Presidents"; but we of the American Republic are happy to be able to say that the decision was in behalf of the "presidential" claimant. The tribunal was to meet at Geneva, which it did, on December 15, 1871, and the claims were to be decided "by a majority of all the Arbitrators."[66] The *Alabama* case was unanimously decided, although the British arbitrator, Sir Alexander Cockburn, then Lord Chief Justice of the Queen's Bench, rendered a separate opinion assigning separate reasons from those stated in the majority opinion.

The contention of the United States was that the conduct of Great Britain was in violation of the law of nations. This, Great Britain denied. As a result of discussion, the representatives of the two countries agreed that—

> In deciding the matters submitted to the Arbitrators, they shall be governed by the following three rules, which are agreed upon by the high contracting parties as rules to be taken as applicable to the case, and by such principles of international law not inconsistent therewith as the Arbitrators shall determine to have been applicable to the case.[67]

The three rules were:

> A neutral Government is bound—
>
> First, to use due diligence to prevent the fitting out, arming, or equipping, within its jurisdiction, of any vessel which it has reasonable ground to believe is intended to cruise or to carry on war against a Power with which it is at peace; and also to use like diligence to prevent the departure from its jurisdiction of any vessel intended to cruise or carry on war as above, such vessel having been specially adapted, in whole or in part, within such jurisdiction, to warlike use.
>
> Secondly, not to permit or suffer either belligerent to make use of its ports or waters as the base of naval operations against the other, or for the purpose of the renewal or augmentation of military supplies or arms, or the recruitment of men.

---

[65] *Malloy's Treaties, Conventions, International Acts, Protocols, and Agreements between the United States of America and Other Powers*, 1776-1909 (Washington, 1910), Vol. I, p. 701.

[66] *Id.*, Art. II, p. 702.

[67] *Id.*, Art. VI, p. 703.

Thirdly, to exercise due diligence in its own ports and waters, and, as to all persons within its jurisdiction, to prevent any violation of the foregoing obligations and duties.[68]

The British Government did not, as already mentioned, accept these rules as rules of international law, but "Her Britannic Majesty," so runs the treaty, "commanded her High Commissioners and Plenipotentiaries to declare that Her Majesty's Government cannot assent to the foregoing rules as a statement of principles of international law which were in force at the time when the claims mentioned in Article I arose." However, "Her Majesty's Government, in order to evince its desire of strengthening the friendly relations between the two countries and of making satisfactory provision for the future," agreed that, in deciding the claims, "the Arbitrators should assume that Her Majesty's Government had undertaken to act upon the principles set forth in these rules."[69] By so doing, Great Britain accepted in advance an adverse decision.

But if those rules were not rules at the time, they were to become so, and they are to be the rules of the future, for the high contracting parties agreed "to observe these rules as between themselves in future, and to bring them to the knowledge of other maritime Powers, and to invite them to accede to them." They have acceded to them in substance if not in form.[70]

The importance of the *Alabama* case lies in the fact that if there be no international law upon which the parties are agreed, they can make the law for the case, so that through their initiative the rules which had not been declared to form a part of international law may, as the rule of right reason, become international law by the agreement of the nations and thus become the municipal law of each and every country so accepting them.

The tribunal . . . has arrived at the decision embodied in the present award. . . .

And whereas the circumstances . . . were of a nature to call for the exercise on the part of Her Britannic Majesty's government of all possible

---

68 *Ibid.*

69 *Ibid.*

70 See Convention (XIII) concerning the Rights and Duties of Neutral Powers in Naval War, signed at The Hague October 18, 1907—Articles 5, 6, 8, 18 and 25.

solicitude for the observance of the rights and the duties involved in the proclamation of neutrality issued by Her Majesty on the 13th day of May, 1861;

And whereas the effects of a violation of neutrality committed by means of the construction, equipment, and armament of a vessel are not done away with by any commission which the government of the belligerent power, benefitted by the violation of neutrality, may afterward have granted to that vessel, and the ultimate step by which the offense is completed, cannot be admissible as a ground for the absolution of the offender, nor can the consummation of his fraud become the means of establishing his innocence;

And whereas the privilege of exterritoriality accorded to vessels of war has been admitted into the law of nations, not as an absolute right, but solely as a proceeding founded on the principle of courtesy and mutual deference between different nations, and therefore can never be appealed to for the protection of acts done in violation of neutrality;

And whereas the absence of a previous notice cannot be regarded as a failure in any consideration required by the law of nations, in those cases in which a vessel carries with it its own condemnation;

And whereas, in order to impart to any supplies of coal a character inconsistent with the second rule, prohibiting the use of neutral ports or waters, as a base of naval operations for a belligerent, it is necessary that said supplies should be connected with special circumstances of time, of person, or of place, which may combine to give them such character; . . .[71]

It will be observed that the above "whereases" were framed by the tribunal in such a way as to lay down the general principles applicable to all the violations of neutrality with respect to the Confederate vessel involved. The tribunal now proceeded to apply them to all of the vessels. But as we are interested at present only in the vessel which has given its name to the arbitration, I quote here merely the award in its behalf:

And whereas, with respect to the vessel called the *Alabama,* it clearly results from all the facts relative to the construction of the ship at first designated by the number '290' in the port of Liverpool, and its equipment and armament in the vicinity of Terceira through the agency of the vessels called the *Agrippina* and the *Bahama,* dispatched from Great Britain to that end, that the British government failed to use due diligence in the performance of its neutral obligations; and especially that it

[71] Sen. Ex. Doc. No. 21, 44th Con. 2d Sess. pp. 147-8.

omitted, notwithstanding the warnings and official representations made by the diplomatic agents of the United States during the construction of the said number '290,' to take in due time any effective measures of prevention, and that those orders which it did give at last, for the detention of the vessel, were issued so late that their execution was not practicable;

And whereas, after the escape of that vessel, the measures taken for its pursuit and arrest were so imperfect as to lead to no result, and therefore cannot be considered sufficient to release Great Britain from the responsibility already incurred;

And whereas, in spite of the violations of the neutrality of Great Britain committed by the '290,' this same vessel, later known as the Confederate cruiser *Alabama,* was on several occasions freely admitted to the ports of colonies of Great Britain, instead of being proceeded against as it ought to have been in any and every port within British jurisdiction in which it might have been found;

And whereas the government of Her Britannic Majesty cannot justify itself for a failure in due diligence on the plea of insufficiency of the legal means of action which it possessed:

Four of the arbitrators, for the reasons above assigned, and the fifth, for reasons separately assigned by him,

Are of opinion—

That Great Britain has in this case failed, by omission, to fulfill the duties prescribed in the first and the third of the rules established by the sixth article of the treaty of Washington.[72]

It is not necessary to say a further word in this connection other than that, as international law was law, as such it measured the right of the United States and the duty of Great Britain, and that the failure of Great Britain to take the necessary preventive measures and to provide judicial remedies, rendered that country liable for a violation of international law; and that the lack of a municipal statute to that effect was no excuse before an international tribunal.

* * * * * * *

There was an aftermath to the *Alabama* case which, although the judgment of a national court, is hardly less important than the award of an international tribunal, and it is to be observed that the opinion of a unanimous court was delivered in the case

[72] Sen. Ex. Doc. No. 21, 44th Con. 2d Sess., at pp. 148-149.

of the *United States* v. *Arjona*[73] by the same Morrison R. Waite, then Chief Justice, who had with great distinction argued the case of the *Alabama* for the United States before the Alabama Tribunal; and, curiously enough, the case in the Supreme Court, as in the arbitral tribunal, turned upon the question of "due diligence," applicable alike in a national as well as in an international tribunal.

The facts of the *Arjona* case are simple. A law of the United States of May 16, 1884,[74] had been passed by the Congress "to prevent and punish the counterfeiting within the United States of notes, bonds, and other securities of foreign Governments." That statute had been violated within the jurisdiction of the United States by one Ramon Arjona. He was tried for having violated this statute within the jurisdiction of the United States, to the detriment of Colombia. The Federal court before which he was tried was divided in opinion, and the case was certified to the Supreme Court of the United States. The question upon which the lower court divided was the constitutionality of the statute which the defendant had violated.

The Supreme Court held that the statute in question was constitutional, and that, indeed, it was the duty of the United States to pass the act in question, and that if the Government of the United States had not passed the act, it would have been remiss in its duty toward the injured nation and toward every other nation of the international community. After citing various articles of the Constitution, the Chief Justice, speaking for the Court, announced its opinion that—

> All official intercourse between a state and foreign nations is prevented, and exclusive authority for that purpose given to the United States. The national government is in this way made responsible to foreign nations for all violations by the United States of their international obligations, and because of this, Congress is expressly authorized 'to define and punish . . . offences against the law of nations.'

What then, is this law of nations, which the Government of the United States would have violated, had it not passed the act

[73] 120 U. S. 479 (1887).
[74] 23 STAT. 22 (1884), 18 U. S. C. § 270 (1926).

in question? "The law of nations"—the Chief Justice said, speaking in behalf of a unanimous court—"requires every national government to use 'due diligence' to prevent a wrong being done within its own dominion to another nation with which it is at peace, or to the people thereof; and because of this, the obligation of one nation to punish those who, within its own jurisdiction, counterfeit the money of another nation, has long been recognized." It is, indeed, interesting to learn from such an authoritative source that the obligation was of long standing, but the importance of the statement lies in the fact that a rule of international law requires each and every member of the international community to enact a municipal statute for the protection of a rule of the law of nations, just as the *Alabama* case, in which Chief Justice Waite had been counsel, decided not merely that the failure to do so, but that the lack of due diligence, rendered Great Britain liable in damages; that is to say, every rule of the law of nations has *in esse* or *in posse* a munipical sanction. Let us follow the Chief Justice in his friendly invasion of the domain of international law:

> Vattel, [he says] in his Law of Nations, which was first printed at Neuchâtel in 1758, and was translated into English and published in England in 1760, uses this language: 'From the principles thus laid down, it is easy to conclude, that if one nation counterfeits the money of another, or if she allows and protects false coiners who presume to do it, she does that nation an injury.'

The Chief Justice here pauses to speak in his own behalf:

> When this was written money was the chief thing of this kind that needed protection, but still it was added: 'There is another custom more modern, and of no less use to commerce than the establishment of coin, namely, *exchange*, or the traffic of bankers, by means of which a merchant remits immense sums from one end of the world to the other, at very trifling expense, and, if he pleases, without risk.'

Vattel himself penetrates the domain still farther, accompanied by the learned Chief Justice:

> For the same reason that sovereigns are obliged [Vattel says] to protect commerce, they are obliged to support this custom, by good laws, in which every merchant, whether citizen or foreigner, may find security.

If commerce is to be protected by a nation, and laws are to be passed for that purpose by every nation, we have in these few lines a duty of due diligence which encircles the world.

So much for the law; now as to its application to the United States.

"No nation can be more interested in this question than the United States,"—the Chief Justice later continues—the meaning of which is that the United States can require of the other nations of the world that due diligence be used in order to protect their money, "their own securities, and those of the states, the cities, and the public corporations, whose interests abroad they alone have the power to guard against foreign national neglect, [which] are found on sale in the principal money markets of Europe." "But"—he continues, applying the rule of law to the United States—"if the United States can require this of another, that other may require it of them, because international obligations are of necessity reciprocal in their nature." For he adds that, "the right, if it exists at all, is given by the law of nations, and what is law for one is, under the same circumstances, law for the other." Therefore, he continues, "a right secured by the law of nations to a nation, or its people, is one the United States, as the representatives of this nation, are bound to protect. Consequently, a law which is necessary and proper to afford this protection is one that Congress may enact. . . . Therefore the United States must have the power to pass it and enforce it themselves, or be unable to perform a duty which they may owe to another nation, and which the law of nations has imposed on them as part of their international obligations."

It is to be observed that the duty does not arise by virtue of the municipal law of the United States. The duty arises from the law of nations—a law superior to municipal law, including in this category the Constitution of the United States which, to the world at large, is a domestic matter. And the judgment in the *Arjona* case is a solemn asseveration on the part of the Supreme Court of the United States that the law of nations is not a law which we accept, but a law which is "imposed" upon us and which we must protect; for, if we do not, we cannot invoke the rules of international law in our own benefit, and while we would not cease to be a member of the international community, we, nevertheless, would not be considered as a member in good standing.

We might well be content to rest our case upon these statements of the Chief Justice, which are also those of his brethren; for the complete reasoning of the Court requiring due diligence in enacting municipal legislation to protect a rule of the law of nations, is the contribution which the *Arjona* case makes to the law of the international community.

However, there is another phase of the case no less worthy of our attention. By Article I, section 8, clause 10 of the Constitution, the Congress is not merely impliedly, but expressly authorized "to define and punish . . . offences against the law of nations." This authorization does not *make* the law of nations a part of our law; it *recognizes* the existence of the law of nations as a part of our law without action on our part, the law being—again to quote Chief Justice Waite—"imposed" upon the United States from their inception, as upon every state of the international community. Indeed, the law of nations, existing before the birth of the United States, became "imposed" upon us the moment the United States came into being. It was not created by the United States; it was not adopted by the United States; it could not be adopted because it was already the law of the United States *ex jure necessitatis;* and it cannot be abrogated by the United States because it was not made by the United States. Therefore, the United States cannot create international law; the most it can do is to define and to enforce it; but the expression "to define" international law is in itself a recognition of its existence, and the definition, it may be said, is only to make that express which is implicit. But that does not, indeed cannot, mean that the definition which the Government of the United States may make of international law is acceptable to the other nations. If it be correct, it is binding, not because it is the act of the United States, but because the definition of international law made or proposed by the United States is in accordance with, to use Victoria's phrase, "a consensus of the greater part of the whole world, especially in behalf of the common good of all."

This is indeed much, but it is not all. The statute creating a liability within the jurisdiction of the United States does not need to mention that it is passed to render effective the law of nations, because the law of nations is the law of the United States, whether it be so stated or not. As this phase of the case arose, it was considered and likewise decided by the Supreme Court. Let us, however, allow the Chief Justice to speak in behalf of the Court, numbering his questions and answers in the paragraph of the opinion dealing with this phase which is, as it were, a link in the chain of the argument.

1. Whether, in enacting a statute to define and punish an offence against the law of nations, it is necessary, in order 'to define' the offence, that it be declared in the statute itself to be 'an offence against the law of nations.'

2. This statute defines the offence, and if the thing made punishable is one which the United States are required by their international obligations to use due diligence to prevent, it is an offence against the law of nations.

3. Such being the case, there is no more need of declaring in the statute that it is such an offence, than there would be in any other criminal statute to declare that it was enacted to carry into execution any other particular power vested by the Constitution in the Government of the United States.

4. Whether the offence as defined is an offence against the law of nations depends on the thing done, not on any declaration to that effect by Congress.

This last is a short and weighty sentence implying that in matters international the Congress of the United States is a mere legislature of the international community for the enactment of a municipal statute in order to create a municipal sanction for the protection, or redress of a violation, of a rule of the law of nations.

5. As has already been seen, it was incumbent on the United States as a nation to use due diligence to prevent any injury to another nation or its people by counterfeiting its money, or its public or *quasi* public securities.

6. This statute was enacted as a means to that end, that is to say, as a means of performing a duty which had been cast on the United

States by the law of nations, and it was clearly appropriate legislation for that purpose.

A break in the quotation must be made to call attention to the phrase "cast on the United States," not "made by the United States."

7. Upon its face, therefore, it [the statute] defines an offence against the law of nations as clearly as if Congress had in express terms so declared.

Seven is said to be the perfect number, and the decision of the Supreme Court in the *Arjona* case can be said to be equally perfect.

Indeed it would almost seem that *United States* v. *Arjona* was, as it were, a case not actually arising in practice, but stated by the Court in order to show the students of international law that the law of nations exists without an affirmative act on the part of the respective countries; that this law of nations so imposed "casts" a duty upon every civilized nation to enact municipal laws to protect a right under the law of nations, thus complying not only with a particular duty of the country in question, but a general duty under international law; that a failure so to comply, renders the nation so failing liable in damages to the nation injured; and that the failure to use due diligence either in passing the municipal law, or in preventing the violation of international law, renders the nation liable under the law of nations, because the municipal statute should have been in existence at the time of the injury—for liability arises even though a subsequent statute be enacted. The injury looks to the past; the statute to the future.

This was the predicament in which England found itself in the reign of Queen Anne, and this was why the passage of a statute with a remedy under the statute, was not regarded as a compliance with the duty which England owed to the Russian Ambassador at the very moment of his arrest. The injuries of the past are not cured by subsequent statute.

To state it all in a word: International law should be, and is today, we may happily say, the law of every nation in the civilized world. It may have, and in some instances does have, a specific and international sanction. But whether or not it has such a sanction, it nevertheless involves the duty on the part of each nation to pass appropriate and adequate laws providing a municipal remedy for any and every violation of international law, whether in peace or in war, within its jurisdiction—that is to say, within its own territory where its jurisdiction is exclusive, or on the high seas where jurisdiction is common to all nations. But the consideration of this duty raises an important issue. A sanction cannot be provided for any law unless that law is properly formulated—at least in general terms.

Now the formulation and adequate statement of international law can only mean the codification of international law—a world code for a world law in clear and unmistakable but general terms—leaving to each nation the duty to enact municipal statutes most apt, in its opinion, to comply in full measure with its obligations under the law of nations.

"From all that has been said," to quote again the language of Victoria, "a corollary may be inferred, namely: that international law has not only the force of a pact and agreement among men, but also the force of a law; for the world as a whole, being in a way one single State, has the power to create laws that are just and fitting for all persons, as are the rules of international law. Consequently, it is clear that they who violate these international rules, whether in peace or in war, commit a mortal sin; moreover, in the gravest matters, such as the inviolability of ambassadors, it is not permissible for one country to refuse to be bound by international law, the latter having been established by the authority of the whole world." [76]

---

[76] Scott, *op. cit.*

CHAPTER III

FRANCISCO SUAREZ

His Philosophy of Law and of Sanctions[1]

WHEREIN does Francisco Suárez differ from Francisco de Vitoria? If they do not differ, we can not claim that Suárez had a hand in the founding of the modern law of nations; he could at most only be considered as confirming what Victoria had already proclaimed. He did indeed confirm what Victoria had stated; but that is not all. He has added a something, and that something gave to the conception of the great Dominican nothing more nor less than a philosophy of law and of the modern law of nations. Indeed, this is so evident that Dr. Jan Kosters,[2] a distinguished countryman of Grotius and a judge of the Supreme Court of the Netherlands, who has devoted himself to this problem, says that after the labors of Suárez the fruit of the international tree was ripe for plucking. And we in our own behalf have ventured to add, on a former occasion, that it was the hand of a Netherlander, the hand of Grotius, that plucked it.[3]

Here we have a threefold relationship. First the expounder; second the philosopher; and third, the compiler, or, if that term be looked upon as being belittling, the purveyor of the ideas of others, or rather, a popularizer in the best sense of the word. And as a popularizer the services of Grotius to international law should never be overlooked. The modern law of nations of

[1] Reprinted with slight modifications from *Georgetown Law Journal*, March, 1934, pp. 405-518.

[1] J. Kosters, in *Fondements du Droit des Gens*, published in the *Bibliotheca Visseriana* (Leyden, 1925), Vol. IV, p. 32.

[3] James Brown Scott, "Suárez and the International Community," *Addresses in Commemoration of His Contribution to International Law and Politics* (Catholic University of America, Washington, 1933), pp. 45-6.

which Victoria was the expounder, Suárez the philosopher, and Grotius the systematizer, is the contribution of what we may call, and indeed must call, the Spanish School of International Law. For if Grotius was not a Spaniard by blood, he was a Spaniard in his conception of international law, and so far as the basic principles of his system are concerned, he was indubitably a member of the Spanish School.

The contributions of Suárez to the epoch-making exposition of Victoria are the analysis and definition of the general and specific kinds of law, their origin, their nature, their various forms of categories: the law natural in its several manifestations, the law of the state in its individual capacity, and the law of the states in their international capacity—in other words, the law of nations.

Both Victoria and Suárez were churchmen, and, in the highest and best sense of the word, they were theologians. They were also jurists, because the conception of theology of that day was an all-pervasive science embracing the conduct of men and women.[4]

Victoria was a practical man as well as a theorist, and a profound student of law in its various aspects. But when he found himself face to face with the American problems thrust upon his country by the western voyage of Columbus, he deemed it his duty to furnish a solution, and in furnishing the solution, he dealt with conclusions rather than with the premises leading

[4] For the sake of comparison we may repeat here the view of Victoria quoted previously (*supra*, p. 66), as expressed in the words of his Reading *De Potestate Civili:* "The duties and functions of the theologian extend over a field so vast, that no argument, no discussion, no text, seem alien to the practice and purpose of theology. And this may account for the fact that the lack of able and sound theologians is as great as—not to say greater than—the lack of orators which is mentioned by Cicero, and which he explains by saying that men who are distinguished and skilled in every science and in all the arts are very rare. Theology, indeed, is the first of all those sciences and studies which the Greeks call Θεολογία.

Suárez, in the Preface to his *De Legibus,* expresses a somewhat similar view in different language: "For just as theologians should ponder concerning God for many other reasons, so also should they ponder concerning Him, for this reason: that He is the final end toward Whom rational creatures tend and in Whom their sole felicity consists. It follows, then, that sacred doctrine has this final end in view, and that it also sets forth the way to attain that end; since God is not only the end and, as it were, the goal, towards which all intellectual creatures are drawn, but also the cause whereby the goal is reached."

to such conclusions. With the solution his work was complete; his task was finished. Yet even if we accept the conclusions and the reasoning by which they could be applied, not merely to a single concrete case, but to all concrete cases of a like nature, when and as they might present themselves, we still would need a philosophy which would justify and integrate the abstract principles behind the conclusions. This philosophy was the contribution of Suárez, although it may not have been his conscious purpose to complete theoretically what Victoria had begun practically.

If it may not be said that Victoria passed the torch of the new learning in matters international to the hand of Suárez, there was, nevertheless, an interval of but two years between the demise of the founder of the modern law of nations and the birth of him who was, to reiterate what can not too often be stated, to furnish law with its indispensable elements, and to state and define the different kinds of law, assigning each to its place, in such a way as to leave as his legacy to the world a law with a philosophy and a philosophy of law. Although Suárez never stood in the presence of the *maestro,* he studied at Salamanca and grew up in its noble traditions. St. Thomas Aquinas had become, as it were, through Victoria, the patron saint of the university, so that Suárez lived, in very fact, his impressionable years in an atmosphere absent elsewhere—the atmosphere of Victoria, enlarged and enriched by the spirit of Aquinas. This atmosphere of Victoria was very real, because the doctrines which he had developed and taught during the twenty years of his professorate at Salamanca were in turn professed with the earnestness of disciples by those who had sat at the feet of the master. And truly it may be said that these doctrines not merely entered into, but were indeed the very foundation of what was to be known, in centuries to come, as the "Spanish School of International Law."

And so it happened that, when Suárez himself was ready to add his incomparable contribution to the Spanish School, he found a law of nations already in existence, not wholly lacking in philosophy—for none can deny that Victoria was a philosopher as well as a jurist—but nevertheless lacking a complete philosophical development.

The philosophy of Victoria was, however, for an occasion, or rather to bring a concrete situation—arising from the discovery of the New World—within the law of Christendom, thus universalizing it; whereas the purpose of Suárez was to state the law universal and its elements in the abstract, with sufficient reference to concrete instances to give it a substance and a body. With Victoria, the philosophy of law was subordinated to its application; with Suárez, the *desideratum* was the creation of a philosophy which would permeate not merely one form of law but all law, and would therefore apply not to a single, but to every concrete situation. Each, as it were, stands by himself; each is independent of the other; but together, through the combination of the concrete and the abstract, they gave, to nation and to nations, law and its philosophy.

Victoria's reputation as an international lawyer depends upon his application of the general principles of justice in relation to the one great concrete fact of his day and generation—the discovery of the Americas.

The reputation of Suárez, on the other hand, does not depend upon his treatment of any single concrete situation of his own day or of any other day. His statement of law and its philosophy was in such terms as to apply equally to his day or to any other day.

Through the discussion of a concrete situation, Victoria formulated the principles of the modern law of nations and pointed the way to their philosophic conception; through the discussion of theoretical positions, Suárez developed, we may say, a philosophy of law applicable to concrete situations. From a different approach, they reached a common goal—the establishment of a single and universal standard of right and wrong in the relations of individuals within a state, in the relations of states with one another and in the relations of the international community composed of these individuals and of these states.

* * * * * * *

Now Suárez has given us three masterpieces dealing with law, as such, with its different branches and with the fundamental principles inherent in each. The first of these masterpieces, the one with which we are immediately concerned, is the *Tractatus de Legibus ac Deo Legislatore,* a large volume of twenty books, published at Coimbra in the year 1612, Suárez being then *prima* professor of theology at the University of Coimbra and its crowning glory, as Victoria had been previously at Salamanca; the second, the *Defensio Fidei Catholicae adversus Anglicanae Sectae Errores,* published in 1613, also at Coimbra, the occasion for which was the oath of allegiance which James I of England and VI of Scotland had exacted from his Catholic subjects, unjustly in their opinion, in the opinion of their Church and, we may add, in the opinion of posterity; and the third of the philosophical trinity was the *Opus de Triplici Virtute Theologica,* left in manuscript at his death in 1617 and published four years later simultaneously at Coimbra and Lyons.

It may seem strange to the uninitiated that the portion of the latter work dealing with Charity is devoted to war, but this was entirely proper according to the theology of his Church, which considered it to be an act of charity to reclaim the erring from the evil of their international ways by an act of force, if such were necessary. In this connection, it may be said in passing that the philosophical treatment of war by Suárez is, to all intents and purposes, similar to, though not identical with, the concrete treatment of Victoria, thus demonstrating beyond peradventure that, whether implicit or express, the conception of each, at least in the matter of war, was in essence the same.

* * * * * * *

For immediate purposes we need only examine certain portions of the vast treatise *De Legibus*—those dealing with the specific phases and classifications of law, their differences, and therefore their different applications. Let us begin as Suárez begins, with the origin and authority of all law, and first with the *Proemium,* or, in the language of the present day, the Introduction.[5]

[5] The quotations from Suárez dealt with in the present volume are from a provisional English translation, in manuscript, of the Latin text of selections from his

Law is of God, whether derived directly or through a human legislator, and, this being the case, "the authority for all laws must ultimately be ascribed to Him."

To turn for a moment to the third book, "What are the elements of law"? They are three in number: the first, "its binding force with respect to the conscience," which Suárez called "its directive force"; second, "its coercive force," by virtue whereof a violation of the law is punishable; and lastly, "the force by which a definite form is laid down for contracts and similar legal acts," so that an act contrary to the prescribed form is invalid.

Now law has a twofold nature. It is *lex* or *jus*. Of each of these in turn.

Law in the sense of *lex* Suárez first defines in the terms of St. Thomas, for although St. Thomas was a Dominican and the great glory of that order, he was adopted as its own by every order of the Catholic Church; and at the present day, by the Encyclical of Pope Leo XIII, under date of August 4, 1879, and a brief of exactly a year later, the doctrine of St. Thomas is declared to be the doctrine of the Catholic Church.[6]

---

three masterpieces *De Legibus ac Deo Legislatore, Defensio Fidei* and *De Triplici Virtute Theologica,* which translation, revised where necessary, will appear in a volume of the "Classics of International Law" in the near future, accompanied by a photographic reproduction of the Latin texts in a separate volume of the series. It is therefore impossible to give for the quotations footnote citations to the English translation, and it seems undesirable to give references to the original editions of the Latin texts—from which the translations are made—as such texts are not only difficult to read, but difficult of access.

---

[6] "Now above all the Doctors of the Schools towers the figure of Thomas Aquinas, the leader and master of them all, who, as Cajetan observes, 'because he had the utmost reverence for the Doctors of antiquity, seems to have inherited in a way the intellect of all.' [*On II. ii,* qu. 148, art. 4, *in finem*]."—Leo XIII, Encyclical *Aeterni Patris,* August 4, 1879; in *Acta Sanctae Sedis* (Rome, 1879), Vol. XII, p. 97 *et seq.*

"We, for the glory of Almighty God and the honour of the Angelic Doctor, for the increase of the sciences, and for the common benefit of human society, declare by Our Supreme Authority, that St. Thomas Aquinas is Patron of Studies in Universities, Colleges, Lyceums, Catholic Schools; and We desire that he be so held by all. . . ."—Leo XIII, Brief of August 4, 1880; *ibid.,* Vol. XIII, p. 56 *et seq.*

The views of Pope Leo XIII were confirmed by each of his distinguished successors: ". . . the capital theses in the philosophy of St. Thomas are not to be placed in the category of opinions capable of being debated one way or another, but are to be considered as the foundations upon which the whole science of natural and divine things is based. . . ." Pius X, *Motu Proprio Doctoris Angelici,* June 29, 1914;

Now this St. Thomas as a youngster was "a dumb ox" to his fellow students. However, to his master, Albertus Magnus—now a saint of the Church—he was even then a youth with a marvelous future. "You call him a Dumb Ox," he cried: "I tell you this Dumb Ox shall bellow so loud that his bellowings will fill the world." [7]

What, then, is the definition of St. Thomas? "Law," he said, "is a species of rule and measure in accordance with which one is induced to act or is restrained from acting." This is, however, only a point of departure for Suárez. The definition seemed, for his purposes, to be "too broad and general," for, without modification or explanation, law so defined would apply not only to human beings—generously defined by Suárez as "rational creatures"—but also to other creatures, said by human beings to be less rational. Again—for Suárez had one of the keenest minds of the Jesuit order, noted for keenness and for discrimination—the definition of St. Thomas was, in his opinion, too broad and

---

in *Acta Apostolicae Sedis, commentarium officiale Annus VI* (1914), Vol. VI, p. 336 *et seq.*

"We are happy to recall that the philosophy of Aquinas was revived by the authority and at the instance of Leo XIII; the merit of Our Illustrious Predecessor in so doing is such, as we have said elsewhere, that if he had not been the author of many acts and decrees of surpassing wisdom, this alone would be sufficient to establish his undying glory. Pope Pius X of saintly memory followed shortly afterwards in his footsteps, more particularly in his *Motu Proprio Doctoris Angelici*. . . .

"Let everyone therefore inviolably observe the prescription contained in the Codex of Canon Law that 'the study of philosophy and theology and the teachings of these sciences to their students must be accurately carried out by professors [in seminaries, etc.] according to the arguments, doctrine and principles of St. Thomas which they are inviolately to hold'; and may they conform to this rule so faithfully as to be able to describe his in very truth as their master." Pius XI, Encyclical *Studiorum Ducem*, June 29, 1923, *ibid.*, Annus XV, Vol. XV, p. 309 *et seq.*

The provisions of the canons mentioned above are as follows:

"*Canon* 589: Religious who have already studied their humanities should devote themselves for two years at least to philosophy and for four years to theology, following the teaching of St. Thomas (cf. *canon* 1366 § 2) in accordance with the instructions of the Holy See."

"*Canon* 1366 § 2: The study of philosophy and theology and the teaching of these sciences to their students must be accurately carried out by professors [in seminaries, etc.] according to the arguments, doctrine, and principles of St. Thomas which they are inviolately to hold."—*Codex Iuris Canonici, Pii X Pont. Max. iussu digestus, Benedicti Papae XV auctoritate promulgatus.* (Rome, 1917) *Canon* 589, p. 170; *Canon* 1366 § 2, p. 398.

---

[7] G. K. Chesterton, *St. Thomas Aquinas* (New York, 1933), p. 74.

too general, because, taken without modification or explanation, it "would relate not only to moral matters, but also to artificial matters, not only to the good and upright, but also to the base." Suárez, however, found a final and a grave "obstacle," as far as his purpose was concerned, to the acceptance of this definition, for, he said, "it would follow that counsels are to be included under law," whereas his opinion was that "according to the faith, counsels are clearly distinct from precepts," from which he draws the conclusion that "they are not included under 'law,' strictly speaking."

What, then, was Suárez' conception of law? "That which pertains to customary conduct [*mores*]," by which definition Suárez contracted, as it were, "the description given by St. Thomas, so that it runs as follows: law is a measure, so to speak, of moral acts"; for, although law may otherwise meet the three requirements, absence of the moral element, we add in our own behalf, from any and every definition of law as applicable to human beings, is fatal.

What, in a word, is the definition of law according to the moral system of Suárez? We do not need to speculate. He says it squarely and distinctly within the compass of a single sentence—"strictly and absolutely speaking, only that which is a measure of rectitude, viewed absolutely, and consequently, only that which is a right and virtuous rule, can be called law." With the humility becoming a commentator, may we not express the hope that one day this definition may find its place not only in every municipal statute, but in the law of nations?

So much at present for law as a rule of action.

But what of *jus,* in which the moral element not only enters but predominates? *Jus,* strictly speaking, Suárez defines as "a certain moral faculty which every man has, either over his own property or with respect to that which is due him." Illustrations? "The owner of a thing is said to have a right"—that is, *jus*—Suárez continues, "in that thing, and the laborer is said"—to give the second illustration by which Suárez drives home his definition—"to have that right to his wages by reason of which he is declared worthy of his hire." For this phase of the subject he had even higher authority than that of St. Thomas, which authority Suárez himself intimates.

What, then, is the distinction between *lex* and *jus*? *Lex* may justify possession; but *jus* is not merely a matter of law—it is the right itself. Where *lex* is appropriate, *jus* is also appropriate; but *jus* has a further implication. From the etymological standpoint, *jus* and *lex*, if not synonymous, have necessarily a point in common. "*Jus*," Suárez informs us, is derived "from *jubendum*" and "*lex* rests on ordering (*jussio*), or command." The consequence? It is that, so far as an order or a command is concerned, the two may seem to be synonymous, but, in the language of Suárez, "the word *jus* has come to possess certain other connotations which have not been transferred to the term *lex*." Of this he gives a number of illustrations. "The act of a judge is thus wont to be designated by the term *jus*." What are the reasons? "Because it ought to be performed in accordance with the laws (*leges*), or because it sometimes seems to establish a law (*lex*), . . .; so that the judge, when he exercises his office, is said to declare the law (*jus dicere*)."

The outstanding theologians were, it would seem, as much at home with the Roman law as with the law of their Church; indeed, both were of Latin origin. But perhaps it is well, thus early in the discussion of Suárez' conception of law in its various phases and aspects, to show the nature and the extent of this familiarity.

Where does he find this function of the judge in relation to law? In a "title of the *Digest*: 'If any one fails to obey him who declares the law.' "[8] In behalf of the law of his Church, Suárez adds: "Moreover, in the canon law[9] we find the words: 'Outside of his own territory, he who declares the law may be disobeyed with impunity' "—a statement which we shall see is fundamental with Suárez, when he treats of domicile.

But if *jus* is to be taken as a command, to the extent that it is synonymous with *lex*, it has nevertheless an ethical implication, whereas *lex* has a merely physical or material content—a distinc-

[8] *Digest*, II. iii.

[9] *Sext*, I. ii. 2.

tion pointed out by St. Thomas, who appears to have had in mind the Roman law and who, according to Suárez, says that "even the art itself by which one determines what is just, is sometimes called *jus*."[10] To enforce this distinction, Suárez himself appeals to the Roman law,[11] "in which Ulpian quotes with approval the definition of Celsus" to the effect that "*jus* is the art of the good and the equitable." Whereupon Suárez comments that "this definition would be suited, not so much to law (*lex*) itself, as to jurisprudence (*juris prudentiae*)," adding: "unless 'art' is taken in a broad sense, as referring to any method or measure of operation."

What, then, is the conclusion of Suárez on this phase of the question? "Through usage," he says, "the term *lex* is properly applied both to written and to non-written [law], so that *jus* in so far as it refers to *lex* is used interchangeably with that term, and the two words are considered as synonyms." However, this does not mean that the two terms are wholly synonymous. They are only the same so far as they go together; but *jus* advances from the material domain of "command" to enter that of "justice," as distinguished from *lex*.

Is there then a distinction between *jus* and "the equitable and the good"?—a question which arises if we consider, as Suárez does, that "*jus* is precisely the same as that which is just, while the latter"—meaning that which is just—"is, in turn, precisely the equitable and the good." Let us first examine the meaning of "equity." According to Suárez, "in one sense, it stands for natural" equity, which, in his opinion, "is identical with natural justice." In Aristotle's conception, it is "the emendation of that which is [legally] just"; but it is rather, in the words of Suárez, "the source or rule thereof." The Latin term "*aequitas*" may be taken, however, "in another sense . . . as being a prudent moderation of the written law (*lex*)," that is, it transcends "the exact, literal interpretation" of the written statute. "In this sense," Suárez continues, "*aequitas* is spoken of . . . as being opposed to

[10] *Summa*, II. ii, qu. 57, art. 1, ad 1.

[11] *Digest*, I. i. 1, § 1.

jus in its strict meaning." This, it may be said in passing, is the modern conception of equity.

Considering equity in this sense, Suárez holds that "the terms 'equitable' (*aequum*) and 'good' (*bonum*) are applied . . . to that which does indeed of itself possess these qualities, even though it may appear to be at variance with the letter of the law (*lex*)." Stated in another way, the judge may temper his application of the law by a judgment *ex aequo et bono,* on the basis of right reason and justice, putting into effect that ancient maxim of equity: "The letter killeth but the spirit maketh alive."

In a few phrases Suárez now states the whole philosophy of equity: "In the interpretation of the laws, the good and the equitable should always be regarded; even if it be needful at times to temper the rigor of the words, in order not to depart from what is naturally equitable and good."

With this as a background, Suárez comes to close quarters with *"jus,"* saying that he will use it "in its second and proper connotation," so that the term "will become synonymous with (*lex*) but only in so far as we shall now be speaking of *lex,* too, in a general manner."

What, then, is law? To this question which we put Suárez himself replies that it "is a kind of rule, establishing or pointing out, in regard to its own subject matter or the operation with which it is concerned that mean which is to be preserved for the sake of right and fitting action." Here we have *jus* in disguise, that is to say, implied, without express mention, but nevertheless completely permeating the definition. It is a universal rule having, as Suárez says, "relation to all persons, in due proportion." And summing it all up, he gives his definition in a single, brief, and weighty sentence: "Law is a common, just and stable precept, sufficiently promulgated." It is common in that it applies to all; it is just in that it is equitable and moral; it is a precept, meaning a rule of action; it is stable, because of its permanent nature; and above and beyond all, it is not something secret, for it must be made known and in such a way that, to paraphrase another ancient maxim, ignorance of it will be no excuse.

It will already be evident that we are dealing with the subject of law as treated by one who, although he was not a member of the legal profession in the strict sense of the term, was nevertheless, in the theory of law, a jurist to his fingertips.

* * * * * * * *

The second of the books of *De Legibus* is for us Suárez' *magnum opus,* dealing as it does with the eternal law, the natural law and the *jus gentium,* in the consideration of which he assumes his rightful place as the founder of the philosophy of law in its various phases, including the law of nations. For this reason, our task will be a somewhat close analysis of the second book, and, without ceasing to be an analysis, it will rely upon and reproduce in no small measure the very language of Suárez.

Let us begin with the "eternal law," for the reason that it rightly occupies the "first place" with Suárez, "on account of its dignity and excellence," and for the further reason, which must be stated in his very words—because it is his fundamental conception, without which his system would not be, indeed could not be, what it is—that "it is the source and origin of all laws."

Next of the "natural law" and of the link between the two. "Natural law," he says, "is the first system whereby the eternal law has been applied or made known to us," and this law of nature, as it is often called, "is made known to us," Suárez continues, "in a twofold way, first through natural reason, and secondly through the law of the Decalogue written on the Mosaic tablets."

And the "law of nations," for which Suárez uses the term *"jus gentium,"* the only term by which it was known in his day, "is of all systems the most closely related to the natural law."

These categories and their inter-relations are appropriately set forth by Suárez by way of introduction to the second book.

In the third chapter, Suárez develops his idea of the eternal law, saying that it "is a free decree of the Will of God, Who lays down the order to be observed either generally, by [the separate] parts of the universe with respect to the common good or else specifically, by intellectual creatures in their free actions." Here we have what may be called its human application.

The eternal law may be looked at from two points of view. In the first place, being eternal, it is "independent of external promulgation," and in this sense it is without "relation to creatures existing for the moment." It is, in short, apart from all things created. It is the source as well as the law; it is timeless and ageless. It is, in other words, the first cause.

From the second point of view, this eternal law is "promulgated and binding at the same time," and it may be called "divine" in so far as it has a "temporal relation to creatures existing at the time," the term "divine" connoting "adequate external communication and promulgation." The promulgation, Suárez adds, may not be necessary to divine law, but for human knowledge of it there must be "some revealing token or sign whereby it is adequately promulgated," and, being thus promulgated, it is a divine and visible law and the means of application of the eternal law to the affairs of men.

The divine law being related to or a part of the eternal law and revealed from time to time, its binding force "proceeds," Suárez says, "immediately from" the eternal. And since it is applicable to human beings, it may be called "human law"—but only in its application, not in its nature. Now there is a human law which is not divine, in that it is made by human beings and, derived from that source, its binding force is not divine; for the human law is not eternal but "something created and temporal, inasmuch as this law is formed and perfected in the mind and will of man," and therefore is "a law of man and not of God Himself." Nevertheless, "human law is an effect of eternal law," since it is only law "by reason of its participation [in the eternal]"; in other words, human law, to be law, must be in accord with the eternal verities, or, as we have previously said, the first cause; or, in the Greek conception, it must conform to what they were pleased to call "design in nature."

Human law has, nevertheless, its own binding force, to the extent that "it is dependent upon principles of the eternal law." And the example is: the precept that obedience is due to superiors." Human law, however, is to be righteous, that is to say, it is to be just and it is to be moral. Therefore it should, in Suárez' language, "conform to the eternal," from which it follows that the human law is related to the eternal law, although not in the same direct sense as is the divine law, which may be defined as the eternal law made evident. Now the immediate source of the divine law is the eternal law, without the intervention of a human agency, while the human law is not only administered, but is formulated by men, "the latter," in Suárez' language, "being not only an incidental cause . . . that is, not merely establishers and appliers of this law; but also the essential cause—that is, the creators of the law itself." What is the result? The force and efficacy of the human law comes "directly from the will of the human legislator." And Suárez sets forth in two sentences, which deserve to be called "classic," the obligation of the divine and human law:

> 1. In the case of the divine law, the obligation is derived immediately from God Himself, since in so far as that law exists in man, it has no binding force save as it manifests the divine reason, or will.
>
> 2. In human law, however, the obligation is not derived immediately from God; for in so far as human law exists in those who are subject thereto, it has an immediate relation to the will of the prince who has the power to create a new law, as distinct from the divine law, and from his will the obligation directly emanates, although fundamentally this obligation proceeds in its entirety from the eternal law.

But the difference is more apparent than real, as is also stated in classic terms by Suárez:

> All men necessarily behold within themselves some sort of participation in the eternal law, since there is no rational person who does not in some manner judge that the honorable course of action must be followed and the base avoided; and in this sense, it is said that men have some knowledge of the eternal law.

It may be asked, according to the conception of Suárez, and indeed of Christendom, is not man the handiwork of God? And what could be more natural than that he should be, at least in some degree, a reflection of his Creator? But it is not given—to paraphrase Suárez—to every man to see the divine both in and through the human law.

We now pass with Suárez to the second division, "natural law," which he defines in a preliminary way as consisting "in a true judicial act of the mind." This brief definition, however, he feels should be expanded. The natural law is not evident as are the ground beneath us and the heavens above us; for the natural law may be called, he immediately says, "the natural light of the intellect, inherently adapted for prescribing what must be done . . . since men retain that law in their hearts, although they may be engaged in no [specific] act of reflection or judgment." The discovery of the natural law may be by means of deliberate reflection, but it may also be instinctive; in either case it is, as Suárez says, the result of "the natural light of the intellect." It is a thing inherent in man, in that it is in the hearts of men because written there by God Himself—on the authority of St. Paul—and, for us of the United States, on the lesser authority of Alexander Hamilton. For does not Hamilton say, in his reply to the "Westchester Farmer," that human rights "are not to be rummaged for among old parchments or musty records. They are written, as with a sunbeam, in the whole volume of human nature, by the hand of the divinity itself, and can never be erased or obscured by mortal power."[12]

Natural law, as we have said, is inherent. So also is conscience. "Nevertheless," says Suárez, "the two are different. For the term 'law' has reference to a rule respecting those things which should be done and framed in general terms; whereas conscience is a practical dictate in a particular case, so that it is the application of the law to a particular act, so to speak, rather than [the law itself]." Natural law is the general standard; conscience is the standard of the individual.

Let us state in a single sentence the obligation of the natural law. As an emanation of the eternal law, the law natural carries with it an obligation proceeding from the divine will, that "men shall be bound to obey that which right reason dictates."

Now what of human law, which, for present purposes, is of

[12] *The Works of Alexander Hamilton,* Edition by Henry Cabot Lodge (New York, 1903), Vol. I, p. 113.

two kinds? Both are human law in the sense that they are not divine. The first is custom or the common law. Neither of these is made by a particular person but grows by human action. The human law considered in this general sense carries with it its own obligation, and this obligation, as will appear later, flows from the natural law itself, and has an inherent sanction. Secondly, there is human law in the specific sense, that is, the law of the legislature, or, as we would say, the statute. This also has an inherent obligation and therefore an inherent sanction; for the obligation, unlike the statute, is not artificial; although inherent, it should be made express, in order that the obligation may be legally enforceable.

There is, however, a further distinction going to the very essence of things. A statute makes a thing a crime and therefore fixes a punishment for its violation. A statute makes wrong the act which it condemns, whereas in the domain of the natural law, a thing is in essence good or bad, and the natural law does not make it bad but prohibits it because it is bad, in other words, because it is inherently evil. In this sense the natural law partakes of, and indeed is, divine law. What is the result? The natural law is a moral law and therefore "embraces all precepts or moral principles which are plainly characterized by the righteousness necessary to virtuous conduct." The converse is also true, as we have said, in that the natural law prohibits things essentially evil. From the statement of Suárez there are two immediate and inevitable conclusions, in the first of which he states and defines the way in which the law of nature is revealed. It is made evident, as we would expect from what Suárez has already said, by "natural illumination," and the consequence is that "the natural law is binding in conscience," for the judge in the forum of conscience is natural reason itself.

Now it is a truism among writers on international law that the law of nature is immutable. But Suárez was not content with truisms. The natural law being synonymous with rational nature, it "cannot of itself lapse or suffer change" but will, as Suárez says, endure as long as the human being is possessed of reason and freedom of will. Natural law, therefore, exists and it continues to exist; but it applies to conditions which are not immutable. The precept is unchangeable; its application may vary from age to age. For in Suárez' own language, "the natural law discerns the mutability contained in the subject matter itself," from which it follows that the mutability existing in the nature of things is, as it were, a constant factor and, again to quote Suárez, the natural law "adapts its own precepts to this mutability, prescribing . . . a certain sort of conduct for one condition, and another sort of conduct for another condition," so that Suárez is justified in logically drawing the conclusion from his premises that "the law in itself remains at all times unchanged, although according to our manner of speaking and by an extrinsic process of metonymy, it would *seem*"—we emphasize the word—"after a fashion, to undergo change."

There are certain positive commands of natural law, and there are certain things which are permitted, conceded or allowed, or, in the language of Suárez, things "permissive, negative, or concessive." With the things prescribed we have already dealt, an example being those things which are prohibited by the natural law as being inherently evil or commanded by it as being intrinsically good and "necessary to virtuous conduct." In the second group which partakes of the nature of a permission and not a command—"there fall many things which . . . are permissible, or conceded, to men." What are these things? "A community of goods, human liberty and the like." And here Suárez proceeds to state how such things, being merely permissible, may change without violating the law of nature. For example, he instances changes which are "in accordance with the demands of reason." "Nakedness is natural to man," according to Suárez. This nakedness does not "require covering in the state of innocence; whereas, in the fallen condition of [human] nature, natural reason imposes a different requirement. So also liberty is natural to man." Why? "Since he possesses it by the force of natural law; yet the law of nature does not forbid the loss of his liberty." We may ourselves advance an example: a captive might under the ancient conception be put to death, or if his life were spared he might be deprived of his liberty; and neither would have been contrary to the law of nature. This is a first group of examples.

There is a second dealing with another phase of the subject—the "foundation" of a right not absolutely prescribed by natural law, the foundation being "in a natural disposition." This is the case of a son inheriting from an intestate father, according to the *Digest*.[13] The example given is of so frequent occurrence that it may not seem to need comment; yet, as Suárez uses it in order to establish a fundamental principle of large implication, he should be heard in its behalf and in his own words: "For the natural law, although it does not absolutely prescribe that this shall be so, does incline toward this [arrangement], which follows from it naturally, so to speak, unless an impediment arises from some other source." In like manner, he instances by way of example the credence given to two witnesses. Proof being needed, two witnesses are considered sufficient for the requirements, and this custom, according to Suárez, may be said "to pertain to the natural law," in its permissive rather than in its prescriptive phase, "unless," he adds, "for special causes some other [requirement] is added, or imposed [in substitution]." Here the Bible may be quoted in his behalf; for is it not said: "In the mouth of two or three witnesses every word may stand."[14]

Suárez now takes up certain "precepts of natural law, . . . dealing with pacts, agreements, or obligations." The first two are truly "introduced through the will of men," and the obligations he has in mind are also those created by the human will but made binding by the natural law. The examples he gives are laws for the "observance of vows, . . . whether these be made in simple form or confirmed by oath." They form a special class. But the principle involved applies to other contracts and also the rights to which they give rise.

Such are, it is believed, the stock examples of natural rights; the duties and obligations of which are stated in three simple Latin words, *Pacta sunt servanda*. With this natural precept of

[13] XXXVIII. vi. 7, at end.
[14] St. Matthew, xviii, 16.

three words, law and order and fair dealing are possible; without it, unfair dealing, leading, it may be, to anarchy. It is the foundation of a governed world; for, if solemn agreements are not to be kept, there is no such thing as law and order, natural or human. Indeed there are many jurists—among them international lawyers of repute—who regard these three words as stating the whole obligation of the law natural with all of the proper and reasonable consequences which flow from such obligation. Even the positivists accept the phrase, unconscious it may be that in so doing they are stamping with their approval the obligation of natural law and its necessary or reasonable consequences; in other words, by admitting the obligation of natural law they recognize, perhaps unwittingly, the existence of a natural jurisprudence.

In order that there may be no doubt about the matter and its importance, it may be said that there is a consensus of opinion in the civilized world that, if the common rights of men are not natural rights, they are, even if "acquired," so fundamental as to be beyond the power of prince, legislature, or even the people themselves to suppress.

So much for precepts of the natural law—or at least their consequences—in which the hand of man is visible. There are others equally binding, as Suárez says, because of their "subject-matter, and independently of any prior consent by human will." These are affirmative—"positive precepts of religious devotion to God, of filial piety, of mercy, and of almsgiving to one's neighbor"—and negative, of which examples are those "against killing, against slander, and similar prohibitions." In so far as the precepts introduced by the will of man are influenced by human will, they are mutable to that extent, whereas the precepts independent of human will are, as Suárez himself says, "immutable." The latter precepts are concerned with timeless truths, the former with "the human power of free-will," which is itself "exceedingly changeable," and frequently requires "correction and alteration." This simple statement of Suárez is of immense importance, as it recognizes the change in law from time to time, to meet the changing conditions upon which the progress and the civilization of the world depend; in other words, we have a rigid law as regards the fundamentals of right and wrong but a variable law in their application to changing human conditions. It follows as a necessary consequence from the immutability of the natural law as such that "no human power, even though it be the Papal power"—it is to be borne in mind that Suárez is speaking—"can abrogate any proper precept of natural law, nor truly and essentially restrict such a precept, nor grant a dispensation from it."

He advances four proofs in behalf of this positive assertion. As Suárez is considered the last of the schoolmen—meaning the last who had something worth saying and said it in the manner of the schoolmen—the proofs in behalf of the assertion under consideration are given in his own words as a perfect example of his mastery of the scholastic method.

> 1. The first proof of this assertion is drawn from the statements made in the preceding chapter; for it has been shown [in that chapter] that the natural law, in so far as its precepts are concerned, is by its very nature unchangeable; and men cannot change that which is unchangeable; therefore, . . .

This proof is confirmed in the true scholastic manner "by the fact that the natural law, in all its precepts, relates to the natural qualities of mankind; and man cannot change the nature of things; therefore, . . ."

Suárez now passes to the second proof, in which the assertion in question is proved by the fact that:

> 2. In the case of every precept of natural law, God is the law-giver; and man cannot change a law that God has established, since an inferior cannot prevail as against his superior.

The next proof is the argument that

> 3. The natural law is the foundation of human law, therefore, human law cannot derogate from natural law; [since], otherwise, it would destroy its own foundation, and, consequently, itself.

These three proofs would seem to be unanswerable; but Suárez, being a schoolman, is not content to convince; his purpose is to overwhelm his adversary. Therefore he continues:

4. If human law could derogate from natural law, it would be possible for the former to make an enactment in opposition to the latter, since one can conceive of no other way of changing natural law; but [human law] cannot make such an enactment; therefore, . . .

To readers of his day, this method of argument would seem the natural way of proceeding, but having pity, as it were, on us moderns, who have fallen into strange ways, Suárez, after having proved his major premise, calls our attention specifically to the minor premise, and incidentally clinches his argument beyond all peradventure of dispute. "The minor premise is proved thus: what is contrary to natural law is intrinsically evil; therefore the human law in question would relate to an intrinsically evil matter, and in consequence would not [truly] constitute either *jus* or *lex*." This would indeed be unfortunate; for if it is neither, it is nothing in the realm of law.

But still Suárez is not content. For his proof of the minor premise, he must have a confirmation and he finds it in "the fact that, for this [same] reason, a custom"—mark the word—"opposed to natural law cannot make a legal rule." Hitherto he has been dealing with the syllogism, its parts and its consequences, but in order to make assurance doubly or trebly sure, he invokes the authority of the *Decretals*[15] and "the Gloss thereon," to the effect that "the natural law is immutable in so far as concerns its commands and prohibitions." To us this would seem sufficient, but Suárez must have another authority, and he finds it in a similar passage "in the Gloss on *Decretum,* I. v. 1, where Gratian"—himself the compiler of the *Decretum*—"says that the natural law is unchangeable; [a statement] which he repeats in . . . *Decretum,* I. vi, last canon."

There is, however, a second brand of precepts of natural law which constitutes an exception to the assertion which Suárez has so convincingly proved. For there are, as he has already informed us, certain precepts of the natural law depending for their binding force "upon a prior consent of human will" and upon its efficacy "to issue in some action." This kind of precept "may sometimes be subjected to human dispensation." Why?

[15] I. iv. 11.

Because such a dispensation does not involve "a direct and absolute abolition of the obligation of natural law" but merely a remission, which affects the subject-matter of the precept. The remission which brings about the change "is not contrary to natural law," because it depends not upon a change of the law itself but upon a change in human volition. This being the case, a superior may, in this sense, alter the obligation of the natural law, but only in remitting its obligation in the special manner thus indicated by Suárez. The essence of the transaction is the remission of a duty or an obligation. Such remission may be, and usually is, by a superior to whom the duty or obligation is due. On the other hand, the private individual may, in certain instances, take such action in his own behalf, as in the case of one who remits "the natural obligation arising from a promise," or the "obligation arising from a mutual contract by effecting a donation": in plain English, the remission of a debt or indebtedness. In this case, the law upon which the obligation depends still remains, but the subject-matter having changed hands, the obligation ceases. The "dispensation," to use the technical expression, is, as Suárez rightly says, "from fact rather than from law."

But the change in subject-matter may be brought about by laws as well as by individuals, superior or private. The example of this which Suárez gives is derived from human law, and he here instances the "*jus gentium* or the civil law," that is to say, the law of nations—or the municipal law of a single nation. Through either of these there may be "effected in the subject-matter of the natural law a change of such sort that, by reason of it, the obligation imposed by natural law will also change."

Let us take an example—not merely a change, but a succession of changes in the subject-matter brought about by the *jus gentium*. There is the precept, "Thou shalt not kill"—a natural precept, if ever there was one. The precept presupposes that there is not just cause for taking life. But suppose a war breaks out—to use the most common example in antiquity and one which is not wholly a stranger to our own day. A life for a life: he who would kill may himself be killed, even after capture. This was both recognized and regularized by the *jus gentium*—the change making that legal which otherwise would not have been so under the natural law. This, however, is but the first change. Later the procedure was not to put prisoners to death but to retain them as captives, depriving them permanently of their natural right to liberty, that procedure being more serviceable, inasmuch as a living slave was more profitable than a dead enemy. This, too, was recognized and approved by the law of nations. Still later, the prisoner was allowed—or others in his behalf—to purchase freedom from slavery (or some other form of captivity) by the payment of a round sum technically known as "ransom money." Again the change of subject-matter entered into the law of nations. Finally, prisoners are today exchanged for prisoners, as it is apparently to the advantage of each of the contending parties to get rid of what might at times be an incumbrance, and to have returned to them the one-time prisoners. However, the element of profit is not overlooked. Private soldiers are exchanged for private soldiers and officers for officers—but only officers of the same rank. Here we have an example, or rather a series of examples, running through countless ages, bearing out the truth of Suárez' statement.

As to the basis in reason of changes of whatsoever kind which may affect the obligation of the natural law without changing the nature of the law, we must assuredly quote the exact language of Suárez, generalizing the question as it does and adding an interesting and a priceless illustration taken from the first authority in the Church after St. Paul, and one to whom international law is forever indebted. "And finally, the rational basis of the assertion in question is that such a mode of change is not inconsistent with the necessary and changeless character of the natural law; and that, for the rest, it is convenient and frequently necessary for men, in accordance with the various changes of estate which befall them." Suárez now invokes the spiritual authority of St. Augustine in the form of a material illustration: "In this connection, too ,one may fittingly apply the familiar illustration drawn from Augustine, that just as the science of medicine lays down certain precepts for the sick, and others for the well, certain ones for the strong, and others for the weak, although the rules of medicine do not therefore undergo essential change, but merely become multiple in their number, so that some serve on one occasion, and others, on another occasion; even so, the natural law, while it remains [in itself] the same, lays down one precept for one occasion, another, for another occasion; and is binding [in one of its rules] at one time, and not binding previously and subsequently, and this without undergoing any change in itself [but merely] because of a change in the subject-matter."

There is a precept of the natural law with which we of the United States have had a long and painful but a chastening experience: liberty for the white; slavery for the black; liberty, now, fortunately, for all human beings. Of "liberty" Suárez says: "Liberty, rather than slavery, is [a precept] of the natural law." The reason? That "nature has made men free in a positive sense, so to speak, with an intrinsic right to liberty, whereas it has not made them slaves in this positive sense, properly speaking." The American Declaration of Independence set forth the same principle in recognizing that "all men are created equal," with a right to "life, liberty and the pursuit of happiness." Now, liberty, in the conception of Suárez, was a natural right—indeed, a precept of the law of nature. Nevertheless it was a right, Suárez says, which man might renounce, and in the case of punishment, society might renounce it in his behalf. In that sense, therefore, slavery or a form of servitude is permissible by the law of nature. Today, fortunately, we no longer avail ourselves of this permission as regards slavery, and indeed the individual can not, of his own free will, make himself a slave. He can only be deprived of his liberty by due process of law, as Suárez later implies, and then solely as a means of punishment, or for the good of society, as in the case of insane persons.

"Nature," Suárez continues in the same passage, "has conferred [upon men] in common dominion over all things, and consequently has given to every man a power to use [these things]." "But nature," according to Suárez and according to writers generally, does not confer "private property rights," to be exercised by individuals to the exclusion of the other members of the community. Nevertheless, ownership of private property is today the rule. Community of property, to be sure, existed under natural law; but was it prescribed by natural law? It may or may not have been so prescribed, in the opinion of Suárez, but while common ownership continued, there was, in his language, "a positive precept of natural law, to the effect that no one should be prohibited or prevented from making the necessary use of the common property." This was so in the days before private property; and indeed it is still so, as Suárez points out, "with regard to those things which are common, and for so long as they are not in any way divided."

It would seem that the high seas constitute the best illustration for Suárez' statement that "no one may be prohibited from the common use of such things, generally speaking, that is, aside from cases involving special necessity or a just cause"—such cases, we may add, as necessary jurisdiction over the marginal waters, and occupation of parts of the sea by belligerents in time of war. What is the application of the natural law after division of community into private property has taken place? "The natural law," Suárez says with admirable brevity, "forbids theft, or the undue taking of another's property."

Let us consider somewhat further the matter of liberty, to which Suárez has already referred and upon which we have made an anticipatory comment. "Nature," he says, "although it has granted liberty, and dominion over that liberty, has, nevertheless, not absolutely forbidden that it should be taken away." What are the reasons which justify its withdrawal? Since "man is lord of his own liberty, it is possible for him to sell or alienate the same." Fortunately this disposition of one's self has gone by the board; in other words, we have here an example of a change in the application of the natural law as the result of the civil law, and that subsequent to Suárez.

As could the individual in Suárez' day, so the commonwealth, made up of individuals, could in his day as well as in ours, alienate liberty, "acting through a higher power, which it"—meaning, of course, the commonwealth—"possesses for the government of man." Is this simply because the commonwealth may possess the physical power? No. It must be "for a just cause." What is this cause? "By way of a punishment." And the whole thing is summed up by Suárez in a single sentence: "For nature also gave to man the use and possession of his own life; yet he may sometimes justly be deprived of it, through human agency."

With a firm hand Suárez draws a distinction between mandatory natural law and the law concerning dominion, whether over self or over property. The former "comprehends rules and principles for right conduct which involve necessary truth, and these," he continues, "are therefore immutable." And the reason is that these rules and principles of the mandatory natural law "are based upon the intrinsic rectitude or perversity of their objects," that is, they command or prohibit a thing because it is good or bad, whereas the civil law—meaning the law applicable within a nation—or the law of the international community makes a thing good or bad by the very fact that it commands or prohibits it.

Thus far of the mandatory natural law.

"The law concerning dominion"—whether over liberty or property—"is merely the subject-matter" of the mandatory law, Suárez meaning thereby that the existence of a certain fact or "a certain condition or habitual state of things," when recognized, is protected by the mandatory natural law. Thus, as an example, when natural law permitted a change of dominion by the division of community into private property, the mandatory natural law stepped in with the command that private rights should be respected.

The succeeding passage deals with the higher rights, and is quoted without a break, in order to show the manner in which Suárez considers and safeguards such rights, permitting their change under natural law yet protecting the new rights brought into being because of the change. "It is evident," he proceeds, without a pause, "that all created things, and especially those which are corruptible, are characterized through nature by many conditions that are changeable and capable of being abolished for many causes. Accordingly, we say of liberty and of any similar lawful right, that even if such a right has been positively granted by nature, it may be changed by human agency, since it is dependent in the individual persons, either upon their own wills, or upon the state, in so far as the latter has lawful power over all private individuals and over their property, to the extent necessary for right government." This is in essence a philosophy not only of law but of government.

Suárez now passes to a consideration of the two points of view from which natural law may be regarded: the first, natural law, as such; and the second, as it may find its expression in a positive law. In the later case, the positive law, in so far as it includes natural law within its terms, is only declaratory as it can neither make nor unmake the law natural. It is, in the words of Suárez, "a reminder of the natural law." It is "declarative," just as were, to use Suárez' illustration, "the moral precepts of the Decalogue in the Old Law." The same may also be said of those human laws involving natural justice, of which Suárez gives a trio of interesting examples: the first, that a "deposit" is to be returned; the second, that a promise must be "fulfilled"—which would fall under the rubric *Pacta sunt servanda;* and the third, contrary to the unfortunately well-nigh prevailing view of the present day, "that a wife must not be separated from her husband."

Thus in a word the natural law may be declared by the positive law, or it may be considered as it is in itself and, Suárez adds, "as it is conceived or dictated by right reason"—which the learned St. Germaine had said, in his *Doctor and Student,* written and published before Suárez was born, is the English for natural law.

But simple as this may seem when stated by Suárez, he himself felt, as must we who only dabble in the law of nature, that "many natural precepts require a great deal of exposition and interpretation in order that their true sense may be established."

There are various reasons why this should be so. Among those which Suárez mentions are the fact that "human actions, in so far as concerns their righteous or wicked character, depend to a great extent upon the circumstances and opportunities for their execution." In English we have a colloquial expression which means much the same thing: "Circumstances alter cases"—the more so as natural law permits the good and prohibits the bad because they are good and bad. This being the case, we must inquire, Suárez continues, "into the conditions and circumstances under which the act concerned is essentially good or evil," which inquiry—still in the words of Suárez—is "the interpretation of a natural precept with respect to the true sense of that precept."

Now there are two processes which, to a certain extent, are similar and may often be confused. But Suárez had no intention that either he or his reader should misunderstand the distinction between "equity" and "interpretation"; for, while "interpretation," as distinct from "equity," applies to every law (natural, municipal, or international), ἐπιείκεια which we shall render as *aequitas,* to avoid the familiar "equity" of chancery in English law, "has no place in any natural precept," as such, "for the law of nature is inherently good and perfect of itself," and a thing perfect can not be perfected by *aequitas.* More than one authority prior to Suárez had apparently confused *"aequitas"* and "interpretation," and the errors of his predecessors and opponents serve, as it were, to light Suárez on his course.

Take, for example, the precept concerning the "return of a deposit," cited by no less an authority than Cajetan, who appears to have considered such a transaction as a case of *"aequitas";* but in the opinion of Suárez, what happens is that "we make an interpretation to the effect that it—the precept—is not binding when the return of the deposit would be contrary to justice or to charity." But this interpretation is not, he informs us, *aequitas.* In this view of things, there is the clear implication that justice and charity are inherent in the natural law. In the words of Suárez, "right reason lays down not an absolute dictate that deposits must be returned, but a dictate that they shall be returned only under certain implied conditions required by the principles of justice and charity." This interpretation does not affect the universal character of the rule of natural law but implies its universality above and beyond circumstances. In other words, the principle holds; it is the circumstances which change.

Before going further in his discussion of this phase of the question, Suárez considers it well to define ἐπιείκεια—or, as we prefer to say, *aequitas.* It is nothing more nor less than the "emendation of a law, or of that which is legally just." But as natural law is just and is founded upon right reason, which, in turn, is the spokesman of truth, it is clear that natural law cannot be amended. Still dealing with the distinction between "interpretation" and *"aequitas,"* Suárez shows at this point the danger of confusion from another source. Supposing that an obligation of the natural law should be held by proper judicial authority to lapse because of a change in the subject-matter—a situation with which Suárez has already dealt—would this be *aequitas*? No, says Suárez, for "this is the result, not of ἐπιείκεια but of a change in subject-matter." What is the effect of the *aequitas* which Suárez has in mind? It is, in a word, an exemption from the law.

Now this being the case, can there likewise be an exemption from the universal law through interpretation? Suárez answers, as we would expect, in the negative, adding that "a dictate of right reason . . . is imposed universally." This does not mean that with changing conditions it may not lapse under certain conditions, but it does mean that as long as the circumstances remain unaltered and the law therefore universal, there can be no exemption from it.

As an illustration of the universality which he has in mind, Suárez takes the simplest of examples of philosophical science, the case of a human hand, which science decrees should have only five fingers—although not in an absolute sense but in a sufficiently limited sense to permit of exceptions. However, until human hands generally have more or less than five fingers, the decree is universal, that is to say, there can be no change in the application of natural law until the conditions themselves change —in this case, a finger more or less. Under such circumstances, the decree, like natural law, would hold and be applicable unless the majority of hands had more or less than five fingers.

It is obvious, therefore, as Suárez proceeds to point out, that in those natural precepts which "are always binding, there is no place for interpretation, since there is no place for variation."

The case is different, however, with reference to precepts which are "not binding for all occasions." The question then arises as to whether the determination of the circumstances under which they are not binding is a matter of *aequitas*. When the natural law in question is expressed in terms of positive human law, then the existence or extent of the obligation may be determined, both by interpretation and *aequitas,* and may even be subject to dispensation. This, however, is a matter of positive law and hence Suárez says, "has no bearing on the question in hand."

Again, the obligation may be determined "through natural reason itself," continues Suárez; but in this case, it is not *aequitas* which is involved, "since there is no exception from the law nor emendation of the precept." There is rather a "simple understanding," which is neither an exception nor an emendation; in other words, an understanding of the law is based not upon *aequitas* but upon the use of reason.

"In the case of positive law" containing a prohibition, to which Suárez now turns, "interpretation by ἐπιείκεια . . . does not refer to the act forbidden by the law; nor to any obscurity in the words of that law," it being here assumed that the "act is one forbidden on the basis of its very form, and that it is comprised within the terms of the law, in their strict sense." On the other hand, the question may arise as to what was the intent of the lawmaker, and this is a case when true *aequitas* comes into play. In that event the process should serve to reveal the intention of the lawmaker, for human law is the expression of a human intention, presumed to be just, as otherwise it is not law.

To drive home again his view that *aequitas* has "no place in the natural law," as such, Suárez here definitely and finally separates it from the natural law by the statement that "this procedure, however, has no place in the natural law, because it"—meaning the natural law—"is founded primarily, not upon the will that prohibits, but upon the nature of the inherently evil act itself."

The difference between human and natural law is this: In the human law, we look for the intent of the lawgiver; in natural law, there is no intent—there is a command, a permission, or a prohibition. It may happen that neither the command nor the prohibition is expressly stated, in which case the one or the other is discovered through the application of right reason; but that is a process of understanding, not of seeking the intention of the lawgiver, as is the case with human law.

* * * * * * * *

Suárez has thus far dealt largely, if not wholly, with natural law, mentioning incidentally the law of the state and the law of that larger community of states, to which law he gives the name of *jus gentium*. Let us for a moment consider the implications of Suárez' conception of the law of nature. In his legal system natural law is to be looked upon as the foundation upon which he is to erect his structure of justice, national and international. National justice expressed in the form of law and applying to individuals within the state is, as it were, the first story of the structure, upon which international justice, binding alike individuals as such and individuals grouped in states, can be said to rest. International law, therefore, is based, so to speak, on two firm foundations. But the more fundamental of these foundations is natural law, the law of the human being as such, which he inherits but does not make, for it is the basis of the law of the individuals forming the state, with such additions as may be made by the proper agency of the state from time to time to meet their special needs. These additions measure, as it were, the extent to which the law of the state is the work of human hands. The *jus gentium,* though not identical with the law of nature, is like it in its generality. For does not Suárez say, speaking of this *jus gentium,* in the opening lines of the seventeenth chapter of Book II, that it has such "a close affinity with the natural law . . . that many persons confuse it therewith, or hold that the *jus gentium* is a part of the natural law; and, furthermore, even in those aspects wherein the two are distinguished, the kinship is very close and the *jus gentium* constitutes an intermediate form, so to speak, between the natural and the human law, a form bordering upon the first of these extremes." But it is also like the non-statutory law of the single state in so far as it is made slowly, and it may be unconsciously, through usage and custom. There is, however, a further element which enters into its making, the agreements of the states—which, in Suárez' lifetime, had not attained the proportions of our day and of our world.

But even though the three forms of law may be distinct, they are one in that the standard of each and all is, or should be, the universal test of right and wrong; and it is the glory of Suárez that to this world, ruled by systems of law—which are in essence, but not in form, the same—he gave an acceptable legal philosophy.

With Suárez the *jus gentium,* which he proposed to analyze, was an existing thing; and that there might be no doubt upon this point in the mind of the reader who happened to thumb the pages of this seventeenth chapter, he proceeds to enumerate the authorities by whom the *jus gentium* was assumed to be "an established fact," as demonstrated by "their very frequent use of the term." What are these authorities? The *Digest* and the *Institutes* of Justinian, the *Decretum* of Gratian, St. Isidore's *Etymologies,* and, in addition, "the Doctors of both canon and civil law," and also St. Thomas and the theologians. In other words, Suárez invokes the consensus of intelligent opinion of the ancient and the mediaeval world in behalf of the existence of a *jus gentium* which had taken moral form in the hands of Victoria, and which was to take a philosophic form in the very tractate of Suárez which we are now discussing.[16] The law of nations is for Suárez a law in the strict legal sense of the word. But there are, as he has already observed, two kinds of law. There is *lex* on the one hand, and *jus* on the other; and, as *jus* is the concomitant of *gentium*—indeed is that upon which *gentium* rests —it is essential that Suárez state in even more precise form the definition of *jus* and the distinctions between its various connotations.

Now this *jus* is, to quote Suárez' exact language, "an equivocal term," and because of that he continues, "its various meanings

[16] Suárez' words on the question of authorities are so enlightening as to his sources that the reader may prefer to have before his eyes a literal translation of the text: "The existence of the *jus gentium* then, is assumed by all authorities to be an established fact, so we gather, from their very frequent use of the term. For the *jus gentium* is often mentioned in the Civil Law in *Digest,* I. i, 2, and *Institutes,* I. ii, and in the *Decretum,* I. i; and following Isidore (*Etymologies,* Bk. V., chap. ii. [V. vi.]); by the Doctors of both Canon and Civil Law, in connection with these and other passages; and by St. Thomas (II. ii, qu. 57, art. 3) and the theologians."

must be distinguished, that we may employ it only in that acceptation which pertains to our purposes." What are these meanings? The first which Suárez mentions is *jus* in the sense of a "moral faculty over or relating to some thing." Now in this meaning, the faculty in question is a right in the sense that it involves "true dominion or merely a partial dominion," which faculty is, according to St. Thomas, "the true object of justice." "*Jus*" was not only equivocal in Suárez' day; it is such in our own. It is "*recht*" in German, meaning "right" in one sense and "law" in another, and each of the two names in German for the law of nations contains the word *recht* (*völkerrecht* and *internationales recht*). In French, *jus* takes the form of "*droit*," whether it be the *droit des gens* or *droit international*—the exact equivalents of the two German expressions. The same thing may be said of the Italian "*diritto*"—*diritto de gente* and *diritto internazionale*. In Spanish, Suárez' native language, the term is "*derecho*"—*derecho de gentes* and *derecho internacional*. But we must not omit the name by which the law is called in the land of Grotius—*volkenrecht* and *internationaal recht*. In English there is, alas, but a single term, "law," whether it be the law of nations or international law, and it may be that the Anglo-Saxon conception of law has lost something of the connection with right which the Romance languages, as well as the Teutonic, preserve—at least in form, if not in substance—through the use of a term which means both right and law.

It is to be observed that in the foreign terminology, in languages other than English, there is at least a moral implication because of the presence of "right," whereas the English term "law" raises no such implication and has in itself no essential connection with right or justice. For the English term is akin not to *jus* but to *lex*[17]—which is but a rule of action without any necessary reference to the moral qualities of right and justice—a fact which may account for the statement we often hear

[17] It seems generally to be conceded that the English "law" is of Teutonic rather than Latin origin, and hence that it is not, as was one time believed, a derivation from *lex*.

(too often, indeed), that a court is a place where law, not justice, is administered.

But to return to Suárez and his analysis of *jus*. This *"jus,"* which may at times mean "right" he now adds, "sometimes means law." Law, in the view of Suárez, is "the rule of righteous conduct," and, so conceived, *jus* is that "which establishes a certain equity in things," and therefore this definition constitutes "the rational basis" for accepting *jus* as "law." Upon whose authority? That of St. Thomas himself. For the "rational basis" is synonymous with law, and again the authority is that of St. Thomas. From which it follows, according to Suárez, that we must speak of the first sort of *jus,* that is, the "moral faculty" involving dominion as "practical" (*jus utile*); and the second *jus* as "law," "in relation to righteousness" (*jus honestum*): or, Suárez continues, we may speak "of the first as 'real' (*jus reale*) and of the second as 'legal' (*jus legale*)." What was the consequence, if not the avowed purpose, of these distinctions? To establish that *jus* in one sense is right in practice or, as Suárez says, right in the "real" sense, and that in the sense of law, it is not right itself but related to righteousness and is primarily legal rather than ethical.

The further consequence of this twofold kind of law in the sense of *jus* is, as Suárez says, its division "into the natural law, the *jus gentium* and the civil law." This threefold division naturally suggests a definition of the sense in which Suárez is to employ each of the terms. "For the *jus utile,"*—*jus* in practice—he proceeds, "is termed natural when it is granted by or originates within nature." The example of Suárez is "liberty," which "may be said to spring from the natural law." The same *jus utile* appears in a different guise within the state, being civil law. And the example? "The right of prescription." It is now the turn of the *jus gentium;* for the *jus utile* is called the law of nations, "when founded upon the common usage of mankind." As illustrations Suárez cites "the right of passage over public highways, or the right to enslave, introduced by war."

This threefold division of *jus,* which Suárez has been discussing, relates "to the object of justice," as may be inferred, he says, "from a passage in St. Thomas,"—which passage, it may be stated, deals with the relationship between the *jus gentium* and the *jus naturale*.[18]

Now Suárez, although no man had a clearer conception of right and wrong, was primarily engaged in formulating a philosophy for law. Therefore he adds, "we are speaking of the *jus gentium* . . . rather as a species of law." This being the case he turns from the *jus utile* to the second conception of *jus*, that of *jus legale*, which is also wont to be divided into natural, civil, and international law.

This conception of law as law we would expect to be confirmed, and in this case, as in many others, it is confirmed by the *Digest* of Justinian.

We here encounter Ulpian's trouble-making definition that "the natural law is shared in common with brute creation, while the *jus gentium* is peculiar to man." The twofold authority, derived in each case from Ulpian, is found in the *Digest*[19] and in the *Institutes*,[20] of which Suárez makes a paraphrase rather than a quotation: "The natural law is that which nature teaches to all animate creatures; for it does not pertain exclusively to the human race, but is shared in common with all animate creatures born on land or sea, and to all birds as well."[21] From the point of view of man, it is not agreeable to share law or, indeed, anything else, with the rest of the animate world. We do not know the view of other animate creatures on the question of this association, but no less a person than Lord Bryce[22] has said that the acceptance of the doctrine of evolution tends to rehabilitate rather than annihilate Ulpian's generosity to brute creation. Nevertheless it is but fair to say that this passage has caused jurists and commentators for many a century untold hours of time in an

[18] II. ii, question 57, art. 3.

[19] *Digest*, I. i. 1, § 3: *"Ius naturale est, quod natura omnia animalia docuit: nam ius istud non humani generis proprium, sed omnium animalium, quae in terra, quae in mari nascuntur avium quoque commune est."*

[20] *Institutes*, I. ii: *"Ius naturale est, quod natura omnia animalia docuit: nam ius istud non humani generis proprium est, sed omnium animalium, quae in caelo, quae in terra, quae in mari nascuntur."*

[21] This quotation follows the *Digest* more closely.

[22] Rt. Hon. James Bryce, *Studies in History and Jurisprudence: Essay on the Law of Nature* (New York and London, 1901), p. 588.

attempt to explain why animals should share with men in the law natural; and Suárez himself felt obliged to meet the question. Even Grotius, in his younger days, as is evidenced by the Commentary *On the Law of Prize,*[23] was generous to animals, but upon reflection he subsequently excluded them from natural law in his Three Books *On the Law of War and of Peace.*[24]

The question, although interesting, is unimportant for our present purpose and we need not here attempt to solve it; in any event, it could fairly be solved only by a conference of the parties in interest, which might be dangerous to the proponents of *homo sapiens.*

The proponents of Ulpian's view, having given the law natural to both men and animals, restricted the *jus gentium* to the human race, Suárez invoking, in behalf of this view, the statement from the *Digest* that the law of nations "is that used by the human race,"[25] the distinction between the natural law and the *jus gentium* thus being that the latter "is common only to men in their mutual relations." However, the writers show the two forms of law as closely related, for in a passage from the *Digest*[26] the *jus gentium* is considered to be "that [law] which natural reason has established for all mankind, and is uniformly observed by all men." Upon this Suárez makes the penetrating comment that "thus it is clear that the *jus gentium* is held to be natural as well." To what extent? "In a special sense, peculiar to mankind." For examples of its special and peculiar application to man, Suárez' authority is again the *Digest*[27]: "Piety toward God; obedience to one's progenitors and to one's country; the repulsion of violence and injury."

Admitting that there are actions "common . . . to men and to brutes," Suárez observes that they are of a material nature and that "the natural law forbids in man, many things from which the brutes are not restrained by natural instinct." The difference

[23] Chap. ii.

[24] Bk. I, chap. i, n. 11, § 1.

[25] *Digest,* I. i. 1, § 4: *"Ius gentium est, quo gentes humanae utuntur."*

[26] *Ibid.,* I. i. 9: *"quod vero naturalis ratio inter omnes homines constituit . . . vocaturque ius gentium.*

[27] I. i. 2, 3.

between the two creations is the difference between instinct and reason.

While admitting the close relationship between the *jus gentium* and the natural law, Suárez rejects the views "of certain theologians" that the precepts of the *jus gentium* share with those of the natural law a quality of "intrinsic necessity." This involves also the rejection of the opinion that the law of nations "differs from the natural law [only] in that the latter is revealed without reflection, or at least with the simplest sort thereof, while the precepts of the *jus gentium* are deduced by means of many and rather intricate inferences." To Suárez, the natural law was revealed by right reason, whether this right reason was of an instinctive nature or a process of profound reflection, while the precepts of the *jus gentium* arose not so much by a conscious reasoning as by unconscious usage.

But having rejected the view which credits the *jus gentium* with intrinsic necessity, Suárez, in his usual thorough manner, states his reasons for this rejection, the first being that numerous things spoken of as coming under the *jus gentium* nevertheless "are not characterized by the intrinsic necessity" in question, and to reinforce this statement, he gives as examples "division of property" and "slavery."

Still further to differentiate the *jus gentium* from the natural law and to give the law of nations its proper and distinct place in the legal hierarchy, he dissociates the *jus gentium* from the "primary moral principles" and their necessary conclusions, since, he continues, "all these principles and conclusions are included under the natural law strictly so-called"; and the confirmation of this is a truth which we, with Suárez, believe worthy of repetition—"that all the precepts written by God in the hearts of men, pertain to the natural law." The authority is also that which he had previously invoked, St. Paul's *Epistle to the Romans,*[28] to which Suárez adds—"all precepts which may clearly

[28] ii. 14-15: "For when the Gentiles, who have not the law, do by nature those things that are of the law; these having not the law are a law to themselves:

"Who shew the work of the law written in their hearts, their conscience bearing witness to them, and their thoughts between themselves accusing, or also defending one another."

be inferred by reason from natural principles are written in [human] hearts," this time not contenting himself with a mere "therefore" but completing the syllogism for less acute minds than his: "therefore all such precepts pertain to the natural law."

On the other hand, the precepts of the *jus gentium* are not written in the human heart, but are "introduced by the free will and consent of mankind, whether in the whole human community or in the major portion thereof." Here we have a statement of vast implications, to be later elaborated by Suárez, but which he does not at the moment enlarge, contenting himself with dissociating these precepts from those "written in the hearts of men by the Author of Nature." And this enables him to add that the precepts of the *jus gentium* are "a part of the human, and not of the natural law."

But there was another distinction between the *jus gentium* and the natural law—that the precepts of the *jus gentium* "should follow, not as a manifest conclusion [from natural principles], but rather from some source less certain" and that therefore they are, as Suárez puts it, "dependent upon the intervention of human free-will, and moral expediency rather than upon necessity"—and necessity was a prime characteristic of the natural law. Suárez has many a time pointed out that natural law forbids a thing because it is evil or commands it because it is good. Not so, however, with human law, including the *jus gentium*. Herein lies another distinction; for under the *jus gentium* the subject-matter of the precept is not necessarily either good or evil in itself but is made so by the command or prohibition of the *jus gentium*, and both command and prohibition are of human volition, not of divine origin. In a word, the natural law is necessary in the nature of things; the *jus gentium* is advantageous, expedient, and even necessary, but only from the human point of view.

In the preceding passages Suárez has been distinguishing natural law in general from the *jus gentium*. There are, however, two general divisions of natural law: the one concessive, the other mandatory; and there are likewise the same classifications of the *jus gentium*. If one classification of the law natural is to be distinguished from the law of nations, so also is the other. Therefore let us pause a moment and consider these two classifications of the natural law. Among the actions which properly take place under the natural law, there are many which are "permissible," that is to say, concessive and not mandatory or prescribed, nor, as Suárez points out, "are their contraries prohibited." As examples of the concessive phase of natural law, Suárez refers to "the right to take a wife"—in this more enlightened age, he would have added, as well, the right to take a husband—or "the right to retain and preserve one's own liberty"; for action under either of these rights "is honorable and is permitted" but is not prescribed. There is another twofold classification of the natural law—one being positive or affirmative, that is, mandatory; the other negative in the sense that it is non-prohibitory, "as may be seen," Suárez says, "from the words of Covarruvias,"[29] a distinguished jurist and statesman of Spain, whose authority he invokes in this classification.

The concession or the prohibition may come from the natural law, but there may also be a concession which is derived from human law. Nevertheless, if a right to do a certain act is once conceded by the human law, any obligation which results therefrom is, to quote Suárez, "natural," and that age-old maxim of the natural law comes into play—*Pacta sunt servanda.* The proof of this simple but immensely important statement is contained, says Suárez, speaking in the first person, in four examples from St. Isidore of Seville, "the examples concerning the occupation of abodes, buildings, fortifications and defences through just warfare." Why should the law applicable be the law natural? Because all these actions, Suárez says, are "permitted by the natural law," and an act permitted by the natural law implies a natural obligation upon the person "to refrain from violating such rights when possessed by another person," the obligation being under "natural legislation," that is to say, natural law.

Because of the fundamental nature of this passage, a mere

[29] On *Sext,* rule *peccatum,* pt. ii, § 11, n. 3.

paraphrase of it is not sufficient. It should and indeed must be quoted in its entirety:

In the first place, this is clearly proved, I think, through the first four examples of Isidore, that is, the examples concerning the occupation of abodes, buildings, fortifications and defenses through just warfare; for the law applying to all of these acts is the natural law, that is to say, they are all permitted by the natural law; and in like manner, the obligation incumbent upon one person, to refrain from violating such rights when possessed by another person, pertains to natural legislation. It is only the actual exercise of these rights which may be said to come within the field of the *jus gentium,* by reason of the custom of all nations. And this exercise [of rights] is a matter pertaining to fact, and not to law.

The right under a concession may, as we have seen, come from the natural law; but if the right under the law natural is concessive, the exercise of the right is volitional and human and therefore within the *jus gentium*. There is, however, an obligation to refrain from violating the right in question, and this obligation, like the right itself, comes under natural law. In a word, the natural law is both a source and a sanction for the right; and the putting of such a right into execution comes under the *jus gentium* only because it depends upon the human will, which has become crystallized, as it were, in what Suárez calls "the custom of all nations."

Suárez refers also to the eighth, ninth and tenth examples from St. Isidore, relating "to peace, truces and ambassadors"; for the conclusion of peace and truces and the sending of ambassadors are governed by rules arising from human agreement, but the power or the right to contract, and the obligation which may arise from the treaty or covenant or contract, or whatever form the agreement may take, demands this "good faith and justice" which, in Suárez' own words, "have regard to the law of nature." *Pacta sunt servanda.*

There are, however, rules regarding the exercise of these rights and powers—an exercise which is volitional on the part of men and nations; and such rules concerning the exercise of these rights, having been agreed upon by all or nearly all nations, are of the *jus gentium*. But, continues Suárez with natural law uppermost in his mind as the wellspring, so to speak, of human law, "actual use" of these powers is not law; it is "the effect of law." And the proof of this is simple and logical, as it is indisputable: "For the law under discussion"—meaning natural law—"does not spring from such use; on the contrary, the use has its source in the law."

By way of summarizing, Suárez concludes with certain fundamental distinctions between the *jus gentium* and the natural law, and as this summary forms a transition to the discussion of the agreement between the two, Suárez should speak in his own behalf and in his exact language:

> From what has thus far been said, the conclusion seems to follow that the *jus gentium*, properly so-called, is not contained within the bounds of the natural law, but that, on the contrary, it differs essentially therefrom; for although it agrees with the natural law in many respects, nevertheless [the two kinds of law] are distinct from each other owing to their characteristic moral difference.

Now as to their agreement. We again quote the language of Suárez; for what can be better than his own summary of his doctrine?

> They agree, indeed, because, in the first place, both are in some manner common to all mankind. And on this ground each may be called [a law] of nations (*gentium*), if we are to insist upon words alone. The characteristic of being common to all nations is evident in the natural law, and for that reason the law of nature itself is called, in the *Digest* (I. i. 9), the law of nations (*jus gentium*)—as may be noted in the wording of many laws. However, this name is more properly bestowed upon the system of law introduced by the custom of nations. On this point, consult the *Institutes* (I. ii, § 4 [I. ii, § 2]).
>
> In the second place, the two kinds of law in question agree in that just as the subject-matter of the *jus gentium* has application to men alone, so also the subject-matter of the natural law is peculiar to mankind, either in its entirety, or in great part, as is, perhaps, sufficiently evident from what we have said in Chapter xvii. Consequently, many examples which are placed by the jurists under the heading of the *jus gentium* because of this characteristic alone, belong only nominally to that system of law, strictly viewed. . . .
>
> In the third place, the *jus gentium* and the natural law agree, in that both systems include precepts, prohibitions, and also concessions or permissions, as has been made sufficiently clear in Chapter xviii.

After having discussed not only the distinctions but also the points in which natural law and the *jus gentium* agree, Suárez passes to the points of difference between the two great systems. In general, it may be said that the differences are fundamental and, though numerous, they may be combined into one all-embracing difference: the law of nature is a law of necessity; the *jus gentium* is a desirable law. The one exists to meet the necessity; the other is made to conform to human desire. Natural law is of a higher will—indeed, the highest of wills—whether it be in the phrase of the Greeks, "design in nature," or whether it be God, the Creator. Man has no part in its formulation. In the *jus gentium* human will not only enters but is the controlling factor —not the will of any one man and not the will of any number of human beings in isolation or in a single group, but the will of individuals grouped into states. It is the law of many peoples, if not of all peoples; it is the law of many states, if not of all states. Or, to express it in terms of man and society, it is the consensus of the will of humankind or the consensus of the international community.

Natural law, then, is of supernatural origin and it is immutable until human nature itself changes. The *jus gentium* is based upon, and indeed is, the expression of the common will and desire of human beings; it is changeable as are their common will and desires, and grows, not out of the natural inherent necessity of human nature, but out of the necessities arising from organized society.

The all-embracing difference with which we have just dealt refers particularly to the affirmative precepts of both the law natural and the *jus gentium*.

There are, however, negative precepts. In the law natural, a thing or an action is prohibited because it is inherently wrong in itself, whereas, as we have said (in the language of Suárez), the negative precepts of the *jus gentium* do not forbid anything on the ground that it is evil in itself. Rather, he says, the *jus gentium* "not only points out what is evil, but constitutes [the forbidden matter as] evil," with the result "that it does not forbid evil actions on the ground that they are evil, but prohibiting them, causes them to be evil." In this regard the two systems are as far apart as the North and the South Poles. These are indeed "real" differences and also "essential" differences. To sum it up in a word: "accordingly, in these ways, there is a distinction between the natural law and the *jus gentium*."

The second difference pointed out by Suárez we have implied, but as Suárez states it expressly and briefly, it should be given in his own words: "The two systems under discussion," he goes on to say, "likewise differ in that the *jus gentium* cannot be immutable to the same degree as the natural law; for immutability springs from necessity, and therefore, that which is not equally necessary cannot be equally immutable, a point which will be expounded more fully in the following chapter." Here we have absolute universality, arising from universal necessity, and relative universality, arising from social necessity, that is, from the needs of society and therefore subject to change as society is subject to change.

But even when these "two systems of law seem to agree," as Suárez puts it, "they are not absolutely similar." The reason may seem to be evident, but it is conclusively so after Suárez' statement—"for in its universality and general acceptance by all peoples, the natural law is common to all, and only through error can it fail of observance in any place." On the contrary, however, "the *jus gentium* is not observed always by all nations, but [only] as a general rule by almost all: as Isidore states."

This is indeed an important statement, and the conclusion which Suárez draws is even as important: "Hence that which is held, among some peoples, to be *jus gentium,* may elsewhere, and without any error, fail to be observed." We here have an admission that international law need not be so universal as natural law, because social necessities may differ from continent to continent, if not from state to state. Europe may have a series of policies separate and distinct from those of America; and as there may be what we Americans would call special rules of international law in Europe for European conditions, so there may be special rules of international law for American conditions. However, as the European conception of the law of nations was the original basis of international law, the exceptions to such law would of necessity deal with what we may call local conditions and differences in other parts of the world; so that, to the extent of these local differences, there might come into existence what could be, and indeed is, at times called, for example, an American international law, although the rules peculiar to it would be few in number and would be additions to, rather than derogations from, the general law of nations.

In a final statement on this phase of the subject Suárez more than implies another difference between the law natural and the *jus gentium*. "The natural law is that law which does not spring from [human] conjecture, but from the evidence of nature, as Cicero has pointed out." And the second term of the syllogism: "Hence, every law that does not arise in this way is positive and human." The conclusion of this informal syllogism is so natural with Suárez and with the schoolmen that it frequently is not stated as such, in the hurry of writing: "And the *jus gentium* is of this latter variety, because it came into existence not through [natural] evidence, but through probability and the common judgment of mankind." Suárez ends with a "therefore," which we complete: Therefore the *jus gentium* is positive human law.

We now pass with Suárez to the differences between the *jus gentium* and the civil law, Suárez saying that the civil law has its precepts in written form, whereas those of the *jus gentium*—at least in his day—could be said to be unwritten. Again speaking of his day, the precepts of the *jus gentium* were "established through the customs, not of one or two states or provinces, but of all or nearly all nations." Here we have an all-important phrase, "of all or nearly all nations." A custom has to have a beginning, and that may be in the usage of one state, in which case it binds that state only and could appropriately be called a civil or national custom. The custom becomes international when more states adopt it, and if practised by many—though not necessarily all—states, it becomes a precept of the "*jus gentium* properly so-called." Thus isolated usage may grow into the custom of many, if not all, and the evidence of this general custom is the practice of nations. In a single sentence Suárez sums up the differences not only between the *jus gentium* and the natural law but also between the *jus gentium* and the civil law. The law of nations, he says, "differs from the natural law because it is based upon custom rather than upon nature; and it is to be distinguished likewise from civil law in its origin, basis and universal application." It is neither the law of a Supreme Being nor is it the law of emperor, of king, of prince or of legislature or other enacting body; it is, so far as custom is concerned, human usage and on a universal scale. Customs may, however, be local, in that they apply to a group of communities, and thus they deviate from the general rules of international law (as we may suppose in the case of Europe and America; for we of the Western World might have a custom, or a series of American customs, enlarging the content of international law in the Americas to the extent of the customs in question). This localization of international law, if the term be permitted, may also occur—oftener in our day than in Suárez' day—by the conclusion of treaties or conventions binding only the contracting parties, be they few or many. Often, however, the provisions of such treaties subsequently enter into the practice of many nations and to the extent of that practice, irrespective of the treaty, become general international law instead of regional law.

As this conception of what we may call regional international law is a matter of far-reaching implications, we feel justified in turning aside for a moment to consider a present movement which, unconsciously perhaps, has for its purpose the carrying into effect of this conception of Suárez.

Mr. Alejandro Alvarez, a distinguished publicist of the Republic of Chile, is the leading exponent, not merely in his own country but in America and in the world at large, of regional schools of international law. In an address on "The New International Law," delivered by him before the Grotius Society in

1929 and published in the *Transactions* of that society for 1930,[30] he says:

In the course of the nineteenth century, certain countries, notably the Great Powers, established special doctrines with respect to certain matters, in which their national interest ordinarily exerts a large influence. This is what is known as national International Law, or simply *schools* of International Law. These schools are the following: the French school, the Italian school, the German school, the North American school, the Russian or Slavic school, and the Japanese school. But all are attached to one or the other of the two great preceding schools: the United States with England form the *Anglo-Saxon school* and the other countries form the *Continental school.*

At the end of the nineteenth century, a great new school [of international law] commences to develop: the *Pan-American school.* It consists of doctrines relating both to American and to universal interests that are professed by all the nations of the New World, and that differ from those of the two preceding schools. It is American International Law.

Hence, the nations of America find themselves in a special situation with regard to International Law which I have already indicated more than once: namely, the United States professes the principles of the Anglo-Saxon school, while the Latin countries profess the principles of the Continental school; but, on the other hand, the United States and the Latin countries have a common body of doctrines which are peculiar to them.

In advance of the meeting of the International Commission of Jurists at Rio de Janeiro, held in 1927, the American Institute of International Law, created in 1912—of which Mr. Alvarez was one of the founders and Secretary-General—undertook the codification of "American International Law," at the request of the Governing Board of the Pan American Union, upon motion of its Chairman, then Secretary of State Hughes.[31] Some thirty

[30] *Transactions of the Grotius Society* (London, 1930), Vol. 15, pp. 35, 44. For further expressions of Mr. Alvarez' views on the matter in hand, see *Le Droit International Américain* (Paris, 1910), note 3, pp. 5-6; *The Monroe Doctrine* (New York, 1924), pp. 26-31; *Considérations générales sur la codification du droit international américain* (Rio de Janeiro, 1927), pp. 15-30. For an opposite point of view, see Manoel Alvaro de Souza Sa Vianna, *De la non Existence d'un Droit International Américain* (Rio de Janeiro, 1912).

[31] The text of the Resolution of the Governing Board of the Pan American Union, adopted January 2, 1924, is as follows:

"Whereas the Fifth International Conference of American States adopted a vote of thanks for the results achieved by the American Institute of International Law; and

projects were adopted by the American Institute at its session of 1924 in Lima, Peru. From the second project, entitled "General Declarations," we quote the following paragraphs:[32]

2. The American Republics declare that matters pertaining especially to America should be regulated in our Continent in conformity with the principles of universal International Law, if that be possible, or by enlarging and developing those principles or creating new ones adapted to the special conditions existing on this Continent.

3. By American International Law is understood all of the institutions, principles, rules, doctrines, conventions, customs, and practices which, in the domain of international relations, are proper to the Republics of the New World.

The existence of this Law is due to the geographical, economic, and political conditions of the American Continent, to the manner in which the new Republics were formed and have entered the international community, and to the solidarity existing between them.

American International Law thus understood in no way tends to create an international system resulting in the separation of the Republics of this hemisphere from the world concert.

Whereas one of the purposes for which the American Institute of International Law has been established is to secure a more definite formulation of the rules of international law; and

Whereas the codification of the rules of international law is the most important task intrusted to the International Commission of Jurists; and

Whereas the labors of the American Institute of International Law will be of great service to the International Commission of Jurists in the fulfillment of the task assigned to it: Be it

Resolved by the governing board of the Pan American Union, To submit to the executive committee of the American Institute of International Law the desirability of holding a session of the institute in 1924 in order that the results of the deliberations of the institute may be submitted to the International Commission of Jurists at its meeting at Rio de Janeiro in 1925."—*Codification of American International Law* (Pan American Union, Washington, 1925), p. 15.

In the letter transmitting this unanimous resolution of the Governing Board, its Chairman, Secretary of State Hughes, said:

"The Commission of Jurists, provided for by the Santiago resolution, is called upon to perform a very great international service. I feel convinced that in the performance of this service the American Institute of International Law can be most helpful. I hope, therefore, that the suggestion submitted by the governing board of the Pan American Union may have the approval of the executive committee of the American Institute of International Law. The establishment of such close cooperative relationship will serve to advance the work which the commission is called upon to perform and will thus bring us nearer to the accomplishment of the purpose for which the International Commission of Jurists was established." *Ibid.* at pp. 15-16.

---

[32] *Ibid.* at p. 26.

On March 2, 1925, Secretary Hughes, as Chairman of the Governing Board of the Pan American Union, laid before the Governing Board the various projects, saying:[33]

> There are 30 of these projects covering a wide range of subjects dealing with the American international law of peace. They represent the labors of distinguished jurists of this hemisphere. . . . It is natural, as is pointed out by the executive committee of the American Institute of International Law, that the law to be applied by the American Republics should, in addition to the law universal, contain not a few rules of American origin and adapted to American exigencies, and that the old and the new, taken together, should constitute what may be called American international law, without derogation from the authority of the law which is applicable to all nations.

* * * * * * * *

But as our French friends say, *retournons à nos moutons.*

Suárez himself regarded the foregoing distinctions between the *jus gentium* and the natural and civil law as of such importance that he reinforced them by citing and analyzing the best of authorities, the *Institutes* of Justinian and the *Etymologies* of St. Isidore, and joined to these the great name of St. Thomas. "The foregoing seems," literally to quote Suárez, "in my judgment"—note the personal appeal—"to be the opinion of Justinian, as expressed in the *Institutes*. . . . 'The *jus gentium,* indeed, is common to all the human race, for because of imperative usage and human needs the nations of the earth have established certain laws for themselves.' "[34] Upon this passage, Suárez comments that "the phrases 'imperative usage' and 'have established' are to be carefully weighed; for the latter implies that the law in question was established, not by nature, but by men; and the phrase 'imperative usage' indicates that it was introduced, not by a written instrument, but through custom."

And St. Isidore,[35] he says, "holds the same view," defining natural law as " 'that which is common to all nations, in that it exists everywhere through natural instinct and not through any formal enactment.' " With this Suárez agrees, saying that

[33] *Ibid.* at pp. 1-2.
[34] *Institutes,* I. ii, § 2.
[35] *Etymologies,* Bk. V., chap. iv.

"herein he supports our own statement" and indicates "that the *jus gentium* is not based upon natural instinct alone."

But this is not the only support which he derives from Isidore; for the latter, in a later passage in which he gives examples of the *jus gentium,* maintains that this system of law "is called the *jus gentium* because almost all nations make use of it." [36]

Now for the commentary of Suárez on these two passages. St. Isidore, he says, is here defining the *jus gentium,* "indicating that it is a system of law common to all nations, and constituted not through natural instinct alone, but through the usage of those nations." This, however, is but part of the penetrating comment. The rest has to do with a single word, but one of surpassing importance. "Neither," says Suárez, "should the little word 'almost' be lightly passed over, for it shows that there is no altogether intrinsic and natural necessity inherent in this law, and that it need not be absolutely common to all peoples, even aside from cases of ignorance or error; but that, on the contrary, it suffices if nearly all well ordered nations shall adopt that law." And to put the matter beyond dispute Suárez laconically adds that "St. Thomas appears to be of the same opinion."

It is evident that Suárez was deeply in earnest, because he uses in this connection the first person, disregarding the impersonal style in order to commit himself to these views, which he rightly thought were fundamental and incontestable.

But authorities, great as they were, were not enough for Suárez on these matters, the import of which none realized better than he. There were, he said, "several examples" upholding the same view, and the first of these was "the custom of receiving ambassadors under a law of immunity and security." This custom, "if considered in an absolute aspect, does not spring from any necessity of the natural law." This is a general statement and we would expect Suárez to furnish proof in the best scholastic manner: "Some particular community of men might fail to have within its territory, any ambassador of a foreign community; or it might be unwilling to admit such ambassadors";

[36] *Ibid.*, chap. vi.

nevertheless, the admittance of these representatives of foreign powers is an obligation imposed by the *jus gentium*. What would be the result of a failure to comply with this obligation? "To repudiate those ambassadors would be a sign of enmity, and a violation of the *jus gentium*, although it would not be an injury committed in contravention of natural reason."

So it was in the time of Suárez. But to us of today, ambassadors and diplomatic agents are so much the rule that the refusal to admit them would seem to be unnatural.

But what is the conclusion which Suárez draws from his example of ambassadors? "Accordingly," he continues, "even assuming that they are indeed admitted on the basis of some implied agreement"—note that the agreement need not be express, but is equally binding if implied—"it would be contrary to the natural law not to respect their immunity." And the reason? "That such an act would be contrary to justice and plighted faith. Nevertheless, this assumption," Suárez adds, "and this implied agreement, in the case supposed, would have been introduced by the *jus gentium*." This passage is an interesting commentary on the reason why diplomatic agents were appointed, and on their immunity from the jurisdiction of the country to which they are accredited and in which they reside—an immunity which is necessary to them in the performance of their many and varied duties. Now the immunity arises out of an agreement, express or implied, between the parties, but the obligation to respect the immunity, whether express or implied, is necessary if the ambassador is to perform his official duties. Therefore, the violation of the obligation is a violation of that good faith which is the very essence of the natural law and finds expression in the classic phrase, *Pacta sunt servanda*. We here have a sanction, not for the agreement but for the obligation arising out of the agreement, to violate which is a violation of natural law, which violation renders the nation so violating it responsible. Why, we may ask. Because the natural law applies equally to all nations, and the nation disregarding it can not but be guilty before both God and man, irrespective of the existence or nonexistence of a municipal statute, which exists, however, today in all civilized nations—at least as regards the immunity of ambassadors and other diplomatic agents.

Suárez now furnishes a second example, also of a universal nature, that of "any contract or commercial agreement." In connection with this there are three points to be distinguished: first, "the specific method of making the contract." This is a matter which "ordinarily pertains to civil law," and, as Suárez maintains, "is frequently decided in accordance with the will of the contracting parties," provided, of course, that their will "conflicts with no existing legal rule."

So much for the first point. The second is "the observance of the contract after it has been made." As we would expect, Suárez at once observes that this "pertains to the natural law." *Pacta sunt servanda.*

Now for the third point—"the liberty to contract commercial agreements with [any] man not actively hostile or unfriendly in sentiment"—or, as we would say today, "freedom to contract," a freedom derived, Suárez informs us, "from the *jus gentium.*" But why should this be so? Because the making of such agreements is not "an obligation imposed by natural law considered in itself"—the action being one of volition—since "a state might conceivably exist in isolation and refuse to enter into commercial relations with another state, even without unfriendly feeling."

So much for the natural law on this point. "But," says Suárez, "it has been established by the *jus gentium* that commercial intercourse shall be free, and it would be a violation of that system of law if such intercourse were prohibited without reasonable cause." Here we have Suárez aligning himself with Victoria, who proclaimed not only that freedom of commercial intercourse was a natural right, but that the natural right could and should have a municipal sanction in case of its violation, and that if the sanction did not exist, the nation failing to comply with this international duty in this respect would be responsible in damages and liable to suit in the court of the prince.[87] Today

[87] Francisco de Vitoria, *De Indis,* pp. 151-4.

the liability is the same, but the suit is in a Permanent Court of International Justice at The Hague.

In the Roman law, which Suárez knew so well, and in the parlance of the jurists, of the canonists, and of the theologians, the term *jus gentium* was used in a twofold sense; or, as he puts it, was viewed in two different aspects:

first, as the law which all the various peoples and nations ought to observe in their relations with each other.

This is the international law of which Suárez speaks as one of the founders, reaching back in origin through the centuries, and today the modern law of nations.

Now for the second of the two aspects of the *jus gentium,* which is

as a body of laws which individual states or kingdoms observe within their own borders, but which is called *jus gentium* because these laws are similar [in each instance] and are commonly accepted.

What is the difference between these two classes? Suárez answers this question immediately: "The first interpretation seems, in my opinion,"—he here observes in his own behalf —"to correspond most properly to the actual *jus gentium*"—again we interpolate, the modern law of nations—"as distinct from the civil law, in accordance with our exposition of the former."

What, now, of the second kind of *jus gentium?* It "involves," in Suárez' definition, "certain precepts, usages, or modes of living, which do not, in themselves and directly, relate to all mankind," —as do the principles of international law proper—"neither do they have for their immediate end, so to speak, the harmonious fellowship and intercourse of all nations with respect to one another." The usages of this kind of *jus gentium* are, on the contrary, he continues, "administered in each state by its own courts, according to appropriate rules." In other words, although this law is essentially local law, applying within different localities, it is similar and may even be identical in form and provision. Indeed, Suárez himself continues that these provisions "are of such a nature that, in the use of similar customs or laws, almost all nations agree with one another," that is, we may say, all nations of the civilized world which have, or ought to have, a similar standard. If they are not identical, "at least, they resemble one another, at times in a generic manner and at times specifically, as it were."

Recurring now to the first aspect of the *jus gentium,* Suárez declares it as his opinion that it corresponds "most properly" to the law of nations, as such, "as distinct from the civil law," and to tie the matter up with what he has just said, he adds that "the examples mentioned above concerning ambassadors and commercial usage, also pertain to this first aspect."

But there were other matters which pertained to the *jus gentium* in the sense of the law of nations, and therefore Suárez refers next to "the law of war," which he considers likewise a part of international law, properly so called, "in so far as that law rests upon the power possessed by a given state or kingdom, for the punishment, avenging or reparation of any injury inflicted upon it by another state." This is, of course, the law of nations and the law of war of Victoria. War does not seem to Suárez to be inevitable; if it were, it would fall within the province of the natural law. The fact remains, however, that the power to make war might not have existed in an injured state, had men "established some other mode of vindication, or entrusted that power to some third prince and quasi-arbitrator with coercive power." Most wars are condemned within a few years after their conclusion; and at the present day we are attempting to condemn them before they happen, not only by outlawing war but by having at the disposal of the parties in dispute proper remedies, beginning with good offices and terminating with the Permanent Court of International Justice at The Hague, although none of the remedies is endowed with coercive power other than that of public opinion. Nevertheless, they may properly be counted as in direct line of descent from Suárez' "third prince and quasi-arbitrator."

But this peaceful procedure was, unfortunately, not in favor in Suárez' day, war being generally considered easier and more in conformity with nature, at least animal nature, and this being the case, the bellicose method of settling disputes "has," he would have us believe, "been adopted by custom, and is just to the extent that it may not be rightfully resisted,"—meaning that in a just war, undertaken for the reparation of an injury received, the party who had committed the injury and resisted the just claims of what we may call the defendant state, was in the wrong. Without dwelling upon the matter—which is a separate topic, and amply covered by Suárez in his Disputation on Charity—the only justification for war, in the opinion of enlightened theologians, from St. Augustine down, was that between equal states there was not, and could not be, in the then state of affairs, a court of the superior. We of today have, as already indicated, solved the difficulty by creating a court of the superior, the superior in this instance being none other than the international community, and to this supreme tribunal all states of the world may appeal for a redress of their legal wrongs. It is not impossible that the future—less familiar than we with the past—may ask how enlightened theologians could ever have considered a resort to force as a permissible and even a just remedy.

We have seen that Suárez' *jus gentium* is made up very largely of custom. Nevertheless he was not unaware that treaties also came under the law of nations. Indeed he expressly says, "treaties of peace and truces may be placed under the head of the *jus gentium*"—meaning, in the strict sense of the term, our modern law of nations. And since the instruments themselves formed a part of the law of nations, so offers to make them, voluntary though they be, "should be heeded, and not refused, when duly presented, and for a reasonable cause." But the obligation created by the voluntary agreement "pertains rather to the natural law," on the simple theory that good faith exists between nations as well as between individuals and therefore requires the execution of international as well as of individual contracts.

We may repeat that while a treaty, as an agreement, is under the law of nations, good faith is a principle—indeed it is a first principle—of the natural law; therefore the violation of the obligation created by the treaty is a breach not only of international but of the natural law. Such a violation of the natural law is an offense not merely against the nation involved but against all nations, as all are bound by and are beneficiaries under the law natural, and it is a right of every nation to insist that the law of nature should be respected and that therefore the obligation under the law of nations—which "pertains to the natural law," as Suárez says—should be observed in its entirety. Now an obligation on the part of one nation creates a right on the part of another, and the right, like the obligation from which it flows, is under the protection of the law natural. It follows, therefore, that if the rights of one nation under natural law can be violated, then the rights of all nations under natural law are endangered and the maxim *Pacta sunt servanda* becomes but empty words.

Let us, however, recur for a moment to another form of obligation in connection with treaties of peace,—a matter which Suárez has already mentioned—that of agreeing to negotiate them when an offer is made. The compliance with such an offer "is to a great degree in harmony with natural reason." However, in his opinion, it receives "additional support from custom itself," and not only from custom but also "from the law of nations, thus becoming a matter of strict obligation." This is of no small importance, for many and many a war would have been terminated in its earlier stages had the acceptance of an offer of peaceful settlement been considered as compulsory.

These observations lead up to a series of conclusions which, taken together, are not only a classic but perhaps the most memorable passage in the history of the law of nations. It has been customary for writers on international law to quote the passage in its entirety, but, while this may the better display its literary beauty, it nevertheless fails to disclose its many unsuspected implications. Therefore we shall quote it sentence by sentence.

1. The rational basis of this branch of law [the law of nations], indeed, consists in the fact that the human race, howsoever many the various peoples and kingdoms into which it may be divided, always

preserves a certain unity not only as a species, but also, as it were, a moral and political unity called for by the natural precept of mutual love and mercy, which applies to all, even to strangers of any nation.

This is a suggestion of the international community, and the reason why this community exists is to be found in the existence of states, separate and independent of one another and yet linked one to the other. It is a political community, because the states are political groups of human beings; it is a social community, because human beings are essentially social and unite in society; and it is a moral community, and will always be such, because the progress of man is measured by his conception and understanding of the moral law, towards whose perfection the path of civilization leads him.

2. Therefore, although a given sovereign state, commonwealth, or kingdom, may constitute a perfect community in itself, consisting of its own members, nevertheless, each one of these states is also, in a certain sense, and viewed in relation to the human race, a member of that universal society; for never are these states, when standing alone, so self-sufficient that they do not require some mutual assistance, association and intercourse, at times for their greater welfare and advantage, but at other times because also of some moral necessity or lack, as is clear from experience.

There is, it is believed, no better statement of the interdependence of nations to be found in the books, and comment would be as impertinent as it is superfluous.

3. Consequently, such communities have need of some system of law whereby they may be directed and properly ordered with regard to this kind of intercourse and association; and although this law is in large measure provided by natural reason, it is not provided in sufficient measure and in a direct manner, with respect to all matters; therefore, it was possible for certain special rules of law to be introduced through the practice of these same nations.

This implies that the law of nations reinforces and extends the law of nature, which is revealed through natural reason. And is it too much to hope that one day, however far in the future it may be, the law of nations may respond as does the law natural to the everlasting fundamentals of our human nature, which can not change without our ceasing to be enlightened men and women?

4. For just as in one state or province law is introduced by custom; so among the human race as a whole it was possible for laws to be introduced by the habitual conduct of nations, and all the more because the matters comprised within this latter system of law are few, and very closely related to the natural law, and most easily deduced therefrom in a manner so advantageous and so in harmony with nature itself, that while this derivation [of the law of nations from the natural law] may not be self-evident, that is, not essentially and absolutely required for moral rectitude, it is nevertheless quite in accord with nature, and universally acceptable for its own sake.

Here we have the origin, the process and the consequence of lawmaking in and for the international community. Is this not the emanation of a noble mind and of a great heart, and the hope of the world—that it may be governed in the future, as never in the past, by the high standard of right reason?

It would be scant courtesy to Suárez if we should utter a word of criticism. It is permissible, however, for the sake of comparison, to reproduce again in this connection a passage from Victoria's Reading *On the Civil Power*,[38] setting forth his conception of an international community:

International law has not only the force of a pact and agreement among men, but also the force of a law; for the world as a whole, being in a way one single state, has the power to create laws that are just and fitting for all persons, as are the rules of international law. Consequently, it is clear that they who violate these international rules, whether in peace or in war, commit a mortal sin; moreover, in the gravest matters, such as the inviolability of ambassadors, it is not permissible for one country to refuse to be bound by international law, the latter having been established by the authority of the whole world.

It is not for us to compare the passages from a moral standpoint. Nor is it our purpose to consider them as literature, although they are both admirable, with the scales inclining, at least in our opinion, towards Victoria. If the two passages, however, be compared from the standpoint of international law, the statement of Suárez is seen to lack that sense of ultimate com-

[38] *De Potestate Civili*, § 21. English translation from Scott, *op. cit.*

pleteness which always seems to have been in the mind of Victoria; his is not merely an international community with law, but it is an international community with the power to create law and to punish the violations of that law. It may well be that the presence of law in Suárez' community implies both the right consciously to create and the power to preserve that law inviolate; but neither the right nor the power is express, as in the case of Francis of Victoria's international community. For does not Victoria say expressly that the *jus gentium* has "the force of a pact and agreement among men"? Whereas Suárez implies in the succeeding chapter of this very book that the law of nations may have been introduced simply through "usage and tradition, . . . and without any special and simultaneous compact or agreement on the part of all peoples." This conception of Suárez looks to an unorganic association; Victoria's conception looks to an organized society, with a law of nations having the force of a pact, the obligations of which are enforceable, not merely under the law of nations, but under the natural law.

Our Daniel Webster, as Secretary of State, had in mind—unconsciously, it may be—the Victorian conception of a pact and an agreement; for his international community is the organic community of Victoria rather than the inorganic community of Suárez, as appears from an instruction from Mr. Webster, as Secretary of State, to Mr. Thompson, Minister to Mexico, under date of April 15, 1842. "Every nation," Secretary Webster says, "on being received . . . into the circle of civilized governments, must understand that she not only attains rights of sovereignty and the dignity of national character, but that she binds herself also to the strict and faithful observance" —we interpolate, *Pacta sunt servanda*—"of all those principles, laws, and usages, which have obtained currency among civilized states." [39]

To return to Suárez' *jus gentium*, properly so called. How did it come into being, or, rather, the question which he has in mind is, how could it have come into being? To which he

[39] John Bassett Moore, *A Digest of International Law* (Washington, 1906), Vol. 1, p. 5.

answers that it "could have been gradually introduced throughout the whole world . . . simply through usage and tradition," and, enlarging upon and emphasizing the matter, he adds, "by means of tradition, propagation and mutual imitation among the nations." And fundamental though it is, this law, as we have seen, could have been introduced, in Suárez' conception of the international community "without any special and simultaneous contract or agreement on the part of all peoples." With Victoria, as has been indicated, the international community is by the very existence of states an organic community, with the power to make laws to prevent the violation of the obligations which every state has by reason of its existence and membership in the community. With Suárez, the law of the international community was simply the product of "usage and tradition" rather than of "pact and agreement" among nations.

But to continue our analysis of Suárez' *jus gentium,* which, in its various parts, "has such a close relationship to nature, and is so advantageous to all nations, individually and collectively, that it has grown almost by natural process with the growth of the human race." Had the body of law in question been indispensable in the nature of things, it would have been natural law. It was not thus indispensable but it was and is "advantageous," not merely to one nation but to all nations, whether considered "individually" or "collectively," and its growth might therefore be considered as well-nigh a natural process by those who looked at results rather than at the process. Although it is not natural law, it exists, Suárez points out, like natural law, in unwritten form. The reason for his view? The law of nations is not dictated by a legislator but "has, on the contrary, waxed strong through custom." Today, we may add, that which was formerly unwritten is, to an ever greater extent, becoming written international law.

Passing now from the *jus gentium,* properly so called, to the term as used by Suárez in the second sense, that is to say, as denoting the existence of uniform laws in the various states, "the source of the great similarity of the forms in which it exists" is, he says, "easy to explain." It was indeed so to him but not to preceding generations, inasmuch as the term *jus gentium* appears to have been used by Roman lawyers as synonymous with the natural law, which the peoples of all states were credited with using. The Romans therefore introduced and applied this *jus gentium,* which we would call natural law, to the transactions of foreigners settled among them, who could not use the civil law of the Romans, because its application was limited to the Romans themselves. The "new wine in old bottles" had the traditional result.

But to Suárez and his explanation of the similarity in local laws. "The resemblance," he says, "is not always perfect," as it consists "only in a general and common rational basis." Whence and what is this common basis? While it is "not derived from natural law," it is "so closely related" to it and is "so thoroughly in accord or harmony with nature that through it the individual nations could easily have been led to adopt the rules in question." And a further and final explanation is to be found in "tradition, and a mutual imitation," which Suárez supposes began with the beginning of the human race.

Returning now to the *jus gentium* properly so called, Suárez invokes the very words of St. Thomas, "that the precepts of the *jus gentium* are conclusions drawn from principles of the natural law," differing, therefore, from the precepts of the civil law, which are not, as in the case of the *jus gentium,* "general conclusions" but "specific applications of the natural law." Is there, in fact, any difference in this respect between the civil law and the *jus gentium* in its primary sense? The answer which Suárez makes to this question is the opinion of Soto, to the effect that the rules of the *jus gentium* are here considered as general conclusions of the law natural, "not in an absolute sense and by necessary inference, but in comparison with the specific applications of civil and private law."

Now in the civil and private law, one of two events must occur, Suárez says, and the first is that "a merely arbitrary specific application is made of the sort concerning which it is said that, 'Whatever pleases the prince has the force of law.'" Given the conception of the state in which the majority controls the prince, this would seem to be strange doctrine for Suárez to profess. But he explains in the succeeding clause that he is not here supporting the unlimited arbitrary power of the prince, for he declares that an application in such terms is not due to the fact that the prince's will "alone suffices as a rational basis, but because that particular decision might reasonably have taken one of various forms." Then, too, "there is frequently no ground on which one form"—of specific application—"should be preferred to another," and it is for this reason alone that the decision is said to be made by the princely will "rather than in accordance with reason."

Now the second of the events arises in a situation calling for a choice, in which case reason is weighed with reference to particular and material circumstances, so that, as Suárez puts it, "the decision thus results from the surrounding circumstances rather than from the substance of the matter in hand." Again we meet, in classic language, a famous colloquial expression "circumstances alter cases."

So much for the precepts of the civil and private law.

Now for the law of nations, the precepts of which are, as Suárez has already said, "of a more general character." Why? Because, as the *jus gentium* is the law of all, or of most nations, it must perforce take into consideration "the welfare of all nature," and since it is, as Suárez has so often pointed out, very closely related to the law of nature, it must be in conformity with nature's "primary and universal principles." Hence it is that such precepts are Suárez' conception of what are properly "called conclusions drawn from natural principles"; but this conception is supported by a further and unanswerable argument —that "their appropriate character and moral value are immediately made manifest by the force of natural reason; an appropriateness and value which have induced men to introduce the customs in question (as the Emperor Justinian has said) more because of the pressure of necessity than because of their own wills." The difference here is between an absolute, and a controlled and human necessity.

In relation to law in general, what then, is the character of the law of nations? This is not an impertinent question, for even to this day there survives an argument as to the legal nature of international law. But to Suárez, the greatest legal philosopher of his day, and, as a great authority puts it, the "prince of modern jurists," the matter was not open to argument. To him the *jus gentium* had every characteristic of true law. "We conclude," he says, "that equity and justice must be observed in the precepts of the *jus gentium.*" Why? To which question, implicit in his argument, he answers: "For such observance is included in the rational basis of every true law, . . . and the rules pertaining to the *jus gentium* are indeed true law." But this was not the whole of Suárez' conception of human laws which, as he has repeatedly said before, are laws only if and in so far as they are in conformity with the natural law. The rules of the *jus gentium,* he continues, are "more closely related to the natural law than are those of civil law." At which point we meet the "therefore" of the syllogism, introducing a conclusion from his fellow-countryman Covarruvias, "it is impossible that these precepts of the *jus gentium* should be contrary to natural equity." And we add in our own behalf that this passage should be inscribed in letters of gold in every Ministry of Foreign Affairs of every state of the international community. If this were done, international law would become, through the ages, a human inspiration as well as a human necessity, not only truly legal but as moral as it is admittedly social.

The great Victoria was not averse to corollaries;[40] indeed, we have quoted on previous pages one of the very greatest of his corollaries—that upon which the municipal sanction of the law of nations depends. In this respect, as well as in others, Suárez was like the *maestro,* although he did not invariably label his corollaries as corollaries. In the present instance, a corollary is inferred by Suárez from the preceding discussion and it is as important as any of his text. The corollary is "that the *jus gentium* is subject to change, in so far as it is dependent upon the consent of men," differing in this respect, as repeatedly said, from natural law.

[40] *Supra,* p. 59.

Now there are in the *jus gentium* two elements. One is the relationship to or derivation from natural law—and to the extent that the law of nations is thus a part of the natural law, its rules may partake of the immutability of the law natural. And the other element is human consent. In so far as this second element is involved, the making and unmaking of the law of nations lies within the power of man. But this power to change the law of nations is to be exercised by society in general or by the majority of the international community, as, in the conception of Suárez, this law was largely a matter of universal custom. The power, however, is not to be exercised by private authority, except in so far as the individual may, if he so desires, renounce rights which are conceded to him by the law of nations, just as rights conceded or permitted by the law of nature may also be renounced. As in Suárez' day it was possible for "a given person" to "make himself a slave by renouncing his natural liberty," so also, under the law of nations, "a religious may renounce the ownership of temporal goods, and even the capacity for such ownership." But such changes, whether in the law of nature or of nations involve only what Suárez calls "negative" precepts, that is, those which permit, but do not positively require, or prohibit, an act—as in the case of a "religious" renouncing the natural right to take a wife. Indeed the same right of renunciation exists as regards rights "individually granted by the civil or canon law."

What, however, of the prohibitions, or positive precepts of the *jus gentium*? On what ground are they subject to change when, as we know, the positive precepts of the natural law are immutable? The reason here is easy to understand, inasmuch as things are intrinsically good or bad under natural law, whereas under the law of nations they are only good or bad in so far as the law makes them so.

There is a second reason, which also goes to the root of things: "the obligation imposed by the *jus gentium*," as Suárez holds, "does not spring from reason alone, apart from human obligation of every sort." If it did, the *jus gentium* would be nothing more nor less than the natural law in the Anglo-Saxon guise of the rule of reason. Nor does the fact that the law of nations "has its source in general custom" alter the view, because custom is not essentially a thing of reason.

It would be inconsistent with reason if the law of nature should be subject to change, since it is the perfection of reason; but the law of nations, being man-made, is to that extent imperfect, because man's reason is imperfect, and therefore "it is not absolutely inconsistent with reason that the said law should be subjected to change." There is, however, an extremely important proviso to this concession on the part of Suárez—that the change must "be made on sufficient authority." This power to change the law of nations was likewise conceded by Victoria, with the same proviso, but expressed in more perfect form, because Victoria was dealing not only with changes in the law of nations but with the very formation of that law. Instead of the "sufficient authority" of Suárez, the authority of Victoria, in his dissertation *On the Indians,* was that of the "consensus of the greater part of the whole world, especially in behalf of the common good of all," [41] a passage which recalls the classic language of the Reading *On the Civil Power,* in the twenty-first section, that international law has been established "by the authority of the whole world." [42] Therefore it would not be permissible for one group of nations or a minority of nations to attempt to establish an international law for the whole world, although they may establish a special rule of conduct for their own guidance and to meet their own special conditions. Neither may they derogate from the generally established international law, since, as Victoria says, "it is not permissible for one country to refuse to be bound by international law." [43]

There was a difference in this respect, however, between the *"jus gentium"* proper and the secondary *jus gentium* in the sense of the civil law common to several or many nations, and Suárez brings out the distinction with such clearness that it can not possibly be stated better than in his own words: "In this con-

[41] *De Indis,* p. 153.
[42] *Supra,* p. 59.
[43] *Ibid.*

nection, I must note, furthermore, that a given change may be effected in the *jus gentium* in one way, with respect to that phase of the said law which is common merely in that several nations agree upon the suitability of certain precepts." What is the process involved in such a change? This *jus gentium*, which is "intrinsically . . . nothing more or less than civil law," can be "changed by an individual kingdom or state" at its will, but only, of course, "to an extent affecting that state alone." So much for the *"jus gentium"* used with respect to the law not of nations but common to certain nations. What, now, of the *jus gentium* or law of nations proper? "When one is dealing with that phase of the *jus gentium* [law of nations], which is common owing to the usage and customs of [all] nations, in so far as there exists among them any fellowship or intercourse," then, says Suárez, "changes are far more difficult." This is because the *jus gentium* in its primary sense involves law common to all nations and appears to have been introduced by the authority of all. "So that," continues Suárez, "it may not be annulled without universal consent." Here the two great luminaries of the Spanish School of International Law are in accord.

However, as Suárez has repeatedly said, a change in the law of nations would not be inconsistent with reason, and in the present passage dealing with this subject, the doctrine of mutability in international law has received its classic form and perfection. "Nevertheless," he goes on to say, "there would be no inherent obstacle to change in the subject-matter of such law, if all nations should agree to the alteration, or if a custom contrary to [some established rule of this law of nations] should gradually come into practice and prevail." However, such an event, he concludes, "although it might be conceived of, as not contrary to reason, yet seems impossible, practically speaking." Suárez does not mean that international law may not under certain conditions, and as an exception to his general rule, be changed by a state with reference to its own subjects, such a change affecting that state, and that state alone. However, this is dangerous doctrine, for if international law is the law universal, then the citizens and subjects of every state should have a right to its protection; and the circumstances must be special indeed to justify an attempt on the part of any nation to change the law of nations, even on its own behalf, especially if the change abolishes, restricts, or reduces a right acquired under, and therefore guaranteed by, the law of nations. But having thus questioned, and, as it were, limited the doctrine, let us quote Suárez' exact words, both as to the exception and the example: "In another sense, a given community may ordain that, within its own territory and among its own subjects, the law in question shall not be observed, such an instance being conceivable and practical.[44] For it was thus that the rule of the *jus gentium* [law of nations] as to the enslavement of prisoners taken in a just war, was changed in the Church." In the example, the change, it is to be said, neither abolishes, restricts, nor reduces, but rather increases, the rights of human beings.

Civil law, Suárez has shown, is readily subject to change, and he now adds that it is "subject to change in its entirety," and herein he points out an important difference between it and the *jus gentium;* for the latter, he continues, "is said to be subject [to change], not in the whole, but in part." The reason for this distinction is that it does not relate to "an absolute power of change, . . . that is, not to the mutable nature of these two bodies of law themselves," since, in so far as this quality is concerned, both are "inherently mutable." The distinction is rather "in accordance with the moral power and usage of men." In point of fact, Suárez declares the distinction is of a somewhat limited nature, since neither the law of nations nor the civil law "is mutable, in a general sense," the implication being that it would not be possible for all the peoples of the world to agree at the same time upon the complete change or abolition of either form of law. Thus the civil law, in the case of a particular precept, may be mutable without qualification, for the reason that the civil law is not universal, "whereas," Suárez holds, the

[44] In the General Treaty of the Inter-American Arbitration, concluded at Washington January 5, 1929, the second Article reads in part as follows:

"There are excepted from the stipulations of the treaty the following controversies: (a) Those which are within the domestic jurisdiction of any of the Parties to the dispute and are not controlled by international law; . . . ."

precepts "of the *jus gentium* may be abrogated only in part." The reason for this limitation on change in or abrogation of the *jus gentium* Suárez has already indicated, stating that it can occur only through the agreement of "all nations," or through general custom. And if such unanimity, or near unanimity, is required for the change or abrogation of a single precept of the law of nations, it is inconceivable that the law as a whole should become subject to change or abolition. Even if it were conceivable or possible to deprive the states of the world of the common law of nations at one fell blow, it would be impossible for them to live without law; indeed, it would be well-nigh impossible for them to create a new *jus gentium,* as it were, offhand. The result could but be a world of anarchy, and not of law.

* * * * * * * *

The thirty-second chapter of the third book of the tractate *De Legibus ac Deo Legislatore* is a formal answer to the query "whether the municipal laws of any kingdom or domain are binding on the men of that domain when they are dwelling outside its territorial limits."

In the first place Suárez states that the question involves four subdivisions—and in our own behalf we may add that it opens up the entire question of jurisdiction and the extraterritoriality of law. As a preliminary step he indicates the way in which a person "may be related to a given domain or diocese," for Suárez, great as a jurist, was first and foremost a churchman. In the first subdivision, the type of relation to the domain in question is "as a permanent inhabitant" of that domain, one who, in other words, is physically dwelling in the country. This relationship is ordinarily indicated by the unqualified term "inhabitant." In the second, says Suárez, "at the opposite extreme," is the person "who has neither of these relations with the domain in question," that is to say, who is neither an inhabitant nor possesses a fixed dwelling place in the country. The third subdivision relates to "a permanent inhabitant" in the country, one "having his domicile therein," but who is "dwelling abroad at the time." Finally, there is a fourth category and Suárez designates as a member of this "a temporary denizen of the said domain" but one who has "neither domicile nor origin therein," —would would say a "transient."

We may eliminate with Suárez the first and second of what he calls the "situations"; for the first deals with the national always present within the country, and the second deals with the national always absent from the country. In the first case, therefore, the question of the binding obligation of the law is obvious, and in the second, as Suárez says, "it is clear that there is no possibility of legal obligation," because the national in this case is completely and permanently outside the jurisdiction of his country, and there is "no title existing under which the status of a subject may be imposed." Suárez here seems to mean by the "status of a subject," not the status of nationality as such but rather that of allegiance begotten of actual presence in the country of the prince. Therefore it is that Suárez devotes most of his attention to what he calls "the third and fourth points."

First of all he considers the question which he has stated at the beginning of the chapter in its relation to the third of the classes which he has described, and a person of this class, "although he is at the time living or traveling outside the boundaries of his own state, always remains a subject," provided that "he does not change his domicile." We thus see that in Suárez' day, as in our own, the question of domicile was a thorny but important one in relation to matters of nationality, allegiance and jurisdiction.

In this connection Suárez refers to "the saying that the law binds all subjects and all parts of the community"; and from this point of view the law is binding in the case in question. Now there was confirmation of this in considering the opposite side of the picture, namely, the case of the inhabitant of some other domain who, "while dwelling in this one"—the kingdom under consideration—"is not bound to observe the laws of the latter kingdom, a fact which seems to be expressly defined in the Canon law," but a fact which Suárez would accept, be it said, only on condition that the inhabitant in question be considered as "under the obligation of observing the laws of his own domain;" for if this were not the case, an anomalous situation would arise in which the foreign inhabitant dwelling in the kingdom which Suárez has in mind "would be free, solely on account of his absence, from the obligation of obeying the laws of either country," and this situation he rightly characterizes as "absurd."

Suárez, as we have said, was a theologian dealing with lay questions, and it was but natural that he should frequently rely upon theological examples. In this particular section he confirms the general principle by illustrations drawn from the Church, especially that of persons in a diocese subject to the jurisdiction of the bishop as distinct from inhabitants of the territory subject to the prince. In other words, Suárez invokes both the temporal and the spiritual law, as the matter in hand may suggest.

In the present instance, the first confirmation is, as we have seen, a lay example. To clinch the matter, however, Suárez invokes the authority of his Church and uses a clerical illustration. He supposes that "a bishop makes a rule" for a diocese, requiring that persons within the diocese and subject to his jurisdiction, "who enjoy a benefice must reside therein during a given period of time under pain of a given punishment or censure." If this is the case, the bishop "so binds the holders of such benefices, where-ever they may be, that if they do not return to the diocese within the prescribed time," they suffer a penalty. This he lays down as a general rule, subject to the exception that the offending person is neither ignorant of the rule nor unable to comply with it. The result is that such "a provincial statute is binding upon those belonging to a diocese, even while they are traveling elsewhere"; and the conclusion, applicable alike to civil as to ecclesiastical law, is that "the same is true of any similar law."

It might be, and indeed it was not infrequently stated, Suárez admits—on the basis of reading equalled by few, if any, in his order—"that no law is binding outside the limits of the country of the lord or prince by whom it is decreed," from which it follows that "the inhabitants of that country, generally speaking, do not sin if they violate the law in question while they are outside of this territory." "Such," according to Suárez, was "the common opinion of the Doctors." This conclusion, he informs us, is deduced from a passage in *Sext*,[45] according to which a person "living outside a particular diocese," who disobeyed a law, although made by the bishop thereof, did not "incur the sentence stipulated for that law." To this conclusion, however, Suárez had a ready and an unanswerable reply; it was to the effect that "in the passage under discussion, the reference is not to the binding authority of the law, but rather to the censure," or, as a layman of our day would say—to the penalty. That is to say, the law is none the less applicable to the individual because he is outside of the jurisdiction of the country, but the penalty can not be imposed until he returns. The question, therefore, is one of jurisdiction. Suárez, however, states the matter in words that can not be paraphrased and therefore he must, in this, as in many other instances, speak in his own behalf: "for the imposition of a censure pertains not to the directive"—that is to say, to the commanding—"but to the coercive power of the law." This is because "the superior or judge may not punish outside of the territory, although he may issue orders and impose obligations." In other words, the power of the superior in the case of the subject living outside his territory is limited to the issuing of orders and the imposing of obligations, but the superior may not penalize the failure to obey or fulfil the orders.

As bearing upon this phase of the question Suárez analyzes a decision of the Pope that *"he who declares a law may be disobeyed with impunity outside* [*his own*] *territory,"* Suárez adding that a declaration of a law is "the same as passing sentence [upon its violation]." But "the intention of the Pope, without doubt, was to assert that the statute in question was not [actually] violated by the subject in the situation posited." The reasons are twofold. The sovereign, in this or any other case, could not impose a penalty outside of his own jurisdiction and if he attempted to do so, the result would be not only that the provision con-

[45] I. ii. 2. *Sext* (or *Liber Sextus Decretalium*) is the sixth book of the *Decretals* (*Corpus Juris Canonici*), being an addition to the collection of five books of *Decretals* compiled by Gregory IX. The *Sext* was prepared by a committee of canonists under Pope Bonifice VIII. It includes papal constitutions subsequent to 1234, notably decrees of the two oecumenical councils of Lyons, and was published in 1298.

cerning a penalty would be invalid, but that the actual provision of the law itself would have no force as regards the subject outside his jurisdiction. In other words, as far as the absent subject was concerned, the penalty would be void and likewise the law. This interpretation of the Pope's decision Suárez appropriately applies to the Church, "so that the person who, under the supposed circumstances does not obey the statute, is not contumaciously disobedient to the Church," and as a logical conclusion this is furthermore "an indication that the person in question is not bound by that statute, even with respect to its directive force." The schoolman, in the best sense of the term, appears in the succeeding sentence, in which Suárez sets forth his conclusion—and a very important one for him as a Churchman and for the Christian world of the Catholic persuasion: "[The truth of] the antecedent is evident," he says, "since if the said subject were contumacious he might accordingly be excommunicated, and consequently would incur a legal censure. For excommunication," in what Suárez calls "the more probable opinion," could be inflicted upon an absent subject "dwelling in a foreign territory." Therefore the conclusion to be drawn from the Pope's statement is that just as the liability to a censure—that is, a penalty—"does not bind an absent person, neither does a law."

This, however, is the temporal phase. How about the conscience? "Although the statute in question may have been published without any [provision as to] censure or penalty, but simply with the force of a directive law binding in conscience, [nevertheless] it will not be binding upon absent subjects." But suppose an attempt were made to add a censure to the law? Still it would not be binding. Why? Because "its power to lay an obligation upon the conscience is not enlarged [or diminished] by reason of the censure." Why should this be so? The matter is important and indeed fundamental. "[The imposition of] a censure rather assumes the existence of jurisdiction and the power to bind; and when the [provision for] a censure is added, the jurisdiction [of the law] is not for that reason diminished or restricted." Neither, we may add in our own behalf, is the jurisdiction of the law extended by reason of the addition of a penalty, for jurisdiction is exercisable within, and only within, the domain of the government, whether it be territorial or spiritual, to which the person involved is subject.

There is a relation of measure between the jurisdiction and the domain; for the one may not be extended beyond the bounds of the other. However, Suárez continues, "all the authorities"—in this as well as in other cases—"do not agree as to the rational basis for the assertion in question." Some seek to justify the conclusion to which they come on the ground that the intent of the legislator was merely to "bind the subjects living within his own territory." Some opponents contended, moreover, that in this case the conclusion which "we"—meaning Suárez—"have laid down is true, only if the law is couched in general terms, since in that case, no other—that is to say, no more extensive—intent on the part of the lawmaker, is expressed; and therefore, if the legislator declares in express terms that he wishes to bind [all] subjects, wherever they may be, then" according to dissenting opinion, "the law is binding even upon subjects outside of the territory." However, Suárez meets this argument by referring again to the decision of the Pope which he had just cited, that "he who declares a law may be disobeyed with impunity outside [his own] territory," on which Suárez comments that the words of the Papal text "indicate a defect not merely of will, but also of power, a fact which is self-evident," but for which he nevertheless invokes the *Digest*[46] and "the commentators," who are "commonly agreed upon this point."

The conclusion of Suárez would seem to be sufficiently clear, but the matter was so important, so far-reaching and fundamental that, having stated and met the reasons set forth by the dissenters, he now proceeds to give in unequivocal terms the true reasons for the conclusions which he has maintained—"the jurisdiction of any one state or prince does not include the power of making laws which shall be valid outside the state or kingdom." This is the fact, but Suárez was not content with fact unless expressed in terms of philosophy and therefore he implies a philosophical analogy. "Just as in philosophy," he says, "we are accus-

[46] II. i. 20.

tomed to say that an action does not continue outside [its] sphere of activity, owing surely to a defect of power and not of will; even so the activity of jurisdiction in the making of any law is limited to a [specific] territory, and hence"—the inevitable conclusion of the schoolman—"that law is not binding outside those territorial limits." And with another "therefore" he ends the entire discussion: "it is clearly to be inferred, that the lawgiver can not bind a subject outside the existing boundaries [of the state], even if he has the specific intention of doing so and expressly states that intention in the words of his [law]."

We now come to a mooted question which Suárez proceeds to discuss: "When a prince may punish a delinquent subject outside of his own territory." The conclusion which Suárez has just reached should in general, he maintains, be considered "as referring to the peculiar directive obligation imposed by law upon the conscience," this being the "proper and immediate effect of law." But if one were considering the matter from the viewpoint of "coercion by means of a penalty, it is the opinion of the jurists that when a subject has committed a crime outside of the state," the prince might inflict a punishment upon him only under certain specific circumstances; that is to say, when the penalty was applicable, not in the place where the crime was committed—namely, outside of the prince's jurisdiction—but only after the erring subject has returned to the realm of the prince. The penalty is thus not, as Suárez says, "imposed *ipso jure,* but its imposition is contingent upon the subject's return to the sphere of jurisdiction within which the law applies. This is a statement of principle, but to Suárez the principle must always be based upon the reason of things. In the present instance, he gives as the rational basis for the doctrine which he has laid down "that under the conditions specified the penalty is not imposed outside of the state, but within the same." This can scarcely be denied; but it was the custom of Suárez to probe deep and he therefore further develops the reason behind the principle. "It is," he continues, "assumed that this punishment must be imposed by human agency." To this assumption there can hardly be a dissent, since it is not within the province of human lawmakers to provide for spiritual punishments. Now "judges do not inflict punishment," he adds, "or exercise power upon persons who are dwelling abroad, but only upon those who return to the country." [47]

But what of the Papal decision, which Suárez has examined and explained, and which, in effect, declares that a law promulgated within a territory may be disobeyed with impunity outside of that territory? Does this decision conflict with the view just set forth? Suárez meets this question by reiterating that the meaning of the decision was merely that a law containing a penalty could not be operative outside of the jurisdiction of the lawmaker and hence, if a subject outside of that jurisdiction committed an offense against the law, he could not be considered guilty under the law as long as he remained outside of the jurisdiction in question. This is quite a different situation from that involved in the return of the offending subject, in which case, Suárez concludes that a penalty may properly become operative upon such return.

We should, however, have the exact language of Suárez on a matter of such importance—the "difference [is] between a law imposing a punishment *ipso facto,* and a law merely declaring a punishment that is to be imposed"; or, to carry the distinction further, as Suárez adds: "the first kind of law of itself inflicts a penalty and thus necessarily extends its binding character and power of execution outside its own territory." Such an extension would be unreasonable because the only way by which the punishment of such a law could be inflicted is "by obliging the guilty person to execute the penalty upon himself," which, as Suárez points out, "is impossible." And it is not only impossible, but it is illogical, as he immediately demonstrates, "for if [the law in question] cannot compel one to, or restrain one from an action, much less will it be able to compel one to the execution of the penalty."

Now the situation is quite different as regards a law "which imposes a penalty that is to be inflicted by a judge," the reason

[47] For an application of this principle to a case of our day, see the leading case of *The Trial of Earl Russell* (before the King in Parliament), L. R. (1901), App. Cas. 446.

being that such a law "is by the very nature of the case, a statute binding the judge to act in accordance with it, rather than a statute binding upon the criminal; and the judge dwells within the territorial limits of the state"—and these territorial limits are likewise the limits of his jurisdiction. Here Suárez has reached the heart of the matter and a final and utterly convincing argument on the territoriality of crime. For it would indeed be a curious state of affairs and a lamentable confusion of jurisdiction if judges were able to follow offenders and try offenses wherever committed.

It was the practice of the schoolmen, as it must be of every logical and successful disputant, not merely to meet the objections which had already been advanced but to foresee and overturn those which might have been or might be advanced. Therefore Suárez in the present instance overcomes an imaginary opponent and in so doing saves himself from a possible later attack by one less imaginary. The manner in which he handles the supposed opponent is so perfect an example of the logical method of Suárez that it must be given in his own words:

> The objection may be raised that the [guilty] subject is also bound in conscience to submit to the punishment in question. Our reply is that the said subject, strictly speaking, is not bound by this law until after sentence has been passed, when he is assumed to be already within the limits of the state.

An extraterritorial crime, to be punishable within the state of the person committing it, must be a crime not only according to a law but a crime intrinsically—or as Suárez says, "essentially"—evil in itself; or it must be sufficiently forbidden in some other way than by the law of the prince imposing the penalty. For this law, as already pointed out, "can not [itself] prohibit the deed, outside of the limits of the state"; and the result of this is that the law in question "cannot designate any penalty" for the offense, "unless the deed is for some other reason assumed to be evil or sufficiently prohibited." There is an age-old example which may illustrate the doctrine of Suárez, although he himself does not employ it. We have cited it in previous pages, but its aptness at this point warrants a re-citation. It is none other than piracy under the law of nations, which is a law not merely for the international community, as such, but for each and every nation or state. Now as the jurisdiction of any nation, within the limitations of international law, is universally admitted upon the high seas, and as piracy is prohibited under the law of nations, it may be punished by any nation as a violation of its own law, and the penalty of death inflicted under the law international. Thus piracy meets precisely the conditions which Suárez has laid down, for it is evil in itself, irrespective of the law of any one country; and not only is it evil in itself, but it is, in Suárez' very words, in "some other way sufficiently forbidden"—that is, by the law of nations.

In dealing with the extraterritoriality of crime, Suárez—and perhaps the reader—has for the moment lost sight of the topic of his narrative, so to speak, namely, the subject living outside the territorial limits of the state, as described in the third of the categories with which he began the present chapter. He now recurs to this temporary resident abroad and states that by "living outside the territorial limits of the state . . . he does not lose his status as a subject in the essential sense." There is, however, a temporary change in his status, "that is to say," in the words of Suárez, "he ceases to exercise it"—meaning his status as subject —"in relation to the laws of [his] country, since he is living beyond the range of their [normal] operation." Applying this principle to the doctrine which he has been discussing, Suárez declares that "outside of the territory no one is bound when the agent"—in the sense of the person performing the act—"and the object acted upon, and the action itself, are entirely without the limits of the state"; but the case is different if one or the other of these elements of the situation is within the territory of the state in question. The inference which Suárez draws is, in fact, that "if the agent is outside, while the object with respect to which he offends is inside," then "the obligatory force of the law may be applicable." Here Suárez cites an authority in whom, as we have already noted, he felt no small confidence. It is none other than Covarruvias, to the effect that "a law is not binding outside the limits of the state, unless the subject-matter of the law has in view the welfare of that same state." Speaking in the first person, Suárez says: "In my opinion, this is the true doctrine."

But Suárez felt that a certain elucidation and a qualification of this "true doctrine"were necessary, and he therefore informs us that, "strictly speaking, the proposition in question is not limited by the said doctrine, since offenses contrary to a law of the sort under discussion should be considered as having been committed, not without, but within the territory [of the lawmaker]." There are two legal conditions under which the act might be committed: in one case the law may be affirmative; in the other, negative. Let us suppose that a law directs that a certain act be performed within the state which Suárez has in mind. If the person to whom the law applies fails to act in compliance with the law, that is, fails to perform the act within the jurisdiction in question, then, even though he is outside of that jurisdiction, the offense may be considered as occurring within the state, since it redounds to the injury of the state. What, on the other hand, of a law which prohibits some act; in other words, the negative law which Suárez has mentioned as the second of the legal conditions? If the prohibition is disregarded by a national of the state, even though he be living abroad, and an injury to the state results therefrom, then, in the opinion of Suárez, the offense is clearly consummated in that state. The example which he gives is perfect of its kind, and one for which professors of the criminal law have, if we may speak from our own experience, an especial weakness. Thus, "a person corporeally outside the limits of the state or kingdom would, if he shot an arrow and thus killed a man within those boundaries, be clearly held to have sinned in the territory of the said state," and having committed such an act he would not merely transgress the law but would incur "in consequence," Suárez continues, "a liability to the censure"—in the sense of penalty or punishment—"if the latter should be provided for by the law in question."

But what of the situation in regard to *enclaves*—to use a term of the law of nations—or, as Suárez says, "with respect to exempt localities when they are otherwise enclosed within a state"?

Having in a previous work [48] dealt with the matter in some detail, Suárez here contents himself by stating "simply" that "the same assertion does indeed hold true with respect to localities of this kind"; and he adds that this is also the view of the canonists.

But notwithstanding the authority of this view, Suárez as usual decided to enforce his statement by an example. "The same view is supported," he says, "by the laws above cited, in so far as it may be inferred from them that a prelate can not exercise his jurisdiction within the exempt territory." This illustration he considers as applicable to every superior; for, as the locality is withdrawn from the territory, so the jurisdiction over the locality is also withdrawn from the territory, unless there be special exceptions under the law. And Suárez concludes by quoting once more the decision of the Pope with reference to the prince and his jurisdiction, that *"he who declares a law may be disobeyed with impunity outside [his own] territory."*

In a later portion of the same book (chapter xxxiii of Book III of the *De Legibus*), Suárez considers a further phase of the binding force of law, and in this phase of the matter he discerns, as he says, "three elements," which, in his opinion, "must be distinguished in every law." The first of these is "its binding force with respect to the conscience." This Suárez called, speaking in the first person, "its directive force." The second element he termed "its coercive force," and this he defines as that force "by means of which one may be punished according to law"—which we would term a sanction, in the language of modern jurisprudence. And the third element, a matter of form rather than of substance, is "the force by which a definite form is laid down for contracts and similar legal acts." This is possibly less important than the two preceding elements; yet it is often vital to the enforceability of an act legal in substance, though, unless the condition is complied with, not legal in form.

The question which Suárez prefixed to this chapter, "whether the domestic laws of any domain are strictly binding upon aliens while they are living therein," he considers in relation

[48] *De Censuris* (Coimbra, 1603).

to these three elements since, in his opinion, they give rise to "some peculiar difficulties."

On these matters there was a twofold divergence of opinion, but, after all, there was similarity if not identity in the basis of each of the views, namely, "that non-resident foreigners (*peregrini*) are not subjects." The reason for this similarity? "The status of subjects," he says, "in so far as moral direction and obligation are concerned, is to be acquired only through domicile, or at least through quasi-domicile." This may be the legal point of view, nevertheless "the law of a locality," he adds, "is binding in conscience upon aliens and guests as long as they dwell therein," the reason being that residence confers jurisdiction, and so long as individuals reside in the locality in question, its laws create an obligation on the part of such residents to observe them. The view of Suárez in favor of assuming jurisdiction over resident aliens and guests is that a law, to be law, must be of general application within the jurisdiction in which it is applied and therefore binding "for the period of their residence, on all persons actually living therein."

This may be admitted. But what of transients? It would seem that they should be included, for the purpose of jurisdiction, in the term "residents"; for they are actually within the community, even when in transit.

In behalf of the view which he had stated as a personal one, Suárez advances three proofs which make it of universal application. The first of the three proofs is one of "the final cause." Here Suárez considers what would be the result if the law were not applicable to the alien and native alike, stating that, if such inequality existed, "disputes and scandals would result." He thus reaches the conclusion, from his viewpoint of the "final cause," that "it is morally necessary for the good government of a province, locality or territory that the laws made for the same should have this [universally binding] effect; for it is necessary to the peace and good morals of that locality"—or, we may add, of any locality—"that aliens should conform to the customs of its people" as long as they live in the same jurisdiction.

Having stated the principle, Suárez indicates the authority, which is none other than the *Decretum,* and that greatest of teachers, "experience." And, as a schoolman, he concludes on the basis of these premises that "since laws are established with a view to the common welfare, peace and good morals of the country, it is necessary that they should possess the [universal] force in question."

After dealing thus with the final cause or purpose—or, as the Greeks put it, design in nature—Suarez passes to the second of his proofs, to be found in the "efficient cause," that is to say, the means or channel by which the purpose is carried out; in other words—and especially in our day—the legislative power.

Since the state, as Suárez has said more than once on the authority of no less a person than Aristotle, should be a perfect community, it rests with the chief executive, as we would say, or, as Suárez says, with the "civil governor . . . to preserve his state and to safeguard its morals," for which purpose the executive in question is presumed to have the necessary power; and, having this power, he exercises it in the making of laws "which are binding upon all living within his domain." "It is on this ground," Suárez continues, "that he is empowered to punish aliens who commit crimes" within his jurisdiction. But this is not enough for Suárez. By "aliens"—as he has been using the term—we would understand foreign persons actually resident within the domain. However, Suárez here enlarges his conception to include within the power of the civil governor the right "to bind by his laws all persons engaged in activities within his realm," provided, of course, that such compulsion on his part "is necessary to the welfare of that realm." In short, the law in question would apply not only to permanent alien residents within the country, but also to temporary residents and even to transients.

In the two preceding proofs, Suárez has considered the matter primarily from the point of view of the act of the state in which the aliens reside. Now he turns to the third proof, which pertains to foreigners within the state. "The same truth," he declares, "is evident from the standpoint of the aliens" and "there are grounds sufficient to justify their subjection to such an extent that they may be bound by the laws of the territory." Suárez does not mean that foreigners should be assimilated to natives nor, on the other hand, that they are to be discriminated against. The duration or degree of subjection, in Suárez' opinion, is not determined by the length of stay in the country. On the contrary, the degree of subjection is the same regardless of the length of residence, "the sole requirement for that subjection being actual sojourn and presence, even though that sojourn may be of short duration."

There then follows a passage in which Suárez displays that keenness, that subtlety, that penetration of thought which characterizes him when at his best, and there can be no doubt that it is not merely the philosopher, or indeed the jurist, but also the *litterateur* as well as the logician who speaks: "For just as a man in changing his domicile from one place to another, by that very act manifests his will to be bound permanently by the laws of that [new] territory, or else become bound in consequence of his act and despite his will to the contrary; even so any person who wills to sojourn in a given locality for a brief time, by that very act manifests or should manifest a will to subject himself temporarily to the government of that territory in everything relating to general customs and laws." So much for the *litterateur*. Now for the logician: "This statement is confirmed by reversing the argument. For an inhabitant of any territory, withdrawing from it for a brief period, at once and throughout that period ceases to be bound by the laws thereof, according to the argument of the preceding chapter; and, consequently, during that time, he is not actually a subject. Hence the converse will also hold true; for the principle is the same, and equity demands that in both cases equality—that is to say, due proportion"—here the Greek wins over the Latin—"shall be observed."

Here Suárez pauses to consider the question of "scandal" in its relation to the obligation of the alien. He was of the opinion that the mere desire to avoid scandal was not the true basis of the obligation, although granting that it "accidentally increases the obligation." What, then, is its real relationship to the obligation? "At the most an occasion or motive," Suárez answers, "which impels the legislator to make the law." But suppose this occasion or motive has lapsed. Does the obligation survive? Yes; because the obligation is not due to scandal: the obligation is due to the law, and therefore, as long as the law exists, the obligation exists, "just as," Suárez says, "the carrying of arms is forbidden, to prevent quarrels, and women are forbidden to adorn themselves in one way or another,"—we quote Suárez as a good churchman, giving his exact words in order on this occasion to disassociate ourselves from his personal opinion—"to avoid scandal." But, as he said above, "the obligation to abstain from these acts exists," not because of the scandal, but *"per se,* by reason of the laws themselves." Of course, in this connection, strangers are bound to conform to the same extent as the subjects, "not only for the sake of avoiding scandal, but also because of the law itself and because they are under a sufficient obligation to obedience, as has been explained." Here we have again a cleancut expression of the opinion of Suárez that residence is a fundamental element of jurisdiction.

This does not mean, however, that aliens should be in all respects subject to the same law as are the residents of the country in which they may happen to sojourn. They should, however, be subject to law, and it is the province and the right of the lawmaking power of the country to determine the content and application of the law affecting them. In the opinion of Suárez, non-residents might have a "peculiar mode of living," or be "located in a given place" and therefore "in many matters, they may require separate statutes." To this extent they are, he says again, subjects, "by the mere fact of their sojourn." There is, however, a twofold requirement: that the special laws applicable to foreigners "be just and expedient, not only to the locality in question, but also to the non-residents themselves," observing, as Suárez discriminatingly says, "a due proportion between the two," in order that they may thus "satisfy every qualification for placing the non-residents under a valid obligation."

Turning now to the coercive element of law, Suárez maintains that it applies not merely to natives and to foreigners who may be domiciled in the country, but to temporary residents, or even to transients. For a transgression of a law of the country renders persons of each and all of these classes equally liable to punishment, "either through a judge or through [the force of] the law itself, if it involves a penalty *ipso facto.*"

Why does Suárez, it may be asked, mention specifically a penalty *ipso facto*? Because in his opinion, and he so says, the "directive power would not be efficacious unless coercive power were annexed thereto." Furthermore, the alien is bound not only in conscience, but in law, to obedience, and this being the case, in transgressing law, "he commits an offence" both in the territory and against the state, and in consequence, "by reason of this offence also he remains subject to the coercive power of the commonwealth in question." This rule was subject, however, to one limitation, that "the non-resident foreigner shall not be superior in rank to the author of the law in question," that is, the sovereign power of the state, "since no superior can be subjected to an inferior by coercive authority." Nor, it may be added, in our own behalf, may sovereigns equal in authority, or their representatives, be subjected one to the other, since the inequality of superior to inferior is lacking.

This means that a sovereign, or his official representative (that is, ambassador) coming within the jurisdiction in question is not subject to the laws, because being equal, he is not inferior, and, according to the conception which Suárez upholds, it is only the inferior who is obliged to yield to coercive authority. This, it may be stated in passing, is international law as approved by the centuries.

It may also be said in passing, without dwelling upon what is self-evident, that a statute may be enacted to punish offenses which, as Suárez says, "may be committed in the future." Such is the case with most laws; indeed they should not be retroactive.

Suárez now proceeds to discuss the third of the three elements with which he began this chapter, that of form, giving concrete examples, such as a will or a contract made within a given territory which, as he had previously said, without pausing to give examples, should follow the laws of the realm in all such matters. The will or the contract of an alien subject would clearly be void, Suárez says—and it should be void—if not made in the form prescribed by the laws of the land. The reason for this is the universality of law within the jurisdiction to which it applies, for if it were not universally applicable, it would cease, in so far as the exception is concerned, to be a law, but would to that extent become a privilege, and, according to Suárez, the alien is not accorded a privilege any more than is the native inhabitant. Therefore the law of the country "obliges all persons in that locality to observe also the form of procedure which it prescribes; and, just as it includes the power to punish, so also it includes the power to invalidate."

Suárez had previously cited a will of an alien by way of example. He now proceeds to the question of taxes as a further illustration; for is anything—in the words of our Franklin—more certain than death and taxes? Not inappropriately, therefore, Suárez asks "whether a foreigner is bound to pay them"—meaning taxes. Fortunately for us citizens, he confines his attention to "a foreigner," and answers his own question in the affirmative. If the alien owns property within a given country, upon which, according to the laws obtaining in that country, a tax is due; or, as Suárez adds, if he performs any act in that place which is subject to tax by the laws of the country, "then there will be an obligation to pay that tax, . . . generally speaking, and"—a proviso which we would expect in all of the principles which Suárez lays down—"assuming that the tax is a just one." The case is otherwise with regard to those taxes "which are of a personal nature." Thus, to give a further example, which Suárez no doubt had in mind but which he did not himself cite, a foreigner temporarily resident in a given locality, would not be subject to a poll tax, although if during his sojourn he purchased a house or lands, or entered into a transaction subject to the internal revenue laws of the realm, he would be subject to taxes in the same manner as in the case of natives of the country.

There are many and interesting examples which could be cited in addition to those which Suárez has given; and although they were sufficient for his purpose, a few others which are of interest in our day and in our country are mentioned to show that Suárez did not write for his day but for all time, just as he wrote not for his own country but for all countries.

Let us take the case of foreigners who come to our shores but who, by the laws of the United States, can not themselves become naturalized citizens.[49] We shall also suppose that they have a child born after their arrival. That child is, by virtue of the Fourteenth Amendment to the Constitution,[50] an American citizen because the child is born within and subject to the jurisdiction of the United States. Such also is the nationality of a child born in American jurisdiction of foreign parents in transit through the United States. In both these cases the laws of the country apply to the foreigner as to the native, in that their children are American citizens if born within the United States. This is citizenship *ex jure soli.* As a result of the law, in many foreign countries, where nationality depends upon *jus sanguinis,* the child born in the United States of foreign parents might have a double nationality. Thus under the law of countries adopting the test of blood relationship, the child in question would have not only American nationality but the nationality of his parents as well.

It is pertinent to reconsider for a moment the view of Victoria, who held that a child should and could have only the nationality of the place of birth;[51] for does he not say explicitly that the child in question has the nationality of the country in which he is born,

---

[49] Act of May 6, 1882 [22 STAT. 61 (1882), 8 U. S. C. § 363 (1926)]:
"That hereafter no State court or court of the United States shall admit Chinese to citizenship; and all laws in conflict with this act are hereby repealed."

[50] "Sec. 1. All persons born or naturalized in the United States, and subject to the jurisdiction thereof, are citizens of the United States and of the State wherein they reside. No State shall make or enforce any law which shall abridge the privileges or immunities of citizens of the United States; nor shall any State deprive any person of life, liberty, or property, without due process of law; nor deny to any person within its jurisdiction the equal protection of the laws."

[51] *De Indis,* pp. 153-4: "If children of any Spaniard be born there and they wish to acquire citizenship, it seems they can not be barred either from citizenship or from the advantages enjoyed by other citizens—I refer to the case where the parents had their domicile there. The proof of this is furnished by the rule of the law of nations, that he is to be called and is a citizen who is born within the state (*Code,* VII. lxxii. 11). And the confirmation lies in the fact that, as man is a civil animal, whoever is born in any one state is not a citizen of another state. Therefore, if he were not a citizen of the state referred to, he would not be a citizen of any state, to the prejudice of his rights under both natural law and the law of nations."

and, if he did not have this nationality, he would be stateless, because he could not have the nationality of a country in which he was not born? This view, it may be said in passing, has two great virtues. It gives every human being a single nationality, and leaves no human being without a nationality.

We have ourselves instanced on a previous page [52] the exemption of a sovereign from the laws of a foreign country within whose jurisdiction he may happen to be, as an illustration of the rule that a law, to be binding, must be the law of a superior. It is therefore a consequence of the immunity of the sovereign from the laws of the country in which he happens to sojourn that in the case of a child born to an ambassador or minister or diplomatic agent (to use an all-inclusive term)—who is, as the agent of the foreign sovereign power, exempt from the jurisdiction of the country to which he is accredited or through which he happens to pass—such a child is born a citizen or subject of the country of the ambassador, minister, or diplomatic agent in question.

* * * * * * * *

Custom played a large part in the growth of law, and indeed it was and continues to be the source of much of the law, especially in the case of the law of nations. It is not surprising, therefore, that Suárez devoted an entire book (the seventh of his *De Legibus*) to custom, its origin, its nature and its effects.

Custom, Suárez says, both preceded and followed law. It preceded it inevitably because custom is the unwritten law and custom antedated writing; and it followed law because custom is ever with us. Speaking of "law" in a formal sense, Suárez says, "it is certain . . . that the written is the principal form of law," and he adds that from it "custom derives in great measure its strength and meaning." In custom three terms are first to be noted: *usus, mos, consuetudo,* which are "closely kindred in meaning" and the result of "free—that is, properly human—action." The word "free" is of no small importance, because it implies voluntary action, and without voluntary action custom, as

[52] *Supra,* p. 209.

such, can not arise, as Suárez demonstrates more fully in a later passage.

As three terms are used, there must be a difference between them, however closely they may be allied. Thus *usus* (and indeed so it is with the English equivalent) applies "equally to a general habit of action and to single actions"; but the term "*mos* . . . may not properly be applied to a single action as *usus* may be, but only to a repetition of like actions." Differing in definition, they are, however, "practically the same" in their relation to the general subject of custom, St. Thomas ascribing to both the same meaning—"the repetition of a voluntary action." Custom is a thing of two elements, Suárez says: one being "formal custom," a "series of repeated actions," identical with "usage" in that both are voluntary and matter of fact; the second element is the "after effect of repeated acts." In a merely material sense, the distinction is more apparent than real, inasmuch as each element is, after all, a matter of fact. Therefore Suárez passes to the spiritual conception inherent in another phase of the second element of custom. His exact language is—"a second after effect is one of the moral order, a faculty compelling the performance of a certain action or nullifying another obligation." This he calls "customary law or a legal rule introduced by custom." But it is not every custom which creates "a legal rule," in confirmation of which he immediately adds that "an evil custom . . . creates no legal force; nor does one that grows out of the observance of a law—although it is spoken of as custom." For, in truth, what is implicit in a law is part of the law and therefore not custom. Therefore, "to limit our definition," continues Suárez, "to that custom of fact which is capable of introducing law, we must include in it . . . the note that the custom is an authorized repetition of actions that contravene no established law." Thus the custom of fact, which in the usual course of events can introduce law, must not be in opposition to the laws already in existence; for the custom which Suárez has at present in mind is only, as we have seen, that "authorized repetition of actions that contravene no established law"; or again, it must be custom "in which all the conditions required by the law are fulfilled."

There are exceptions, of course, to this statement, and these, as we shall see, Suárez takes up in subsequent pages. While custom is a thing of practice, there is practice and practice. There must be "public practice" of the community, in order that custom may generate law and its strict obligation. Therefore the converse is true. "Private practice of a person," or indeed "of a family," is not sufficient to establish a "legal rule." In a word, the custom which "suffices to introduce law must be drawn from the general practice of the people," that is, of "the community as a whole"; or, as in the case of the law of nations and the international community, "of all, or the greater part of its members." That is to say, custom is the generator of law; and in the sense in which the term customary law is used by Suárez, it is popular law as distinct from legislative law. In the Anglo-Saxon system, it becomes "common law."

Suárez has before defined the term *jus,* but in connection with "custom," he finds it necessary to consider this term afresh. Therefore he says that it "has two meanings," the one signifying "the faculty of use," that is to say, "ownership or quasi-ownership"; while in the second sense *jus* is defined by Suárez as "a right that carries the power to bind and command: . . . the right of law or legal right." This is law in the strict legal sense of the analytical school of jurisprudence—a command imposed by a superior, with a penalty for disobedience; and the rights under this law are not natural rights but the rights of man-made law.

Suárez observes that in his two definitions of *jus* lies the distinction between "custom" in the legal sense and "prescription"; for prescription may arise from private use by an individual and therefore is not general custom, which arises only from public use; hence prescription can not generate law but can only confer a right of ownership—in other words, *jus* in the sense first defined by Suárez. Instead of introducing a legal rule, "prescription" confers rather "a right of ownership or one of a similar kind"; and he renders the definition more explicit by examples such as "the use or enjoyment of some material thing, as a house, an article of clothing; or, of an immaterial thing, as, the exercise of jurisdiction or the right of suffrage." The contrast is further brought out by Suárez' statement that "a custom of the people is essential for the kind of *jus* which is law"; whereas in general "usage of a private person is sufficient for prescription," although the community "as a moral person" may at times exercise in its own behalf a prescriptive right.

Further illustrating the distinction between custom and prescription Suárez says that "for the validity of a true, legal custom . . . the consent of the community, or of the sovereign against whom the prescription is in a certain sense obtained is necessary." The consent of the community is unnecessary, however, in the case of prescription against a private person, that is, prescription in the ordinary sense of the term. In the first instance, Suárez is speaking of prescription against the community or against its sovereign by the community, which is not prescription in the usual legal meaning of the term; in the second case he is referring to prescription, as such, that is, against private individuals, in which case consent is not necessary, and here again Suárez proves himself to be a lawyer as well as a theologian. The prescription against the community—that is to say, against the sovereign authority of the community—establishes custom if the community consents to it; the prescription of a private individual does not. In custom, as in prescription, time is an element, but it differs in duration. The length of time for prescription, Suárez says, "is fixed by law." On the other hand, there is no time limit in the matter of custom; "rather," says Suárez, "that period suffices which gives time for manifesting the consent of the sovereign or of the people."

In the conclusion stated in the third chapter of Book VII, Suárez, for the benefit of lawyer as well as layman, distinguishes the various kinds of custom in the legal sense, saying that from the "variety of custom arises a variety and multiplicity in customary law." We shall group the varieties in numbered paragraphs.

1. "If the community is ecclesiastical its custom will introduce ecclesiastical law." But suppose that, in the words of Suárez,

"the custom be that of the whole Church." The result will be the creation of "a general rule of canon law concerning which" —as he well knew—"there are many decrees." If the custom were that of a whole ecclesiastical province, there would result what might be termed a national ecclesiastical law of custom; while if the custom were that of a particular bishopric, "then the law" would be, so to speak, "synodal or diocesan"; should it be "of a private chapter or community, the law will be, as it were, municipal."

Thus far Suárez the theologian. Now for Suárez the lawyer:

2. "The same sort of relation will hold true," he continues, "of the civil customs." Thus it is that, "if the custom be that of one kingdom, it will be, so to speak, that of the realm," and may introduce a civil law applicable to the entire country. If, again, the custom applies to one province, but not to others, it may bring into being what we might call a "provincial" law, or, if we are to speak of still narrower limits, those of the city or town, then the custom arising within such a municipality may introduce municipal law.

Now for the third category of legal custom, that giving rise to—

3. "General civil law," that is to say, law arising from similar customs in different countries, with the result that these laws, in howsoever many different jurisdictions they may apply, are the same. It is such a general civil law which was often termed the *jus gentium,* meaning not laws between the states but similar laws within the states; "and," observes Suárez, "even though their laws are sometimes alike in respect of a certain custom, they observe not one, but many customs which are like one another; just as in various kingdoms there will be many laws that are alike, but the law of one is not binding on the subjects of any other."

This category of customs arises within different communities and relates to matters of national concern. And however numerous these different communities with identical customs may be, the customs are not, in the international sense, universal since they deal with internal and not international matters; if they were international they would be, in the conception of Suárez, a part of the law of nations, which, in Suárez' day and in our own, was custom not within nations but between nations.

Having distinguished custom of fact from custom of law and having also distinguished the varieties of customary law arising within a country, Suárez now makes what he terms "a third principal division of custom," and under the first head is "that which is according to law"; the second, that which is "beyond the ambit of the existing law"; and the third, "that counter to law." This threefold division applies to custom in relation to the three branches of law, to "the natural law, to positive divine law, and to human law."

Let us confine our attention for the moment to the application of these three division of custom to the natural law. On this point Suárez says positively that "no custom . . . can exist outside of the ambit of that law." A particular custom may, of course, be spoken of as being "in accord with the natural law, since it proceeds from it, and through it the natural law is observed," but since custom can not exist outside of natural law, a usage which is contrary to that law and violates it is not, in the words of Suárez, "worthy of the name of custom." Indeed, he says, in no uncertain terms, "it rather merits that given it in the language of the laws—corruption." Hence such a so-called custom can "have no effect on law, either by abrogating or introducing it"—and this on no less an authority than St. Thomas Aquinas—"since the law of nature is, as we have seen, immutable and so cannot be abrogated."

There is another kind of custom which may in a sense be outside the natural law, in that it consists, as Suárez points out, of "actions that are, according to a probable opinion, indifferent" to the law natural; or it may consist of "good actions, which although they are approved by the natural law or enjoined by it as to mode or manner . . . are not absolutely enjoined as to performance." In this sense, custom is related not to the mandatory or prohibitory phases of natural law but to its concessive phase.

What, we may now ask, is the relation of custom to the law

of nations? It may be in conformity therewith, but in such a case it is "an extension of universal custom and is consequently the same law and not a new one." But may a custom be contrary to the *jus gentium*? This is quite another matter. Certain jurists held that such a custom could not "introduce law." But to Suárez the matter was but one of terminology; if the term "*jus gentium*" was used in the sense of international law, there was no difficulty. "I believe, therefore," he says in the first person, "it must be agreed that it is not absolutely inconceivable that a part of the law of nations should be cancelled by custom." The reason was that the law of nations, although related to the natural law, was not natural law and therefore that what is "contrary" merely to the law of nations, as such, is not intrinsically wrong as would be the case were it contrary to natural law. A familiar example here meets us, that "respecting the slavery of prisoners captured in war." This was a practice introduced by the *jus gentium* but one which, Suárez says "may be"—we are glad to add "is"—"abolished by custom." But such abrogation by custom can apply only to part of the law of nations, because "it is morally impossible that the whole of this law could be abolished." Why? To bring about a total abolition all nations would need to concur in "a custom contrary to the *jus gentium*"—meaning the law of nations in its entirety. But indeed, as Suárez points out, "such uniformity in any matter is rarely attained," and in the matter in hand there is an additional and special reason why uniformity would be rare, in that the *jus gentium* is in close harmony with nature. Man, we may observe, rarely departs from nature, and then only at his peril.

This does not mean, however, that an individual nation may not under special circumstances adopt "a custom contrary to the *jus gentium*." In such a case, the citizens or subjects of the nation in question would be bound by the custom; but the custom may not prejudice the rights of any other nation or the rights of its subjects, for while a nation can renounce the exercise of a right for itself or for its people, it may not renounce the right in behalf of another nation.

Suárez reinforces his opinion on this point by an example as up to date today as it was in his—the use of highways. "If," he says, "in some territory passage over highways were permitted only upon irksome conditions, such a custom could not extend to foreigners who allow such passage without such conditions." This is not only a matter of equal treatment but of reciprocity. There are, we may add, certain minor restrictions of traffic which would not constitute "the irksome conditions" of Suárez. Thus, the American motorist on the English highways will find that the customary traffic rules of the country require him to keep to the left instead of to the right. This requirement may sometimes be "irksome" to him personally—accustomed as he is to the American rule, "keep to the right"—but it is not in violation of the law of nations. However, if the cause for a restriction of this nature should cease to exist, it is the view of Suárez that the restriction itself would then be unjust, for it would be "contrary to the natural law to extend such a custom to foreigners."

Suárez, trained as a schoolman, had what we must call an ingrained habit of meeting and forestalling objections to any and every solution; and it is permissible to say that many a modern solution could not withstand this test of the schoolman's logic. It was generally admitted, according to Suárez, that a "prince may not exact anything contrary to the *jus gentium,* because his jurisdiction is inferior thereto," and it might therefore be argued, "neither can the custom of one nation derogate from the *jus gentium,* because the custom is no more powerful than the law of one sovereign." But Suárez is ready with a reply. What the prince might not do alone, the prince, with that most fundamental of elements of Suárez' society—the consent of the people—might do; and indeed Suárez is of opinion that, even without the consent of the prince, the community might establish a rule contrary to the *jus gentium* "by common consent and custom." This is a matter of such importance that it is well to examine closely what Suárez has in mind. He is not dealing with an untrammelled right of nations to unmake the law of nations at their will. What he does have in mind is relief from the application of a certain rule of the law of nations which might be unsuitable under conditions peculiar to a particular country. Thus, speaking of the ruler as a prince—and meaning thereby a prince who governs his country for its own good—he says: "I maintain that a prince may, perhaps, enact a law contrary to the *jus gentium* by departing therefrom in the non-observance of some rule which is deemed inexpedient in his territories and for his subjects." Now for his example, which makes clear the conception of Suárez. "For example," he continues, "he"—meaning the prince—"might enact not a law against slavery, but one that all men should be free, or something similar." It should be added that under the law of nations of Suárez' day, slavery was still permitted; therefore a ruler might not enact a law directly abolishing it; or, as Chief Justice Marshall said in the *Antelope case,*[53] no single nation may make a law of nations. The most that the prince could do would be to derogate from the law of nations by the passage of a law applicable only within his domain and to his own subjects, that "all men should be free"—an act on his part not in opposition to natural reason or the proper government of the state. For it is by these two factors that the propriety of such a law must invariably be tested.

This is but an incident by way of illustration. The right of the prince is not limited to this example for just as he might enact a law contrary to a municipal custom of his realms, so also he may, Suárez says, "make a rule contrary to that portion of the *jus gentium* which affects his government." The reason? The law of nations is, by "its universality alone," not "the stronger or more immutable with respect to his subjects; it is only so with respect to [his relations with] other nations."

The right to hold slaves was, in Suárez' day, a universal right, but the prince had the power to renounce it on behalf of his subjects. Fortunately all civilized nations have today seen fit to take the same action.

The people of a state may renounce a right which it possesses under the law of nations, but they can not renounce a right of other nations, because such renunciation is and must always

[53] 10 Wheat. 66 (1825).

depend upon the consent of the people to whom the right belongs.

"Custom of fact" is a series of actions as distinct from a rule which may arise from a series of actions: the one being a matter of fact; the other a matter of law. Thus Suárez looks upon custom of fact as "a form of observance of a pre-existing law." The repetition of actions (which is called "custom of fact") must be in conformity with the law, as otherwise it would constitute a series of illegal actions; and therefore, in the main, custom is conformity with law already in existence. It is not always, perhaps, a direct observance of the law in the sense that the actions are permitted merely with a view to complying with the law. Nevertheless they are, as Suárez says, a form of observance, in that they comply with, and are not contrary to, the law already in existence.

In a word, in Suárez' conception, custom of fact as distinct from custom which has become law is to be looked upon not as making but as evidence of the law; and in behalf of Suárez, a statute of the Permanent Court of International Justice[54] may be invoked, prescribing among the principles which the court shall apply "international custom, as evidence of a general practice accepted as law." Custom as thus conceived is a matter of evidence, rather than of the introduction of law; or, stated in still another way: it is the fulfilment and not the creation of law. "Wherefore," continues Suárez, "Baldus . . . truly says that a custom in harmony with law is not regulative in character but one which is imitative of the law, or, as it were executive."

What happens to custom, however, if the law of which the custom of fact is evidence should be abrogated by another law? Suárez replies on the authority of the Gloss[55] and of Panormitanus[56] that the custom which grew out of the observance of the law is then "abolished also, even if no mention is made of it." This could only be so if the custom is looked upon as a part of the law. If the case were otherwise, the custom would

[54] Statute of the Permanent Court of International Justice, Article 38, § 2.
[55] On *Sext.* I. iv. 1.
[56] On *Decretals,* I. iv. 11, n. 21.

be independent of the law and therefore would continue to exist notwithstanding the abrogation of the law. Indeed, custom of fact may be said to confirm the law, or, as the statute of the Permanent Court of International Justice puts it, it may be "evidence of the law." Or as Gratian,[58] the authority upon which Suárez relies, held: "Laws are established when they are promulgated; confirmed when they are approved by the practice [*mores*] of those who use them,"—a matter which Bartolus[59] explains by saying that "such custom confirms the law not directly, but by holding back or prohibiting, that is, the opposite custom and the abrogation of the law." And as Suárez puts it, "this sort of custom"—meaning custom of fact—"may be said to bear aid to the law . . . since the custom makes easier the observance of the law, and, in a certain sense, [the law itself] less liable to change." There is thus a protective function of custom of fact in its relation to law.

But, in addition, custom may be said "to interpret the law, indeed it is called in the law *'an excellent interpreter of the law.'*" The reason? Because "it"—custom—"indicates in what sense the law was originally made and received."

Those who have read, and especially pondered, Suárez, have a suspicion that there is no limit to the depth and subtlety of his exposition; but a merciful man at heart, he relieves our apprehensions by coming to a "finally" in his discussion "of another effect" of custom of fact, namely, "the extension of law"; and the illustration he takes is of his calling: that "a law may be made originally for laymen only" but that, as a result of custom, "clerics" follow it and it becomes a law for them as for laymen.

Turning now to custom according to law, Suárez points out that it may be defined in two senses: first in the sense that it "exists by force of law and by its command"; and secondly, "in the sense that it is modelled on the law, in its likeness, that it imitates it." Although both senses relate to custom according to law, it is the first of these conceptions of custom with which

[58] *Decretum*, I. iv. 3.
[59] On *Digest*, I. iii. 32, n. 4.

Suárez wishes at present to deal. Recurring to the matter of interpretation, which he had already mentioned, Suárez continues that "such custom does not really extend law except by way of the interpretation that it may give to the words of the law." And he draws a distinction, saying that in the example of the clerics above given the custom is not according to the law, in the interpretive sense. Why? Because "it does not proceed from the civil law, but from the free will of those who wished to perform what the civil law prescribed, even if they are not bound thereby."

Another "finally"—in this case a "lastly". Suárez divides custom "into positive and privative or negative custom." Now "positive usage" is the origin of the former, consisting, to the extent that it is custom of fact, "in a certain repitition of actions," but, in so far as it is custom of law, "it sets up an inclination and an obligation to act," whereas a "negative custom" is negative in the sense that it is passive in character, originating "from non-usage"; but "to the extent that this non-usage is frequent and continuous," it assumes the characteristics of custom, being indeed "of a quasi-positive nature"; and to this extent it approaches the custom of law, for where "it establishes some legal rule," it fosters, as in the case of the positive custom, "an inclination and obligation to refrain from action."

But whatever form custom may assume — chameleon-like though it seems betimes to be—it must always possess as a constant element, a moral character. For as law can not truly be said to exist unless it be moral, so custom of any kind or variety can not establish a legal obligation unless it be a moral custom.

From the beginning, the conception of the Spanish School was that of the morality of law, and therefore the custom with which its members dealt could not be immoral—or indeed unmoral—for morality, in their conception, was the essence of good law whether natural, statutory, or customary.

Suárez having hitherto dealt in some detail with the effect of custom upon law, now turns to the opposite phase of the matter, as it were,—the effect of law upon custom, and the first of these effects is the annulment of custom by law in one way or another.

Of these ways there are no less than three, and Suárez ventures to add a fourth. First there is abrogation of custom by law; then prohibition of custom by law; third, condemnation of custom; and the fourth, which he has attempted to add—and which, as a matter of fact, he does add—is "an unqualified opposition to custom."

First of abrogation, which is not necessarily "equivalent to a condemnation" of custom, because the abrogation may occur, not because the custom is of an unreasonable nature but merely because "it pleases the lawmaker" to abrogate the custom, on the ground that this course is the "more expedient" under existing conditions. Law should look to the greater rather than to the lesser expedient.

In the case of prohibition, not merely the existing custom but that which "is to be established," is prohibited; in other words, the law not merely prohibits the present custom but checks its introduction in the future.

Now for condemnation, which the law may accomplish in either of two ways: "by a purely declaratory law; and by a law passed to quiet a doubt." If the custom is condemned by a declaratory law, it would be on the ground that the custom is obviously so "base as to be contrary to natural or divine law"; or else because it is not merely "useless" but "harmful to general welfare." Let us suppose, however, that it is not clearly evident whether the custom is good or bad. In this case, the law which condemns it will, as Suárez states, "quiet a doubt." Such a condemnation is "unquestionably" within the province of human law and "especially" of the canon law; and may be in the highest degree proper in the interest of good morals.

The fourth of the ways in which law may affect custom Suárez has previously referred to as "opposition"; but he now uses a different term for the sake of precision, namely, "interruption." How can this be brought about? The interruption of a custom can only be "by the whole community in which the custom has been followed." Such a view is in conformity with the doctrine of government by majority, for which Suárez firmly stands. "For," he says, "the acts of a few private individuals do not annul the consent of the community," and therefore they "can not destroy a general custom." If, however, the community has delegated power to a chief executive (whether prince or president), then the interruption—or, to use another term employed by Suárez, "suppression"—of the custom might be brought about through "the public authority of the one holding the necessary power," not necessarily by a direct abolition of the custom but by decreeing a public punishment for an individual who had observed the custom, thus indicating that the custom, in the language of Suárez, "was not in accord with the will of the Prince."

These matters were, in a way, preliminary to the more profound examination of custom which we would expect from Suárez; and with the preliminaries out of the way, he is now ready to consider "the matter and form in the constitution of a custom." As regards the former—meaning the matter—he finds that custom and human law are similar, if not identical: "in so far as the custom is a juridical entity its matter is the same as that of written human law." The difference between them is rather one of form, or, in Suárez' words, "in the mode of expression through which they exist."

As a result of the labor of lawmakers throughout the centuries, certain definite prerequisites of form and expression have come into use for written statutes, but, as Suárez points out, "in the law of custom, there is no special form, sensible and external." There is indeed nothing except those actions which constitute custom, and these, continues Suárez, "in so far as they are tokens of consent, may be called the unwritten words by which this kind of law is engraved upon the memory of men."

There is an additional distinction which arises in the comparison between custom and written law. The statute does not go into effect until it is promulgated. Not so with the custom, for which "no promulgation is required"; and the reason for this is stated with maximlike brevity—"custom, through the usage itself, is its own public manifestation and promulgation."

Suárez now turns to another phase of the relation between custom and law: what is the result if a private custom is in conflict with a general law? This brings us again to the question of prescription; for, as Suárez points out, an exemption from the obligation of the law might result from obtaining a prescriptive right through custom, since the acquistion of this right "may change the matter" of the law and thus "terminate the obligation of that law." To illustrate this, Suárez refers to the fact that "a private custom can exempt, or rather remove the obligation of the law from, a certain person." Here, however, what happens is not a "derogation from the general law, but an abolition of its subject-matter"; and a change of subject-matter as a result of change of circumstances, as Suárez had already pointed out, and as he here reiterates, may even affect the natural law. From which fact the principle which he has just stated gained, he felt, a notable support.

So much for private custom and its effect on law through prescription. But may such a custom have a direct effect on law, or, in the words of Suárez, may it "derogate from the general law by abating its obligation directly and of its own force"? The answer to this question is an unequivocal denial, stated in the first person. "This we maintain is impossible." Why? "Because a private custom of breaking the law never excuses the fault; on the contrary, it rather increases it."

This does not mean, however, that law can not be changed by a group of individuals, although it does mean that individuals acting alone can not change the law. Not every group of individuals, however, has the power in question. Thus a legal custom, in Suárez' language, can not be "introduced by any community whatever, but only by one possessing the capacity for legislative authority over itself; or, at least, by a community of sufficient perfection to be the subject of the law properly so-called."

What is this community? The *civitas,* or state. The reason for this limitation on the introduction of legal custom is, in simplest terms, that law derives its consent from the community, the general rule in such a matter being that only the majority, not the minority—much less the individual—can act for the people, whether in the making of law or in the formation of custom or the unmaking of either; because, as we have ourselves said, custom is popular law. In the words of Suárez, "the consent, therefore, of the majority of the community is also to be held as that of the whole community, and sufficient, consequently, for the establishment of custom."

In this case, it is sufficient that the custom be of itself a public one; and in the case of custom, as of other law, ignorance is no excuse, provided that knowledge may be had, and is had, by the majority. How is the majority, or the major portion, to be computed? Fortunately Suárez found that there was "a general agreement on this point," the majority or major portion consisting "only" of "such persons as can give consent to a legal custom." This excludes infants and all mentally defective persons. Suárez, celebrated as he was and living in the world but, as it were, not a part of it, curiously had observed that this perfect community consisted not merely of men but of men and women. He was aware, as are we of what is termed a more "modern" age, that "some would also exclude women entirely, on the ground that they can exercise no legislative authority." And as far as the United States are concerned, it is proper to add, the Nineteenth Amendment to the Constitution has ended that myth. Over three centuries ago, however, Suárez, speaking of the exclusion of women, and of men below the age of twenty-five, declared in words which can not be too often quoted, as they do him infinite credit: "Some would also exclude women entirely, on the ground that they can exercise no legislative authority. Among men, they exclude all below the age of twenty-five years. However, I cannot find any basis in law or any justification"—mark the words —"in reason for the exclusion of the last two groups." Francisco Suárez is rightly considered as a great theologian and philosopher, and a no less great jurist, and these qualities his various works demonstrate beyond the possibility of successful contradiction, but in the quotation which we have just made of his exact language, Suárez proclaims himself as a feminist in a day when feminism was hardly a dream, let alone a hope.

In his discussion of the state, which we do not dwell upon in this connection, it may be observed that Suárez is the outspoken advocate of consent in law, law being made by the consent of the people when it is not directly made by them. Here, however, is a short passage, which may be considered as a resumé of the doctrine applying to custom. After saying that custom can only exist through a succession of actions, he then gives as a reason that "the custom in question requires the consent of the people, and of the Prince"; and he adds that "such a multiplication of actions will be held sufficient as will make known the consent of the people"—mark again the words, for Suárez is even today the formidable advocate of government by compact—"and the tacit approval of the Prince."

If the contention of Suárez be correct that it is only the people, and a majority of them, who can make custom, it follows necessarily that a single individual can not make custom, even though he be a judge, for a judge is authorized not to make, but to declare and apply law. The matter is of such moment, owing to the widespread objection and opposition to judge-made law, that the language of Suárez on this point is more than ordinarily important. "If the judge," he says, "rendering the opinion is not a sovereign Prince, and so does not possess legislative authority, his decision, even if it is given more than once, or if it is repeated by different judges of the same rank, does not, on the mere ground of the number of acts performed, have the effect of making law."

In law made by custom, as in all kinds of law, there must be a standard, and the standard is that the custom be founded in reason and not in error. "For if it has been established through error," Suárez says, then it would follow that, "upon discovery of the error, there disappears the apparent reason which might justify such a custom." What, then, is the consequence? "The custom itself lapses also, because it cannot exist without reason." And then follow within a modest compass further examples of what may be termed Suárez' "purple patches": "Wherefore, even though the custom will seem to stand and to establish law before the error is detected, it will do so only from an erroneous conscience; for when the truth is known, the force of the custom vanishes. It was never, therefore, true law, but merely thought to be such; and the same is true of the custom itself."

Suárez now passes from error in fact to error in law, in its effect on custom, and here again he must be allowed to speak for himself. "An error in law," he says, not less than an error of fact, "removes the element of consent in the establishment of law. For in those customs which in no way touch existing law, there can be no error as to law, save by the misapprehension that their subject-matter is either forbidden or enjoined."

There is a further passage, in which Suárez lets himself go, if such an expression be permissible in the case of so distinguished a person:

> I shall say no more than that there is a much stronger reason why in the case of custom fear should be a bar to validity: and that the reason is that for a custom mere actions are not sufficient; it is essential that those actions be performed with the intention of introducting custom, which intention is commonly tacit rather than expressed. But when the actions are done solely from fear—when they would not be done except under its compulsion—they lack that intention; nor can such an intention be morally presumed, since the fear in itself, in a certain way, excludes it. Thus a frequency of actions done solely through fear, is never a sufficient evidence of the public consent of a whole people to the establishment of a custom. There is the additional consideration that the Prince cannot be presumed in such a situation to give his consent, since he does not manifest a will that his subjects be forced to adopt customs of that kind under unjust fear. And if he himself brings force and fear to bear [upon his people], he commits an injury, since he has no right to wring from his people a consent by which they are to be bound. . . .

However broad a legal custom may be according to the classification which Suárez has made, the purpose and result of such a custom are to establish law where there was no law before, in contradistinction to the custom of fact; however, "not every unwritten law," Suárez points out, "is a law of custom" but only that which "has its origin in the customs and usages of a people." There might, as he says, be unwritten law established by the Prince, or by another executive—such as an officer of the Church—and subsequently it might continue to be observed "solely through the usage and tradition of his subjects." Herein lies the distinction between tradition and custom, and herein again we come upon a "purple patch," in which Suárez reiterates his faith in people and their government:

> . . . For a legal custom proceeds either from a free people, and hence, one having supreme power, and therefore, the power of enacting law; or, from one having a Pastor or Prince by whom it is governed. In this latter case, if a legal custom is thought of—as it should be—as proceeding not from a people apart from its sovereign but from the people jointly with its Prince, that is, a people that shares in some sufficient way in the legislative power of the Prince, either by possession of the power to make its own municipal laws or statutes, or by the approval of custom, whether this approval be made manifest by law itself or declared through tacit will: a custom, I say, proceeding from a people so united with its superior, proceeds from one in which clearly the power of legislation resides. . . . It is to the will of the people that the Prince (so to speak) conforms himself, by granting the people permission, as it were, to introduce such legal custom as it may wish; or, by approving of the popular intention, or confirming it.

What a pity that the views of Suárez did not prevail in his day and generation! Yet what a blessing it is that these views—although not through Suárez—are today as commonplaces in every civilized country of the world.

In a previous passage Suárez had referred, although not in detail, to the element of intention in voluntary custom, for, in his view custom, to establish law, must not only be voluntary but must conform to the intention of those by whom it was established; and the evidence of this will and intention of the people and of the obligation which springs from this custom and to which they must, in his view, consent, is, he says, "the custom of fact itself," that is to say, the series of actions by which the customary law is established; in a word, the evidence of the legal custom is the fact of the custom.

There are other means which are and should be used in testing the validity of custom. There is the test of reason, and the test of "sufficient usage." If a custom is in conformity with reason and if it has been established for an adequate period of time, we may safely assume that it is conducive to the public welfare and therefore that it should have "the binding power of law." The test of reason is an inherent and therefore a natural test, whereas the test of time is, we may say, artificial in that it is wholly arbitrary. The question which needs consideration here, then, is: what is an adequate period of time? The answer of Suárez is based on the authority of "prudent men," who, he says, "realizing this need, hold that a period of ten years is sufficient" for the establishment of a legal custom. Suppose, however, that the prince should not be in the country during this period or during a part of it? His absence would not affect the matter, for Suárez maintains that the ten-year period would suffice, irrespective of the presence or absence of the Prince. For, after all, the custom is that of the people, not of the ruler, and, while the latter might give his consent to custom if he were present in the country or even seek to oppose it if not present, the mere continued usage over an adequate period of time, by the people, who are themselves the source of power, is sufficient.

In the case of a custom as to which there may be a doubt, there are, Suárez says, four criteria. If the custom be "of long standing" —Suárez has just referred to the period of ten years—and is in the interest of "the general welfare, and imposes . . . a burden" —in other words, a duty, which assuredly would not be imposed if the people were not in favor of the custom—or if the observance of the custom is by "the major part of the people," then "we have," Suárez says, "sound evidence that the custom has been introduced out of a deliberate desire for the obligation that is established" or is being established by it. This is the first criterion.

The second is enlightened public opinion—that of "prudent and God-fearing men." If such men think ill of those who violate the custom, "or if the people generally are scandalized" at its non-observance, again "we have," Suárez says, "another strong indication of an intention on the part of the people to introduce customary law."

The third criterion concerns not the people but their prelates and governors, who, if they "gravely censure and punish those who do not follow the custom," thus supply "another important token of the binding character of the custom."

And "fourthly" and finally—and this is the supreme criterion—if the subject-matter with which the custom deals is so advantageous to the community as to make it essential for the public welfare that the custom be binding, then any doubt concerning it is disposed of: clearly the custom has been introduced for the good of the people. For the all-inclusive test of law, whether it be written or customary, is, after all, that the subject-matter of each and every variety be "morally sound, adapted to the public good, and, finally, reasonable"; for "reason," Suárez finely and impressively says, "is, as it were, the soul of both kinds of law."

It need not be said that Suárez has shown himself to be a consummate jurist and master in the legal forum. But he was also a churchman, and the forum of conscience was never absent from his thoughts. And if the written law is to be moral and its morality tested by conscience, so should custom be binding in conscience, for it is law—indeed, he expressly says in this passage, "it is true law"—and the obligation of customary law is, he adds, to be "judged" precisely as in the case of the written law, "according to the character of the subject-matter," if the will of the people has not otherwise provided.

There is therefore a sanction in the forum of conscience. Can custom provide a material sanction? The answer of Suárez is in the affirmative, to the effect that there may be a penal sanction, "for," he says, "what absurdity in reason can be shown in the possibility of a custom binding under a [physical] penalty as well as under [the moral one of] the stain of guilt?"

After having discussed the question of the abrogation of custom by law, Suárez reverses the question and asks whether a law may be abrogated by custom. His answer is in the affirmative; for the authority to abolish law, as well as to make law, is primarily in the people, and if through them a custom is established which is contrary to a given law, the law falls before the will of the people. The exercise of this power, however, is usually through the government which the people have established, and this power, Suárez says, "must be explained as resulting from a union of the people with their Prince and lawmaker," the reason being, Suárez adds, "that this power to put aside a law, as it exists in the people taken alone, is rather a factual than a legal one." The rôle which the prince plays in the matter is, we might say, that of a silent partner who supplies the legal formalities and has the "power to tolerate and give consent to the popular will."

Now, whether the people make their laws directly or whether they have delegatd their powers of lawmaking to their representatives, the effect is the same in so far as the abolition of laws by custom is concerned. It is sufficient, as Suárez observes, "that they have a capacity for law," and that the custom which is to abrogate the law should "be introduced by those to whom the law is to apply." The reason for this is that the repudiation of a law is not a matter of jurisdiction on the part of those in power nor is it a matter of the public authority which they exercise. It is "rather one that proceeds from those under a duty of obedience to the law," that is to say, a law should be repudiated only by those to whom it applies, and not by those who execute it.

A custom contrary to a law introduced by the people does not "actively," as Suárez says, abolish law. Rather the custom is the voice of the people demanding that "the superior . . . abolish the law." And woe betide him if he is deaf to the voice of his fellow-countrymen! The action of the people, therefore, is, as Suárez puts it, the manifestation of "an intention not to have or retain the law in question, or"—again in the language of this champion of liberty—"to resume the earlier status of freedom from legal obligation" in the matter in hand. And the intention itself, he concludes, "is sufficiently manifest from the agreement and constancy of the people in actions to that end"; for custom, does it not spring from the agreement and constancy of the people in action?

We now come upon a passage in which Suárez anticipates—unconsciously, of course—the action of the people of the United States in regard to the Eighteenth Amendment to the Constitution of the United States, forbidding the manufacture and sale of intoxicating liquors. His language here is, if we may say so, in point:

> From a public custom made up of actions in violation of law, especially from such a custom when it is tolerated, there results such an ignorance of the law that the offense comes to be regarded as less serious; or, if not ignorance of the law, such an insensitiveness to the unlawfulness of the act, is induced as lessens the gravity of the fault, and, consequently, of the liability to punishment.

Indeed we might here rest the case in behalf of customs made up of actions in violation of law; but Suárez felt the matter to be —as do we of the United States—of more than passing importance. Therefore he adds:

> The example of the violation of the law by great numbers of people presents a very strong temptation, as it were, drawing the violator on by a vehement desire and passion; and this fact must usually be accounted as a mitigating circumstance in individual violations of the law.

As we are inditing these lines, the Supreme Court of the United States has rendered a decision which in effect has quashed some thirteen thousand suits for violations of the law, on the ground that the Eighteenth Amendment itself having been repealed, there is no liability after repeal for its violation, although the violation in question took place while the Eighteenth Amendment was still in effect.[60] This would seem to be a concession to "vehement desire and passion." In delivering the opinion of the Supreme Court, Mr. Chief Justice Hughes expressed in stately and unforgettable language the fundamental conception of the Spanish School that the source of power is vested in the people. "The question," in the language of the learned Chief Justice, "is not one of public policy which the courts may be considered free to declare, but of the continued efficacy of legislation in the face of controlling action of the people, the source of the power to enact and maintain it. It is not a question of the developing common law. . . . Prosecution for crimes is but an application or enforcement of the law, and if the prosecution continues the law must continue to vivify it. The law, here sought to be applied, was deprived of force by the people themselves as the inescapable effect of their repeal of the Eighteenth Amendment. The principle involved is thus not archaic but rather is continuing and vital—that the people are free to withdraw the authority they have conferred and, when withdrawn, neither the Congress nor the courts can assume the right to continue to exercise it."

And, because of its unfortunate appositeness to present conditions in our beloved country, we again invoke Suárez: "With

---

[60] United States *v.* Chambers *et al.,* 291 U. S. 217, 226 (1934).

respect to the community in general, the multitude of offenders gives rise to the occasion for a lapse in the execution of the penalty, for the reason that it is not easy to punish so large a number without scandal, or without causing great disorder and very serious harm to the community. Neither is it expedient to punish some, and not others, since this also would give rise to scandal through charges of favoritism. Even when punishment can, for a particular reason, be visited upon some persons, these are usually few in number, and immunity is the rule with the generality of the people." It is with a deep sense of humiliation that we mention a form of violation of law in these United States —a violation so often unpunished, that it has almost come to have the power of customary law and which bears the opprobrious title of "lynch law."

Without quoting the maxim *Cessante ratione legis, cessat ipsa lex,* Suárez compresses within three paragraphs the entire philosophy of the cessation of custom:

> If . . . the matter is so changed that the reason and end of the custom disappear, not only in some particular respects, but in general, then the obligation of the custom will lapse also.
>
> Indeed, should the change in circumstances be such that the purpose for which the custom was introduced does not so much disappear as work to vicious effect, then there may be a positive duty not to observe the custom. This would be the case should the custom begin to be a moral occasion of sin, or be otherwise harmful to the general good of the commonwealth. The same will be true, if, in some particular case, the reason for the custom not only ceases simply to be, but produces opposite effects. This principle we have shown to be true of written law, and it is equally applicable to custom.
>
> Finally it is clear that this is the only way in which custom can of itself cease to exist; since it is not dependent upon any other cause as an active principle to preserve it, as it were, in being. For although the custom may depend upon the will of the sovereign, the fact that he does not revoke it is enough for its preservation; and the same is true also of the popular will, in so far as the custom is dependent upon it. . . .

* * * * * * * *

It was to be expected that Suárez contemplated a sanction for each of the various kinds of laws with which he has dealt. It might, however, be a sanction differing from that of Victoria, because Victoria was dealing with law in a specific and concrete case. Now Victoria stated the sanction by implication, if not in unmistakable and incontrovertible terms, the sanction resting upon the natural authority of the state, by appropriate legislation, to protect all human beings within its jurisdiction—whether in their individual or in their united capacity—in the enjoyment of their rights and the performance of their duties under the law of nations; and, failing to do so—failing, that is, in its duty, both national and international, and in what we of today call "due diligence"—the state was to be liable, before the international community, in damages for such negligence.[61]

The difference between Victoria and Suárez is that Victoria stated the sanction as a fact and Suárez states it as a philosophy.

Suárez was dealing with law in general as well as with law in its several branches. It was therefore natural that he should contemplate a sanction which would be general in its nature, instead of specific. That sanction was to be for him as a first principle. And the natural law being the basis of his system, the sanction was therefore rooted in the natural law.

The natural law being universal, the sanction would also be universal; otherwise there would not be a complete sanction for the law natural. If there be a right and if there be a duty under the law natural, the sanction protecting the right and enforcing the duty should, like the law, be natural. Now the obligation

[61] *De Jure Belli,* pp. 172, 181. ". . . princes have authority not only over their own subjects, but also over foreigners, so far as to prevent them from committing wrongs, and this is by the law of nations and by the authority of the whole world. Nay, it seems to be by natural law also, seeing that otherwise society could not hold together unless there was somewhere a power and authority to deter wrongdoers and prevent them from injuring the good and innocent. Now, everything needed for the government and preservation of society exists by natural law, and in no other way can we show that a State has by natural law authority to inflict pains and penalties on its citizens who are dangerous to it. . . .

". . . For instance, if French brigands made a raid into Spanish territory and the French King would not, though able, compel them to restore their booty, the Spanish might on the authorization of their sovereign, despoil French merchants or farmers, however innocent these might be. This is because, although the French State or sovereign might initially be blameless, yet it is a breach of duty, as St. Augustine says, for them to neglect to vindicate the right against the wrongdoing of their subjects, and the injured sovereign can take satisfaction from every member and portion of their State. . . ."

under a rule of law, whether it deal with the law natural, civil law, or the law international, was assimilated by Suárez to the natural law. The reason? That good faith is a natural principle, and in his conception an obligation under any category of law would be incomplete unless the obligation were executed in good faith. Therefore, with Suárez, the obligation to execute a human compact or agreement made under any form of law was a *natural* obligation, requiring compliance of the state or the community through a municipal statute or, as we would say, a municipal sanction.

This conception is vastly important, so important that it must be considered in all its various implications. So far as temporal things are concerned—for we are not dealing in this connection with the divine law as such—the natural law is, in Suárez' conception, the fundamental law underlying all man-made law. It is the law conformable and conforming to human nature and, we would add, to the dignity of the human being, as such; and as human beings are scattered throughout the world, it is a universal law. Now good faith is an inherent element—indeed, the essence—of the natural law, and therefore any and every obligation, whether it arises from the natural law itself or, through intervention of the human being, from the law of the state or from that of the international community, is *natural* in the sense that its execution is required by good faith. Hence, in the system of Suárez, the obligation, however it arises, flows directly from the law natural or indirectly from the natural law through the law of the state or the law of the states, and is thus a natural obligation.

There is here, however, a further observation to be made. If the obligation belongs to the natural law, the legislation to carry it into effect is either of the states individually or of the states collectively as they form the international community. In other words, the obligation in essence is one of good faith; its execution is a thing separate and distinct, the latter being municipal and requiring municipal action whether the obligation be national or international. In short, the obligation is one thing, the execution is another thing, but together they are natural law in action.

To approach the matter from another angle and, by what may seem a restatement, clear up any possible misconception, the obligation, when created, becomes an obligation under natural law, and, as every obligation is thus an integral part of the natural law, it should be carried out in good faith—which is an all-pervading principle of the natural law. Hence it is the unescapable duty of every state under the law of nature to supply the appropriate measure or means for carrying into effect the obligation: thus, for example, it is universally a duty to execute any and every agreement properly entered into in good faith. If the agreement is made within the state, the obligation, like the law to enforce its execution, is national. If the agreement is between states, the obligation is international, separate and distinct from the statutory or municipal law which may be necessary to carry it into effect. And here we catch, as it were, a glimpse of the sanction, in the form of a municipal statute, *in esse* or *in posse,* to carry into effect an international pact or agreement creating an obligation under the law of nature.

Why should "a pact and agreement," to quote Victoria, require a sanction? Because the conception of a universal law controlling human beings in all their actions would be imperfect if the obligation imposed upon human beings were not to be executed, since the law universal would then be but a series of precepts in the abstract; it would not be precepts in action. And the precept in action requires a municipal sanction to carry it into effect. Whether the obligation arises from a contract between two or more individuals, whether it be a compact of groups of individuals or whether it be that most formal of agreements known as a treaty or convention, to which all of the states of the world may be parties in an international conference, the natural element of good faith permeates each and every one and requires the execution of the obligation. Although we as yet have no international legislature, nevertheless we have and have had from time out of mind a rule of international law flowing from the natural law, and binding the groups of human beings which we are pleased to call states. The rule is a Latin maxim, *Pacta sunt servanda.*

We have the precept and the obligation to carry it into effect; the one without the other is incomplete. It is therefore the manifest duty of every community to provide the sanction by which good faith in all human legal relations is observed, whether these relations be between individual and individual, between individual and community, or between state and state—in a word, however they may arise.

There can be no association of human beings except upon a moral basis, because man is a moral animal; and the first, indeed the greatest, of the foundations of human society is good faith. How can people associate except on terms of good faith? And good faith, is it not the prime natural principle in the relationship of human beings?

As man is a moral being he differs, we are prone to think, from the brute creation in that he possesses a conscience. The conscience of man is an individual thing; the conscience of nations, if the expression be permissible, is enlightened public opinion. And public opinion is, or must be in the long run, moral opinion, for it is but the expression of the collective conscience of moral and human beings.

This is Suárez' philosophic demonstration of the Victorian sanction.

In the conception of Suárez there is no rule of law which does not create a natural obligation, whether the immediate transaction out of which the obligation arises be between individuals, between individuals and states, or between state and state. Put, then, in terms of the lawyer, there is no rule of law, national or international, which does not create a natural duty and a legal obligation, and, if legislation on the part of a state does not enforce and render that obligation effective by providing the means to carry it out, the state itself is recreant in its duty.

To repeat, there is no rule of law without a legal obligation, the obligation being a consequence of law, and made explicit by the statute which creates it; but although the obligation is, as it were, the creature of statute, its ultimate source is the natural law, and the duty to put it into effect carries with it the further duty to display due diligence in its execution—duties which arise from the natural principle of good faith, present in the heart and conscience of every human being.

Indeed, to violate good faith is to violate the moral law, which is, in essence, the law of nature "written in the heart of man," as it were, "with the finger of God."

THE STATE

THE DOCTRINE OF TYRANNICIDE
Its Development and Application

Baltimore became the absolute lord, viceroy, seigneur, and proprietor of the province of Maryland. In his "style," . . . he and his successors continued to employ the form "Absolute Lord and Proprietary of Maryland and Avalon, Lord Baron of Baltimore."

Baltimore was a lord of Maryland by divine right, quite as much so indeed as ever was a Stuart the king of England; and he possessed . . . even fuller powers in Maryland than the king himself possessed or at least exercised at home. . . .

He exercised his prerogatives at a time when Charles II and James II were on the throne and when conditions were favorable to the enforcement of the divine right of proprietors as well as the divine right of kings. But just as the revolution of 1689 in England destroyed the divine right of kings in all its manifold phases, so the revolution of the same year in Maryland destroyed in its even more extravagant manifestations the divine right of proprietors there.—Charles M. Andrews, *Our Earliest Colonial Settlements* (1933), pp. 148-9, 155.

We hold these truths to be self-evident, that all men are created equal, that they are endowed by their Creator with certain unalienable Rights, that among these are Life, Liberty and the pursuit of Happiness.—That to secure these rights, Governments are instituted among Men, deriving their just powers from the consent of the governed—That whenever any Form of Government becomes destructive of these ends, it is the Right of the People to alter or to abolish it, and to institute new Government, laying its foundation on such principles and organizing its powers in such form, as to them shall seem most likely to effect their Safety and Happiness.—*Declaration of Independence of the United States of America, July 4, 1776.*

CHAPTER IV

SUÁREZ ON THE STATE

If we are properly to understand the Catholic conception of the law of nations—the law to be applied, that is, to the relations between states—we must also understand the Catholic conception of the state and its government, a government in which the people is the source of power, for this conception has been of vast influence on human relations between as within the states. In addition we must examine the Spanish theory of tyrannicide, its classic precedents and its modern developments, because this theory, while not held exclusively by members of any one creed or at any one time or place, has played no small part in the establishment of states and their governments, past and present.

The views of Suárez on the origin of law, its various questions and their distinctions and resemblances, we have considered. Had he done nothing more, the world would be possessed of a novel heritage. But in a way, the views of Suárez upon law and its various categories were in the nature of those of a judge leisurely pointing to the conception of man in society and that form of society we call the state, or which we ourselves would prefer to term the status of organization.

Hitherto we have proceeded, as it were, from book to book of the *De Legibus;* indeed our course has brought us to the end of the volume. We now retrace our steps, in order to consider in Book III the fundamental questions concerning the lawmaking power in its relation to the state.

1. In the first of the four chapters of the third book, Suárez presents the question: Does a legislative power exist in men? And he indicates that the question should be considered whether men possess naturally the power to command other men, binding the

latter by human laws. The reason for doubting that they have such power lies in the fact that man is by nature free and subject only to his Creator, so that, in consequence, human principalities are contrary to the order of nature, including as they do an element of tyranny.

Suárez lists various arguments in support of this doubt drawn from comments on historical characters, from the doctors, from the Scriptures and from reasoning.

2. However, the first conclusion of Suárez is that the institution of "civil magistrates endowed with the power of ruling over men" is "just and thoroughly in accord with human nature." One proof of this conclusion is drawn from the fact that God Himself set up such governors over the Jewish people; for this form of government, though it was in fact directly derived from Him, did not transcend natural bounds, and was such that it could justly be established by ordinary means. Hence the power of the kind possessed by these governors is in conformity with nature, in so far as it may be necessary for the proper government of the human community. This view is also confirmed by human custom as recorded and commanded in the Scriptures.

3. Now this first conclusion of Suárez may also be supported by reasoning derived from Aristotle and other authorities and based upon two principles. "The first principle," says Suárez, "is this: Man is a social animal, and cherishes a natural and right desire to live in a community." But there are two forms of community: the imperfect, or domestic; and the perfect, or political.

The former is a natural in the highest degree, and—so to speak —fundamental, being based upon three relationships: that of man and woman; that of parent and child; that of master and servant. From these relationships, the first community of men arises; perfect in a domestic sense, but imperfect politically. The political community is composed of many households, and exists in order that the arts and offices needful in human life may be practised, that knowledge may be more widely disseminated, that there may be peace among men, and that injuries may be warded off, or avenged. Thus Cicero said: "Nothing in human affairs is more pleasing to God the Ruler [of all], than that men should live one with another in an orderly and perfect society, called *civitas* (a city state)." Such a society may consist of one city state, or it it may extend into a kingdom embracing many cities; the latter arrangement being still more advantageous to mankind, for reasons similar to those already stated, although it is not equally necessary.

4. "The second principle," continues Suárez, "is this: in a perfect community, it is needful that there shall exist a power to which the government of the community pertains; and this principle would seem to be self-evident, by the very nature of its terms. For, as Solomon says (*Proverbs,* xi [14]), 'Where there is no governor, the people shall fall.'" But nature is never deficient in that which is necessary. Therefore, since the perfect community is in accordance with natural law and with reason, so also is the power necessary in accordance therewith. This Suárez confirms by analogy with other social relationships among human beings; since there is a head or governing power in the relationship of man and woman, in that of parent and child, and in that of master and servant, and since such subjection is natural and just, as in indicated by various Scriptural passages; similarly, a proportionate governing power is needful in the case of a political community.

5. Suárez then goes on to discuss the *a priori* reason supporting the second principle, a reason already noted by St. Thomas, that: "It is impossible for a body to be preserved without a [governing] principle whose function it is to procure and strive for the common good of that body." Here we have a manifest truth in the case of the natural body, and one taught by experience in the case of the political body. The basis, in turn, of this *a priori* reason, is the fact that each private member strives for its private good, whereas such is not always the mode by which the common good is to be attained. It is thus natural and necessary that there be a civil magistracy—in other words, a man, or multitude of men, in whom there is vested the governing power; for men are not naturally governed, in their political affairs, by the angels, nor by the direct intervention of God.

6. Suárez nows turns to his second conclusion: "A human

magistrate, if he is supreme in his own order, has the power to make laws suitable to his sphere (*sibi proportionatas*); that is to say, civil or human laws which he may both justly and validly establish, by virtue of natural law, provided that the other conditions necessary to law are observed." Various philisophers, theologians and doctors are cited in defense of this conclusion. It is also supported by reasoning to the effect that civil magistrates are a necessity in the state, and for the government thereof, as has been demonstrated already. Now one of the most necessary acts for such a government is the establishment of laws (a fact proved by Suárez in a preceding book of the *De Legibus*); and it is a self-evident principle of law that he who is endowed with any office is also endowed with every power necessary to its proper exercise; and therefore, political magistrates possess the law-making power.

7. From all of this, there follows an inference that the said power to establish laws is equivalent to that human magistracy which is vested with superior jurisdictional power of a state. In support of this inference, Suárez refers to his proof (in Book I) that the legislative power in question pertains to a perfect jurisdiction. And continuing his argument he declares that only the prince or magistrate possesses the power which is directed to a public act, relates to the community in its entirety, and is characterized by a binding and coercive efficacy; yet these qualities are necessary to law, says Suárez, here citing various other authorities, and earlier remarks of his own. Therefore it is that only a magistrate with superior power over the state, has also the power to establish human or civil laws; and finally, such superior power is not of a despotic sort, being rather one which calls for a civil subjection; accordingly, it is a jurisdictional dominion, of the sort found in a prince or a king.

8. Certain jurisconsults, however, limit the inference above set forth, saying that it applies to those common laws which embrace a kingdom, but not to municipal laws nor to special statutes.

9 and 10. Suárez answers that this limitation is not necessary, save in case of a misunderstanding as to the terms involved. He holds that the inference in question is to be accepted in a universal

and unlimited sense. In the two present sections he presents arguments in proof of this contention, and in opposition to the arguments of the authorities who would impose the limitation. And he sums up this part of the discussion with the statement that, "the legislative power, even as it is a power of *imperium*, is also and similarly a power of jurisdiction."

11. Returning, then, to the reason for doubting the existence of a legislative power in men, as set forth in Section I—that man is by nature free and subject to no one, save only his Creator—Suárez concludes that the consequent there laid down [1] is false; for though man may be born not subject to the power of any human prince, he is nevertheless born capable of such subjection; and although nature may not directly subject him, this subjection is not opposed to the precepts of natural law; on the contrary, it is in accord with natural reason that a human state should be subject to some one, even if natural law itself would not, acting of itself, bring about political subjection, apart from the intervention of the human will. However, Suárez promises that he will later return to the matter, and he now proceeds to refute the four confirmations of the argument supporting the doubt. In refuting the first—that which relates to certain historical characters—he makes, among other remarks, an admission that kingdoms, and other forms of government, have in point of fact often arisen or been usurped through tyranny and violence; but he denies that such circumstances were due to the intrinsic nature of principates, or that kingdoms have arisen thus from the very beginning.

12. In refuting the second confirmation—drawn from the Doctors of the Church—Suárez interprets, for example, Gregory's statement that "power of this kind was introduced through sin, and seized by usurpation." Now according to Suárez, Gregory referred to governing power in its coercive aspect; for our Suárez holds that directive power was probably destined to exist among men even in the state of innocence, since there are a hierarchy and a principate for the angels themselves. And he continues: "The

[1] *i.e.*, "human principates are contrary to the order of nature, and include an element of tyranny."

argument which we have presented may be applied even to the state of innocence; for the foundation [of that argument] is not in sin, nor in any irregular conduct, but in the natural state of man, who is a social animal and by nature demands a communal mode of living, while a community must necessarily be ruled through public power."

13. As to the third confirmation—based upon certain Scriptural passages—Suárez contends that the powers ascribed to God, by Isaiah,[2] in the words, "For the Lord is our judge, the Lord is our lawgiver, the Lord is our king," do not necessarily preclude the existence of similar powers in a human degree and vested in human judges, lawgivers and kings. Again Suárez interprets the words from the *Epistle of Saint James*[3] "There is one lawgiver, and judge, . . . [that is able to destroy and to deliver]," not as a denial of human ability to give law and to pass judgment, but as a rebuke to those who judge rashly and also usurp the offices of judges and legislators; for these words, according to Suárez, mean that he who is a lawgiver is also a judge, so that he who is not a lawgiver ought not to usurp the office of judge.

As to the fourth confirmation—drawn from reasoning—this is to be refuted in a subsequent part of the work, dealing with the binding force of human law, with which we have already dealt.

In what man does the said power to make human laws reside, directly and by the force of nature?

1. This is the important thesis of the second chapter of the third Book. The reason for asking the question is that any one of three answers might be given: First, that the power under discussion exists directly and naturally in certain individuals; second, that it exists thus in all individuals; and third, that it exists thus in men viewed as a whole. Suárez, however, rejects the first answer, since there are no men who are by nature superior to the rest,—this would appear to be the force of his first argument, in the light of the context, although the Latin is decidedly ambiguous:

[2] xxxiii. 22.
[3] iv. 12.

quia neque omnes sunt aliorum superiores; nor do certain persons naturally possess the legislative power to a greater degree than other persons, on any ground apart from natural superiority, inasmuch as no reason presents itself in this connection in favor of some persons as compared with others. The second answer Suárez also rejects: first, because if it were correct, all the laws derived from such power would be common to all men; secondly, because no source can be found, from which the power would have flowed into every man—for it could not have been given by men (who may not give that which they do not possess), and it could not have been granted by God (for in that case it would have been incapable of undergoing transference and would have remained with all men in a process of perpetual succession).

2. Here Suárez pauses to quote and refute an opinion upheld by certain canonists, who maintain that the power in question exists by the force of nature in some supreme prince upon whom it has been conferred by God, and that it must dwell always in some such prince, by a process of succession. On this point Suárez declares that the passages from the Gloss on canon law, cited in defense of this opinion, have, as we would suspect, been misinterpreted, and that the opinion is founded upon no authority or other valid basis, a view which his later remarks will make still clearer.

3. Therefore, "In whom or in what," Suárez inquires, does the "power to make human laws reside?" "It should be asserted," Suárez replies, "that the power in question exists by the sole force of nature, not in any individual man, but in men, viewed as a whole. This conclusion is commonly accepted and indubitably true." And Suárez cites, in its defense, a number of authorities,—among them St. Thomas, various other theologians, and the *Digest.* Then Suárez proceeds to prove the first and negative part of the conclusion—"the power in question exists by the sole force of nature, not in any individual man"—reasoning thus: it is a self-evident fact, and one which Suárez has touched upon elsewhere, that "all men are by the force of nature born free, so that no person is [naturally] endowed with political jurisdiction over another person; even as no one is [thus] en-

dowed with dominion over another; nor is there any reason why such dominion should be bestowed by nature upon certain persons with respect to others, rather than conversely." We would almost think that we have here the source of our own Declaration of Independence. But to Suárez, who next disposes of the argument that this natural power can be traced back to Adam, and derived from him either on grounds of primogeniture or in accordance with his will, for Adam's power was economic or domestic, and not political. Later, when families began to multiply, each man possessed this same power over his own family. "But," says Suárez, "political power does not arise until several families have begun to congregate in a single perfect community. Therefore, just as this [form of] community arose, not as a creation of Adam nor solely through his will, but through [the will] of all who have agreed to its existence—government by consent of the governed, to refer again to the American Declaration of Independence—even so we can not say, with any foundation for the statement, that by the force of nature Adam held political primacy over such a community; for there are no natural principles from which to draw an inference of this sort, inasmuch as the sole force of natural law does not render it the due of a progenitor that he should also be king over posterity." Neither is the power in question ascribed to Adam by the Scriptures. These state that God gave man dominion over the other animals, but they do not say that He gave man dominion over other men. "Therefore," Suárez concludes logically and wisely, "the power of political dominion or rule over man, has not been bestowed immediately by God upon any man in particular."

4. Thus it is easy to prove the second and affirmative part of Suárez' conclusion, none other than the assertion that "the power in question exists by the sole force of nature . . . in men viewed as a whole." For it has already been proved by Suárez that this power does exist in men, that it does not exist in specific individuals nor in any one specific individual, nor, we add, in all men viewed as individuals; therefore, it must exist in men viewed as a whole. It should be noted at this point, however, that a multitude of men may be considered in either one of two phases.(1) A

multitude may be simply an aggregate of men devoid of any order or any physical or moral bond uniting them. In this case it is not, properly speaking, a single political body, and consequently does not need one head; so that the power in question is to be conceived of as not existing in the multitude,—at least, not strictly and formally, but, at the most, in a quasi-potential sense (*quasi radicaliter*). (2) In its second aspect, however, a multitude of men may be considered as being "congregated in a single political body, through a special act of will, or common consent, by means of one bond of fellowship, and with the purpose of aiding one another in the attainment of a single political end." In this sense, they form one united mystical body, which requires a head; so that, in the case of such a multitude, the power in question exists by the force of nature; nor would it be possible for men to congregate in this manner on condition that they should not be subject to this power. "For it is impossible to conceive of a single political body, apart from political government and from subordination thereto. It is impossible because, in the first place, such unity is derived, to a great degree, from subjection to one and the same rule, as well as to some common and superior power. Moreover, and secondly, if this were not the case, that body could not be directed to a single end and a common good. Consequently, it would be repugnant to natural reason to assume the existence of a human assemblage, united by means of one political body, yet devoid of a common power which the individual members of the community were bound to obey. Therefore, if that power does not exist in any specific person [or persons], it must reside in the community as a whole." Here we have the political power of mankind established by a syllogism.

5. There is, however, another point which must be noted in this connection. This natural power does not necessarily reside in a single group of men comprising all existent mankind, throughout the entire world. Such an organization of all men into one and the same political community is not necessary; indeed, it would scarcely be possible, and still less would it be expedient. If, as Aristotle says, it is difficult to govern rightly an execessively populous state, it would therefore be much more difficult to govern

aright the whole world. Accordingly, Suárez believes that the power in question was never—or, at most, was for a very brief period—thus vested in a single assemblage made up of all mankind. For, "shortly after the creation of the world, men began to divide themselves into various commonwealths, and in each [of these] the said power existed in a distinct manifestation." St. Augustine is here quoted as attributing the first establishment of such a commonwealth to Cain, and the first after the flood, to Nimrod. Suárez was an idealist, but he kept his idealism within the bounds of the practicable. His international community is not a single and a world state, but a community of separate and independent states, yet each and all dependent upon the international community.

6. In Section 6, Suárez continues in the same vein: "Therefore, we . . . conclude that this power of making human laws . . . never existed as one and the same power with respect to mankind as a whole, but was divided for the respective communities in accordance with the establishment and division of the communities themselves." This conclusion, in turn, leads to another: that such civil power never existed in any one specific person—not, at least, before the coming of Christ—with respect to the whole world. For it was never agreed by all men that this universal power should be conferred on any given individual; neither it is recorded that God bestowed such a grant of power on any person; nor was this power ever obtained by an individual, through war, nor in any similar way. All this, however, confirms rather than contradicts what Suárez himself has elsewhere said on the *jus gentium*. "For even though the whole of mankind may not have been assembled into one political body, being —on the contrary—divided into various communities, nevertheless, in order that those communities might afford mutual aid one to another, and in order that justice and peace might be maintained in their mutual relations (a condition which was requisite to the good of the whole), it was necessary that they should accord mutual observance—by a common pact and agreement, as it were—to certain common laws; and these are the laws which are called the *iura gentium*, and which were introduced—as we

have said—by tradition and by custom, rather than by any specific enactment." And Suárez concludes the chapter with the remark that this is the twofold law—both individual (*proprium*) and common—mentioned by Gaius, as he is quoted in the *Digest*. The third chapter of the third Book of the *De Legibus* was the reply to the query, "Was the power to make human laws given to men immediately by God, as the Author of nature?"

1. The reason for this question may be the deduction, apparently following upon what Suárez has already said, that the power involved is derived from individual men, through their own consent, and thus vested in the whole community made up of these individuals. He briefly discusses the reasons for and against this inference.

2. Suárez begins by expounding the "common and true opinion," to the effect that the power in question is given directly by God, as the Author of nature, but in such a manner that men have a quasi-disposition of the matter involved and may render a certain subject—that is, person—capable of wielding the power. In support of this opinion, Cajetan, Covarruvias, Victoria and Soto are cited. It may also be supported by reasoning; for, as Suárez has previously demonstrated, once men "will" to assemble in a political community, they are powerless to prevent the existence of the jurisdiction in question; and this defect of power indicates that such jurisdiction can not arise proximately from the will of man as its efficient cause. The example of a husband's dominion over his wife, when she has by her own will entered into the marriage, is cited by way of comparison. St. Paul is next quoted, in confirmation of the true opinion; for he has said that, "there is no power but from God . . . Therefore he that resisteth the power, resisteth the ordinance of God;"[4] consequently, the power under discussion is also from God; and hence, it proceeds immediately from Him, since it does not proceed primarily and immediately from some other source. As always, the reasoning of Suárez is not only close, but unanswerable.

[4] *Romans*, xiii, 1, 2.

In addition to these citations and to the argument based on defect of power, Suárez adds a second argument drawn from reason, that the said power involves many acts which would appear to exceed human power, as it exists in men viewed individually; and this fact indicates that the former power proceeds not from men, but from God. These acts, as enumerated by Suárez, are four in number, and the one which appears most particularly to pertain to divine power, is the act of binding the conscience.

4. The opinion laid down in Section 2, however, is composed of two parts, one of which is clear and undoubtedly true, while the other requires explanation. The first part is: the power in question proceeds from God as its primary and principal Author. Of this statement the arguments above set forth are sufficient proof; yet Suárez adds two more: (1) this power exists in the very nature of things, as a good and necessary factor for proper habits in human nature; and therefore, it must flow from the Author of that nature; (2) those who wield such power in the human community, are ministers of God, so that this power which they administer is one which they have received from God; and therefore, God is not only the chief, but also the original (*proprius*), Author of the power. The second of the two parts is the assertion that God confers that power immediately.

5-7. Suárez devotes the remainder of the chapter principally to an exposition of this second part of the opinion which he accepts. He declares that, in the first place, the power in question is granted by God, for the conservation and proper government of mankind, as a necessary consequence of the nature of things; for there has been no revelation of any special act or concession, apart from that of creation, by which the power was conferred. Secondly, Suárez enters into a lengthy comparison of man's natural power over the members of his body, with the power of the political community over its various members. In the former case, the power must originally be bestowed upon man by the Author of nature; the corporeal father intervenes by an act of generation, but it is not necessary that he should specifically will that the child shall possess the said power over his body; for that is a consequence which follows naturally, through the providence of the Author of nature; and in this sense, then, it is rightly asserted that He immediately bestows the power. Similarly, the will and consent of men intervene in their assemblage into a political community; but when that community, or mystic body, is once formed, its power over its members is a natural and necessary consequence, derived from the Author of nature. Thirdly, Suárez emphasizes the fact that the power under discussion is decidedly a mutable power, and one that is very dependent upon the will of men; and by the consent of the community, or in some other just manner, it may be transferred to some particular person, or to another community. Accordingly, such power can not be the result of a special act of institution, since in that case it would depend entirely upon the will of the one who established it, and would not be subject to change by inferiors; on the contrary, it is a power derived from nature and from the Author of nature, and therefore it is characterized by all the mutability befitting to the rational nature and conducive to the common good.

We now pass, in the summary of Chapter IV, Book III, to the "Corollaries of the Doctrines Above Set Forth."

1. The preceding chapter, as Suárez says, leads us to several very important inferences. The first is that "although the power in question"—*haec potestas*, evidently referring to the power of establishing human laws, which is the subject of the three preceding chapters—"is, in an absolute sense, derived from the law of nature, its specific application to a given form of power and of rule results from the human will." In order to prove this inference, Suárez calls attention to the doctrine, supported by Plato and by Aristotle, that there are three fundamental forms of political government: monarchy (or rule by one sole head); aristocracy (the rule of the superior few); democracy (the rule of the many and of the common people). There are also various possible forms of government composed of a mixture of two or all three of these simple forms. Now natural law does not oblige men to choose any particular one of these forms, but leaves the choice to the human will; and this, in spite of the fact that mon-

archy is the best form. This latter statement Suárez proves by citing Aristotle and—in connection with this citation—by drawing an analogy with the government of the universe, which should be the best form; by pointing out the example of Christ in the establishment and government of His Church; and, finally, on the basis of the comparatively frequent use of the monarchical form of government, among the nations. Moreover, actual experience shows that there is much variety in the forms of government chosen, and in the mixture of elements in these forms. The conclusion of Suárez' argument is in favor of the first inference. "This entire matter, then, is," he contends, "dependent upon human counsel and human will. Accordingly, it must be inferred that individual human beings possess by the force of nature and partially—so to speak—the capacity to establish or bring about a perfect community; while, from the very fact that they estabilsh it, the entire community becomes endowed with the power under discussion"—that is, the power of establishing human laws. "Nevertheless, the law of nature does not make it obligatory, either that this power be exercised directly by the community as a whole, or that it continue to reside therein for all time. On the contrary, it would be exceedingly difficult, from a practical viewpoint, if such were the case, since untold confusion and difficulty would result, were laws to be made by universal vote; and therefore, the said power is assigned directly by men to [be exercised in accordance with] one of the specific modes of government above-mentioned . . ."

2. The second inference is that "civil power, whether it resides in one man, or prince, by a legitimate and ordinary right, has been derived from the people and the community, either directly or indirectly; and this cannot fail to be the case, if the power is to be just." This inference can also be proved on the basis of what Suárez has previously said. "For," he continues, "the power in question resides directly in the community, by the force of nature; and therefore, in order that it may come to reside in any individual, as—for example—in a supreme prince, it is necessary that it be conferred upon him by the consent of the community." It thus appears beyond peradventure that the

government of Suárez' choice is government by consent of the governed, a phrase with which all citizens of the United States are familiar. But to continue his argument, and his imposing array of proofs, for he now advances another proof based upon an enumeration of all the titles by which an individual can attain such power. First, there is the case in which a king has been granted the power directly by God Himself. Such instances exist—Saul and David thus received their power—but these cases are extraordinary and supernatural, and not in accord with the common and ordinary course of providence; for revelation was involved in the making of the grant, whereas, ordinarily, men are ruled in civil matters simply by natural reason; such instances do not comply with the phrase used above, "By a legitimate and ordinary right." And at this point several passages from the Scriptures which might seem to conflict with Suárez' view are interpreted by him in such a way that the conflict does not arise.

3. Turning now, in the third section, to the second of the various titles which he is enumerating, Suárez declares that the power under consideration may reside in the king through hereditary succession. He points out, however, that this power through succession must eventually be traced back to someone who did not receive it thus, so that the right of succession is not the ultimate source for the power. Neither did this person to whom we finally trace the power, possess it inherently, by the force of natural law. We conclude with Suárez that he, too, received the supreme power directly from the state.

4. A third title to royal power is that based upon war. But the war must be just, in order to confer a true title and a true dominion. In this connection, Suárez, after citing several authors on the subject of tyranny, says: "Therefore, when possession is taken of a kingdom solely by means of unjust force, true legislative power does not dwell in the king. Nevertheless, it can come to pass, in the course of time, that the people give their consent and sufferance to such a principate; and, in that case, the power in question will [once again] be traced back to an act of transmission and donation on the part of the people." Then, too, even when a state not formerly subjected to a king is made subject to him,

through a just war, some fault on the part of the newly subjected state must have existed, in order that the war be just; consequently, the state is under an obligation to obey this new king, and to consent to the subjection; so that, in this situation also, the consent of the state—either expressed or due—is involved. And, in any case, it is in general assumed that the king who is waging the just war is already endowed with the royal power, the act of subduing the guilty state being, in a sense, an extension of that power; therefore, all the royal power of the said king may ultimately be traced back, not simply to the just war, but to just election, or the consent of the people. To the uninitiated this would indeed seem to be a triumph of logic as much as of reason.

5. So much for the affirmative proofs of the second inference. Suárez now undertakes to answer certain objections that may be made with regard to this inference. The objections are: (1) the inference would lead, in turn, to the conclusion that royal power is derived solely from a human right (*jus*), a conclusion which would seem to be in conflict with the Scriptural passages, "By me kings reign," and "For he is God's minister," etc.; (2) the inference would also lead to the conclusions that the kingdom is superior to the king (since the latter has received his power from the former), and that, consequently, the kingdom may, if it so wishes, depose or change its king (an assertion which is held to be entirely false). Here Suárez cites conflicting authorities in regard to the first objection. His own position is that, if one is speaking strictly of royal power as such and in so far as it resides in a particular individual, such power of political government is undoubtedly derived from God, but it is nevertheless vested in the individual by a grant of the state, as was shown above; therefore, in this sense, the power can be said to be derived from a human right. And, moreover, the very fact that the government of the state is monarchical is due to man's establishment of the government in that form; hence, the principate itself was derived from men. Again, the power of the king is greater or less, according to the agreement made between the kingdom and himself; and therefore, this power is, absolutely speaking, derived from men.

6. Continuing his answer to the first objection, and linking

with it an answer to the second, Suárez finds that the two Scriptural passages above quoted lay down two principles: (1) that the power in question, viewed in itself, is derived from God, and is just and in conformity with the divine Will; (2) that the king, when this power has been transferred to him, is God's deputy, to whom obedience is due, by natural law. Here Suárez cites an analogical case of a private individual who sells himself into slavery to another individual, and thus comes under the dominion of the latter. Similarly, once the kingdom has transferred its power to the king, the latter becomes its superior by virtue of this very transference, and the kingdom is deprived of its original liberty. Thus the main part of the second objection is refuted. As for the corollary to the second objection, it may be rejected on like grounds. For, "the king can not be deprived of that power," says Suárez, "owing to the fact that he has acquired true dominion; unless, perchance, he should fall into tyranny, which would afford the kingdom grounds for waging a just war against him."

7. The seventh section develops a third important inference, in so far as the nature of things is concerned, that is, from the viewpoint of the natural and ordinary course of human affairs, there are no civil laws which are universally established, with respect to the whole world, and which are binding upon all men. The truth of this assertion is evident, first, from the very term employed. For in speaking of civil laws, Suárez refers to human laws, relating to a single city or people, as distinguished from the *jus gentium;* and moreover, he refers to laws which may be established by natural power, and it is an inherent requisite of such laws that they be not universal. The *a priori* reason in support of this same inference is that "there is no legislative power having jurisdiction over the whole world, that is, over all men; therefore, there can be no civil law that is thus universal." Of this *a priori* reason Suárez proves the consequent by the argument that a law does not pass beyond the bounds of jurisdiction possessed by the lawmaker; and he holds that the antecedent is clearly true in the light of what has already been said—that is, that such [universal] power is not vested in the whole community

of mankind; neither is there any title by which it can be claimed as a grant from mankind to one individual, so that, "in the [ordinary course of human nature], there is not, never has been, nor—practically speaking—can there ever be a universal human legislative power relating to the whole world." Thus it appears that all the world—or, at least, all parts of it which are not totally barbarous—is governed and bound by civil laws; but the various parts are not all governed and bound by one and the same body of civil laws.

8. Suárez now proceeds to the fourth inference, which relates to the various modes of participation in the power to make human laws. First: this power may be held as a direct gift from God. For (as has been shown in a preceding chapter) it can have no other origin, God being the Author of all good things and—consequently—of all powers; particularly of this power, which—inasmuch as it is necessary to the good conduct of men, and to their proper preservation and government—depends in the highest degree upon the divine Providence; and therefore, the said power, since it is of God, must exist in some recipient as a direct gift from Him, since those who have received it indirectly must trace the receiving of it back to some other source, and this process can not continue *ad infinitum*. Nevertheless, there are two ways in which such power might be derived from God: (1) it might be derived naturally from God as the Author of nature; or (2) supernaturally, from God as the Author of grace. Of the latter mode, Suárez treats elsewhere (Book V), and the former mode has been sufficiently well expounded in his preceding remarks. The same remarks also make it clear that the power in question may be derived directly from men and indirectly from God, and that this, indeed, is ordinarily the case with regard to natural power. For that power, when immediately derived, resides in the community, and is consequently transmitted through the community to kings, or other chief governors, etc. Rarely, if ever, is it retained in the community as a whole, in such a way that it is administered directly by the latter. But, in spite of all subsequent successions or elections, the immediate source of the power will continue to be the community, just as the immediate source

of the Pontifical power will always be God, in spite of successive elections.

9. Suárez now makes a different sort of distinction—also twofold—regarding customary modes of holding power. For power may be ordinary, or it may be delegated. His preceding observations would apply to ordinary power; but, with respect to the second mode, it might be doubted whether the power in question can be delegated. But Suárez cites various authorities who indicate that such delegation is indeed possible.

10. However, Suárez notes that the delegation may take either of two forms. In the first place, power may be delegated merely to enact the law, to declare that it is just and useful, or needful, and to frame its terms; but not to give it binding force, and consequently, not to promulgate it as actual law. Indeed, there is no doubt that legislative power can be and frequently is delegated, although this is a delegation of service rather than of jurisdiction; and furthermore, it is almost a necessity for princes to resort to such aid in the process of lawmaking, since they cannot perform by themselves all the acts needful in that process. It is manifestly clear that Suárez does not include dictators among his "princes."

The other, and strict, mode of delegation, however, is neither so common nor so easily effected. According to this mode, power is delegated to publish a law, and to give it authority and force through one's own will, with no further confirmation or approbation on the part of the delegators.

10 and 11. Bartolus makes a distinction, in this connection, between the community and the prince. He declares that the community may delegate the power in question, when the community itself holds it as ordinary power. Suárez grants that this part of Bartolus' opinion is clearly true. However, Bartolus denies that princes or judges to whom such jurisdiction has been entrusted, can delegate it, for he argues: (1) that when the power was committed to them, their personal labors were required, and that this is a task which they cannot transfer to others; (2) that in their case, the power is merely delegated, not ordinary, wherefore they cannot delegate it anew. Suárez is far from agreeing unreservedly with Bartolus on this second point. He holds that such

a doctrine is false, if it is taken as referring to the Emperor, to kings, or to other princes, to whom the said power of the state has been transferred in an absolute degree; for under those circumstances, the power is not delegated, but ordinary, being perpetual, and proper to them by virtue of their office. After minor arguments to the same effect Suárez adds: "Accordingly, the transfer of this power by the state to the prince is not an act of delegation, but a quasi-alienation,—that is to say, a perfect surrender of all the power that [previously] resided in the community; and therefore, even as the community was able to delegate this power, just so the prince is able." Suárez furthermore denies that any requisite regarding the prince's personal labor accompanies the bestowal of the power upon him; the grant was absolute, and the power was to be exercised by the prince in person or through agents, as he might deem expedient. Thus the Pope, and even bishops, may under similar circumstances delegate their legislative power.

12. The last section of the chapter deals with the cases for which Suárez admits the validity of Bartolus' arguments, that is: the case of magistrates and judges whose power has been delegated to them by the highest authority; or the case of senates, and such like bodies, to whom legislation has been entrusted by a free state retaining supreme power in its own hands. Though even in such cases, special circumstances might render the power in question capable of delegation. On this point, and on the question of what persons actually have the power in question delegated to them, Suárez refuses to commit himself, explaining that ordinary law has set up no rules regarding these matters. The meaning of this is that Suárez was as prudent as he was logical.

CHAPTER V

SUÁREZ' *DEFENSIO FIDEI* AND THE SPANISH CONCEPTION OF TYRANNICIDE

HAVING examined at some length Suárez' views on the origin, nature and exercise of the legislative power in its relation to the state, we are now in a position to consider certain other aspects of the state which are discussed in the *Defensio Fidei Catholicae adversus Anglicanae Sectae Errores.* For present purposes we may confine our attention to but three of the many chapters in this treatise, two in the third book—Chapters 5 and 23—and one in the sixth book—Chapter 4.

In the first of these chapters Suárez considers the question, "Do Christian Kings Possess Supreme Power in Civil or Temporal Matters?"

1. Now the word "supreme," Suárez points out, denies the existence of any superior whom the person, said to have supreme power, is bound to obey. It is to be understood that this interpretation refers to an earthly or human superior. But even so, such a denial may be variously interpreted. For in the first place, we may either deny every kind of subjection to any human superior, whether in spiritual or in temporal matters, or else we may simply deny subjection to such a superior, with respect to temporal and civil matters. It is upon the latter interpretation that the present discussion turns.

2. Of this interpretation, a second division may be made, as there are two sorts of subjection, direct and indirect. For example, the temporal magistrates of a community may be directly subject, in temporal affairs, to the superior power of the temporal sovereign of that community; while, on the other hand, that sovereign may be indirectly subject, in temporal matters, to a spiritual authority concerned with his power only in an indirect

sense, in so far as the exercise of that temporal power affects the ends to which the spiritual power is primarily directed.

3. Thus, there arise two questions in connection with the temporal sovereignty of princes, (1) Is the power of a Christian king supreme in the sense that it recognizes absolutely no human superior, whether directly or indirectly, in temporal matters? (2) Or does such power merely deny the existence of a direct superior in temporal matters? It is the latter question which Suárez undertakes to discuss, in this chapter. "For," as Suárez says, "although . . . there is on this point no dispute between the King of England and ourselves, nevertheless, in view of the fact that he frequently complains, with regard to Catholics, that we deny the jurisdiction of Christian princes and the obedience due them, it has seemed to me that this question should not be overlooked in the present discussion; thus, by its solution, it will become manifest that the royal power of Christian princes in all points which are in agreement with the natural law, is preserved in its integrity, according to Catholic doctrine."

4. In order to prove this statement, Suárez next examines the first opinion to the contrary: that in the Church of Christ, not only the spiritual government, but also the temporal, is monarchical; that the Church therefore has but one supreme temporal prince, who, of himself and directly, possesses supreme temporal power over the whole Church; that this supreme prince is the Pope; and that consequently, no state, king or emperor has supreme power in temporal matters, since there cannot be two supreme heads within one and the same order. Some there be who even add that all rights over kingdoms and rights of dominion were conferred first upon Peter, and then by succession upon the Popes, so that supreme civil power dwells potentially (*in habitu*) in the Pope alone, although he may administer it, either by tacit or by express consent, through other and temporal kings.

5. In support of this contrary opinion Suárez adduces three arguments: (1) The opinion in question would seem to be confirmed by many papal decrees; (2) usage and various effects indicating the existence of such papal power, apparently confirm

the same opinion; (3) Scriptural proofs are cited, held to indicate that Christ had direct temporal power, as well as spiritual, and that he transferred this temporal power to his Vicar (the often quoted injunction, "Feed my sheep," being invoked in this connection); (4) reason shows that it is expedient for the good government of the Church, and for its peace and unity, that there should be one supreme head to minister to both the physical body and the soul of that mystical body which constitutes the Church, for a division of powers leads to infinite and intricate dissensions and disputes.

6. "Nevertheless, it must be stated that Christian kings do possess civil power which is supreme in its own order," and Suárez states it under the subheading, "The true opinion is set forth"; adding, "and that they recognize no other as their direct superior within that same temporal or civil order, upon whom they inherently depend in the exercise of their own power." Consequently, the Church contains no supreme temporal head over the whole body. Therefore all the existing kingdoms or republics are sovereign communities. However, the present discussion does not involve a comparison of one temporal prince with another.

7. In spite of the last statement, Suárez does treat briefly of the question, whether the Emperor is superior in jurisdiction over all Christian provinces and kingdoms, and, in consequence, whether he is the supreme monarch over the universal Church. To this query Suárez answers that the Emperor does not possess such supreme temporal jurisdiction, since—as is probable—he never did possess it, or else he has lost the greater part of it. Thus it is that in addition to the Emperor, there are many temporal kings—such as those of Spain, France and England—who are entirely free from the imperial jurisdiction.

8. Suárez first undertakes to prove his proposition that the Pope does not possess such supreme temporal jurisdiction over the whole Church. In favor of this negative view, he cites, as we would expect, the views of many theologians and jurists, and even those of the Popes themselves.

9. However, the laws promulgated by the latter are a primary

proof. Of the various Papal statements quoted by Suárez, perhaps the most explicit is the one ascribed to Pope Nicholas, that "the Emperor has not seized the pontifical rights, nor has the Pope usurped the title of the Emperor, inasmuch as Christ has thus distinguished between the offices pertaining to the two powers, assigning to each its peculiar acts and distinct dignity."

10. After citing further proofs drawn from the statements of the Popes, Suárez then concludes: "It is, then, sufficiently evident that the Roman Pontiffs themselves have never assumed power of this sort, as will become still more clear from what follows."

11. Secondly, Suárez' proposition—that the Pope does not possess supreme and universal temporal power—is proved by that reasoning of which he was a past master. For no just title, he asserts, can be found by which the Pope might obtain the power in question—a statement, which, in turn, he proves at some length. Indeed Suárez has elsewhere demonstrated that only a perfect human community assembled politically into the body of one state possesses, by natural law, supreme temporal jurisdiction over itself. This is, as it were, the major premise; the minor, that the Church does not possess this sort of political unity; and therefore the inevitable conclusion follows that natural law does not confer upon the Church a direct temporal jurisdiction, supreme and universally applicable to the whole Church. "On the contrary," he maintains, "there are as many supreme temporal jurisdictions as there are political communities which are not members of [another] single kingdom or civil state." Therefore, the further conclusion follows that the title in question, if it existed, would be derived either from positive divine law, or from human law.

12. The title to such power, he continues, by way of further proof, citing chapter, verse and authority for every point, has not been conferred by human law; for it is shown to have been derived neither from an election or popular consent; nor from a just war; nor by lawful succession; nor by donation.

13. But what is the canon of the Church upon this phase of the question? Its laws confer upon the Pope of Rome a legitimate

right and temporal dominion over the Roman kingdom, or patrimony of St. Peter, through the donation of Constantine, the implication being that it is only by title of donation that the Holy Father has direct jurisdiction over that patrimony, though its extent may have been increased by later donations.

14. Now from positive divine right the title could be derived only through donation by Christ, and perserverance through legitimate succession. But Christ did not make this donation. "Therefore, we have no supernatural evidence of such a direct temporal jurisdiction on the part of the Pope; and consequently, the attribution to him of such jurisdiction is without foundation, since he cannot possess it save through some supernatural [title]."

15 and 16. It seems most probable, then, that Christ Himself did not, in His human character, claim for himself an earthly or temporal kingdom, with direct temporal jurisdiction, such as that possessed by the Emperor and by other human princes. After referring to proofs already laid down in another work, as well as to various passages from the Scriptures and from other authorities, Suárez adds an argument drawn from reasoning, namely, "a temporal kingdom was not necessary to Christ for His honor or majesty, and furthermore, it was more expedient for the example set us and for our redemption that He should not claim for Himself such a kingdom."

17. From this conclusion Suárez draws, and proceeds to defend, an inference that Christ did not confer upon His Vicar the power which He Himself did not claim. That Christ was able to do so, without claiming that temporal power for Himself, Suárez admits; but he has inferred that Christ did not confer it upon His Vicar, since He did not claim it, and left upon earth only a Vicar for that spiritual kingdom which He did in fact claim. A second proof of the inference is that Christ exercised perfect spiritual authority, without direct temporal jurisdiction; therefore, He was able to impart to His Vicar that spiritual jurisdiction which was perfect, without any other element that was directly temporal. In the next place, just as it was expedient that Christ Himself should not assume the jurisdiction in ques-

tion, even so was it expedient that He should not confer this jurisdiction upon His Vicar, lest disturbance among the kings of the earth result, or an apparent intermingling of spiritual and temporal matters.

18. From the foregoing statements, which are as premises, Suárez draws "a last argument" in defense of his denial that the Church contains one supreme temporal prince. It is, "that temporal dominion, accompanied by a direct civil jurisdiction over the Church as a whole, was not necessary to the spiritual government of the Church—which is a self-evident fact—nor was it even useful to that same end, but might, on the contrary, have afforded a great impediment thereto; therefore, it is not probable that such [dominion and jurisdiction] were granted by Christ." Therefore it is morally impossible, argues Suárez, for one man to sustain the weight of both the spiritual and temporal phases of universal government.

19. Concerning the objection that the foregoing arguments and conclusions would prove that the Pope and other bishops were unable and indeed ought not to be, at the same time, temporal princes, Suárez in the first place admits it to be true that Christ did not institute or prescribe such a practice. However, He did not actually forbid it, nor do the statements above made prove that it is essentially evil for one and the same person to be an ecclesiastical pastor and a temporal prince. While a temporal charge that is excessive in extent and universal in character may not harmonize with spiritual responsibility, nevertheless, a limited temporal principate may be not only permissible but even expedient to preserve to the Church its splendor and authority, as well as for its necessary expenses, and for similar honorable ends. Thus Christ left this point for human disposition, as regulated by right reason and moulded by the exigencies of the times.

20. Another reply to Suárez' "last argument" is that, even if it be granted that both phases of universal jurisdiction should not be committed to one person, to be exercised at one and the same time, nevertheless both phases might be granted to the Pope potentially (*in habitu*); and that they have been so granted,

with the accompanying condition that His Holiness exercise the spiritual power himself, but the temporal power, ordinarily, through other persons. But Suárez is ready for such a reply and in his own behalf argues that such jurisdiction *in habitu* is not proved to exist by any title or by any convincing argument; and that indeed it would be either irrelevant or extremely offensive.

21. Continuing the argument in the same vein, Suárez then adds as the final argument that, if the Pope did possess such temporal jurisdiction *in habitu* over the whole Church, he would bear the responsibility, not only for the spiritual rule of all the bishoprics, but also for the temporal rule of all the kingdoms of the Church; and this, again, would be a task too great for human strength and capacity, and one contrary to all reason and usage.

22. And returning to the four basic arguments for the opposing opinion, Suárez declares that the first and second relate only to the indirect power of the Pope; the third is derived from a false principle, since Christ did not assume for Himself temporal dominion; and the fourth is likewise faulty, since the Church is not a single temporal commonwealth, as it is a spiritual one, and therefore does not require a directly supreme temporal power, but rather a spiritual one, which may be extended to temporal matters.

Are we not here in the presence of a magnificant admission of the temporal source of temporal power?

Let us now state in brief, indeed summary, form the contention of Suárez, or rather of His Church, that "The Supreme Pontiff may use coercive power against Kings, even to the point of deposing them, if there is adequate cause." This contention is to be found in the twenty-third chapter of the third book of the *Defensio Fidei.*

1. The title of the chapter touches the very heart of the controversy with the King of England.

2. It is indeed true that the Supreme Pontiff possesses coercive power over wicked and incorrigible kings, particularly "schismatics" and "pertinacious heretics." One proof of this statement is the fact that, if the Pope did not possess such coercive

power, the directive power bestowed on him by God would be imperfect and inefficacious whereas nothing imperfect and inefficacious can come from God.

3 and 4. For this truth Suárez finds, as we are now prepared to expect, confirmation in the Scriptures.

5. Suárez then refutes the arguments that might be advanced in opposition to such citations from the Scriptures. In this connection, he says: ". . . why should the words of Paul not have application to Christian kings who are both disobedient and obstinate? . . . is the reason, perhaps, the superior temporal power and dignity of kings? Yet this superiority does not prevent them from coming under the yoke of Christ and the power of the Church."

6. Moreover, the Pope's unique power of binding and loosing (also confirmed by Scripture) includes coercive power.

7. The power to impose the censure of excommunication has indeed frequently been exercised by the Popes.

8. At this point, Suárez cites various instances of acknowledgment, by temporal sovereigns, of the papal power to impose censures of excommunication and interdict.

9. However, the chief question raised in the present instance relates, not to the power of excommunication but to that of temporal punishment, of depriving the king of his royal dominion and power.

10-13. The Pope has power to punish temporal kings, even by means of temporal punishments. Proof of this statement may also be drawn from the Scriptures (the passages which Suárez has already cited; and others, relating to Ananias and Sapphira, to Job and to Paul and a certain fornicator), as well as from the Patristic interpretation of incidents such as that of Paul and the fornicator. Therefore Suárez draws the conclusion that "ecclesiastical correction and punishment consist, not in a spiritual censure alone, but also, at times, in affliction of the body; and accordingly, the pastors of the Church may resort to temporal punishment for the sake of spiritual welfare."

14-16. A second group of proofs is drawn by Suárez from the authority and practice of the Church, which has given its consent to instances of such coercion and punishment and to canon laws imposing penalties of this sort upon temporal princes; for "the Church cannot err," he says, "in matters of faith and morals."

17-21. A third proof, Suárez appropriately enough draws from reasoning. For the possession of such power by the Pope is necessary: (a) for the correction of temporal princes, and for their punishment in order both that amends for injuries may be made and that satisfaction may be given to God and to the Church; (b) for the defense of the subjects, whom wicked kings place in great peril of perdition.

22. For the very same reason—the protection of subjects against spiritual danger—though not by way of vindictive and just punishment, the Pope may free Christian subjects from the dominion of a heathen king. "With the same, or even greater reason, then," says Suárez, "a Christian king"—that is to say, a subject of the Church by virtue of baptism—"may be deprived of his dominion over his vassals; therefore, this ground alone suffices to endow the Pope with the power to turn upon such princes, lawfully depriving them of their kingdoms, and to avail himself, for this purpose, of the sword of other princes, that [the temporal sword] may thus be under [the spiritual] sword, for mutual aid in the support and defence of the Church." Here we have the two swords in action.

Hitherto Suárez, in dealing with the temporal and spiritual power, has been preparing himself, as it were, to attack and overthrow the oath exacted of his subjects by King James the Sixth of Scotland and (unhappily, it may be) the First of England, and particularly the third part of the oath which, in his opinion and that of his Church, exceeded the requirements of civil obedience and was contrary to Catholic doctrine. In order to refute this part of the oath, it was necessary to quote it for the information of the reader. Therefore it follows: "'And I do further swear that I do from my heart abhor, detest and abjure, as impious and heretical, this damnable doctrine and position, that princes which be excommunicated or deprived by the Pope may be deposed or murdered by their subjects or any other whatsoever'."

1. In this connection, Suárez undertakes, in the fourth chapter of Book VI, to examine three points: (1) the doctrine itself, to a discussion of which most of the chapter is devoted; (2) the right of a ruler to exact this oath from his subjects; (3) the conflict between the words quoted and King James' assertion that the oath in question contained nothing in excess of the requirements of civil obedience. Consideration of the first point involves a discussion of the thorny and then much debated question, "Is it permissible for a private person, or for his subjects, to slay a tyrannical king?" Now the term "tyrannical king," may be interpreted as referring either to one who has usurped the royal power unjustly and by force, or to one who is a true, that is, a constitutional, king, but exercises his sovereignty in an unjust and oppressive manner.

2. Choosing the latter interpretation of the term as most befitting the case in hand, Suárez lays down an assertion which he declares to be commonly held and certainly true: "A prince cannot justly be slain on any private authority, either on account of his tyrannical rule, or [simply] on account of any crime whatsoever."

3. The Council of Constance condemned, Suárez points out, the contrary view, when it condemned the proposition that "a tyrant may and should, licitly and deservedly, be slain through the agency of any of his vassals and subjects, even though this be effected by means of secret snares and subtle blandishments or flattery, notwithstanding any oath whatever that may have been taken to him, or any alliance that may have been entered into with him, and apart from any sentence or mandate imposed by any judge whatsoever." It is important to state that the Council of Constance was held in 1415, thus antedating by more than a century the schism of the Church. The doctrine laid down by the Council has therefore no immediate connection with the "Protestant Reformation" of Luther's day. The proposition and the condemnation of it by the Council refer to tyrants in a general sense, and particularly to tyrants in the sense of

lawful kings ruling tyrannically, which is the interpretation with which Suárez is chiefly concerned.

4. In a discussion of the bases of the condemned proposition, Suárez rejects one of these without qualification—the assumption that a king ruling tyrannically may be slain by any subject on private grounds of just vengeance and punishment. His purpose is to eliminate the question of private interest in favor of public good.

5. The other basic assumption Suárez examines at much greater length—that such slaying may take place on the ground of just self-defence, or of just defence of the state. Nevertheless, he prefaces the examination with the warning that this assumption, though it may be a valid argument in some cases, does not apply to the question in hand, "May a king be slain by a private individual solely on account of that king's tyrannical government?" Suárez goes on to say that defense of one's own life when it is violently threatened by the king, but not defense of one's own property, is ordinarily a justifiable ground for slaying the king, "because the right to protect one's own life is paramount, and because such a prince is not involved in a need that obliges the subject to lose his life for the former; on the contrary, the prince himself has voluntarily and iniquitously placed himself in that position of peril." However, the subject might be obliged, even in such a case, by charity towards his country and considerations of the common welfare, to refrain from killing the tyrant.

Suárez holds, it should be added, that the life of a prince is to be preferred to one's own property, because of the dignity of his rank; because he represents God, and acts in His stead, in a unique manner; and because he possesses a certain superior administrative power over all the property of his subjects, such that he may be bound in justice, and required, to make compensation for exceeding that power, but may not be slain for the purpose of resisting these excesses.

6. Defense of the state is a justifiable ground, only when the prince actually wages an aggressive war on the state, tending to its destruction and to the slaughter of many of its citizens

—again, not a case which comes under the question at issue. In the circumstances which Suárez has in mind, any citizen or member of the state, expressly or tacitly set in motion by that state, may defend it in whatsoever way he can.

7, 8, 9. For the sake of completeness, he now proceeds to deal with an application of the foregoing discussion to the case of tyrants in the other sense of the term, that is, usurpers of kingly power. Suárez cites here many authorities tending to prove that a tyrant of this sort may be slain by any private person of the state suffering the tyranny, for the sake of freeing that state, provided: that there is no possible recourse to a superior, by whom a judgment may be passed upon the invader; that the tyranny and injustice be matters of public and manifest knowledge; that the deed be necessary to the attainment of the kingdom's liberty, for if some other and less harsh method is feasible, the tyrant may not be slain at once and without the intervention of a weightier power and an examination of the case; that there shall be involved no treaty or truce or pact between the tyrant and the people, confirmed by oath, "for pacts and oaths must be observed, even when entered into with enemies, unless, perchance, they are clearly unjust and the result of coercion; that it shall not be feared, in consequence of the slaying, that the state will suffer the same evils as, or greater than, those suffered under him; and, finally, that the state shall not expressly oppose the slaying.

10. Suárez admits, however, that certain authorities do not accept this distinction, but hold rather that it is impermissible for a private person to slay a tyrant, whether the latter be a tyrant in his rule only, or in regard to his title as well.

11. Nevertheless, Suárez refutes the arguments adduced in support of this view. To the argument that the Lateran Council referred to tyrants in an absolute and general sense, he replies that this Council did not lay down the universal negative proposition that no tyrant should be slain, but simply condemned a universal affirmative proposition, that every tyrant may be slain, —and this, not in an absolute fashion, but employing many additional terms; so that their statement may be reduced to the

indefinite declaration that not every tyrant may be slain before sentence has been pronounced against him. To the argument that Augustine[1] also made an absolute statement to the effect that it is not permissible to slay any person without public administrative authority, Suárez answers that "the private person who slays a tyrant of this sort does not do so without public administrative authority, inasmuch as he performs the act either by the authorization of the state, which tacitly consents, or by the authorization of God, Who, through the natural law, has given to each individual the power to defend himself and his state from violence, such as is wrought by a tyrant of the kind in question." As for the negative argument that St. Thomas' assertion is, not that a given tyrant is laudably slain by any person whatsoever, but simply—in indefinite terms—that he is laudably slain,[2] Suárez' reply is based on St. Thomas' own language elsewhere in the article cited, that is to say, his use of the indefinite pronoun *aliquis*. Finally, to the last argument —that no malefactor may rightfully be slain, nor one who is in possession be actually dispossessed, without first being heard and judged, nor is evidence of a crime committed sufficient without a sentence—Suárez replies that this rule does not hold for the case in question, which is one of self-defense, not vengeance, and of actual violence, not peaceable possession, "since the state, though it may not undertake war, owing to its inability to do so, nevertheless . . . carries on always an implicit war, for it resists to the extent of its ability."

12. A difficulty now arises in the argument; for the foregoing remarks would seem to imply that there is no difference between the two cases—that involving a lawful sovereign who governs tyrannically, and that involving a usurper—since the same conditions are required in both instances, in order that the slaying may be permissible.

13. To this objection, Suárez replies, first, that the two situations are indeed alike, in that even a tyrant who usurps royal

[1] St. Augustine, *De Civitate Dei*, Bk. I, chap. xvii. Suárez also refers to chaps. xviii, xxi and xxvi.

[2] St. Thomas Aquinas, *On the Sentences of Peter Lombard*, Bk. II, dist. xliv, qu. ii, art. 2.

power cannot justly be slain by any private individual whomsoever, on grounds of vengeance or punishment. The absolute principle of injustice exists in both cases. But the crime involved when the king is a lawful ruler is far more grave, constituting an act of lese-majesty, whereas, in the case of a false ruler, it is simply defense against injustice and a usurpation of jurisdiction. Therefore, it is permissible for a private person to slay the lawful ruler only on the ground of defense, and this ground will not exist, so long as that ruler refrains from actually opening an unjust war against and inflicting actual violence upon his kingdom; while, in the case of a usurper, it is assumed that the state—provided it makes no declaration to the contrary—is tacitly waging a defensive war against the person ruling it by an unjust title and by force, and that it wishes to be defended by any one of its citizens, or even by any foreigner. Consequently, if no other means of defense exists, it is permissible for any one of the people to slay the tyrant. Such a person will indeed be acting with public authorization, or with divine authorization, even as in the case of a lawful ruler; but the difference consists in the fact that the power to slay is understood to be granted to any private person whomsoever, when the tyrant is a usurper, and not, when the tyrant is a lawful sovereign.[3]

14. At this point, however, another difficult question arises, particularly pertinent to the oath under discussion. This aspect has to do with the deposition of a lawful ruler. Now Suárez points out the fact that even the condemnation laid down by the Council of Constance includes the words, "apart from any

[3] We have hesitated to present this argument of Suárez in a more concise form, in view of the context. He would seem to have pointed out *two* differences between the conditions required to justify slaying a lawful ruler who governs tyrannically, and those required for the just slaying of a usurper: (1) in the former case, an act of aggression and actual violence on the part of the ruler is required; in the latter case, the act of usurpation, and the tacit resistance of the kingdom are sufficient grounds; (2) any person whomsoever has the power to slay in the latter case, but not in the former. Perhaps the two differences should be fused into one by interpreting (2) as follows: any person has this power, in the latter case, apart from any special act of violence, any sentence passed against the tyrant, or any similar consideration which would specifically authorize him to slay that tyrant. We may also note that a third difference exists, if we take into account the case of the slaying of either sort of tyrant, when the required conditions do not exist: in such a case, the slaying of a tyrant who is a lawful ruler is a much graver crime.

sentence or mandate imposed by any judge whomsoever," implying that the condemnation of the Council does not extend to cases in which a qualified judge has by just sentence deposed the king; nor can there be applied to such cases the assertion laid down by Suárez—a prince cannot justly be slain on any private authority, either on account of his tyrannical rule, or simply on account of any crime whatsoever—for the slayer will no longer be acting on private authority, and the tyrant slain will no longer be a lawful prince. This principle Suárez applies in greater detail to the case of an heretical prince. Such a prince is, in a sense, deprived of his lordship over the kingdom, by the very fact of his heresy, but the kingdom may not on that ground instantly be taken from him; a condemnatory sentence must first be passed against him; thereupon, he loses all just title to the kingdom, he may be treated altogether as a tyrant, and therefore be slain by any private person whomsoever.

15. The assumption that the punishment of deposition and a sentence depriving a person of his sovereignty may be imposed upon a supreme temporal sovereign was, on assumption, displeasing—indeed very displeasing—to the King of England, but nevertheless, most true, says Suárez, referring the reader to the proofs laid down in the third Book. The question, however, as to what person has power to impose such a sentence now arises. Suárez assumes, briefly, that this power to depose the king may exist either in the state itself, or in the Pope—though in a different manner in the latter case. The state as a whole may depose the king, as a necessary means to defend itself against him, in a public and general council of citizens and nobles; and in so doing the state is supported by the authority of the natural law, and by the fact that such a case must be understood to be an exception, for the sake of necessary self-defence, to the compact by which the state has transferred its power to the king. Among the many authorities whom Suárez quotes, in this connection, is St. Thomas, who, it may be noted, adds the condition that such sentence shall be passed prudently, without resulting in still greater harm to the people.[4]

[4] II. II, qu. 42, art. 2.

16. In the case of the Pope, indeed, this power exists as in a superior having jurisdiction over kings, even though they be supreme beings, as over subjects. If the crimes are spiritual—for example, crimes of heresy—the Pope may punish the king by his direct power, even to the point of deposing him, when the obstinacy of the king and the general welfare of the Church may so require. The Pope may punish temporal sins through his direct power in so far as those crimes are temporally injurious to a Christian kingdom; and by his indirect power, in so far as the tyrannical rule of a temporal prince is always injurious even to the welfare of souls.

17. Suárez adds that a Christian kingdom, when it deposes a tyrant, is in a sense subordinate to the Pope: first, in that the Pope has power to forbid any such kingdom to rise up hastily against its king and depose him, without a prior examination of the case by the Pope himself, in order to avert the moral and spiritual ills, the sedition and the unjust rebellion that might arise; secondly, in that the Pope has the power to take the initiative, and command or force the kingdom to depose its king, when such a course may be deemed necessary for the spiritual welfare of the kingdom, particularly for the avoidance of heresies or schisms.

18. The next question taken up by Suárez is: supposing such a just sentence has been passed against a king, in what manner may that king be punished? Suárez holds that the person who imposed the sentence, or the agent to whom he has committed the charge, may deprive the king of his kingdom, even by slaying him, if no other means of carrying out the sentence can be found and if the sentence is justly extended to include such a penalty; for the power to impose a just sentence presupposes the power to execute, directly or with aid, the punishment imposed. But the condemned king may not be slain straightway, or even forcibly expelled, simply by any private individual, whomsoever. Such an individual must first be generally commissioned to perform the act, either by the sentence itself, or by law. He will then be acting as the minister of the state, in cases in which the sentence has been imposed by the state,

and on the public authority. In like manner, when the sentence has been imposed by the Pope, the expulsion or slaying is to be brought about by those persons whom he has charged with the task; if he does not designate any agent, the legitimate successor to the kingdom will be the proper agent, or, in default of such a successor, the kingdom itself. The doctors, he says, apply the foregoing to heretical kings who have been publicly sentenced.

19. What Suárez has just said raises another point, the fact that one who has justly been condemned to death may not therefore be slain by any private individual whomsoever, acting on his own authority. If this is true of an ordinary criminal, it is, he asserts, far more true in the case of a prince. Neither does the sentence contain of itself a tacit authorization to every person whomsoever to make himself its executor. For—as Suárez once more points out—sentence in the case of an ordinary person does not involve such a tacit authorization, and still less does it do so, when the one condemned is a prince, since prudence and a just mode of execution are always requisite, and since the danger of disturbances and coercion is especially great when a prince is involved. Thus sentence passed by the Pope does not give any and every prince the power to commence a war against the prince condemned; for we assume that the former prince is not the temporal superior of the latter, nor does the papal sentence automatically confer upon him that power to wage war. The legitimate successor alone, Suárez repeats, provided he is a Catholic, and in cases in which the Pope has designated no executor, has such power; if he neglects the task or if there is no such successor, the kingdom as a whole—if it be a Catholic kingdom—receives the power, although this kingdom may ask and receive aid of other princes, in discharging this function. However, the Pope may designate other kings as possessors of the power in question, in which case, they may justly invade the kingdom of the condemned king.

20. Accordingly, Suárez concludes that the third part of the oath under discussion involves: (a) an excessive assumption of power, (b) an injustice against morality, and (c) an error op-

posed to the true and Catholic doctrine. He proves the first charge when he asks by what authority the King compels his subjects to swear that a proposition, which has not yet been condemned by the Catholic Church, is heretical. If the King answers that the proposition has been condemned by the Council of Constance, then, in the first place, he is inconsistent, since he holds that the authority of councils, and particularly of modern councils, counts for nothing; and, in the second place, the proposition condemned by the Council of Constance does not correspond to the proposition against which the oath is directed; for the former makes no mention of "princes who have been excommunicated or deprived of their dignity by the Pope," nor does it contain the words, "through the agency of their own subjects or of any other person whomsoever." If the King is relying on his own authority, he is assuredly guilty of an abuse of power, and of an arrogation to himself of authority to define matters of faith, such as he has criticized the Pope for exercising. Again, the King is inconsistent in that he holds nothing to be of the faith which is not found in the Scriptures; but he does not show that the Scriptures condemn as heretical the proposition in question; nor does St. Paul's exhortation to be obedient to the higher powers refer, Suárez points out, to powers that have been excommunicated or removed by the Pope. Thus, to take such an oath, is, in a sense, to confess that the King has power to condemn propositions, at will, as heretical, and to prescribe to the faithful what they shall believe, "which, on the part of the King, is an abuse and usurpation of spiritual power, and, on the part of those who take the said oath, a virtual profession, so to speak, of false faith."

21. Moreover, in support of the first and second charges, the very words of the oath are a clear proof that it calls not merely for civil obedience, or a profession of such obedience. For civil obedience is of an order far inferior to the Christian faith; and, in this case, the King is requiring Christian subjects to abhor as heretical a proposition which—as was said above—is condemned merely on his own authority. "Wherefore," Suárez says, "it has been sufficiently proved that the oath in question

is, on the part of the King, unjust: inasmuch as it exceeds his power in many ways, and thus constitutes a violent coercion, and a usurpation of another's authority. Again, on the part of the faithful, it is in like manner unjust to take the oath," for they are either swearing illicitly, if they believe the proposition—which is most true and certain according to the true principles of the faith—to be heretical, solely on the authority of the King, or perjuring themselves, if they do not in their hearts believe that it is heretical; and, furthermore, "such a profession involves a special and real injury to the Pope, whose power and [right to] obedience they deny through human fear."

22. The third charge is easily proved. One doctrinal error involved in the oath is the denial of the Pope's power to depose a heretical or schismatic king who is drawing his kingdom into such heresy or schism. Another error—less readily apparent, but implied in the oath—is the imputation to a temporal king of the power to require that his subjects shall swear to beliefs laid down by him in matters pertaining to the doctrines of the faith and the abhorrence of heresies, and—what is more—the implication that in such a case the decision of the king is to be preferred to that of the Pope. This would constitute a virtual profession that a temporal king possesses primacy in spiritual, or ecclesiastical, matters, "and accordingly," so Suárez concludes the chapter, "the profession of the oath in question is clearly a profession of schism and error; therefore, true Catholics are in conscience bound to reject the oath."

CHAPTER VI

MARIANA'S *DE REGE ET REGIS INSTITUTIONE*

WITHOUT referring to Mariana's history of Spain—not merely a history, but one of the glories of Spanish prose—we need only mention that, were he not the greatest of Spanish historians, his tractate *De Rege et Regis Institutione,* appearing in the last years of the sixteenth century, would cause the name of Mariana to be held in grateful remembrance by those who believe that a king or a chief magistrate is but a trustee of his fellow-countrymen, and it would be something akin to execration for those who maintain that the emperor or king rules of his own right as divinely instituted. The tractate whereof we are speaking was not exactly a companion piece of Erasmus' famous admonitions to a Christian prince, but rather a successor pushing the Erasmian doctrine to its logical conclusion, and indeed adding to it. In another respect the two treatises were similar, if not identical, in that Erasmus wrote for a Spanish prince, Charles I of Spain—later to be the Emperor Charles V—while Mariana wrote for a youth later to become King Phillip III of Spain. However, the views of Erasmus concerning the education of his prince have not been the subject of criticism, while the views of Mariana have been condemned in so far as he not only admitted but advocated the doctrine of tyrannicide, although his treatise has otherwise had the good fortune to be commended by a competent Protestant authority as an "excellent mirror for kings," containing "more healthy material for the education of future monarchs than any other existing princely mirror," and being "worthy of all respect, as much from kings themselves, as from their educators." And as Dr. Leutbecher, from whom we have quoted, ejaculates, "Would that all kings were as Mariana wanted them to be!" [1]

We have therefore selected various passages for consideration and comment, as they are of more than passing—indeed of surpassing—interest. The selections are taken from Chapters I, II, V, VI, VII, VIII and IX of the first Book, which deals with the origin of the state, its forms of government, the relation of people as the source of power to their chief magistrates, and the remedies, assuredly drastic enough, although not undeserved, against those who come into power illegally, and those who, legally in office, abuse their trust.

In Chapter I, dealing with man as a "sociable animal," Mariana draws the conventional classical pictures—to a large extent, in the conventional classical phrases—first, of man as a solitary and lawless being (controlled solely and loosely by a natural impulse of respect, within families, for the individual clearly the superior in age); next, of man in a "golden age," leading a simple and peaceful life, which was nevertheless full of material hardships and perils. For God purposely left men more exposed to the elements, less protected from such hardships by instinct, and weaker in many ways, than were the other animals; and He did so with the same motive that He had in giving men speech: namely, that they might be impelled to mutual association, mutual aid and mutual love.

Finally, driven by natural adversities, and by increasing selfishness and violence among men themselves, "those who found themselves oppressed by the more powerful, began to associate in groups united by a mutual bond of fellowship; and to look to some particular individual, outstanding in justice and good faith, under whose protection they might ward off injuries, private or public, might establish an equitable state of affairs, and might bind by uniform laws the high, the low and those of intermediate rank. This was the origin of civil groups and of the kingly majesty, which, in those early times, was obtained

[1] Quoted by Father Augustinus Lehmkuhl, S.J., in his article on Mariana in the *Catholic Encyclopedia,* vol. ix, p. 659.

not through wealth and ambitious devices, but through moderation, innocence and manifest virtue."

Therefore, man should not rail against nature and against Providence, but should on the contrary be grateful to them, for the debilities and needs through which he was led to enjoy the great blessings resulting from a social mode of living. It is in consequence of these debilities and needs that, "there exists nothing [created], more excellent, more pleasing, than man, who has been chastened through discipline, recalled to moderation, and constrained by law and by a superior power."

Chapter II deals with the question whether a state should be ruled by one, rather than by many.

Mariana first summarizes the contents of the preceding chapter, and then describes the kingly majesty which arose with the first civil societies as "a guardian of the multitude, so to speak, preference having been accorded to some one individual who was believed to be outstanding in probity and prudence; a majesty which was attended by no terrifying princely pomp, which—in the beginning—was hedged about with no laws. The goodwill of the citizens protected against dangers, the ruler who dwelt with them under a system of equal rights. Both the state as a whole and private controversies were regulated in accordance with his will and his decisions; for there was no undertaking so grave—provided only it was just—but the individual citizens, and the whole body of citizens as well, hoped that it might be achieved with such a prince as its author."

However, laws were later established, and for a twofold reason. (1) The equity of the prince fell under suspicion, since it is indeed difficult for one individual to view all matters impartially, unmoved by favoritism, hatred or other sentiments. Therefore, laws were promulgated, as a means of insuring impartiality. It is in this connection that Mariana defines a law as, "a rational principle free from every disturbing element, and drawn from the divine mind: a principle which prescribes that which is honorable and salutary, and prohibits the contrary." (2) The increasing depravity of men made it necessary that there should be laws to curb their vices; and not merely the few simple laws which were probably established in the beginning, but a great number of them, increasingly elaborate and severe.

The point in the history of government on which Mariana next touches, is the growth of the original small city states into great empires, owing to various motives—greed, ambition, sometimes resentment of an injury received—which moved their kings to wars of conquest. For example, Ninus, Cyrus, Alexander and Caesar, who were the first to establish great empires, were not legitimate kings; moreover, far from being the enemies of tyranny and vice which they wished to seem, and in spite of the high esteem in which they are held by the common run of mankind, their acts were the acts of robbers.

Mariana now turns to the precise question suggested by the chapter title, the question of whether it is preferable to other forms of rule, and most expedient to human welfare, that a state or province should be ruled by one king; or whether the power and sovereignty should be divided among various persons, —either a few selected from the whole mass, or the entire body of citizens living within the same bounds and under the same laws.

First Mariana presents the arguments in favor of a monarchical form of government. Briefly, these are based upon an analogical form of government as observed in the workings of nature, and in institutions such as the home and the first states (organized when men were nearer to their first and best origins, and had a better perception of the nature of things); upon the fact that a monarchy is best fitted for the preservation of peace, and affords less opportunity for greed, injustice and extravagance; and finally, upon the fact that the power to rule and command is useless when not backed by strength, while such strength exists to a much more adequate degree—whether it be in the shape of wealth, authority, or popular support—when concentrated in one person, than when divided among several or many.

There are, however, certain arguments in favor of democratic forms of government. These Mariana discusses, admitting that weighty authorities yield to their force. For instance, even

Aristotle approves of the rule of one, only in states wherein one man stands out above all the rest in every gift of mind and body. In regard to forms of government, as in all other questions—concludes Mariana—there will be a difference of tastes, and the form which is most excellent will not, simply for that reason, accord with the customs and institutions of all peoples. Neither does he deny that certain perils accompany monarchies, nor that the latter frequently degenerate into tyrannies; but he does hold that these evils are offset by still greater advantages, and that government by one is, on the whole, to be preferred to all other systems.

At this point, Mariana repeats and develops the argument that monarchical government makes for peace—peace among the citizens, a most essential factor to the state, and well worth exposure to peril in its attainment. "For what is more excellent than peace," he exclaims, "through which cities are adorned and embellished, public and private fortunes insured? What is more deadly than war, by which all things are overturned, consumed, and brought to destruction? Small realms wax greater through concord; the greatest perish as the result of dissension." Thus he continues to advance arguments in favor of monarchies, remarking pessimistically that, "among all classes of the people, the vast majority are wicked," so that, when power is placed in the hands of the many, the better part are certain to be submerged by the less worthy; whereas this is not the case, under one good prince. And from Spanish history he cites further examples, demonstrating the inadvisability of a division of power.

However, Mariana adds that his preference is for a monarchy in which the best of the citizens, or "aristocrats," are summoned to give counsel, public and private affairs being regulated in the light of their advice; for it is by following this course of government that the ship of state may be steered into "the longed for port of happiness."

On the other hand, "One can conceive of no graver pestilence than a king who serves his personal inclinations, or governs the public and private affairs of his subjects on the sole basis of his own judgment or that of his courtiers. This fact is clearly indicated by the pitiful fall of great empires, and the unforgettably dire disasters that overtook them. For when the king abandons benevolence and assumes the rôle of a tyrant, when his courtiers rule in his name, he must needs plunge all parts of the state into ruin, and hurl headlong into the gravest disasters, the subjects who trusted in his good faith. Nature has, in truth, provided that certain things of surpassing excellence shall, if they are corrupted, sink into evils of the worst and most loathsome sort. Nor is this of slight weight as an indication that the monarchical power is more excellent than other forms—[this very fact] that monarchy declines into the worst tyranny and the most noxious form of government. For the worst must necessarily be opposed to the best, and the most notorious rule, to that which is most salutary."

The question discussed in Chapter V is the difference between a king and a tyrant. In order that we may the better comprehend the distance which separates the benevolence of a king from what Mariana considers the insane fury of a tyrant, he first enumerates and defines the six forms of government: monarchies (in which the sum of power is conferred upon one man); aristocracies; republics; democracies; oligarchies; tyrannies (the last and worst of these forms, and the antithesis of monarchies). It is unnecessary for our purpose to repeat all of the definitions given by Mariana, but it may be noted that he has apparently listed the six forms in what is, to his mind, a descending order of merit, each good governmental form having its corresponding antithesis.

By way of a preliminary contrast, Mariana remarks that "the tyrant . . . afflicts his subjects with a grievous power which—in many cases—has been seized by violence; or else, even if this power be sound in its origin, it lapses into vice, and particularly, into avarice, lust and cruelty. Furthermore, while the part of a true king is to protect the innocent, repress the wicked, act as a safeguard, and enrich the state in all good things and in felicity, the tyrant, on the contrary, has used the highest power as a license for infinite lust and the enjoyment thereof, considering no wickedness as degrading to him, and finding no crime so grave that he will not undertake to commit it. He overthrows the fortunes of the powerful; he violates the chaste; he slays the virtuous; at one time or another in his life, he engages in every form of wantonness. Again, the [true] king is gentle and tractable, he is easy of access, he lives under equal laws with his fellow-citizens; while the tyrant—since he is distrustful of the [other] citizens, whom he fears—is wont to inspire terror with his royal pomp and exceeding wealth, with the harshness of his manner, with the savage cruelty of his judgments."

There is still more to be said, however, regarding the difference between kings and tyrants; and we must take under consideration the origins, methods, and progress of the two kinds of rule.

After making this general statement, Mariana returns to his discussion of the virtues of the true king. Such a king receives his power from the people. Accordingly, he does not dominate over his subjects as though they were slaves, but governs them as his children. Being loved and defended by his people, he has no great need of guards for himself, nor of mercenaries for foreign wars. Yet he does not disarm the citizens, but on the contrary, endeavors to keep them trained and prepared for times of danger. He is not extravagant; he does not impose heavy taxes (unless they are strictly necessary—for Mariana was an economist as well as an historian—and even in such cases, he obtains the consent of the citizens, through explanation, not through threats or trickery); he does not consider himself the owner of the whole state and of his vassals. Nevertheless he enriches the public treasury, with the spoils of enemies; and in addition to living modestly himself, he will take care that his courtiers and officials do not filch from the public wealth. Thus Mariana points out that Henry III of Castile filled the royal treasury without deceiving or hurting a single one of his subjects; for he declared that he "dreaded the execration of the people more than the arms of enemies." And the true king will admonish the citizens as to their duty by the example of his own life and moderation, rather than by verbal precepts. In fact, a prince can not long deceive his people as to his way of living, since

"Majesty resembles light; for it brings into view and prominence, good deeds and bad, nor does it suffer them to remain hid." The true king will discourage flatterers. He will encourage sincere and honorable men to ascertain all that is said and done in the kingdom which concerns him, and to report to him the truth, however disagreeable that truth may be; for the public welfare will thus be promoted to an extent well worth his personal vexation, "And the roots of truth are bitter, but its fruits are exceedingly sweet." All the deeds of the king should be directed to increasing goodwill among his subjects, their happiness, and their wellbeing. He should not merely govern, but also protect, and guide them, as a shepherd does his flock. "Such," says Mariana, in conclusion, "are the virtues befitting a king; such is the path by which he wins to immortality."

The tyrant, however, treads the opposite course, one which leads to the ruin of the state. In the first place, his power, instead of having been granted to him because of his merits, has been seized by him by means of violence, riches, or ambitious intrigue; or else, if it was originally bestowed upon him by the will of the people, he is wielding it with violence, and is guided not by considerations of the public advantage, but by his own convenience, his own pleasure, and the licentiousness of his vices. At first, Mariana continues, he may display a false gentleness, a false sense of equity and clemency, while he strengthens his position and his resources. But, once that position is established, he breaks forth into every sort of cruelty and vice. Tyrants "strive to inflict injury upon all, to destroy all; but in particular, they attack with all their power those persons who are wealthy and virtuous. They are more distrustful of the good than of the wicked, the virtue of others being always a cause of dread to wicked persons." The cry of the tyrants is: "Whatever is exalted in the kingdom, let it be brought low!" They work to this end either by open violence, or by craft and secret accusations. They exhaust those subjects who remain; they increase the exactions of taxes and tribute; they stir up mutual strife among the citizens; they impose crushing tasks upon their subjects; and thus the people are kept from even aspiring to liberty. But the tyrant himself fears those in whom he inspires terror,—and must take care lest the persons whom he enslaves should rise up to destroy him; and thus he must deprive them of arms, of military exercises and other means of defense. "The tyrant feels fear, to be sure, and the [good] king feels fear. But the latter fears *for* his subjects; the former fears the subjects themselves, for his own sake, lest, forsooth, those whom he governs as if they were enemies, should strip him of his wealth and princely power." So it is that he forbids the citizens to congregate or speak freely, plunging them into the very depths of slavery, in which they are not free even to make complaint. He relies on secret inquisitions, on fraud, on friendship with foreign princes, on barbarian mercenaries, and dares not trust his own subjects.

Throughout this description of the tyrant, Mariana has sprinkled various historical examples. He cites last the case of Tarquin the Proud, whom he depicts as a typical tyrant. He concludes by remarking that such a tyrant overturns the whole state; plunders without respect to the laws, which he does not consider to be binding upon himself; brings every misfortune upon the citizens, when he intervenes in public affairs; wrongfully deprives men of their patrimony in order that he alone may be the owner of all fortunes, and strips the common people of their goods; so that there is no calamity which fails to visit his subjects.

In Chapter VI Mariana asks and answers the question, Is it right to overthrow a tyrant?[2] The tyrant, Mariana would have us believe, thus abhorred by God and man alike, suffers in his own mind and conscience a severe punishment for his sins, although he may seem to enjoy exceeding happiness. He is urged on, by an avenging heaven, to acts that will destroy him.

Accordingly, history—ancient and modern—abounds with examples of tyrants who have met with ruin through the hatred

[2] *An tyrannum opprimere fas sit.* The words seem to have been chosen with special care: *fas* implying a moral and divine sanction, not merely a human or legal permission; *opprimere* meaning to overthrow, or crush, with an implication of killing, although the act is not definitely mentioned.

of their peoples. Mariana proceeds to describe at length one of these instances: the slaying of Henry III of France by the monk Jacques Clément.

Speaking as an historian, Mariana declares that this event was a glorious yet pitiful reminder of the fact that the minds of the people must be kept tranquil, for their minds can not be ruled in the same fashion as their bodies. Such deeds—repugnant though they are, and rarely worthy to be recorded—nevertheless serve as a lesson to princes that their impious daring may not pass entirely unpunished; for the power of princes is weak, once reverence departs from the minds of their subjects. Mariana gives a full—though possibly not an impartial—account of the assassination of Henry. He depicts Henry as a perfidious tyrant; the Duke of Guise and his family as brave and blameless, the very hope of France; and Clément as one who sought to save his country, a youth "of simple spirit and delicate body, whose mind and [bodily] force were nevertheless strengthened by a high power." Of the blow struck by Clément, Mariana exclaims: "Illustrious boldness! Memorable deed!" And, speaking of the consequent slaughter of the monk, he adds: "Thus perished Clément, the eternal glory of France, as many persons have thought." On second thought, it may be said in passing, the phrase *aeternum Galliae decus* disappeared, at the suggestion of Mariana's superiors, from the second edition of the *De Rege et Regis Institutione*. This, it would seem, was the only phrase suppressed in the edition in question, which, curiously enough, appeared in 1603, the very year in which King James VI of Scotland left Edinburgh for London, bringing with him his "divine right of kings."

However, Mariana points out diverse opinions as to the act of Clément. Many persons praised it and considered it an immortal deed. Others—outstanding in prudence and in learning—condemned the act, "denying that it is right for any person acting on private authority, to slay a king who has been acclaimed by the consent of the people, and anointed and consecrated by the sacred oil, according to custom, though his conduct may be depraved and he may have degenerated into tyranny."

Mariana takes up first the arguments and examples in favor of the latter view. There was the case of Saul, whom David not only spared, in spite of the former's wickedness, but avenged against the Amalekite who slew Saul at his own bidding. Again, the Roman Emperors, in the days of their persecution of the early Christian Church, met not with vengeance, but with patience and obedience. St. Paul's admonition to obey the powers constituted by God is also mentioned. Moreover, in addition to the fact that kings have the sanction of God and of the state, there is the danger that a change of government may bring about evils worse than those which already existed, a fact which is also attested by history. It should be observed, too, that the clemency of kings depends upon the attitude of their subjects, as well as upon their own attitude, and that the apparent cruelty of kings may be a necessary harshness resulting from the faults of their subjects. Furthermore, it would interfere with the necessary sentiment of reverence toward kings, if the subjects were persuaded that they had the right to inflict punishment for the sins of the former. Constant turmoil, for real or apparent reasons, would be the result.

So much for the arguments against tyrannicide; but the opposing arguments are no less numerous and weighty. In the first place, the kingly power was originally derived from the state, even hereditary royal power requiring confirmation by the oath of the people for its transference, and the state has retained, not merely certain legislative and other powers, but also the power to recall the king to order, in case of necessity, and even—if he refuses to amend his ways—to deprive him of his principate. Furthermore, history shows that in all times, those who have attempted to slay tyrants have been accorded great praise. Again, there is the argument that a tyrant is like a cruel and savage beast, from whom we should defend our native land, even though it be at great risk to ourselves. For refusal to do so would be even worse than refusal to aid one's mother or wife when they are molested.

These are the arguments in favor of the two opposing views;

and it will not be difficult, says Mariana, to decide what our own view shall be.

He considers first the case of a prince who has seized his power by armed violence, without the consent of the citizens, and without other ground for his claim. Both the philosophers and the theologians would seem to agree that such a prince, being a true tyrant in title and in behavior, may be slain by any person whatsoever, thus undergoing violent deprivation of the power which he violently seized.

But what of the prince whose sovereignty was obtained by popular consent or by hereditary right? Mariana believes that, under these circumstances, "the vices and wanton passions of the prince should be endured up to the point where he becomes heedless of those laws of virtue and modesty which he is bound to maintain." For princes should not lightly be changed, lest the greater evils already mentioned should result; yet they ought not to be permitted to destroy the state, plunder public and private fortunes, hold laws and religion in contempt, and make virtues of arrogance, audacity, and impiety. The means of deliverance from such a prince, however, is in itself a matter calling for careful deliberation. If public assemblies are allowed, a common agreement should be arrived at and adopted, as to the proper course. Moreover, the following steps should be taken: firstly, admonition of the prince (which, if he heeds it and mends his ways, should be sufficient, without more drastic remedies); secondly, a sentence, to be passed by the state (in case the prince does not heed the admonition and no hope of his correction remains), depriving him of his power; and (since war will necessarily follow) the necessary plans for defence, the procuring of arms and money, and finally, if the case should so require and no other means of protecting the state should be adequate, "by this same right of defence and, moreover, by the state's own superior authority, the slaying of the prince by the sword, as a declared public enemy. Furthermore, this same authority shall reside in any private individual who wills to assume it, with no hope of impunity for himself and heedless of his own safety in his attempt to succor the state." If, as often happens, public assemblies are not allowed, the situation is not really different. As long as the state is oppressed by such tyranny, the citizens will have the same right to agree among themselves that it should be stamped out, and he who, acting in accord with the public will, attempts to destroy the tyrant, has by no means acted iniquitously.

There still remains, however, this question: who may rightly be considered a tyrant? Mariana wisely makes no direct attempt to answer the question, apparently leaving it to be decided in each case on the basis of the acts of the ruler involved. He does, however, assure us that there will be no danger, as a result of his doctrine, of a multitude of uprisings against so-called tyrants. For in the first place, the whole people must have protested against the ruler, and the counsel of learned and authoritative men should be sought. And in any case, there are only too few individuals who care to sacrifice their own welfare and their lives in order to free their country. Nevertheless, the possibility of such a punishment will have a salutary and deterrent effect on bad kings; and "the point of chief importance is this: that the prince shall be persuaded that the authority of the state as a whole is greater than his own individual authority," nor shall he give credence to those base creatures who, for purposes of flattery, and with most pernicious effect, make the contrary assertion.

Much of the remainder of the chapter is devoted to a refutation of the opposing arguments already adduced. David, for example, had insufficient reasons for the slaying of Saul, and would not have been justified in so doing. As for the resignation and martyrdom of the early Christians, under the Roman Emperors, these constituted the foundations of the Church's greatness, and were therefore most seemly, although the contrary behavior was not essentially prohibited to them. Here Mariana turns aside for a moment from his answers to the arguments, and reminds us that the course which he has advocated should be followed to the end only in case of necessity. As the final step in his series of refutations, Mariana brings forth and answers one more argument, the fact that the Council of Constance rejected the assertion that "a tyrant may and should be slain by any subject whatsoever, and not merely by open violence, but even through snares and trickery."

Mariana replies that this rejection stands in a decree from which the approval of the Popes was withheld, and that it was passed under peculiar and disturbed circumstances, with reference to a special situation. One of its purposes, indeed, was to rebuke the excuse made for the assassination of Louis Orleans, an excuse in which it was alleged that "it is right to slay on private authority one whose character approaches tyranny (*quasi tyrannum*)." Such an act was indeed not permissible, and especially not, in view of the violated oath which was an additional feature of the case.

Mariana therefore concludes: "This is my opinion, assuredly offered in a sincere spirit. I shall be grateful if anyone can amend my remarks, since, being human, I may have been mistaken in that opinion. I should like to close this discussion with the words of the Tribune, Flavius, who—when he had been convicted of conspiracy against Domitius Nero, and was questioned as to why he had forgotten his oath [of allegiance]—replied: 'I loved you, nor was any one of your soldiers more faithful to you than I, as long as you merited love. I began to hate you when you had become the murderer of your mother and of your wife, a charioteer, an actor, an incendiary.' O, soldierly and courageous spirit!"

To us of today the title of Chapter VII—"Is it permissible to slay a tyrant with poison?"—seems strange and even revolting, but unfortunately in Mariana's day poison had, if not a legitimate, at least a recognized use. In the present analysis we need follow only the general trend of the argument, omitting in the text a detailed consideration of the question of poisoning. A summary of Mariana's views on this question are given, however, in a footnote.

Briefly, according to the argument of this chapter, the lot of the tyrant is indeed miserable, for he must trust in no one, realizing that his slayer would only be committing a welcome and glorious deed; and it is right that he who causes fear should live in fear, right that a gangrened member should be cut from the body which it imperils; but, granting that thus to cut off the tyrant, in open violence, with the sword, is a rightful act, there still remains the question of whether it is right to kill him by means of snares and intrigues. To this question, Mariana replies in the affirmative, remarking that he himself commends the practice of the Spartans, who sacrificed only a white cock to Mars when victory had been won in actual battle, whereas they slaughtered a fat bull for him, if the victory was the result of craft!—as if to say that it is better to preserve one's army unhurt and to conquer by the human qualities of prudence and reason, than to win through the physical strength in which man is surpassed by the beasts.[8]

The eighth chapter answers a question formerly much debated but now looked upon, at least by the enlightened, as settled—"Which has the greater power, the state or the king?"

Mariana discusses this delicate question delicately, but leaves the impression (repeatedly confirmed in the following chapter) that the state may and should retain the ultimate power for itself, in certain essential respects. To be sure, he grants that "the royal power is supreme in the kingdom with regard to all those matters which have been given over to the will of the prince by the custom of the people, by settled institutions, or by fixed law, whether they relate to the waging of war, the administration of justice among his subjects, or the creation of chiefs and magistrates." In such matters, the prince will have a power not only greater than that of other individuals, but greater than the power of the whole; there shall be none to resist him, to demand an account of his acts, to undo what he has done, or even to dispute

[8] Mariana argues that to slay a tyrant by poisoning, however, is a different matter, for, as a rule, it would result in causing the tyrant—howsoever ignorantly—to commit suicide, a death that is contrary to the law of nature: there are certain exceptional cases in which the poison is so strong that it slays the person exposed to it, in some external manner—for example, simply by being poured upon his clothing—and in such cases, since he himself is not caused to administer the poison to himself, suicide is not involved; poisons of this sort have in the past been sent to certain kings in the guise of gifts, and while it is not permissible to present such ostensible gifts to one who does not suspect your enmity, or who believes that a reconciliation has been effected between you, the tyrant has no right to hope for such a friendly attitude from his subjects, so long as he continues to be a tyrant; he should fear even those who bear gifts, for "it is permissible to make an attack against his life by any device whatsoever, provided only that he is not compelled, either knowingly or in ignorance, to be a conspirator in his own death"; most cases of poisoning, however, would come under this prohibited head.

concerning it; for this is the established practice of almost all peoples.

So it doubtless was in Mariana's day, but with the source of power in individuals, and therefore in the people, it would be suicidal on the part of a modern monarch or other chief of state to arrogate to himself alone the authority to declare war. Indeed, in the United States the Congress, by an express provision of the Constitution, is possessed of the exclusive right to declare war and the rôle of the President is merely to proclaim it, after it has been declared by the Congress of the United States. It is also the custom in our day to separate the executive from the judicial power, lest justice be contaminated at its source. And the creation of the principal chiefs and magistrates is, we may say, governed by statute or by custom having the force of law. With us the President can only appoint important officials subject to confirmation by the Senate of the United States of America.

With respect to certain other points, however, Mariana holds that "the authority of the state is greater than that of the prince, provided that the former agrees as a whole upon one and the same opinion." In this class of questions, Mariana includes the imposition of tribute, the abrogation of laws, changes in succession to the kingly power, and any other matters which the people as a whole may have reserved for themselves. Mariana then adds: "Finally, and what is most important, there resides in the state the power to repress the prince in wrongdoing, if he is tainted with vice and wickedness, if—ignoring the true path to glory—he has preferred to be feared by his subjects rather than to be loved by them, ruling through fear a trembling and prostrate people; [if, in short,] he has become a tyrant and continues to pursue this injurious course."

"How may the state subdue a prince who is oppressing it with his depraved conduct," Mariana asks, "and degenerating into open tyranny; how may it even deprive him—if this be necessary—of his principate and his life, unless it does so through a superior power retained within the state itself, when the latter delegated to the king his share of power?"

To a further question whether a state may delegate absolutely all power to its king—depriving itself even of the parts which have been described above as pertaining to the state alone, Mariana wisely and prudently replies that he himself is not interested in whether or not this act of delegation is possible; but simply in the fact that it would be very undesirable either for the state to delegate such power, or for the prince to accept it, since the result would be, in his opinion, that the monarchy would degenerate into a tyranny.

In Chapter IX a question is decided which never should have been raised: whether the prince is free from obligation to obey the laws.

By way of introduction to this theme, Mariana laments the tendency of princes—and we may ourselves add, chief executives in general—to heed flattering courtiers, rather than to remember that nothing is more fortifying to their royal estate than the quality of modesty. They should be conscious of the obedience they owe, first, to God; secondly, to the requirements of honor and righteousness; and finally, to the demands of popular opinion and posthumous fame.

The prince should also bear in mind the fact that the sacred laws on which the public welfare depends, need the confirmation of his example, in order that they may be stable. Moreover, although it is permissible, in case of necessity, for kings to propose new laws, interpret and soften the old, and supply deficiencies in the law as it stands, it is not permissible for them to overthrow the law in accordance with their own whims or adapt it to their wanton desires and private advantage, restrained by no reverence for the customs and institutions of the country; for such behavior is a characteristic vice of tyrants. A prince has no greater power than that which would be vested in the people as a whole, under a popular form of government, no greater power than that which would be held by the chief men of the state, in an aristocracy; and therefore, he should not suppose that he enjoys any greater freedom from his own laws than that which would be enjoyed by the people, or the chief men, under the circumstances mentioned. This is especially true in view of the fact that many laws have not even been decreed by the prince, but have been established by the will of the state as a whole, while the authority of this whole to command or to prohibit, and its sovereignty, are greater than the authority and the sovereignty of the prince. These remarks are illustrated by means of various historical examples; among them, that of Augustus, to whom there was granted a dispensation from any obligation to observe the laws, and who, in spite of his clemency and other good qualities, was therefore a tyrant. In a word, the doctrine is here implied, if not expressed, that a people may not rightfully enslave itself.

Mariana recognized that his views in regard to the binding force of laws over kings might be open to objections and attempted limitations. He concedes, in particular, that there are certain laws which do not apply to the prince and would indeed impede him in the exercise of his princely functions; to these laws, he would not subject the prince. But, on the other hand, there are many laws—for example, those which relate to good moral conduct—by which the prince is bound, since, in spite of his exalted position, he does not cease to be a man and a member of the state. As to the theory that the king is subject to the directive, but not to the coercive, force of the law, Mariana upholds the opposite view, that the king is subject to both the directive and the coercive force of the law. He goes so far as to remark that, with respect to those laws which the state has sanctioned, the prince is indeed bound, as the power of the state is greater than and therefore superior to that of the prince. And in case of necessity, he may even be coerced by the punishment of deposition and death. With respect to the laws which the prince alone and on his own authority has decreed, Mariana is not so severe, leaving the matter of obedience in the hands of the prince himself, with no threat of punishment to coerce him. Nevertheless he concludes the chapter with a description of the advantages to be gained both by the prince and by the state from the former's support of all the laws.

It is well for us to remember that this tractate—*De Rege et Regis Institutione*—was written by a Spaniard and that it was published in 1599.

CHAPTER VII

LE CONTR'UN DE LA BOÉTIE—TYRANNICIDE THROUGH THE AGES

THE most intimate of Montaigne's friends, whose early death the great essayist regarded not only as a personal but as a public loss, was Etienne de la Boétie, like Montaigne a lawyer, and also like him a magistrate at Bordeaux. Deeply interested in things classical, La Boétie wrote in his teens, and apparently for his own pleasure, a *Discours de la Servitude Volontaire*, which passes current under the title of *Contr'un*. Whatever its name, it is in fact a literary exercise in behalf of liberty in which he condemns tyranny in any and all of its forms as ruinous alike to the tyrant, the state and the people. Many years after his death it first appeared in print in a collection published in 1574,[1] and from that day to this it has been a favorite of the advocates of liberty such as De Laminet and of contemners of tyranny, whose names are legion. It is as a primer in the "battle of books" waged on the subject of tyranny in the sixteenth century, and for this reason we present a somewhat extensive abstract of it, which with our subsequent analysis of the famous *Vindiciae contra Tyrannos* will enable the reader the better to understand the doctrine of tyrannicide as it developed in France.

In considering La Boétie's *Discours de la Servitude Volontaire* or *Contr'un*, we should bear in mind that La Boétie followed no set plan in the famous *Discours*, which is remarkable rather for its spontaneous eloquence and rich classical background than for closeness of reasoning. It is therefore characteristic that he begins the *Discours* with a classical quotation, "No good thing is a multitude of lords; let there be one lord, one king."[2] La Boétie

[1] Simon Goulart's *Memoires de l'Estat de France*.

[2] *Iliad*, Bk. II, lines 204-5 (pp. 64-65 of the Loeb edition). Odysseus was speaking thus to the common soldiers when the Greek troops were planning to return home without taking Troy; La Boétie accordingly suggests that we excuse Odysseus in view of the circumstances and interpret his words as conforming to expediency rather than to truth.

is indeed heartily in accord with Odysseus' initial statement, regarding a multitude of lords, but he takes exception to the concluding exhortation. For subjection to one master—he declares—is in itself a great evil, even though subjection to many is a still greater evil. These observations lead us to the brink of a question which La Boétie puts aside for the time being, as not strictly pertinent to the matter in hand, although we are allowed to draw our own inferences as to his attitude. Now this question is: "Are other forms of commonwealth (*républiques*) preferable to monarchy?" In answering this question, he says we might first wish to assure ourselves that a monarchy is indeed a form of commonwealth; since the "common" element in a government given over to one person is scarcely visible!

After partially evading and partially answering this dangerous question, La Boétie, marveling at the indifference of men toward their natural right to liberty, declares that what absorbs his attention for the moment, is the amazing spectacle of great numbers of people, towns, cities and countries, all voluntarily submitting themselves to the miserable servitude imposed by a single tyrant. For these voluntary serfs, he adds, are not coerced by fear of the tyrant's strength, nor by the exigencies of war, as in the case of Athens submitting to the thirty tyrants; nor are they moved by love and gratitude for the good qualities of the tyrant, motives which could at least be partially condoned. Such a willing servitude "not to a Hercules"—be it said—"nor to a Samson, but to a single wretched manikin, often the most craven and effeminate individual of the whole nation,"[8] passes the very bounds of cowardice. What word, indeed—demands La Boétie—can be found for such base conduct, "which nature disowns and the tongue refuses to name"? History—when recording battles

[8] Approximately at this point in the text, Bonnefon in his edition of the *Discours* (Paris, 1922), which we are here using, adds a note suggesting that La Boétie's portrait of a tyrant is partially symbolic and general, partially the representation of an historical figure. He quotes Delornelle to the effect that this historical figure is Nero. (L. Delornelle, *L'inspiration antique dans le "Discours de la Servitude volontaire," Revue d'histoire littéraire de la France,* XVII (17ᵉ année), pp. 34-72). But surely the critics do not mean to say that La Boétie's youthful ardor was aroused to such a pitch simply by the memory of Nero and a vague general conception of tyranny, without reference to specific figures or events of more recent date.

like those of Miltiades, Leonidas and Themistocles—indicates that the defence of liberty is a marvellously powerful motive in war, far more forcible than mere greed, and capable of imparting the greater strength to the physically weaker side; yet we are confronted with the astounding fact that in every country, day after day,[4] thousands of men yield up this rich treasure of liberty to a single individual, and do so not merely without a struggle but even as collaborators in his crimes against themselves. For there is no need of any aggressive struggle against this solitary tyrant; all that is required is that the country shall cease to consent to servitude, and cease to give actual support to his tyranny. Nor is there need for this purpose to sacrifice the assurance of some sort of miserable existence to the doubtful hope of a happy life; for if the fire of tyranny is no longer fed by obedience, services, and other attributes of the people, it will consume itself and die away for lack of fuel, even though no one runs the risk of bringing water to extinguish the flames. But alas! there is one good thing which the people, for all their covetousness, apparently do not desire; and that good, strangely enough, is liberty, without which they must indeed suffer many ills and enjoy but faintly the good things which they actually possess. In a passage which may not be paraphrased, La Boétie appeals to the love of liberty of his own and future generations: "He who abuses you so cruelly has but two eyes, two hands, one body; nor has he any other thing not possessed by the meanest man in all our countless cities, save only the advantages bestowed upon him by yourselves and for your own destruction. Whence has he secured so many eyes for spying upon you, unless you yourselves supply them? Whence, save from you, so many hands with which to smite you? Whence, if they be not yours, has he the feet that trample down your cities? By what means has he gained any power over you, save through yourselves? How would he dare attack you, were it not that he is in league with you? What harm could he do you, were you not receivers for

[4] *en tous pays . . . tous les jours,* one of the phrases scattered throughout the *Discours* which indicate that, despite its classical tone, Nero and other ancient tyrants were not the sole objects of La Boétie's generous wrath.

the thieves who steal your goods, accomplices of the murderers who slay you, and indeed traitors to yourselves?"

La Boétie now returns to the starting point, with the admonition: "Resolve that you will remain in servitude no longer, and behold! you are free." He does not require of the people that they shall violently overthrow the tyrant, but merely that they shall cease to support him, whereupon he will fall of his own dead weight. However—says La Boétie—although it is better to leave incurable diseases alone, and to waste no appeals upon a people who so cling to servitude that their very love of liberty has lost much of its natural force, nevertheless, we may investigate the question, how is it that any people could have come to such a sorry pass.

As a preliminary to this investigation, La Boétie sets forth in some detail the thesis that the love of liberty is indeed natural to man in his original state. For, if men lived in accordance with nature, they would obey their parents and subject themselves to the rule of reason, and they would be slaves to no man; for nature, has she not molded all men on the same pattern, given them the whole world for their common lodging, and bestowed upon them the gift of speech, in order that they might be companions, understanding one another, while she has intended that even certain inequalities should serve to kindle fraternal affection between those who need aid and those able to give aid; and therefore, having made them companions, how can she have destined any of them for servitude to another? If, then, we grant that liberty is a natural gift, would it not follow that the impulse to defend one's liberty is also natural?—an inference which is strengthened by the conduct even of dumb beasts, who, in spite of the fact that they were made for man's service, are so resentful of servitude that they fight bitterly for their liberty and sometimes die as soon as they are made captive.

How, then, has man—born to live free—so forgotten his heritage and the very desire to regain it, that he willingly submits to a tyrant?

Now there are three means—says La Boétie—by which a tyrant may attain his power: election by the people; force of arms;

inheritance. Yet this distinction of method seems of slight significance to the author of the *Discours,* since the manner of reigning is similar in all the three cases: to tyrants raised to power by election, the people are bulls for taming; to conquerors in war, the people are their prey; to the heirs of the kingdom, its inhabitants are their natural slaves.

In any case, La Boétie prefers to examine more subtly the origin of tyrannical power. He therefore asks us to conceive of an entirely new and unprejudiced people, accustomed neither to servitude nor to liberty, but suddenly confronted with a choice between servitude under one man, and a free life subject simply to the laws of reason. Such a people would certainly favor the second alternative.[5] For no community of men worthy of manhood's name will, from their original state, deliberately and voluntarily cast themselves into subjection; they must first be reduced to subjection by one or both of two forces: coercion, and deception. Now coercion may be applied by foreign arms, as when Sparta and Athens were coerced by Alexander; or it may be applied by internal factions, as in the case of the triumph of Pisistratus over the aristocrats of Athens. Deception, La Boétie says, is most frequently self-deception, rather than external, and he adduces a striking example of such self-deception in the bestowal of power upon Dionysius by the people of Syracuse. In a word, the servitude of any people is originally involuntary.

Now custom is the first cause of their voluntary servitude. So swiftly do the victims become oblivious of their right to liberty, and so willingly do they adapt themselves to their new estate, that an observer might suppose them not to have lost their liberty, but to have "won their servitude." And those who are born into this state, carelessly accept it as their natural inheritance. As Mithridates is said to have hardened himself against poison by taking continual small doses, so custom inures us to the bitter poison of servitude; for custom has more power over men than has nature herself. Here La Boétie mentions various peoples who

[5] La Boétie admits that the people of Israel, when of their own accord they made for themselves a tyrant, may be an exception to his rule; but they were duly punished, and he appears to regard the exception with contemptuous indifference.

illustrate the force of environment and custom when working upon man's original nature. He contrasts the free Venetians with the slaves who live under the Sultan's rule. Among classical examples to which he calls attention is the admirable tale of two Spartans about to be delivered into the hands of Xerxes: Now Sparta had refused to pay the homage requested by Xerxes, but a Persian favorite of that monarch advised the two Spartans to seek and profit by the friendship of Xerxes, as he himself had done; to which the Spartans replied that the favorite was incapable of advising them well on this point, since he was acquainted only with that good which he promised—the king's favor—and not at all with the good which the Spartans would not relinquish —liberty; for had the favorite but tasted of its sweetness he would himself counsel them to defend it "tooth and nail." [6] "We never mourn," La Boétie concludes appropriately, "for that which we have never possessed; regret only comes in the wake of pleasure, and recognition of misfortune must ever be accompanied by the memory of bygone joys. It is indeed the nature of man to be free and to will that he be free; yet is his nature also such that it retains the bent given it by his rearing." The love of freedom is native in man—that is, inborn; but servitude may become natural to him, through custom.

This first cause of voluntary servitude, however, can not be entirely depended upon by tyrants. Generations of servitude may banish the desire and the very memory of freedom from the hearts of the many; but there are always some keener spirits who will reject that base estate even in its most luxurious guise and who will persist in the restless search for their lost inheritance as Odysseus searched restlessly on land and sea till he beheld the

[6] Another example given by La Boétie is less striking for the purposes of his argument at this particular point, but more pertinent to the question of tyrannicide. It is the anecdote of Cato the Younger, in his childhood, and the Dictator Sulla. The latter's house was, it seems, always open to Cato, for the two were closely related, and the child observed that judgment was passed there against citizens in a manner more tyrannical than was becoming to a representative of the people. He therefore suggested that his tutor provide him with a dagger, so that he might assassinate the Dictator in his very bedchamber. This speech, La Boétie characterizes as typically Roman, and as a beginning to Cato's career that was worthy of his glorious death.

smoke rising from his own chimney. Thus tyrants take care to crush out enlightenment, learning and frank intercourse among their subjects, lest the latter be roused to their ancient love of freedom. Free action, free speech, and even free thought are stifled. Once again La Boétie illustrates his argument by drawing upon classical mythology and classical history, lamenting, for example, that Brutus and Cassius dared not trust Cicero, the "keenest of spirits" for the public good, to aid them in freeing Rome—and indeed, the whole world— believing that his courage was not equal to his goodwill.

A second cause of voluntary servitude is the fact that, under the sway of tyrants, men easily become cowardly and effeminate; and this fact, too, tyrants are careful to control and exploit. Once more La Boétie resorts to classical illustrations. For example, when explaining why tyrants are urged to take such precautionary measures, he reminds us of Xenophon's much-quoted account of the tyrant's ills—Xenophon saying, among other things, that tyrants do ill to all, and therefore live in fear of all; and that in time of war they hire foreign mercenaries, not daring to put weapons into the hands of their own wronged subjects. A further and an outstanding example of a tyrannical ruse, selected by La Boétie, is the treatment which the inhabitants of Sardes received at the hands of Cyrus after the suppression of their revolt. Cyrus was unwilling either to sack so beautiful a city, or to maintain an army constantly on the spot; so he ingeniously weakened his victims with the pleasant poison of taverns and public amusements of a devitalizing nature! Again the Roman tyrants bethought them of yet another vulnerable point—the mouths of the people. The latter, having been presented with a little wheat, a little wine, a coin or two, burst into pitiable cheers for their oppressor, not realizing that they were merely getting back a little of their own property, and that the tyrant could not have given them that little had he not first taken it away from them. Thus Nero's games and feasts were so missed, that the people were on the point of mourning for the monster himself. All this does not astonish La Boétie, who recalls how, for similar reasons, they had mourned and honored Julius Caesar, that oppressor of law and liberty.

There are still other ways in which tyrants have pampered and hoodwinked the people. They have cloaked great crimes with some small pretense of interest in the public good, as did the Roman Emperors when they assumed the title of Tribunes of the People. Or—like the Kings of Assyria, Media and Egypt—they have kept their subjects in awe by an atmosphere of mystery and symbolism. The very victims of tyrants have aided in the mockery against themselves by spinning miraculous tales about their rulers—such tales as the legend of Pyrrhus' thumb and its healing powers. Withal, the tyrants could not believe in the security of their own irrational position as lone individuals abusing a multitude of men, so that they sought yet another shield in religion, and, attempting to borrow a spark of divinity to protect them in their wickedness, surely they merited a fate worse than that of Salmoneus, the comparatively innocent imitator of Heaven's lightning.

But La Boétie comes now to what he considers the very secret of tyrannical domination, its true support and foundation. In his opinion, this support does not consist in palace guards and armed troops—for indeed, among the Roman Emperors, the number slain by their own archers exceeded the number of those whose guards aided them in escape from danger. Rather does it center in a small group of persons—say, four or five—serving directly under the tyrant, for their own profit. A still larger number is to be found serving under these persons, for similar purposes, and so on, until the number of malefactors has swollen into millions, all the elements of the kingdom having grouped themselves about the original point of infection in the body politic.

La Boétie's transitions are not clear cut, but the reckless greed supporting this complicated structure might be considered, in a sense, as a third cause of voluntary servitude.

Now these countless malefactors are all attached to the string manipulated by a single tyrant, just as—according to Homer's account—all the gods were attached to a chain by which Jupiter could draw them to himself. The tyrant then, enslaves his subjects by means of some of their own number; he uses as guards the very persons against whom, were they not worthless, he would need to be guarded. Such wretches embrace their servitude, and console themselves for their wretchedness by persecuting, not their oppressor, but others among the oppressed. And yet their fellow victims who are not favorites of the tyrant are comparatively fortunate and free, since they have but to obey the monster, while their oppressors must also please him, perverting their energies, their whole lives, their every word and sign and glance, and their very natures, for his pleasure. Indeed, they have nothing that is their own—not even their happiness, their liberty, their bodies, or their lives—though they chose servitude for the sake of riches; for in so choosing, they gave the tyrant strength to deprive them of all their possessions. Pursuing such wealth as they may attain, hoping that they will find in it a means to win his favor and that this favor will in turn enrich them the more, they forget how many who were thus enriched momentarily, lost both wealth and life, and how few retained such wealth. History, ancient and more recent, shows clearly that the majority of persons who have grown rich under the shadow of a tyrant's favor, battening on the remains of others, have eventually fed that tyrant with their own remains. For the wicked accomplices of tyrants, the good men who serve them—such as Seneca, Burrus, Thrasea, and those for whom tyrants profess love or whom they ought to love—such as Poppaea, Agrippina, Messalina, must all alike dread a grisly reward from their master, unless they first slay him—frequently the fate of ancient tyrants, for example, of Commodus. Tyrants have never truly loved nor been loved, since only worthy persons can be friends, friendship being a relation based upon the knowledge of the integrity of the person loved. Moreover, even the element of equality is wanting between the tyrant and his accomplices, so that they lack also the tie of mutual fear and need that makes for honor among thieves. Those who seek tyrannical favor do so without regard to the clear evidence that others—as in the fable of the fox and the lion—have trod the same dangerous path before them, a path which shows no returning footprints. They are lured to their destruction by the glitter of the tyrant's treasures, as the satyr was lured by the Promethean fire, and Petrarch's butterfly by the flame. Moreover, they must fear not only their chosen master, but also his successor; for if they escape the wrath of the former, the latter—be he good or bad—will for one reason or another look upon them with disfavor. Their lives are a continual torment of toil and fear and pretense, for they can not be merry, and dare not be sad. Finally, these tools of tyranny are punished by the people's hatred in life, and by the hatred of posterity after death.

What is the moral of all this? The answer of La Boétie is not that of the man of action but that of the Christian philosopher: "Let us then . . . learn to do good; let us lift our eyes to heaven. . . . For my part, I hold—and rightly hold, since in the eyes of God the all bounteous and supremely gentle, there is nothing else so inacceptable as Tyranny—that in the lower world He has in store for tyrants and their accomplices a special punishment."

* * * * * * * *

Given the importance of the doctrine of tyrannicide, based as it is upon sovereignty vested in the people, we have deemed it advisable to summarize some epoch-making tractates by writers other than Spanish and belonging to different religious denominations, in order that the doctrine which Suárez professed might be revealed as it actually was. For it was not exclusively Catholic or exclusively Protestant, not of one country or of one decade; rather it was of many countries, including Greece and Rome, and indeed of many ages, ages culminating in our own period when the doctrine of the right of peoples to make and unmake their own governments is still the very keystone of that democracy which is essential to true internationalism.

The ancient conception of tyranny is given its most perfect expression by a Greek statesman, a Greek poet and a Greek philosopher.[7]

---

[7] See Professor William Talbot Allison's edition of Milton's *Tenure of Kings and Magistrates* (New York, 1911), Appendix, pp. 159-161. The Appendix is a concise but admirable account of tyrannicide.

First of Solon, the statesman (*circa,* B. C. 638-558):

> Truth it is that I declined the bloody desperate career
> Of tyrannical command, to rule alone and domineer;
> In my native happy land, with arbitrary force and fear;
> Neither have I since repented; unreproach'd, without a crime;
> Placed alone, unparalleled, among the statesmen of the time.[8]

The poet, Theognis of Megara (*circa* B. C. 570-548 or 544), having been deprived of property by a tyrant and forced into exile, thus expressed his indignation:

> Court not a tyrant's favor, nor combine
> To further his iniquitous design!
> But, if your faith is pledged, though late and loath,
> If covenants have pass'd between you both,
> Never assassinate him! keep your oath!
> But should he still misuse his lawless power,
> To trample on the people, and devour;
> Depose or overturn him—anyhow!
> Your oath permits it, and the gods allow.[9]

Finally the philosopher, Aristotle (B. C. 384-322), the founder of political science, who, in his *Politics*[10] refers to the "most typical form" of tyranny, as "the counterpart of the perfect monarchy," and describes it as "just that arbitrary power of an individual which is responsible to no one, and governs all alike, whether equals or betters, with a view to its own advantage, not to that of its subjects, and therefore against their will. No freeman, if he can escape from it, will endure such a government."

The medieval conception of tyranny we may not here consider in detail. It must suffice for present purposes to discuss briefly certain views on the subject set forth by St. Thomas Aquinas, who elaborated and developed so many doctrines of the Middle Ages, expressing them in a form so perfect that they are the doctrines of today and will remain the doctrines of tomorrow.[11]

---

[8] Trans. Frere, Works, III. 356.

[9] *Ibid.,* III. 361.

[10] IV. x. trans. Jowett.

[11] For an account of the views of authors in the Middle Ages on the subject of tyranny and the right of resistance on the part of the people, see Charles Bréchillet Jourdain, *Mémoire sur la Royauté Française et le Droit Populaire d'après les Ecrivains*

Now St. Thomas Aquinas was a contemporary of Louis IX—who personified the good ruler to the people of the Middle Ages—albeit the saint and doctor was somewhat younger than and died before the model king. St. Thomas Aquinas therefore had before his eyes a living example by which to measure the rights and duties of kings. In Part I of the second part of the *Summa Theologica,* St. Thomas asks a question very material to the present matter, which he answers, as was the wont of the schoolmen. The question was none other than "whether the old law enjoyed fitting precepts concerning rulers."[12] St. Thomas must have been very sure of himself and of his views, because, after stating the opponent's case in the form of objections, he then says—as always—in the first person, "I answer"; and his doctrine was, as we have seen, confirmed in the 80's of the last century by the Church of which he is an outstanding member. What is the answer in the present case? "Two points are to be observed concerning the right ordering of rulers in a state or nation." The first point—and indeed the fundamental one—is that "all should take some share in the government: for this form of constitution ensures peace among the people, commends itself to all, and is most enduring, . . ." What is his authority for such a theory of government? The exact reference is *Politics,* ii.6—meaning, of course, the *Politics* of Aristotle, that oldest and yet ever new treatise on the state and its government. "The other point," St. Thomas says, "is to be observed in respect of the kinds of government, or the different ways in which the constitutions are established." Here again he has an authority, and the authority is again that of Aristotle: "For whereas these differ in kind, as the Philosopher states (*Polit.* iii. 5), nevertheless the first place is held by the *kingdom,* where the power of government is vested in

du Moyen Age, as published in the posthumous volume by M. Jourdain entitled *Excursions Historiques et Philosophiques à travers le Moyen Age* (Paris, 1888), pp. 513-58.

A discussion of this account, together with an analysis of various writings on relevant aspects of the subject not included in the present volume, is contained in the forthcoming, *The Spanish Origin of International Law, Part II, The Spanish School and Francisco Suárez.*

[12] Qu. cv, Art. 1.

one; and *aristocracy,* which signifies government by the best, where the power of government is vested in a few." It was the opinion of St. Thomas and of many learned writers and prudent people, before and after his day, that "the best form of government is in a state or kingdom"—St. Thomas himself was inclined to kingship, but with him the king was somewhat in the nature of a presiding officer, for he continues—"wherein one is given the power to preside over all; while under him are others having governing powers." Here was, however, no government of all by one; for St. Thomas immediately adds: "and yet a government of this kind is shared by all." The reason? "Both because all are eligible to govern, and because"—mark the condition—"the rules are chosen by all." We here have government by coöperation and consent as well as by choice or election.

Why, then, is this "the best form of polity"? he asks. It is such, he continues, "being partly kingdom, since there is one at the head of all; partly aristocracy, in so far as a number of persons are set in authority; partly democracy, i.e., government by the people, in so far as the rulers can be chosen from the people, and the people have the right to choose their rulers."

It appears to have been the purpose of St. Thomas to choose the best element from these three forms of government and combine them into a perfect whole. Where did St. Thomas get this conception? The answer to this question follows immediately: "Such was the form of government established by the Divine Law." The proof of this statement is brief, clear and to the point, and shorter than a summary could well be: "For Moses and his successors governed the people in such a way that each of them was ruler over all; so that there was a kind of kingdom. Moreover, seventy-two men were chosen, who were elders in virtue: for it is written (Deut. i. 15): *I took out of your tribes men wise and honourable, and appointed them rulers:* so that there was an element of aristocracy. But it was a democratical government in so far as the rulers were chosen from all the people; for it is written (Exod. xviii. 21): *Provide out of all the people wise* (Vulg.,—*able*) *men,* etc.; and, again, in so far as they were chosen by the people; wherefore it is written (Deut. i. 13):

Let me have from among you wise (Vulg.,—*able*) *men,* etc. Consequently it is evident that the ordering of the rulers was well provided for by the Law."

It is not such a long cry as one would think from this pronouncement of St. Thomas in behalf of popular government to Abraham Lincoln's "government of the people, for the people and by the people."

We have more than intimated that St. Thomas had a penchant for the monarchical form of government. He had; but with decided limitations and with a condition. Now St. Thomas had a habit of stating it all in a single and telling phrase, and then adding a comment in a few words to make assurance doubly sure. The single phrase is: "A kingdom is the best form of government of the people, so long as it is not corrupt." The first half of this statement alone would be a mere generality. Accompanied by the condition, it indicates beyond question that St. Thomas was an open-eyed observer of humanity; indeed, we might say that he was very much of a realist.

Now for his comment, both on the kingdom and the condition: "But since the power granted to a king is so great, it easily degenerates into tyranny, unless he to whom this power is given be a very virtuous man: for it is only the virtuous man that conducts himself well in the midst of prosperity. On whose authority, we may ask? To which St. Thomas obligingly answers: "as the Philosopher observes (*Ethic.* iv. 3)." But again to the comment. "Now perfect virtue is to be found in few: and especially were the Jews inclined to cruelty and avarice, which vices above all turn men into tyrants. Hence from the very first the Lord did not set up the kingly authority with full power, but gave them judges and governors to rule them. But afterwards when the people asked Him to do so, being indignant with them, so to speak, He granted them a king, as is clear from His words to Samuel (I Kings viii. 7): *They have not rejected thee, but Me, that I should not reign over them.*" The meaning of this seems to us to be that the chosen people were given a government with "full"—or, as we would say, unlimited—power, as a sort of punishment, the earlier kings having possessed but limited powers.

There are still not a few in our day who cry out for rulers of unlimited power, sometimes called "dictators,"—a term which perilously approaches "tyrant"; for a dictator may well seem to many to be but a tyrant in disguise.

But let us return to St. Thomas, and the rules to which the king he had in mind should be subject. After having established the manner of election, the Creator determined two points to keep the king within bounds: "first, that in choosing a king they should wait for the Lord's decision; and that they should not make a man of another nation king, because such kings are wont to take little interest in the people they are set over, and consequently to have no care for their welfare." St. Thomas apparently would not have found it difficult to accept our constitutional provision that the President must be a native citizen of the United States and that, as Chief Magistrate instead of king, his duty is not to himself but to the welfare of his countrymen.

Again to quote the exact language of St. Thomas: "secondly, He prescribed how the king after his appointment should behave, in regard to himself; namely, that he should not accumulate chariots and horses, nor wives,"—a direct criticism, it would seem, of one Solomon, and an indirect criticism of monarchs of his and of later days, who married one wife, reserving, apparently, the right to consort with others—"nor immense wealth: because through craving for such things princes become tyrants and forsake justice." The path to tyranny has perhaps never been more clearly revealed. But the path of the virtuous ruler was likewise revealed: "He [the Creator] also appointed the manner in which they were to conduct themselves towards God: namely, that they should continually read and ponder on God's Law, and should ever fear and obey God." Here undoubtedly St. Thomas had in mind his contemporary, Louis IX. However, St. Thomas was not merely interested in kings as such. He saw them in relation to their people, saying: "Moreover, He"—meaning the Creator—"decided how they should behave towards their subjects: namely, that they should not proudly despise them, or ill-treat them, and that they should not depart from the paths of justice." Here we have, in one majestic and immortal paragraph, the portrait, as on two sides of a medal, of the perfect king and of the tyrant.

But St. Thomas was unwilling to deal with the tyrant in general. He particularized him, and he did it, as was his wont, in such a way that it could not be bettered. The rulers, as he had previously said, "were chosen from the whole people; wherefore they had their own possessions, from which to derive a living: and so much the more, since the Lord forbade even a king to have superabundant wealth or to make too much show of magnificance." Why should this be so? Because monarchy and magnificence seemed to the historian to go hand in hand, and too often the greatest magnificance has accompanied the worst of monarchies. St. Thomas discerned clearly the evils lurking in the possession of great wealth by the ruler. "He could scarcely avoid the excesses of pride and tyranny, arising from such things"; moreover, "if the rulers were not very rich, and if their office involved much work and anxiety, it would not tempt the ambition of the common people; and would not become an occasion of sedition."

What was the conclusion which St. Thomas would draw from the above observation? "That right"—referring to the absolute and tyrannical right of ruling as described in *I Kings,* viii. 2—"was not given to the king by Divine institution: rather was it foretold that kings would usurp that right, by framing unjust laws, and by degenerating into tyrants who preyed on their subjects. This is clear from the context that follows." It is apparent that St. Thomas was not acquainted with the unconstitutional maxim that the king could do no wrong—which is another way of saying, the divine right of kings to govern wrong. The relation between the tyrant and the subject was, in the view of St. Thomas, that between master and servant, "since a tyrant rules his subjects as though they were his slaves." This was apparently a deep-seated conviction on the part of the saint. He had spoken of Samuel as warning the people that a king—meaning an absolute monarch—would make slaves of his people. *"But,"* as St. Thomas adds, quoting the exact language of Holy Writ, *"the people would not hear the voice of Samuel."*

What action would St. Thomas permit against a tyrannical government? We do not need to speculate. He himself answers the question in Part II of the second part of his *Summa Theologica*.[13] "A tyrannical government," he says, "is not just, because it is directed, not to the common good, but to the private good of the ruler." Upon what authority would he rely? Again upon that of the Philosopher (*Politics*, iii. 5; *Ethics*, viii. 10); and, as a writer in *The Commonweal* has recently observed: "Aristotelian philosophy, even in its Thomist interpretation, is a good philosophy not only for Christians, but for Arabs, Jews and pagans."[14] But to recur to the text of St. Thomas. "Consequently there is no sedition"—used in the sense of unjustified rebellion against the government—"in disturbing a government of this kind." However, St. Thomas foresees that the ills resulting from rebellion might be greater in certain cases than the benefits. Therefore he qualifies his statement by adding, "unless indeed the tyrant's rule be disturbed so inordinately, that his subjects suffer greater harm from the consequent disturbance than from the tyrant's government." But we would add a query. How can we determine that greater harm than good will result from such a disturbance? We can only learn in such matters from experience, and the world's experience with tyrants has put them out of business. St. Thomas had more than a suspicion of this truth. "Indeed," he declares, "it is the tyrant rather that is guilty of sedition, since he encourages discord and sedition among his subjects, that he may lord over them more securely; for this is tyranny, because conducive to the private good of the ruler, and to the injury of the multitude."[15] There is here implicit the distinction between unjustified rebellion and justified rebellion. Indeed the founders of the first American republic could have invoked St. Thomas, had they needed justification other than the defense of their natural right to "life, liberty and the pursuit of happiness."

[13] Qu. xlii, Art. 2.

[14] Ernest A. Moody in the "Communications" column, May 4, 1934, under the heading, "Scholastic Philosophy."

[15] For the benefit of the reader who may not have St. Thomas' *Summa Theologica* at hand, we quote below the passages which have been discussed in the preceding pages:

"*I answer that,* Two points are to be observed concerning the right ordering of

The views of Victoria, as has more than once been stated, were based upon the doctrine of St. Thomas Aquinas. There is direct evidence of this to the eye of even the casual reader in the frequent references to the *Summa Theologica* contained in the Readings *On the Indians* and *On War.* But there is also indirect evidence throughout the Readings in the similarity between the views of Victoria and those of his great predecessor, even though in the passages of the Readings where these similarities are to be noted, there are no direct references to the writings

---

rulers in a state or nation. One is that all should take some share in the government: for this form of constitution ensures peace among the people, commends itself to all, and is most enduring, as stated in *Polit.* ii. 6. The other point is to be observed in respect of the kinds of government, or the different ways in which the constitutions are established. For whereas these differ in kind, as the Philosopher states (*Polit.* iii. 5), nevertheless the first place is held by the *kingdom,* where the power of government is vested in one; and *aristocracy,* which signifies government by the best, where the power of government is vested in a few. Accordingly, the best form of government is in a state or kingdom, wherein one is given the power to preside over all; while under him are others having governing powers; and yet a government of this kind is shared by all, both because all are eligible to govern, and because the rulers are chosen by all. For this is the best form of polity, being partly kingdom, since there is one at the head of all; partly aristocracy, in so far as a number of persons are set in authority; partly democracy, i.e., government by the people, in so far as the rulers can be chosen from the people, and the people have the right to choose their rulers.

"Such was the form of government established by the Divine Law. For Moses and his successors governed the people in such a way that each of them was ruler over all; so that there was a kind of kingdom. Moreover, seventy-two men were chosen, who were elders in virtue: for it is written (Deut. i. 15): *I took out of your tribes men wise and honourable, and appointed them rulers;* so that there was an element of aristocracy. But it was democratical government in so far as the rulers were chosen from all the people; for it is written (Exod. xviii. 21): *Provide out of all the people wise* (Vulg., — *able*) *men,* etc.; and, again, in so far as they were chosen by the people; wherefore it is written (Deut. i. 13): *Let me have from among you wise* (Vulg.,—*able*) men, etc. Consequently it is evident that the ordering of the rulers was well provided for by the Law.

* * * * * * *

"A kingdom is the best form of government of the people, so long as it is not corrupt. But since the power granted to a king is so great, it easily degenerates into tyranny, unless he to whom this power is given be a very virtuous man: for it is only the virtuous man that conducts himself well in the midst of prosperity, as the Philosopher observes (*Ethic.* iv. 3). Now perfect virtue is to be found in few: and especially were the Jews inclined to cruelty and avarice, which vices above all turn men into tyrants. Hence from the very first the Lord did not set up the kingly authority with full power, but gave them judges and governors to rule them. But afterwards when the people asked Him to do so, being indignant with them, so to speak, He granted them a king, as is clear from His words to Samuel (I. Kings viii. 7): *They have not rejected thee, but Me, that I should not reign over them.*

of St. Thomas. An example of what we may call an indirect reference to St. Thomas occurs in a passage in Victoria's Reading *On War* which is more than a little appropriate to the present topic. This passage we have already examined on an earlier

---

"Nevertheless, as regards the appointment of a king, He did establish the manner of election from the very beginning (Deut. xvii. 14 *et seqq.*); and then He determined two points: first, that in choosing a king they should wait for the Lord's decision; and that they should not make a man of another nation king, because such kings are wont to take little interest in the people they are set over, and consequently to have no care for their welfare:—secondly, He prescribed how the king after his appointment should behave, in regard to himself; namely, that he should not accumulate chariots and horses, nor wives, nor immense wealth: because through craving for such things princes become tyrants and forsake justice.—He also appointed the manner in which they were to conduct themselves towards God: namely, that they should continually read and ponder on God's Law, and should ever fear and obey God.—Moreover, He decided how they should behave towards their subjects: namely, that they should not proudly despise them, or ill-treat them, and that they should not depart from the paths of justice.

* * * * * * *

"The priestly office was bequeathed by succession from father to son: and this, in order that it might be held in greater respect, if not any man from the people could become a priest: since honour was given to them out of reverence for the divine worship. Hence it was necessary to put aside certain things for them both as to tithes and as to first-fruits, and, again, as to oblations and sacrifices, that they might be afforded a means of livelihood. On the other hand, the rulers, as stated above, were chosen from the whole people; wherefore they had their own possessions, from which to derive a living: and so much the more, since the Lord forbade even a king to have superabundant wealth or to make too much show of magnificence: both because he could scarcely avoid the excesses of pride and tyranny, arising from such things, and because, if the rulers were not very rich, and if their office involved much work and anxiety, it would not tempt the ambition of the common people; and would not become an occasion of sedition.

"That right was not given to the king by Divine institution: rather was it foretold that kings would usurp that right, by framing unjust laws, and by degenerating into tyrants who preyed on their subjects. This is clear from the context that follows: And you shall be his *slaves* (Douay, *servants*): which is significative of tyranny, since a tyrant rules his subjects as though they were his slaves. Hence Samuel spoke these words to deter them from asking for a king; since the narrative continues: *But the people would not hear the voice of Samuel.*—It may happen, however, that even a good king, without being a tyrant, may take away the sons, and make them tribunes and centurions; and may take many things from his subjects in order to secure the common weal."—I. II, Qu. cv, Art. 1.

"A tyrannical government is not just, because it is directed, not to the common good, but to the private good of the ruler, as the Philosopher states (*Polit.* iii. 5; *Ethic.* viii. 10). Consequently there is no sedition in disturbing a government of this kind, unless indeed the tyrant's rule be disturbed so inordinately, that his subjects suffer greater harm from the consequent disturbance than from the tyrant's government. Indeed it is the tyrant rather that is guilty of sedition, since he encourages discord and sedition among his subjects, that he may lord over them more securely; for this is tyranny, being conducive to the private good of the ruler, and to the injury of the multitude."—II. II, Qu. xlii, Art. 2.

page.[16] But it is so germane to the subject in hand as to justify a further examination.

Having stated that the prince "only holds his position by the election of the State" and that "therefore he is its representative," [17] Victoria says on the page following, in his discussion of the unjust causes of war, that "neither the personal glory of the prince nor any other advantage to him is a just cause of war." This is an acceptable statement. But it was not Victoria's custom to leave his statements unsupported, even though the truth of them was, as he declares in the present instance, "notorious." Therefore he adds by way of proof: "For a prince ought to subordinate both peace and war to the common weal of his State and not spend public revenues in quest of his own glory or gain, much less expose his subjects to danger on that account." But what if the prince cared nothing for the welfare of the state and its people and committed the very crimes—for they are nothing less—which Victoria has just mentioned? In that event, he places himself outside the pale of the law for, in the words of Victoria, "herein, indeed, is the difference between a lawful king and a tyrant." The meaning of these words is clear to us, but Victoria had no hesitation in emphasizing by reiteration points which he considered fundamental. Therefore he expands his statement on the difference between the constitutional monarch and the tyrant by stating that "the latter directs his government towards his individual profit and advantage, but a king to the public welfare," a political truth for which he could and did vouch the authority of Aristotle.[18]

The advocates of tyranny, if any there be, could find little comfort in these words, but they would doubtless find still less in the three sentences which follow. The first two are gems of that logic and brevity of style of which Victoria was a past master: "The prince derives his authority from the State." There is no denying this if we accept the view already advanced, that "the prince only holds his position by the election of the State."

---

[16] *Supra*, p. 37.

[17] *De Iure Belli*, p. 169.

[18] *Politics*, IV. x.

Now for the second of the brief but unanswerable statements: "Therefore he ought to use it"—meaning princely authority—"for the good of the State."

But this was not all. The tyrant was to be hedged in by a further and unimpeachable rule: "Also, laws ought 'not to be enacted for the private good of any individual, but in the common interest of all the citizens,' as is ruled in can. 2, Dist. 4, a citation from Isidore." Even this did not exhaust Victoria's ammunition against the tyrant. "Again," he continues, "this is the difference between freemen and slaves, as Aristotle says (*Politics,* bk. I, ch. 3 and 4) that masters exploit slaves for their own good and not for the good of the slaves, while freemen do not exist in the interest of others, but in their own interest."

Without mentioning the *Summa Theologica,* Victoria has here expressed, indirectly to be sure, and in his own inimitable manner, but none the less clearly, the doctrine of St. Thomas on the subject of tyrants.[19]

We have already devoted no little attention to the development of the doctrine of tyrannicide in Spain, where it was given expression by Mariana and Suárez, two of the greatest geniuses of that illustrious country. And having considered in *La Servitude Volontaire* of La Boétie the various phases of tyranny, we now

[19] Victoria's views are contained in less than a dozen sentences in the Reading *On War,* and we therefore reproduce them here *in extenso:* ". . . for the prince only holds his position by the election of the State. Therefore he is its representative . . . Neither the personal glory of the prince nor any other advantage to him is a just cause of war. This, too, is notorious. For a prince ought to subordinate both peace and war to the common weal of his State and not spend public revenues in quest of his own glory or gain, much less expose his subjects to danger on that account. Herein, indeed, is the difference between a lawful king and a tyrant, that the latter directs his government towards his individual profit and advantage, but a king to the public welfare, as Aristotle says (*Politics,* bk. 4, ch. 10). Also, the prince derives his authority from the State. Therefore he ought to use it for the good of the State. Also, laws ought 'not to be enacted for the private good of any individual, but in the common interest of all the citizens,' as is ruled in can. 2, Dist. 4, a citation from Isidore. Therefore the rules relating to war ought to be for the common good of all and not for the private good of the prince. Again, this is the difference between freemen and slaves, as Aristotle says (*Politics,* bk. I, ch. 3 and 4) that masters exploit slaves for their own good and not for the good of the slaves, while freemen do not exist in the interest of others, but in their own interest. And so, were a prince to misuse his subjects by compelling them to go soldiering and to contribute money for his campaigns, not for the public good, but for his own private gain, this would be to make slaves of them."—*De Iure Belli Relectiones,* pp. 169, 170.

proceed to examine more in detail such matters as what constitutes tyranny on the part of a ruler, the right of the subject to confine the ruler within the laws which he has taken an oath justly to administer, the remedies of a general nature against the violation of such an oath which the subjects may pursue, beginning with admonition and ending with what the apologists of the divine right of kings would call sedition or rebellion but for which we prefer the term revolution.

For present purposes, the classic examples of tyranny culminating in tyrannicide, or regicide—according to the reader's preference—center in James the Sixth of Scotland and the First of England. Now James proclaimed with exceptional clearness the doctrine of the divine right of kings, of which doctrine both his mother, Mary, Queen of Scots, and his son, Charles the First, King of England and of Scotland, were victims—not to speak of the unfortunate grandson, James the Second of England and the Seventh of Scotland, who fled his kingdoms lest his fate should be that of his ancestors.

It may be of interest to mention that La Boétie was a Frenchman and, as we have said, the intimate, indeed the soul friend of Montaigne, not merely a lawyer by training but a member of the Parliament of Bordeaux. It should be mentioned that other Frenchmen, such as Francis Hotman, also a lawyer, and Théodore de Bèze, likewise a lawyer, took more than a passing interest in the subject of tyrannicide, although lack of space makes impossible here an adequate examination and appreciation of their views. However, one may properly say that the genesis of new ideas—or the revival of old ones with a new application—seems to be the specialty of our French friends; indeed, they not only originate and revive them, but they apply them as well, with astonishing earnestness and with resounding results—witness the French Revolution of 1789!

Among the many treatises more or less like those we have just mentioned, there are two others which were then and are now outstanding. One was also by a Frenchman and is entitled, *Vindiciae contra Tyrannos;* the other was by a Scotchman who may qualify at least as a quasi-Frenchman by reason of the many years which he passed in France. The name of this Scotchman of France was George Buchanan—and in the language of none other than Grotius, *"Scotiae illud numen."*

Now Stephanus Junius Brutus, whose name appears on the title page, may never be identified, but the nationality of the author of the *Vindiciae* is not in doubt. He was French, and French to the core, and whoever he was, he was as staunch a Huguenot as Buchanan was a Presbyterian.

For many years Hubert Languet, a Frenchman by birth—who, like Buchanan, lived in foreign parts, but unlike him, held diplomatic posts—was credited with the *Vindiciae.* One day the tide of credit runs toward Duplessis-Mornay,[20] a leading advocate in his lifetime of Protestantism at home and abroad—so much so that he was even termed the "Protestant Pope"; the next day the tide turns to Languet. Today it favors Duplessis-Mornay, and we therefore refer to him as the author. But whether from the hand of Languet or of Duplessis-Mornay, the book has held its place as a masterly treatise against tyrants in behalf of constitutional government.

Curiously, the *Vindiciae* and the *De Jure Regni apud Scotos* bear upon their respective title-pages Edinburgh as the place of publication and 1579 as the date. There can be no doubt that Buchanan's tractate was published in Scotland, although it was written several years before it was printed; whereas it is said that the treatise of the other—notwithstanding the title page—was printed in that Holland which, after storm and stress, was about to take its place in the world as a federated republic. Whether it was the work of Languet or of Duplessis-Mornay, each may have had Holland in mind, as Languet was a devoted friend and adviser of William the Silent and resided, after the cessation of his diplomatic career, in the land of William the Silent, while Duplessis-Mornay was also in frequent contact with William the Silent and indeed passed much time in his company about the date of the *Vindiciae's* publication. In any

[20] This is the name by which Philippe de Mornay, seigneur du Plessis-Marly, is usually known. The more familiar name is used in the present text.

event, the two treatises were written for a practical purpose and by authors in deadly earnest.

Because the Frenchman's treatise—not to be partial either to Languet or to Duplessis-Mornay—is either directly known to persons interested in the history of political science, or indirectly known, because it is largely embodied in the text of John Locke's two famous *Treatises on Government,* we need only dwell on one phase of the treatise—and that not at length.

The account of Buchanan's treatise will be considered more at length, as it is of special interest to the English-speaking world, and was largely drawn upon by no less a person than John Milton in *The Tenure of Kings and Magistrates,* written in defense of the execution of Charles I. Buchanan's tractate also appears to have had an influence in America in pre-Revolutionary days, being printed at Philadelphia in 1766, within a year of the "Stamp Act." It must, moreover, have been known to Thomas Jefferson, whose hand drafted the Declaration of Independence, because his library is said to have contained a complete set of Buchanan's works.

CHAPTER VIII

VINDICIAE CONTRA TYRANNOS

THE *Vindiciae*, to which we now turn our attention, was also known in England and through Locke its views obtained currency in the American Colonies. An English translation of the tractate was published in London in 1649—said to have been the work of "one William Walker of Darnel, near Sheffield, who cut off the head of Charles I," [1] and this translation—whether by William Walker or not—was republished in 1689 at London in justification of the English Revolution of that year by which the son of James, Charles I, lost his throne.

The Preface to the *Vindiciae* could not have been more happily chosen, being an epistle of "The Emperors Theodosius and Valentinian to Volusianus, Great Provost of the Empire." It is, in but two paragraphs the thesis which Languet or Duplessis-Mornay set himself to justify:

> It is a Thing well becoming the Majesty of an Emperor, to acknowledge Himself bound to obey the Laws. Our Authority depending on the Authority of the Laws, and in very Deed to submit the Principality to Law, is a greater thing than to bear Rule. We therefore make it known unto all Men, by the Declaration of this our Edict, that We do not allow Ourselves, or repute it Lawful, to do anything contrary to this.
>
> Justin in the Second Book, speaks thus of Lycurgus, Law-giver to the Lacedemonians. He gave Laws to the Spartans which had not any; and was as much renowned for his diligent Observing of them Himself, as for his discreet Inventing of them. For he made no Laws for Others, to the Obedience whereof he did not first submit Himself: Fashioning the People to obey willingly, and the Prince to Govern uprightly.[2]

[1] "A Defence of Liberty against Tyrants—A Translation of the *Vindiciae contra Tyrannos* by Junius Brutus," with an Historical Introduction by Harold J. Laski (London, 1924), p. 60.

[2] *Ibid.*, p. 63.

The "Defence of Liberty against Tyrants"—for such is the English version of the Latin title, *Vindiciae contra Tyrannos*—is a full-length reply to four questions which the writer propounds. The first is: "Whether subjects are bound and ought to obey princes, if they command that which is against the law of God." We ourselves summarize a somewhat elaborate argument in a single but all-embracing word—"No."

The second question is: "Whether it be lawful to resist a prince who doth infringe the law of God, or ruin His Church: by whom, how, and how far it is lawful." The answer to this question is more elaborate than the answer to the first but it may be indicated, as would be expected, by the word "Yes."

The third question with which we are chiefly concerned is: "Whether it be lawful to resist a prince who doth oppress or ruin a public state, and how far such resistance may be extended: by whom, how, and by what right or law it is permitted." The answer to this question will appear on subsequent pages.

The fourth, which we merely mention in passing, is: "Whether neighbour princes may, or are bound by law to aid the subjects of other princes, persecuted for true religion, or oppressed by manifest tyranny." Given the third question, the answer to the fourth can not be doubtful as far as oppressed peoples are concerned, inasmuch as nothing could be more agreeable to subjects engaged in resisting their tyrannical princes than to have outsiders espouse their cause and bring it to triumph.

The mere statement of the four parts in which "Junius Brutus"—for so the author styles himself on the title page—divided his tractate shows sufficiently its importance not merely for the reader of the day but for those of us who take an interest in the growth of that liberty of which we were to be the happy possessors. For present purposes the third part is fundamental, going to the very root of government as the enlightened of that day—and indeed of our day—looked at government, the source of which they found in the people to be governed, and indicating the ways and means by which the government, conceived as an agency of the people, could be kept within the lines laid down by them, the king being in this conception merely an agent or trustee.

It will be observed from the statement of the divisions of the tractate that *A Defence of Liberty against Tyrants* is deeply religious, and we can well understand why any tractate on government issued after August 24, 1572, St. Bartholomew's Day, and written by those among its victims who survived, would seek an authority for government higher than the monarch; and the highest, of course, would be, not the people, but the power that created the people. Now the people, in turn, for purposes of law and social order, the ends for which all government was established, should possess the temporal power to choose the means through which their government was exercised and to hold their agent or trustee thus chosen to a strict accountability.

Before St. Bartholomew's Day the authors of tractates on government, and they were legion in France, were careful, whatever their feelings may have been, to refrain from attacking the French sovereign. His majesty's ministers were at fault, the authors assumed, and should be held to the law and punished for each and every violation. They would not have said that the king could do no wrong, but they would attribute the wrong that he may have committed to the bad advice or action of his ministers. The fact is that government and despotism were largely, if not wholly, synonymous, and the jurists and publicists even on the eve of St. Bartholomew's Day were advocates of what we would call despotic government. And it is simple truth that the Huguenots, who were for tolerance—in so far as toleration of their form of religion was concerned—professed a loyalty to the king differing but little, if at all, from the loyalty of his partisans. After St. Bartholomew's Day, with which the name Charles IX, then king, was inseparably connected, and indeed he gloried in the act, the Huguenots came to and expressed the conclusion that they must henceforth hold the king as well as his ministers responsible; and that both king and minister should be servants of the law, the law itself being made, not by the king and his ministers, but by the people, or by their representatives. The monarch, being the creation of the people and under a contract express or implied, should be made to abide by the terms of the contract, to which both people and king were parties. And as a corollary to this conclusion the Huguenots arrived at the further, and for our purposes almost equally important, conception that responsibility for misgovernment rests in large part, if not wholly, upon the shoulders of the monarch.

Now there might conceivably be a breach of contract on the part of the people as well as the king, although if the truth be told, the people have rarely violated the contract. Nevertheless, history is full of the use of force on the kings' part to suppress what they were pleased to call "sedition." And while there are indeed instances in which the people or their representatives have sought to restrain the king within the terms of the "contract," these instances too were but few in number and far apart. Resistance is sedition or rebellion when it is unsuccessful; it is revolution when it succeeds; and, expressing our personal views, we believe that loyalty to the monarch has always been so general that it is almost within the mark to say there has never been unjustified sedition or revolution on the part of the people.

Our purpose, however, is to analyze a few pages of the *Vindiciae contra Tyrannos,* or, as we shall hereafter call it, the "Defence of Liberty against Tyrants." The analysis will deal exclusively with the third part, in which the author expresses his views under certain captions. These headings in the third book show its origin, which we may content ourselves with paraphrasing in briefer form: The institution of the king by the people; The superiority of the people to the king; The contractual basis of royal authority; The right of resistance to tyrants—four headings which were an insult and a challenge to the monarchs of the author's day and which would not be over-palatable to the remnant of kings who sit unsteadily upon their thrones in the days in which we live.

The purpose of the author—whether we call him Junius Brutus, Hubert Languet or Duplessis-Mornay—is in the third part of his tractate to show "that the people set up kings, commit kingdoms to them, and confirm the selection by their suffrages." Why should this be so? To which the first reply is that "God has willed that it should be done in this manner." Why should it be done? "In order that kings should acknowledge that whatever authority and power they possess have been received from the people." This is a clean-cut statement that kings do not create themselves, and that they do not pass on their kingship to others, but that whatever power they have is derivative, not inherent or innate. And the second answer to the query is that kings, being so created, "should, therefore, devote all their thought and efforts to the interests of the people." We here have in a sentence or two the simple fact that the people both create the king and prescribe his duties. Now this would seem to be sufficiently clear without illustration, but in order that the king should be put in his proper place the *Defence* immediately states that the kings should not think "they excel other men through some superiority of nature, as men stand above flocks of sheep or herds of cattle." We would say in our behalf that the comparison is apposite although some kings would consider it discourteous. This, however, was not enough; more was to come: "Let them remember," the author continues, "that they are born of the same stuff as other men and have been raised from the ground to their high station by the suffrages and, as it were, upon the shoulders, of the people, in order that henceforth the burden of the commonwealth should rest in great part upon their own shoulders."

It is to be observed that the author of the *Defence* frequently, if not constantly, refers to the Scriptures in support of his various theses. Now "publicists" of our day on government consider writings of this kind as medieval because the authors vouch Biblical examples in behalf of their views. It is true and indeed only too true that the Old and New Testaments seem to have lost their vogue with writers of today, who prefer science and the quotation of each other to Revelation. Instead of considering this a defect on the part of the so-called medievalists, we believe that they should be commended rather than criticized for so doing, as the authorities to which the medievalists appealed are likely always to be appealed to by all peoples of Christian civilization in moments of storm and stress and revolution. The so-called medievalists were seeking not only an historical but a moral standard, and they found the historical standard in the Old Testament and the moral standard in both the Old and the New. Now the standard of the writers of our day is difficult to determine unless it be the authority of might as exemplified in the power of the state, considered as an artificial person, to impose its will within the territory subject to its jurisdiction without reference to the rights of the people, who, instead of being the source of power, are too often regarded as cogs in the machine of state. Morality and machinery do not seem to have much in common to the modern mind. For ourselves, we are medievalists and feel that the wisdom of the old books cannot "profitably" be replaced by the wisdom of mechanics.

Let us first examine the passage which is fundamental with the author of the *Defence* and upon which he raises the institution of kingship. And with him, let us begin with a quotation from the book of *Deuteronomy,* for the convenience of the modern reader. Now for the convenience of those who are not medievalists it may be stated that *Deuteronomy* is a book of the Old Testament in which Moses says [3] : "When thou art come into the land which the Lord thy God giveth thee, and shalt possess it, and shalt dwell therein, and shalt say, I will set a king over me, like as all the nations that are about me, thou shalt in any wise set him king over thee, whom the Lord thy God shall choose." Upon this the author comments: "You see here that the selection (*electio*) of the king is attributed to God, the investment to the people." So much for what the author considers the statement of fact. What was the process of election and establishment? "The elders of Israel, representing the whole of the people . . . came together at Ramah to meet Samuel; and, wearied of the sons of Samuel, who were unjust judges, and believing that they could by this means wage war more successfully, demanded a king of Samuel." Now Samuel, as was his wont, took counsel with the Lord, Who informed Samuel that "He had chosen Saul to rule over the people"; whereupon Samuel "anointed Saul." The transaction, however, was not complete. Something more was to be done. At first glance, the transaction

[3] Chap. xvii, vv. 14-15.

might have seemed complete when Samuel had presented Saul to the people as their king and "admonished them to be obedient to him"; but as the king is to be for and of the people they would, under these circumstances, have taken no part in his choice other than to say that they wanted the king instead of Samuel's sons, who had been unjust judges. But, the rule of the people is positive; it is not acquiescent. Saul had been divinely designated, but if the designation had completed the transaction, the people would have no share in the actual making of the ruler to whom they were to be obedient. Therefore the divine choice was to be confirmed by the people, not only for their satisfaction, but lest the king, aware of his divine appointment, should become arrogant, as happened to not a few kings who claimed appointment by divine right in later days. As the author puts it, therefore, in order that Saul might know that he was really of the people and that, indeed, he was "established by the people," Samuel ordered an assemblage of the people, and "by acclamation of all the people Saul was declared the appointed king." But even this was not all. The king might have alleged that chance had entered into the matter; therefore, after he had been afforded an opportunity to show "some proof of his valor in relieving Jabesh Gilead from the siege of the Ammonites," he was again in full assembly at Gilgal (a few dissenting to no purpose) confirmed king before God." It is to be observed that a few dissented against his confirmation, but, as the author adds, "to no purpose," since the majority had declared itself. Upon this transaction as a whole the author of the *Defence* addressed his countrymen and his prospective readers: "You see thus that he whom God had chosen and chance had selected from all the rest, was established as king by the suffrages of the people."

It would seem that the intelligent reader could draw from this incident the consequence that the people establishing the king by their suffrages were superior to him whom they had chosen just as the principal is superior to the agent; but as this is a fundamental proposition the author is unwilling to leave anything to chance, and states in his own words the temporal consequences which accompany the establishment of kings: "In a word, all kings were in the beginning elected. Those who to-day appear to accede to their kingdoms by inheritance were necessarily first established by the people." And he continues, "Although the people of certain countries," speaking of his own day, "are accustomed to choose their kings from a particular stock on account of its peculiar merits, nevertheless," he insists, "it is the stock and not the branch that they choose." But what if the stock should degenerate? The author answers: "they may select another," for "those who are next in line for the kingship are not born kings; they rather become such: they are not deemed kings so much as candidates for the kingship."

So much for kingmaking. Now what is the relation between the king and the people? This was a matter of the utmost importance, and it is so treated. For if the king, when elected and consecrated, held his office in his own right, we would have the king responsible only to himself; yet, if he did not govern in his own right, in whose right did he govern and what was his relationship to the governed? The author's statement is clear, to the point, and, in view of his premises, unanswerable: "the whole body of the people are superior to the king." For to the author, as well as to us, it is "evident that he who is established by another is accounted less than he that has established him, and that he who receives his authority from another is inferior to him from whom he derives his authority." And after Old Testament instances, Duplessis-Mornay—whom we may assume for the present to have been the author—comments: "In like manner the people establish the king as minister of the commonwealth."

The principal is therefore superior to his agent. But being the agent of the people, the king must have been "instituted for the benefit of the people," since the contrary would, in the language of logic, be an absurdity. For "you could not say that for the sake of some hundred men, inferior to most of the rest of the community, the whole community was created; rather that the former were created for the latter." In this connection the king is likened to a pilot who "sits at the helm to see that she"—the ship—"be not dashed to pieces upon the rocks or follow the wrong course." He is not the owner of the ship; he is rather "a servant of the ship, differing from the common drudges only in type of work"; and in the view of the author of the *Defence* the king is as a pilot to the commonwealth. As long as the king does well and acts in the interest of the commonwealth, he is respected. Nevertheless, he is but the captain of the ship; he is not its owner. And further, whatever he acquires as king, he acquires "not for himself, but for the kingdom,"—that is, for the people who have established the kingdom,—just as the servant makes acquisitions for his master."

We have said that the king is as a pilot; but he is not even that as regards the commonwealth, for while a ship can not go on without a pilot, people may get on without a king. For, as the author says, "there are many peoples who live without a king; a king without a people, however, you cannot imagine." It is said that kings have many eyes and ears, that they have long heads, and exceptionally swift feet. Admitting that this be so, it is only because "the people concerned lend to the king their eyes and ears, their strength and their faculties, for the use of the commonwealth." That this is so is evident from the fact that if the people withdraw from him "he who seemed of good sight and hearing, robust and vigorous, will grow blind and deaf, and will suddenly collapse." And the conclusion which the author of the *Defence* draws from all this is that the king exists "through, and for the sake of, the people, and without the people cannot stand." Who, then, will not say that "the people are greater than the king"? Assuredly not the author of the *Defence*.

The king, however, cannot act alone. He must needs have his servants, both domestic, for his personal convenience, and official, for the business of his kingship. The one class of assistants is appointed directly by the king and they are responsible only to him, as is the usual relation between servant and employer. The situation is different, however, with the officials who assist royalty in governing. They, like the king, are concerned with the welfare of the commonwealth, and, like the king, they should "receive their authority from the people." Formerly, we are told, they were appointed in public assembly, and it naturally followed that they could be discharged only by the same body. This being the case, they were, like the king, responsible "to the supreme sovereign—the people, upon whom the king himself, and through him his officers, must depend." In later times, it must be admitted, the appointment of ministers and other officers of the commonwealth became less a function of the people and in some instances, indeed, almost if not wholly a function of the king. Nevertheless, whether appointed in one way or another, their fundamental duty was to "preserve the rights and privileges of the people," and, more than this, "to take diligent care that the king commit or omit nothing to their [the people's] damage." They occupy the position of "associates of the king in the administration of justice." The difference between their office and that of the king is merely one of degree, and in essence the responsibility of minister and ruler is the same, for whether the officers of the commonwealth be appointed in one way or another, and even though their immediate responsibility is to the king, their ultimate responsibility is through the king to the people. But we may go, as does the author of the *Defence*, a step farther. The ministers, advisers, officers—call them what we may—of the king are individually inferior to him in degree of rank, as has been stated; but if we consider them all together they assume proportions that overshadow the king himself. This is not a mere matter of measurement; it is a question of purpose as well. The ministers are said to serve the king, but their real duty is to serve the people, to guard and protect the interests of the people. If the king should conduct himself in such a way as to endanger the rights of the people, then it is the duty of the ministers to protect those rights, even against the king; and such protection can be exercised only if the ministers, acting together, are superior in authority and power to the king. Today the form of government has changed in most countries, if not in all: the people are represented not only by ministers but by representatives expressly chosen to protect their rights and advance their interests. But the essence of the doctrine set forth by the writer who signed himself "Junius Brutus" is the essence of the doctrine of government today—that the representatives of the people shall advise and consent to the acts of the ruler, whether he be king or chief magistrate, and shall serve as a check and a stay against the abuse of his authority.

How did the office of king arise? This is a question of some importance, for the origin of an institution is nearly if not always related to its purpose. "In the first place," we are informed, "it is clear that men by nature free,"—a quality with which we as the beneficiaries of the Declaration of Independence are familiar—"impatient of servitude, born rather to command than to obey, would not, save for the sake of some great profit, have chosen subjection to another and have renounced their own natural right, so to speak, to submit to the right of another." Next we are advised not to consider "that kings were chosen to convert to their own uses the goods obtained by the sweat of the many; for every one loves and cherishes his own. Nor were they created that they might squander the public power to their own pleasure; for ordinarily any one hates, or at least envies, his superior." What, then, were they created for? "To protect individuals from each other by the administration of justice, and to defend all from dangers from without by repelling force with force." The king, in the sense of the *Defence,* was to govern. But what does the term "govern" mean? "Simply to give counsel." What is the end of government? "The good of the people." What, then, is the duty of governors and kings? "To take care of the people." Indeed, "royal dignity is, properly speaking, not an honor, but a burden." Nor is it "a privilege," but "a calling." It is not an office which brings immunity, but rather "duty," and finally, history to the contrary notwithstanding, it is "not a license, but a public service." These statements on what royal dignity is, and is not, might seem to have denied all honor to kingship. Yet honor there was, as we are told: "Some honor indeed is attached to the office; one would hardly be willing to partake of such troubles unless they were flavored with some relish of honor." Honor means much, it is true, but will it ease the burden that rests on the royal shoulders? "The common saying is true that if every one knew with how great annoyances the royal diadem was wreathed no one would pick it up if he found it at his feet along the wayside." Bonaparte, it may be remarked in passing, said that he found Charlemagne's crown in the gutter and he picked it up with the point of his sword, although even he was eventually overcome by the "annoyances" with which it was "wreathed."

To return to the question of the origin of monarchs—how, we may ask, did the idea of having kings first occur to human beings? According to the author of the *Defence* the idea appears to have had its inception in the settlement of disputes between individuals "concerning ownership of things" and "between neighboring peoples over boundaries." For the settlement of these controversies "it became customary," the author would have us believe, "to have recourse to some one who would justly and effectively see that the poor suffered no violence from the rich, or the whole people from their neighbors." With the increase of controversies and wars a permanent administrator of justice was chosen, "one for whose valor and diligence all had high regard." As representatives of justice, it was reasonable for kings to be considered as "ordained by God"; and as protectors of the people they were also "established by the people for the benefit of the citizens." Now what is this benefit? The answer is not far to seek. It "consists principally in two things—in the maintenance of justice among individuals and of security against enemies."

It is all very well to say that the king is appointed to administer justice, but what is to be his standard of justice? To state the question in a word, "Does the king depend on law, or law on the king?" In one case we have civil liberty, in the other despotism. In the view of Duplessis-Mornay, it is not the function of kings but rather of magistrates to "discover" laws—"laws which could speak with one and the same voice to all men"; and of these laws the kings were the guardians and administrators. In case the laws did not reach "every contingency" it might indeed seem just that the king should by natural equity supply the law that was lacking. But even the exercise of this duty, if unlimited, might open the way to abuse, for the king is after all but an individual, with the judgment of an individual, and equity in his hands alone might cease to be true equity and even "do violence to the law." Therefore, magistrates and other wise men "were soon associated with the kings by the people."

Thus far we have been dealing with the king as an administrator of the law, but there is another relationship between the sovereign and the law which he administers. Let us suppose that certain of the laws of a commonwealth are so framed—as they should be—that they apply to the king as well as to other inhabitants. The question then arises, Is the king above the law? The answer is emphatically in the negative. "Kings themselves should be obedient to law and acknowledge it as their superior." It might be argued that such an answer means a limitation on the king's activities of governing; but in fact the opposite is the case, for law is an assistance rather than a limitation to the royal governor. It is, we are told, "a kind of instrument by means of which human societies are best ruled and directed to a happy end." This is a statement that needs no demonstration, for it is a mere truism that without law a people must live in anarchy, and there are few indeed who would argue that anarchy as such will bring human societies "to a happy end." It is not difficult, therefore, to accept the statement that "kings were foolish who should think it base to yield to law," just as would be the case with the geometrician who felt it "unbecoming" to employ mathematical rules and instruments. Therefore, we can have no hesitation in agreeing with the maximlike statements that "Law is the soul of the good king; in it is his inspiration, feeling, and life. The king is the organ of the law, the body through which the law exercises its power, fulfils its function and expresses its meaning."

Here the author pauses for a moment to give us three definitions of law so perfect that they may not be paraphrased:

(1) *"Law is the concentrated reason and wisdom of many sages."* On this there is a comment which justifies the wisdom of many as against the wisdom of one: "The many are more clear-sighted and far-seeing than the one; it is, therefore, safer to follow the law than a man, however perspicacious he may be."

(2) *"Law is reason or intelligence unperturbed, and free from the influence of anger, cupidity, hate, or prejudice; nor is it de-*

flected by tears or threats." Law, in a word, is impersonal and impartial, while man, being a creature of emotion as well as of intelligence, is never truly impersonal and rarely impartial, however much he may strive to attain those two qualities: "he is compounded of reason and passion, and he cannot always prevent the latter from gaining the upper hand."

(3) *"Law is the coalescence of a multitude of minds."* Now the mind, we may say, is the dwelling place of the spiritual nature of man, the nature which links him with the divine: in a word, "mind is a parcel of the divine spirit; so that he who obeys the law seems to obey God and to make Him his judge."

Duplessis-Mornay has spoken of the twofold pact in kingmaking. The first we have already mentioned as "between God, on the one hand, and the king and people, on the other"; the second is "between the king and the people." To this he now returns, and his justification of the contract to which both the king and the people are parties is perhaps his greatest service to the liberty of the peoples. We have already related the establishment of Saul and we may content ourselves with two further worthies. The first is David, who "in Hebron made a covenant in the presence of the Lord"—God Himself being present as a witness—then "with the elders of Israel, who represented the whole people"; after which, but not before, he was "anointed king." Here we have a contract of the future king with the people, for it does not matter if the contract was made with the whole people or with the elders rightfully representing them. If the contract were made with the people it would be made with them directly as principal; if with elders having the right to represent them, it would be made by the elders as agents for their principal, the people.

The second of the worthies is Josias, who promised, to quote Duplessis-Mornay, "to observe the commandments, testimonies and precepts." Stated by word of mouth? No—as "comprised in the book of the covenant." And "by these words," Duplessis-Mornay informs us, "are to be understood the laws, which relate now to piety, now to justice." But lest he should be misunderstood on this point, which is of the utmost importance, he adds:

"In all of these passages the covenant is said to have been made with all the people, or with the entire multitude, all the elders, or all the men of Judea."

The purpose of the pact was to create a king, says Duplessis-Mornay, "for the people made the king, not *vice versa*." Now what was this transaction? It was of a threefold nature. First, "the people had the part of stipulator," and, secondly, "the king that of promisor." In what sense are these terms used? The part of stipulator, Duplessis says, "is deemed the more advantageous at law." Why is this so? Because "the people, as stipulator, ask the king whether he will govern justly and according to the laws." So much for the people. What of the other party? "The king promises that he will." Here we have the first two parts of the transaction stated and explained. Now we come to the third part, which is not the least important. "The people then respond," Duplessis goes on, "that they will faithfully obey him." Whatever he does? No—only "while he governs justly." We have here two promises: the first is that of the king, who promises absolutely; the second that of the people, who promise conditionally. But what if the condition is not fulfilled? "The people are lawfully absolved from every obligation." The matter is so important that Duplessis proceeds further to analyze the relationships of one to the other: "In the first covenant or contract," he says, "there is an obligation to piety, in the second, to justice.—In the former,"—meaning the covenant with God,—"the king promises dutifully to obey God, in the latter,"—that is the contract between the king and the people,—"that he will rule the people justly"; or Duplessis continues, in order to prevent any misapprehension in this, the foundation upon which he rears his structure of liberty, "in the one that he will provide for the glory of God, in the other, that he will secure the welfare of the people." In the first contract or compact or covenant, as it is variously called, "the condition is—if you observe my law," meaning the law divine; in the second, the contract, between king and people, "if you render to each his due," which is the justice of the Golden Rule. What is the consequence of "failure to fulfil the various promises? The failure to fulfil the first pact is duly punished by God; failure to fulfil the second"—here we encounter the doctrine of tyrannicide—"is legitimately punishable by the whole people or by those magistrates whose function it is to protect the people."

Now Duplessis-Mornay understands that he is dealing with technical questions, and he proceeds to explain by question and answer what he means by condition, non-observance, and matters of that kind. "Why is it," he asks, "that the king swears first, the people stipulating, unless it is that he thereby accepts a condition"—mark the words—"tacitly or expressly"? And he again puts and answers a question: "And why is a condition attached to a contract unless it be that if the condition be not fulfilled the contract is by that fact abrogated by law?" A third question accompanied by a third answer: "And if through non-observance of the condition a contract is made null at law, who will call that people perjured who refuse obedience to the king when he disregards the condition which he is obligated and able to fulfil and violates the law to which he has sworn?" Yet Duplessis-Mornay is not satisfied, and it takes a fourth question to meet and satisfy the demands of what he must have regarded as the reluctant reader: "On the other hand, who would not regard such a perjured and perfidious king as unworthy of his office?" And the conclusion which he draws from this series of questions and answers is not merely a conclusion, but conclusive, although it also is in the form of a question: "If all these things are true," he says, and in Duplessis' opinion, as well as in ours, they are among the eternal verities, "is it not even more certain that the people should be absolved from the oath which they have taken to the king, if he, who first swore solemnly to them, as an agent to his principal, has broken his oath?"

So much for the express contract; but what of the tacit or implied contract? If no express contract has been made Duplessis-Mornay invokes Mother Nature as a witness to the tacit contract "that kings are established by the people with the condition that they govern well; judges, that they judge justly; military leaders, that they lead forth the army against the enemy."

Duplessis-Mornay has hitherto treated of kings, defining the king as one who "rules and governs a kingdom, acceding to his position either through heredity or through election confirmed by the appropriate rights." He now comes to consider a ruler, called by him a tyrant, who "either has seized the government" by violent means or, "invested therewith in regular manner, rules contrary to right and justice and in violation of the laws and pacts to which he has solemnly bound himself."

There are thus two kinds of tyrants, the one who rules "without title (*tyrannus absque titulo*)," the other, a king who has legally obtained his office but practices tyranny (*tyrannus exercitio*). Until a duly constituted ruler does practice tyranny, however, allegiance is due him, for "when faith has once been given there is no longer opportunity for repentance."

The right against a tyrant without title arises under three legal systems. The first is the "law of nature," which recognizes in the animal creation as well as in man the right to defend life and liberty. Therefore, Duplessis-Mornay says that "he who questions whether it is permissible to resist seems to contend with Nature herself." The second is the law of nations, by which "dominions are defined and boundaries established which everyone is obligated to defend against all invaders," whether the invader be Alexander the Great, Diomedes the pirate, or "a footpad in purloining a clock." Third, there is the civil law, whereby, "societies of men are established under a fixed system" of one kind or another. The justification for resistance to the tyrant in this case is preëminent, almost self-evident, and finely stated: "If any one attempts to violate this law by force or fraud we are all bound to resist him, because he wrongs society, to which he owes everything, and would undermine his country, to which we are devoted by nature, law, and solemn oath; if we neglect this duty we are traitors to our country, deserters from human society, contemners of the law." There is thus a threefold right which permits, indeed commands, the people "to take arms against tyrants." And Duplessis-Mornay adds that "no other reason can properly dissuade us." Nor is this all. "No oath or other pact, public or private, interposes to prevent us." The consequence? Any private person can "eject an intruding tyrant." Hence it is that a person resisting a tyrant without title is not a rebel, for he is defending himself and his country; nor can he be condemned for sedition, for he is resisting one who is himself seditious, and thus safeguarding the commonwealth.

The case is different with a king legally elected, that is, a king with proper title but of improper conduct, who is only to be ejected by magistrates or representatives of the people or by the people as distinct from individuals as such. The reason for the distinction is that the usurper is a tyrant without title and therefore without legal standing, and hence any person may properly take any action against such a tyrant; whereas in the case of a king legally in office but who acts illegally, he can only be resisted by magistrates or other duly constituted representatives of the people—or by the people acting as such under the approval of the law. Here we have foreshadowed, as it were, the impeachment of a later day.

In considering when resistance may properly be opposed to a king guilty of misrule, Duplessis-Mornay would have us bear in mind what he has previously stated,—that princes are men, with the faults as well as the virtues of men. We can not expect perfect princes, and indeed we should consider ourselves fortunate, he says, "if we find mediocre ones." The experience of history vouches—indeed over-vouches—for this statement.

Nor must the prince who has lapsed from grace be called a tyrant if his only faults are that he "does not observe moderation" nor yield to reason, is careless of public welfare or "becomes less diligent in administration of justice or less zealous in warding off war." But he is to be adjudged a tyrant—"an enemy of God and man"—"if he deliberately," to quote, as previously, Duplessis-Mornay's exact language, "upsets the commonwealth," "wantonly perverts lawful rights, or has no regard for oaths and covenants, for justice or piety."

The distinction here is between the weak prince and the malicious tyrant, for although the former might "rightly be deposed, nevertheless he can be endured; but the longer the tyrant is tolerated the more insufferable he becomes." But prudence is to be used in doing what may lawfully be done. For it often happens—then as now—that the remedy is "worse than the disease." Does not the poet of our English tongue advise us to bear the evils which we have, rather than to fly to others we know not of?

A tyrant apparently does not become such over night or at once, and when he begins to act unlawfully, the representatives of the people should admonish him, "not waiting until the evil becomes graver and acquires greater strength. For tyranny is like a hectic fever, which, at first easily cured but detected with difficulty, later becomes easily recognizable but almost incurable."

The admonition is of course a preliminary remedy; but if it does not accomplish its purpose, what then? If the king does not mend his ways, "the crime of tyranny is" then "complete." Only a final—albeit a harsh—remedy remains—"whatever may be done through the law or through just resistance, against a tyrant, can be done against him." What justifies such a remedy? The fact that "tyranny is not a crime merely, but the chiefest, and, as it were, the epitome of all crimes." But what are the specific crimes with which a tyrant is charged?—for "epitome" is a general term. Duplessis-Mornay thus states them: "The tyrant subverts the commonwealth, pillages every one and lays snares for their lives, violates any promise, despising the sanctity of a solemn oath." Indeed his crimes are, as it were, cumulative; for he is as much more vicious than the ordinary bandit, murderer or oath-breaker, as it is more serious to offend against the many or all than against particular individuals." For if, the author concludes, "these private offences are deemed infamous and are punishable by death, is it," he asks, "possible to devise a penalty worthy of a crime so atrocious as tyranny"?

It is customary to consider those who resist kings as rebels, but Duplessis-Mornay reverses the process, so to speak, by placing the tyrant in the rôle of a rebel. The people, and not the king, being the source of power, it follows that if "the tyrant commits a felony against the people . . . he is guilty of treason against the kingdom or empire"—and the republic, we may add—and if he is guilty of treason, then certainly, again to quote the *Defence,* "he is a rebel." But in a sense he is more a rebel than the ordinary individual; indeed we might describe him as an arch rebel, and in the opinion of Duplessis-Mornay he therefore "merits far severer punishment." Now a rebel is always a danger to the state, and therefore magistrates or other proper representatives of the people are in duty bound to call the people themselves to arms.

What is to be the test of the rightfulness or the wrongfulness of the ruler? We have it in asingle phrase,—"whatever tends to the public good is lawful." And here Duplessis-Mornay, a Protestant, calls to his aid no less a person than St. Thomas Aquinas, saint, doctor and unimpeachable authority of the Catholic Church, who, he informs us, "says that since tyrannical government, established not for the public good but for the private good of him who rules, is unjust, its overthrow does not have the nature of sedition." Of course, if the resistance were against a prince legitimately ruling, the status of things would be otherwise; but, says Duplessis-Mornay, "the prince is simply animate law," that is to say, he is "animate law" if he rules according to the law, but if he attempts "to annihilate law," he becomes without further ado an enemy of the commonwealth.

It is in fact as well as in law "the tyrant who is guilty of treason against the commonwealth; and those who, relying upon their own authority and sense of duty, assail the tyrant are protectors of the commonwealth"; for "in such case the latter are acting not as individuals, but as the whole people, not as subjects, but as masters demanding from their agent an accounting of his work."

Why is this of necessity so? Because "everywhere there is between prince and people a mutual and reciprocal obligation: he promises that he will be a good prince; the people promise that if he is such they will obey him."

Immediately following, and indeed in connection with, the foregoing statements, Duplessis-Mornay gives what may be called a masterly summary of his entire doctrine, a doctrine which applied not only to France but especially to Holland, then in a life and death struggle against Philip II of Spain, who had broken his solemn oath to the people of the Low Countries. Here is the summary in full: "The people are entirely innocent of the crime of perfidy if they publicly renounce an unjust ruler or endeavor to overpower by force of arms one who without lawful right attempts to hold the kingdom."

In a previous passage Duplessis-Mornay has spoken of the duties of magistrates, ministers and other officers of state. He now returns to the subject and in words that ring with conviction but are sharpened with the bitterness of disillusion he calls upon the "officers of the kingdom to repress a tyrant," stating that such action is not merely permissible to them but "incumbent upon them as part of their duty." Indeed his words might be humorous were they not so biting; for if the officers do not discharge this duty they can plead no contract as an excuse. The electors, patricians, peers and other nobles (*optimates*) should not think that they were instituted to exhibit themselves, clothed in their robes of state, at the coronation of the king, according to the ancient custom; as if they were acting in a Greek interlude, or playing the parts of Roland, Oliver, Renaldo and other stage personages representing the knights of King Arthur's Table. Nor after the assemblage has been dismissed should they think that they have fulfilled their parts excellently. Such ceremonies are not intended to be executed perfunctorily, or designed for sport—as in children's games when, as Horace describes, they make a king in play. These leaders (*optimates*) should rather know that they are called to a place of work as well as of honor, and that the commonwealth is entrusted to the king as its first and principal guardian and to them as co-guardians. Just as other guardians are appointed to observe the acts of him who holds the place of chief guardian, to demand constant accounting of his administration and watch carefully how he acquits himself of his charge; so likewise officers are appointed to watch the king (who is master only in the sense of having the care of a ward), to see that he does nothing to the detriment of the people. . . . The commonwealth is entrusted as much to their care as to his; their commission is not only that they serve the public interest through their particular offices, but also that they hold him to his proper function. Both he and they have promised to secure the welfare of the commonwealth. If he violates his oath they are not to imagine that they are thereby absolved from their pledge any more than are bishops released from their vows if the Pope defends heresy or seeks to destroy the Church. The more the king becomes an oath-breaker, the more should the officers consider themselves bound to keep their faith. If they act collusively they are to be accounted prevaricators; if they conspire with him, they are deserters and traitors; if they neglect to deliver the commonwealth from tyranny, they are tyrants themselves. On the other hand, if they undertake to save the commonwealth and defend it with all their powers, they are protectors, guardians, and, in a sense, kings themselves."

Would that this passage could penetrate the nurseries of every king, princeling or officer of state of the international community that, when they reach manhood and be installed in their respective offices, it may be as a "lamp unto their feet and a light unto their path!"

* * *

From now on the scene shifts from *la belle France* to the British Isles—Scotland and England first and later the United Kingdom —a transition easy of accomplishment but epoch-making in its results. But it is not such a transition as it may at first sight seem. As we have said, the *Defence of Liberty against Tyrants* first saw the light of day in Scotland, for although it may have been printed in Amsterdam, the title page is of Edinburgh, which seems to show that Scotland was the preferred kingdom for the appearance of this masterpiece—at least in the opinion of its author.

As we have also said, George Buchanan's *De Jure Regni apud Scotos* was published at Edinburgh in the same year. Buchanan's tractate is supposed to have been written some years earlier—in or about 1567. This may or may not be so, but it appears first to have circulated in manuscript. Its influence, however, was to be larger, for not merely did it state the cause of liberty in its extreme form (tyrannicide) for and in Scotland, but in the noble country to the south of the Tweed it was to bear its full fruits in its application to Charles I. In Scotland, the influence of Buchanan was largely theoretical; in England it was practical, and it is only just to say, without questioning the capacity of the great man involved, that Milton's *The Tenure of Kings and Magistrates*—a defense of Charles First's execution—was based, as we have already said, upon Buchanan's tractate.

CHAPTER IX

BUCHANAN'S *DE JURE REGNI APUD SCOTOS*

BUCHANAN explains in his dedication that the *De Jure Regni apud Scotos* was written some years earlier than 1579, the year of its publication at Edinburgh, at a more turbulent time, in an attempt to explain "what right, or what authority both Kings and People have one with another." Having come upon the work at this later date, Buchanan decided to publish it as a testimonial to his own affection for the King to whom he had been a tutor and an admonition to the young monarch of his duty toward his subjects. Among various remarks in this connection, we may particularly note the author's warning to James against "flattery, which is the nurse of Tyranny, and a most grievous plague of a Kingdom." Against this and other dangers, Buchanan hoped that his treatise might guard the King—admonishing him, reprehending him should he fail in his duty, and leading him along the paths where both he and his subjects would find tranquillity in this world and eternal glory in the next.

If the present analysis[1] seems rather lengthy, it is due to the fact that the dialogue is valuable in itself and important because of its influence on subsequent writings concerning government; because an edition of it was printed in 1766, in Philadelphia,

[1] This analysis is based upon an English translation made from the original Latin by "a Person of Honour of the Kingdom of Scotland," and printed in 1721. The Latin text has, however, been used for purposes of reference where the English translation was vague or obviously at fault. Such instances—though one hesitates to remark on the fact after reading the translator's comments on the "snarling critics" of his work—are rather frequent in the English text; though the printer may have been more at fault than the translator. Where the analysis departs in any important respect from the translator's English, the fact is mentioned in a footnote. In preparing this analysis another edition of the translation, that printed in Philadelphia in 1766, by one Andrew Steuart, a Scotchman by birth, was consulted from time to time.

within a year of the repeal of the "Stamp Act"—as we have already stated—and because Thomas Jefferson possessed a complete edition of Buchanan's works; and finally because, in the hurry and bustle of our more modern world, Buchanan's admirable dialogue seems to be overlooked except by the few persons who take more than a platonic interest in the ancient and honorable science of good government. It will be observed that the analysis endeavors, where possible, to preserve the dialogue form into which Buchanan cast his treatise.

The views which Buchanan advances are presumably his views, based upon wide reading, observation and no little reflection. Thomas Maitland, who is the other party to the dialogue, is for the most part a man of straw, or, to vary the figure, a screen upon which Buchanan displays his views. Still the dialogue is by no means a monologue.

The Maitland in question was the brother of William Maitland, of Lethington, the celebrated secretary of Queen Mary, who was generally known as "Secretary Lethington" and was the eldest son of Sir Richard Maitland. William Maitland, it may be noted, was described by no less a person than Queen Elizabeth as the "flower of the wits of Scotland."[2] His brother, Thomas, with whom we are now concerned, is said later to have repudiated the sentiments attributed to him by Buchanan in the dialogue. This repudiation is somewhat weakened, however, by the fact that Maitland had already subscribed to the sentiments in question in a poem which appears in the *Delitiae Poetarum Scotorum*.[3]

Of Buchanan it is sometimes said, and with much truth, that he was as much a Frenchman as he was a Scot, or perhaps more of a Frenchman. He had passed many years in France, some twenty-six or seven in all, studying and teaching in Paris and Bordeaux and later in Portugal. George Buchanan, however, was a Scotchman by birth, born in the parish of Killearn in Stirlingshire some time in February of the year 1506. Upon

[2] For further particulars concerning William Maitland of Lethington, see article in *Dictionary of National Biography*, vol. xii, pp. 821-7.

[3] *George Buchanan, Glasgow Quatercentenary Studies, 1906* (Glasgow, 1907), p. 452.

graduating from the University of St. Andrews, he repaired to France in 1527 to continue his studies. Ten years later he returned to Scotland. Within a decade he was again in France, this time teaching in Paris. Later he repaired to Portugal but, becoming involved in difficulties over religious matters, he eventually sailed for England in 1552. The following year found him again in Paris, however, and again he remained abroad for a long period, for the most part in France, although he passed some time in Italy. About 1561—the date can not be fixed precisely—he returned to Scotland, and in the ensuing years he played no small part in the grim but stirring events in that country which were to have such a vast influence on history. During this period he became principal of St. Leonard's College, St. Andrews, and was tutor to no less exalted personages than Queen Mary and her son James, whom he is said to have birched into an excellent classical scholar.

Both in Scotland and abroad he was welcomed by scholars and persons of distinction because of his vast learning and what may fittingly be called a world-wide reputation. Among his students was Montaigne, who always retained a kindly feeling for his instructor. Indeed it is not too much to say that in the world of ideas he was among the most preeminent in his day, for does not Hume Brown, Royal Historiographer of Scotland, Professor of Ancient (Scottish) History in the University of Edinburgh, author of the standard history of Scotland, say in his life of Buchanan: "For continental scholars and men of letters in the latter half of the sixteenth century the most distinguished person then living in the British Islands was the Scottish humanist and reformer, George Buchanan."[4] Hume Brown, it may be added, approved the statement of a continental scholar that Buchanan possessed "French grace combined with Scottish solidity."[5]

That Buchanan was competent to pass judgment on forms of government and the merits and demerits of kings is evident both from his distinguished political career and the famous and in-

[4] *George Buchanan, Humanist and Reformer* (Edinburgh, 1890), vol. 1, p. 1.
[5] *George Buchanan, Quatercentenary Studies, 1906* (Glasgow, 1907), p. xxviii.

deed long standard history of Scotland which he wrote with his own hand in Latin. And of his *De Jure Regni apud Scotos* it may be said that it was the authoritative statement on the doctrine of tyrannicide for the next century or more. Indeed, it was relied upon by those who supported and defended the execution of James' son, Charles I.

The Dialogue opens with a few introductory remarks in which BUCHANAN relates how he came to ask of Thomas MAITLAND (lately returned from France), "what was the opinion of the Frenche or other nations with whom he had conversed in France," concerning the murder of Darnley and the apprehension of Mary Queen of Scots.[6]

MAITLAND admits that the position of a Scot abroad is indeed disagreeable, since on the one hand he meets with the abhorrence felt toward the author of the "horrid villainy" (Darnley's murder)—an abhorrence which redounds to the unpopularity of the whole Scotch nation, and, on the other hand, he is liable to equally horrified blame for the "atrocious cruelty" involved in bringing to punishment for that crime not merely a woman but a woman who is Queen of Scotland.

But no!—says BUCHANAN—if the first deed was truly so horrible, severity in punishing it can not be reproved. One of these two acts must be praised, while the other is blamed.

MAITLAND confesses that, for his part, he will be glad to see the murderer brought to justice, but adds that he is fearful lest the nations of Europe, "especially such as live under kingly Governments," will not relish the fact that the avengers "have taken order with the chief Majestrate, and put contempt upon Sovereignty."

BUCHANAN thus perceives that his interlocutor is troubled, not so much by his own scruples, as by the need of satisfying the scruples of foreign judges. Now these judges, BUCHANAN divides into three groups. (1) The most pernicious is that composed of the ministers to the lusts of tyrants; a group who consider as

[6] In fact, Buchanan rather stresses at this point the importance of foreign opinion, in that it is apt to be relatively free from prejudice, fear and similar emotions. In other portions of the Dialogue, however, and particularly in the concluding pages, he appears to resent foreign criticism of Scotch domestic policy.

just and lawful all deeds whereby they may gratify kings, who have left themselves no liberty to speak or act independently of the lusts of others, who share in the responsibility for the murder and grieve, not—as they would seem to do—for the Queen's misfortune, but for the peril to their own security and the loss of the hoped for rewards. These persons, indeed, should not so much be satisfied by reasoning as chastised by law and by force of arms. (2) The second group is made up of persons who "are all for themselves," and who are malicious only in that they grieve "for their own domestic damages," rather than for the public calamity. These persons, again, stand in need not of reasoning, but rather of comfort for their losses. (3) The third group of critics, however, is composed of "the rude multitude," who are simply aghast at all novelties; "for how much any thing done doth incline from an ancient custom, so far they think it is fallen from justice and equity." Such persons may be won over by argument, since they are for the most part willing to be instructed and "weaned from their errour," and since, if they are asked in the midst of their protests what they think of the punishment of Caligula or Nero or Domitian, there will in all probability be "none of them so addicted to the name of *King*" as to deny that the punishment in these cases was just.

Maitland objects that the persons interrogated would cry out that they were not complaining of the punishment of Tyrants, but were "grieved at the sad calamaties of lawful Kings."

Buchanan answers that any one who protests in these terms will easily be persuaded to change his opinion, once he clearly understands the difference between a Tyrant and a King. The further objection advanced by Maitland (to the effect that not all men will admit that Tyrants are justly killed; and that some authorities even make Kings liable to legal penalties, while they preposterously maintain that Tyrants are sacred persons) is postponed for discussion elsewhere. For the present, the Dialogue turns upon the proposition set forth by Buchanan: "Let us then conclude these two to be contraries a *King* and a *Tyrant*." This proposition leads in turn to the corollary that whoever explains the origin and causes of the creation of Kings, together with the duties of Kings toward their people and of people toward their Kings, will very nearly have explained the nature of a tyrant.

II. *On Kings.*) Buchanan accordingly agrees to set forth, not so much his own conception of a King, as the conception formed by the ancients, whose opinion will have the more authority in that it is not colored by any prejudice connected with the case under discussion. Putting certain preliminary questions to MAITLAND, which the latter answers, he gradually ascertains by this Socratic procedure:

(a. *The origin and causes of the creation of Kings.*)—"Do you not think," asks BUCHANAN, "that the time hath been, when men . . . as strangers did wander to and from without laws, or certain dwelling places, and did assemble together as their fond humors did lead them, or as some commodity and common utility did allure them?" Having secured an affirmative answer from MAITLAND,[7] he puts another question: Which seems the more agreeable to nature, "the vagrant and solitary life, or the association of men civilly incorporate"? To MAITLAND's reply in favor of the latter, on the ground that utility first brought men together, BUCHANAN takes partial exception, inasmuch as he does not consider utility to be "the first and main cause of the association of men." This is often an efficacious factor, but there is a more ancient and sacred bond, consisting in an instinct of nature, a desire for association with one's kind which is independent of all the "allurements of utility."

MAITLAND regards this view with favor, but feels the need of a definition of the term "nature," which—he confesses—"I do often use rather out of custom, than that I understand it."

The definitions of "nature" and "law of nature" which BUCHANAN therefore gives are worth bearing in mind throughout his discourse. He says: "At present I would have no other

[7] Maitland, citing both the testimony of nature and that of history, mentions among other things the kind of life described by Homer in the passage to which Grotius (*De Jure Praedae*) also refers—a life in which every man "ruleth his own house, wife and children."

Maitland calls utility "the mother almost of justice and equity," a quotation from Horace (Satires, I. iii. 98), which Grotius also cites.

thing to be understood thereby, than the LIGHT *infused by God into our minds,* for when God formed that creature . . . which might have dominion over the other creatures, he gave not only *eyes* to his Body, . . . but also he produced in his mind a certain LIGHT, whereby he might discern things filthy from honest; this *light* some call *nature,* others the *Law of nature,* . . . and I am fully persuaded, that *nature* doth never say one thing, and *wisdom* another. Moreover, God hath given us an abridgment of that LAW, which might contain the whole in a few words, viz. *That we should love him with all our soul, and our Neighbours as our selves. . . .*" Accordingly, God Himself was the Author of human society, and Buchanan agrees with Cicero that nothing done on earth is more acceptable to Him, "than the associations of men legally united, which are called Civil Incorporations, whose several parts must be as compactly joined together, as the several members of our Body," each part having its proper function that it may cooperate in producing the good of the whole. Elaborating this metaphor, BUCHANAN declares that civil bodies require a physician even as our physical bodies do, and asks MAITLAND to supply a name for this civil physician.

MAITLAND suggests the name of "King."

BUCHANAN accepts the suggestion, and furthermore calls attention to the fact that we have found no better name than this, by which to designate God in his paternal care over us.

(b. *The function of a King.*)—BUCHANAN also mentions other titles by which a King may be designated: "Father," "pastor of the people," "leader," "Prince," "Governour"—all names indicating that Kings are ordained, not for themselves, but for their people. This brings him to the next point in his description of Kings (a point closely bound up with the causes for their creation); their function. This function, as he has already suggested, is analogous to that of a physician; in other words, it is the care of the civil body's health, and is of a twofold nature, involving both the preservation of health when the body is well, and the restoration of health when the body is attacked by sickness. MAITLAND is correct—continues BUCHANAN—in supposing that while the physician of physical bodies is charged with reducing bodily humors to the proper temperate state, the task of the civil physician is the reduction of habits of conduct to a corresponding state. To this condition of temperance or moderation—when it is found "in publick matters, and mens mutual commerces"—we may assign the name "Justice."

(c. *The manner of creating Kings.*)—So intimately connected is the matter of the kingly function with that of the choice and creation of Kings, that BUCHANAN enters upon this phase of the discussion without any formal introduction of the topic. It is his belief—in which MAITLAND concurs—that the ancients willingly conferred the government upon any citizen who seemed to exceed all others in equity and prudence. Where there is no such citizen, it is still possible to elect as lawful King some person not perfectly endowed with royal virtues, but outstanding for noble descent or warlike valor. To be a King, however—BUCHANAN once more brings his friend to the same conclusion, by the Socratic method—one must be skillful in the art of government, even as other physicians must be skillful in the art of medicine; and the art of government consists, not so much in a bare knowledge of civil laws, unaccompanied by practice, as in the faculty—acquired through practice—to govern well and rationally.

MAITLAND, asked to supply a name for this governing faculty, or civil art, replies: "It seems you would call it prudence; Out of which, as from a fountain or spring, all laws, provided they be useful for the preservation of humane society, must proceed. . . ."

Agreed—says BUCHANAN. Moreover, a person possessing perfect prudence of this sort is a King by nature and not by suffrage, one to whom a free power over all things might be resigned.

(d. *The restriction of Kings by laws. Is this injurious to the kingly authority?*)—BUCHANAN continues, however, with the assertion that if, for lack of such a man, we are obliged to choose as King that person who comes nearest to such excellence, we do not give him arbitrary power over all things but appoint law as his Colleague, that his lusts may be bridled. Thus, if ignorant, he will be shown the way by law; and if he wander out of the way, law will bring him back to it.

"Of the cause of creating Kings," says MAITLAND, "of their name and duty you have fully satisfied me . . . yet there is one thing which in all your discourse did not a little offend me . . . *viz.* that you seem somewhat injurious to Kings." Moreover, MAITLAND has seemed to detect the same fault in his friend when hearing the latter praise the ancient Commonwealths and the City of Venice.

BUCHANAN replies first to the last part of this accusation, asserting that he praised, not so much the form of government, as the equity of the form; since it matters little what we call the chief in authority, "provided . . . he is placed in the magistracy for the maintenance of equity; for if the government be lawful, we must not contend for the name thereof." Thus he returns to his former assertion, that Kings were first instituted in order to maintain equity. If they had so exercised their power as to preserve it in this noble form, they might have kept an unlimited sovereignty perpetually; but, because they abused the authority which was ordained for the public utility, "laws were made by the people, and Kings constrained to make use, not of their own licentious wills in judgment, but of that right or privilege which the people had conferred upon them." Accordingly, this sole injunction was laid upon Kings, "otherwise free, that they should conform their actions and speech to the prescripts of laws." In this connection, BUCHANAN quotes the saying that, *"A King should be a speaking law, and the law a dumb King."*

MAITLAND again protests at the lack of due respect for sovereignty shown by his friend's argument, and asks who would choose to be King if that position involved simply perpetual trouble in the care of other people's affairs, neglect of one's own interests, and the ordering of all one's life in accordance with rules laid down by others.

"Consider, I pray you," answers BUCHANAN, "in how great an errour you are, who do think that Kings were created by people and nations, not for justice, but for pleasure, and do think there can be no honour, where wealth and pleasures abound not;

wherein consider how much you diminish their grandeur." He —BUCHANAN—relates various anecdotes showing that the majesty of great rulers consists, not in vain ostentation and service received from others, but in rendering services to their people.[8] Next, he cites the sources from which he draws his conception of this form of government, or which support such a conception, and dwells particularly upon a passage from Cicero's *De Officiis,* quoting these statements among others: "It seems . . . that of old, well-bred[9] Kings who were created . . . for executing of justice; for . . . the people . . . betook themselves to some one who was eminent for virtue, who whilst he kept off the weakest from injuries, establishing equity . . . hemmed in the highest with the lowest, by equal laws to both. And the reason of making laws, was the same as of the creation of Kings; for it is requisite that justice be always equal, for otherwise it were not justice. If this they did obtain from one good and just man, they were therewith well pleased; when that did not occur, laws were made, which by one and the same voice might speak to all alike . . . those were usually chosen to govern of whose justice the people had a great opinion."

(e. *The making and interpretation of laws. Are these acts a part of the kingly office?*)—MAITLAND being as yet imperfectly convinced, BUCHANAN summarizes and elaborates what he has already said in his discussion of Kings, and carries his interlocutor with him step by step. This process leads them to a more detailed consideration of the making and interpretation of laws. They agree that civil precepts, like the precepts of medicinal art, can not cover the entire ground relating to the health of nations. New problems may arise in a new age, with respect to which the King should call to council some of the most prudent citizens. Again, questions may rise out of the past,

[8] Perhaps the most striking incident described here by Buchanan is the story of Philip of Macedon and the old woman who petitioned him to hear her cause. Receiving the answer that "he had no leisure," she replied, "Then cease to be a King." Phillip, a King "victorious in so many battles, and conqueror of so many nations, admonished to do his duty by a poor old wife, obeyed, and acknowledged that it was the duty of Kings so to do."

[9] *Bene morati,* for which the Loeb translation, "of high moral character," is perhaps preferable; or, more precisely still, "of right moral conduct."

necessitating conjecture and calling for the testimony of witnesses; and regarding these points, the King may be obliged to rely upon the skill of lawyers and the judgment of judges. For he will not be able to discharge his other duties, or find needed time for rest, if he himself attends to every private cause arising among his subjects. At first glance, to be sure, it would seem that the King himself, like a skillful physician, might sometimes be called upon to deal with cases not provided for by set rules, and might find it necessary to impose upon his subjects—whether through persuasion or against their wills—new laws advantageous to them; all of which he should be enabled to do by his skill in the art of government. Furthermore, it might be argued that while the law is inexorable, the King is a possible source of mercy for those who have erred. However, the King who may be left free from the bonds of law is a King of ideal excellence, such as we imagine rather than behold in actual life; so that it is inexpedient to leave the health of the nation entirely to the control of rules laid down to Kings who are susceptible to such emotions as "love and hatred, which drive the minds of men to and fro in judging."

Thus, when BUCHANAN asks what was the pattern set before the minds of those who first made laws the cue has already been given for MAITLAND's reply:

". . . they in council had [10] an Idea of that perfect King, and . . . did express a certain Image, not of the body but of the mind, according to that foresaid Idea as near as they could. And would have that to be in stead of Laws which he is to think might be good and equitable."

BUCHANAN [11] finds the reply acceptable, and reminds his interlocutor that this ideal King, as already described, was "firm and stedfast against hatred, love, wrath, envy, and other perturbations of the mind"; that laws seem to have been made according to

[10] *habuisse*. Our English text has "hands," obviously a misprint.

[11] Our next ascribes three consecutive speeches, of which this is the second, to Maitland. The edition of Philadelphia, 1766, and the Latin text, both ascribe the second speech to Buchanan. This sort of error occurs not infrequently in the English edition of 1721.

this Idea of a King; and that, accordingly, "A good King . . . is no less severe and inexorable than a good law." To Maitland's plea that the severity of both should, if possible, be tempered, he responds, inflexibly: ". . . God desires not that mercy be shewed even to the poor in judgment, but commandeth us to respect that one thing which is just and equal, and to pronounce sentence accordingly."

MAITLAND at last assents on this point, but he asks: "Seeing therefore it is not lawful to loose Kings from the bonds of laws, who shall then be the lawgiver?" Urged to suggest his own solution, he continues: ". . . I think the King himself."

BUCHANAN, however, objects: "On the contrary, I for my part see no difference between leaving the King free and unbound by laws, and granting him the power to command the laws.[12] For no man will willingly lay bonds and fetters upon himself." Moreover, he knows not whether it is better to leave a man free of all bonds, or to fetter him merely with bonds which are of no avail, which, indeed he may fling off when he so desires!

MAITLAND here warns BUCHANAN lest, in conceding the helm of government to laws rather than to the King, he make of the latter a Tyrant.

BUCHANAN replies that he would merely have the people empowered to prescribe to the King whose authority is derived from them, a model by which he is to govern; and that he would have these laws imposed not by force but by a common council acting in conjunction with the King.

On this point, MAITLAND definitely disagrees, for he is unwilling to grant so much power to the people, that *"beast with many heads."* Neither is he satisfied by the explanation that the deliberations are to be conducted by a select number out of the various estates, not by the people as a whole, though the preliminary decrees (once they have been drawn up) shall be laid before the people. For the very dangers which make us fear to trust the

[12] The Latin reads: *Ego contra nihil interesse video, Regemne liberum & solutum legibus relinquamus, an ei tribuamus legum jubendarum potestatem.* Our English text can not be followed for this sentence, which it mistranslates. It is slightly misleading with respect to the immediately following sentence also.

King, contends MAITLAND, are multiplied when we add to his authority that of the counsellors, since they, too, are men. He argues that, "The more . . . you adjoin to the King as assessors there will be a greater number of fools. . . ."

BUCHANAN retorts that many persons together see and understand more than one person alone, even though he be more prudent than any one of them; and that, furthermore, the mingling of various qualities which we find in a multitude tends to produce that moderation of temperament which is necessary to every kind of virtue.

Turning from the making of laws to their interpretation, MAITLAND asks what is to be done in those cases where the laws seem to clash, or where for some other reason there is need of the King as a kindly interpreter.[18]

BUCHANAN—so he reminds his friend—has already contended that it is the King's duty, in cases where he clearly sees what is just and good, to provide that the actual laws and their interpretation shall conform to the ideal model on which they were based; but there are other questions of interpretation usually deferred to judges, and MAITLAND apparently desires to defer these, also, to Kings, thus exceeding their own most imperious claims.

MAITLAND urges that interpretation by one good man is better than prolonged contention among subtle and crafty men.

We have already granted—replies BUCHANAN—that if this one man were sufficiently good, the ideal King, he might be granted the power in question, and all others. But if we grant such power of interpretation to a King less excellent than the ideal, we are restoring to him the immoderate power which we have just agreed he should not possess. BUCHANAN speaks at length of the harm that may easily result from endowing imperfect Kings with this power of interpretation; and when MAITLAND expresses doubt that any King would, in point of fact, be so imprudent as to abuse the power thus, the other declares that

[18] Here again (pp. 210-211) the English edition has confused the order of the speakers, so that the careful reader must resort to the Latin, in order to follow the Dialogue properly.

history records actual examples of such abuse, and himself cites the examples of the Pope and of the Emperor Caligula. (It is in this connection that he speaks of "that *Roman Jupiter* of ours . . . I say *Pope Julius* the Third, who seems contended with C. Caligula, a most wicked wretch, for preheminence of impiety.")

MAITLAND objects that the ancients, at least, can hardly have considered this power of interpretation to be so great a thing, since the Roman Emperors granted it to lawyers. Moreover, the very fact that they were able to grant the power to others indicates that they had the right to exercise it themselves, had they so wished, and had the pressure of other affairs allowed.

BUCHANAN's reply is, first: that the wicked Roman Emperors—having been chosen by the soldiers indeliberately, or else having usurped the imperial power—were not Kings as the term is defined in this Dialogue; and secondly: that the danger resulting from their grant of interpretative power to the lawyers was not particularly great, since there were judges set above the lawyers and since these judges were not bound to accept the lawyers' rulings, while the Emperor was over all, and the interpreters' fear of punishment might well have been greater than their hope of reward for fraud.

(f. *Review of preceding remarks. Buchanan's representation of King has not detracted from their majesty, but exalted them.*) BUCHANAN here suggests another review of what has been said, and also remarks: "We seemed to be at accord sufficiently concerning the origin and cause of creating Kings, and making Laws, but of the Lawgiver not so: But at last, though somewhat unwillingly, you seem, in my opinion, to have consented, being compelled by the strength of the truth." [14]

MAITLAND admits that he is still uneasy at having allowed BUCHANAN, in his discourse, to deprive Kings not only of the power to command laws but also of the power to interpret them.

BUCHANAN answers that, of the many affairs not to be com-

[14] *Sed visus es mihi tandem, etsi subinvitus, tamen vi ipsa veritatis coactus, consensisse.* In translating this sentence, we must depart a little from our English text, which renders it incorrectly.

prehended within laws, he has laid a part on ordinary judges, a part on the King's council by the King's consent; and marvels that MAITLAND, "good advocate of Kings," does not rejoice that they should thus be given aid in bearing their burdens.

MAITLAND is, indeed, willing to accept these auxiliaries, but he would have such persons serve, rather than command; he would have them show the way, rather than lead it and thus deprive the King of every power other than that of assenting to them. Accordingly, he urges that they leave the subject of Kings and turn to a discussion of Tyrants, before his friend shall have deprived the King of his every honor and dignity.

BUCHANAN, however, is not content to let matters stand thus. It is MAITLAND, he declares, who is calumniating Kings, while BUCHANAN himself defends them. He argues, first, that he would not have the King an idler any more than he would wish a master-builder to be idle. Secondly, MAITLAND is attempting to deprive the King of the ministers and friends whom BUCHANAN would attach to him, not as keepers but as helpers. Again, MAITLAND wishes to surround the King with knaves who will aid in making him formidable to his subjects, while BUCHANAN would guard him, not with the fear, but with the love and goodwill of his subjects, "which arms alone do make Kings invincible"—a point stressed, we may say, in other treatises on Tyranny, including Mariana's. Furthermore, BUCHANAN now reveals his purpose of attributing to Kings all the authority and greatness they could prudently desire, by assigning to them one power, greater than that of "all the conventions of all estates met for making of laws." For laws, after all, may be and frequently are broken as regards their spirit, even while the letter of the law is obeyed, so that many illnesses may spring up in the body politic as a result of a legislative attempt to cure one sole affection; but through the kingly power which Buchanan has in mind, it is possible to rid the whole body of all its evil humors. Now what is this power? It is that of a good example, set by the nation's ruler. The passage from Claudian quoted in this connection includes the following exhortations: ". . . If thou commandest [what] ought to be done by all, and to be obeyed, obey the same first thy self: Then will the people become the more observant of equity, nor will refuse to bear any burden, when they see their King himself obedient to what he commands. The whole world doth act conform[ably] to the example of a King. The laws of Kings prevail not so much to incline mens minds unto obedience, as the conversation of the Rulers. . . ." Nor is this an exaggerated picture—says BUCHANAN—of the influence of kingly example; for the people tend both to admire sincerely all that is done by the King, and to imitate even when they do not admire, in order to flatter him. Here he proceeds to lay down the traditional admonitions: "Let therefore a King carefully consider, that he is set on the Theatre of the world, and for a spectacle proposed to all, so as no word or deed of his can be concealed. The vices of Kings can never be kept secret. For the supream light of Fate suffers nothing to lie hid in obscurity, and Fame enters into all secret places, and finds out obscure corners. O how much doth it concern Kings to be circumspect on all hands! feeling neither their vices nor their virtues can be concealed, nor yet without a great universal change of affairs." BUCHANAN goes on to cite Numa Pompilius [15] as an example illustrating his conception of a virtuous king. He speaks, next, of the various reasons which should move the Princes of a later age to serve as models for their subjects: advantages of birth and education; hope of honor in this life, and hope of reward in the next. He compares such a model King to the brazen serpent of Moses, which healed the people of their serpents' wounds when they looked on it; for one "may reckon a good King amongst the greatest benefits of God; who alone . . . doth relieve a Kingdom of all its troubles, . . . in whose image so great a force is presented to the minds of his subjects, that it doth easily perform what the prudence of lawyers, the science of Philosophers, and the experience of so many ages in collecting their several arts could never perform." Such, then, "is the true representation of a King," says BUCHANAN, "not that

[15] The second legendary king of Rome (715-672 B. C.). Elected by the Roman people, he enjoyed, according to Livy (I. xviii), "a great reputation for justice and piety," and was "deeply versed, so far as anyone could be in that age, in all law, divine and human."

of a King guarded with weapons of war, ever fearing others, or making others afraid, by his hatred towards his people measuring his people's hatred against him." Far from speaking contemptuously of Kings, BUCHANAN attempts to guard them with their own innocence and the love of their peoples, rather than with the terror of arms, and would set them in a position of eminence, freedom and honor. "What acclamation," he demands, "or what triumph can be compared with this daily pomp? or if God in human likeness should come down into earth what greater honour could be given Him by men, than that which would be given to a true King, that is to the lively image of God? . . . What do you think of this representation of a King?"

MAITLAND agrees that "nothing can be said or imagined more magnificent," but feels that such Kings will be hard to procure, unless this be done through careful education. Education, indeed, is of great importance for all conditions of life; but special care should be taken—seeing how great is the influence of princes—"that the tender minds of Kings be rightly principled, even from their very infancy." However, MAITLAND fears that the Kings whom the dialoguists have in mind will scarcely be persuaded to pattern themselves after BUCHANAN's model, but will rather be deceived by "the false shew of honour," even as the Trojans—according to some poets—fought for a false likeness of Helen, while the true Helen was left in Egypt. In like manner, impotent Tyrants embrace the false representation of a Kingdom, and "if any do admonish them, that the true Helena for whom they imagine to fight is elsewhere concealed, they would call him mad."

BUCHANAN, approving this simile, remarks that Tyrants could not be better punished than by being allowed to behold "that true daughter of Jupiter," in whose place they have set the false Helen. Accordingly, he quotes Persius' imprecation: "O supream Father of the Gods, be pleased thus to punish cruel Tyrants . . . let them see what vertue is, and let them pine away for sorrow, because they despised her." [16]

[16] *Satires,* III. 35-38.

III. *Thus we come to the discussion of Tyrants.*—BUCHANAN suggests that, "we proceed in the same footsteps for finding out a Tyrant, wherein we did insist in seeking out a King.

(a. *The name of "Tyrant," and its connotations.*)—He considers, first, the very name of "Tyrant," although he brushes aside the etymological questions relating to it.[17] The ancients —he says—used this term to denote those "who had the full power of all things in their hands," and applied the name not only to their heroes and most famous men, but to Jupiter himself

How—inquires MAITLAND—has a name once so honorable come long since to be accounted odious?

BUCHANAN replies that a word may through circumstances acquire an unpleasant meaning, though there be no evil in the word itself. The infamous individuals who bore the name of tyrant in later times so polluted the title that men "thought it a more light reproach to be called an hang-man than a Tyrant"; while conversely, base names may be rendered illustrious by virtuous men. The Tyrant may be the true head of a lawful government. Indeed, it would seem that the terms "King" and "Tyrant" were used among the ancients—though presumably in different ages—with one and the same meaning. BUCHANAN's theory is that the term "Tyrant" is the older; that when this name (through its associations) grew wearisome, it was replaced by the term "King," together with a more gentle form of government; and that when Kings also began to degenerate, laws were introduced for the purpose of keeping their lusts within bounds.[18]

[17] The English text might momentarily mislead the reader at this point, owing to an obvious misprint. For, "I therefore think it now necessary," we must read, "I therefore think it not necessary."

[18] An attempt to discuss Buchanan's view in this place would lead us far afield. It may be of interest, however, to consider the etymology of the word "tyrant." A. H. Greenidge (*Tyrannus* in Smith's *Dictionary of Greek and Roman Antiquities*, London, 1891, Vol. II, p. 914 b) says that the word Τύραννος "has not yet been satisfactorily explained by a Greek etymology, and Boeckh's conjecture that it was a foreign word and came to the Greeks from Lydia or Phrygia, where it is found frequently in inscriptions, is extremely probable." It is, again, probable (according to Liddell and Scott, *A Greek English Lexicon* . . . Eighth Edition, Oxford, 1901) that it was first used in the Homeric Hymns, viii. 5, where it appears in connection with the god Ares.

The latter authority defines it as meaning *"an absolute sovereign,* unlimited by

(b. *The differences between Tyrants and Kings.*)—BUCHANAN purposes to discuss and compare the two forms of government—i.e., the government of Kings combined with that of laws; and "the worst king of Tyranny wherein all things are contrary to a Kingdom." Accordingly, he once more calls attention to what has already been said regarding the creation of Kings, their offices and duties, and their cooperation with law. He then points out a primary difference between Kings and Tyrants, in that he who receives a government not by the will of the people but by a fraud, is a Tyrant. There are many other points of difference, since "the government of Kings is according to nature, but that of Tyrants is not." BUCHANAN runs through these points briefly, referring to Aristotle for a fuller treatment. "A King," says BUCHANAN, "doth rule his subjects and reign over them by their own consent. Tyrants reign over them nill they, will they. A Kingdom is a principality of a free man among free men: Tyranny is a principality of a Master over his slaves. For defence of a King's safety the subjects watch and ward, for a Tyrant forrainers do watch to oppress the subjects. The one beareth rule for the subjects welfare, the other for himself."

---

law or constitution," and tells us that "it first began to be used in the time of Archilochus" who flourished *circa* 700 B. C. Archilochus' use of the word corresponds then, roughly, to the first despotic era (7th and 6th centuries) which prepared the way for the free constitutions of the next succeeding centuries. Greenidge says of the rulers of this period: "The demagogue who united military prowess with zeal for the popular welfare was the most ordinary type of despot; this character is found chiefly exemplified by the pretenders who in the 7th and 6th centuries rose to the throne through opposition to the ruling oligarchies, such as Orthagoras at Sicyon, Cypselus at Corinth, Theagenes at Megara, and Pisistratus at Athens."

Τύραννος came into common use two centuries later, during the time of Theognis, Pindar, and Herodotus, when, as Liddell and Scott say, "free governments having superseded the old hereditary sovereignties (βασιλεῖαι) all who obtained absolute power in a state were called Τύραννοι, *tyrants,* or rather *despots;* for the term rather regards the irregular way in which the power was *gained,* whether force or fraud, than the way in which it was exercised, being applied to the mild Pisistratus, but not to the despotic kings of Persia."

The implications which the word carries in its derived forms in modern languages are not, however, to be regarded as post-classical accretions; "the word soon came to imply reproach" say Liddell and Scott; and the references which they give to Plato and Sophocles can easily be supplemented by others to Aristotle and all the later writers.

"What," asks MAITLAND, "do you say of those who have gotten . . . the supream authority by force and without the people's consent, and yet for many years did so rule that the people were not weary of their government?" For what do such rulers lack to make them just kings except "the people's suffrages"?

BUCHANAN replies that even these persons are Tyrants, owing not only to their method of acquiring their power, but also to the fact that their benignancy suggests the ostentatious bounty of robbers, being directed to their own security rather than to the welfare of the people; so that, once they are secure, they turn back to their old ways. Yet Tyrants of this sort may perhaps be endured, if it is impossible to uproot them without still greater injury to the commonwealth.[19] He adds, however, that those persons who bear rule not for their country's good but for their own self-interest, who have regard not for the public advantage but only for their own pleasure and lust, who rely for the stability of their authority upon the people's weakness, and "think that a Kingdom is not a procuration credited to them by God, but rather a prey into their hands,"—those persons are not joined to us by any civil bond, or bond of humanity, but should be accounted the greatest enemies of God and of all men. "By how much Kings are raised above other men, so much should they imitate the celestial bodies, which having no good offices of ours given to them, yet do infuse on human affairs a vital and bountiful vertue of heat and light." The very titles which the dialoguists have agreed to confer upon Kings—father, shepherd, etc.—indicate that Kings are under this obligation. And as for those rulers who usurp the name of King, and who, instead of discharging their obligations, adopt the contrary course, acting always for their own gain and oppressing the people, are they to be accounted Kings, whatever pomp they may assume?

They are not to be so accounted—answers MAITLAND—but rather as beings beyond the pale of human society.

"Within what limits," asks BUCHANAN, "do you circumscribe human society?"

---

[19] Our English text is again misleading at this point, due to its omission of a negative word.

"Within the hedge of law," replies MAITLAND; adding that they who transgress these limits are publicly and justly punished.

But what of those persons who never once enter within these limits?—is BUCHANAN's next query.

Such persons—says MAITLAND—"should be accounted enemies to God and men, and reckoned amongst wolves, or some other kind of noisome beasts, rather than amongst men." He goes on to describe the treatment which these creatures should receive from all true men; for beings thus inhuman—whatever their resemblance to humankind in countenance, gesture and speech—are no more to be called men than are satyrs, apes and bears.

BUCHANAN perceives that his friend now understands the differences between Kings and Tyrants, as the terms were used by the wisest ancients. He adds, however, to what has already been said, a vivid description of the torments endured by Tyrants in their fear-haunted lives, comparing them to devils who rejoice in torturing men while they themselves are undergoing perpetual torture; or to the master of a storm-tossed ship who must depend for his safety upon a hostile crew. "They are afraid of enemies abroad, and of their subjects at home, . . . of their domesticks . . . and near relations . . . they have always war . . . or else they are still in fear thereof. Neither do they expect aid anywhere but by a mercenary way, they dare not hire good men, nor can they trust bad men; what then in all their life can be to them pleasant?" Even when asleep, they are tormented by terrifying dreams, and nature's season of rest and relaxation is turned into one of horrors and punishment.

(c. *The application of the foregoing statements to the situation in Scotland.*)—Even if all these assertions be true—objects MAITLAND—what do they prove for present purposes? "For they who have the power to chuse what Kings they please, in them is the power to bind by laws such as they have chosen. But you know that our Kings are not chosen, but born Kings. To whom I have always though it to be no less hereditary, that their will and pleasure should stand for law, than the Kingdom itself." Several great authorities, according to MAITLAND, support him in this view; for example, the Jurists affirm that, "by the royal law which is made for the government of Kings, all the people's power is so transmitted into them, that their will and pleasure should be accounted for laws." In this connection, he cites the threat made by a certain Emperor, of abolishing the whole science of jurists by one edict.

The author of that threat—retorts BUCHANAN—was the wicked Caligula,[20] who was no man, and far less a King, save in shape. As for the royal law mentioned by MAITLAND, what evidence is at hand regarding its nature or establishment? The Roman Emperors did not reign according to this law, since appeals were made from them to the people. The ordinances of certain Tyrants cannot be considered to have been laws. And in any case, if there has ever been such a law, it should be considered as "an example proposed . . . for caution, but not for imitation."

MAITLAND repeats his contention that it is all very well to address admonitions of this sort to peoples having the power to elect the best Kings, but that the ancestors of the Scottish Kings received from the Scots such right and authority that those early rulers and their posterity acquired perpetual empire and authority over that people; and thus BUCHANAN's counsel comes too late, since nothing is "left to those that are made slaves, but to be punished for other men's folly," and to lighten the punishment by propitiating their masters with patience. Moreover, the royal law concerning which BUCHANAN is so dubious, could not have been made in favor of tyranny since it was approved by Justinian, an exceedingly just Prince.

BUCHANAN admits the greatness of Justinian, although history records that he was not perfect: but, on the other hand, there was among the chief compilers of the Justinian Code a very

---

[20] The nickname of the Emperor Gaius Caesar (12-41 A. D.), who began his reign with moderation but soon became a monster of cruelty and vice. The reference here is apparently to a passage in Suetonius' *Lives of the Caesars* (IV. xxxiv) in which that Roman writer says of Caligula that "with regard to lawyers, too, as if intending to do away with any practice of their profession, he often threatened that he would see to it, by Heaven, that they could give no advice contrary to his wish." —Loeb translation, by Professor John C. Rolfe.

wicked man, Tribonian,[21] who might well have been guilty of distorting the law in order to flatter the Prince. BUCHANAN then adds: "But let us return to our own Princes, . . . of our own only I speak, for if I shall digress to speak of foreign Princes, I fear lest our discourse become . . . prolix. . . ."

MAITLAND discreetly agrees that foreign affaris are not very pertinent to their discussion.

Accordingly, BUCHANAN—beginning "at the first principles"—reminds his friend that the Scottish Princes were originally chosen for their virtues; and points out the fact that the Scotch have been known to call to account and punish, with the greatest severity, both wicked Kings and the murderers of good Kings. He relates in this connection various incidents in the history of Scotland.

But MAITLAND objects: "I do not so much enquire at present what some time hath been done, as by what right Kings reign amongst us."

Very well—answers BUCHANAN—first we must ask whether these Kings were created by the people's will or against it. If the latter had been the case, the people would have had the right to cast off—when they themselves had grown sufficiently strong—the yoke which had been thus violently imposed; for law and nature agree "that whatever is done by force and violence, may be undone by the like violence." Even if the people had, as MAITLAND suggests, been induced by fear or through fraud to surrender themselves into such slavery, the same principle applies and the pact thus made can be dissolved. For there is a law, drawn from Nature's spring, allowing "restitution to be fully made to such as are by fraud circumvented. . . . What assembly . . . of men can require more justly to have restitution, than a whole people, to whom the wrong is done . . . ?"

MAITLAND confesses that this law does indeed justly apply in the case of private persons. However, he cuts short this part of

---

[21] A famous fifth century Roman jurist and the chief legal minister of the Emperor Justinian. He was at one time charged with having prostituted his office for gain, as related by Procopius (*History of the Wars*, Bk. I, chaps. xxiv and xxv).

the debate with the assertion—supported by historians—that the sovereignty of the Scotch Kings was probably granted to them by the people's will.

BUCHANAN comments that this grant can not have been made without some great cause.

MAITLAND replies that the cause was weariness of ambitious strife and intestine wars; but he admits that this strife was more pernicious to the Kings themselves than to the people.

"It seems, then," remarks BUCHANAN, "that Princes rather for themselves than for the good of the people desired to establish the Kingdom in their own family." Yet the people would scarcely have bestowed so great a benefit on these Kings, without receiving some concessions in return, for they would have been worse off than before. These concessions, BUCHANAN implies, consist in a moderation of the King's power by law, a moderation which strengthens the very power that it limits. Now the Scottish people—whose royal family, as MAITLAND himself points out, has been one of the most enduring in Europe, and this apparently because of the moderation of supreme authority—can not have been so fearful or foolish as to surrender themselves into slavery, *i.e.,* to a kingly power unmitigated by law.

Nevertheless—protests MAITLAND—if the people actually were blind or careless as to their own good, would they not be justly punished for their folly?

In BUCHANAN's opinion, it is not probable that the people were guilty of such weaknesses. He cites various facts drawn from Scottish history and Scottish custom to prove that the Kings of Scotland received from the ancestors of the present day Scots, not a boundless power, but one restricted within certain limits; and that, "further, there was the confirmation of a long time, and the usurpation of a perpetual right by the people, never reprehended by a publick decree." Thus, while MAITLAND fears that it is difficult to persuade Kings to yield to these laws, BUCHANAN believes that it is no less difficult to persuade the people to cede their age-old right. If the obstinacy of both forces comes to the point where arms are taken up, such contentions are apt to be long indeed and attended "with very great damage of the people, but with the utter overthrow of Kings. For from this spring do flow all the destructions of all kingdoms."

So much for the arguments based upon ancient Scottish history. BUCHANAN then remarks: ". . . if I had reasoned with you according to the rigour of the law, I might have gained my point in a far more compendious way." If he were reasoning thus, he would ask: "Do you not approve the definition of law set down by lawyers, who say that law is, that which the people have approved when it has been proposed to them by him to whom the prerogative of proposal belongeth?"[22] MAITLAND answers in the affirmative, and BUCHANAN continues: ". . . the faults of the laws being found out, they may be amended or abrogated by the Lawgivers." This same reasoning applies to the creation of Kings by the laws and suffrages of the people, except "that the law concerning our Kings was made several ages before and when any doth enter into the Kingdom, there useth to be no new law made, but the old law is approven and ratified." BUCHANAN recapitulates in this connection several points already agreed upon by dialoguists; for he asserts that the approval of Kings who are such by birth, and even the choice of new Kings, involves a certain risk for the people, owing to the scarcity of men completely worthy of absolute sovereignty, so that, to protect themselves against the risk, the people must have laws to modify this sovereignty, laws which should be the very image of that ideally worthy King.

(d. *On the judgment and punishment of Tyrants.*)—Turning from this part of the discussion—on which the dialoguists are now in accord—BUCHANAN devotes his attention to the question of the punishment of Tyrants. "If then," he demands, "a King break all the bonds of laws, and plainly behave himself as a publick enemy, what think you should be done in this case?"

MAITLAND wavers here between the view to which he has been brought by BUCHANAN's discourse, that such a King should be placed without the pale of human society; and, on the other

[22] Our English text does not translate the verbs satisfactorily in this question, so that it has been altered slightly in the quotation here given.

hand, the strength of custom, which might be more injurious when defied than when tolerated. A still stronger objection than that based on custom, an objection more potent "than all the arguments of Philosophers," is the fact that Scripture apparently confirms the form of government characterized by BUCHANAN as tyranny.

As to the first objection, BUCHANAN retorts that his friend attempts to confirm Tyranny by Tyranny, for the Tyranny of custom is one against which Herodotus has warned us,[23] as we might well be warned by more modern examples. As to the argument based upon Scripture, BUCHANAN holds that the Kings referred to by MAITLAND were in reality Tyrants, whom the people asked to have over them in place of lawful Kings like Samuel, and who not only differed from but were the very opposite of the kingly pattern prescribed by the Lord.

And what—persists MAITLAND—shall we say of Paul's admonition to pray for the safety of Princes,[23a] seeing that the Princes whom he recommends to our prayers—his Epistles are almost contemporary with them—are "the most cruel that ever were, Tiberius, Caligula, Claudius, Nero"?

BUCHANAN replies that the authority of Paul is indeed weighty, but that his meaning must be carefully interpreted in the light not only of his words but also of the circumstance attendant upon his writing. A number of passages from Paul are quoted and BUCHANAN comments upon them, saying—for example—that Paul admonished us to pray for all men; that the end of this praying was not the King's safety, but the Church's tranquillity, that certain words of Paul's writings do refer to true and lawful magistrates, but not to Tyrants; that though we ought to pray for wicked Princes, it does not follow that their vices should be left unpunished; and that Paul was writing for a very specific purpose—the chastisement of certain persons who rashly denied that authority was necessary for Christians. Paul, then, is speaking not merely of Magistrates, but of

[23] Apparently a reference to the passage (Bk. III. 38) in which Herodotus, describing the conflict between customs of different peoples, cites Pindar's famous maxim, "Custom is the king of all things."

[23a] *I Timothy*, ii. 1 and 2.

Magistracy, and furthermore, of every form of lawful Magistracy. BUCHANAN agrees "that there is need of Magistracy even in the best Commonwealths, and that we should in every way honour the same;" that if any man thinks otherwise, we should consider him a madman worthy of all punishment, "for he doth plainly contravene the will of God revealed to us in the Scriptures." But Paul lays down no objection to the punishment of Tyrants such as Caligula, Nero and Domitian. BUCHANAN here anticipates the argument "that wicked Princes are also ordained by God." God may indeed set up a wicked man to punish wicked men, but God is not therefore the author of evil, or wickedness, whereas He is the Author of punishment for the wicked. Even so a wicked man may be chosen by a good Magistrate as a hangman, the latter's function being undeniably a part of the public office, but no impunity is hereby granted the wicked man for his misdeeds. Returning, then, to Paul's exhortations, why should they be interpreted as referring only to Kings and not to other Magistrates? And if they refer to all Magistrates, shall the immunity from laws be extended to all these, or granted to Kings only? When Paul commands that all shall be subject to the higher powers, he must include other Magistrates than Kings, unless we are to suppose that Paul considered those Commonwealths which have no kingly government as being without power.

In spite of these arguments, MAITLAND clings to his belief that Paul referred, in his exhortation to obedience, to such cruel Tyrants as Nero. This belief is also supported by Jeremy's advice to the Jews, that they should obey the King of Assria.[23b]

To the latter point, BUCHANAN retorts that this advice applied to one specific case. If, then, any one should argue that all Tyrants must be obeyed, "because God by his Prophet did command his people to obey one Tyrant," it may be replied that, by the same reasoning, all Tyrants ought to be killed, because Ahab was killed at the command of God by the captain of his host.

[23b] *Jeremiah*, xxvii. 6 *et seq.*

MAITLAND, reserving his opinion on this matter, asks: "What do you bring from Scripture, why Tyrants may be lawfully killed?"

In the first place—replies BUCHANAN—the express command is given that wickedness and wicked men be cut off, no exception being made of rank or degree; and there is no passage of Scripture sparing Tyrants more than private persons. Secondly, Paul's definition of powers is not entirely applicable to Tyrants, since they use their authority not for the benefit of the people, but to gratify their own lusts. Furthermore, Paul grants great power to Bishops, whose function he compares to that of Kings (though he would have neither sort of magistrate absolutely free of the other, but would subject Bishops civilly to Kings, even as he would subject Kings to the spiritual admonitions of Bishops); and nevertheless, these Bishops to whom so much authority is granted are not exempted from punishment for crimes, by any law, human or divine. Even the Pope (that Bishop of Bishops!) for all his self-exaltation is held to be liable to vice and punishment in his capacity as a man, although he is said to be infallible as Pope. Here BUCHANAN leaves for a moment the field of Scriptural interpretation, and points out the fact that it is no blot upon any office or trade if an officer or member of the trade be punished; on the contrary, such individual punishments uphold the dignity of the group as a whole. In BUCHANAN's opinion, "if Kings would . . . measure their own greatness rather by duties of virtue, than by the impunity of evil deeds, they would not be grieved for the punishment of Tyrants, nor think that royal Majesty is lessened by whatsoever destruction of Tyrants, but rather be glad that it is purged from a most filthy blot of wickedness; especially seeing they use to be highly offended with robbers, and that very justly, if any of them in their malefices pretend the King's name."

MAITLAND, assenting to this, asks his friend to pass on to the other point which he has mentioned, and on which, to be sure, BUCHANAN has already touched: "in what time and to whom Paul wrote" the words in question.

BUCHANAN answers: first, that the time was during the infancy of the Church, when it was particularly important that no member of the Church should give an opening to those who sought occasions for reproaching it; secondly, Paul's admonitions were adapted for a specific group of people, a group consisting largely of the humble, poor and weak—many of them strangers in the Empire—a group unfitted for the helm of public affairs, and inclined to exaggerate the claims of Christian liberty. If, on the other hand, Paul had been writing in later days, when Princes also professed Christianity, his assertions would certainly have included a denunciation of Tyrants.

BUCHANAN then turns his attention to another point: the argument that God sets Tyrants over wicked peoples in order to punish them. This is true; but God also stirs up the avengers of tyranny, for He—being the Father of all alike—commands that all wickedness shall be cut down, without any exception of rank.

Again, BUCHANAN feels that his opponents may seek to find negative support in the Scriptures, asking if he can supply a Scriptural example of a King punished by his subjects. He admits his inability to do this, but adds that the mere absence of such an instance in Holy Writ does not imply that punishment of this kind is criminal. "For that servitude was never received, nor will the nature of things so fruitful of new examples suffer the same to be received, that whatever is not by some law commanded, or recorded by some famous example, should be accounted for a great crime and malefice." To this demand for a Scriptural example, one might reply: Where in the Scriptures is such punishment reprehended? And in any case, the relation of the Jewish Kings to their subjects is not exactly pertinent to the question in hand; for these Kings were given to the Jews by God, and it was therefore just that He who gave them as Kings should punish their misdeeds. But, in the case of the Scotch, BUCHANAN maintains "that the people, from whom our Kings enjoy what ever privilege they claim, is more powerful than their Kings; and that the whole people have that same privilege over them, which they have over every one in particular of the whole people. All the rights and privileges of foreign Nations, who live under lawful Kings do make for us; all the Nations which are subject to Kings chosen by themselves, do commonly agree herein, that whatever privilege the people hath given to any, the same they may require very justly." BUCHANAN mentions various historical examples of the actual exercise of this right by foreign nations, for he would not have it seem that the Scots have usurped a new privilege against their Kings. Had he been treating, however, of the Scots only, "the matter might have been handled in a few words."

MAITLAND begs to know how this could have been done.

Passing over a number of instances which might have been classified as obsolete tales, BUCHANAN calls to mind a more modern incident, that of the killing of the cruel James III, a deed condoned by all the Estates in a public convention. After comparing this with a similar occurrence recorded in Roman history, BUCHANAN asks: Does it not seem, then, that those persons who publicly decreed that there should be no punishment of a certain deed already done, were in effect passing a law applicable to any future repetition of that deed?

MAITLAND admits that all this may have some weight among the Scots, but he is still preoccupied with the need to satisfy foreign critics, who may blame the very decrees invoked as arguments by BUCHANAN, more than they blame the crime in question. He therefore desires to know what BUCHANAN can say in order to establish the equity of the law supporting the views above set forth.[24]

For his friend's sake, BUCHANAN somewhat reluctantly consents to stand at the bar and plead before foreigners for a law approved from the earliest times of the Scottish Kingdom by constant practice, a law which is necessary for the people's sake, not unjust for kings, highly honorable, but not at last accused of being illegal! Accordingly, BUCHANAN in his turn puts these questions to the critics of the law: What do they find in it

[24] The reference is evidently to the general law permitting the punishment of Tyrants, the existence of which we may infer from the decrees condoning a particular deed of this sort.

worthy of reprehension? Do they object to the cause owing to which the law was found desirable; or to the law itself? The cause was the wish to repress the unjust lusts of kings, and "Whoever doth condemn this, must likewise condemn all the laws of all Nations, for all laws were desired for the very same cause." And if, on the other hand, it is contended that the law itself is wrongful and that Kings ought not to be liable to laws, such a contention is inexpedient—obviously so for the people, since it confers upon Kings "a promiscuous license, . . . for making havock of all;" and inexpedient for the Kings themselves as it is inexpedient for a madman that his bonds should be loosed, or for a sick man that he should be given a drink which he craves but which will harm him. For it is true that not all Kings are of unsound mind, even as it is true that not all of the people are thus unsound; and nevertheless, the laws speak to all. Good Kings have no need to fear laws, and even wicked Kings, if they once regain their right minds, will realize that these legal restraints are beneficial to them, while the men who have flattered and indulged their lusts are their worst enemies. Just so a sick man who hates the restraining hand of the physician is grateful to that same physician, when health has returned.

MAITLAND here admits that restraints should indeed be applied to such unsound Kings, "For there is no monster more violent and pestiferous than man, when . . . he is once degenerate into a beast."

And in how many ways—exclaims BUCHANAN—does he become a beast! To mention only two of the monsters which appear in man, he is liable to wrath and lust; and whoever looses a King or any other man from all restraint, looses these two cruel monsters. Thus Aristotle has said: ". . . he who obeyeth the law, doth obey both God and the law; but he that obeyeth the King, doth obey both a man and a beast." [25]

MAITLAND advances two objections, at this point: (1) the statements made above are not consistent with what has already been agreed upon—that the voice of the King and the voice of the

[25] *Politics,* III. xi. 4.

law should be one and the same; for BUCHANAN now attempts to make the King subject to the law; (2) the main point of the debate has been missed—for who is to call to account a King that has become a Tyrant, since a privilege without strength will scarcely avail to control such a King?

BUCHANAN answers these objections by drawing a comparison between, on the one hand, a proclamation first uttered by a Magistrate and later taken up by a Herald, so that the voice of the two is the same voice, while he who first utters the words is nevertheless greater; and, on the other hand, the King, the law, and the people. The law—as BUCHANAN leads MAITLAND to admit—is greated than the King, for the former serves to restrain the latter, and not *vice versa;* while the whole people is greater than the law, being the author of the law and having the power to abrogate it; yet the voice of all three is the same. As for the question of calling the King to judgment, it would be a simple matter to deduce from BUCHANAN's previous remarks the conclusion that the people is greater than the King, but he chooses to introduce an entirely different proof: that the thing for whose sake another thing is made is the better of the two; and the King, having been constituted for the good of the people, or of society, the latter is accordingly better—and, by the same token greater—than the King; therefore, the King may be called to judgment before the people.

MAITLAND again objects: "But when shall we hope that the whole people agree unto that which is right?

BUCHANAN replies that this is a consummation scarcely to be expected and is by no means necessary. But a law or a magistrate must be of advantage to the greater part of the people, and must be set up by the greater part; and such a magistrate may be judged by them.

MAITLAND, who begins to perceive that all these things may indeed be done by a people, still doubts that, in actual practice, a people will do such things: "For the greatest part . . . hateth novelty."

But—answers BUCHANAN—no novelty is involved in this matter, since "it hath been of old, that a King should answer in judgment before Judges." He refers to certain historical examples, such as that of the Arbiters to whom appeal was made by contenders for the Kingdom, among the Persians and others.

With respect to the Arbiters, MAITLAND approves the argument; but when BUCHANAN applies it to ordinary Judges, also, his friend protests that, "apprehending, restraint and punishment is carried on by the more powerful against the weaker." Is the King, then, to be called before Judges over whom he himself has supreme power to judge?

BUCHANAN reminds his interlocutor that there exists in the people an even greater power, which includes that jurisdiction over Kings that Kings have over others.

MAITLAND admits that such power does exist in the whole people or in the greatest part thereof; and even in those persons, or in the greatest part of those persons, to whom the people shall transmit that power. Yet the greatest part of the people is in one way or another corrupted; while some of the people hold the name of "King" to be sacred, even when it is applied to a wicked ruler; and again, there are others too slothful to defend what they know to be the just and lawful cause.

Such persons—replies BUCHANAN—do not form so large a group as one might suppose. For the wrongs done by Tyrants affect many, their good deeds reach but few. Moreover, the fidelity of the latter group is an unstable thing. Finally, these persons are not in any case to be accounted among the true subjects, who are made up of those who obey and defend the laws; so that, if "subjects be reckoned, not by number, but by dignity and worth, not only the better part, but also the greater part will stand for their liberty, honesty and safety." However, all this discussion as to what the people will or will not do is not pertinent to the question in hand, namely, What may lawfully be done? (which is not the same as, What is going to be done?)

Turning, then, to the discussion of judicial sentences, BUCHANAN leads MAITLAND to admit that in lesser matters—such as an inheritance considered to be unjustly detained by the King—sentence may be passed against the King's proxy; and this—says BUCHANAN—is the same as passing sentence directly against the King. Is it not consequently absurd that the greatest license and impunity should be granted the King in the gravest matters, such as parricide and treason? This leniency would seem to support the old proverb, "Laws are very like spiders webs, which hold flies fast, but let bigger beasts pass thro'." The argument that judgment can not be passed against a King by a man of inferior rank is thus rendered ridiculous, since the practice is clearly permissible in disputes regarding land and money. The same argument is again refuted by the fact that the greatest peers next to the King must, if justice is to be properly observed throughout the realm, be liable to such sentences; yet they do not protest that this liability derogates from their dignity. More than all this, judges can not really be inferior to any man coming before them, inasmuch as God Himself has communicated to them His own dignity. Indeed, even the Popes, whose majesty Kings have recognized as far above their own, have submitted to the judgments and sentences of Cardinals. After all, it is not the judge viewed as an individual who condemns or absolves, it is the law; and to the law Kings should yield obedience. In this connection, BUCHANAN reminds us that such illustrious Emperors as Theodosius and Valentianus, as well as the tyrant Nero, himself, gave evidence of the fact that their majesty seemed to them enhanced rather than debased by observance of the laws.

MAITLAND perceives that BUCHANAN's arguments have a more authoritative foundation than he had at first supposed, since they are drawn from Kings, Emperors and Councils of the Church; but he asks for further explanation of the statement that "it is not man but the law that judgeth." [26]

BUCHANAN accordingly repeats a conclusion already agreed upon, that the voice of the person proclaiming the law, and the voice of the law are one and the same; while the judge nevertheless has his authority from the law, and not *vice versa.* The strength of a sentence is thus derived from the law, and merely the utterance of the words is derived from the judges; and this is so true that the sentence pronounced by a judge in accordance

[26] The two separate but consecutive speeches assigned to MAITLAND at this point by the English text, are simply one speech made by him.

with law is ratified, whereas his sentence when not thus lawful is rescinded; therefore, when the King is condemned by a judge, he is condemned by the law. BUCHANAN goes on to point out the further conclusion that, in such a case, the King is also condemned by his own voice.[27] "Why then"—he continues—"do we so much weary ourselves concerning a judge, seeing we have the King's own confession, that is to say, the law?" Another point relating to this same "wearisome" question of who may judge a King is the fact that in the passing of judgment, no respect should be had of persons; rather must judgment be passed with regard to the crime committed, no heed being given to the rank, influence, and other characteristics of the culprit, characteristics extraneous to that crime and to the question of guilt or innocence; therefore, what can it matter whether the accused be a King or merely a poverty-stricken citizen?

MAITLAND, however, has yet another question to raise: "What if the King will not willingly compear, nor by force can be compelled to compear?"

Such a King—says Buchanan—should be treated as other malefactors are treated, under similar circumstances; in other words, resort must be had to arms. "Nor is there almost any other cause of all the warres betwixt Nations, People, and Kings, than those injuries which, whilst they cannot be determined by justice, are by arms decided." Moreover, in answer to MAITLAND's objection that wars with foreigners and wars with one's own King—to whom one has sworn allegiance—are two very different things, BUCHANAN retorts that the pact made between the King and the people is mutual, the King having first promised to rule in equity and justice; consequently, when the King is faithless to his part of the covenant, the subjects are freed from the obligation into which they, on their side, formerly entered; and therefore, a King who acts in a manner tending directly to the dissolution of that society for whose continuance he was created, is a tyrant, and not only lacks just authority over his people, but

[27] The English text is again in error here, and the Latin must be used for any attempt at verification.

is also their enemy, with whom a just and lawful war may be waged for grievous injuries. "Now a lawful war being once undertaken with an enemy," adds BUCHANAN, "and for a just cause, it is lawful, not only for the whole people to kill that enemy, but for every one of them." Consequently, he asks: "May not every one out of the whole multitude of mankind assault, with all the calamities of war, a Tyrant who is a publick enemy, with whom all good men have a perpetual warfare?"

MAITLAND admits that all Nations seem to have held very nearly this opinion, and cites historical instances of its support by individuals or single nations or even the whole world. Even wicked men are not void of this hatred of tyrants, as was revealed by Caligula's Ministers, after his slaughter, for they stilled in admiration their tumultuous inquiries as to the identity of the slaughterer, when Valerius Asiaticus cried out: "I wish I had killed him." "For there is so great force in an honest deed, that the very lightest show thereof being presented to the minds of men, . . . fierce fury doth languish, and madness nill it will it doth acknowledge the sovereignty of reason." Even those persons who are crying out against present events in Scotland, approve these ancient deeds, indicating that they are now moved more by private reasons than by concern for the public welfare! Perhaps the surest witness of all, however, is the conscience of the Tyrants, which causes them to fear perpetually from others—and particularly from good men—the hatred and violence with which these others are threatened by themselves. Nevertheless, though MAITLAND grants the logical force of BUCHANAN's arguments, he still fears the possible results of accepting BUCHANAN's doctrine. "For if it shall be lawful for any man to kill a Tyrant, see how great a gap you do open for wicked men to commit any mischief, and how great a hazard you create to good men . . . For he that shall kill a good King, or at least none of the worst, may be not pretend by his wicked deed some show of honest and lawful duty?" Or even if a good subject attempts—whether vainly or successfully—to slay a wicked Prince, great and terrible confusion may be the consequence. Not all good men will approve the deed; and some persons who approve, will not defend the doer, but will prefer an imperfect tranquillity to the struggle for liberty.

BUCHANAN here takes occasion to remind his friend that they have already spoken of Tyrants who govern with due moderation, whether through the free suffrages of the people, or after acquiring sovereignty by force or fraud. Against such Tyrants, no man shall, with BUCHANAN's approval, resort to violence. Furthermore, BUCHANAN has merely explained what may lawfully or what should properly be done in certain situations; he is not exhorting that such action shall in point of fact be taken in any case. For the actual undertaking should be accompanied by good counsel, prudence, courage, and—in general—the proper circumstances. If the attempt be made rashly and under improper circumstances, he will not be to blame, any more than a physician will, when he has prescribed the proper remedies for a disease, and these remedies are unseasonably administered by another hand.

MAITLAND has one more question that must be answered, before he can rest content: "Are there any Church censures against Tyrants?"

BUCHANAN refers him to Paul's prohibition, laid down in the First Epistle to the Corinthians,[27a] against "any fellowship either at meat or discourse with openly lewd and flagitious men." If Christians obeyed this prohibition, such lewd men might perish—unless they repented—of hunger, cold and nakedness.

MAITLAND doubts, however, that a people who allow their Rulers such great liberty would agree to that punishment of Kings.

Nevertheless—says BUCHANAN—the ecclesiastical writers, without exception, have so interpreted Paul's prohibition. Moreover, it may be compared with the interdiction from fire and water imposed by temporal rulers. But the secular judge merely sentences the body to death; while the ecclesiastical judge can

[27a] Chap. v. 9-12.

expel the culprit from the fellowship of the good and can banish his soul, after death, to the fellowship of devils, so that one would suppose this ecclesiastical judge to be possessed also of the simple power to impose this sentence of bodily death.[28]

IV. *Concluding Remarks*—BUCHANAN now concludes that enough has been said in behalf of the equity of his cause. The remainder of his discourse he devotes to putting the foreign critics of Scotland in their place. The sturdy Scot apparently forgets the artificial framework of his Dialogue, which he opened with his own request for enlightenment as to the valuable opinion of foreign countries regarding Scottish affairs, and declares that he has spoken more fully than he had intended and than the subject warranted, solely for the sake of his friend. Among other peppery remarks, he points out the fact that it is unjust for foreign nations to be displeased because Scottish ideas of government differ from their own (which, in turn, differ from one another). He adds that the Scots have indeed but a little Kingdom; yet they "have enjoyed it these two thousand years free of the Empire of foreign Nations." They created lawful Kings, upon whom, as upon themselves, they imposed equal and just laws; and it is impudent of other nations—who can scarce defend their own governments—to attempt to weaken that of their neighbor. Moreover, the good order of Scottish government is in point of fact an advantage to her neighbors, as well as to herself. Again, she does not curiously enquire into the laws of other nations; so why should they interfere with her observance of her own well-tried laws? As to their complaint that the Scotch are seditious, it might be answered that this is no concern of others, and that the Scotch are seditious at their own peril; but BUCHANAN goes further and denies that any nation is less seditious than Scotland. "Many contentions have fallen out . . . yet the main business hath been still kept safe. Our contentions never were . . . with the destruction of the people, nor with the

[28] The English translation—inadequate in this passage taken as a whole—is actually in error at this particular point, where it translates a question as an assertion and thus reverses the force of the argument.

hatred of our Princes; but only out of love to our own country and desire to maintain her laws."

The dialogue which BUCHANAN opened is closed by MAITLAND: "As for me, you have abundantly satisfied me: But if I can satisfy others also, I shall think I have received much good by your discourse, and my self eased of very much trouble."

CHAPTER X

DIVINE RIGHT AND TYRANNICIDE

The Stewart Experiment

PART I

Queen Mary and Her Son James

In 1561, when Mary Stewart, then Dowager Queen of France, returned to Scotland, after an absence of thirteen years and a nominal reign of some nineteen years, mostly *in absentia* she was anxious to try her wiles—which appear to have been wellnigh irresistible—upon one John Knox, the then leader of the militant Presbyterians of Scotland. An interview accordingly took place between the Queen and John Knox on the 26th of August, 1561, within a week of her landing, at which time the leaders of Catholicism and Protestanism in Scotland stood face to face. Upon that interview the fate of both might depend, and also the fate of Scotland. We give an account of the interview in the language of Professor Hume Brown, the most distinguished of Scotch historians and who also happened to be the author of the standard Life of Mary's determined and inveterate opponent, John Knox:

"And so, Madam, ye may perceave that subjectis ar not bound to the Religioun of thair Princes, Albeit thei ar commanded to geve thame obedience."

"Yea," quod sche, "but none of thai men raised the sweard against thair Princes."

"Yit, Madam," quod he, "ye cane not deny but that they resisted; for these that obey nott the commandiments that ar gevin in some sort resist."

"But yit," said sche, "thei resisted not by the sweard?"

"God," said he, "Madam, had not gevin unto thame the power and the meanes."

"Think ye," quod sche, "that subjectis having power may resist thair Princes?"

"If thair Princes exceed thair boundis," quod he, "Madam, and do against that whair for they should be obeyed, it is no doubt but they may be resisted, evin by power. For thair is neather greattar honour nor greattar obedience to be gevin to kings or princes then God hes commanded to be gevin unto father and mother: But so it is, Madam, that the father may be stricken with a phrensye, in the which he wold slay his awin childrene. Now, Madame, yf the children aryese, joyne them selfis togetther, apprehend the father, tack the sweard or other weaponis frome him, and finallie bind his handis, and keape him in preasone, till that his phrenesy be over past; think ye, Madam, that the children do any wrang? Or, think ye, Madam, that God wilbe offended with thame that have stayed thair father to committ wickedness? It is even so," said he, "Madam, with Princes that wold murther the children of God that ar subject unto thame. Thair blynd zeall is no thing but a verray mad phrenesie; and, thairfor, to tack the sweard frome thame, to bynd their handis, and to cast thame selfis in preasone till that thei be brought to a more sober mynd, is no disobedience against princes, but just obedience, becaus that it aggreith with the will of God! . . .

"Weall then I perceave that my subjectis shall obey you, and not me."

"God forbid," was the reply, "that ever I tack upoun me to command any to obey me, or yitt to set subjectis at libertie to do what pleasest thame. Bot my travell is that boyth princes and subjectis obey God. And think not," said he, "Madam, that wrong is done unto you, when ye ar willed to be subject unto God: for it is he that subjects people under princes and causses obedience to be gevin unto thame; yea, God craves of Kingis that thei be as it war foster-fatheris to his Churche, and commands to be nurrisis to his people. And this subjectioun, Madam, unto God, and unto his trubled Churche, is the greatest dignitie that fleshe can get upoun the face of the earth, for it shall cary thame to everlasting glorie."

Mary's retort was as vehement and decided as any utterance of Knox's own.

"Yea, but ye are not the kirk that I will nureiss. I will defend the Kirk of Rome, for I think it is the true Kirk of God."[1]

This was in 1561. Several centuries later a Queen of the United Kingdom of Great Britain and Ireland, Victoria by name—seated upon the throne because a drop of blood from Mary Stewart flowed in her veins, with a generous contribution of the Hanoverian variety—said to Lord John Russell: "Is it true, Lord

[1] P. Hume Brown, *John Knox—A Biography* (London, 1895, 2 vols.), vol. ii, pp. 164-5, 165-6, citing *Works*, ii. 281, 282, 283.

John, that you hold that a subject is justified, in certain circumstances, in disobeying his sovereign?" "Well," replied the noble and courageous lord, "speaking to a sovereign of the House of Hanover, I can only say that I suppose it is."

Between these two dates and these two women the doctrine of tyrannicide flowered and bore the fruit of civil liberty, both in Scotland and in the United Kingdom of Great Britain and Ireland.

It is not for us to go at length into the stormy career of Mary, Queen of Scots, or to attempt to decide the undecidable. The fact is that this inexperienced and high-spirited woman found herself between two fires and was bound to be scorched whichever way she turned. Her determination to uphold the Catholic faith, in which she was born and bred, aroused the fierce opposition of the Calvinists who, being of the Scotch Presbyterian variety, were least open to compromise or suggestion. One or other of the religious factions was to obtain the upper hand. The supremacy of one or the other—for both could not succeed—was uncertain. The scales tipped, betimes, from one side to the other. If Queen Mary had not made colossal mistakes—and any mistake was wellnigh fatal under those circumstances—she might have sustained herself at the expense of allowing equal rights to Presbyterians and Catholics, but government by favorites of one party would naturally displace the other, whichever that party might be. Now her government through Rizzio, her Italian secretary, who had become—if not so called—Secretary of State, annoyed both parties. He was murdered and those who took part in the murder came to power.

She had previously married her cousin, Henry Stewart, Lord Darnley—like her a great grandchild, on the mother's side, of Henry VII, Mary being in addition the daughter of James V, the late King of Scotland. This marriage is looked upon by Hume Brown as a master stroke, inasmuch as it united the heirs, and, were a male child born, he would have a double and unquestionable claim to the English throne upon the death of the Virgin Queen Elizabeth. That is what actually happened.

Upon the birth of her son James on June 19, 1566, Mary said

to her husband: "My lord, he is so much your own son that I fear it will be the worse for him hereafter." [2] In this she was a prophetess. And she risked another prophecy which was also realized: "This is the son who shall first unite the two kingdoms of Scotland and England." [3] Would she had foreseen her own danger as clearly as she foresaw the destiny of her son and heir!

Of her husband, Darnley, there is little or nothing to be said to his credit. He had taken part in the murder of Rizzio. Darnley in turn was got out of the way principally by the Earl of Bothwell, and it would seem that Mary herself—if not an actual party to the murder—was not ignorant of the plot. In any event, within three months and six days she married the Earl of Bothwell. This was too much for the Scotch stomach to stand. Mary was obliged to sever her relations with Bothwell. The opposition to her ways—of life as well as government—overcame her supporters, under the command of Bothwell himself, at Carberry Hill on the 15th of June, 1567—one month from the day in which Mary and Bothwell had celebrated their marriage—at which time she was made prisoner and taken, under guard, to Holyrood and thence to the Island of Lochleven, by way of Leith.

One June 20th, a casket containing letters was captured on its way to Bothwell, who had requested it—letters which were incriminating to Bothwell, else he would not have desired them, and unfortunate, if not so incriminating, for Mary. Three days later a committee of three of her opponents—Lord Lindsay, Lord Ruthven and Sir Robert Melville—waited upon her at Lochleven and secured her signature to an instrument of abdication in favor of her infant son James, destined to be the Sixth of Scotland and the First of England. Approximately a year later, in May, 1568, Mary escaped and her army of supporters was defeated at Langside, on the outskirts of Glasgow, by an army under Moray, her illegitimate brother, who, upon her abdication, had been made regent. The defeat was crushing and hopeless. With a few of her supporters Mary crossed the border into England, where for

[2] *King James's Secret:* Negotiations between Elizabeth and James VI. Relating to the Execution of Mary Queen of Scots, from the Warrender Papers, edited by Robert S. Rait and Annie I. Cameron (London, 1927), p. 1.

[3] *Ibid.*

the next twenty years she was to live, and finally to die.

Now Mary had been invited by her cousin Elizabeth to England—apparently in the belief that she would not be able to accept. Elizabeth did not want her but when Mary was in her power, she wanted her still less. Indeed, on three separate occasions Elizabeth actually offered to return her to Scotland, provided that Mary be immediately put to death on reaching her native land. *"O tempora! O mores!"*

On July 15, 1568, Queen Mary began her imprisonment at Bolton Castle in north Yorkshire, and from time to time she visited—not as an inspectress, it may be said, but as an inmate—many a strong castle of England, the last being Fotheringay.

Unfortunately for Queen Mary, while still in Bolton Castle, she asked Elizabeth, as stated by Hume Brown in his *History of Scotland,*[4] that "her complaints against her rebellious subjects might be heard." This was, be it said, a "false move," and it resulted in her continued imprisonment and eventually in her death.

There were three parties in issue. "For Elizabeth," Mr. Hume Brown says, "the one question to be considered was how to end the controversy between Mary and her subjects with the greatest advantage to England. As for Mary, she had too good reason to shrink from a curious scrutiny into her relations with Bothwell and Darnley. Nor were the allies of Moray [the regent and the third party to the conference] in a position to be specially eager for the revelation of the whole truth, since two of their number —Morton and Lethington—had been directly concerned in Darnley's murder."

The Commissioners, beginning their deliberations at York, ended up at Hampton Court, where Elizabeth, whom Queen Mary had expected to be "a friendly arbiter," actually assumed the rôle of a judge "between two unwilling litigants."[5] No one of the three parties was disinterested, least of all Elizabeth as judge. The decision, as summarized by Hume Brown, was that "nothing had been alleged against them [Moray and his allies]

---

[4] P. Hume Brown, *History of Scotland* (Cambridge, England, 1911), vol. ii, p. 103.
[5] *Ibid.*, p. 102.

which might 'impair their honour or allegiance'; and, on the other hand, Mary was given to understand that nothing had been produced against her 'whereby the Queen of England should conceive or take any evil opinion' of her."[6] Adopting as we do Mr. Brown's conclusions, we quote them literally: "With such meaningless words the conference closed; but its practical conclusion was of momentous consequence for the future of Scotland. Mary was retained a prisoner in England, and Moray was sent home with hands strengthened to administer the government in the name of James VI."[7]

Least of all should Queen Elizabeth, who considered herself the chief party in interest, have been appointed arbiter or judge, for, given her situation, it was difficult to render a judgment which would not be in the interest of herself and of her subjects; for, with all her faults, the reign of Elizabeth, outstanding in English history, was, as she conceived it and as confirmed by history, in the interest of her people.

If Mary had made a mistake in crossing the border, and perhaps a greater mistake in asking Queen Elizabeth to pass upon the merits of her conduct in Scotland, Elizabeth was determined to make no mistake in the relation of Mary to herself. For Elizabeth viewed everything from her own standpoint and from that of her people and she was indeed in a trying situation. Mary was in a way her guest. In England she was a charge and in Scotland a menace, while, if allowed to proceed to the continent, she would doubtless have remarried; and an invasion of England from the continent—which was later actually attempted—was what Elizabeth had to fear.

As Mary in Scotland, so Elizabeth in England had troubles of her own. Elizabeth had declared for Protestantism, as the majority of her people seemed inclined that way; but there was a strong, intelligent and determined Catholic minority. There was before her, therefore, the possibility of an insurrection. As Hume Brown states it, "reasons of State overbore whatever natural feelings Elizabeth may have entertained towards the unhappy fugi-

---

[6] P. Hume Brown, *op. cit.*, vol. ii, pp. 103-4.

[7] *Ibid.*, p. 104.

tive."[8] Therefore Elizabeth had to choose between the horns of a dilemma: to get rid of her unwelcome guest by returning her to Scotland—where she would have been a menace (but which nevertheless Elizabeth had tried to do, as we have seen, on three separate occasions, although with the understanding that Mary's life should be taken when she had crossed the border); or as the Scotch were unwilling to accept their Queen on those terms, to continue Queen Mary in confinement until such time as it pleased Queen Elizabeth to take the life of her royal guest.

As the years passed, the situation was made more difficult by the question of the attitude of James, now growing up and actually reigning—for since his thirteenth year, he had been king in fact as well as in law, although it was not until 1583 that he began to govern in reality. What might Elizabeth expect the attitude of this young man to be toward his mother, and especially toward the taking of her life?

Now James also found himself in an embarrassing position. If he had been a true Scotchman and had inherited the qualities of his mother instead of those of his weakling father, there is no doubt whatever, from the history of Scotland, that the only answer to any attempt of Queen Elizabeth to take the life of his mother would have been not by word of mouth or of writing but in "an armed coat of mail." Under those circumstances, to put Mary to death would have created an implacable enemy to the north and doubtless a joint invasion from the north and the continent, with an outbreak of the Catholic Party in England. But James was not of an heroic build. He was obsessed with the idea of succession to the English throne and obsessed also with the idea that his own mother stood in his way.

Now Queen Elizabeth too had an obsession—that it was in her interest that she should not die before Mary, as in that case the Catholic Party in England would proclaim Mary as queen. Why? Because she had the misfortune to be descended in direct line from Henry VII—as was her cousin Elizabeth, if Henry Eighth's marriage with Ann Boleyn was to be considered legitimate.

[8] *Ibid.*, p. 102.

It was therefore, strangely enough, in the personal interest of the two royalties concerned that Mary should die. But even between royalties the question of murder is a delicate one, not to be treated directly and personally by them. It is but fair to repeat that Elizabeth was in an uncomfortable position. She was a Protestant and responsible for the acceptance of that religion by the majority of her people. She was unmarried and she was no longer young and, with Queen Mary out of the way, James VI of Scotland was in direct line of hereditary succession. James therefore was, so to speak, the heir apparent. But if Mary escaped, remarried and had an heir by a crowned head, there might be a further claimant to the throne. Queen Elizabeth and her advisers, as we have intimated, were anxious to have Queen Mary removed from the contest for succession, as a Catholic claimant could but lead to civil and religious strife. Hence Elizabeth's anxiety to know definitely the attitude that the son would take toward the execution of his mother, particularly since he was known to have relations not only in England with the Protestants but on the continent with Catholics, so that by one or the other, or if possible by both, elements—for James was a past master in the difficult and dangerous art of intrigue—he would become king of the Protestants and king of the Catholics, his own ambition and the constant element in his wavering policy being to succeed Queen Elizabeth upon the throne of England, thus uniting the kingdoms in his own person. This Elizabeth well knew; were she but convinced, therefore, that James would not take his mother's death amiss, she would no longer need to hesitate in deciding Queen Mary's fate.

Outwardly King James affected a natural feeling of filial devotion toward his mother, and, in consequence, of opposition to her death, but for a reason of his own which will shortly appear. Inwardly he resented a life which he conceived to stand in his way. As soon as Elizabeth was assured of this inward feeling and that he would take no hostile action, the question of Mary's death was settled once and for all. But for the sake of public appearances—for, as we have intimated, even royalty was careful of appearances—it was deemed desirable that Queen Mary should be involved in a plot to take the English Queen's life. Therefore, Queen Mary was given every opportunity to be a party to a Catholic conspiracy against the life of the Virgin Queen. The net was drawn and Mary caught. On October 14 and 15, 1586, at Fotheringay Castle, a so-called trial was had, in which she defended herself magnificently, but the decision was reached in advance and for this reason her defence was not, and could not be, of avail. On February 8, 1587, the unfortunate Mary paid the penalty of her rash act in crossing the border and entrusting herself to her cousin Elizabeth.

As anticipated, King James acquiesced, after some show of indignation, and now only Elizabeth stood in his way to the throne. But how did Elizabeth know in advance that James' indignation would be only on the surface? By word of mouth from Scotchmen in a position to speak—the Master of Gray, in the favor and high employment of King James, and one Archibald Douglas—and in addition from the handwriting of James himself, supplemented by a special emissary, who accompanied the embassy to Elizabeth in order outwardly to protest against the taking of Queen Mary's life.

We have spoken of James' outward unwillingness to have his mother harmed. It would be better, however, to let His Majesty, King James, state in his own words his attitude as revealed in two long letters. First, his inward and real opinion, contained in a letter to Queen Elizabeth's favorite for the time being, the Earl of Leicester, written from "Holyroodhouse" and under date of "15th December, 1586," and the later letter written on the eve of the condemnation of King James' mother. The Earl of Leicester is addressed as "Richt trusty and wellbelovit cousing." After stating that he had "no tyme throught the hasty dispeshe [dispatch] of this bearer to ansour in this letter" that which "Mr. Archibald wrote to me in your name," he proceeded with a few words of eulogy of his own character: "But to my first purpos, this farre shortlie may I say, I am honest, no changear of course, altogether in all thingis as I professe to be, and quhosomevir will affirme that I had ever intelligence with my mother sen [since] the Master of Grayis being in England, or ever thocht to preferre her to my selff in the title or ever delt in any uther foreyne course, they lie falselie and unhonestlie of me."[9] Next for the special purpose: "But speciallie how fonde and inconstant I were if I shulde preferre my mother to the title let all men judge. My religioun ever moved me to haite her course althogh my honour constraynis me to insist for her lyffe. Thairfore I pray yow suspend your judgement of me least your credulitie in suche reportis do harme ws bothe."[10] And James' signature is in keeping with the time-serving content and tone of the letter—"Your most loving and asseured friend James R."

On the 15th of December—the same day as the letter to Leicester in which King James explicitly stated that he preferred to his mother's well-being his title to the Kingdom of England—he wrote a friendly letter to Queen Elizabeth: "As for me, I knowe well aneugh, how hardlie ye are preassed by the objecting the perrell of your owne lyffe unto yow [*i.e.*, by those who urge that your own life is in danger], and thairfore I never blamed your selff directlie of thir procedingis"—meaning her advisers. "I pray yow then, Madame," he continued, "to accompt me your most honest and steadfast friend, since I never did nor shall deserve any uther opinioun to be conceaved by yow of me." And this friendly epistle, on the eve of his mother's death, is signed, "Your most loving and affectionat brother and cousing."[11]

Passing from the official instructions given by James to the Master of Gray, under date of 17th December, 1586—to cause the public to believe that the son was deeply interested in his mother's welfare, Queen Elizabeth already having been warned of his inward feelings in the letter to Leicester and that to herself—we come to His Majesty's letter of the 26th of January, 1587, in which he informs his royal correspondent, Queen Elizabeth, of the danger to their class if she should be a party to what we would call tyrannicide. The letter has the further advantage of stating clearly and definitely, and within a short compass, that doctrine of the divine right of kings which he had foisted upon his

[9] *King James's Secret*, pp. 101-102.
[10] *Ibid.*, p. 102, note 1.
[11] *Ibid.*, p. 99.

countrymen—and subsequently was to foist upon the English people—much to the detriment of his offspring: "Madame and dearest sister," he begins, and after a labored introduction and an eulogium upon his own plain speaking, comes to the point:

. . . Quhat thing, madame, can greatlier touche me in honoure, that both is a King and a sonne, then that my nearest neihboure being in straittest freindshippe with me shall rigouruslie putt to death a free sovereaigne prince and my naturall mother, alyke in estaite and sex to hir that so uses her, albeit subject I grant to a harder fortoune, and touching hir nearlie in proximitie of bloode? Quhat lau of Godd can permitt that justice shall strikke upon thaime quhom he hes appointid supreame dispensatouris of the same, under Him, quhom He hath callid Goddis, and thairfore subjectid to the censoure of none in earth, quhose anointing by Godd can not be defylid be man unrevenged by the authore thairof, quho being supreme and immediatt lieutenant of Godd in heaven cannot thairfore be judgit by thair equallis in earth?

Quhat monstruous thinge is it that souveraigne princes thaime selfis shoulde be the exemple giveris of thaire ouen sacred diademes' prophaining? Then quhat shoulde move you to this forme of proceiding—supponin the vorst quhiche in goode faith I looke not for at youre handis—honoure or profeitt? Honoure vaire [were] it to you to spaire quhen it is least lookid for, honoure vaire it to you—quhiche is not only my freindlie advyce but my earnist suite—to take me and all other princes in Europe eternally beholdin unto you in granting this my so reasonable request, and not—appardon I pray you my free speaking—to putt princes to straittis of honoure quhair throuch youre generall reputatione and the universall—allmost—mislyking of you may daingerouslie perrel both in honour and utilitie youre persoune and estate.[12]

Upon this correspondence Sir Robert Rait, Principal and Vice-Chancellor of Glasgow University and formerly Historiographer-Royal for Scotland, comments: "James still preferred his title to his mother. We cannot be sure whether he had given private instructions to Sir Alexander Stewart or not—his treatment of Stewart suggests that he had—but there can be no doubt that he deliberately gave Elizabeth to understand, as his communications with Leicester had implied, that, though he would deeply resent his mother's execution, he was not prepared to take offensive action to avenge it."[13] To this we may add a comment in our

[12] *Ibid.*, pp. 179, 180-181.
[13] *Ibid.*, p. 178.

own behalf, in the nature of a query as to the depth and sincerity of his resentment: Was not Queen Mary as good as dead?

Queen Elizabeth died on March 24, 1603—although not before having kept King James for some years on tenterhooks to know whether she would designate him as her heir to the English throne. She did, however, so designate him—or, what was the same thing in those days, she was declared to have designated him, and Burghley, now the Earl of Salisbury, who had always been in favor of James' succession and in constant communication with him, dispatched a messenger to convey the joyful news that Elizabeth was dead, and "Long live the King." It is not for us to attempt to picture His Majesty's emotions. His mother had not died in vain; Queen Elizabeth too was dead. Upon two deaths he thus mounted the throne of England, which was, it may be said, as dear to him as his own life, and to obtain which he had intrigued, now with the Catholics, now with the Protestants, deceiving each in turn, when it seemed to his advantage to do so.

But when he turned his back upon Scotland—to revisit it only once in the twenty-odd years of his kingship below the Tweed—he might well have looked upon himself as the greatest diplomatist of his time—if intrigue of the basest kind be taken as the standard of diplomacy, or if "diplomacy" and "duplicity" be taken as synonyms.

If Elizabeth was not punished during her lifetime for the murder of Queen Mary—for it was a murder—her people were punished by the reign of his double-dealing and double-crowned Majesty, King James; and because of his conception of state and of church his family also suffered. His son and heir, Charles I, was to lose his head and his grandson was to flee his kingdom, and although there still is an attenuated drop of Stewart blood in the present ruling family of the United Kingdom of Great Britain and Ireland and the Dominions Beyond the Seas, it is submerged in the Hanoverian stream, which at present is disguised under the name of Windsor.

* * * * * * * *

The reason for our interest in the conduct—or rather misconduct—of His Majesty, James I of England and VI of Scotland, is that the theory of government which he had imposed upon his Scottish realm gave rise to a far from bloodless "battle of the books," to which were parties not only His Scottish and English Majesty but the Pope of Rome as well, and which called into the fray two such bookmen and redoubtable controversialists as Robert, Cardinal—now Saint Robert—Bellarmine and Francisco Suárez. Indeed it may be said that these great controversialists were merely the vanguard.

What kind of a ruler was James I of England? We know what he was as King of Scotland. What was his conception of kingship? How did it become a matter of international concern? As Scotland had been the center point of Europe during Queen Mary's short and troubled career, so with King James' accession, the center was transferred from Scotland to England. As a matter of fact, the realization of what we call tyrannicide was exemplified to a wellnigh unbelievable degree in the fortunes—or rather misfortunes—of his family. His mother was a victim of the resistance of subjects to a legally born and reigning Queen—although the execution in this case was not by the people whom she had misgoverned, but by her cousin of England; and indeed this same tyrannicide was as a stepping stone by which James mounted the English throne. His son—doubly Charles I, of Scotland and of England—paid the penalty with his head (the tyrannicide in this case not being exercised in foreign parts, but by his own people) for his father's obsession with the doctrine of the divine right of kings to govern—in our own behalf we may say, to govern wrong. His grandson, James VII of Scotland and the Second of England, saved his head, but not his crown, by flight. And that we may see how important and far-reaching beyond the lives of Mary and of Charles, who suffered for it, was the doctrine of tyrannicide, vesting sovereignty in the people, with the inalienable right of resistance and the overthrow of any tyrannical monarch or chief magistrate and the government of which he is the evil and presiding genius we might state that its realization in the person of the Stewarts substituted parliamentary government for kingcraft in England, justified the independence of these United States, inspired the French Revolution and today is the foundation of the rule and the practice of holding chief magistrates responsible for the lawful conduct of their governments and calling them to account—by legal means, if possible; by force, if necessary—for misconduct. In the United States, impeachment seems as yet to be a sufficient deterrent; in other countries, overthrow by revolution; and in extreme cases tyrannicide by means of a firing squad.

Now the source of this unexpected and beneficent development is none other than the "battle of the books," to which we have referred, arising immediately out of the oath of supremacy of 1605 which James and his Parliament imposed upon his subjects, with special reference to his Catholic subjects. As the controversy with which we are concerned arose out of the oath of allegiance above mentioned, we quote it in its entirety:

> I. A. B. do truly and sincerely acknowledge, profess, testify and declare in my conscience before God and the world, that our sovereign lord King James is lawful and rightful King of this realm and of all other his Majesty's dominions and countries; and that the Pope, neither of himself nor by any authority of the church or See of Rome or by any other means with any other hath any power or authority to depose the King, or to dispose any of his Majesty's kingdoms or dominions, or to authorize any foreign prince to invade or annoy him or his countries, or to discharge any of his subjects of their allegiance and obedience to his Majesty, or to give licence or leave to any of them to bear arms, raise tumult or to offer any violence or hurt to his Majesty's royal person, state or government or to any of his Majesty's subjects within his Majesty's dominions. Also I do swear from my heart that, notwithstanding any declaration or sentence of excommunication or deprivation made or granted or to be made or granted by the Pope or his successors or by any authority derived or pretended to be derived from him or his see against the said King, his heirs or successors, or any absolution of the said subjects from their obedience, I will bear faith and true allegiance to his Majesty, his heirs and successors, and him or them will defend to the uttermost of my power against all conspiracies and attempts whatsoever, which shall be made against his or their persons, their crown and dignity, by reason or colour of any such sentence or declaration or otherwise, and will do my best endeavour to disclose and make known unto his Majesty, his heirs and successors, all treasons and traitorous conspiracies, which I shall know or hear of to

be against him or any of them: and I do further swear that I do from my heart abhor, detest and abjure, as impious and heretical, this damnable doctrine and position, that princes which be excommunicated or deprived by the Pope may be deposed or murdered by their subjects or any other whatsoever: and I do believe and in my conscience am resolved that neither the Pope nor any person whatsoever hath power to absolve me of this oath or any part thereof, which I acknowledge by good and full authority to be lawfully ministered unto me, and do renounce all pardons and dispensations to the contrary: and all these things I do plainly and sincerely acknowledge and swear, according to these express words by me spoken and according to the plain and common sense and understanding of the same words, without any equivocation or mental evasion or secret reservation whatsoever: and I do make this recognition and acknowledgment heartily, willingly and truly, upon the true faith of a Christian: so help me God. Unto which oath so taken, the said person shall subscribe his or her name or mark.[14]

As far as James was personally concerned, the question involved was merely the divine right of kings, that is to say, their superiority to their people and to all forms of government, his contention being that they held their office by grant from, and were responsible to, Almighty God. The laws originating in the Parliaments of Scotland and of England, upon his recommendation and approved by him, were the laws of the land, binding upon his subjects and upon foreigners residing temporarily or found within the territorial limits of his Scottish Kingdom or other domain, save that of France; for the Frenchmen—logical people that they are—could not understand how a person could exercise the authority of a king over a domain from which the ancestors, through whom he claimed, had been expelled for wellnigh two centuries!

The sovereign power of King James being, in his opinion, exclusive within his domain, it applied to matters spiritual as well as temporal. There was an objection, however, to such a spiritual jurisdiction, which objection was sponsored by His Eminence Cardinal Bellarmine, both Saint and Doctor of the Church of which he was, and always will be, a conspicuous ornament.

[14] *Select Statutes and other Constitutional Documents Illustrative of the Reigns of Elizabeth and James I* (1558-1625), edited by G. W. Prothero (Third Edition, Oxford, 1906), pp. 259-60.

Pope Paul V stoutly claimed the right to exercise temporal power in behalf of the spiritual welfare of the members of the Catholic Church in foreign jurisdictions such as King James' dominions; and this question of the power of the Pope was admirably presented, as we already know, by Francisco Suárez in his *Defensio Fidei,* where it received what may be called its classical form and shape.

The question then at issue was whether the Catholics of King James' domain could be properly obliged to take the oath of allegiance in a form inconsistent with their religious belief, and, if King James should penalize them for not taking the oath, whether the hoary—and we would say, were it not undignified, the bewhiskered—doctrine of the divine right of kings could stand in the way of the application of the doctrine of tyrannicide, equally ancient and sanctioned by time—applicable, albeit in modified form under another name, in the day and generation in which we live and move and have our being.

Now King James claimed sovereignty within his dominions, his conception of sovereignty being derived from Bodin's *Six Books of the Republic,* published in 1576, exactly two centuries before the American Revolution, which deprived the successors of King James of any and every vestige of sovereignty in the so-called thirteen Colonies which became the original thirteen States of the United States.

King James' refutation of the doctrine of tyrannicide was taken from the *Apologia pro Regibus,* which had appeared in 1581 from the pen of one Adam Blackwood, a Scotchman domiciled in France, and a member of the Catholic Church; and His Majesty likewise borrowed from *De Regno et Regali Potestate adversus Buchananum, Brutum Boucherium, et reliquos Monarchomachos,* published in Paris in 1600, from the pen of one William Barclay, another Scotchman of the Catholic faith and, like Blackwood, also domiciled in France. So that, if the "royal bird" were plucked of his plumage, there would be little visible to the naked, as well as the literary eye, but a wearisome repetition of off-stated and already outworn doctrines.

It is of more than passing importance to mention that the three "source books" from which King James derived his arguments (Bodin's, Blackwood's and Barclay's disquisitions) had appeared, one and all, while King James was King of Scotland and busy plotting in Edinburgh for his succession to the English throne. The question then, as far as he was concerned, was not of English origin, nor was it connected with the so-called "gunpowder plot" of 1605.

We are already familiar with what may be called a "royal" statement of King James' views, being written in his own hand to Queen Elizabeth, another royal personage, which views were later expressed in different ways with painful and irritating elaboration in his various tractates and in his addresses to the Parliament and on other occasions.

He first burst into print, it may be said, in the *Basilikon Doron,* published in 1598, anonymously written for the edification of his eldest son, who, had he lived the span of life allotted to his father, and even to his younger brother, would have been king both of Scotland and England. In 1599 it was reissued under King James' name. It is, as it were, the mirror of the perfect prince, the portrait being that of James himself—or as he would have others think he was. It deals, of course, with His Majesty's theories of government, but as these are treated at length in *The Trew Law of Free Monarchies,* we need only quote a passage from the *Basilikon,* wherein he admonishes Prince Henry, his son, to love God "first, for that he made you a man; and next, for that he made you a little GOD to sit on his Throne, and rule ouer other men."[15]

In *The Trew Law of Free Monarchies* King James displayed himself and his views on government at large. As Prince Henry was then living, he was probably the cause of the remark which James makes in *The Trew Law:* "As the Fathers chiefe ioy," so the parent says, "ought to be in procuring his children's welfare, reioycing at their weale, sorrowing and pitying at their euill, to hazard for their safetie, trauell for their rest, wake for their sleepe;

[15] *The Political Works of James I*—Reprinted from the Edition of 1616, with an Introduction by Charles Howard McIlwain (Cambridge, Massachusetts, and London, 1918), p. 12.

and in a word, to thinke that his earthly felicitie and life standeth and liueth more in them, nor in himselfe; so ought a good Prince thinke of his people."[16] Of a truth! But where is the good prince to be found other than in books such as this one of King James?

Now His Majesty was very generous with his views on statecraft. He set them forth from time to time in various publications,[17] but just as we preferred to quote King James' views on the divine right of kings as they were confided in a letter in his own hand to Queen Elizabeth, in which he spoke as King to Queen, so we deem it advisable for our purposes to prefer his statements, not as a controversialist with Cardinal Bellarmine but as King of England in his measured expressions of opinion to his English Parliament. For his views, however personal, were views of what he conceived to be his duty as king, contained in an address to Parliament, which he considered—and so stated—as inferior to him and subject to his royal will. In this harangue, as it may appropriately be called, the King of England stated clearly and unmistakably his conception of kingcraft and declared the duty of his Parliament to be that of an advisory rather than a legislative body, in language which must have made the members of that body—whether Parliament or Council—"gape and stare." The language of King James is so important that we feel that we should interpose as little of our own as possible, lest we attribute to him that which may have been implicit but not actually expressed. The harangue is given in authoritative form in McIlwain's *Political Works of James I,* which we have already cited, and its material portion is at the disposition of any readers who may care to possess themselves of the *British Historical & Political Orations from the XIIth to the XXth Century,* in the Everyman's Library.

What is this state of monarchy of which we have been discoursing? In what may be considered as King James' version of government—wellnigh contemporaneous with his so-called version of the Bible—he informed the members of Parliament—and us incidentally—that "The State of MONARCHIE is the suprem-

[16] McIlwain, *op. cit.,* p. 56.

[17] These are reproduced by McIlwain, *op. cit.*

est thing vpon earth: For Kings are not onely GODS Lieutenants vpon earth, and sit vpon GODS throne, but euen by God himselfe they are called Gods."[18]

So much for what we may call the "royal exordium."

But there are monarchies and monarchies and James described one which supported his own conception. However, let the royal orator speak for himself: "There bee three principall similitudes that illustrates the state of MONARCHIE: One taken out of the word of GOD; and the two other out of the grounds of Policie and Philosophie. In the Scriptures Kings are called Gods, and so their power after a certaine relation compared to the Diuine power. Kings are also compared to Fathers of families: for a King is trewly *Parens patriae,* the politique father of his people. And lastly, Kings are compared to the head of this Microcosme of the body of man." Why are kings justly called gods, we may ask? To which King James replies: "for that they exercise a manner or resemblance of Diuine power vpon earth." His demonstration was satisfactory to himself and to his royal brethren and sistern. This is his language: "For if you wil consider the Attributes to God, you shall see how they agree in the person of a King. God hath power to create, or destroy, make, or vnmake at his pleasure, to giue life, or send death, to iudge all, and to be iudged nor accomptable to none: To raise low things, and to make high things low at his pleasure, and to God are both soule and body due."[19]

We may admit that this to the Christian of mediaeval—and even modern—days is an adequate statement of divine attributes. Now for the similitude: "And the like power haue Kings: they make and vnmake their subiects: they haue power of raising, and casting downe: of life, and of death: Iudges ouer all their subiects, and in all causes, and yet accomptable to none but God onely."[20] This is indeed a royal "mouthful." But there was more to come; for James saw his kingdom but as a chessboard. "They haue power to exalt low things, and abase high things, and make of

[18] McIlwain, *op. cit.*, p. 307.
[19] *Ibid.*, pp. 307-8.
[20] *Ibid.*, p. 308.

their subiects like men at the Chesse." But again, this is not all: "And to the King is due both the affection of the soule, and the seruice of the body of his subiects: . . . For to Emperors, or Kings that are Monarches, their Subiects bodies & goods are due for their defence and maintenance." [21] This would seem to us of today a large order.

Next to his comparison of the king to *paterfamilias:* "Now a Father may dispose of his Inheritance to his children, at his pleasure: yea, euen disinherite the eldest vpon iust occasions, and preferre the youngest, according to his liking; make them beggers, or rich at his pleasure; restraine, or banish out of his presence, as hee findes them giue cause of offence, or restore them in fauour againe with the penitent sinner: So may the King deale with his Subiects." [22] So he may do, but at his peril. Witness Charles I and his son, the second of the English Jameses!

Finally, there is a comparison of the king to "the head of this Microcosme of the body of man." Now "the head of the naturall body," His Majesty informed his Parliament, "hath the power of directing all the members of the body to that vse which the iudgement in the head thinkes most conuenient." Thus, in managing the body, the head may "apply sharpe cures, or cut off corrupt members, let blood in what proportion it thinkes fit, and as the body may spare." Even James, however, felt that there might be some limitation in this doctrine of blood-letting, since, if carried to an extreme, it might result in a monarch bleeding his kingdom to death and thus having nothing left to reign over. Therefore he admitted that "all this power" was "ordeined by God *Ad aedificationem, non ad destructionem.*" [23]

King James prided himself upon his knowledge of theology, and it was not strange, therefore, that he should conclude this phase of his remarkable observations on royal power by an "Axiome of Diunitie, That as to dispute what God may doe, is Blasphemie; but *quid vult Deus,* that Diuines may lawfully, and doe ordinarily dispute and discusse; . . . So is it sedition in Sub-

---

[21] McIlwain, *op. cit.,* p. 308
[22] *Ibid.*
[23] *Ibid.,* pp. 308-9

iects, to dispute what a King may do in the height of his power."[24] On that subject, in the opinion of James, the occupant of the throne was alone competet to hold forth. "Iust Kings," he assured his no doubt astonished listeners, "wil euer be willing to declare what they wil do,"—and not, it is to be observed what they ought to do or what they may do—"if they wil not incurre the curse of God."[25] Upon this phase of his conception of royal authority he had unequivocal views. "I wil not be content," he asserts emphatically, "that my power be disputed vpon." This is but the logical conclusion; for, if it be blasphemy on the part of a mortal to challenge or criticize the acts of a God, is it not equally blasphemous for a subject to dispute what kings "may do," when "kings are justly called GODS"? Outrageous, and even ridiculous, as this doctrine may seem to us, there can be no doubt that to King James it was a matter of fundamental importance and of the greatest gravity; and the reason for this was that, in his conception of government, the monarch loomed large and his subjects were seen as through the wrong end of a telescope, inconsequential beings whose importance consisted, not in their humanity but in the fact that they were *his* subjects. King James is perhaps the completest example in history of the great "I am."

To return for a moment to his denial of the right of subjects to criticize their rulers, we may note a further statement, which he doubtless intended to be a concession, but which is in fact a further evidence of the royal ego: "I shall euer be willing to make the reason appeare of all my doings, and rule my actions according to my Lawes"[26]—a standard which was designed to give him the least possible difficulty, since the laws which were to govern his actions were to be his own.

It seems that the question of grievances had arisen in the Parliament, and, as the presentation of grievances by subjects, might easily imply a criticism of the royal government, it was to be expected that King James would have something to say regarding it. He did, and his comments were three in number. "First," he

---

[24] *Ibid.*, p. 310.
[25] *Ibid.*
[26] *Ibid.*

instructed the members of Parliament that they were not to "meddle with the maine points of Gouernment." On what ground? "That," declared James royally, "is my craft: . . . to meddle with that, were to lesson me." [27]

Referring to his "sixe and thirtie yeeres" of government—we would be more inclined to say misgovernment—he capped this part of his instruction on the subject of grievances by the arrogant announcement: "I must not be taught my office." [28]

The second of his royal orders—for such they were in fact, if not in form—on the question of grievances runs thus: "Secondly, I would not haue you meedle with such ancient Rights of mine, as I haue receiued from my Predecessors, possessing them, *More Maiorum.*" Things such as these, he informed his listeners, he "would bee sorie should bee accounted for *Grieuances.*" [29] There was perhaps more frankness than usual in this statement, for we can well imagine that James would have experienced no little sorrow if his subjects had had the temerity to question the "ancient rights" which he claimed.

Now whatever he may have been—and he was many things without which the record of history would be a happier one—he was no fool, and he realized that it would be well to touch up his doctrine here and there with a semblance of political wisdom. Therefore, to justify his statements, he added a platitude which is as gospel to the orthodox and conventional and as anathema to the radical: "All nouelties are dangerous as well in a politique as in a naturall Body." His next two remarks are a revelation of a childish and overweening conceit: "And therefore I would be loth to be quarrelled in my ancient Rights and possessions: for that were to iudge mee vnworthly of that which my Predecessors had and left me." [30] Obviously, humility of spirit was not one of his qualities.

Finally, he warned his subjects to beware of presenting grievances on matters concerning which there was no possibility of a

---

[27] McIlwain, *op. cit.*, p. 315.
[28] *Ibid.*
[29] *Ibid.*
[30] *Ibid.*

favorable answer being given. "For it is an vndutifull part in Subiects," he told them, "to presse their King, wherein they know beforehand he will refuse them." [31] It was not until some years later that a monarch on the other side of the English Channel was to sum up the theory of the divine right of kings in a phrase destined to be as immortal as it is infamous: *"L'Etat, c'est moi."* But although King James, in all his writings, never attained this perfect expression of his theories, he stated it in his own—albeit a less striking—manner. "For if the King want," he explained to Parliament, "the State wants, and therefore the strengthening of the King is the preseruation and the standing of the State." [32] Here the monarch, in the person of King James, and the state, in the kingdoms of Scotland and England, are merged in a single personality. How delighted James would have been if his devious mind could have stumbled upon the compact phrase of Louis XIV, *"L'Etat, c'est moi"!*

Having thus expounded his theory, King James reinforced it with a phrase which was nothing less than a threat: "Woe be to him that diuides the weale of the King from the weale of the Kingdome." [33] But a single comment may be made on this warning: Herein lies the essence of all that is tyranny, of kingship above and beyond all human law. There can be no doubt that King James visualized his own office as subject to no legal restraint whatsoever; indeed he informed Chief Justice Coke, who argued for the supremacy of the law in all matters, that such a doctrine would mean that he (the king) would be "under the law, which it is treason to affirm." [34]

The dispute with the Chief Justice on the relation between the king and the law was, it should be added, of long standing. The learned judge firmly stood his ground for many years, but eventually lost his office in consequence of his courageous conduct. The conflict was brought to a head in 1616, largely as a result of the Chief Justice's action on the question of the right of the

[31] *Ibid.*
[32] *Ibid.*, p. 318.
[33] *Ibid.*
[34] *Dictionary of National Biography* (London, 1908), vol. x, p. 608.

king to appoint a Scotchman to a living, which question arose in action against the Bishop of Coventry in *Colt & Glover* v. *Bishop of Coventry & Lichfield,* Hobart, 140. Because of his interest in the matter, King James directed the judges to stay action until they learned His Majesty's pleasure. But the judges, in an opinion by Coke, had first flatly denied the King's request. Whereupon, they were immediately summoned into his royal presence, to be upbraided and lectured with great severity. After a stormy session, the twelve judges were severally asked whether they would not obey in the future. Overawed by the scene in which they had just been unwilling participants, eleven of the judges promptly promised obedience. But Coke was not of the eleven and replied that when the case came before him, he would decide it as became an upright judge.

On June 20, 1616, King James expressed what may be called his definitive views on the subject. The matter of the relation between the crown and the law was, he declared, "no subject for the tongue of a lawyer, nor is it lawful to be disputed. . . . It is presumption and high contempt in a subject to dispute what a king can do, or say that a king cannot do this or that; [he must] rest in that which is the king's will revealed in his law." [35]

Speaking as King of England, in the performance of his royal duty as he conceived it, he impressed upon his subjects their duty not only to obey him as sovereign but to accept his interpretation of the laws of the realm, and his will itself as law. There can be little doubt that in his own judgment King James was himself the repository of all of the powers of government, that he believed himself to be possessed of a divine right to rule as he pleased and endowed also with the wisdom of Solomon.[36]

[35] Dictionary of National Biography, vol. x, p. 611.

[36] "There are some, to tell the truth, who do not hesitate to compare James with Solomon, and even to think him superior in the circumstances of his birth. Solomon, they will tell you, was the son of David, who was formerly the musician of Saul; but then James was the son of Lord Darnley, who *killed* the musician David, not long after he had found him inside the Queen's bedchamber with the door bolted, as Buchanan relates. James was therefore the more illustrious in the matter of parentage, and is consequently often called the Second Solomon, notwithstanding that it is doubtful whether he was actually the Son of David the musician." Quoted from John Milton's *Pro Populo Anglicano Defensio contra Salmasium,* Chapter II, in *The Life of John Milton* by David Masson (London, 1877), vol. iv, p. 260.

Fortunately the judgment of the world has long since passed upon and finally condemned both his judgment of himself and his theory of government.

* * *

The oath which we have produced was but a part—although a most important part—of the legislation enacted by which James VI of Scotland celebrated his ascent to the throne of Elizabeth as James I of England.

His Majesty's policy in Scotland had been, as we have already said, to use both the Catholics and the Protestants for dynastic purposes,—inclined to conciliation to please the Catholics, and upholding Protestantism to satisfy Elizabeth. The Catholics were optimistic—unduly so, as they were soon to learn. However, on the 16th of April, 1603, within a few weeks after King James' accession to the English throne, Father Garnet, then the leading Catholic in England, wrote to Father Parsons, the leading English Catholic abroad, whose habitat was Rome rather than London: "Since my last to you of the sixteenth of March, there hath happened a great alteration, by the death of the Queen." In what did this alteration consist? "Great fears were: but all are turned into greatest security; and a golden time we have of unexpected freedom abroad. . . ." Father Garnet adds: "The King's coming is uncertain." Father Parsons' correspondent was soon to learn that James' policy was to be certain,—even more certain than that of Queen Elizabeth. "Great hope," he further added, "is of toleration; and so general a consent of Catholics in his proclaiming, as it seemeth God will work much. . . ."[37]

These "great expectations" in reference to James' "coming" were justified by a statement to the French Ambassador upon his arrival in London, in which His Majesty, after observing that he was brought up as a Protestant—which, of course, His Excellency the Ambassador knew—added that "he was no Puritan and would always allow the Pope first place among bishops."[38]

[37] James Brodrick, *The Life and Work of Blessed Robert Francis Bellarmine* (London, 1928), vol. ii, p. 148, quoting from Stonyhurst archives, *Anglia* A. vol. iii, p. 32.

[38] *Ibid.*, quoting from De Beaumont to Henry IV, 23 July 1603. In the Dépêches de Mons. de Beaumont, King's Library, British Museum.

Apparently James was in matters religious, before he found himself firmly seated on the English throne, "all things to all men," that is, all things to Catholics and Protestants alike. But as early as July, 1603, he is reported as saying "in broad Scots" to a nobleman: "Na, na, gud fayth, wee's not neede the papists now."[39] In "mother English," this Scots' phrase means that, assured of the support of the English churchmen as well as of the despised Puritans, he could afford to persecute the Catholics, whom, it hardly need be mentioned, he found to be in the minority. Indeed, within a few days after his arrival in London, His Majesty gave strict orders that the persecutions carried on by Elizabeth, under what the historian Gardiner calls the "abominable system,"[40] were to be continued.

Unfortunately in this matter His Majesty did not—as was so often the case—change his mind; for on February 22, 1604, he informed his new fellow countrymen that he "had never intended, nor given any man cause to expect that he would make any innovation in matters of religion."[41] The "matters of religion," as he understood them, were at once made clear by the unmistakable words of the proclamation:

> We do hereby will and command all manner of Jesuits, Seminaries, and other priests whatsoever, having ordination from any authority by the laws of this realm prohibited, to take notice, that our pleasure is, that they do, before the nineteenth day of March next ensuing the date hereof, depart forth out of our realm and dominions; . . . admonishing and assuring all such Jesuits, Seminaries, and priests, of what sort soever, that, if any of them shall be, after the said nineteenth day, taken within this realm, or any our Dominions, or, departing now, upon this our pleasure signified, shall hereafter return into this realm or any our Dominions again, that they shall be left to the penalty of the laws, here being in force concerning them, without hope of any favour or remission from us.[42]

Thus the Acts of Queen Elizabeth were to be enforced against Catholics and increased in their severity. It is to be observed that

[39] Brodrick, p. 149, quoting from Copley's Declaration, in Tierney-Dodd, vol. iv, app., n. 1, p. i. Cf. Bishop Goodman's remarks, *The Court of King James I,* Brewer's ed. vol. 1, p. 87.

[40] *Ibid.*, quoting from S. R. Gardiner, *History of England,* vol. 1, p. 97.

[41] *Ibid.*, p. 149, quoting from Rymer's *Foedera,* vol. xvi, p. 572.

[42] *Ibid.*

King James' proclamation, with its implications, was issued before the Gunpowder Plot (which is ordinarily supposed to have been the inciting cause of the legislation against the Catholics).

Furthermore, Richard Bancroft, then Archbishop of Canterbury, in a pastoral letter of 1604, thus summarized a speech which His Majesty had recently delivered to the Privy Council:

> His most excellent majesty hath with the admiration of all that heard him most fully, rarely, and resolutely declared himself touching such courses as he wisheth should be held with popish recusants, being most desirous to rid his Kingdom of these pestiferous adversaries, to which purpose he hath dealt very thoroughly and privily both with the lords of his right honourable privy council, and with his judges; expecting likewise that we who are bishops should not be negligent in discharging of our duties, for the furthering and effecting of so royal and so religious a designment.[43]

We ordinarily speak of people as "good, bad or indifferent." But to King James of England all Catholics were bad, and according to His Majesty there were three degrees of badness, or rather, to use his own language: "Three sorts—1°. Papists old, rooted and rotten—small hope to reclaim them—rather superstitious than seditious—left to the old laws. 2°. Novelists, apostates, the greatest danger—most malignant—to be sifted by oaths both before and after. 3°. The youth, the future tense of the papists—take care of marriages and christenings—nip them in the bud—the beginning of procreation the action." [44]

The nature of the laws which His Majesty had in mind, and which were actually enacted, can be divined. They were one and all, it may be said in a single phrase, inconsistent with the nature and the dignity of the human being.

Professor McIlwain, a distinguished political scientist of our day, who has specialized in King James and his political views, says that the oath of allegiance was "England's answer to the Jesuit challenge contained in Bellarmine's theory of the Pope's

[43] *Ibid.*, p. 171, quoting from *Documentary Annals of the Reformed Church of England*, Oxford, 1839, vol. ii, pp. 77-78.

[44] *Ibid.*, from *Common Journals*, vol. i, p. 265—quoted from Tierney-Dodd, vol. iv, p. 69.

indirect power." [45] But he adds that it was in reality the "answer which tacitly accepted one-half of Bellarmine's theory, the separation of the spiritual from the secular."

In this conception of the oath, Mr. McIlwain's statement has the approval of Father Brodrick, who says that "Bancroft's device" (the Bancroft in question being the Archbishop of Canterbury, with whose views we are familiar)—which played no small part in the framing of the oath and the provisions which accompanied it—"was a variation of the old theme, *divide et impera,* and it met with extraordinary success." [46] Does not the Catholic historian Lingard inform us that "Archbishop Abbott and Sir Christopher Perkins, a conforming Jesuit," [47] drew up the oath? Indeed Lingard further says that it "effectually broke the power of the Catholic body in England, by dividing them into two parties marshalled against each other." [48]

The greatest of modern historians, Leopold Ranke—whose knowledge of the Papacy was unrivalled among Catholics as well as Protestants—says that by acceptance of the oath of allegiance, "the supremacy of the king would be actually acknowledged, and the connection of the English Catholics with the Papacy dissolved." [49]

We are dealing with a matter both abstract and practical and with international implications, and, as we shall later see, the solution of the problem redounds to Cardinal Bellarmine's credit, through the separation of the two powers of which the Cardinal was the leading and successful advocate.

First let us consider the part of the oath upon which both Catholics and Protestants could agree, quoting Father Brodrick's language in behalf of his Church: "The oath was a clever blend of perfectly legitimate declarations with highly controversial ones.

---

[45] Charles Howard McIlwain, Introduction to *The Political Works of James I* (Cambridge, Massachusetts, and London, 1918), p. xlix.

[46] Brodrick, *op. cit.,* vol. ii, p. 176.

[47] *Ibid.,* John Lingard, *History of England* (London, 1883), vol. vii, p. 91.

[48] *Ibid.,* p. 90.

[49] *Englische Geschichte,* vol. 2, p. 55, in *Leopold von Ranke's Sämmtliche Werke,* vol. 15, Leipzig, 1877. The English translation seems to be at fault at this point, since it gives "practically acknowledged" instead of "actually acknowledged," involving a world of difference.

All Catholics were quite at liberty to recognize in James their 'lawfull and rightfull King'; moreover they were bound by their faith to 'abhorre, detest, and abjure as impious and hereticall, this damnable doctrine and position that Princes which bee excommunicated or deprived by the Pope may be *murthered* by their subjects or any other whatsoever'; and they certainly had a duty in conscience 'to disclose and make knowne unto his Majesty all treasons and traiterous conspiracies against him.' "[50] These were the legitimate and acceptable parts of the oath.

Now for the controversial ones. "But on the other hand,"—to quote again from Father Brodrick—"how could any Catholic of those days 'truly and sincerely acknowledge, professe, testifie and declare that the Pope, neither of himself nor by any authority of the Church and See of Rome, or by any other meanes, hath any power or authority to depose the King'? And still less, how could any Catholic 'abhorre, detest, and abjure as impious and *hereticall,* this damnable doctrine and position that Princes which bee excommunicated or deprived by the Pope may be *deposed* by their subjects or any other whatsoever' "?[51]

We find ourselves here confronted by two theories: the one of a united Christendom; the other of a Christendom broken by the Reformation. The conflict was between the old state of things and the new. The Catholic point of view is stated, it would seem, with fairness by Father Brodrick in a single paragraph following his analysis of the oath, which we have quoted:

All the Popes of medieval times had been allowed by the common consent of Christendom a certain authority over monarchs, which included, in special circumstances, the right of deposing them. At the beginning of the sixteenth century the vast majority of Catholic theologians admitted the existence of these rights, though they carried on vigorous disputes among themselves as to their origin, their nature, their limits, and the advisability of exercising them. . . . Consequently the Catholics of England were being forced to affirm on oath that for three whole centuries the Papacy had been usurping rights which in no way belonged to it, and to condemn as heretical and impious a theory which had behind it all the weight and learning of the Church's greatest theologians. It is

[50] Brodrick, *op. cit.,* vol. ii, p. 176.
[51] *Ibid.*

beside the point to say that the theologians were wrong in forgetting that the medieval theocracy had passed away never to return. They may have been, but what really matters is that they taught what they did teach. To condemn such teaching as impious and heretical might, in the circumstances, be considered as tantamount to condemning the whole doctrinal and disciplinary basis of Catholicism.[52]

Now what was Bellarmine's conception of the Pope's spiritual and his "indirect power"? In a word, Bellarmine denied that the Popes had received from God directly any power over temporal matters, and asserted that the direct power which they did receive from Him pertained immediately to things spiritual, with only an indirect application to temporal affairs. In Bellarmine's subtle Latin the conception runs as follows:

Asserimus Pontificem ut Pontificem etsi non habeat ullam mere temporalem potestatem, tamen habere in ordint ad bonum spirituale summam potestatem disponendi de temporalibus rebus omnium Christianorum.[53]

The sense in which the Cardinal understood what is called the "Bellarmine theory" is stated in two short sentences: "The spiritual and temporal powers in the Church are related in the same way as spirit and flesh in man. For flesh and spirit are as it were two republics which may be found united or apart."[54]

But the matter is too important to be dismissed with a few lines, even by the Cardinal himself. The indirect power was not of his discovery or creation, and it shows his integrity that he seemed to take pleasure in unearthing its advocates in times past instead of having it ascribed to himself. But in any event, he was its great advocate and, as already said, it is often called, not unjustly, the "Bellarmine theory."[54a]

---

[52] Brodrick, *op. cit.*, p. 176.

[53] *Ibid.*, vol. i, p. 262.—We declare that the Pope in his papal capacity even though he possesses no purely temporal power, nevertheless does possess supreme power to order the temporal affairs of all Christians for purposes of spiritual welfare.

[54] *Ibid.*, p. 263.

[54a] We have already referred to Victoria's views on this subject, but it is not inappropriate to quote his exact language at this point: "The Pope has temporal power only so far as it is in subservience to matters spiritual, that is, as far as is necessary for the administration of spiritual affairs. This is also the view of Torquemada . . . and of all the doctors. And the proof of it lies in the fact that an art to which a higher end pertains is imperative and preceptive as regards the arts to which lower ends pertain (*Ethics*, bk. 1). But the end of spiritual power is

What, then, does Cardinal Bellarmine mean by the "indirect power" as distinguished from the "direct power"? "The Pope," says this faithful son of the Church, "has not the same kind of right to depose temporal princes, even though they might deserve to be deposed, as he has to depose bishops, that is as their legitimate, ordinary judge."[55] What then? "Nevertheless, he may," the Cardinal continues, "as the supreme spiritual authority, dispose of kingdoms, taking away the power from one monarch and conferring it on another, if such a change be necessary for the salvation of souls."

Now "with regard to legislation," the Cardinal holds, "the Pope as Pope cannot ordinarily make any civil law, nor can he confirm or render void any law made by secular princes, because he is not their political suzerain." Again, what then? "Nevertheless, he may do all these things should the salvation of souls require that a particular civil law be passed and the Prince be unwilling to pass it, or that a law be abrogated as harmful to

ultimate felicity, while the end of civil power is political felicity. Therefore, temporal power is subject to spiritual power. This is the reasoning adopted by Innocent in *X*, 1, 33, 6; and it receives confirmation from the consideration that, whenever anybody is entrusted with the charge of any office, he is impliedly granted everything without which the duties of the office can not rightly be discharged (*X*, 1, 29, 1). Inasmuch, then, as the Pope is a spiritual pastor by Christ's commission and the discharge of the duties of this office can not be hindered by the civil power (there being no lack in the provision of things necessary either by God or by Nature), it is beyond doubt that power over things temporal has also been left to him so far as is necessary for the government of things spiritual. And on this principle the Pope can infringe civil laws which tend to breed sinners, just as he has infringed the laws with regard to prescription by a party acting in bad faith, as is clear from *X*, 2, 26, 20. And on this principle also, when princes are at variance with one another about some right of sovereignty and are rushing into war, he can act as judge and inquire into the claims of the parties and deliver judgment, a judgment which the princes are bound to respect, lest those numerous spiritual evils should befall which are the inevitable results of a war between Christian princes. And although the Pope does not do this or does not do it often, it is not becausee he can not, . . . but because, for fear of scandal, he wishes to prevent the princes from thinking his motive is ambition or because he is afraid of a revolt from the Apostolic See on the part of the princes. And on this principle the Pope can sometimes depose kings and even set up new kings, as at times has been done. And certainly no one rightly calling himself Christian should deny this power to the Pope. . . . It is in this sense, also, that those numerous rules are to be interpreted which say that the Pope has both swords. The earlier doctors make the same assertion, as also does St. Thomas in the second book of the *Sententiae*, . . ."

[55] *Ibid.*, p. 264.

religion and the Prince be unwilling to abrogate it." What is his authority for such a doctrine? "That is an excellent rule of jurisprudence which says: 'When about one and the same matter the laws of Emperor and Pope are found to be in opposition, if the matter in question is concerned with the salvation of souls, as involving danger to them, then the Imperial law is abrogated by that of the Pope; if, on the other hand, the affair is one of purely temporal interest, the Papal law cannot cancel the Emperor's. . . .' "[56]

Returning to "judicial sentences," this saint and doctor of the Church concludes, so far as this phase of the subject is concerned: "The Pope as Pope has no power to decide purely civil cases which might be brought to his notice." What, then, is the Pope's jurisdiction? "If, however, the spiritual welfare of souls is involved, he can act as a temporal judge supposing that there is no one else to assume the office. This might fall out when two supreme rulers are at war, or when those whose duty it is to act as judges refuse to give a decision. Pope Innocent III had the circumstance in mind when he wrote, *jurisdictionem temporalem solum casualiter Pontificem exercere.*"[57]

Now Bellarmine considered that there were two states—the temporal and the spiritual: that is to say, the ordinary states, with which we are all familiar, and the Church—meaning, of course, the Catholic Church. The end of the temporal—which in this connection may more properly be called secular—state is material happiness. On the other hand, the Church is a perfect society in the same sense but its end is spiritual. The conclusion which Bellarmine, and it is believed any churchman, would draw is that the end of the spiritual commonwealth is superior to that of the secular state and that, if there is to be dependence, the material should be subordinated to the spiritual. But let us see how Bellarmine handles this phase of the question. "That political power, not only as Christian but as political, is subordinate to ecclesiastical power, is proved by a consideration of their respective ends." For, he continues, "a temporal

[56] Brodrick, *op. cit.*, p. 264.
[57] *Ibid.*

end, such as that of the State, must obviously be subordinate to spiritual ends, because temporal happiness is not the ultimate purpose for which men were made and therefore must be directed towards that purpose, which is eternal happiness." The authority of the "Philosopher" is invoked: "As Aristotle says in the first chapter of his *Ethics,* faculties are subordinated according to the subordination of their ends." [58]

But to continue with Bellarmine. "Now, Popes and princes, priests and people, together make one great Christian Republic which is the Church"—meaning, of course, Catholic Christendom. "We are all one body, says St. Paul, and in every body the members are mutually connected and dependent one upon another. It cannot, in reason, be asserted that the organs of spiritual power are dependent on the organs of temporal power and therefore the relation of dependence must be the other way about." This is a very direct route to a desired end. By way of illustration, the Cardinal now proceeds to enforce his doctrine by "a plain sign," that is to say, "the fact that if the temporal administration hinders spiritual good, the prince is obliged, in the judgment of all men, to change that form of administration, even though temporal prosperity may suffer by the change." [59]

Now no state can be perfect unless it possess the power required to attain its end. Concerning the spiritual power of the Church there was no question, but what of its temporal power? This question Bellarmine answers by means of an analogy. "Each state," he declares, "because and in so far as it is perfect and self-sufficing, has a right and a duty . . . to compel other independent states to change their methods of administration." But the right and the duty do not stop there, for he proceeds to add that the state in question might even depose a ruler of the recalcitrant state "and set up someone else in his place, if that is the only means by which it can protect itself from aggression." [60] The logic is perfect; but what of the facts? "The history of Napoleon Bonaparte is a good modern illustration," [61] says Father

[58] *Ibid.,* p. 265.
[59] *Ibid.,* pp. 265-6.
[60] *Ibid.,* p. 266.
[61] *Ibid.,* p. 266, note.

Brodrick, reinforcing the Cardinal's argument in regard to the spiritual power.

Now for the second half of the analogy. "Still stronger is the right of the spiritual State, the Church, to command and compel the secular State to change its policy and depose its prince, *quando aliter non potest bonum suum spirituale tueri. . . .* Christians are not obliged to tolerate the rule of a non-Christian or heretical king when his government is a plain menace to their religion."[62] This time Father Brodrick is silent; but we may add our own illustration to the argument. The "glorious revolution," as our English friends call the "deposing" of James II, was due to the unwillingness of his Protestant countrymen to have a Catholic as successor to the throne, as would have been the case if his newly born son (to be known in history as the "Old Pretender") had succeeded him; but he did not succeed his father, because the English Protestants took—perhaps unwittingly—a leaf from the book of the Catholic Bellarmine, and since they were the beneficiaries of his doctrine, we may be pardoned for citing a Protestant incident of the "Bellarmine theory." But we should not overlook the authority of Bellarmine, who said that it was the duty of Christians to "repudiate" the rule of a non-Christian or heretical king "for if human law comes into conflict with the law of God, it is obviously the law of God that must be obeyed. . . . On the other hand, that this man or that should be king of the State is a mere matter of human law."[63]

Times change, new conditions spring up and render many an axiom of the past inapplicable to the present not to speak of the future. So it is with certain phases of the Bellarmine theory, since tyrannicide has taken on a constitutional aspect and makes

[62] Brodrick, *op. cit.*, p. 266.

[63] *Ibid.*, pp. 266-7. There is an interesting passage cited by Brodrick from Leibnitz, who invokes Hobbes in behalf of the "Bellarmine theory"; "Has the Pope [he asks] the power of deposing kings, and of absolving their subjects from their oath of allegiance? It is a point that has often been discussed; and Bellarmine's arguments, which deduce from the Pope's supposed spiritual jurisdiction, a jurisdiction at least indirect over temporalities, have not appeared contemptible even to Hobbes himself. In fact, it is certain that whoever has received from God power to procure the salvation of souls has a power of repressing the tyranny and ambition of the great, which destroy such a multitude of souls."—*De Jure Suprematus* (*Op.* t. IV, pars. iii, p. 401.)

not merely monarchs but presidents careful to keep their activities within the constitutions and laws of their respective countries and therefore in conformity with, instead of in opposition to, not only material happiness but spiritual wellbeing. As Pope Pius IX said as recently as 1871:

> Altogether different from such a social order is the condition of affairs at the present day, and only malice could confuse things and times so unlike; as if an infallible decision concerning a principle of revealed truth, had any affinity with a right which by the will of Christendom the Popes were in duty bound to exercise when the common good demanded it. It is as clear as the day that malice alone is the explanation of such an absurd idea as that of including the [theory of the deposing power in the doctrine of infallibility]. No one any longer gives such an idea a second thought, least of all the Supreme Pontiff himself.[64]

Yet even in 1605, when the oath of allegiance was put into effect, the question of the right of the Supreme Pontiff to depose Europeans monarchs was an academic rather than a living issue. As Father Brodrick says: "If the King"—meaning James I of England—"knew anything of Papal diplomacy, he must have been perfectly well aware that he stood in no danger of deposition at the hands of the Pope. The time for such action, as far, at least, as the sovereigns of non-Catholic countries were concerned, was long past, and James must have known that it was past." [65]

But while this phase of the "indirect power" of the Pope is now and was even in the day of King James an academic question, there is another phase of the "indirect power" of the Pope which has had a remarkable and unexpected development and which is of very first importance in the realm of international law and relations. For it often happens that a principle intended for one purpose unexpectedly becomes the source of an unforeseen development. Just as from the oppostion to the doctrine of the divine right of kings sovereignty became vested in the people and the system of democratic government ceased to be a theory and became a reality, so it is with the Bellarmine theory. The indirect intervention for spiritual purposes has become in modern practice

---

[64] Brodrick, *op. cit.*, vol. i, p. 268, quoting from *La Civitià Cattolica,* serie viii, vol. iii, fasc. 508, 12 agosto 1871.

[65] Brodrick, vol. ii, p. 193.

direct intervention under the law of nations, as a result of the recognition by Protestant as well as Catholic countries, of the Papacy as a *societas perfecta*. Today, in a word, the Church is recognized as a state, with the legal rights and duties of a state, including the right of direct intercourse with all other states for the purpose of protecting its interests throughout the international community. Instead of an exclusive Christendom we are dealing with an all-inclusive international community made up of duly recognized and independent states or nations.

This conception is of such fundamental importance in the matter of human relationships, both spiritual and temporal, that we feel justified in developing it and showing its application to the international community through the treaty-making power.

Now there are of necessity relations between these independent nations and there is likewise of necessity a law to govern those relations. What is this law? International law, under which each and every nation has a right to protect its citizens or subjects. And the Papacy, although a state for spiritual purposes, is nevertheless a state, and although its subjects are scattered throughout the entire international community and are also subjects of the secular states in which they reside, the Papacy has a right to intervene in behalf of the spiritual welfare of those subjects and to protect them in the enjoyment of their spiritual rights by all legal means at its disposal. In an age of intolerance —and none were less tolerant than the Protestant states, among them Great Britain, whose statutes depriving Catholics of the rights of citizens were in force indeed until the first quarter of the last century had run its course—protection could not be recognized in its completeness, for intolerance stood in the way not only of equality within the states but also of equality of the states toward one another. Fortunately, tolerance has come, and this twofold equality exists in our day, and it exists because of the universal acceptance of the *societas perfecta,* whether the *societas* be spiritual or temporal, with a treaty or convention or concordat not only for temporal relations but for the regulation of matters spiritual.

Now for the application. Not the least interesting example is that of the treaty of October 8,1782, negotiated by John Adams, Minister of the United States to the Netherlands, in behalf of a *societas* far from *perfecta* at the time but which has since become the *societas perfecta* known as these United States of America, the treaty stipulating for the exercise of the religious rights of his fellow countrymen in Holland.

> There shall be an entire and perfect liberty of Conscience allowed to the Subjects and Inhabitants of each Party, and to their Families; and no one shall be molested in regard to his worship, provided he submits, as to the public demonstration of it, to the Laws of the Country: . . .[66]

Here we have liberty of conscience and the free exercise of religion for the citizens or subjects of the contracting parties. The Treaty of 1858 between China and the United States of America includes a provision in regard to freedom of worship not only to citizens of the United States but to Chinese converts as well. In other words, freedom of conscience and religious worship are regarded as acquired, if not inherent, natural rights. The provisions of the pertinent article of this treaty are:

> The principles of the Christian religion as professed by the Protestant and Roman Catholic churches, are recognized as teaching men to do good, and to do to others as they would have others do to them. Hereafter, those who quietly profess and teach these doctrines shall not be harassed or persecuted on account of their faith. Any person, whether citizen of the United States or Chinese convert, who according to these tenets, peaceably teach and practice the principles of Christianity, shall in no case be interfered with or molested.[67]

By a treaty concluded between the same parties in 1868, it is provided that

> The 29th Article of the treaty of the 18th of June, 1858, having stipulated for the exemption of Christian citizens of the United States and Chinese converts, from persecution in China on account of their faith, it is further agreed that citizens of the United States in China of every religious

[66] Art. IV of Treaty with the Netherlands of October 8, 1782, *Treaties and Other International Acts of the United States of America*, edited by Hunter Miller (Washington, 1931), vol. 2, p. 63.
[67] Article XXIX of Treaty of Peace, Amity, and Commerce with China of June 18, 1858, MS., U. S. Department of State, Treaty Series, no. 46.

persuasion, and Chinese subjects in the United States, shall enjoy entire liberty of conscience, and shall be exempt from all disability or persecution on account of their religious faith or worship in either country. . . .[68]

A further treaty concluded October 8, 1903, between the same parties stipulates that

> The principles of the Christian religion, as professed by the Protestant and Roman Catholic Churches, are recognized as teaching men to do good and to do to others as they would have others do to them. Those who quietly profess and teach these doctrines shall not be harassed or persecuted on account of their faith. Any person, whether citizen of the United States or Chinese convert, who, according to these tenets, peaceably teaches and practices the principles of Christianity shall in no case be interfered with or molested therefor. No restrictions shall be placed on Chinese joining Christian churches. Converts and non-converts, being Chinese subjects, shall alike conform to the laws of China; and shall pay due respect to those in authority, living together in peace and amity; and the fact of being converts shall not protect them from the consequences of any offence they may have committed before or may commit after their admission into the church, or exempt them from paying legal taxes levied on Chinese subjects generally, except taxes levied and contributions for the support of religious customs and practices contrary to their faith. Missionaries shall not interfere with the exercise by the native authorities of their jurisdiction over Chinese subjects; nor shall the native authorities make any distinction between converts and non-converts, but shall administer the laws without partiality so that both classes can live together in peace.
>
> Missionary societies of the United States shall be permitted to rent and to lease in perpetuity, as the property of such societies, buildings or lands in all parts of the Empire for missionary purposes and, after the title deeds have been found in order and duly stamped by the local authorities, to erect such suitable buildings as may be required for carrying on their good work.[69]

These three treaties have been selected from many as showing the growth of intervention through the treaty-making power, for the removal of inequalities in the spiritual as distinct from the material domain, which means, if it remove inequality in one

[68] Article IV of Treaty of Trade, Consuls, and Emigration with China, July 28, 1868, MS., U. S. Department of State, Treaty Series, no. 48.

[69] Article XIV of Treaty as to Commercial Relations with China, October 8, 1903, MS., U. S. Department of State, Treaty Series, no. 430.

phase of the spiritual domain [70] may remove it in each and every phase.

"Bellarmin, sur ce point là, tout au moins, redevient tout à fait à la mode." [71]

* * *

We have set forth, perhaps in more than sufficient detail, the views of His Majesty James I on the doctrine of the divine right of kings, as to which Father Brodrick somewhat picturesquely says: "It was not merely that monarchical power in general was divinely ordained, but that James Stuart was monarch of the particular country called Scotland by right divine, and did every man, woman, and child from John o' Groats to the Tweed yearn for a Republic, they would be yearning for something as much forbidden as the apple coveted by Eve." [72]

As we have also set forth in what is believed sufficient detail Cardinal Bellarmine's views on the indirect power—which King James considered inconsistent with his overlordship of the Kingdoms of England, Scotland and Ireland, of which he was the recognized sovereign, it would seem fitting that we should state, at least in outline, Cardinal Bellarmine's views on the origin and the nature of civil government. Here, as in connection with the indirect power, again we place under contribution his *Controversiae,* and particularly the section of that work known as *De Laicis*. In a word, the Cardinal's theory was that government was of God but that its institution was of man.

"Political power considered in general," he says, "not descending in particular to Monarchy, Aristocracy or Democracy, comes directly from God alone." [73] This was not a mere statement of opinion, for, in the Cardinal's view, it followed "of necessity from the nature of men," and therefore the power in question "derives from the natural law." [74] Now "this power resides . . . immedi-

[70] James Brown Scott, "The Government of the United States and American Foreign Missionaries"—*American Journal of International Law,* 1912, vol. 6, pp. 70-82.

[71] Brodrick, op. cit., vol. i, p. 268, quoting E. Amann in the *Revue des Sciences Religieuses* (Université de Strasbourg), Jan. 1927, p. 547.

[72] *Ibid.,* vol. ii, p. 154.

[73] *De Laicis, or the Treatise on Civil Government by Robert Bellarmine,* translated by Kathleen E. Murphy (New York), p. 24.

[74] *Ibid.*

ately in the whole state," for although it is of Divine origin, "Divine law gives this power" to no particular man. The consequence of this is that, until positive law decrees to the contrary, "there is no good reason why, in a multitude of equals, one rather than another should dominate."[75] Nevertheless, there must be organization for, in the Cardinal's opinion, "human society ought to be a perfect State"[76]—as we have already seen. "Therefore," he continues, "it should have the power to preserve itself, hence, to punish disturbers of the peace."[77] To sum up in a few phrases, the views of Cardinal Bellarmine, the political philosopher, not in his language but nevertheless in words representing his thought, the civil state took its origin from human agreement; its purpose is temporal peace; its laws are the creation of human reason, and vary according to circumstances. This is the sum and substance of modern political doctrine.

There is, however, one further matter considered by Cardinal Bellarmine, to which it will not be inappropriate to refer. If there is a civil state, there must be a civil government, and government has from earliest times implied the appointment of one or more to govern, as distinct from the remainder of the individuals making up the state. How were these governors or chief magistrates appointed and what was the nature and the tenure of their office? "By natural law," the Cardinal affirms, the power of government "is delegated by the multitude to one or several."[78] Why was such a delegation necessary? Because "the State cannot of itself exercise this power." But the power of government having been delegated to a particular person, did it become his permanent possession? Bellarmine's answer to this was an unequivocal denial: The matter of the form of government was a matter of positive rather than of natural or divine law, that is to say, it was to be determined by the laws of each particular state. It is "evident," he declares, that it "depends on the consent of the

[75] *De Laicis*, p. 25.
[76] *Ibid.*, pp. 25-6.
[77] *Ibid.*, p. 26.
[78] *Ibid.*, p. 26.

people to decide whether kings, or consuls, or other magistrates are to be established in authority over them."[79] This, it may be said, was not an original contribution by the Cardinal—and he made no claim as to its originality. Members of his own Church had more than once expounded it; but for present purposes we may content ourselves with quoting, for the sake of comparison, a passage from Victoria's Reading *On the Civil Power,* delivered in 1528:

> The State, then, possesses this power by divine Disposition; but the material cause in which, by natural and divine law, power of this kind resides, is the State itself, which by its very nature is competent to govern and administer itself, and to order all its powers for the common good. The proof of this fact is as follows: since by a natural and divine law there must be a power for the government of the State, and since—if common, positive, and human laws are laid aside—there is no reason for depositing that power in one person rather than in another; it necessarily follows that the community is self-sufficing and that it has the power to govern itself.[80]

Now the power of government having been delegated to a certain individual or individuals, the question then arises, was such delegation irrevocable? There were some who held that it was, but Bellarmine was not numbered among them. "If there be legitimate cause," he asserts, "the people can change a kingdom into an aristocracy, or an aristocracy into a democracy, and *vice versa,* as we read was done in Rome."[81] In a word, the people of the state could—and did—make the government, and then could also unmake or remake it.

The passages which we have quoted from Cardinal Bellarmine are *loci classici.* Many an American, having by heart the Declaration of Independence, would be astonished if he should learn that in substance, if not in form, the truths which Thomas Jefferson—who drafted the Declaration—held to be "self-evident" are to

---

[79] *Ibid.,* p. 27.

[80] James Brown Scott, *The Spanish Origin of International Law*—Part I, *Francisco de Vitoria and His Law of Nations*—(Oxford, 1934), p. lxxvii.

[81] *De Laicis,* p. 27.

be found in the section on *De Laicis* of Cardinal Bellarmine's famous *Controversiae.*[82]

What did our Jefferson have before his eyes? The very passage from the Cardinal to which we refer is contained in Sir Robert Filmer's *Patriarcha*—left in manuscript at his death in 1653, published in 1680, a copy of which was in the library of Thomas Jefferson and is now contained in the "Jefferson Collection," purchased by the Congress of the United States to form the nucleus of the new Library of Congress, the original Library having been burned by the British when they captured the city of Washington in 1814.[83]

The Bellarmine theory of the *societas perfecta* of both the Church and State was to become merged in international law and modern political theory and indeed it is a milestone in the development of modern international law; and the Bellarmine theory of the source of power as vested in the people of the State is the foundation of Democratic government throughout the world.

[82] Bellarmine's *De Laicis sive Saecularibus* is the third part of a long dissertation called *De Membris Ecclesiae,* the other two parts of which discuss the clergy and the religious. It was published in the first volume of the *Controversiae,* the first edition of which appeared at Ingolstadt in 1586.

[83] Sir Robert Filmer thus quotes "passages" from Bellarmine:

"2. To make evident the Grounds of this Question, about the *Natural Liberty of Mankind,* I will lay down some passages of Cardinal *Bellarmine,* that may best unfold the State of this Controversy. *Secular or Civil Power* (saith he) *is instituted by Men; It is in the People, unless they bestow it on a Prince. This Power is immediately in the whole Multitude, as in the Subject of it; for this Power is in the Divine Law, but the Divine Law hath given this Power to no particular Man—If the Positive Law be taken away, there is left no Reason why amongst a Multitude (who are Equal) one rather than another should bear Rule over the rest?—Power is given by the Multitude to one man, or to more by the same Law of Nature; for the Commonwealth cannot exercise this Power, therefore it is bound to bestow it upon some One Man, or some few—It depends upon the Consent of the Multitude to ordain over themselves a King, or Consul, or other Magistrates; and if there be a lawful Cause, the Multitude may change the Kingdom into an* Aristocracy *or* Democracy. Thus far *Bellarmine;* in which passages are comprised the strength of all that ever I have read, or heard produced for the *Natural Liberty of the Subject.*"

The quotation is made from the Jefferson copy of Filmer (which has been marked with a lead pencil in the margin opposite the above text): *Patriarcha; or the* **Natural Power** *of Kings. By the Learned Sir Robert Filmer Baronet . . . London, Printed for Ric. Chiswell in St. Paul's Church-Yard, Matthew Gillyflower and William Henchman in Westminster Hall,* 1680.

The Jefferson *Patriarcha*—a first edition—is bound up with a copy of Filmer's *Observations,* dated London, 1696.

CHAPTER XI

DIVINE RIGHT AND TYRANNICIDE

The Stewart Experiment

PART II

Charles I

On the 30th day of January, 1648, the theory of tyrannicide was put into practice, not by a mere criticism and dethronement or expulsion but by the decapitation of the sovereign whose official title was "Charles, By the Grace of God King of England, of Scotland, of France and of Ireland, and Defender of the Faith." We do not need to go into minute details; suffice it to say that Charles, second son of King James VI of Scotland and of his royal spouse, Princess Anne of Denmark—the eldest son, Henry, having died before his father—sat at the feet of his royal father imbibing the doctrine of the divine right of kings, and later sought to impose upon the dominions whereof he was sovereign his father's conception of statecraft.

Now King James had himself weathered the storm—indeed it is proper to say the storms—of his English career; but the son was overwhelmed by force of arms, tried by a specially constituted tribunal for his many and varied sins against the state, and sentenced to death.

Now there was a time in England when power was considered to be vested in the Crown, but, as Sir Edward Coke, the implacable enemy of the Stewarts, whimsically but truly maintained, law, like Magna Carta, "is such a fellow that he will have no sovereign." Parliament, moreover, which had come into being through Magna Carta, slowly but surely encroached upon what the sovereigns considered their lawmaking power, and by the time of "good Queen Bess," the power had actually passed to the Parliament. King James' theories of government were irreconcilable with a lawmaking Parliament and his reign was one of crimination and recrimination.

In Charles' reign the Parliament had not only become conscious of its supremacy but insisted upon asserting it, and the resistance of the King to the supremacy of Parliament and his attempt to bend Parliament to his will by force of arms caused what is known as the "Great Rebellion." Then too, admitting that King Charles was a high-minded, Christian gentleman in his private life—as was not always the case with the Stewarts—his royal word, experience had unfortunately shown, could not be trusted in public affairs. Government, he insisted was his prerogative, and he was set upon governing—with the Parliament, if it obeyed his will, or without the Parliament if it opposed him. For this and many other reasons the Parliament had lost confidence in him. He in turn attempted to govern without Parliament. His efforts to raise revenue without representation failed in England as a later sovereign's attempt was to fail in the New World. In plain terms, Charles was looked upon as a tyrant and the only certain and effective remedy against him, in the opinion of Cromwell and his party, was tyrannicide, the tyrannicide as set forth and justified by John Milton in his pamphlet, "The Tenure of Kings and Magistrates: Providing That it is Lawfull, and hath been held so through all Ages, for any who have the Power, to call to account a Tyrant, or wicked King, and after due conviction, to depose and put him to death; if the ordinary MAGISTRATE have neglected or deny'd to doe it. And that they, who of late, so much blame Deposing, are the Men that did it themselves."

On January 1st, the Commons resolved that King Charles was guilty of treason and on the 6th of the same month they established a High Court of Justice to try the King. Some two weeks later the trial of Charles Stewart took place in Westminster Hall. It is recorded that the royal prisoner laughed aloud when he heard himself called a traitor, demanding to know by what authority he was tried. He was soon to discover that it was no laughing matter; for he was told by Bradshaw, the president officer of the court, that the trial was by authority of the people of England, to whom Charles owed his election as sovereign. It appears that the retort of the royal prisoner—that he was King by inheritance and not by election—had little weight with the court.

On the 26th of January, Charles was found guilty of the charges and the court unanimously decided upon his execution. On the following day the prisoner came before the court for the last time to hear his sentence. The court considered itself competent to such a degree that it refused his request to be heard before the Lords and Commons.[84]

It must be said to his credit that he that bore himself with great dignity, and that "nothing in his life became Charles like the leaving it," in front of Whitehall, on January 30, 1648.

There is a very close connection between the trial of Charles and his execution on the one hand, and Milton's pamphlet on the other, which was to be—and it was—a defense of the High Court of Justice in having King Charles stand trial. From internal evidence, the "Tenure" seems to have been written between January 8th and January 27th, the very day when Charles heard his sentence. It was of course *un livre de circonstance* but it was the result of much preparation in advance; for Milton, deeply interested in the troubled period of Charles' reign, was veering toward republicanism. At the time of composing the pamphlet, however, he could not be said to be an opponent of monarchy, although he was a convinced enemy of the doctrine of the divine right of kings—to govern wrong. Later he became an outspoken enemy of monarchy and a staunch defender of the Commonwealth. In any event, *The Tenure of Kings and Magistrates* was his defense of tyrannicide and it is still the greatest defense of that doctrine in the English language. A dozen years later, on the eve of the Restoration, he published a pamphlet the title of which, like that of the "Tenure" is a statement of its aim, its purpose, its content, and its author's final views: *A Free Com-*

[84] Whether Charles should or should not have been executed may, from the legal and from other points of view, be open to discussion, but in the matter of his deposition posterity is in full agreement with those who overthrew him and his government.

monwealth—"The Ready and Easy Way to establish a Free Commonwealth, and the Excellence thereof, compared with the Inconveniences and Dangers of readmitting Kingship in this Nation."

Now Milton had convinced himself to such a degree of the righteousness and importance of the cause which he espoused that during the years of the Commonwealth he was to be deaf to the voice of the muse. The period of the Commonwealth was the period of his prose, and so intent was he on doing his duty as he measured it, that, warned by his physician to renounce the work upon which he was engaged, lest he lose his sight, he preferred his duty as he saw it to his eyes; and thenceforth the sun and the moon and the stars were to him but a recollection.

The "Tenure of Kings and Magistrates," to which we now turn, was a pamphlet of fifty-seven pages; but the portion essential to our purpose is of even lesser compass, and rather than paraphrase an admitted masterpiece, we have arranged Milton's views in their order in some eighteen numbered paragraphs.

1. No man who knows ought, can be so stupid to deny that all men naturally were borne free, being the image and resemblance of God himselfe, and were by privilege above all the creatures, borne to command and not to obey: and that they livd so, till from the root of *Adams* transgression, falling among themselves to doe wrong and violence, and foreseeing that such courses must needs tend to the destruction of them all, they agreed by common league to bind each other from mutual injury, and joyntly to defend themselves against any that gave disturbance or opposition to such agreement. Hence came Cities, Townes and Commonwealths.

2. And because no faith in all was found sufficiently binding, they saw it needfull to ordaine some authoritie, that might restraine by force and punishment what was violated against peace and common right.

3. This autoritie and power of self-defence and preservation being originally and naturally in every one of them, and unitedly in them all, for ease, for order, and least each man should be his owne partial judge, they communicated and deriv'd either to one, whom for the eminence of his wisdom and integritie they chose above the rest, or to more then one whom they thought of equal deserving: the first was calld a King; the other Magistrates.

4. Not to be thir Lords and Maisters (though afterward those names in som places were giv'n voluntarily to such as had bin authors of inestimable

good to the people) but, to be thir Deputies and Commissioners, to execute, by vertue of thir intrusted power, that justice which else every man by the bond of nature and of Cov'nant must have executed for himselfe, and for one another.

5. And to him that shall consider well why among free persons, one man by civill right should beare autority and jurisdiction over another, no other end or reason can be imaginable. These for a while governd well, and with much equitie decided all things at thir owne arbitrement: till the temptation of such a power left absolute in thir hands, perverted them at length to injustice and partialitie.

6. Then did they, who now by tryall had found the danger and inconveniences of committing arbitrary power to any, invent Lawes either fram'd, or consented to by all, that should confine and limit the autority of whom they chose to govern them: that so man of whose failing they had proof, might no more rule over them, but law and reason abstracted as much as might be from personal errors and frailties.

7. When this would not serve but that the Law was either not executed, or misapply'd they were constraind from that time, the onely remedy left them, to put conditions and take Oaths from all Kings and Magistrates at thir first instalment to doe impartial justice by Law: who upon those termes and no other receiv'd Allegeance from the people, that is to say, bond or Covnant to obey them in execution of those Lawes which they the people had themselves made, or assented to.

8. And this oft times with express warning, that if the King or Magistrate prov'd unfaithfull to his trust, the people would be disingag'd.

9. They added also Counselors and Parlaments, not to be onely at his beck, but with him or without him, at set times, or all times, when any danger threatn'd to have care of the public safety.

10. It being thus manifest that the power of Kings and Magistrates is nothing else, but what is onely derivative, transferrd and committed to them in trust from the people, to the Common good of them all, in whom the power yet remaines fundamentally, and cannot be tak'n from them, without a violation of thir natural birthright.

11. To say, as is usual, the King hath as good right to his crown and dignitie, as any man to his inheritance, is to make the subject no better then the Kings slave, his chattell, or his possession that may be bought and sould, and doubtless, if hereditary title were sufficiently inquir'd, the best foundation of it would be found but either in courtesie or convenience.

12. But suppose it to be of right hereditarie, what can be more just and legal, if a subject for certaine crimes be to forfet by Law from himselfe and posterity, all his inheritance to the King, then that a King for crimes proportionall, should forfet all his title and inheritance to the people: unless the people must be thought created all for him, he not for them,

and they all in one body inferior to him single, which were a kinde of treason against the dignitie of mankind to affirm.

13. To say Kings are accountable to none but God, is the overturning of all Law and government. For if they may refuse to give account, then all covnants made with them at Coronation: all Oathes are in vaine, and meer mockeries, all Lawes which they sweare to keep, made to no purpose; for if the King feare not God, as how many of them doe not? we hold then our lives and estates, by the tenure of his meer grace and mercy, as from a God, not a mortall Magistrate, a position that none but Court parasites or men besotted would maintain.

14. *Theodosius* the younger, Christian Emperor and one of the best, causd it to be enacted as a rule undenyable and fit to be acknowledgd by all Kings and Emperors, that a Prince is bound to the Laws; that on the autority of Law the autority of a Prince depends, and to the Laws ought submit. Which Edict of his remaines yet unrepealed in the Code of *Justinian*. l. i. tit. 24. as a sacred constitution to all the succeeding Emperors.

15. How then can any King in Europe maintaine and write himselfe accountable to none but God, when Emperors in thir own imperiall Statutes have writt'n and decreed themselves accountable to Law. And indeed where such account is not fear'd, he that bids a man reigne over him above Law, may bid as well a savage beast.

16. It follows lastly, that since the King or Magistrate holds his autoritie of the people, both originally and naturally for their good in the first place and not his owne, then may the people as oft as they shall judge it for the best, either choose him or reject him, retaine him or depose him though no Tyrant, meerly by the libertie and right of free born men to be govern'd as seems to them best.

17. We may from hence with more ease, and force of argument determin what a Tyrant is, and what the people may doe against him. A Tyrant whether by wrong or by right comming to the Crowne, is he who regarding neither Law nor the common good, reigns onely for himself and his faction.

18. And I ask by what conscience, or divinity, or Law, or reason, a State is bound to leave all these sacred concernments under a perpetual hazard and extremity of danger, rather then cutt off a wicked prince, who sitts plotting day and night to subvert them: They tell us that the Law of nature justifies any man to defend himself, eev'ng against the King in Person: let them shew us then why the same Law may not justifie much more a State or whole people, to doe justice upon him, against whom each privat man may lawfully defend himself; seeing all kind of justice don, is a defence to good men, as well as a punishment to bad; and justice don

upon a Tyrant is no more but the necessary self-defence of a whole Common wealth.[85]

Such is the sum and substance of *The Tenure of Kings and Magistrates.*

There is a further statement, in the nature of a corollary, contained in Milton's *Pro Populo Anglicano—Defensio contra Salmasium,* which should be quoted to give his matured conception on the matter of kings and government:

I should wish all to note this again and again, on the authority of God himself in this text (Deut. xvii. 14), that all peoples and nations have always had the free choice of either continuing the form of Government that pleased them, or changing it into another. Of the Hebrews God says this expressly; of other nations He does not deny it: but farther it is implied that the Republican Form was thought by God more perfect than Monarchy, as human things are, and of more use to his own people.[86]

Until the rights and duties of governments were adequately defined and specific laws passed by the proper legislative body, the monarch might be kept within bounds either by such law as existed or—the law failing—by fear of just punishment through tyrannicide. As little by little the source of power was either recognized in the people, or their right to participate in the government was made a fact, the duties of the king were prescribed not merely in the oath which he took at coronation but also by statute. Now the violation of a statute was the violation of a positive law, and the monarch or chief magistrate in constitutional governments may himself be taxed with such a violation of the law. However, the control of the people over their government may be and often is exerted on lesser grounds than that of the violation of a statute, as, for example, when the government in office no longer responds to the needs or desires of the people. The result is the fall of the ministry on the ground that they no

[85] John Milton, *The Tenure of Kings and Magistrates,* edited with an Introduction and Notes by William Talbot Allison (New York, 1911), pp. 9-15, 19, 53.

[86] Masson, *op. cit.,* vol. iv, p. 259. Quoted from Chapter II of Milton's *Pro Populo Anglicano Defensio.*

longer truly represent the majority of the people. This sort of vicarious punishment keeps the English monarch on the throne.

In France there have been various examples of tyrannicide. Among the more recent was the removal of Louis XVI from his kingship and his execution on January 21, 1793. To other French monarchs of the past century the milder form has been applied, Revolution and uprising forced Charles X to flee in 1830, as Louis Philippe was forced to flee in 1848. In 1870 the Emperor Napoleon III was overthrown. No physical harm was done to him, however, as he surrendered both himself and his army to the Germans at Sedan. Under the Third Republic no less than three Presidents have been forced to resign: President Jules Grèvy (1887) and Alexandre Millerand in 1924; and President Casimir Perrier resigned in 1895 because not able to carry out his policies, due to the opposition of the French Parliament. The number of French ministries which have been overthrown is almost legion.

Among the most spectacular instances of tyrannicide and its results in our days are the overthrow of the government of the Czar Nicholas of Russia in 1917, with the advent of the present Soviet Government, and the deposition of the Sultan of Turkey, the overthrow of the Turkish Empire, the removal of the capital from Constantinople to Angora and the establishment of a Republic under the distinguished soldier and statesman, Mustapha Kemal, resulting in the transformation of the sick man of Europe into the young man of Asia.

By the Constitution of the United States, tyrannicide in modified form is a constitutional remedy, Section 4 of Article II providing that

> The President, Vice President and all civil Officers of the United States, shall be removed from Office on Impeachment for, and Conviction of, Treason, Bribery, or other high Crimes and Misdemeanors.

Article I, Section 2, paragraph 5, of the Constitution provides that the House of Representatives "shall have the sole Power of Impeachment," the reason being that the House of Representatives, as the popular branch of the Congress, should indict an official guilty of unworthy acts.

By the sixth paragraph of Section 3 of Article I,

"the Senate shall have the sole Power to try all Impeachments. When sitting for that Purpose, they shall be on Oath or Affirmation. When the President of the United States is tried, the Chief Justice shall preside: And no Person shall be convicted without the Concurrence of two thirds of the Members present."

Within the lives of persons now living, Andrew Johnson, seventeenth President of the United States, was impeached for alleged maladministration. He failed of conviction by a single vote—a fortunate fact, as his policy today is looked upon not only as constitutional but as that of a statesman. We have given this example lest we be subject to the accusation of omitting one of the rare instances when the right of the people to act against their ruler was abused—or in danger of abuse. Yet it is better to have a good rule, though it may conceivably be subject to misapplication. Even the Golden Rule could be misinterpreted by those interested in its misinterpretation!

The classic example of the tyrant in the Western World is that of Maximilian, Emperor of Mexico. He was an Austrian archduke, seated on the throne of Mexico by the armed forces of Napoleon III, who wished to placate the Emperor of Austria because of the then recent war between France and Austria, in which the latter country was worsted; and in addition, to form a Latin confederation in opposition to the United States. We here have an illustration of a tyrant who came tyranically into office. Unaccepted by the people, his reign continued to be tyrannical. In the end the Mexican people were able to assert their right to overthrow the government imposed upon them. Maximilian's forces were defeated. He himself was captured and passed before a firing squad on June 19, 1867.

In some American Republics a President who has come into office legally, but has fallen on evil ways and has attempted to remain in office illegally in violation of the laws of the country, has been overthrown by force of arms. So it is that tyrannicide, whether in its milder form in the United States, or in its extreme form in Mexico or in one form or the other in the American Republics, has not yet run its course, in this our Western World.

Like all great doctrines of government, it may be misused, but the fact remains that it is the ultimate means whereby the people, as the source of power, may exercise that power and cause their will to prevail. Indeed the motto of one of the states of the American Union—and not the least—is *"Sic semper tyrannis."*

THE LAW OF WAR

Its Philosophic Justification by Suárez

CHAPTER XII

SUÁREZ ON WAR

The third of Suárez' contributions to international law is *De Triplici Virtute Theologica, Fide, Spe et Charitate,* left in manuscript but published in 1621, four years after his death. Now the third of the three theological virtues is charity; and it may seem strange that war should be treated under this caption. The fact, however, is that war is force used in order to redress an injury, to recover damage, to place, so far as possible, the injured parties in the position they would have occupied had war not resulted from the injury, and to administer punishment according to the nature of the injury. It is considered by the Church of which Suárez is an accredited authority that it is an act of charity to bring the erring back to and within the fold. From this standpoint war is a benefit; it is helping those who either can not or will not help themselves; it is an act of charity.

So much by way of introduction.

We are now ready to deal with the thirteenth disputation, on the subject of war. Naturally we would expect Suárez to begin with a definition of the topic on which he is to discourse, and we are not disappointed, for the opening lines of the disquisition give the definition: "An external contest at arms which is incompatible with peace abroad is properly called war, when carried on between two sovereign princes or between two states." [1] It is to be observed that this definition refers to what is sometimes called "public war," to distinguish it from what was out of date even in

[1] The quotations from *De Bello* here used are taken from a provisional English translation of the Latin text, which translation, together with selections from *De Legibus ac Deo Legislatore* and *Defensio Fidei* will appear in a volume of the "Classics of International Law." See *supra,* p. 131, note 5.

Suárez' time, "private war," that is to say, war begun and carried on by individuals, not in the interest of the state but for their own private advantage. It is also to be observed that the purpose of war is to restore peace; and assuredly peace is as charity to a war-stricken world.

But to return to the definition of war in its various aspects. The definition which Suárez has given is of a general nature and contemplates what we may call an "external war." Force may, however, be used within the state and, although it is not war in the sense in which Suárez has just defined the term, it is nevertheless a contest by means of armed force. Thus he says that "when it"—meaning an armed contest—"is between a prince and his own state, however, or between a state and its citizens, it is termed sedition." There may, however, be a contest to which only private individuals as such are parties. Then "it is called a quarrel (*rixa*) or duel (*duellum*)." What, then, in the opinion of Suárez, is the difference between these three categories of warfare? "The difference," he says, "appears to be material rather than formal, and we shall discuss them all,"—for which he had the best of models—"as did St. Thomas [2] and others" whom he also mentions.

For a moralist—and Suárez was assuredly one—we would expect the primary consideration to be whether war is right or wrong, or, as he himself says, "whether war is intrinsically evil." First stating the contrary view, as was the wont of the schoolman, he then sets forth his own conclusion that "war, in an absolute sense, is not intrinsically evil, nor is it forbidden to Christians." To this conclusion there are, he admits, four objections, the fourth of which he discusses at some length. Following Suárez' example, we dwell upon the fourth, which, in his own language, is that "war, morally speaking, draws in its train an infinite number of sins; and a given course of action is considered in itself evil and impermissible, if it is practically always accompanied by untoward circumstances and harm to one's neighbors." But this was not the whole of the objection, for there was a confirmation of it

[2] II. II, qq. 40, 41, 42.

to the effect that "war is opposed to peace, to the love of one's enemies and to the forgiveness of injuries."

It might seem that Suárez had raised for himself a difficult objection which would indeed need a reply. By way of reply, he appeals for the reason of the thing to St. Augustine[8]—the greatest authority of his Church, it is said, after St. Paul—who deemed it "advisable to avoid war in so far as is possible, and to undertake it only in cases of extreme necessity, when no alternative remains." This is, however, but half of the answer, as St. Augustine also holds that "war is not entirely evil, since the fact that ills follow upon war is incidental and since greater ills would result if war were never allowed." So much for reason.

Now for the confirmation of the argument upholding the fourth objection. War is not opposed, Suárez says, "to an honorable peace" but "to an unjust peace, for it is more truly a means of attaining a real and secure peace"—what he desired for his day as we also desire not only for our day but for all future time. But what of the admonition to love our enemies? "War," replies Suárez, "is not irreconcilable with a love of one's enemies; for whoever honorably wages war hates, not individuals, but the actions which he justly punishes."

But there are two kinds of war, aggressive and defensive, and, speaking of the latter, Suárez says that it may not only be permitted but "sometimes even commanded." The reason is that "the right of self-defence is natural and necessary." This is the law regarding individuals. But, adds Suárez, "the same is true of the defence of the state, especially if such defence is an official duty."

Now of aggressive warfare. This is not, in the opinion of Suárez, "an evil in itself, but may be honorable and necessary." What is the reason?—for Suárez always sought a reason. "In order to ward off injuries and to hold enemies in check"; for without such wars states could not "be preserved in peace." And the authority for this far-reaching statement? Warfare for such a purpose "is allowed by natural law; and even by the law of the Gospel, which derogates in no way from natural law." But

[8] *On the City of God*, Bk. XIX, last chapter.

Luther was apparently of the other opinion, holding that war was a divine punishment and that it was unlawful "to resist the punishment of God"; to which Suárez replies that this statement "is indeed ridiculous; for God does not will the evils [against which war is waged], but [merely] permits them; and therefore, He does not forbid that they should be justly repelled."

What, now, are aggressive and defensive wars?—for the two may not always be readily distinguished. Suárez here cites an example which we reproduce: "If enemies seize the houses or the property of others, but have [themselves] suffered invasion from the latter, that is no aggression but defence"; for "if anyone tries to oust me from possession of my property, it is lawful for me to repel force with force." In a word, this is a matter of protection of property unlawfully seized. What is the legal basis for this? The act in question "is not an assault, but a defence, and may be lawfully undertaken even on one's own authority." Suppose, however, that the injury has been committed and the property seized "and redress is sought through war." In such case "the war is aggressive." As a concession to the infirmity of man, he is allowed to defend the property in his possession against attack: a universal rule of criminal law. It is also, Suárez informs us, "the common opinion of the Doctors" and the jurists.

Admitting that war is legitimate, to be honorable it must be carried on in accordance with three conditions: First, it "must be waged by a lawful power"; secondly, "for a just cause and on just grounds"; and thirdly, "a prescribed and uniform mode of procedure must be observed at its beginning, during its prosecution and after victory." Now war may have a just cause, but its consequences at best are evil and to mitigate these consequences there must be rules for its beginning, conduct and end.

Suárez now passes to a consideration of these conditions and asks who may lawfully declare war. This question could only arise in connection with aggressive warfare, for everyone, whether individual or state, has the right of self-defence, without permission or declaration. Who, therefore, may declare aggressive war? Relying upon St. Thomas Aquinas,[4] Suárez grants this right only

[4] II. II, qu. 40, art. 1.

to "a sovereign prince who has no superior in temporal affairs, or a state which retains for itself a like jurisdiction." By what law? Natural law. War can only be declared by the prince, because in him is vested the duty, and therefore the power, to defend the state from harm.

The second reason is fundamental, assimilating as it does warfare to a judicial process; and as a judge may only decide a question if he have jurisdiction of the parties, so the prince, acting as a judge in his own behalf and in behalf of his people, can only execute, as it were, a judicial decision against those of whom he has "jurisdiction." The matter is so important, going as it does to the very root of war and its justification, that we quote the exact language of Suárez somewhat at length. "Just as the sovereign prince," he says, "may punish his own subjects when they offend others, so may he avenge himself on another prince or state which by reason of some offence becomes subject to him; and this vengeance cannot be sought at the hands of another judge, because the prince of whom we are speaking has no superior in temporal affairs;" and therefore Suárez concludes, "if that offender is not prepared to give satisfaction, he may be compelled to do so by war."

Here we have in plain and unmistakable terms what we may call a "war suit" through force, or to combine the two in a single phrase of three words, "a force suit" between princes or states, just as we have within states a lawsuit for the purpose of redressing injuries. The subject has already been discussed by Victoria, as we have seen, but the conception of war as a force suit is of such fundamental and far-reaching consequences that we consider it again and in detail. It is to be observed that the entire procedure set forth in Suárez' tractate *On War* is based upon an analogy between the civil suit within the state and the international suit between states by means of war. And if the analogy is to hold, this means, of course, that the cause of war must be just, because a suitor within a state could have a judgment rendered in his favor only if the cause of his suit were just. And the only reason why the theologians, up to and through the period of the Reformation, allowed war to be justifiable is that it was in its nature a legal remedy and because—a matter of the utmost importance—between equal states there could not be, as within the state, a court of the superior. The prince, therefore—for the chief executive is ordinarily referred to as prince—acted as a judge, for the claim, when rejected by the defendant state, was laid before him and passed upon by him with the aid of his counselors; and if after careful examination the case were found to be just—meaning "just" in the sense that the court within the state, if it could accept jurisdiction, would render judgment in its behalf—then the prince should—indeed must, in accordance with judicial procedure—pass judgment, place the complaint before the offending state and demand satisfaction. In lawsuits within the state the plaintiff first seeks redress directly from the defendant and, on the latter's failure to comply, brings a lawsuit, and obtains judgment and execution against him. To follow the analogy—which is complete, in spite of different conditions of procedure—let us assume that the defendant state refuses satisfaction. The prince in question then proceeds to execution, that is, to use the force of war. The lawsuit from within becomes the force suit without and between the states.

We shall see in later portions of the tratate that each step of the process within the state is parallelled in the force suit between the states. For example, if the suit, whether between states or within the state, be for property which has been misappropriated, seized or carried away, the judgment will be either for the return of the property or for just compensation for the value thereof and, in addition, the costs of the suit, that is, the expenses of the legal proceeding. If the suit be of a criminal nature, that is, one involving punishment for an injury rather than mere reparation for property, reparation which is deemed proper in the opinion of the prince as judge can be exacted. And this is not all; for just as in criminal procedure within the state the convicted party may be bound over to keep the peace, so in the force suit between the states, the guilty state may be bound over, not only to redress the injury but to keep the peace, if need be, by erection of fortifications, or indeed occupation of the territory. These things will appear in the course of the analysis of the tractate, but, in the language of the day, a "preview" will but add to the appreciation of Suárez' subsequent development of the theme.

It is further to be added that, although Suárez was both a moralist and a theologian, he was also a lawyer to his fingertips, because in his day law was an integral branch of theology, the theologians alone having a philosophy of law and the practising lawyer merely a precedent or text of the law,—as we have already said in the previous section on Victoria and indeed in that on Suárez. And it should be repeated in this connection that the only justification for war during the Middle Ages was the absence, as already stated, of a court between the states for the redress of an injury received. Fortunately, the difficulty in the way of a court of the superior between equal states has been overcome by an agreement of the states in the form of a treaty, whereby, in 1921, there was installed in the Peace Palace at The Hague, as we have seen, a court before which all "princes," presidents and chief magistrates, irrespective of nomenclature, may present their controversies and have them decided by due process of international law, as the suits within states would be decided by due process of municipal law.

We now return to the text of Suárez and we immediately find ourselves on familiar ground. Suárez says that he has used the expression "or a state," in addition to that of "prince," in order that he "might include every kind of government"; for his reasoning is intended to apply to all governments. However, he had in mind, as was natural in those days, the monarchical régime, in which the power of the state had been transmitted "to some one person," so that the state—meaning the people—conferred upon the monarch as their agent the exercise of sovereign powers, the sovereignty, however, remaining within the people. The state may not "declare war" without the monarch's "consent." We said that we were on familiar ground, and in behalf of this statement we quote,—"unless the prince should chance to be so negligent in avenging or defending the state, as to cause public and severe injury to that state, for, in such a case, the commonwealth as a whole might take vengeance and deprive the sovereign of the authority in question"; in other words, exercise the right of tyrannicide.

But the prince, as well as the state, which Suárez has in mind, is not of the inferior variety; for a prince or state with a superior, "cannot justly declare war without the authorization of that superior." If in his case there is, so to speak, a court of the superior, he must appeal to it.

Suárez ranged far and wide in his search for authorities and it is to be expected that he would not overlook Victoria. Indeed at this very point he recalls to us that certain illustrations concerning inferior princes had been set forth by Victoria, in his disquisition *On the Law of War.*[5] The first of these illustrations was to the effect that an inferior prince was not forbidden to declare war in his own behalf, if he had enjoyed such a right from time immemorial. With this Suárez agrees, although he limits the limitation, so to speak, by stating that inferior princes should not be allowed to declare war against another inferior under the jurisdiction of the same monarch, the reason for this being that between two such contestants the court of the superior is available.

There was, however, a second limitation of Victoria, which is concerned with the case in which the superior prince is negligent in avenging the wrong suffered by inferior rulers within his domain. In this case, Victoria held that the inferior prince might take matters into his own hands. Suárez agreed in part, but not wholly, indicating his view that "this course of action is not [entirely] commendable," for the reason that, even as a private individual might, upon his own authority, protect himself but could not avenge an injury done him, so also a subordinate state might not properly undertake to avenge injuries. Therefore, in the opinion of Suárez, permission to exact private vengeance "must not be granted to a portion of a state or to a private person, save only within the limits of a just defense."

But there may arise an occasion in which an inferior sovereign may be—and indeed is—obliged to take action before he can appeal to his superior; in the words of Suárez: "If the matter

[5] *De Iure Belli*, p. 169.

is pressing, and [direct] recourse [to the sovereign] is not immediately possible."

Having dealt with an imperfect state, Suárez asks "what is a perfect state; or what is a sovereign prince." What is the test of the perfect state or perfect prince? "It is the mark of supreme jurisdiction when before such a prince or in such a state there meets a tribunal in which all litigated cases of the realm are terminated, and from which there is no appeal to any superior tribunal." All other states and princes are imperfect.

On previous occasions, we have taken examples from the United States. We are now in a position to appeal to the British Commonwealth of Nations to illustrate Suárez' statement that "not all the states which are subject to the same king"—in the case of the British Commonwealth, their common king is his present Majesty, King George V—"are necessarily of the imperfect sort."

In addition to perfect and imperfect states, there were states of unbelievers and of Christians and the question naturally arose in the mind of a faithful son of the Church as to what the duty of the Pope should be toward Christian monarchies. Now these monarchies, supreme though they be in the temporal realm, are also subject to a supreme monarch in spiritual matters; or, to quote Suárez' exact language, "although he [the Pope] has no direct power in temporal affairs outside of his own domain, nevertheless [he] does possess such power indirectly." What, then, is this indirect power? The Pope has by virtue thereof "a right to require that a cause of war be submitted to his [judgment], and the power to pass [thereon] a sentence, which the parties in question are bound to obey, unless his decision be manifestly unjust." Why should the Pope possess such authority, we may ask. Because, Suárez says, it "is certainly necessary for the spiritual welfare of the Church and for the avoidance of almost infinite evils." For our purpose, the next sentence states a further reason of great importance, citing the Spanish theologian Soto: "War between Christian princes is rarely just, since they have at hand another means of settling their common disputes," meaning, of course, resort to the Pope as the supreme arbiter of the Catholic princes and states. As has more than once been mentioned, there is today for all of the states of the world another tribunal to which resort may be had in controversies which, if not adjudged, may lead to war,—indeed, there are two tribunals, the Permanent Court of Arbitration and the Permanent Court of International Justice, both at The Hague and located in Mr. Carnegie's Peace Palace.

If we recur to history, we find that the intervention of the Pope in disputes of Christian princes and states was not so frequent as we would like, and the reason that Suárez gives is one which had previously been stated by Victoria,[6]—"lest perchance greater evils result." And while it may be that princes are not obliged to appeal to the Pope for the settlement of their difficulties, Suárez warns them nevertheless that they "should take care lest they themselves be a cause of the fact that the Pope dares not intervene; for in that case they will not be free from blame."

Suppose that a war is declared, but without lawful authority. Though its cause be just, it is in itself unjust and opposed to charity. The reason? In the language of the judge, it is waged "without lawful jurisdiction, and is consequently illegitimate." If its cause is legitimate—that is, legal—it would seem logically to follow, and it is the opinion of Suárez, that such a war entails "restitution for all [resulting] damages." In the case put by Suárez, it follows that a participant in a war declared without legal authority may properly recover his own property but that he would be "liable for all injuries and losses inflicted upon others." And rightly so, for war without the required declaration is an illegal act and its consequences are illegal and therefore subject to reparation.

We may suppose that such a war had been waged in spite of a Papal prohibition,—by a Christian king or prince "subject only to the Pope." What is the situation? If the Pope had not only prohibited the war but had remanded for his own decision as a judge the dispute which caused it, then the prince is without right to declare the war, since there is a judge available for its decision. The case is different, however, if the prohibition is without intention to adjudicate the cause, since in that case, if

[6] *Supra*, p. 8.

the prince were strictly bound by the prohibition, he might be left without recourse against the state which had injured him. In a word, the simple prohibition by the Pope, without judgment or intention to judge, does not deprive the prince of "his own jurisdiction and power."

But let us further suppose that the Pope not only forbids war but declares it to be "opposed to the spiritual welfare of the Church," and thereby "deprives the prince of all right to make war." Here we have a perfect example of the exercise of the indirect power of the Pope. In such circumstances, the prince who insists on waging the war "will sin against justice" and will be bound to make restitution. The validity of such a prohibition on the part of the Pope, Suárez informs us, is always with the proviso "that he is truly acting for the common good."

In Section III of the Disputation, we come to the question "whether it is permissible even for clerics to declare war and to engage therein." The answer which Suárez gives, is somewhat long, but for present purposes the reply to this question may be in a few words. When Suárez wrote, there were two kinds of ecclesiastical princes and dignitaries of the Church, one kind possessing temporal sovereignty in addition to their spiritual offices, and the other kind having no temporal power. The question which Suárez has raised can apply only to aggressive war, inasmuch as an ecclesiastical prince—like any other prince, or indeed individual—would have the right to defend himself and his property against attack. The question therefore is: may the ecclesiastical prince declare aggressive war? Assuredly, if he is "sovereign in temporal affairs." But the case is otherwise with the princes who are "not sovereign in temporal affairs." To them self-defense only is permitted, and if the question of offensive war arises they "may easily have recourse to their supreme head."

Speaking of Churchmen, as distinct from "ecclesiastical" sovereigns, Suárez says that although they are not forbidden "by divine law" to engage in war, "nevertheless, by ecclesiastical law they are forbidden to do so." However, the Supreme Pontiff possesses, and may exercise, the right of dispensation. But it is to be said, however, that by the law and practice of war—both of

Suárez' day and of ours—a cleric taking part as a combatant in a war is to be treated as a layman.

It was the custom to exhort and encourage the combatants to acts of bravery, and, while this might be considered as an incentive to homicide, it was not necessarily held to be forbidden. However, as far as the Church was concerned, the exhortation was to be strictly limited to advice to the soldier to bear arms with fortitude.

Suárez has been discouraging of war in its various aspects; but he now comes to the fact which determines whether a war is just or unjust,—a fact which is indicated in the heading of the fourth section of the disputation on war: "What is a just cause of war, from the viewpoint of natural reason?" Suárez was well aware that from the dawn of history, one of the greatest of human errors had persisted—that might makes right. "There was," he says in the opening lines of the section, "an [old] error current among the Gentiles, who thought that the rights of nations were based on military strength, and that it was permissible to make war solely to acquire prestige and wealth." To the reasonable man this "error" should be at once apparent; and it is hardly a compliment to the human race that it is still mistakenly accepted as a truth by all too many—in our day. Suárez minces no words in denouncing it as "a belief which, even from the standpoint of natural reason, is most absurd."

Having disposed of the "error," he comes to grips with the matter in hand, saying "that there can be no just war without an underlying cause of a legitimate and necessary nature," a truth which he characterizes as "indubitable and clearly evident." War was a grave matter, and therefore it could only be justified as the redress for a "grave injury which cannot be avenged or repaired in any other way." There was no doubt upon this point; for it was the consensus of opinion of all the theologians as well as of other authorities. Now to Suárez reason was to the essence in every statement of principle and doctrine. Therefore he supports his conclusion by a series of reasons, the first being that war is permitted solely to preserve the state from injury, and since war itself brings injury in its train and is opposed to the welfare of the human race, it can only be justified on the ground that it protects from a greater injury. Consequently, if the wrong which furnishes the just cause of the war ceases to exist, "the justice of war would also cease to exist."

The second reason is that war despoils men "of their property, their liberty and their lives," and it would be wholly "iniquitous" if this were done without a just cause. In a word, war can not be made a justification for murder.

It is to be borne in mind, unless stated to the contrary, that the warfare with which Suárez is dealing is aggressive war, and, as such, ordinarily waged against non-subjects. For aggressive war to be just, therefore, the non-subjects must have committed a wrong affecting the subjects of the war-waging power. Why must this be so? Because, according to what Suárez has said, jurisdiction must be obtained over the foreigner before the prince can act as his judge and punish him.

Now the scholastic conception of war is that it is just on one side and wrong on the other. If such things as "ambition, avarice and even vainglory or a display of ferocity" were to be regarded as legitimate causes of war—which is the modern attitude, it would seem, of some states—the "war would be just on both sides,"—a supposition, Suárez goes on to say, "entirely absurd; for two rights contrary to each other cannot [both] be just."

But it is not enough that the prince should assume jurisdiction —for there are causes and causes, and, to quote a legal phrase of which Suárez does not avail himself on this occasion, *De minimis non curat lex* (the law does not take heed of trifles). In other words, the cause must be "serious and proportionate to the losses which the war would occasion." And as Suárez says, employing his ever ready analogy, a judge can punish only offenses "which are opposed to the common peace, and to the welfare of the realm."

The matter is to be carefully weighed, because what in itself may be slight may give rise to grave consequences.

There are, however, as many justifications of war as there are what Suárez calls "grave injuries." He groups these causes under three heads. The first is seizure of another's property, and a refusal to restore it; the second, denial by the prince, with no reasonable cause, "of the common rights of nations, such as the right of transit over highways, common commercial rights, etc."; and the third, any "grave injury to one's reputation or honor." The injury in each case may be to the prince or to his subjects, inasmuch as the "prince is guardian of his state and also of his subjects;" or the injury may be to foreigners residing within the prince's territory and therefore under his protection. But what is the situation if the injury is inflicted upon allies or friends? Here the same test for the justification of war applies as in the case when the injury is inflicted upon the prince or his subjects, that is to say, the injury must be sufficiently grave. Furthermore, the war in behalf of the ally should be undertaken only when the latter "consents thereto, either expressly or by implication." This is in effect a prohibition of intervention in behalf of parties who do not expressly invite such intervention. "Wherefore," says Suárez, "the assertion made by some writers, that sovereign kings have the power of avenging injuries done in any part of the world, is entirely false, and throws into confusion all the orderly degrees and divisions of jurisdiction." What is the reason for this statement? "Such power," we are told, "was not [expressly] granted by God and [its existence] is not to be inferred by a process of reasoning."

As regards the injury inflicted, two arguments may be invoked in order to justify a declaration of war. The first is that "reparation for the losses suffered should be made to the injured party." Here we have the judicial analogy implied in the terminology of Suárez. The second argument is that "the offender may be duly punished" if he refuses to give just satisfaction. Here again we have the judicial analogy. Now to carry his judicial analogy to its conclusion, Suárez says that "just as within a state some lawful power to punish crimes is necessary to the preservation of domestic peace; so in the world [as a whole], there must exist, in order that the various states may live in mutual harmony, some power for the punishment of injuries inflicted by one [state] upon another"; and this power is that of an acknowledged "superior." The consequence, therefore, is that "the power in question must reside in the sovereign prince of the injured state, to whom, by reason of that injury, the opposing [prince] is made subject; and consequently war, of the kind in question, has been instituted in place of a tribunal administering just punishment." Here we have the philosophical defense of war, in the absence of a tribunal of the superior between states.

In the manner of the schoolman, Suárez foresees objections. The first is that war is contrary to the Bibical admonitions, *To no man rendering evil for evil,*[7] and *Revenging not yourselves.*[8] the reply of Suárez is a triumph of scholastic logic. "The passages quoted," he says, "refer to acts performed by private authority and with the intention of doing evil for its own sake, to another." The case, however, is different when, instead of the individual acting in his own behalf and for his own benefit, war is proclaimed and conducted under legitimate and public authority for the common good. Then such acts "are not only not prohibited," but they are "even necessary," and he triumphs with a phrase from the New Testament, *For he beareth not the sword in vain, for he is God's minister to work vengeance upon evildoers.*[9]

So much for the objection by the theologians. Now for the one which might be raised by men of law—for Suárez was as ready to meet one as the other—the legal lights claiming that if the prince is to adjudicate in the case of an injury committed against him (the prince) or his people, then "the same party in the same case is both accuser and judge." This contention was not without foundation, "since the prince who has been wronged, assumes the rôle of judge by [his] act of aggression," that is, his aggression against the guilty party.

But this was not all of the legal argument. For private individuals may not be permitted to avenge themselves because of the possibility that they would "exceed the bounds of moral justice; and yet the same danger exists in the case of a prince who avenges himself for injuries to himself or his state."

Suárez' answer to this objection consists not of mere legal

[7] *Epistle to the Romans,* chap. xii, v. 17.
[8] *Ibid.,* v. 19.
[9] *Romans,* chap. xii, v. 4.

argument and, if we may use the term, hairsplitting, but is fundamental and based upon sound reason and equally sound common sense. "Our reply is"—he says, granting a certain measure of validity to the objection in order that he may the more completely rebut it—"that it cannot be denied that in this matter [of public vengeance], one and the same person assumes, in a measure, the rôle of accuser and that of judge; even as we perceive that God, to Whom there is some analogy in the public authority, assumes this double rôle." Suárez was writing in 1612, before the world had reached the conception of a court of the nations for the settlement of their disputes. But why was it essential to human welfare in the then state of affairs for the prince to assume a rôle that was at once judicial and punitive? The reason was that only too often "the offender" was obstinately unwilling "to give satisfaction," and if this unwillingness brought him into subjection to the injured party, he might, in the words of Suárez, "impute his own misfortune to himself."

Now we have seen that the objection relied in part upon an analogy between the private individual and the prince in the matter of avenging and punishing one who had committed an injury. But Suárez immediately punctures, so to speak, this analogy by stating that the individual acted according to his own unaided judgment, and, since no man is perfect, it was easily possible that he would "exceed the just limits of vengeance." With the prince whom Suárez had in mind, the situation was different because "public authority is guided by public counsel, to which heed must be paid, and consequently [authority of this sort] may more easily avoid the excesses induced by personal inclination." But this was not all for, while the private individual sought his own private good, the avenging power exercised by the prince "has for its end not private but public good."

But the weakness of the opposing argument by analogy was revealed by Suárez' brief but masterly examination of the fundamental bases of the whole doctrine of the prince's power to adjudicate in international cases wherein the public good of the commonwealth was involved. "An act of vindicative justice," Suárez declares, "is an exercise of that jurisdiction which private individuals do not possess, and cannot obtain through an offense committed by another." So much for the statement of principle.

Suárez' examination proceeds by way of argument as logical as it is irrefutable: "For if they could possess it"—meaning jurisdiction—"there would be no need of recourse to the public power of jurisdiction, since certainly, if this power of jurisdiction had its roots in men as individuals, the latter could not transfer it to magistrates, but would be obliged to keep it themselves; [a course of action] which would be opposed to the natural law, and to the proper governance of the human race."

But what, it might be argued by the opposition, was the individual to do if he could not obtain redress "through public authority"? Does this destroy the rule which Suárez has laid down? There is a maxim saying that the "exception proves the rule," and this, it would seem, is the view of Suárez. He was dealing with general principles, not with individual cases, and the mere fact that sometimes the private individual might find it difficult to secure justice did not weaken the validity of the rule.

Again and again throughout his disputation on war, Suárez emphasizes by repetition, restatement and the power of logic that a war begun without a just cause was essentially and wholly evil, involving a sin both against charity and against justice, and subjecting the offender to liability to make full reparation for all the harm he has caused.

But even when the justice of the cause was indisputable, Suárez counseled the prince against hasty action, for if the prince begins war, "even with just cause, while exposing his own realm to disproportionate loss and peril, then he will be sinning not only against charity, but also against the justice due to his own state"; and the reason why such an act would be a sin in spite of the justice of the cause of war, is that "a prince is bound in justice to provide for the common good of his state, rather than for his personal welfare; otherwise, he will become a tyrant." The illustration is to us touched with humor. "So a judge," Suárez explains, "who hanged a criminal deserving of execution but very necessary to the state, would act in a manner opposed to his official obligations, and, consequently, to justice." Perhaps fearing that this illustration might meet objections from the literally minded, he added another: "In the same way a physician would sin against the justice required in his profession if he should give medicine which would heal some immediate disease but would cause more serious ones to follow."

But if the commonwealth be composed of several kingdoms, it may be objected that the advantage of the whole may be to the detriment of one or the other. This is answered by the old principle of the greatest good to the greatest number; also "the defence of one results in the benefit of another and [in this way, the principle of] equality is preserved." To take an example from the United States of America. If the United States were engaged in an unfortunate war and the conditions of peace required that one or more states of the Union be ceded, the terms of peace, hard as they were, would be complied with, because it would be in the interest of the United States that the war should end, even upon disadvantageous terms. If, on the other hand, in the case put, the United States should go to war in the interest of one or other state of the Union and victory crowned their arms, the Union might be more powerful in the future than in the past,—which, as Suárez says, is in itself extremely advantageous to each of the kingdoms involved.

To take another example from the history of the United States. In 1861, some twelve of the southern states, as we call them, attempted to secede. The Government of the United States resisted, and after four years of Civil War, the Union was preserved. The war was of great detriment to the south, which had sought to secede, but the preservation of the Union has resulted in a future advantage to the whole which compensated for the temporary loss.

There is another question which the prince must consider in balancing the good and the evil of war: whether he is reasonably sure to win it. Suárez would not insist that he be absolutely sure, because he says that "from a human standpoint, it is almost impossible of realization," and the urgency of circumstances may make it inadvisable "to await such a degree of certitude." Again, if absolute certainty were required, a weak power, obliged to be certain of victory, would never be able to attack a stronger power; thus the thirteen British Colonies which declared themselves independent States of the Union, would never have become independent if they had waited until they were assured in advance of victory. On the basis of these general principles, Suárez lays down certain rules, the first being that a prince should "attain the maxim certitude possible regarding victory." This was not all; for he ought also to weigh "the hope of victory against the risk of loss." Yet, as in the illustration which we have just given, a strong degree of certitude may be "impossible of attainment"; in which case, Suárez would only require the prince to feel that "the outcome for which he hopes and which accords with the needs of the state and of the general welfare, is the more probable." Let us suppose, however, that even this probability does not exist, but the cause for undertaking war is of the utmost urgency for the common weal. Then, says Suárez, the prince before embarking on hostilities should feel "that the chances [of victory or defeat] are equal."

This latter statement, of course, applies more to a defensive than to an offensive war, for "if the war is offensive in character" and the chances are even or doubtful, then, says Suárez, "in almost every case, that war should be avoided. What is the test of these conclusions and rules? "The principles of conscience and justice."

The question may arise "whether Christian princes can wage war for reasons beyond the dictates of natural reason." The first reason for war alleged by those who answered in the affirmative—is "a refusal to accept the true religion." But reserving a discussion of this question to a later disputation, Suárez answers here and now that this ground is "fallacious."

The second of the grounds is—we quote the language of Suárez in the matter—"that God may be avenged for injuries done to Him through sins against nature, and through idolatry." But Suárez' immediate answer is that "such an opinion is false," and the reason immediately following is that "God did not give to all men the power to avenge the injuries done Him by them."

There is, however, a third ground, "that unbelievers are not true owners of their possessions," or that the Emperor "or—at least—the Supreme Pontiff has direct temporal lordship over the whole world." As we have seen, Victoria met and disposed of these arguments in his Reading *On the Indians,*[10] and it will be interesting to follow the argument of another great Spanish theologian on the same subject. His first statement is positive and blunt,—"all such claims are vain inventions."

But Suárez was not only to dispose of the argument by arbitrary pronouncements, for he immediately proceeds to give a logical foundation for his view, presenting the matter to the reader from the standpoint of the unbeliever, and saying that "even if we grant that such a title does indeed exist, still it would be impossible either to demonstrate its existence to the satisfaction of infidels, or to force them to believe in the validity of such dominion; and therefore, they could not be forced to obey." Furthermore, if the Pope or the Emperor were supreme overlords, they could wage war even against Christian princes—which the princes in question would have found as little to their liking as the infidels.

Suárez had already dealt with the question of the power of the Pope, but he here restates his view in a manner even more effective. "Wherefore," he asserts, "it must be observed that although the Pope indirectly has supreme power in temporal affairs, nevertheless the existence of such temporal power is always based, essentially, upon the assumption of direct power in the spiritual realm." This being the case, the indirect power of the Pope "does not essentially extend to unbelievers, over whom no direct spiritual dominion exists even in the Pope himself." This was a general statement, and therefore Suárez carefully used the word "essentially" (*per se*), because, since circumstances sometimes alter cases, there might arise "incidentally" (*per accidens*) causes in which the Papal authority could be exerted directly upon "barbarians."

Victoria had also treated the allegation that the barbarians were incapable of self-government; and again it is interesting to follow the examination of Suárez on the same point. Those who held this view claimed that the requirements of the natural

---

[10] *Supra*, pp. 2, 4-9.

order demanded that "men of this condition should be governed by those who are more prudent," vouching for this argument the statement by Aristotle[11] concerning men born to be slaves,—a doctrine greatly appreciated and set forth at length by one Sepúlveda, of unhappy memory.

Such a contention was difficult to maintain, and it assuredly was without general application, Suárez himself saying, in language which shows his open mind and his appreciation of good qualities even in races and beliefs other than his own, that "there are many unbelievers more gifted by nature than are the faithful," and he even adds, "better adapted to political life." Pushing the point home, he continues that it is not enough that the people be "of inferior natural talents"; they must be of such a low nature and on such a low plane that they "live uniformly more like wild beasts than like men." Admitting that there might be such peoples, action might be taken, not because of their religion or lack of religion but rather in order that they "may be organized in human fashion, and justly governed." Here we have the mandate of our day, which had already been announced and adequately stated by Victoria.[12] In any event, if war were to be undertaken against such savages, it should be defensive rather than offensive.

The authority of Aristotle had been invoked by Suárez' opponents on the question of war against inferior peoples. Suárez feels it only just to Aristotle, as well as to the cause which he himself advanced, that the meaning of the Philosopher should be explained, war being only permissible, according to this elucidation, to subdue a people "as different from the rest of mankind as is the body from the soul." However, those who have relied on Aristotle strike a snag in Suárez, who declares that if the ground in question actually exists, it "is valid not only for Christians, but also for every sovereign who wishes to defend the law of nature."

Now Suárez has started out to examine the question whether there is any legitimate cause for war beyond the dictates of

[11] *Politics*, Bk. I, chaps. i, ii.

[12] *Supra*, p. 31.

natural reason, and he reaches a general and negative conclusion which he supports by three special conclusions, the first being that no ground for war exists "so exclusively reserved to Christian princes that it does not have some basis in, or at least some due relation to, natural law, being therefore also fitted for princes who are unbelievers."

The second of the conclusions is of a very special nature, permitting Christian princes to defend the innocent and to avenge injuries committed against them. The illustrations which he advances in support of the general principle are highly theological, allowing war to be waged against a prince who would keep his people from accepting the Christian faith when they had expressed a desire to do so. But apparently the same rule does not work in behalf of those who wish to embrace, let us say, the Mohammedan faith, the reason being, from the Christian and theological point of view, that the prevention of the acceptance of Christianity is a real evil, whereas the prevention of the acceptance of Mohammedanism would not constitute an evil; and we would expect that Suárez would apply the rule in favor of the law of Christ, that any people "willing to listen [to the Gospel]" should be aided under such circumstances.

Now for the third conclusion. Suárez, although a theologian, was also a man of reason and a broadminded humanitarian and he maintained that the preceding considerations, being founded on natural reason, were applicable likewise "to a certain extent and in due proportion . . . to unbelievers." For this view he gives an explanation which proves that if men of Suárez' stamp could have had their way, the Reformation might never have occurred. If any one state, he says, "wishes to worship the one God and observe the law of nature, or to listen to preachers who teach these things, and if the sovereign of that state forcibly prevents it from doing so, there would spring up in consequence a just ground for war to be waged by some other prince," and the "other prince" might even be "an unbeliever and guided solely by natural reason," the war in question being "a just defence of innocent persons."

In the conception of Suárez, the law of nature was essentially the law of God; hence, any people who lived in accordance with the law of nature were living in accordance with the law of God, and such people were not to be penalized because they were not Christians, inasmuch as the Gospel of Christ had not been preached to them. Moreover, the nation which worshipped "the one God" possessed the right and the privilege to lay its beliefs before less fortunate peoples. This right is, in a word, the right to send missionaries.

Admitting that war to be legal should be just, what is the degree of certitude concerning its justice which is required of those who wage it? Now Suárez deals in trinities; and there is a trinity of individuals who wage a war, "to wit:"—as Suárez says—"the sovereign king and prince; the leading men and generals; and the common soldiers." Absolute certitude is not of this world in the moral sciences or in the causes of war. Therefore "practical certitude" satisfies Suárez,—"a certitude which may be summed up in the statement: 'It is lawful for me to make war.' " Therefore the test seems to be, is this cause of war—whatever it may be—"just in itself?" or, in other words and in Suárez' language: "This thing which I seek through war is [rightfully] mine."

First, of the prince who can rightfully make war, not of his own irresponsible will, but only after diligent examination of the "cause of the war and its justice," for war is a serious matter and "of the gravest character," and the diligence which Suárez would require is the due diligence of a judge, proportionate to its importance. We are again in the presence of the judicial analogy; and the diligence of a judge in a lawsuit should be the diligence of a prince in a force suit. The reason for this was obvious to Suárez—as it no doubt will be to his readers—that, if the prince were not held to this standard of criticism, "the rashness of princes would easily result in universal disturbance." But the diligence would be useless if the prince were not bound to act in accordance with the results of a diligent and impartial investigation.

Let us suppose, as does Suárez, that a king claims a city as belonging of right to him or as coming to him by inheritance, and let us suppose also that this claim conflicts with that of another monarch. If upon investigation the claim is clearly established, "it will be evident," says Suárez, "what decision [should be made]." Here the prince acts more as a fact finder than as a law finder. If, however, the claim of each seems to have equal validity, the king should then act "as a fair-minded judge." If after fair and adequate examination, he is of the opinion that his own claim "is the more credible," he may then, "even justly, prosecute his own right." The reason? "Because," says Suárez the lawyer, "the more credible opinion should always be preferred in handing down decisions." If, on the other hand, the more credible opinion is that of the other side, the prince, acting as a fair-minded judge, may not rightfully declare war.

But a diligent investigation by a fair-minded judge may result in finding that the claims are equally credible. In this case, the ancient legal maxim comes into play, "Possession is nine points of the law"; so that, if the opposing party is in possession, he ought to have the preference.

We are pleased to observe that the views of Suárez are—as we believe they should be—in accordance with those of Victoria, upon whom he relies, who required of the prince in possession, when doubt should arise, that as a judge he "diligently" investigate and, should he fail to do so, the other party to the dispute might force him so to do; for, as Suárez, agreeing with Victoria, says, "the principles of justice and sound judgment do indeed demand that such an investigation be made."

But it may happen that no one is in possession of property sought by belligerents, and that the doubts and probabilities balance each other. The property in question is what the jurists call *res nullius*. "The common opinion seems to be," says Suárez, "that either one" might seize the property in dispute and that the right of the first excluded the right of the other. But until such seizure were completed, if this common opinion were correct, we would be confronted by the paradox of a war just on both sides. The reason alleged is that in such a case a judge could award the property according to his discretion to either one or other of the litigants. However, Suárez did not accept this opinion, but, as is the case throughout the disputation, when dealing with a controverted point, he speaks in the first person: "I am unable to persuade myself that a judge may act thus in the case supposed." For if the right to possession were doubtful, the judge could not award the property to either party, and in such a case it should be divided between the claimants. But suppose that such division could not be made—or at least not to the satisfaction of both parties. King Solomon at one time encountered a similar difficulty but decided it differently; for as Suárez—not Solomon—insisted, the parties "must either divide between them the thing in dispute, or cast lots for it, or settle the matter in some other way." "But if one party should attempt to seize the whole possession to the exclusion of the other party," he would by so doing wrong the other claimant, who may in such a case seize by force, resulting in war, "the entire disputed possession."

But it may be asked whether, in cases of dispute over property or other rights, "sovereign princes" are bound to submit the dispute to the decision "of good men,"—a question of arbitration—obligatory or voluntary. We here find ourselves in the presence of one of the most perfect "purple patches" of Suárez, although perhaps not equalling his magnificent demonstration of the international community in *De Legibus ac Deo Legislatore.* The answer which he gives to the question is in the affirmative, that "princes are bound to avoid war in so far as is possible and by honorable means," and arbitration "is plainly the best means of decision, and therefore should be employed." Now for the purple patch: "It is impossible that the Author of nature should have left human affairs, governed as they are by conjecture more frequently than by sure reason, in such a critical condition that all controversies between sovereigns and states should be settled only by war; for such a condition would be contrary to wisdom and to the general welfare of the human race; and therefore, it would be contrary to justice. Furthermore, [if this condition prevailed,] those persons would regularly possess the greater rights who were the more powerful; and thus [such rights] would have to be measured by arms, which is manifestly a barbarous and absurd [supposition]."

It must, however, be observed that a sovereign prince, according to the opinion of Suárez, is not obliged to accept and permit the decision unless he has participated in and agreed to the appointment of the judges of the tribunal. In a word, the arbitration of Suárez is not obligatory, but with the consent of both sides. Rightly enough, he informs us that in his day arbitration was "a most rare occurrence"; that the prince of his day did not often consider it with favor, and for a reason which is not absent from our day—that "an opposing sovereign holds the foreign judges in suspicion."

Now Suárez was so in favor of—indeed it may be said he was obsessed with—the judicial analogy to which we have so frequently referred, that he inclined to the opinion that the prince could be adequately informed by his learned and competent advisers as to the right and the wrong of the case, with the result that he could act in his own behalf, and therefore arbitration, while it might be convenient, was not essential. If the premise of Suárez is true, then his conclusion would be acceptable, but true impartiality is hard to find on one side or the other in matters of pith and moment when the interests of the entire state may be involved.

As the passage in which Suárez expresses his opinion on this phase of the subject is, as it were, appended to the passage which has preceded it, we quote it in full:

> It should be noted that a sovereign prince, if he is acting in good faith, may ascertain his own rights through prudent and learned men [of his own choice]; then he may follow their judgment (if by it his rights are made clear to him); and under these circumstances he will not be bound to abide by the judgment of other [and foreign arbitrators]. The reason in support of this statement is that the rights in question must be judicially ascertained in the same manner as a just decision of a court; and in the latter sort of decision, [only] two objectives are involved. One is an examination of the cause and a determination of the rights of both sides; for which process, not jurisdiction, but knowledge and discretion, are necessary. For since this decision is not sought through war; but on the contrary, a substitute for war [i.e., a judicial inquiry]

is employed, there is no occasion to call in any arbitrator. The other objective is the enforcement of the right after it has been made clear. For this jurisdiction is indeed required; but such jurisdiction is inherent in a sovereign prince when in other respects he is sufficiently certain of his right. In that case, then, there is no reason binding him to await the judgment of another, although he ought to accept just settlements if they are presented to him.

We now come to the second group of persons who are concerned with the justice of war, "generals and other chief men of the kingdom." When called upon to give counsel, they are obliged to examine diligently into the truth of the matter before they venture an opinion; and if they fail to do so, they may be charged, in Suárez' opinion, with any injustice that there might be in the war. As to their responsibility when not called upon for consultation or advice, there might be a difference of opinion, one view being that they were under no more obligation to inquire into the merits of the war than would be private soldiers. But Suárez again turns to Victoria for what seems to us a more enlightened view, that is to say, "that such generals are bound in charity to inquire into the justice of the war." For what reason? "In order to give warning when it shall be necessary."

Now we come to the third and most numerous group of persons included in the material trinity—the common soldier. Since soldiers were in the usual course of things unlikely to be called upon to give counsel and advice, they were not bound to investigate the justice or injustice of the war and therefore might with a clear conscience go to war when called upon unless, even without investigation, it was "clear to them that the war is unjust."

In these days of a growing public opinion, we may be inclined to the belief that the "common man" is as much entitled to examine into the right and wrong of an international dispute as are his so-called "superiors." But in Suárez' day, the opinion was commonly held—and indeed it is still held by many—that the judgment of the prince and of his advisers was to be accepted without question. There is, it must be added, a justification for this view, in that subjects are often not in a position, either through lack of education or other qualifications, to examine into and decide difficult questions, and for this reason it is held to be the better course for them to obey their superiors. The merits of this state of things need not be discussed here, but it may be said in passing that a public opinion which depends wholly upon the views of the ruler and his counselors is not the enlightened public opinion which brings force to bear upon questions national and international and is therefore the hope of the future.

Suárez, to confirm his view that the subject should accept the opinion of the prince, turned again to the now familiar judicial analogy, saying that it was "confirmed by the fact that the official subordinate of a judge may execute a sentence without any previous examination, provided that sentence is not manifestly unjust." There was some difference of opinion on this matter, Sylvester maintaining that when soldiers had doubts, they should dispel them by making inquiries. But they might, under these circumstances, be caught between two fires; for, if they doubted the justice of the war and disobeyed orders, they would suffer the penalties for disobedience, and, on the other hand, if they obeyed orders, they might feel themselves guilty of "unjust slaughter and plundering," for "justice," Pope Adrian maintains, "imposes a more rigorous obligation than that of obedience." Suárez felt the force of this argument, but he met it by stating that the soldier's doubt "in such a case is not practical but speculative" and the speculative doubt was not for the soldier to indulge in.

Theirs not to make reply,
Theirs not to reason why,
Theirs but to do and die.

From a practical point of view, moreover, it would not do to have soldiers entering battle in a doubtful or half-hearted mood, for the reason that "it would become impossible for princes to defend their rights, and this would be a serious and general misfortune."

Stating his own opinion among the conflicting views, Suárez declares that soldiers who have no knowledge of the right and wrong of a particular war need not concern themselves about its justice or injustice. If, however, there were arguments abroad on the subject and the soldiers should encounter these and feel them so valid that they deemed the justice of the war extremely doubtful, they would be justified—and indeed bound—"to inquire into the truth in some way."

The world of today is not disposed to approve of the use of mercenaries in war, but it was still common in Suárez' day—and indeed for many years thereafter—and concerning these soldiers hired to fight it was the common opinion that they should examine into the justice of a war before enlisting—an opinion for which confirmation was to be found in the *Decretals*[13] and in the *Digest*,[14] to the effect that "he is not exempt from blame who thrusts himself, with peril to another, into affairs that do not concern him." St. Ambrose[15] too, is called upon to support this view by the statement that "no one ought to assist one party to the prejudice of another."

As a corollary to this view, it might also be said that "Princes who are kinsmen or friends may not assist one another until they have duly examined the cause."

But the opinion concerning the duty of mercenaries was open to objection, since it would involve an examination by every single soldier; and it may be admitted without argument that many soldiers were not in a position to get at the facts and form an enlightened opinion concerning them.

Again, mercenaries sometimes enlisted, not for any particular war but in the general service of a prince. What should they do when a war broke out after their enlistment, since they had bound themselves to fight and had, as Suárez puts it, given "their consciences into the keeping of the prince's conscience"? It would seem that in this case the soldier is bound by the prior rather than the subsequent obligation, unless the injustice of the war is manifest to him.

Here Suárez pauses to take up a related matter which is a burning issue in this very year of 1934—the question of the sale of arms to belligerents. Where the justice of the war is doubtful,

[13] *Sext*, V. vii, rule 19.
[14] *Digest*, L. xvii. 38.
[15] *On Duties*, Bk. III, chap. ix, and cited in *Decretum*, II. xiv. 5, 10.

arms may be sold to the combatants, yet the sale is accompanied by the risk that if the purchaser of the arms proves subsequently to have an unjust cause, the seller has incurred liability for the injury of the belligerent who has justice on his side. This leaves the neutral who wishes to profit in the wars of others—without endangering himself or his soul—in something of a quandary. In short, he must either sell to one party only, assuming the dangerous task of judging the merits of the controversy, incurring the enmity of the other party, and, in short, losing his neutral status—for the neutral, as a neutral, should not and indeed can not assume the rôle of friend to one belligerent and of enemy to the other—or, if he treats both parties alike, furnishing arms to both, he can not avoid the consequence that he has contributed in no small measure to the waging of an unjust war, often doing more harm, as Suárez says, than the soldiers themselves.

What is the solution for this perplexing question? Today we are approaching an answer, and indeed the United States of America have recently taken steps to prohibit trade in "arms or munitions of war" with two republics at war in the Western World. This is only a step, but it is a step in the right direction.

To refer again to the general question of the attitude of soldiers, Suárez says, in reaching his conclusion, that he does not find that mercenaries differ in fact from subjects, and in this connection he invokes the authority of Victoria, who speaks, as Suárez says, merely of soldiers, without distinction between mercenaries and subjects; but since the question of responsibility in the matter of the justice of the war is a moral one, Suárez, following Victoria, lays down the rule that if the soldier has a merely negative doubt as to the justice of the war, he may take part in the war without examining the question, upon the responsibility of the prince into whose service he has entered, who is presumably of a good reputation. This, says Suárez, is clearly Victoria's opinion and is upheld by other Thomists.

But the doubt of the soldier may be positive and if the arguments on both sides seem to have equal weight, then, in Suárez' opinion, the soldier before enlisting should inquire "into the truth of the matter." For the case is one of conscience, and the soldiers should not depend on themselves alone in so important a matter. They should therefore "consult prudent and devout men." If the soldiers form "a single political body" and are under their own chiefs, they may safely follow the judgment of their chief or prince.

After deciding under what conditions war is just, Suárez asks what is the proper mode of conducting war. Here again we are in the presence of a trinity,—"its commencement; its prosecution, before victory is gained; and the period after victory." And the three classes of persons which he has previously considered are likewise to be distinguished in this conenction: "the sovereign prince; the intermediate group of leaders; and the soldiers of the lowest rank."

Now these persons are to be considered in certain specific relationships:

> First, with respect to the enemy; that is, how may they lawfully conduct themselves toward the enemy?
>
> Secondly, with respect to one another. How should the king conduct himself toward his soldiers?
>
> Thirdly, [and again with respect to one another,] how should the soldiers conduct themselves toward the king?
>
> Fourthly, how should they conduct themselves toward other persons, for example, those persons at whose houses the soldiers are quartered during the march?

Leaving the first relationship, as the most important, for later treatment, Suárez takes up the others in a few paragraphs. As regards the fourth, we may quote without comment the admonition which Suárez himself quotes from John the Baptist:[16] *Do violence to no man . . . and be content with your pay.* The military leaders of intermediate rank and the princes themselves "are bound, by virtue of their office, to prevent such acts in so far as they are able. If they fail to do so, the whole duty of making restitution falls upon them, after the soldiers."

Suárez now takes up the second and third relationships, saying that as kings pay wages to the soldiers, the latter are bound because of such payment, "to discharge all the duties pertaining to

[16] *Luke*, chap. iii, v. 14.

their position," and this involves on their part "brave conduct, even to such a degree that they shall not take to flight, nor desert their stations or fortifications." As regards the soldiers' conduct toward each other, they should in the first place observe "the ordinary rules of justice" and "they are especially bound after victory to make a just distribution of the booty." However, as the laws of different countries differ as to the distribution of booty, Suárez does not discuss these laws, which in general are established "by use and custom."

Recurring now to the first and most important of the relationships which Suárez has listed—namely, the relationship with the enemy—he states that before declaring war, it is the duty of the prince to inform the opposing state that a just cause of war exists, "and to seek adequate reparation therefor." What is the result if adequate reparation is offered? The prince, whom we shall now call the plaintiff, must accept the offer from the opposing state, which we now call the defendant, and "desist from war," as in the case of a lawsuit. If, however, the defendant refuses to give satisfaction, the plaintiff may resort to war, since he could not in Suárez' day go to court.

What is the reason for this important conclusion? Any other method of entering into war, says Suárez, "would be unjust" and the consequent war would also be unjust. This reason is, as we would expect, based on the judicial analogy, which, we now see, is a shibboleth of Suárez. "For where a full and sufficient satisfaction is voluntarily offered, there is no ground for violence; especially since reason demands that puntive justice be exercised with the least possible harm to all, provided, however, that the principle of equality be observed. Moreover, one sovereign has no coercive power over another sovereign, unless the latter acts unjustly and is, accordingly, unwilling to give satisfaction."

The question arises whether the so-called satisfaction must be given before the outbreak of war, or whether it may properly be tendered during the course of the war. Suárez is of the opinion that the time of the offer is less important than the offer, and that in either case the satisfaction, when tendered, should be accepted, provided that it includes damages for the injuries and losses which have been incurred by the plaintiff belligerent, but in any event, the satisfaction demanded should not be excessive. "In short," Suárez continues, "the right to make war is an odious thing and the punishment inflicted through war is of the severest kind; therefore, that punishment ought to be inflicted as sparingly as is possible."

But the satisfaction, whenever offered after the outbreak of war and with a view to stopping the war, should be complete. Of what must the complete satisfaction consist? Suárez sets this forth, in what we may call a bill of particulars, in the following ample passage: "All property unjustly withheld shall be restored; secondly, reimbursement must be made for all expenses due to injuries inflicted by the enemy, so that, once the war has been begun, a claim may justly be made for all its costs, to date; thirdly, something may be demanded as a penalty for the injury inflicted, for the war has the character of punitive as well as of commutative justice; and finally, a demand may justly be made for whatever shall seem necessary to preserve and also to guard peace, in the future, since the chief end of war is to establish [such] a future peace."

What is the *rationale* involved in this bill of particulars? The reason for it is that "the state of war has its rightful source in justice and that, consequently, if war is made contrary to justice, there arises from that fact an obligation to make reparation [for this injury]."

The question arises as to what losses the enemy may be made to suffer in order that the plaintiff belligerent may obtain victory. The answer is that "hardly anything done against the enemy involves injustice, except the slaying of the innocent."

What damages may a victor with a just cause inflict upon the defeated defendant? The answer is based upon the standard of the righteous judgment at law, for here as elsewhere, there is always in the background the judicial analogy. And the damages should include "all the losses by the state in question throughout the war, *i.e.,* the deaths of men, conflagrations, etc." For this statement Suárez invokes the authority of Sylvester[17] and Vic-

[17] Word *bellum*, Pt. I, qu. 9.

toria[18] that "movable goods captured by soldiers during the war are not to be reckoned by the prince as part of the restitution. For this rule has become a part of the *ius gentium,* through common custom. The reason underlying it, is that, since the soldiers' lives are exposed to dangers so numerous and so grave, they should be allowed something; and the same is true of their prince." We of the United States have adopted the pension and soldier bonus system instead of reward by booty.

But suppose certain individuals among the defendant and defeated enemy should stand out as peculiarly guilty of misconduct. Suárez says they may "with justice, be put to death; and, although the slaying of a great multitude would be [thus] permissible only when there was most urgent cause, nevertheless, even such slaughter may sometimes be allowed, in order to terrify the rest, as is indicated in the following passage from *Deuteronomy: When the Lord thy God shall deliver the city into thy hands thou shall slay all that are therein of the male sex, with the edge of the sword, excepting women and the children, etc.* This is a harsh disposition, based upon the thirteenth and fourteenth verses of the twentieth chapter of *Deuteronomy,* which we should look upon as a special permission to the Jews and not to us Gentiles. Suárez as a righteous judge was anxious to temper the justice of the Old Testament with the mercy of the New. He admits that by the *ius gentium* all property of the enemy, both movable and immovable, might pass to the victors and he enumerates his authorities.[19] He contents himself by saying of these authorities that "a just equality must be preserved, and care must be taken for the future peace," Why? we may ask. To which the ever ready answer is the necessity "to preserve in war, the same quality as in a righteous judgment; and in such a judgment, the offender cannot be visited with every sort of punishment nor deprived of all his property without any restriction, but may be punished only in proportion to his fault."

[18] *De Iure Belli,* p. 184.

[19] *Digest* XLIX, xv. 24, 28; *Code* VIII. liii. 36; *Decretum,* I.i. 9 and 10. Ambrose, *On Abraham,* Bk. I, chap. iii. St. Thomas, *De Regimine Principum,* Bk. III. Covarruvias (on *Sext,* rule *peccatum,* Pt. II, § 13 [Pt. II, § 11, n. 6-7]. *Deuteronomy,* chaps. xi and xx. Abulensis, *On Deuteronomy,* qu. 3.

Doubts may arise as to title to movable and immovable property in possession of the enemy but belonging to third and therefore innocent parties—in other words, the property of neutrals. The case is especially clear with immovables, which remain the property of the neutral and should return to his possession. In the case of movable property, the law seems to be against its return, but putting aside positive law for the moment, Suárez takes the case of property acquired by theft, in which case the title never vested in the thief, and therefore must in Suárez' opinion, "incontestably" be returned to the "former owners." Turning now to positive laws, Suárez says that some of them seem to allow ownership of such neutral movable property to the soldiers who capture it, on the theory that possession of it by the enemy vests title in the enemy, and therefore the former owners lose their title to the property.

Now damages might legally be inflicted upon the enemy, and the question arises: Who are enemies in this sense, or in other words, who are the guilty and who are the innocent? "By the natural law, as it were," Suárez says, "the innocent include children, women, and all unable to bear arms; by the *ius gentium,* ambassadors; and among Christians, by positive [canon] law [20] religious persons, priests, etc." These we would call noncombatants, and Suárez adds to the list pilgrims and travelers, "since they form no part of the state and therefore are not reckoned among the enemy unless they are allies in the war." In the opinion of Suárez, it is a general rule that the innocent should be exempt from damages inflicted by the victor, if restitution and satisfaction may be obtained from the guilty, for the principle of equity clearly imposes this rule. But it might happen that complete satisfaction could not be obtained from the guilty, and in that event the innocent among the enemy were liable, Suárez held, for the portion of the reparation required to make the satisfaction complete, even at the expense of their liberty. At first sight it might seem unjust that innocent individuals should suffer for the misdeeds of the guilty, but Suárez was viewing the defendant state as a whole, and in these circumstances the innocent

[20] *Decretals,* I. xxxiv. 2 and *Decretum,* II. xxiii. 4 [II. xxiv. 3. 25].

must suffer for the deeds of the guilty. But while the latter of the old laws might permit depriving the innocent and guilty alike of their liberty—in other words, enslaving them—the law of nations had introduced among Christians the custom that prisoners of war should not be enslaved, although they might be held as prisoners until "sufficiently punished or redeemed by a just ransom." In the opinion of Suárez, liberal indeed for his day, this custom as applied to ordinary Christians he would likewise extend to what were then called apostates and heretics.

In the days of Suárez, Christians granted immunity to ecclesiastical persons and property, as he says "both because of reverence, and because these persons or goods seem to form a kind of spiritual realm distinct from the temporal state and exempt from temporal jurisdiction." But the Church should not be made a cloak for hostile action. Men might retreat to it for protection of their lives, "but if an enemy use a church as a citadel or as a defensive camp, that church may be attacked and burned, even if some disadvantages follow therefrom; for such disadvantages would be of an incidental nature (*per accidens*)."

But there was a definite limit to the damages to be inflicted upon innocent persons, and that limit stopped short of death, unless their death occurred "incidentally (*per accidens*)," when the act involving their death was "necessary in order to secure victory." Here Suárez the humanitarian speaks, saying that "the slaying of innocent persons is intrinsically wicked."

At this point, Suárez draws an important and proper distinction between life and other possessions. "For the latter," he says, "fall under human ownership, and the state as a whole has a higher right to them than single individuals; hence, individuals may be deprived of such property because of the guilt of the whole realm. But life does not fall under human ownership, and therefore, no one may be deprived of his life save by reason of his own guilt."

In a previous passage, Suárez has already defined innocent people, but for present purposes he now adds to his previous definition "those who are able to bear arms, if it is evident in other respects that they have not shared in the crime nor in the unjust war." What is the justification for including these in the ranks of the innocent? The fact that they are non-combatants. And Suárez sums it all up by first referring to a judicial analogy and then to the moral law. First of the analogy. Human beings should not be slaughtered indiscriminately, "since in a criminal trial, particularly, there should be sufficient proof, and since, indeed, he who is not proved guilty, is presumed to be innocent." Now for the moral law. "Finally, it is a moral certainty that, among a whole multitude, some may be found who neither consented to the war, nor gave any assistance in it, but who, on the contrary, urged the acceptance of peace; and therefore, all may not be indiscriminately slain."

"These arguments," he concludes, "prove beyond a doubt that after victory has been attained, those only who are clearly guilty may be slain."

In the warfare of Suárez' day whole cities were unfortunately given over to slaughter, "either on account of the enormity of the offence, or for the correction [by example] of other cities; since, to be sure, upon such occasions it is scarcely possible to distinguish the innocent from the guilty, except through age and sex." No doubt Suárez was reluctant to admit this rule, even as Victoria had reluctantly felt obliged to admit it. And this reluctance must have been all the greater because both of them had in mind the unspeakable sack of Rome by the imperial army of Charles V. But having admitted the rule, Suárez limited it as much as possible by stating immediately that "the case will be otherwise after the cessation of combat, and the attainment of victory."

In support of this opinion, Suárez instances the burning of cities and destruction of fortresses in which, of course, there are innocent men, women and children—innocent in the sense that they are not combatants, since they take no part in the warlike operations. The death of such innocent persons is not sought, indeed, but is, as Suárez puts it, an "incidental consequence" of the legitimate end of war, that is to say, the winning of the war.

So the matter stands and such has been the invariable practice of belligerents. Suárez, however, regarded the matter as of practical as well as theoretical importance and as a schoolman follows his conclusion with six arguments which might be opposed to the general rule which he has just laid down, following these six objections by six answers effectually disposing of them. It is, however, sufficient for us to repeat, as said before, that the conclusion is in accordance with practice and is allowable at the present day.

We are to suppose that the prince has obtained a just victory. What may he then do?—everything with the property of the enemy, provided he spare their lives, which is essential to the preservation of an undisturbed peace in the future." What is the justification for such a rule? It is that "war is permissible, especially for this reason, namely, as a road, so to speak, to honorable peace." As within the state the malefactor may be bound over to keep the peace, so the international malefactor may be bound over to keep the peace in the future by the seizing of its cities, provinces, etc.

Suárez has laid down the conditions under which war may be just; yet even though all these conditions are present, there is a possibility that the war in question "may have some evil aspect" which will nullify, so to speak, what would otherwise be a just war and make it contrary to charity. As an illustration Suárez refers to a situation in which the conditions he has set forth are fulfilled, but in which war is actually "rooted in hatred," and is therefore from its very motive essentially unjust and opposed to charity. But what is the situation when both the parties voluntarily rush to war "without just cause"? From the point of view of abstract justice and in the sight of God, there could be no doubt, in the opinion of Suárez, that such a war was homicide and therefore "opposed to justice." But as regards the parties themselves, we may consider that they have entered into an agreement, as it were, by virtue whereof they surrender their own rights and "join in a pact to the effect that the victor shall acquire the property of the vanquished," and this being the case, the question of restitution would not arise between them, the conqueror becoming the true owner of such property, since he possesses it by will of the former owner. For a like reason it might be argued that there was no obligation to make reparation, but Suárez considers the argument on this point doubtful as regards property, saying—"we do not not deny that the opposite opinion may be correct; and much less do we deny that it is [morally] safe."

What of stratagems in the course of war? They are permissible according to St. Thomas,[21] as stated by Suárez, "in so far as relates to the prudent concealment of one's plans; but not with respect to the use of active deception."

Is it permissible to break an agreement with the enemy? The answer of Suárez is, as we would expect, founded upon the maxim which is with him, as it were, a text, *Pacta sunt servanda.* Reparation, therefore, should be made by the belligerent breaking faith. Of course the agreement must have been made voluntarily by the parties and not under duress; but if one party violates the agreement, the other is released, and the same holds true in case of a change of circumstances, resulting in an inability to keep the promise without grave injury. The rule *rebus sic stantibus* is applicable. In such a case, the other belligerent should be informed that, for the reasons stated, it is impossible to keep the promise. Such a declaration, he says, is, however, seldom to be permitted.

Is fighting permissible on feast days? Yes, says Suárez, "in cases of urgent necessity."

We now come to a matter which was the subject of much discussion before and during Suárez' time, "whether or not a Christian prince sins, in calling to his aid infidel sovereigns, or, conversely, in giving them aid in a war which is otherwise just." The classic example was the alliance made with the Turks by Francis I of France, in his war with Charles V, Holy Roman Emperor. We here have an opportunity of testing the breadth and the accuracy of Suárez' conception of war, as he answers that "such an action is not in itself a sin." His authority? Examples drawn from the Scriptures, involving David[22] and the *Maccabees.*[23] His further reason is of his day—we trust it is not

[21] II. II, qu. 40, art. 3.
[22] *Kings,* chap. xxviii.
[23] *Maccabees,* chaps. viii and xi.

of ours and that it shall never take place in the future: "It is permissible in war to employ the aid of wild animals, so why not that of unbelievers?" The whole question is, we hope, entirely academic today, and yet within the period of our history in America savage Indians were called to the aid of the British, the French and even of the Americans in their contests with one another on the American Continent.

The question of trade in contraband has always troubled belligerents and an acceptable settlement or compromise is still awaited. Granting that contraband may be supplied to belligerents, the view of Suárez is as sane as it is logical. "It is permissible," he says, "to sell arms to unbelievers for use in just wars; hence it is permissible to aid them."

In Section VIII is a reply to the question, "Is sedition intrinsically evil?" the answer depending on which party to the sedition be asked. Suárez, however, views it from the standpoint of an impartial observer. First of his definition of "sedition." It is, he says, "the term used to designate war carried on within a single state, and either waged between two parts thereof or between the prince and the state." For the first of these, our present term is "civil war" and for the second, "rebellion" or, if successful, "revolution."

Now Suárez was, as we have said, looking at the matter impartially, and it was his belief that the aggressor in sedition within the state was always in the wrong, whereas justice was on the side of the defense. The reason? Because there is no legitimate authority on the part of the aggressor to declare war, since the authority to declare war "resides in the sovereign prince."

But if the right of sedition be denied to a part of the state which has been injured, what is its remedy? In the opinion of Suárez, it lies through the courts exactly as in the case of an injured individual.

We now come to a phase of the question which smacks of tyrannicide. Let us suppose, says Suárez, that the sedition—or, as we prefer to call it, rebellion or revolution—is against the prince; "it is not intrinsically evil," although it "be aggressive."

But the conditions for a just war must exist, in order that it may be righteous. One condition which, in his opinion, would justify the war is when the prince is a "tyrant"—a situation which may occur in one of two ways: "In the first place, the prince may be a tyrant respecting his [assertion of tyrannical] dominion and power; secondly, he may be so merely in regard to his [acts of] government."

Suárez has already discussed the question of tyrannicide—for such is the technical name for this situation—in a most able manner in his masterpiece, *Defensio Fidei Catholicae adversus Anglicanae Sectae Errores.* But the matter is of such importance and apparently is such an integral part of the conception of Suárez, that he could not discuss the question of war without dealing with it, saying: "When the first kind of tyranny occurs, the whole state, or any portion thereof, has the right [to revolt] against the prince. Hence, it follows that any person whatsoever may avenge himself and the state against tyranny. The reason supporting [these statements] is that the tyrant in question is an aggressor, and is waging war unjustly against the state and its separate parts, so that, in consequence, all [those parts] have the right of defence. Such is the opinion expressed by Cajetan;[24] and the same conclusion may be derived from a passage in St. Thomas'[25] works." In the case of the first of the two kinds of tyrants which Suárez has described, the prince is as a usuper and any person may proceed against him in the interest of the state. In the second case, he is a lawful prince, acting unlawfully, and in this event, individuals as such may not take action against him if they do not represent the state, but "the state as a whole, however, may rise in revolt against such a tyrant," and this uprising would not be a case of sedition in the strict sense, assuming, indeed, that the word sedition is ordinarily used with an evil connotation." What is the reason for the distinction which Suárez draws? "The state, when it granted him"—meaning the prince—"his power, is held to have granted it upon these conditions: that he should govern in accord with the public weal,

[24] *On* II. II, qu. 64, art. i, ad 3.

[25] *On the Sentences,* Bk. II, dist. xliv, qu. 2, art. 2.

and not tyrannically; and that, if he did not govern thus, he might be deposed from that [position of] power.

In this connection Suárez again invokes, as well he might, the authority of St. Thomas.[26]

Suárez was not unaware of the possibility of abusing the right of rebellion, and he therefore admonished his readers that war against a ruler who was not a tyrant was sedition in the worst sense, and "intrinsically evil"; and that, if a prince had just cause to proceed against sedition in his state, he might rightfully do so. But Suárez concludes that "in the absence of those conditions, that same war is entirely unjust."

The concluding section (No. IX) of the tractate *De Bello* is an elaborate and detailed answer to the question posed by Suárez himself: "Is a private war, that is to say, a duel, intrinsically evil?" The question which Suárez raised and elaborately answered was one of his day. Dueling was then the fashion with the man of honor, although it is difficult for us of today to understand the relation of the duel to the honor of the individual; for assuredly dueling was a matter of skill, and the most honorable man in the world could not hope to overcome a scoundrel skilful either with pistol or sword.

Suárez, however, felt obliged to deal with what was a common custom of his day, but his elaborate argument can be stated in a few words: The person who challenges is an aggressor, and the person challenged is not obliged to accept. If he does, he takes his life into his own hands, but shares the rôle of aggressor with the challenger, since he is under no obligation to accept, and can not claim that acceptance of the challenge is an act of self-defense. Even if the person challenged is unjustly accused or condemned and accepts the challenge as a means of vindication, Suárez does not consider his acceptance an act of self-defense, for "calumny," he declares, "is not repelled by violence, but by the manifestation of truth." Furthermore, Suárez points out, if this procedure were permissible, any one might readily persuade himself that he was unjustly accused in court and that he might therefore properly slay his accuser.

[26] *De Regimine Principum*, Bk. I, chap. vi.

In our day dueling is fortunately illegal in most, if not all countries, and Suárez considered it illegal if it did not have the sanction of the prince, who represented the supreme legal authority of the state. Nevertheless the occasion would be rare indeed when the prince would be morally justified, in Suárez' opinion, in permitting a duel.

If, however, a private armed contest were approved by the public authority, if it were "for a public cause" and if it fulfilled in every other respect the requirements of a just war, it might be justified, Suárez held, "for in that event it has the nature of a war—at least, war of a limited sort—rather than that of a duel." This is, in effect, a justification strictly limited by Suárez to the few instances in which the private combat might have the approval of the state and in which all the rules and requirements of a just war were observed. Thus, if two belligerents should decide to reduce their war to a contest between a few combatants instead of between armies—as in the classic case of the *Horatii*—such a contest, in reality a part of the war, would have the approval of Suárez in that it would minimize the evils of war. In our own behalf, be it said, it would seem of no small advantage if the combatants were chosen in the future from the statesmen responsible for the war—beginning with the chief executives—who would thus be brought to a lively realization of what war means.

CONCLUSION

CHAPTER XIII

CONCLUSION

As we have said in the Foreword, both Victoria and Suárez have spoken for themselves. The subjects upon which they discoursed were to some extent identical: Victoria was dealing with a concrete case—the effect of the discovery of America upon the law which should govern the international relations of Spaniards and barbarians alike; Francisco Suárez discoursed in the abstract—at least without reference to any particular event, such as the discovery of America and the relations of the Europeans to the barbarians "recently discovered." The topic fundamental with both was necessarily the "state," its origin, its source, its attributes in relation to the people composing it—who are nothing more nor less than men, women and children in organized society.

Victoria had delivered a Reading on the state, under the title of *De Potestate Civili* at the University of Salamanca in 1528, some four years before his first Reading *On the Indians.* Suárez treated of the state as an integral part of his *Defensio Fidei,* here departing from his usual practice and applying his doctrines to a specific instance. For the occasion was concrete in the sense that it required Suárez to define the powers of King James I of England with regard to the spiritual rights of his subjects, a question which caused Suárez—as Victoria—to consider in general, and indeed in detail, the origin, the nature and the attributes of the state in the concrete case before him.

In the conception of each of these great internationalists, the state is not a thing of itself. It is not spontaneously generated. It is a human organization. The people united themselves into a state which we prefer to call the status of organization. This organization, although human in its fabrication, is nevertheless of divine ordination; for it is in accordance with the law of nature, which itself is of divine origin. The people, therefore, uniting themselves into a group or a community or a state, determine the nature and the form of their organization and government, which, according to their preference, may be monarchic, aristocratic, democratic or mixed. But the form of organization created by the people may be changed by the people, if they come to the opinion that they have made a mistake in their previous form of government—for "to err is human," we only too well know.

Within each state—at least in the period with which we deal—there was a political system, a system of government. And a judicial system, courts of the prince—to use the expression then common, also existed in each of the states or communities in which disputes between citizens and subjects should be determined without a resort to private warfare, although self-defense was permissible in the face of urgent danger to life or to property, as it is today. There was likewise a social system with various classifications and gradations, inasmuch as free born men were equal only in theory and unequal in practice.

And outside, and indeed above the social and political organization, there was also a religious organization which, at the date of the discovery of America in 1492, was coterminous with Christendom.

Within the state thus conceived as an organization, there was a sanction through the courts for each municipal rule of law, the decisions being executed by the authority of the prince as chief magistrate.

Now the state, just as the individual, could not exist and prosper in isolation. This was the conception of Victoria, who set it forth in lines destined to be forever memorable in the literature of the law of nations:

> International law has not only the force of a pact and agreement among men, but also the force of a law; for the world as a whole, being in a way one single state, has the power to create laws that are just and fitting for all persons, as are the rules of international law. Consequently, it is clear that they who violate these international rules, whether

> in peace or in war, commit a mortal sin; moreover, in the gravest matters, such as the inviolability of ambassadors, it is not permissible for one country to refuse to be bound by international law, the latter having been established by the authority of the whole world.

These lines contemplate an organized international community supported, in the words of Victoria, "by the authority of the whole world." It is a community with the power to create laws, laws that are binding upon every nation, binding because they have the authority of the world behind them.

Likewise to Suárez the existence of states as isolated and unrelated entities was impossible, for he also saw the world as an integrated if inorganic international community:

> The rational basis of this branch of law [the law of nations], indeed, consists in the fact that the human race, howsoever many the various peoples and kingdoms into which it may be divided, always preserves a certain unity not only as a species, but also, as it were, a moral and political unity called for by the natural precept of mutual love and mercy, which applies to all, even to strangers of any nation.
>
> Therefore, although a given sovereign state, commonwealth, or kingdom, may constitute a perfect community in itself, consisting of its own members, nevertheless, each one of these states is also, in a certain sense, and viewed in relation to the human race, a member of that universal society; for never are these states, when standing alone, so self-sufficient that they do not require some mutual assistance, association and intercourse, at times for their greater welfare and advantage, but at other times because also of some moral necessity or lack, as is clear from experience.
>
> Consequently, such communities have need of some system of law whereby they may be directed and properly ordered with regard to this kind of intercourse and association; and although this law is in large measure provided by natural reason, it is not provided in sufficient measure and in a direct manner, with respect to all matters; therefore, it was possible for certain special rules of law to be introduced through the practice of these same nations.
>
> For just as in one state or province law is introduced by custom; so among the human race as a whole it was possible for laws to be introduced by the habitual conduct of nations, and all the more because the matters comprised within this latter system of law are few, and very closely related to the natural law, and most easily deduced therefrom in a manner so advantageous and so in harmony with nature itself, that while this derivation [of the law of nations from the natural law] may

not be self-evident, that is, not essentially and absolutely required for moral rectitude, it is nevertheless quite in accord with nature, and universally acceptable for its own sake.

There was, however, an essential difference between the international community of Suárez and that of Victoria. To the former, the community of states was inorganic. It existed because the states existed and had need of relations, one with the other, of "mutual assistance, association and intercourse." But the community which he had in mind was not an organized community, with law-making and law-enforcing powers. The laws of the international community of Victoria were created because the community had "the power to create" them, just as it had the power, backed by the authority of the world, to enforce them. The international community of Suárez was governed by laws introduced slowly, unconsciously, by custom, in his own words, "by the habitual conduct of nations."

We of today are not infrequently pleased to consider ourselves as originators, specially in matters international; but in point of fact the two great modern conceptions of the international community are the conceptions of Victoria and of Suárez. The one—an organized community—the statesmen of the world had in mind when they developed the vast and complicated machinery of Geneva. The other—that of an inorganic community, a gradual development growing out of the mere coexistence of states—has found expression in the international machiney set up at The Hague. The choice of the future lies between the two.

In both a sanction is contemplated. In the one, it is a legal and a physical sanction, the authority of the world supported by law and expressed through physical means. In the other, the sanction is a moral and spiritual force which, also supported by law, is based fundamentally, however, not upon physical action but upon the moral principle which underlies all human relationships, good faith.

Let us consider for purposes of illustration how each of these types of sanction would operate in a specific case. Lest it be thought that we deal with impracticable matters, it may be supposed that a given nation owes the United States certain sums of money which it declines to pay, a situation which may seem to be not wholly unrelated to present-day facts. Now if the world were a closely organized community of nations, with the authority and power to enforce its rules, the position of the United States as a member of such a close organization would be analogous to that of the creditor within the state, who would seek a judgment through the proper authorities and have the judgment executed by the sheriff in his behalf. So the United States might do in seeking to recover their debt, if the international machinery necessary were actually in operation. However, it can not be again said that the machinery for execution against an international debtor is still a matter of words rather than of facts.

Let us therefore turn to another alternative, that which might be possible in the international community which we have termed inorganic. We may suppose that the United States has brought its case before the Permanent Court of International Justice at The Hague and has secured a favorable judgment. There remains the question of execution. In a word, how can the United States collect? There would seem to be, in the inorganic community of nations, no provision, no international sanction available. But there may be—indeed there should be—a municipal sanction for international law. Now if the debtor nation has property in the United States, why could not the United States through its own courts attach that property in satisfaction of the debts which it could not otherwise collect? It may be argued that the property would be insufficient in amount—and this might conceivably be the case—but in most instances there would be not only ships in our harbors but goods in our warehouses, balances in our banks and investments in our industries and lands belonging to the debtor nation which could be attached without difficulty and which would go far toward meeting—and indeed in most cases would exceed—the amount of the debt. But what, it may be asked, would be the attitude of the debtor nation? Would it not protest against such seizures? To be sure, it might protest, but it is difficult to see upon what legal ground it could base its protests if the United States had merely collected what was owing to them by due process of law, employing a municipal sanction in an international matter in which there was no international sanction available. Reprisals on the high seas, even occupation of lands if necessary, and judicial decisions with seizure of the property of the debtor within the plaintiff state are acts of coercion but not of war. At least that is the claim of the large states.

But to return to Victoria and to Suárez. In both, the essence of the system of international law was equality among nations as among individuals. Both, however, were not merely theorists but practical humanitarians. Equality there should be between nations, as such, but what of those imperfect communities which were not in a position to organize themselves in such a way as to protect their own interests? Both maintained that a responsibility for such imperfect communities lay with more advanced peoples and they charged the latter with the task of assisting the backward states to a position in which they would be able to look after their own welfare and interest—a charge which was to be carried out solely in the interest of the imperfect community and not in that of the guardian state. The world has recently rediscovered this doctrine, has equipped it with a modern set of rules and has christened it the "mandate."

As we have said, Victoria was interested in the application of his system to a specific situation, that which arose in the new Spanish possessions beyond the seas. Suárez, on the other hand, except in his *Defensio Fidei,* developed his system in the abstract without a specific situation in mind and with only sufficient concrete illustrations to support his arguments. Indeed his purpose was not to apply the law which he expounded but to furnish it with a philosophy. Now it is not possible to evolve a philosophy for any one branch of law without considering other branches of law, and therefore the task which Suárez set himself was to develop not only a philosophy of the law of nations but a philosophy of law in general. This being the case, he analyzes at length, not only the definitions of law, but the sources and the purposes of law, and he examines, with the knowledge of a lawyer, the care of a philosopher and the standard of a moralist, all branches of law—the divine law, the law of nature and the relation of human reason thereto, human law, the *ius gentium* and customary law, giving to each due importance in the philosophical structure which he was evolving.

The international doctrines of Victoria and Suárez have stood the test of centuries and of posterity's critical eyes. They still stand as they will stand in the future, holding up to a troubled and doubting world what we may call the three international virtues—justice, good faith and equality. The sum and substance of their messages, simple, timeless and founded upon the eternal verities, is stated by each in a series of brief passages, some of which we have just quoted but which can not be quoted too often, and which require neither explanation nor comment.

First, the passages chosen from Victoria:[1]

Title by Discovery. There is another title which can be set up, namely, by right of discovery; and no other title was originally set up, and it was in virtue of this title alone that Columbus the Genoan first set sail. And this seems to be an adequate title because those regions which are deserted become, by the law of nations and the natural law, the property of the first occupant (*Inst.*, 2, 1, 12). Therefore, as the Spaniards were the first to discover and occupy the provinces in question, they are in lawful possession thereof, just as if they had discovered some lonely and thitherto uninhabited region.

Not much, however, need be said about this third title of ours, because, as proved above, the barbarians were true owners, both from the public and from the private standpoint. Now the rule of the law of nations is that what belongs to nobody is granted to the first occupant, as is expressly laid down in the aforementioned passage of the *Institutes.* And so, as the object in question was not without an owner, it does not fall under the title which we are discussing. Although, then, this title, when conjoined with another, can produce some effect here (as will be said below), yet in and by itself it gives no support to a seizure of the aborigines any more than if it had been they who had discovered us.—*De Indis,* Section II.

[1] For an admirable treatment of Victoria's contribution to international law, see the lectures delivered by Professor Camilo Barcia Trelles at The Hague Academy of International Law in 1927, as printed in the *Recueil des Cours* of the Academy, vol. 17, p. 117. These lectures, the title of which is *Francisco de Vitoria et l'École moderne du Droit international,* have since been published in book form in Spanish under the title *Francisco de Vitoria, Fundador del Derecho Internacional Moderno* (Universidad de Valladolid, Publicaciones de la Sección de Estudios Americanistas, Serie Quinta, Número III, 1928).

The Law of Nations and Natural Law—Freedom of Travel. I will now speak of the lawful and adequate titles whereby the Indians might have come under the sway of the Spaniards. (1) The first title to be named is that of natural society and fellowship. And hereon let my first conclusion be: (2) The Spaniards have a right to travel into the lands in question and to sojourn there, provided they do no harm to the natives, and the natives may not prevent them. Proof of this may in the first place be derived from the law of nations (*jus gentium*), which either is natural law or is derived from natural law (*Inst.*, 1, 2, 1): "What natural reason has established among all nations is called the *jus gentium*." For, congruently herewith, it is reckoned among all nations inhumane to treat visitors and foreigners badly without some special cause, while, on the other hand, it is humane and correct to treat visitors well; but the case would be different, if the foreigners were to misbehave when visiting other nations.—*De Indis,* Section III.

Freedom of Trade. The Spaniards may lawfully carry on trade among the native Indians, so long as they do no harm to their country, as, for instance, by importing thither wares which the natives lack and by exporting thence either gold or silver or other wares of which the natives have abundance. Neither may the native princes hinder their subjects from carrying on trade with the Spanish; nor, on the other hand, may the princes of Spain prevent commerce with the natives. This is proved by means of my first proposition.—*De Indis,* Section III.

"Man is not a wolf to his fellow man." And, in sum, it is certain that the aborigines can no more keep off the Spaniards from trade than Christians can keep off other Christians. Now, it is clear that if the Spaniards kept off the French from trade with the Spaniards, and this is not for the good of Spain, but in order to prevent the French from sharing in some advantage, that practice would offend against righteousness and charity. If, then, there can be no just legal ordinance to this effect, it also can not be accomplished in actual fact (for the injustice of a law consists solely in the execution of the law). And, as is said in *Dig.*, 1, 1, 3, "Nature has established a bond of relationship between all men," and so it is contrary to natural law for one man to dissociate himself from another without good reason. Man is not, as Ovid says, "a wolf to his fellow man, but a man."—*De Indis,* Section III.

Rights of Foreigners. If there are among the Indians any things which are treated as common both to citizens and to strangers, the Indians may not prevent the Spaniards from a communication and participation in them. If, for example, other foreigners are allowed to dig for gold in the land of the community or in rivers, or to fish for pearls in the sea or in a river, the natives can not prevent the Spaniards from doing this, but they have the same right to do it as others have, so long as the citizens and indigenous population are not hurt thereby. . . . For if the Spaniards may travel and trade among them, they may consequently make use of the laws and advantages enjoyed by all foreigners. —*De Indis,* Section III.

Nationality. If children of any Spaniard be born there and they wish to acquire citizenship, it seems they cannot be barred either from citizenship or from the advantages enjoyed by other citizens—I refer to the case where the parents had their domicile there. The proof of this is furnished by the rule of the law of nations, that he is to be called and is a citizen who is born within the state (*Cod.,* 7, 62, 11). And the confirmation lies in the fact that, as man is a civil animal, whoever is born in any one state is not a citizen of another state. Therefore, if he were not a citizen of the state referred to, he would not be a citizen of any state, to the prejudice of his rights under both natural law and the law of nations. Aye, and if there be any persons who wish to acquire a domicile in some state of the Indians, as by marriage or in virtue of any other fact whereby other foreigners are wont to become citizens, they can not be impeded any more than others, and consequently they enjoy the privileges of citizens just as others do, provided they also submit to the burdens to which others submit.—*De Indis,* Section III.

Missionaries. Christians have a right to preach and declare the gospel in barbarian lands.

. . . If the Indians allow the Spaniards freely and without hindrance to preach the Gospel, then whether they do or do not receive the faith, this furnishes no lawful ground for making war on them and seizing in any other way their lands.—*De Indis,* Section III.

Mandates. Although the aborigines in question are . . . not wholly unintelligent, yet they are little short of that condition, and so are unfit to found or administer a lawful state up to the standard required by human and civil claims. . . . It might, therefore, be maintained that in their own interests the sovereigns of Spain might undertake the administration of their country, providing them with prefects and governors for their towns, and might even give them new lords, so long as this was clearly for their benefit. . . . Let this, however . . . be put forward without dogmatism and subject also to the limitation that any such interposition be for the welfare and in the interests of the Indians and not merely for the profit of the Spaniards. For this is the respect in which all the danger to soul and salvation lies.—*De Indis,* Section III.

Conscientious Objectors. If a subject is convinced of the injustice of a war, he ought not to serve in it, even on the command of his prince.—*De Iure Belli,* paragraph 22.

The Law of Nations, Natural Law and General Consent. And, indeed, there are many things in this connection which issue from the law of nations, which, because it has a sufficient derivation from natural law, is clearly capable of conferring rights and creating obligations. And even if we grant that it is not always derived from natural law, yet there exists clearly enough a consensus of the greater part of the whole world, especially in behalf of the common good of all. For if after the early days of the creation of the world or its recovery from the flood the majority of mankind decided that ambassadors should everywhere be reckoned inviolable and that the seas should be common and that prisoners of war should be made slaves, and if this, namely, that strangers should not be driven out, were deemed a desirable principle, it would certainly have the force of law, even though the rest of mankind objected thereto. —*De Indis,* Section III.

International Community and Sanctions. Society could not hold together unless there was somewhere a power and authority to deter wrongdoers and prevent them from injuring the good and innocent. Now, everything needed for the government and the preservation of society exists by natural law, and in no other way can we show that a state has by natural law authority to inflict pains and penalties on its citizens who are dangerous to it. But if a state can do this to its own citizens, society at large no doubt can do it to all wicked and dangerous folk, and this can only be through the instrumentality of princes.—*De Iure Belli,* paragraph 19.

The Authority of the Whole World. International law has not only the force of a pact and agreement among men, but also the force of a law; for the world as a whole, being in a way one single State, has the power to create laws that are just and fitting for all persons, as are the rules of international law. Consequently, it is clear that they who violate these international rules, whether in peace or in war, commit a mortal sin; moreover, in the gravest matters, such as the inviolability of ambassadors, it is not permissible for one country to refuse to be bound by international law, the latter having been established by the authority of the whole world.—*De Potestate Civili,* Section 21.

Compulsory Acceptance of Peaceful Settlement. If one party wants to settle and make a division or compromise as to part of the claim, the other is bound to accept his proposal, even if that other be the stronger and able to seize the whole by armed force; nor would he have a just cause of war.—*De Iure Belli,* paragraph 28.

Arbitration by the Pope. And on this principle also, when princes are at variance with one another about some right of sovereignty and are rushing into war, he [the Pope] can act as judge and inquire into the claims of the parties and deliver judgment, a judgment which the princes are bound to respect, lest those numerous spiritual evils should befall which are the inevitable results of a war between Christian princes. —*De Indis,* Section II.

The passages from Suárez are also fourteen in number:[2]

Law Defined. Strictly and absolutely speaking, only that which is a measure of rectitude, viewed absolutely, and consequently, only that which is a right and virtuous rule, can be called law.—*De Legibus ac Deo Legislatore.*

Eternal Law. The eternal law has first place, on account of its dignity and excellence, and because it is the source and origin of all laws.—*De Legibus ac Deo Legislatore.*

Natural Law Made Known. Natural law is the first system whereby the eternal law has been applied or made known to us. . . .

The natural law is made known to men in a twofold way, first through natural reason, and secondly, through the law of the Decalogue written on the Mosaic tablets. . . .—*De Legibus ac Deo Legislatore.*

What Pertains to Natural Law. All the precepts written by God in the hearts of men, pertain to the natural law, a fact which may be gathered from the words of Paul (*Romans,* chap. ii, vv. 14-15): and all precepts which may clearly be inferred by reason from natural principles are written in [human] hearts; therefore, all such precepts pertain to the natural law.

Examples of Natural Law. The commands relating to restitution of the property of another, or the return of a deposit, or observing good faith, or telling the truth, or similar matters . . . pertain in the highest degree to the province of the natural law.—*De Legibus ac Deo Legislatore.*

Natural Law and Promises. It should be further noted that, among the precepts of natural law, there are certain ones, dealing with pacts, agreements, or obligations, which are introduced through the will of men. Such are the laws relating to the observance of vows and of human promises, whether these be made in simple form or confirmed by oath; and the same is true of other contracts, according to the particular characteristics of each; and true, also, of the rights or duties arising therefrom.—*De Legibus ac Deo Legislatore.*

Natural Law and Observance of Contracts. In the case of any contract or commercial agreement . . . the observance of the contract after it has been made . . . pertains to the natural law. . . .—*De Legibus ac Deo Legislatore.*

Treaties of Peace and Truces. Likewise, treaties of peace and truces may be placed under the head of the *ius gentium* in the strict sense of the term; not in so far as relates to the obligation to observe them after

[2] An illuminating discussion of Suárez' system of international law is contained in lectures delivered by Professor Camilo Barcia Trelles at The Hague Academy of International Law in 1933, under the title *Francisco Suárez (1548-1617), Les théologiens espagnols du XVIe siècle et l'école moderne du Droit international,* which are printed in the *Recueil des Cours* of the Academy, vol. 43, p. 389.

they are made, since this obligation pertains rather to the nautral law; but in so far as [offers to make] such treaties should be needed, and not refused, when duly presented, and for a reasonable cause. . . .—*De Legibus ac Deo Legislatore.*

The Law of Nature, Good Faith and the Ius Gentium. With regard . . . to peace, truces and ambassadors, . . . all the [rules] on these points have their foundation in some human agreement, in which both the power to contract [a treaty or convention] and the obligation arising from that treaty or convention and demanding good faith and justice, have regard to the law of nature. Only the exercise [of these powers] may be termed a part of the *ius gentium* owing to the accord of all nations with respect to the exercise of such faculties, generally speaking. And this actual use [of the powers in question] is the effect of law, and not law itself; for the law under discussion does not spring from such use; on the contrary, the use has its source in the law.—*De Legibus ac Deo Legislatore.*

Equality. It remains that we explain in what manner the computation of this "major portion" should be made, or of what persons it is composed. There is a general agreement on this point, that there should be reckoned in this number only such persons as can give consent to a legal custom. All infants are, therefore, excluded, and all persons mentally defective. Some would also exclude women entirely, on the ground that they can exercise no legislative authority. Among men, they exclude all below the age of twenty-five years. However, I cannot find any basis in law or any justification in reason for the exclusion of the last two groups.—*De Legibus ac Deo Legislatore.*

Rationale of International Law. The rational basis of this branch of law [the law of nations], indeed, consists in the fact that the human race, howsoever many the various peoples and kingdoms into which it may be divided, always preserves a certain unity, not only as a species, but also, as it were, a moral and political unity called for by the natural precept of mutual love and mercy, which applies to all, even to strangers of any nation.—*De Legibus ac Deo Legislatore.*

The Universal Society. Therefore, although a given sovereign state, commonwealth, or kingdom, may constitute a perfect community in itself, consisting of its own members, nevertheless, each one of these states is also, in a certain sense, and viewed in relation to the human race, a member of that universal society; for never are these states, when standing alone, so self-sufficient that they do not require some mutual assistance, association and intercourse, at times for their greater welfare and advantage, but at other times because also of some moral necessity or lack, as is clear from experience.—*De Legibus ac Deo Legislatore.*

Intercourse of Nations. Consequently, such communities have need of some system of law whereby they may be directed and properly ordered with regard to this kind of intercourse and association; and although this law is in large measure provided by natural reason, it is not provided in sufficient measure and in a direct manner, with respect to all matters; therefore, it was possible for certain special rules of law to be introduced through the practice of these same nations.—*De Legibus ac Deo Legislatore.*

Laws of the International Community. For just as in one state or province law is introduced by custom: so in the human race as a whole it was possible for laws to be introduced by the habitual conduct of nations, and all the more because the matters comprised within this latter system of law are few, and very closely related to the natural law, and most easily deduced therefrom in a manner so advantageous and so in harmony with nature itself, that while this derivation [of the law of nations from the natural law] may not be self-evident, that is, not essentially and absolutely required for moral rectitude, it is nevertheless quite in accord with nature, and universally acceptable for its own sake. —*De Legibus ac Deo Legislatore.*

These passages contain the fundamental concepts of the modern law of nations—a law resting upon a Latin foundation and formulated in a Catholic atmosphere by Spanish theologians and publicists.

We have observed that both to Victoria and to Suárez the international community was a community, not of large and small states or of powerful and weak states, but of equal states. The principle of equality was therefore fundamental to both, but Suárez carried it, as we have seen, to its logical and what we may call its modern conclusion by denying any legal reason or justification for inequality between men and women:

It remains that we explain in what manner the computation of this "major portion" should be made, or of what persons it is composed. There is general agreement on this point, that there should be reckoned in this number only such persons as can give consent to a legal custom. All infants are, therefore, excluded, and all persons mentally defective. Some would also exclude women entirely, on the ground that they can exercise no legislative authority. Among men, they exclude all below the age of twenty-five years. However, I can not find any basis in law or any justification in reason for the exclusion of the last two groups.

As Suárez stood for equality of men and women, Victoria, by adopting the principle of *jus soli,* necessarily stood for the principle of nationality. Appropriately the New World has taken up the equal and single nationality of Victoria and the larger equality of Suárez at the Seventh of the Pan American Conferances held in Montevideo in 1933, when the American Republics adopted an equal nationality convention [3] without a dissenting vote, and a quadruple equal rights treaty.[4]

* * * * * * * *

We have endeavored to set forth the international doctrines of the Catholic Church as conceived by two great teachers and doctors of the Church, St. Augustine and St. Thomas Aquinas—doctrines which were given their international application and legal philosophy by two outstanding teachers of a later day, Francisco de Vitoria and Francisco Suárez.

May the teachers of the present and future ground their instruction upon the doctrines of these great teachers of the past; for, in the words of Pius XI addressed to an assembly of teachers as recently as the first of August, 1934, teachers are indeed "greater artists than painters or sculptors," who only work with inanimate materials, while the labor of teachers is to "form souls"—the souls, we venture to add in our own behalf, not merely of men but of nations.

---

[3] In the material portion ,Article 1) of the Stevens Nationality Convention the signatories declare that:

There will be no distinction based on sex as regards nationality, in their legislation or in their practice.

[4] The material portion (Article 1) of the Stevens Equal Rights Treaty reads as follows:

The contracting states agree that upon the ratification of this treaty men and women shall have equal rights throughout the territory subject to their respective jurisdictions.

Both the convention and the treaty are open to the adherence of all nations.

www.ingramcontent.com/pod-product-compliance
Ingram Content Group UK Ltd.
Pitfield, Milton Keynes, MK11 3LW, UK
UKHW041448071026
15587UKWH00010B/664

9 781584 778219